ISBN 978-0-9828971-8-8

10-digit ISBN 0-9828971-8-9

Library of Congress Control Number 2013906091

Published in the USA

First paper back printing April 2013

The text type was set in Arial Unicode

Indus Writing in ancient Near East

-- Corpora and a dictionary

S. Kalyanaraman Sarasvati Research Center 2013

Table of contents

Indus Writing in ancient Near East

Corpora and a dictionary

"*Spoken words are the symbols of mental experience and written words are the symbols of spoken words. Just as all men have not the same writing, so all men have not the same speech sounds, but the mental experiences, which these directly symbolize, are the same for all, as also are those things of which our experiences are the images.*"[1]

Validating this Aristotle's insight, Indus writing is composed using symbols of spoken words. The symbols are hieroglyphs of meluhha (mleccha) words spoken by artisans recording the repertoire of stone, mineral and metal workers.

Mohenjo-daro seal showing composite animal and fish

The writing results in a set of catalogs of metalworking of bronze age.

Evidence of this competence in metallurgy which evolved from 4th millennium BCE of bronze age, is provided in corpora of metal ware catalogs and a dictionary of meluhha (mleccha).

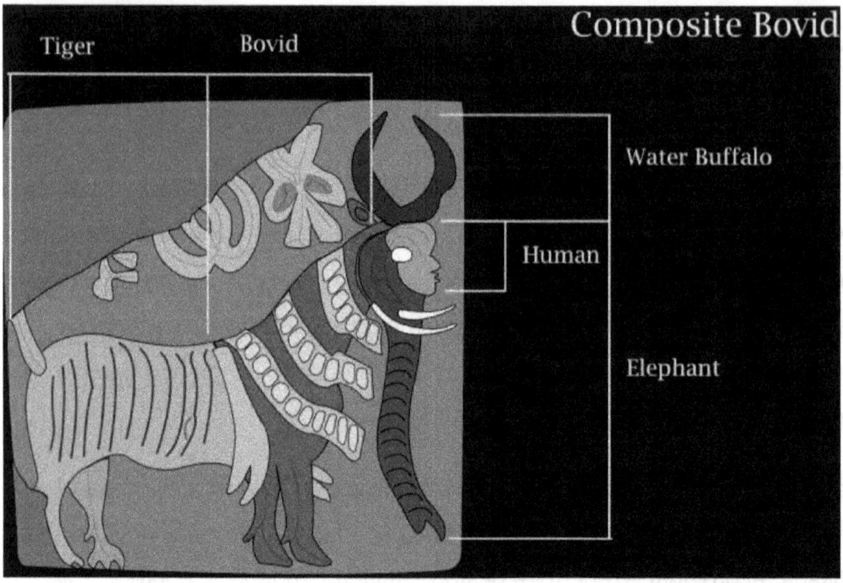

An art historian's component analysis of ligatured animal glyph on seal m0299.[2]

The component glyphs in the two Mohenjo-daro seals are: 1. antelope; 2. bull; 3. fish; 4. water buffalo; 5. human face; 6. elephant; 7. bovid; 8. tiger; 9. snake's hood (tail); 10. scarves on neck.

Read rebus, the composition glyph denotes a metal-/(mineral) stone-work catalog: 1. *tagara* 'antelope'; rebus: *tamkāru, damgar* 'merchant' (Assyrian); 2. *ḍangar* 'bull'; rebus: *ḍangar* 'blacksmith' (Hindi); 3. *ayo* 'fish'; rebus: *ayas* 'metal' 4. *kaṇḍ* 'water buffalo'; rebus: *kaṇḍ* 'stone (ore)'; *kaḍaio* = Skt. sthapati a mason] a bricklayer; a mason 5. *mũhe* 'face' (Santali) ; rebus:*mũh* metal ingot (Santali) 6. *ibha* (elephant); *ib* 'iron'; rebus: *ibbo* 'merchant'; 7. *pasaramu, pasalamu* 'an animal, a beast, a brute, quadruped' (Telugu); rebus: *pasra* 'smithy' (Santali); 8. *kola* 'tiger'; rebus: *kol* 'working in iron'; 9. *paṭam* , *n.* < *phaṭa*. 'cobra's hood' (CDIAL 9040). Rebus: 'sharpness of iron': *padm* (obl.*padt-*) temper of iron (Kota)(DEDR 3907); *patam* 'sharpness, as of the edge of a knife' (Ta.); 10.*dhaṭu* m. (also *dhaṭhu*) m. 'scarf' (WPah.); rebus: *dhātu* 'mineral' (Skt.), *dhatu* id. (Santali).

The key to the rebus reading method is paralleled 1. on Susa ritual basin with a ligatured 'goat-fish' and 2. on Warka vase with antelope and tiger denoting tin and iron ingots delivered to the temple with ligatured 'reed-scarf' standard.

Indus writing was a principal tool of economic administration for account-keeping by artisan and trader guilds and did not record literature or, history. Some sacred ideas and historical links across interaction areas between India and ancient Near East, may be inferred from the writing.

Hieroglyphic method

Some examples of hieroglyphs in Indus writing may be cited to explain the cipher which is a modified logo-graphic method which may be called a logo-semantic method. Many logo-phonetic systems are logo syllabic, that is, phonetic glyphs denote syllables. In a logo-semantic system like Indus writing, hieroglyphs denote words or sememes (smallest meaningful units of meaning). Sememe is derived from the Greek: σημαίνω (sēmaino), "mean, signify".

Seal impression, Ur (UPenn; U.16747); dia. 2.6, ht. 0.9 cm.; Gadd, PBA 18

(1932), pp. 11-12, pl. II, no. 12; Porada 1971: pl.9, fig.5; Parpola, 1994, p. 183; water carrier with a skin (or pot?) hung on each end of the yoke across his shoulders and another one below the crook of his left arm; the vessel on the right end of his yoke is over a receptacle for the water; a star on either side of the head (denoting supernatural?). "The whole object is enclosed by 'parenthesis' marks. The parenthesis is perhaps a way of splitting of the ellipse. An unmistakable example of an 'hieroglyphic' seal."[3]

This hieroglyph is normalized as a 'sign' (Glyph 12) on Indus Writing corpora.

kuṭi 'water carrier' (Te.) Rebus: *kuṭhi* 'smelter furnace' (Santali) *kuṛī* f. 'fireplace' (Hindi); krvṛl f. 'granary' (Wpah.); kuṛī, kuṛo house, building'(Ku.)(CDIAL 3232) kuṭi 'hut made of boughs' (Skt.) guḍi temple (Telugu)

Ligatured glyph 15. Thus, the 'rim-of-jar' glyph connotes: furnace account (scribe). Together with the glyph showing 'water-carrier', the ligatured glyphs of 'water-carrier' + 'rim-of-jar' can thus be read as: *kuṭhi kaṇḍa kanka* 'smelting furnace account (scribe)'.

Combined rebus reading: *ayakāra* 'iron-smith' (Pali)

m0482A One side of a two-sided tablet m1429C One side of a prism tablet. ayo 'fish' (Mu.); rebus: aya '(alloyed) metal' (G.) *kāru* a wild crocodile or alligator (Te.) Rebus: *khār* a blacksmith, an iron worker (cf. bandūka-khār) (Kashmiri)

m1162 Text 2058 Ligatured glyph of three sememes: 1. *meḍ* 'body'(Mu.); rebus: 'iron' (Ho.); *kāḍ* 2 काड् a man's length, the stature of a man (as a measure of length); rebus*:* *kāḍ* 'stone'; Ga. (Oll.) *kanḍ*, (S.) *kanḍu (pl. kanḍkil)* stone; 2. *aḍar* 'harrow'; rebus: *aduru* 'native metal'. *ibha* 'elephant'; rebus: ibbo 'merchant' (Gujarati)

Listed by Koskenniemi and Parpola and cited by Diwiyana[4]. Ligatured glyph of three sememes: 1. *meḍ* 'body' (Mu.); rebus: 'iron' (Ho.); 2. *kuṭi* 'water carrier' (Te.) Rebus: *kuṭhi* 'smelter furnace' (Santali); 3. खांडा [*khāṇḍā*] *m* a jag, notch, or indentation (as upon the edge of a tool or weapon); rebus: *khāṇḍā* 'metal tools, pots and pans'.

4th millennium Indus writing pre-dates all known writing

The potsherd h1522 discovered in Harappa on the banks of River Ravi by archaeologists of HARP (Harvard Archaeology Project) is dated to ca. 3500 BCE. Citing this find, the report quoted one of the excavators, Richard Meadow: "...these primitive inscriptions found on pottery may pre-date all other known writing."[5] As the hieroglyphic writing system evolved, the impact was also evidenced in Susa, with the foundation of a settlement on the banks of Karkheh and Dez Rivers dated to 5th millennium BCE.[6] The interactions between Elamite, Persian and Parthian empires of Iran and seafaring merchants of Meluhha can be re-evaluated in the context of the evidence provided by Indus writing[7]. Discussing 3rd millennium BCE cultural relationships of Indus valley with the Helmand and Baluchistan, Cortesi et al[8] refer to artifacts found at Shahr-I Sokhta and nearby sites (Iranian Seistan) presumably imported from Baluchistan, Mundigak (Kandahar, Afghanistan) and the Indus domain and indicating local adaptation of south-eastern manufactures and practices.[9]

The invention of writing was necessitated by the inventions of alloys during the Bronze Age. Arsenical-copper alloy was replaced by tin bronzes in 3rd millennium BCE in the Ancient Near East and in the region where Indus writing was in vogue. "The Early Bronze Age of the 3rd millennium BCE saw the first development of a truly international age of metallurgy… The question is, of course, why all this took place in the 3rd millennium BCE… It seems to me that any attempt to explain why things suddenly took off about 3000 BCE has to explain the most important development, the birth of the art of writing… As for the concept of a Bronze Age one of the most significant events in the 3rd millennium

was the development of true tin-bronze alongside an arsenical alloy of copper…"[10] Arsenical bronze occurs in the archaeological record across the globe, the earliest artifacts so far known have been found on the Iranian plateau in the 5th millennium BCE.[11]

Arsenical bronze and tin bronze

A tough problem in evaluating the preference for tin bronze is the difficulty of identifying the sources of tin from circa 4th millennium BCE. I suggest that, consistent with the identification of the source as Meluhha, tin may have been obtained by the panning method, similar to the method adopted in early times for sourcing gold.

"Tin ore occurrences discovered recently at Nurango in Bihar, Tosham near Delhi, Bastar district in Chattisgarh and the Koraput district in Oridda have not shown evidences of ancient mining or smelting, although there is interesting, simple, low-technology exploitation of the ores today. It is possible that the majority of the tin needed, and probably arsenic minerals as well, would have been brought from far away…Recent tin production by tribals using a simple technology give us some indication of how the metal may have been won in the remote past…The simple mining and metallurgical methods followed even now by Bastar and Koraput tribals in Chattisgarh and Orissa, central India, could be an indication of the methods used in the past. These tribal people produce considerable quantities of tin without any external help, electric power or chemical reagents, enough to make a modern metallurgist, used to high technology, wonder almost in disbelief…The ore is localized in the black pebbles of cassiterite which outcrop in stream beds etc. and there are other indicators, in the vegetation. The leaves of the sarai tree (shoria robusta) growing on tin-rich ground are often covered in yellow spots, as if suffering from a disease. (The leaves were found to contain 700 ppm of tin on analysis!). Wherever the tribals find concentrations of ore in the top soil, the ground all around the area is dug up and transported to nearby streams, rivers or ponds – in fact to any source of

water large enough to allow the washing process to take place to separate the tin ore from the soil...The ore is smelted in small clay shaft furnaces, heating and reducing the ore using charcoal as the fuel...The charcoal acts as both the heating and reducing agent, reducing the black cassiterite mineral into bright, white tin metal. The tin metal flows down through a hole made at the bottom of the furnace. At the end of each day, all the metal is collected and a crude refining is carried out by remelting the metal in an iron pan at about 250 degrees C The molten tin is then poured into the stone-carved moulds (Fig. 11.9) to make square- or rectangular-shaped tin ingots for easy transportation. The primitive technology being used here now amply demonstrates the methods by which the ancient Indians could have smelted tin...The prehistoric inhabitants not only discovered the art of extracting copper metal from the ore but also learned alloying to make various articles of daily use and weapons...The history of this (tin) industry is at present unknown, but it is likely that such sources of readily available ore were exploited from a number of locations in central eastern India where tin mineralization occurs more or less at surface."[12]

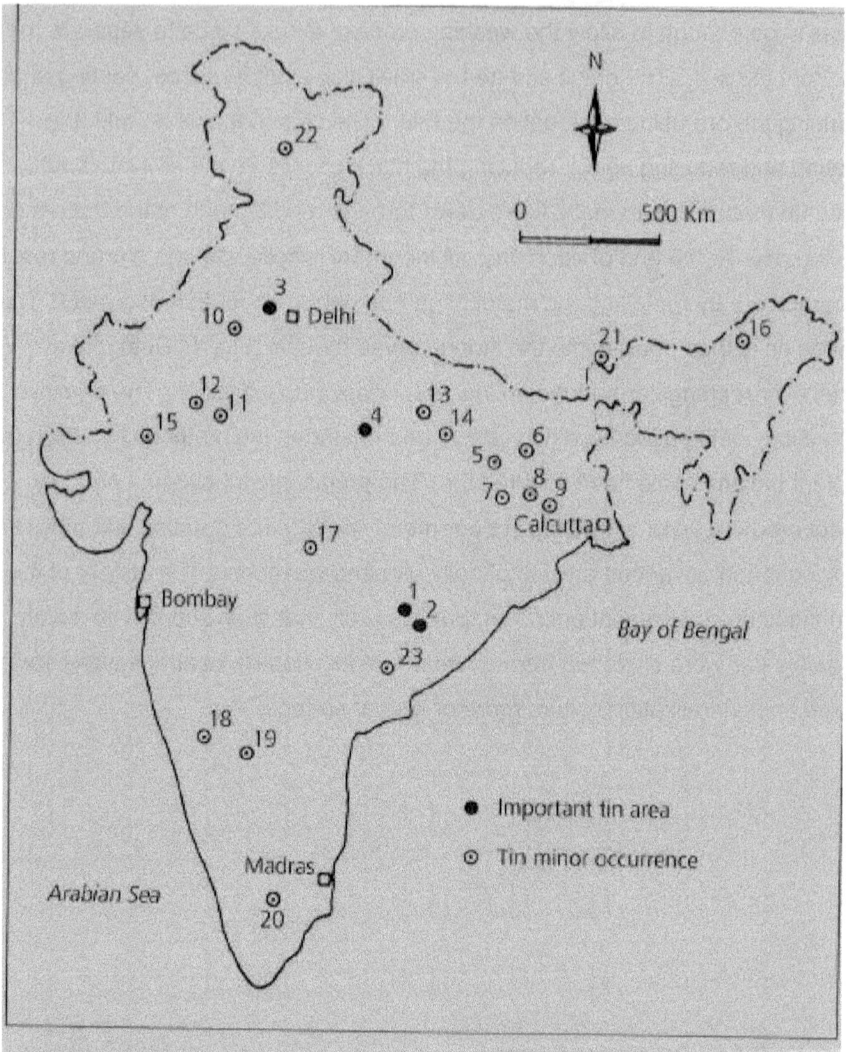

Fig. 11.2 Occurrence of tin in India. 1 Bastar; 2 Koraput; 3 Tosham; 4 Nurango; 5 Chakrabanda; 6 Kalikpar; 7 Paharsingh; 8 Purulia; 9 Bankura; 10 Jhunjhunu; 11 Soniana; 12 Nathadwara; 13 Almora; 14 Pauri-Garwal; 15 Banaskanta; 16 Rangavalley; 17 Goberwahi; 18 Dumble-Dharwar; 19 Makargavi; 20 Kadavur; 21 Sikkim; 22 Udhampur; 23 Aduamunda: (From Babu 1994, p. 37)

Occurrence of tin in India (After Fig. 11.2 in TM Babu).

Tribals panning for cassiterite mineral in the remote jungles of central India. (After Fig. 11.4 in TM Babu).

The ore is carried to the water pond or stream for washing in bamboo baskets (After Fig. 11.5 in TM Babu).

The ore is washed using bamboo pans, to concentrate cassiterite mineral (After Fig. 11.6 of TM Babu)

Base of small brick and mud furnace for smelting tin (After Fig. 11.7 of TM Babu) The shape of this furnace is comparable to the shape of iron smelter discovered in Malhar dated to ca. 18th cent. BCE

Damaged circular clay furnace, comprising iron slag and tuyeres exposed at lohsanwa mound, Period II, Malhar, Dist. Chandauli.[13]

Molten tin poured into stone-carved mould to make square or rectangular tin ingots (After Fig. 11.9 in TM Babu).

The Indus hieroglyphic writing system had a significant role in advancing cultural interactions with the Ancient Near East. The context provides for a review of development of glyptic art, adaptation of metallurgical practices, trade in minerals and metals by seafaring merchants traversing an expansive cultural area from Rakhigarhi in Sarasvati river basin to Haifa in the Levant. Trade loads were conveyed to trade agents across a vast area extending from Rakhigarhi in the east to Altyn-tepe in the northwest, using caravans and from Daimabad in the southwest to Susa in the northwest, navigating the Persian Gulf using the famed Meluhha boats. Susa in Khuzistan province of southwestern Iran is located on Karkeh river which converges with Tigris-Euphrates river system at the Shatt al-Arab. Susa was continuously occupied from around 4000 BCE until the end of the 13th century CE and was in contact with Dilmun and Meluhha between 4th and 2nd millenniums BCE. Use of hieroglyphs for tablets was a revolution in the mode

of thought of early inventors of the bronze age. Using the rebus method of the type used on Narmer palette, use of hieroglyphs together with their rebus rendering provided the facility for accounting for a large number of types of transactions (mining, smelting, ingot-making, forging, turning, i.e. re-processing used metal). Hieroglyphs of writing systems were also improvised. Sets of hieroglyphic ligatures were created to communicate messages involving multiple transaction types. For example, when a bronze-age smith's role had to be described, three hieroglyphs were ligatured to communicate that the smith was also a merchant and a turner (with a forge/workshop).

Tabernae montana as a hieroglyph

Warka stone (alabaster) vase dated to c. 3000 BCE, has relief decoration in four registers.[14] On top register are glyphs of a goat and a tiger/jackal above two glyphs (which may denote bun-ingots out

of a furnace). On bottom register are shown *tabernae montana* sprouts. The second and third registers of the vase seem to show a procession of metal workers and animals bringing alloyed metal ingots in pots.

Tell Abraq axe[15] with epigraph ('tulip' glyph + a person raising his arm above his shoulder and wielding a tool + dotted circles on body).

tabar = a broad axe (Punjabi). Rebus: tam(b)ra 'copper' tagara 'tabernae montana', 'tulip'. Rebus: tagara 'tin'.

[quote] The site of Uruk, modern Warka, is located in southern Iraq about 35 kilometers east of the modern course of the Euphrates river. Settlement at the site began in the Ubaid period (5th millennium BC). In the Uruk period (4000-3000 BC) the site was the largest in Mesopotamia at 100 hectares. Uruk continued to grow in the Early Dynastic period (2900-2350 BC), reaching a size of about 400 hectares. After the end of the Early Dynastic period, the city declined in size and significance until the Ur III period (2100-2000 BC), when the ruling dynasty pursued new building projects in the Eanna precinct. It is to this period that the massive ziggurat still visible today dates. Uruk declined again after the Ur III period, and was resettled in the Neo-Assyrian (883-612 BC) and Neo-Babylonian periods (612-539 BC). [unquote] [16]

These flowers are identified as tulips, perhaps Mountain tulip or Boeotian tulip (both of which grow in Afghanistan) which have an undulate leaf. There is a possibility that the comb is an import from Bactria, perhaps transmitted through Meluhha to the Oman Peninsula site of Tell Abraq.

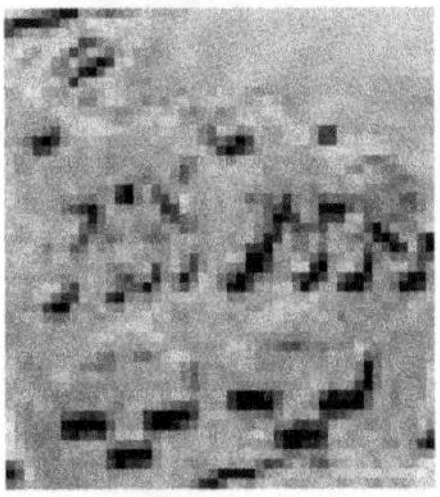

kand 'fire-altar' (Santali) The pair of composite glyphs together with ram and tiger glyphs may read as: tin ingot, *tagara kand mũh* and *kol kand khōṭ,* 'alloyed ingot'. An allograph for kand: kŏnḍ क्रंड् or kŏnḍa क्रंड । कुण्ड m a deep still spring (El., Gr.Gr. 145); (amongst Hindūs) a hole dug in the ground for receiving consecrated fire; cf. ạgana-kŏnḍ (p.

16*b*, l. 34) (Rām. 631). kǫ̆ṇḍu or konḍu । कुण्डम् m. a hole dug in the ground for receiving consecrated fire kōda कौंद । कुलालादिकन्दुः f. a kiln; a potter's kiln (Rām. 1446; H. xi, 11); a brick-kiln (Śiv. 133); a lime-kiln. (Kashmiri)

A pair of *khōṭ* 'alloyed ingots' are shown atop the fire-altars. An allograph for mũh 'ingot' (Santali) : kōḍ कोड् m. a kernel (Kashmiri) खोट [khōṭa] A lump or solid bit (as of phlegm, gore, curds, inspissated milk); any concretion or clot. (Marathi) Rebus: L. *khoṭ*f. ' alloy, impurity ', *°ṭā* ' alloyed ', awāṇ. *khoṭā* ' forged '; P. *khoṭ* m. ' base, alloy ' M.*khoṭā* ' alloyed ', (CDIAL 3931)

kol 'tiger' (Kon.) Rebus: kol 'iron' (Ta.)

tagara 'ram' (Ta.) Rebus: *damgar* 'merchant' (Akk.) (Top register, ahead of the two storage jars with ingots).

pasaramu, pasalamu = quadrupeds (Telugu); pasra 'smithy, forge' (Santali) (Third register).

tagaraka *tabernae montana* (Skt.) Rebus: tagara 'tin' (Ka.) (Fourth register).

Thus, the vase describes two types of metal ingots being carried into the treasury: ingots of tin, ingots of iron.

That a metal ingot is being carried is reinforced by the head of an ox shown together with a pellet between its horns.

This depiction may be seen between the two storage jars filled with the ingots.[17]

On the top register, a scarf atop a post is shown behind two adorants standing on two 'frames of buildings' and atop a ram. The male adorant carries in his hands a glyphic comparable to the glyptic shown on the Susa ritual basin flanked by two antelope-goat composite hieroglyphs. If this glyphic denotes tamar, 'palm tree, date palm' the rebus reading would be: tam(b)ra, 'copper' (Pkt.)

The frames of buildings used in the glyphic composition are hieroglyphs: *sãgāḍā* m. ' frame of a building ' (M.)(CDIAL 12859) Rebus: *jangaḍiyo* 'military guards who accompanies treasure into the treasury" (G.)

tagara 'ram' (Ta.) Rebus: *damgar* 'merchant' (Akk.) (Top register, ahead of the two storage jars with ingots).

dhatu 'scarf'; rebus: dhatu 'mineral' (Santali) dhātu 'mineral (Pali) dhātu 'mineral' (Vedic); a mineral, metal (Santali); dhāta id. (G.) H. dhāṛnā 'to send out, pour out, cast (metal)' (CDIAL 6771).

A pair of reeds as standard. *sangaḍa* 'pair', *kāḍ* काँड् । काण्ड: m. 'the stalk or stem of a reed, grass, or the like, straw', *khōṭ* 'blob atop standard' *dhatu* 'scarf'.

The rebus reading of the pair of reeds in Sumer standard is: *khānḍa* 'tools, pots and pans and metal-ware', *khōṭ* 'alloyed ingots',

dhatu 'mineral (ore)'.

Ko. goṇḍ knob on end of walking-stick, head of pin (DEDR 2081). Rebus: kǒṇḍu or konḍu । कुण्डम् m. a hole dug in the ground for receiving consecrated fire (Kashmiri) H. *gõṛā* m. 'reservoir used in irrigation '. (CDIAL 3264). अग्निकुण्डम्. A pool, well; especially one consecrated to some deity or holy purpose. (Sanskrit) *Kur.* xoṇḍxā, xõṛxā deep; a pit, abyss. *Malt.* qonḍe deep, low lands. (DEDR 2082).

The glyphs in the composition of a pair of scarved posts are:

sangaḍa 'pair' (Marathi) Rebus: jaṅgaḍ 'entrustment articles'. The pair of pegs denote the pair of minerals dealt with: *tagara,*'tin' and *kol,* 'iron'. The pair of reed stalks read rebus: *sangaḍa kāṇḍa* 'entrustment articles' of 'tools, pots and pans, metal-ware'.

goṇḍ 'knob on end of walking-stick, head of pin' (Ko.); *khũṭ* peg, post'. Allograph: *kõdā* खोंड [khōṇḍa] m A young bull, a bullcalf. (Marathi) Rebus 1: kǒṇḍu or konḍu । कुण्डम् m. a hole dug in the ground for receiving consecrated fire (Kashmiri) Rebus 2: A. *kundār*, B. *kũdār*, *°ri*, Or. *kundāru*; H. *kũderā* m. ' one who works a lathe, one who scrapes ', *°rī* f., *kũdernā* ' to scrape, plane, round on a lathe '.(CDIAL 3297).

dhatu 'scarf'; rebus: 'cast mineral' (Santali); (cf. H. dhāṛnā 'to send out, pour out, cast metal)

The pegs or posts may be joints of stalk or reeds: *kaṇḍa* -- m.n. ' joint of stalk, stalk (Pali); *kāḍ* m. ' stalk of a reed, straw ' (Kashmiri); *kāḍ* n. ' trunk, stem ' (Marathi); Or.*kāṇḍa, kāṛ* ' stalk (Oriya); *kāṛā* 'stem of muñja grass (used for thatching) (Bihari); *kānā* m. ' stalk of the reed Sara ' (Lahnda)(CDIAL 3023). Rebus: *kāṇḍa* 'tools, pots and pans, metal-ware'.

Thus the combined glyphs of *goṇḍ* knob, *kāḍ* reed, *dhatu* scarf read rebus: *kũdār* 'turner'; *konḍu* 'consecrated fire'; furnace' (Santali); *kāṇḍa* 'tools, pots and pans, metal-ware'; *dhatu* 'mineral ore'.

medhi (f.) [Vedic methī pillar, post (to bind cattle to); BSk. medhi Divy 244; Prk. meḍhi Pischel *Gr.* § 221. See for etym. Walde, *Lat. Wtb.* s. v. meta] pillar, part of a stūpa [not in the Canon?].(Pali) What are often referred to as 'temple poles' of Inanna may thus connote: the following glyphic readings:

sangaḍa 'pair' [A word associated with the pair of storage jars, pair of 'reed' glyphs, pair of vases – glyphs shown on Warka vase.]

meḍhi 'pillar'.

dhatu 'scarf'

The rebus readings for these glyphs are:

jangaḍa 'entrustment articles' (of) *dhatu* 'iron ore'.

dhatu 'minerals' (cast in) *kaṇḍa*, furnace (fire-altar, consecrated pit). khondu id. (Kashmiri) kŏnḍ क्ंड् 'a hole dug in the ground for receiving consecrated fire' (Kashmiri) kunḍa 'consecrated fire-pit'. Allograph: koṇḍi knot of hair on the crown of the head (Telugu) Allograph: konḍu spine (Kashmiri) *kaṇḍa* 'nodule of stone ore'.

The pair of 'reed' glyphs can thus be read rebus: *sangaḍa* 'entrustment articles': *dhatu.kūdār kāṇḍa* 'iron ore turner tools, pots and pans, metal-ware'.

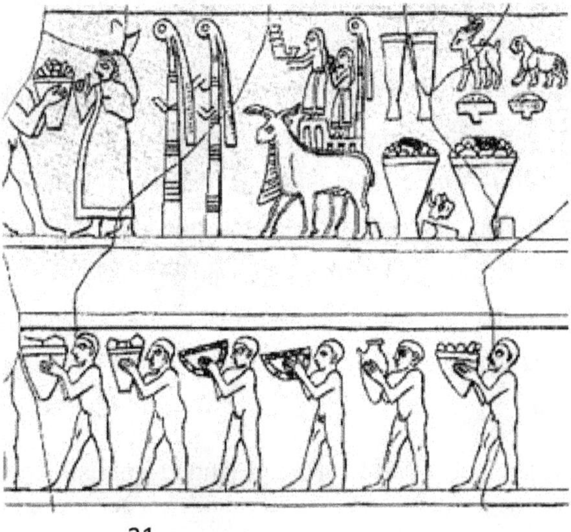

The word *kole.l* has two meanings: smithy, temple. Thus, the pair of 'reeds' signify sacredness associated with a temple.

kunḍa 'pot; rebus:

'consecrated fire-pit'. The 'U' glyphic is a semantic determinant to emphasize that this is a

temple with a smithy furnace and a consecrated fire-pit. The structural form (*sangaḍa* 'frame of a building') within which this sign is enclosed may represent a temple: kole.l 'temple, smithy' (Ko.); kolme smithy' (Ka.) The ligatured sign may thus be read: *sangaḍa kunḍ* to mean 'entrustment articles (of) consecrated fire-altar or furnace'.

The naked person is offering a large storage jar with ingots of smithy to a person who carries on the left hand face of a bull. ḍangar 'bull' ḍāṅgar 'cattle'; rebus: *ṭhākur* ' blacksmith ' (Maithili) [The bull head carried by the person is a phonetic determinant of the identification of the person's title or profession.]

Allograph: damgar 'merchant' (Akkadian).

The person stands in front of two poles surmounted by two scarves.

Thus, the scarfed composition denotes the *damgar* 'merchant' and female (*kola*, smithy) attendant, offering *dhatu,* 'mineral', and *tam(b)ra* 'copper' from *kand*, 'furnaces (consecrated fire-altars)'. The top register of the vase records this offering on a tall storage jar containing ingots and a cob. The cob is kolmo 'seeding, rice-plant'(Munda) rebus: kolami 'smithy'; (Telugu) mũh ' ingot' (Santali).

Allograph of Maithili. *ṭhākur* 'blacksmith' : Pk. *ṭhakkura* -- m. 'Rajput, chief man of a village'; P. *ṭhākar* m. landholder, ludh. *ṭhaukar* m. ' lord '; Ku. *ṭhākur* m. ' master, title of a Rajput '; N. *ṭhākur* ' term of address from slave to master ' (f. *ṭhakurāni*), *ṭhakuri* 'a clan of Chetris' (f. *ṭhakurni*); A. *ṭhākur* 'a Brahman', *ṭhākurānī* 'goddess'; B. *ṭhākurāni, ṭhākrān, °run* ' honored lady, goddess '; Or. *ṭhākura* ' term of address to a Brahman, god, idol ', *ṭhākurāṇī* ' goddess '; Bi. *ṭhākur* ' barber '; Maithili. *ṭhākur* ' blacksmith '; Bhoj. Aw.lakh.*ṭhākur* ' lord, master '; H. *ṭhākur* m. ' master, landlord, god, idol ', *ṭhākurāin, ṭhākurānī* f. ' mistress, goddess '; G. *ṭhākor, °kar* m. ' member of a clan of Rajputs ',*ṭhakrāṇī* f. ' his wife ', *ṭhākor* ' god, idol '; M. *ṭhākur* m. ' jungle tribe in North Konkan, family priest, god, idol '; Si. mald. "*tacourou*" ' title added to names of noblemen '; Garh. *ṭhākur* ' master '; A. *ṭhākur* also ' idol ' (CDIAL 5488).

sangaḍa 'pair' (Marathi) Rebus: jaṅgaḍ 'entrustment notes' indicates entrustment

into the treasury by *jangaḍiyo* 'military guards who accompanies treasure into the treasury" (G.)

A seal made in Susa with Indus writing

9801Susa

Susa, Iran; steatite cylinder seal.Cylinder seal carved with an elongated buffalo and a Harappa inscription circa 2600-1700 BCE; Susa, Iran; Fired steatite; H. 2.3 cm; Diam. 1.6 cm; Jacques de Morgan excavations, Susa; Sb 2425; Near Eastern Antiquities; Richelieu wing; Ground floor; Iran and Susa during the 3rd millennium BC; Room 8.

Marshall comments on a Susa cylinder seal: "...the occurrence of the same form of manger on a cylinder-seal of bone found at Susa leaves no doubt, I think, that this seal either came from India in the first instance, or, as is suggested by its very rough workmanship, was engraved for an Indian visitor to Susa by an Elamite workman...One of these five (Mesopotamian seals with Indus script) is a bone roll cylinder found at Susa, apparently in the same strata as that of the tablets in Proto-Elamitic script of the second period of painted ware. Scheil, in *Delegation en Perse*, vol. xvii, assigns this group of tablets and painted pottery to the period of Sargon of Agade, twenty-eighth century BCE, and some of the tablets to a period as late as the twenty-fourth century. The cylinder was first published by Scheil in *Delegation en Perse* ii, 129, where no precise field data by the excavator are given. The test is there given *as it appears on the seal*, and consequently the text is reversed. Louis Delaporte in his *Catalogue des Cylindres Orientaux...du Musee du Louvre*,

vol. I, pl. xxv, No. 15, published this seal from an impression, which gives the proper representation of the inscription. Now, it will be noted that the style of the design is distinctly *pre-Sargonic*: witness the animal file and the distribution of the text *around the circumference* of the seal, and not parallel to its axis as on the seals of the Agade and later periods…It is certain that the design known as the animal file *motif* is extremely early in Sumerian and Elamitic glyptic; in fact is among the oldest known glyptic designs. But the two-horned bull standing over a manger was a design unknown in Sumerian glyptic, except on the small round press seal found by De Sarzec at Telloh and published by Heuzey, *Decouvertes en Chaldee*, pl. xxx, fig. 3a, and by Delaporte, *Cat.* I, pl. ii, t.24. The Indus seals frequently represent this same bull or bison with head bent towards a manger…Two archaeological aspects of the Susa seal are disturbing. The cylinder roll seal has not yet been found in the Indus Valley, nor does the Sumero-Elamitic animal file motif occur on any of the 530 press seals of the Indus region. It seems evident, therefore, that some trader or traveler from that country lived at Susa in the pre-Sargonic period and made a roll seal in accordance with the custom of the seal-makers of the period, inscribing it with his own native script, and working the Indian bull into a file design after the manner of the Sumero-Elamitic glyptic. The Susa seal clearly indicated a period ad quem below which this Indian culture cannot be placed, that is, about 2800 BCE. On a roll cylinder it is frequently impossible to determine where the inscription begins and ends, unless the language is known, and that is the case with the Susa seal. However, I have been able to determine a good many important features of these inscriptions and I believe that this text should be copied as follows:

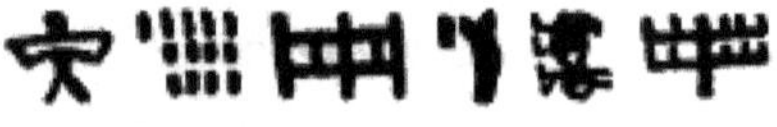

The last sign is No. 194 of my list, variant of No. 193, which is a post-fixed determinative, denoting the name of a profession, that is 'carrier, mason, builder', ad invariably stands at the end. (The script runs from *right* to *left*.)"[18] The seal's chalky white appearance is due to the fired steatite it is made of. Craftsmen in the Indus Valley made most of their seals from this material, although square shapes were usually favored. The animal carving is similar to those found in Harappa works. The animal is a bull with no hump on

its shoulders, or possibly a short-horned gaur. Its head is lowered and the body unusually elongated. As was often the case, the animal is depicted eating from a woven wicker manger.[19]

9852 Telloh

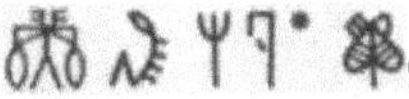9851 Telloh

This piece can be compared to another circular seal carved with a Harappa inscription, also found in Susa. The two seals reveal the existence of trading links between this region and the Indus valley. Other Harappa objects have likewise been found in Mesopotamia, whose sphere of influence reached as far as Susa.

The manufacture and use of the seals

Cylinder seals were used mainly to protect sealed vessels and even doors to storage spaces against tampering. The surface of the seal was carved. Because the seals were so small, the artists had to carve tiny scenes on a material that allowed for fine detail. The seal was then rolled over clay to produce a reverse print of the carving. Some cylinder seals also had handles.

Sources:Amiet Pierre, L'Âge des échanges inter-iraniens : 3500-1700 av. J.-C., Paris, Éditions de la Réunion des musées nationaux, 1986, coll. "Notes et documents des musées de France", p. 143 et p. 280, fig. 93.
Borne interactive du département des Antiquités orientales.
Les cités oubliées de l'Indus : archéologie du Pakistan, cat. exp. Paris, Musée national des arts asiatiques, Guimet, 16 novembre 1988-30 janvier 1989, sous la dir. de Jean-François Jarrige, Paris, Association française d'action artistique, 1988, pp. 194-195, fig. A5.

http://www.louvre.fr/en/oeuvre-notices/cylinder-seal-carved-elongated-buffalo-and-harappan-inscription

 Louvre Museum; Luristan; unglazed, gray steatite;

short-honed bull and 4 pictograms

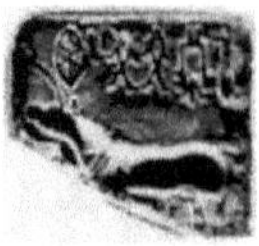

steatite; perhaps Iraqi bull, the standard are

Iraq from an museum; glazed site; the one-horned below a six-sign inscription.

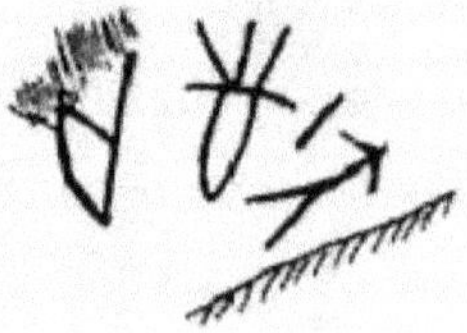

4 Foroughi collection; Luristan; medium gray

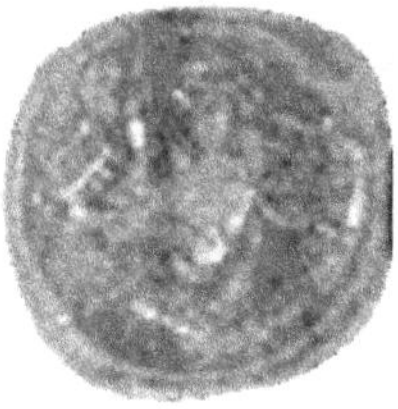

steatite; bull, crescent, star and net square; of the Dilmun seal type.

TextFailaka; unglazed steatite; an arc of four pictograms above the hindquarter of a bull.

Textseal, impression, inscription; Failaka; brownish-grey unglazed steatite; Indus pictograms above a short-horned bull.

seal, impression; Qala'at al-Bahrain; green steatite; short-horned bull and five pictograms. 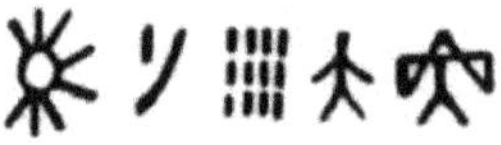 Found in association with an Isin-Larsa type tablet bearing three Amorite names.

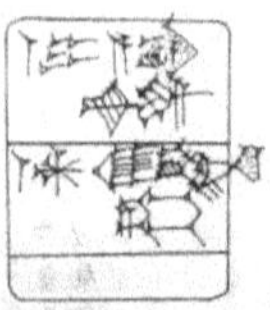

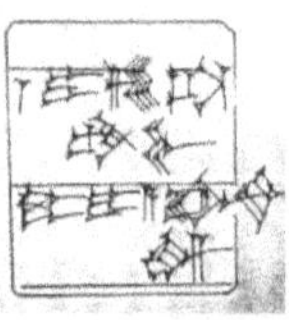

Qala'at al-Bahrain; ca. 2050-1900 BC; tablet,

found in the same level where 8 Dilmun seals and six Harappa type weights

were found. Three Amorite names are: Obverse. Janbi-naim; Ila-milkum; Reverse. Jis.i-tambu (son of Janbi-naim). The script is dated to c. 2050-1900 BCE.

Qala'at al-Bahrain; light-grey steatite; hindquarters of a bull and two pictograms.

urseal2  9832 Ur Seal; BM 122187; dia. 2.55; ht. 1.55 cm. Gadd PBA 18 (1932), pp. 6-7, pl. 1, no. 2

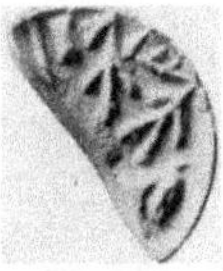

urseal3  9833 Ur Seal; BM 122946; Dia. 2.6; ht. 1.2cm.; Gadd PBA 18 (1932), p. 7, pl. I, no.3; Legrain, Ur Excavations, X (1951), no. 629.

urseal8Seal; BM 118704; U. 6020; Gadd PBA 18 (1932), pp. 9-10, pl. II, no.8; two figures carry between them a vase, and one presents a goat-like animal (not an antelope) which he holds by the neck. Human figures wear early Sumerian garments of fleece.

urseal9Seal; BM 122945; U. 16181; dia. 2.25, ht. 1.05 cm; Gadd PBA 18 (1932), p. 10, pl. II, no. o; each of four quadrants terminates at the edge of the seal in a vase; each quadrant is occupied by a naked figure, sitting so that, following round the circle, the head of one is placed nearest to the feet of the preceding; two figures clasp their hands upon their breasts; the other two spread out the arms, beckoning with one hand.

urseal10 Seal; BM 120576; U. 9265; Gadd, PBA 18 (1932), p. 10, pl. II, no. 10;

bull with long horns below an uncertain object, possibly a quadruped and rider, at right angles to the ox (counter clockwise); "...there is, below, a bull with long horns roughly

depicted, but above is a rather uncertain addition, which is perhaps an attempt to show one (possibly two) more, in a couching position, as viewed by turning the seal round until the face of the standing bull is downwards. If this is intended, the head of the second bull is turned back, and it is not, perhaps, quite impossible that the remaining part of the design is meant for a bird, such as is fairly often seen perched upon the back of a bull in Sumerian art, a device which has not yet been certainly explained." (C.J. Gadd, Seals of Ancient Indian Style Found at Ur', in: G.L. Possehl, ed., 1979, *Ancient Cities of the Indus*, Delhi, Vikas Publishing House, p. 118).

urseal11Seal; UPenn; a scorpion and an elipse [an eye (?)]; U. 16397; Gadd, PBA 18 (1932), pp. 10-11, pl. II, no. 11 [Note: Is the 'eye' an oval representation of a bun ingot made from bicā, sand ore?]

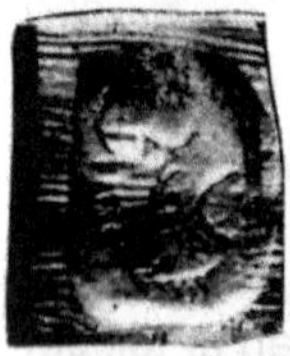

Rectangular stamp seal of dark steatite; U. 11181; B.IM. 7854; ht. 1.4, width 1.1 cm.; Woolley, Ur Excavations, IV (1956), p. 50, n.3. Scorpion.

Seal impression, Ur (Upenn; U.16747); dia. 2.6, ht. 0.9 cm.; Gadd, PBA 18 (1932), pp. 11-12, pl. II, no. 12; Porada 1971: pl.9, fig.5; Parpola, 1994, p. 183; water carrier with a skin (or pot?) hung on each end of the yoke across his shoulders and another one below the crook of his left arm; the vessel on the right end of his yoke is over a receptacle for the water; a star on either side of the head (denoting supernatural?). The whole object is enclosed by 'parenthesis' marks. The parenthesis is perhaps a way of splitting of the ellipse

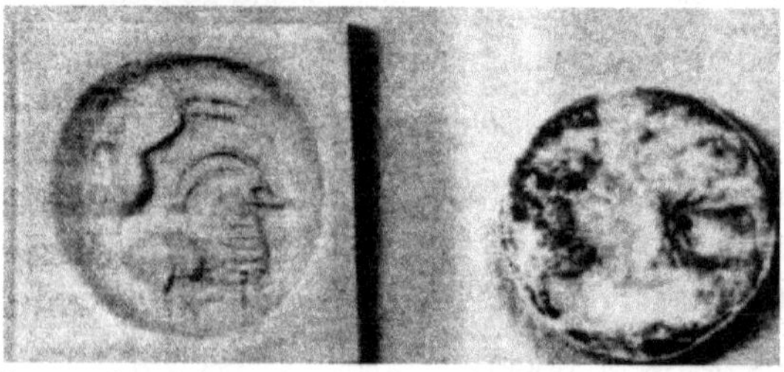

(Hunter, G.R., JRAS, 1932, 476). An unmistakable example of an 'hieroglyphic' seal. meḍha 'polar star' (Marathi). Rebus: 'iron' (Ho.)

Bahrain seal: two antelopes

Bahrain seal: four antelope heads emanating from a star. Dotted circles on the obverse.

meḍha 'polar star' (Marathi). மேடன் mēṭaṉ , *n.* < மேடம்[1]. The planet Mars, as the lord of the sign Aries (Tamil) மேடாதிபன் mēṭātipaṉ , *n.* < *mēṣādhipa.* Agni, as riding a ram; அக்கினிதேவன். (W.) மேண்டம் mēṇṭam , *n.* < *mēṇḍha.* Ram; ஆடு. (பரி. அக.)

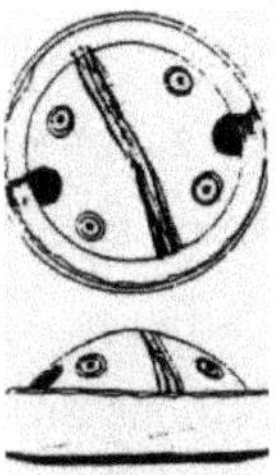

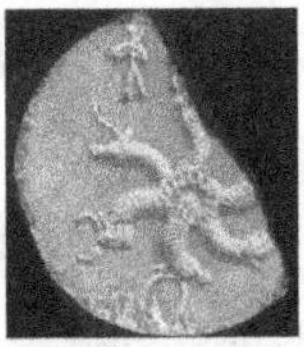

'iron' (Ho.Mu.) Allograph: meḍh 'ram'.

m417 six heads from a core. This hieroglyphic composition finds a parallel on a Dilmun seal:

Dilmun seal from Barbar; six heads of antelope radiating from a circle; similar to animal protomes in Failaka, Anatolia and Indus. Baṭa 'six' (G.); rebus: bhaṭa furnace (Santali)

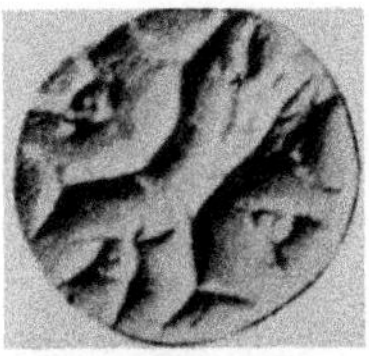

urseal13 Seal; BM 122841; dia. 2.35; ht. 1 cm.; Gadd PBA 18 (1932), p. 12, pl. II, no. 13; circle with center-spot in each of four spaces formed by four forked branches springing from the angles of a small square. Alt. four stylized bulls' heads (bucrania) in the quadrants of an elaborate quartering device which has a cross-hatched rectangle in the center.

urseal14Seal; UPenn; cf. Philadelphia Museum Journal, 1929; ithyphallic bull-men; the so-called 'Enkidu' figure common upon Babylonian cylinders of the early period; all have horned head-dresses; moon-symbols upon poles seem to represent the

door-posts that the pair of 'twin' genii are commonly seen supporting on either side of a god; material and shape make it the 'Indus' type while the device is Babylonian.

 urseal159845 Ur [The last glyph on top line looks like an animal with a long tail – as seen from the back and may have been the model for the orthography of Sign 51 as noted in Mahadevan corpus].

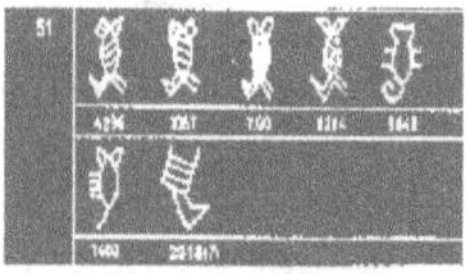

Variants of Sign 51. Seal impression; UPenn; steatite; bull below a scorpion; dia. 2.4cm.; Gadd, PBA 18 (1932), p. 13, Pl. III, no. 15; Legrain, MJ (1929), p. 306, pl. XLI, no. 119; found at Ur in the cemetery area, in a ruined grave .9 meters from the surface, together with a pair of gold ear-rings of the double-crescent type and long beads of steatite and carnelian, two of gilt copper, and others of lapis-lazuli, carnelian, and banded sard. The first sign to the left has the form of a flower or perhaps an animal's skin with curly tail; there is a round spot upon the bull's back.

urseal16  9846 Ur Seal impression; BM 123208; found in the filling of a tomb-shaft (Second Dynasty of Ur). Dia. 2.3; ht. 1.5 cm.; Gadd, PBA 18 (1932), pp. 13-14, pl. III, no. 16; Buchanan, JAOS 74 (1954), p. 149.

urseal17 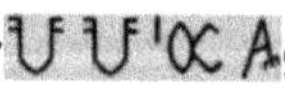 9901 Prob. West Asian find Seal impression, Mesopotamia (?) (BM 120228); cf. Gadd 1932: no.17; cf. Parpola, 1994, p. 132. Note the doubling of the common sign, 'jar'.

urseal18  9902 Prob. West Asian find Pictorial motif: Pict-45 Bull mating a cow. Seal and impression (BM 123059), from an

antique dealer, Baghdad; script and motif of a bull mating with a cow; the tuft at the end of the tail of the cow is summarily shaped like an arrow-head; inscription is of five characters, most prominent among them the two 'men' standing side by side. To the right of these is a damaged 'fish' sign.cf. Gadd 1932: no.18; Parpola, 1994, p.219.

urseal6 Cylinder seal; BM 122947; U. 16220 (cut down into Ur III mausolea from Larsa level; U. 16220), enstatite; Legrain, 1951, No. 632; Collon, 1987, Fig. 611.Humped bull stands before a plant, feeding from a round manger or a bundle of fodder (or, probably, a cactus); behind the bull is a scorpion and two snakes; above the whole a human figure, placed horizontally, with fantastically long arms and legs, and rays about his head.

A symbolism of a woman spreading her legs apart, which recurs on an SSVC inscribed object. Cylinder-seal impression from Ur showing a squatting female. L. Legrain, 1936, *Ur excavations, Vol. 3, Archaic Seal Impressions*. [cf. Nausharo seal with two scorpions flanking a similar glyph with legs apart – also looks like a frog].

Mohenjo-daro. Sealing. Surrounded by fishes, lizard and snakes, a horned person sits in 'yoga' on a throne with hoofed legs. One side of a triangular

terracotta amulet (Md 013); surface find at Mohenjo-daro in 1936. Dept. of Eastern Art, Ashmolean Museum, Oxford.

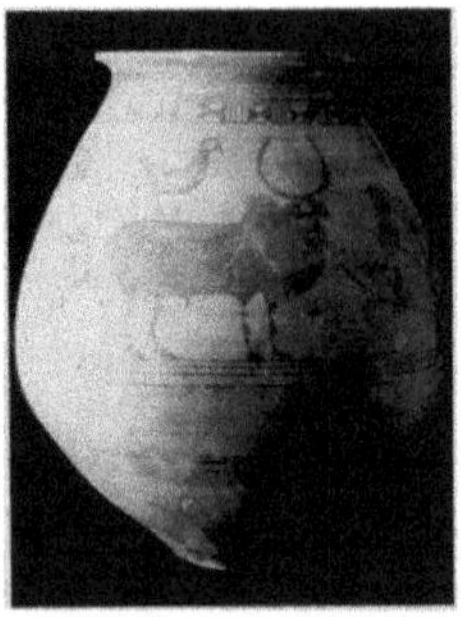

A zebu bull tied to a post; a bird above. Large painted storage jar discovered in burned rooms at Cat. No. 8. Nausharo, ca. 2600 to 2500 BCE. Cf. Fig. 2.18, J.M. Kenoyer, 1998,

A fish over a short-horned bull and a bird over a one-horned bull; cylinder seal impression, (Akkadian to early Old Babylonian). Gypsum. 2.6 cm. Long 1.6 cm. Dia. [Drawing by Larnia Al-Gailani Werr. Cf. Dominique Collon 1987, *First impressions: cylinder seals in the ancient Near East*, London: 143, no. 609] Tell Suleimeh (level IV), Iraq; IM 87798; (al-Gailani Werr, 1983, p. 49 No. 7).

Cylinder-seal impression; a griffin and a tiger attack an antelope with its head turned back. The upper register shows two scorpions and a frog; the lower register shows a scorpion and two fishes.Syro-Mitannian, fifteenth to fourteenth centuries BCE, Pierpont Morgan Library, New York. [After Fig. 9 in: Jack M. Sasson (ed.), *Civilizations of the Ancient Near East*, p.2705].

Rhinoceros, elephant, lizard.Tell Asmar (Eshnunna), Iraq. IM 14674; glazed steatite; Frankfort, 1955, No. 642; Collon, 1987, Fig. 610.

Hieroglyphs from a vase in Tell Asmar (29-27th cent. BCE). Pair of tigers, pair of zebu; a person holding two snakes; eagle and lion attacking a zebu.

Seal from Shortugai incised with an antelope and two other pictographs. "...Shortugai in Oxus basin, on the Kokcha-Amu Darya doab, has revealed the existence of a Harappa colony for carrying out trade in lapis lazuli.

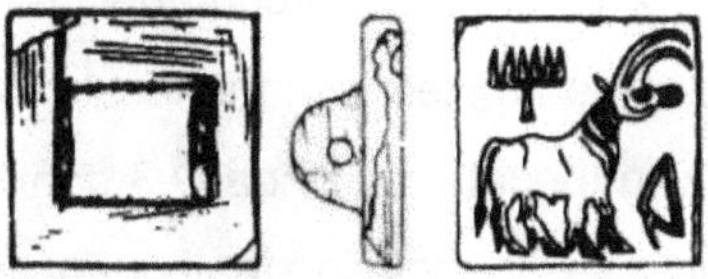

Apart form typical Harappa pottery, a seal bearing the script has also been found to confirm the trading character of the colony." (Six decades of Indus Studies in: BB Lal and SP Gupta, eds., *Frontiers of the Indus Civilization*, Fig. .8, p. 9].

Ur, Iraq; BM 123195; clay, half missing; Collon, 1987, Fig. 613. Probably originated in the east (exact location unknown).

A person with a vase with overflowing water; sun sign. C. 18th cent. BCE. [E. Porada,1971, Remarks on seals found in the Gulf states, *Artibus Asiae*, 33, 31-7].

"The main importance of a seal found in 1980 in Maysar-1 (Weisgerber, 1980), is the fact that the Makan/Oman civilisation used seals, as did the great cultures of the Nile, Euphrates/Tigris and Indus. But it is also a convincing proof of contact between Meluhha and Makan. On three sides six animals are engraved: two caprides, an ibex and a wild goat; a zebu cow and a scorpion; a dog and again a wild goat. In our context the zebu cow is the most important. Together with the humped bull painted on a jar from Umm an-Nar (Bibby, 1970:

280) it demonstrates the presence of these animals in the Oman peninsula during the third millennium BCE. This again proves contact with India.

Harappa control over the Oman Sea

"Recently Oman has yielded the first signs of the use of tin in the region. The analysis of a sword from Hili, dated to the mid-3rd millennium, shows a tin content of 6.5%, and a mold of a tap hole (?) associated with the remains of a furnace held metal with a tin content of 5%. The furnace is dated after the tree-ring calibration of a radiocarbon analysis (MC 2261) to circa 2225 BC...it is clear that the tin was added to the copper and it is also clear that it did not come from Oman itself. At Umm an-Nar artifacts with tin contents on the order of 2% were recovered; the tin must have been mixed with the local copper...Meluhha...the use of tin is attested already in the late 4th or early 3rd millennium at Mundigak III in southern Afghanistan. Tin appears only in small quantities in artifacts from Sahr-i-Sokhta in eastern Iran and at Tepe Yahya in southern Iran...In the Indus Valley, the copper-tin alloy is known at Mohenjodaro.

"...Oman's trade with southeastern Iran and Baluchistan is well attested...Among the products attributed to Meluhha, lapis lazuli and carnelian are found in sites and tombs of the 3rd millennium. We can suggest with reasonable certainty that the tin used in Oman was in transit through Meluhha and that the most likely source was western Afghanistan. The discoveries of tin in artifacts at Hili, though singular, are important because the site lies in an area clearly involved in long-distance trade. However, there is no clear evidence that the site was a way-station on the route which brought tin from Afghanistan to Mesopotamia. Therefore the presence of tin at Hili indicates only that it was transported in the Gulf area, where it was also used to fill local needs.

"The collective indications are that western Afghanistan ws the zone able to provide the tin used in Southwest Asia in the 4th and 3rd millennia...In order to elucidate the questions raised by our findings, a project aimed specifically at tin--its sources and metallurgy-- should be organized." (Serge Cleuziou and Thierry

Berthoud, Early Tin in the Near East, in: *Expedition*, Vol. 25, No. 1, 1982, pp. 14-19).

"Oman peninsula/Makkan lies half way between the two main civilization centres of the third millennium Middle East: Mesopotamia and the Indus valley... an increasing influence of Harappa civilization on Eastern Arabia during the last two centuries of the third millennium. This influence seems to strengthen during the early second millennium where proper Harappa objects are found all over the Oman peninsula: a cubic stone weight at Shimal, sherds of Harappa storage jars on several sites including Hili 8 (period III). Maysar and Ra's Al-Junayz bears a Harappa inscription and Tosi (forth.) has emphasized the importance of this discovery for knowledge of Harappa control over the Oman Sea." [Serge Cleuziou, Dilmun and Makkan during the third and early second millennia BC, 143-155 in: Shaikha Haya Ali Al Khalifa and Michael Rice (eds.) *Bahrain through the ages: the archaeology*, London, KPI, 1986.]

(Not illustrated) "A new seal from Hajjar in Bahrain now gives the same evidence, its shape being nearly identical with the Maysar-1 seal. Among its three engravings are a short-horned bull and an insription in Indus Valley script (Weisgerber, 1981: 218, fig. 54)." (Gerd Weisgerber, Makkan and Meluhha--third millennium BCE copper production in Oman and the evidence of contact with the Indus Valley, in: Parpola, Asko and Petteri Koskikallio (eds.), *South Asian Archaeology 1993,* Helsinki, Suomalainen Tiedeakatemia, 1994).

(Not illustrated) "(At Padri, Gujarat) A of the most significant discoveries is a copper fish-hook, which is 14 cm long and weights 41 gm. A copper fish-hook of such a magnitude has not been reported from any other site so far... The other material equipment include a seal on a stud handle engraved with fish motif, Harappa letters engraved on pot-sherds, cubical chert weights, micro steatite beads, beads of terracotta, carnelian, agate, etc."

Early Harappa bowl. Fish. [After Fig. 23.35 in, Asko Parpola, New correspondences between Harappa and near Eastern glyptic art, in: in B. Allchin, ed., *South Asian Archaeology,*

1981, Cambridge].

Seal impression; Dept. of Antiquities, Bahrain; three Harapan-style bulls

An Early Dynastic II votive plaque from the Inanna temple at Nippur VIII (after Pritchard, 1969: 356, no. 646). "It has something very Harappa about it also in the lower part depicting two 'unicorn' bulls.

Nippur; ca. 13th cent. BC; white stone; zebu bull and two pictograms

Tree in front. Fish in front of and above a one-horned bull. Cylinder seal impression (IM 8028), Ur, Mesopotamia. White shell. 1.7 cm. High, dia. 0.9 cm. [Cf. Mitchell 1986 Indus and Gulf type seals from Ur: 280-1, no.8 and fig. 112; Shaikha Haya Ali Al Khalifa and Michael Rice, 1986, *Bahrain through the ages: the archaeology*, London: 280-1, no.8 and fig. 112]. cf. Gadd, PBA 18 (1932), pp. 7-8, pl. I, no.7;; Parpola, 1994, p. 181; fish vertically in front of and horizontally above a unicorn; trefoil design

Terracotta sealing depicting an inscription, 2600 BCE, Western UP, Saharanpur (After Manoj Kumar Sharma). [Source: Page 32 in: Deo Prakash Sharma, 2000,

Harappa seals, sealings and copper tablets, Delhi, National Museum].

Stamp seals in Metropolitan Museum of Art, New York. 49.40.1 to 3. All three samples show a bull.

"Rendered in strict profile, standing before what might be an altar, the bull is by far the most popular motif in the Indus Valley glyptic art; there is virtually no v ariation in either the style or the iconographic details among the individual examples. The shoulder of the bull is emphasized by an upside-down doubly outlined heart shape that has been interpreted as painted decoration on the body of the bull, but is more likely an artistic convention for representing the muscles of the bull's shoulder."[After Fig. 38 in Holly Pittman, 1984, p. 84].

Mohenjo-daro. Silver seal (After Mackay 1938, vol. 2, Pl. XC,1; XCVI, 520). Two silver seals at Mohenjo-daro, two copper seals at Lothal and at Ras al-Junayz in Oman are rare uses of metal for making seals.

Stamp seal and a modern impression: unicorn or bull and inscription,, Mature Harappa period, ca. 2600–1900 B.C. Indus Valley Burnt steatite; 1 1/2 x 1 1/2 in. (3.8 x 3.8 cm)

http://www.metmuseum.org/toah/ho/02/ssa/ho_49.40.1.htm

Manuscripts in Schoyen Collection

Some manuscripts available in the Schoyen Collection. Located mainly in London and Oslo. URL http://www.nb.no/baser/schoyen/contentnew3.html "The Schøyen Collection comprises most types of manuscripts from the whole world spanning over 5000 years. It is the largest private manuscript collection formed in the 20th century. The whole collection, MSS 1-5245, comprises 13,010

manuscript items, including 2,172 volumes. 6,510 manuscript items are from the ancient period, 3300 BCE – 500 CE. For scholarly research and access the collection is a unique source, uniting materials usually scattered world wide to two locations only. These MSS are the world's heritage, the memory of the world. They are felt not really to belong to The Schøyen Collection and its owner, who only is the privileged, respectful and humble keeper, neither do they belong to a particular nation, people, religion, culture, but to mankind, being the property of the entire world. In the future The Schøyen Collection will have to be placed in a public context that can fulfil these visions...The Schøyen Collection is located mainly in Oslo and London. Scholars are always welcome, and are strongly encouraged to do research and to publish material."

Source:http://www.nb.no/baser/schoyen/intro.html#1.1

Included in the 6,510 manuscripts from the ancient period, 3300 BCE - 500 CE are the following epigraphs which are closely associated with the script of the Sarasvati Civilization.

MS 249 Unidentified Minoan text. Knossos, Crete, 16th cent. BCE, Linear A script?

MS in Minoan on clay, Knossos, Crete, 16th c. BC, 1 black roundel, 3,0x2,7 cm, 4 characters of late Minoan I Linear A script, 2 impressions (1,6x1,0 cm) on opposite edges by an amygdaloid seal with head of papyrus plant.

Provenance: 1. Possibly the archive in the West Wing of the Knossos Palace (16th c. BC - ca. 1950); 2. Erlenmeyer Collection, Basel, CMS no. 120 (until 1981); 3. Erlenmeyer Foundation, Basel (1981-1988); 4. Christie's 5.6.1989:99.

Commentary: The famous Linear B script

of the Mycenean kings, consisting of syllabic signs, ideograms and numerals, resisted decipherment for a generation. When Michael Ventris deciphered it in

1952, the achievement was called the "Everest" in classical archaeology. The language was archaic Greek. Linear A, the earliest script of Europe, has so far

resisted all attempts of decipherment, partly because the language is unknown, and the material small, ca. 700 copies only, while Linear B is known in 12,000 - 13,000 examples. This roundel is the only one in private ownership. Outside the Greek museums, they are, in fact, represented in 2 Italian museums only. KN Wc 26 in Erik Hallager: The Knossos roundels, BSA 82(1987).

This MS has signs which are comparable with the signs on epigraphs of Sarasvati-Sindhu Civilization.

MS 4625 Cylinder seal with a scene of drinking from a straw, Pakistan ca. 1500-500 BCE

Seal of hard red stone, Coast between Indus and the Persian Gulf, Pakistan, ca. 1500-500 BC, 1 cylinder seal matrix, diam. 1,3x3,2 cm, figure sitting left, holding a long straw from his mouth to a pot with bulbous body and narrow neck, resting on a stand; behind him a servant holding up a fan; behind the servant another standing person grasping a small quadruped. Above and below him 3 other quadrupeds. Between the 2 main figures a solar disc with rays and a crescent and a full moon combined.

Provenance: 1. Found in Baluchistan?, Pakistan (1965); 2. The Waria Collection, Dadu, Pakistan (ca. 1965-2001).

Commentary: Drinking beer from a straw is known from Sumer ca. 2700 BC on, but usually a big pot from which a number of persons are all drinking through their own straws. The fan is known in Iranian seals of ca. 1300-1100 BC. While the scene as a whole is Near Eastern, the dress and anklets of the servant is clearly of Indian type. The iconography combined is thus unique.

MS 4602 Indus Valley cylinder seal, ca. 3000 BCE depicting a palm tree and a man between two lions with wings and snakeheads, holding one arm around each, two long fish below, and one fish jumping after one lion's tail or the tail of a sitting monkey above it

Seal matrix on creamy stone or shell, Indus Valley, Pakistan, ca. 3000 BC, 1 cylinder seal, diam. 2,0x3,7 cm, in fine execution influenced by the Jemdet Nasr style of Sumer.

Provenance: 1. Found in Mehrgarh, Pakistan; 2. The Waria Collection, Dadu, Pakistan (-2001).

Commentary: Similar fish can be found on Indus Valley pottery from the period and later

http://www.nb.no/baser/schoyen/5/5.6/index.html#4602

MS 4617 Pakistan, ca. 2200-2000 BCE

White steatite, 1 square seal matrix, 4,3x4,3x1,9 cm, 6 Indus Valley signs in a formal script of high quality, unicorn standing left facing an altar, with loop handle.

Provenance: 1. The Waria Collection, Dadu, Pakistan (-2001).

Commentary: This seal is among the largest extant. The execution is representing Indus art at its best. The Indus script is still undeciphered, as is the Linear A script from Crete and the Rongo-Rongo script from Easter Island, which has numerous signs in common with the Indus script.

MS 4619, Pakistan, ca. 2200-1800 BCE

White coated grey steatite, Mohenjo-Daro?, Indus Valley, Pakistan, ca. 2200-1800 BC, 1 round seal matrix, diam. 2,3x1,5 cm, 5 Indus Valley signs, bison left eating from a trough, with double loop handle.

Context: Only 2 more round seals with inscriptions are known, both with bison and from Mohenjo-Daro (M-415 and M-416).

Provenance: 1. The Waria Collection, Dadu, Pakistan (1960'ies-2001).

MS5059 Pakistan, ca. 2200-1800 BCE

White steatite, Mohenjo-Daro, Indus Valley, 2200-1800 BC, 1 square stamp seal matrix, 3,4x3,4x1,7 cm, 9 Indus valley signs

Provenance: 1. Found in Mohenjo-Daro (ca. 1950-1970); 2. The Waria Collection, Dadu, Pakistan (-2001).

MS5061 Pakistan, ca. 2200-1800 BCE

White steatite, Mohenjo-Daro, Indus Valley, 2200-1800 BC, 1 square stamp seal matrix, 2,4x2,5x1,2 cm, 3 Indus valley signs

Provenance: 1. Found in Mohenjo-Daro (ca. 1950-1970); 2. The Waria Collection, Dadu, Pakistan (-2001).

MS5062 Pakistan, ca. 2200-1800 BCE

White steatite, Mohenjo-Daro, Indus Valley, 2200-1800 BC, 1 square stamp seal matrix, 2,7x2,7x1,6

cm, 4 Indus valley signs

Provenance: 1. Found in Mohenjo-Daro (ca. 1950-1970); 2. The Waria Collection, Dadu, Pakistan (-2001).

MS5065 Pakistan, ca. 1800 BCE

MS Indus Valley language on copper, Mohenjo-Daro, Indus Valley, ca. 1800 BC, 1 square stamp seal matrix, 1,3x1,3x0,9 cm, 3 Indus valley signs in script

Provenance: 1. Found in Mohenjo-Daro (ca. 1950-1970); 2. The Waria Collection, Dadu, Pakistan (-2001).

Commentary: There is only one similar seal known, from Lothal (L-44).

Parallels from Mesopotamia , Anatolia and other contact areas.

Administrative tablet with cylinder seal impression of a male figure, hunting dogs, and boars, 3100–2900 B.C.; Jemdet Nasr period (Uruk III script)
Mesopotamia Clay; H. 2 in. (5.3 cm)

The seal impression depicts a male figure guiding two dogs on a leash and hunting or herding boars in a marsh environment. Cylinder seal and modern impression: hunting scene, 2250–2150 B.C.; late Akkadian period Mesopotamia Chert; H. 1 1/16 in. (2.8 cm) This seal, depicting a man hunting an ibex in a mountain forest, is an early attempt to represent a landscape in Mesopotamian art. It was made during the Akkadian period (ca. 2350–2150 B.C.), during which the iconographic repertory of the seal engraver expanded to include a variety of new mythological and narrative subjects. The owner of the seal was Balu-ili, a high court official

whose title was Cupbearer.

http://www.metmuseum.org/toah/ho/02/wam/hod_41.160.192.htm

Shaft-hole axhead with a bird-headed demon, boar,and dragon, late 3rd–early 2nd millennium BCE Central Asia (Bactria-Margiana) Silver, gold foil; 5 7/8 in. (15 cm) "Western Central Asia, now known as Turkmenistan, Uzbekistan, and northern Afghanistan, has yielded objects attesting to a highly developed civilization in the late third and early second millennium B.C. Artifacts from the region indicate that there were contacts with Iran to the southwest. Tools and weapons, especially axes, comprise a large portion of the metal objects from this region. This shaft-hole axhead is a masterpiece of three-dimensional and relief sculpture. Expertly cast in silver and gilded with gold foil, it depicts a bird-headed hero grappling with a wild boar and a winged dragon. The idea of the heroic bird-headed creature probably came from western Iran, where it is first documented on a cylinder seal impression. The hero's muscular body is human except for the bird talons that replace the hands and feet. He is represented twice, once on each side of the ax, and consequently appears to have two heads. On one side, he grasps the boar by the belly and on the other, by the tusks. The posture of the boar is contorted so that its bristly back forms the shape of the blade. With his other talon, the bird-headed hero grasps the winged dragon by the neck. The dragon, probably originating in Mesopotamia or Iran, is represented with folded wings, a feline body, and the talons of a bird of prey."

Stamp seal, quatrefoil/maltese cross with infill, whip or snake

MS on grey steatite, North Syria/North Iraq/Iran, 5th millennium BC, 1 square stamp seal, 3,0x3,5x0,6 cm, 1 pictographic sign on reverse, pierced through.

Provenance: 1. Erlenmeyer Collection, Basel (before 1958-1981); 2. The Erlenmeyer Foundation, Basel (1981-1997); 3. Sotheby's 12.6.1997:6.

Stamp seal, standing male figure between two horned quadrupeds bak to back and head to end

MS on speckled dark-olive steatite or chlorite, North Syria/Iraq/Iran, 5th-4th millennium BC, 1 circular stamp seal, diam. 8,4x1,3 cm, pierced through.

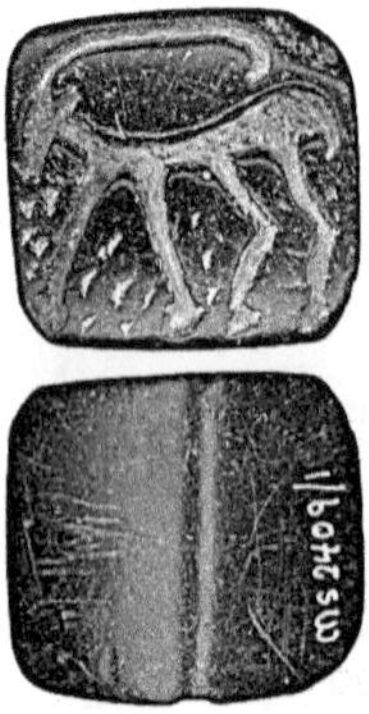

Provenance: 1. Erlenmeyer Collection, Basel (before 1958-1981); 2. The Erlenmeyer Foundation, Basel (1981-1997); 3. Sotheby's 12.6.1997:10.

Commentary: The earliest stamp seals of Sumer had various geometric patterns, later more elaborate designs and illustrations like the present seal, as a proof of identity and ownership. These can, together with the counting tokens, possibly be considered forerunners to the pictographic script of ca. 3200 BC. http://www.nb.no/baser/schoyen/5/5.6/#2411

Stamp seal, large ibex walking left

MS on black steatite or chlorite, North Syria or Anatolia, 4th millennium BC, 1 rectangular gabled stamp seal, 4,7x5,1x1,3 cm, pierced through.

Provenance: 1. Erlenmeyer Collection, Basel (before 1958-1981); 2. The Erlenmeyer Foundation, Basel (1981-1997); 3. Sotheby's 12.6.1997:8.

MS 4631 Bulla-envelope with 11 plain and complex tokens inside, representing an account or agreement, tentatively of wages for 4 days' work, 4 measures of metal, 1 large measure of barley and 2 small measures of some other commodity

Bulla in clay, Adab, Sumer, ca. 3700-3200 BC, 1 spherical bulla-envelope (complete), diam. ca. 6,5 cm, cylinder seal impressions of a row of men walking left; and of a predator attacking a deer, inside a complete set of plain and complex tokens: 4 tetrahedrons 0,9x1,0 cm (D.S.-B.5:1), 4 triangles with 2 incised lines 2,0x0,9 (D.S.-B.(:14), 1 sphere diam. 1,7 cm (D.S.-B.2:2), 1 cylinder with 1 grove 2,0x0,3 cm (D.S.-B.4:13), 1 bent paraboloid 1,3xdiam. 0,5 cm (D.S.-B.8:14).

Context: MSS 4631-4646 and 5114-5127are from the same archive. Only 25 more bulla-envelopes are known from Sumer, all excavated in Uruk. Total number of bulla-envelopes worldwide is ca. 165 intact and 70 fragmentary.

Commentary: While counting for stocktaking purposes started ca. 8000 BC using plain tokens of the type also represented here, more complex accounting and recording of agreements started about 3700 BC using 2 systems: a) a string of complex tokens with the ends locked into a massive rollsealed clay bulla (see MS 4523), and b) the present system with the tokens enclosed inside a hollow bulla-shaped rollsealed envelope, sometimes with marks on the outside representing the hidden contents. The bulla-envelope had to be broken to check the contents hence the very few surviving intact bulla- envelopes. This complicated system was superseded around 3500-3200 BCE by counting tablets giving birth to the actual recording in writing, of various number systems (see MSS 3007 and 4647), and around 3300-3200 BC the beginning of pictographic writing.
Exhibited: The Norwegian Intitute of Palaeography and Historical Philology (PHI), Oslo, 13.10.2003-06.2005.

MS 2963

ACCOUNT OF MALE AND FEMALE SLAVES

MS in Old Sumerian on clay, Sumer, ca. 3300-3200 BC, 1 nearly cubic tablet, 5,2x6,2x4,5 cm, 5 compartments in primitive pictographic script, fine cylinder seal impressions on all sides made prior to writing of 2 men walking left,

carrying ostriches, a basket between them and wine amphorae above.

Context The tablets MSS 2963, 3149-3151, 4510 and 4511, are all nearly cubic i form, MS 4511 being 4,8x4,8x4,5 cm. There is nothing similar in any public collection apart from 1 in Berlin. They possibly derive from the bulla-envelopes with counting tokens inside (cf. MSS 4631-4632, 4638, ca. 3700-3200 BC). The cubic tablets might represent the next logical step, the adding of pictographs representing the commodities involved, and adapted from the spherical shape of the bullas, to cubic shape, before being reduced to a thinner and more handy tablet. The 2 earliest cubic tablets (MSS 4510 and 3151) are ideonumerographical from Uruk V period, ca. 3400 BC, next to the protopictographical texts Uruk VI, the earliest continous writing know, predating the Tell Brak and Kish tablets (ca. 3200 BC, and the Uruk IV tablets (ca. 3200-3100 BC).

Commentary: The present tablet is the earliest written evidence of slavery, see collection 24.13

MS 2645 Indus valley script, and old akkadian illustration. North West Afghanistan, ca. 21st cent.

This seal links Indus Valley and Old Akkadian civilizations. The seal is of blue stone, North West Afghanistan, ca. 23rd-21st c. BC, 1 cylinder seal, 3,9x2,7 cm, 5 Indus valley signs, illustration standing archer aiming his bow at a falling boar, in the style of the best Old Akkadian art in Sumer.

Harappa, potsherd.

Experts believe that this seal may have been used by a merchant from the Indus Valley who was living in Bahrein or Babylon. This seal was found in the Mesopotamian city of Babylon. The seal shows a bull and has a short inscription in the Indus Valley script. However, it is not square like seals from the Indus Valley. It is round with a knob on the back, which is more like seals from the Gulf island of Bahrein which date from about 2000 B.C. Other seals like this were found in the Sumerian city of Ur. A copy of a square, Indus-type seal with a picture of a bull was also found at Ur. However, this seal had an inscription in cuneiform script rather than in the Indus Valley script.

Harappa, seals, sealings and other miscellaneous objects of faience, stone, etc. selected for the Burdin Fine Arts Exhibition

http://www.photocentralasia.com/specialex/specialexphotos06.html

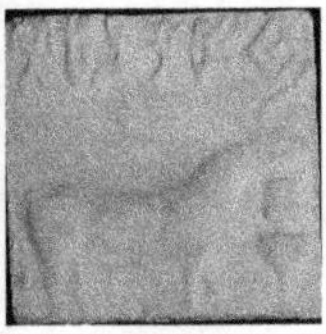

Seal impression. Royal Ontario Museum, Canada (No ROM number)

Unicorn seal ROM 996.74.5 Royal Ontario Museum, Canada

A group of six steatite seals, each with a depiction of an ox before an altar beneath a row of

pictographic symbols; the reverse with a pierced boss.

http://www.asianartresource.co.uk/mall/asianartresourcecouk/products/product-823937.stm

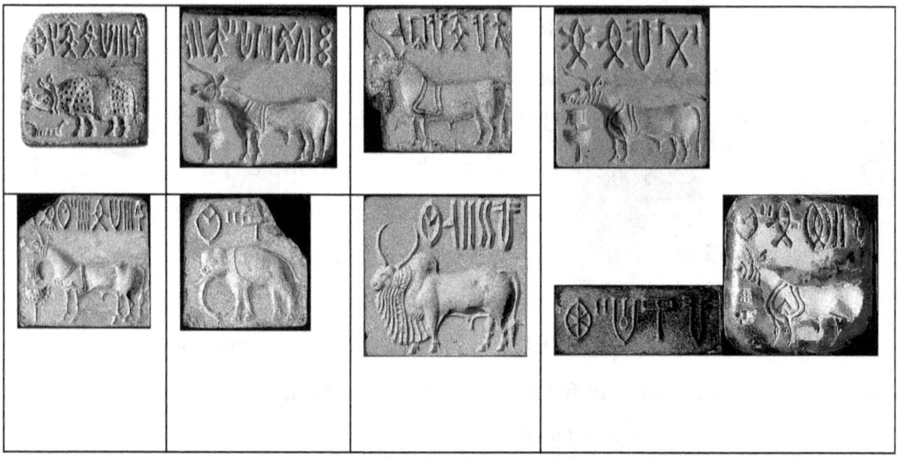

(British Museum1892-12-10, 1) Steatite seals

in the British Museum

Impression of an Akkadian cylinder seal (ca. 2350-2100 BCE) variously interpreted as potting or cheese-making (after Boehmer 1965: no.693). Another interpretation could be that a man is offering a sword to the eagle-person. The three animals following this man could denote some metallurgical objects. The brazier is inscribing a vessel at the top-left.

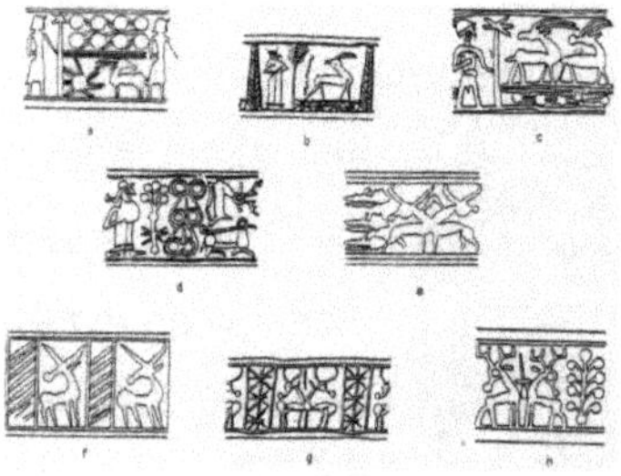

Metal artifacts of the Bronze Age from southern Turkmenia. a,c.d Altin-depe; b Anau; e Ashkhabad; f Daina (After fig. 30 in: V.M. Masson and V.I. Sarianidi, 972, *Central Asia: Turkmenia before the Achaemen**ids*, New York, Praeger Publishers) Lead and arsenic was often added to the bronze. Some objects from Namazga-depe contained as much as 8-0 lead and in one case the artifact was even made of brass (an alloy of copper and zinc). Twin moulds were used for casting; precious metals including gold and silver were also used. There are analogies of metal artifacts in the Harappa assemblages; for example, flag daggers without a midrib which were quite atypical for Hissar, were very widespread both in southern Turkmenia and in the Indus Valley.

Artifacts including golden head of bull. Southern Turkmenia, Margiana, Bactria: 4-7 golden head of bull and seals from Altyn depe (Developed Bronze Age); 8-21 seals and amulets of Bactria and Margiana (After Fig.4 in L.P'yankova, Central Asia in the Bronze Age: sedentary and nomadic cultures, in: *Antiquity* 68 (1994): 355-372).4.4 golden head of a bull with a turquoise sickle inlaid in the forehead; 4.5: steatite plate with an image of cross and half-moon.

Procession of animals. Bronze dish found by Layard at Nimrud: circular objects are decorated by consecutive chains of animals following each other round in a circle. A similar theme occurs on the famous silver vase of Entemena. In the innermost circle, a troop of gazelles (similar to the ones depicted on cylinder seals) march along in file; the middle register has a variety of animals, all marching in the same direction as the gazelles. A one-horned bull, a winged griffin, an ibex and a gazelle, are followed by two bulls who are being attacked by lions, and a griffin, a one-horned bull, and a gazelle, who are all respectively

being attacked by leopards. In the outermost zone there is a stately procession of realistically conceived one-horned bulls marching in the opposite direction to the

animals parading in the two inner circles. The dish has a handle. (Percy S.P.Handcock, 1912, *Mesopotamian Archaeology*, London, Macmillan and Co., p. 256). Cf. pasaramu, pasalamu = quadrupeds (Telugu); rebus: pasra = smithy ! (Santali) Smithy for varieties of minerals and metals, indeed.

"Of lasting significance were attempts to lighten the disk wheels, as first seen on a third-millennium seal from Hissar IIIB (fig.2). On it, the central plank, through which the axle passes, is narrowed to a diametral bar; the flanking planks of the Hissar. Depiction of a wheel on a seal from Hissar IIIB. 3rd millennium BCE (After Figure 2, Littauer and Crouwel, 979). tripartite wheel are eliminated, and the former bonding slats are turned into sturdy transverse bars between the diametral bar and the felloe. This crossbar wheel is also clearly illustrated in the second millennium BCE, fixed on a revolving axle; it has remained in use with simple carts in various parts of the world.

Cylinder seal impressions: (a) Nuzi (D. Stein); (b) Ugarit (Schaeffer-Forrer 1983); (c) Alalakh (Collon 1982); (d) Alalakh (Collon 1982); (e) Nuzi (D. Stein); (f) Nuzi (D.Stein); (g) Ugarit (Schaeffer-Forrer 1983); (h) Alalakh (Collon 1982).The styles are: juxtaposed antelope, humans and trees framed by geometric patters. The styles have prehistoric roots in Mesopotamia and glyphs such as an antelope with its head turned, jointed animal heads are also seen in Harappa inscription motifs.

Tepe Yahya

Grooved lid (exterior and interior). Tepe Yahya. 10.5 cm. wide.

Combatant serpent and eagle vessel from Nippur. Scale = 15 cm.

Plaque from Agrab, Diyala valley.

Humped bull.

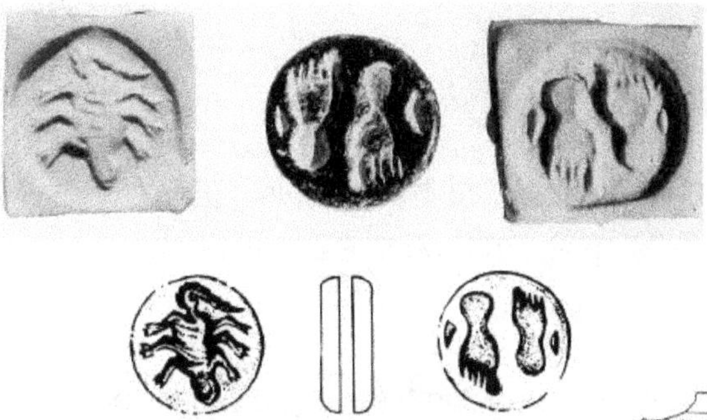

Disk seal (glyptic catalogue no. 58; 15 mm in dia. X 8 mm) Excavations at Tepe yahya, 3rd millennium, p. 154 Double-sided steatite stamp seal with opposing foot prints and six-legged creature on opposite sides.

Stamp seal impression on plain red ware sherd with Harappa inscription

(Fig. 10.63).

Tepe Yahya. Cylinder seal reconstructed from 7 fragments. Two rampant caprids against a stepped platform surmounted by tree with third caprid and four-sided crosses (Fig. 10.27)

Tepe Yahya circular steatite stamp seal with pierced knob and horned caprid and bovid (Fig. 10.55 in: CC Lamberg-Karlovsky and DT Potts, 2001, Excavations at Tepe Yahya, Iran 1967-1975, Peabody Museum of Archaeology and Ethnology, Cambridge, Massachusetts.)

Gulf Type seals

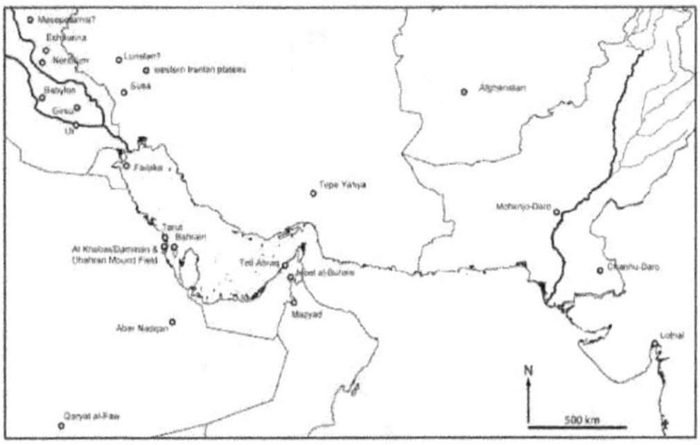

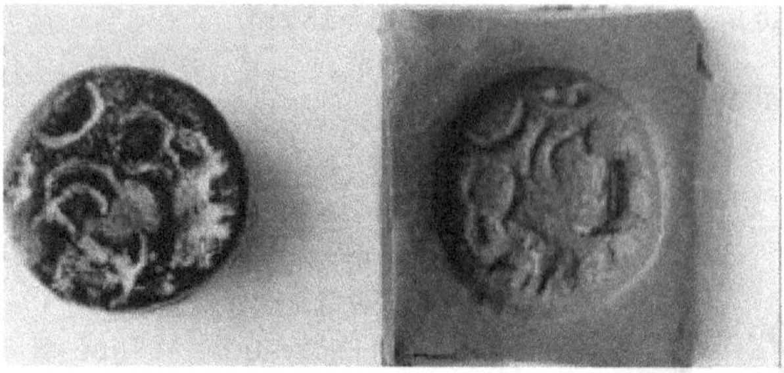

Gulf Type seals come from Bahrain, the Indus Valley (Mohenjo-Daro and Chanhu-Daro), Iran (Kerman, Luristan, Susa and the western Iranian plateau),Kuwait (Failaka), Mesopotamia (Ur, Girsu, Babylon) and the UAE (Tell Abraq).

Gulf seal with bucranium (top center), anthropomorph (left), grid, and scorpion (right), as well as bird (Kjaerum 1983: 37). Kjaerum, Poul. 1983. Failaka / Dilmun, the Second Millennium Settlements, Vol. 1:1, The Stamp and Cylinder Seals. Jutland Archaeological Society Publications XVII:1. Moesgard, Aarhus: Jysk ArkaeologiskSelskab.

(Distribution of Gulf and Dilmun Type seals demonstrates geographical vastness of the underlying network of exchanges. After Fig.13 Steffen Terp Laursen, 2010)

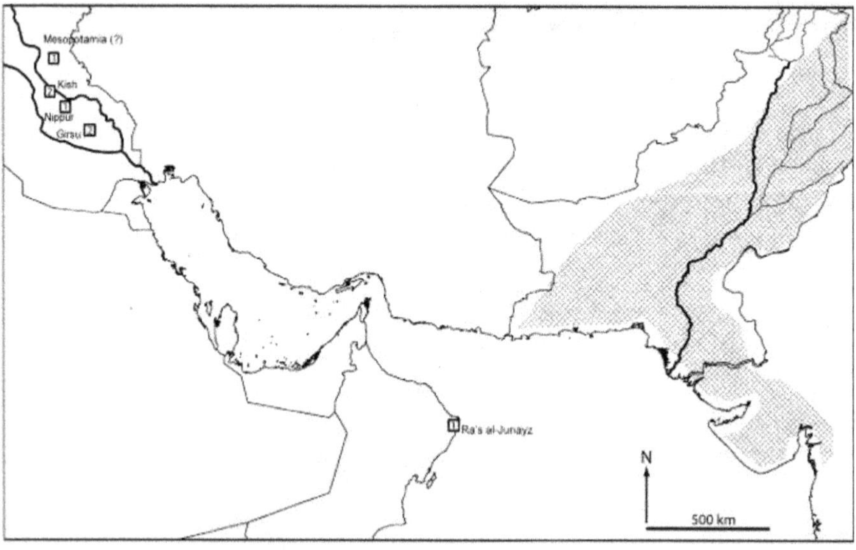

(Classic square Indus selas. Kish (2): Langdon 1931: 593 and Mackay 1925:679; Nippur (1): Gibson 1976: 26-28; Girsu (2): Thureau-Dangin 1925: 99 and Amiet 1988: 195 no. 1; Ra's al-Junayz (1): Cleuziou & Tosi 1988: 12 and 21, fig. 18.1; 1990: 14 and 23, fig. 18; Mesopotamia unspecified (1): Brunswig, Parpola A & Potts 1983: 102-105 no. 1 pl. I/1. After Fig.14 Steffen Terp Laursen, 2010)

104

105

106

107

108

109

110

111

112

113

114

116

(Twelve of the Gulf Type seals previously unpublished. After Fig. 17in Steffen Terp Laursen, 2010)

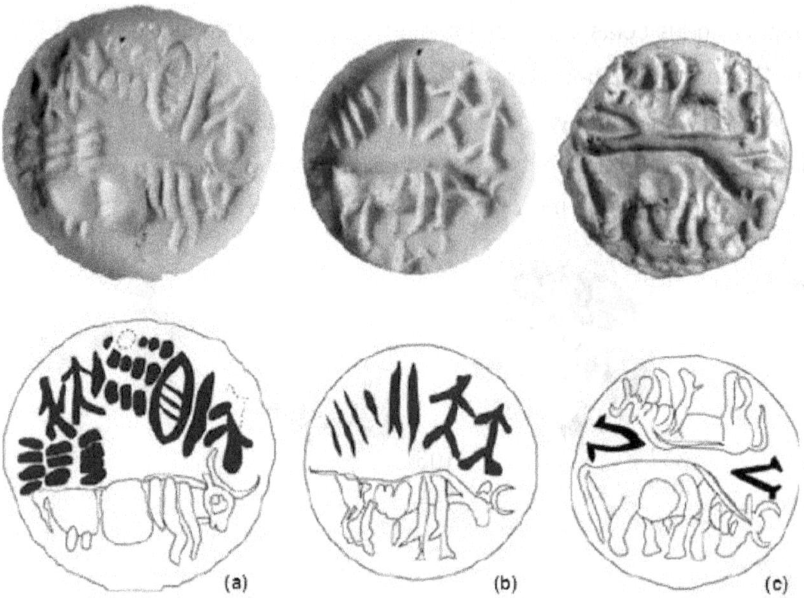

(Impressions and drawings of Gulf Type seals with Indus text and bull motif found in Early Dilmun burial mounds of Bahrain: a. 10; b. 11; c. 56 of Table 1. After Fig. 1 Steffen Terp Laursen, 2010 where 121 seals are analysed.)

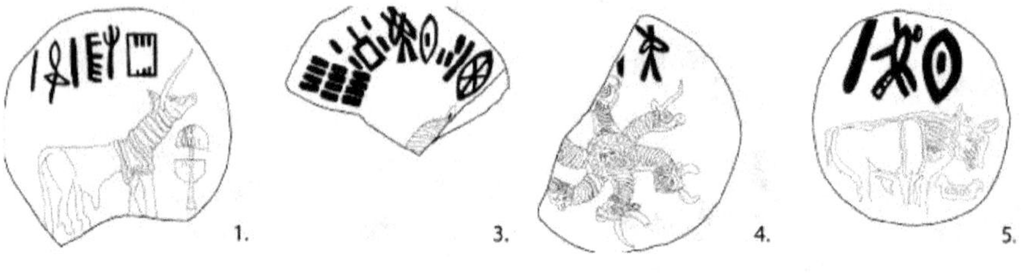

(The lower Indus seals from Mohenjo-Daro and Chanhu-Daro: 1. After Mackay 1943: pl. LI/23; 3. And 4. After Marshall 1931: pl. CXIV/478 and pl. CXII/383, respectively; 5. After Mackay et al. 1937-38: pl. XCVL/500. Impression drawings after Fig. 8 Steffen Terp Laursen, 2010)

(Inscribed seals. 2. After Marshall 1931: pl. CX/309; 16-21, 23 and 24. After Gadd 1932: pl. I/2-5 and pl. III/15-18; 22. After Sarzec & Heuzey 1884-1912: 321-322 and pl. 30.3a-b; 25.Langdon 1932:p.48; 26. After Hallo & Buchanan 1981: no. 1088; 27. After Buchanan 1981: no. 1089; 7. After Kjaerum 1994: fig. 1725; 8. After Srrivastava 1991: fig. 55; 9. After Al-Sindi 1999: no. 182; 56. After Al-Sindi 1999: no.160; 6. After Kjaerum 1994: fig. 1726; 13. After Kjaerum 1983: no.279; 12. After Kjaerum 1983: no. 319; 28. After Winkelmann 1999; Abb.2; 15.

After Amiet 1973: pl. 23a-b; 14. Amiet 1972: pl. 153/1643. Impression drawings After Fig. 10 Steffen Terp Laursen, 2010)

“The innovative group of risk-taking entrepreneurs that were instrumental in transmitting Indus Valley sealing, writing and weight technology into Dilmun culture must at first have been composed of break-away Harappans (c. 2100 BCE), followed by a combination of Dilmunite and accultured Harappans merchants (c. 2050 BCE) attracted by the emerging social elite to the rising centre of trade on Bahrain…with the emergence of the Dilmun Type seal around 2000 BCE the stamp seals became heavily institutionalized, as testified by the standard three groves and four dots-in circle ‘brand’ on the reverse.”(Steffen Terp Laursen, 2010, p.131)

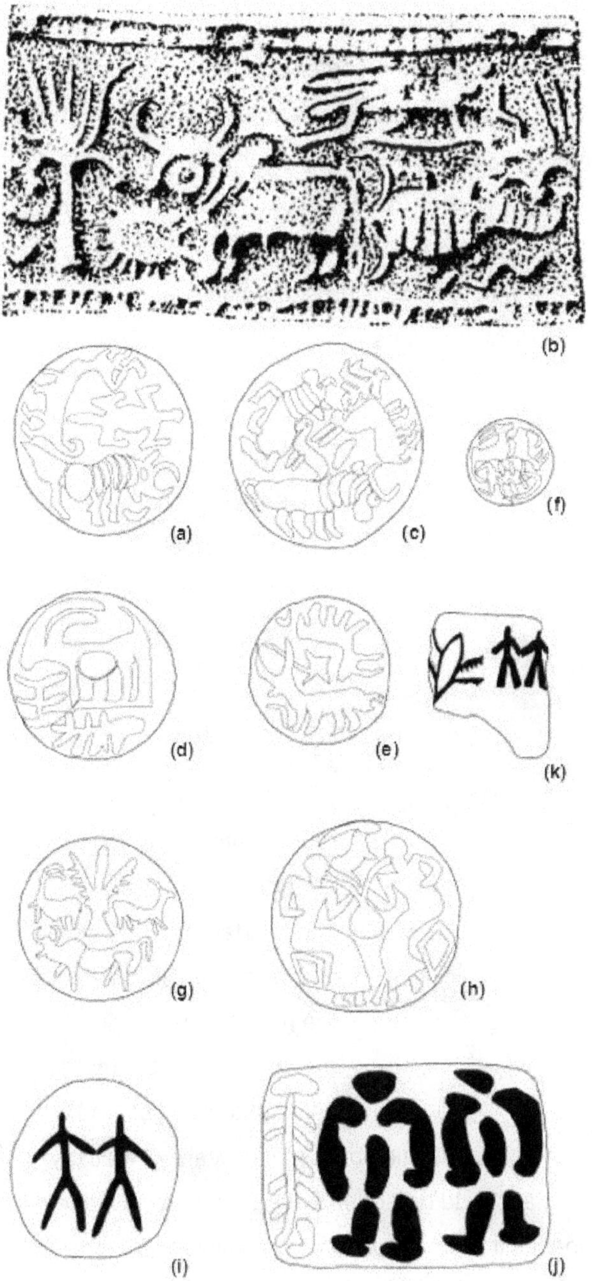

(b. impression drawing of a cylinder seal from Ur with a humped bull and a 'bale of fodder' (Gadd 1932: pl. I/6, courtesy of Gregory L. Possehl; c. an example of a seal with Indus-inscribed bull without inscription; d-f. examples of Gulf Type seals

from Bahrain. D. depicts two palm branches below a quadruped; 3. Depicts two quadrupeds and a pair of crescents while in the center a 'comet' or 'shooting star' can be identified by its long tail; f. depicts a scorpion below a pair of quadrupeds; 9. Mesopotamian styled 'vulture' above a bull in profile; h. 'two men drinking scene'; i. pseudo-'twins' sign, after Cleuziou 2003: fig. 6/2; j. from Ra's al-Jinz RJ-2 with pseudo-'twins' sign, after Cleuziou 2003: fig.6/1; k. fragment of a 'cylinder seal' from Mohenjo-Daro with a 'twins' sign and another 'sign', after Shah&Parpola 1991: 179, M-1370. All drawings After Fig.10 Steffen Terp Laursen, 2010) .

(Inscriptions in Indus and Indus-related characters of Gulf Type seals as seen on the impression. Note abundance of 'twins' signs. After Fig.10 Steffen Terp Laursen, 2010)

"The assumption that these round stamp seals came from an Indus Valley site…was later sustained by Mackay who, with specific reference to the round variant, added: 'it is extremely probable that slight variations distinguished objects of the same type from the different cities of the Indus Valley' (Mackay 1948: 343), thereby, suggesting, as Gadd had done before, that the round form could very sell have been a special trademark of some unexplored Harappa community. "[20] The 'pseudo-twin' glyphs are read rebus: *dul* 'pair + body'; rebus: casting (metal) + iron, that is 'cast iron'.

Seals from Failaka

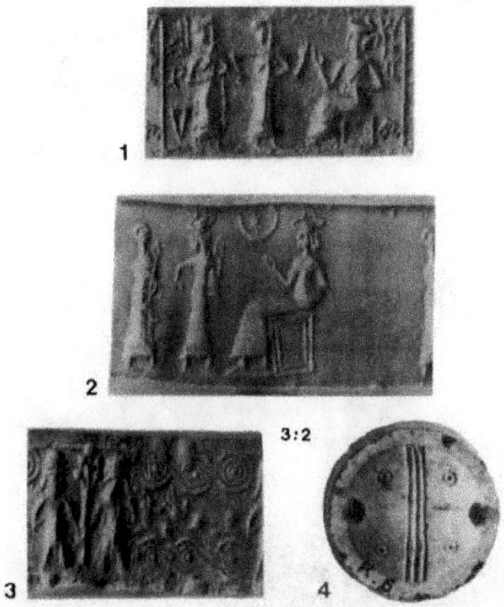

5

7

6

8

10

9a

2:1

11

9b

12

14

15

13

16

2:1

17

18

19

20

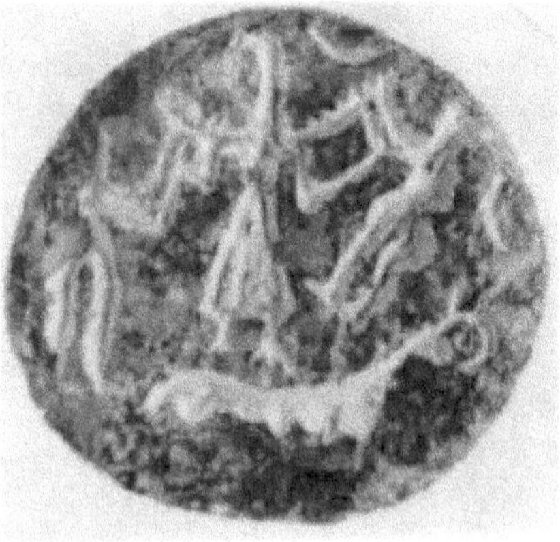

21

22

23

Source: P. Kjaerum, 1980, Seals of 'Dilmun-type' from Failaka, Kuwait, PSAS 10: 45-53.

Mesopotamian trade with Dilmun, Magan and Meluhha

Products imported into Ur from Dilmun Late third and early second millennium BC	Products imported into Ur from Magan *Late third millennium BC*	Products imported into Ur from Meluhha Mid-third to mid-second millennium BC
lapis lazuli	timber and wooden objects	Timber and wooden furniture
cornelian	a type of onion (?)	Copper
semi-precious stones	copper	Gold dust
ivory and ivory objects	ivory	Lapis lazuli
copper	gold dust	Cornelian
silver	cornelian	Birds (including peacock)
'fish-eyes'	semi-precious stones	Multi-coloured ivory birds
red gold	diorite	Cornelian monkey
white corals	red ochre	Red dog
various woods	goats	
dates		
[Except for the dates		

and 'fish-eyes', all the commodities came to Dilmun from elsewhere for onward shipment; cf. Tilmun: Edzard et al., 1977, p. 157-8; Groneberg, 1980: 237).	[Cornelian and ivory were being shipped from further east; copper and diorite were local]. Akkadian kings claimed to have campaigned in Magan and taken boody. (Potts, D., 1986).	(Ratnagar, 1981: 66ff.) Texts refer to it as the land of seafarers.

(P.R.S. Moorey, 1994, Ancient Mesopotamian Materials and Industries, Oxford, Clarendon Press.)

Oman and Bahrain

Harappa control over the Oman Sea

"Oman peninsula/Makkan lies half way between the two main civilization centres of the third millennium Middle East: Mesopotamia and the Indus valley... an increasing influence of Harappa civilization on Eastern Arabia during the last two centuries of the third millennium. This influence seems to strengthen during the early second millennium where proper Harappa objects are found all over the Oman peninsula: a cubic stone weight at Shimal, sherds of Harappa storage jars on several sites including Hili 8 (period III). Maysar and Ra's Al-Junayz bears a Harappa inscription and Tosi (forth.) has emphasized the importance of this discovery for knowledge of Harappa control over the Oman Sea." [Serge Cleuziou, Dilmun and Makkan during the third and early second millennia BC, 143-155 in: Shaikha Haya Ali Al Khalifa and Michael Rice (eds.) *Bahrain through the ages: the archaeology*, London, KPI, 1986.]

An indus seal from the excavation of the salūt early bronze age tower. Location of wādī Salūt, Oman (in relation to indian civilization area).latitude. 23.0444444°, longitude. 57.6472222° a stone seal, to be considered an import from indus valley, has

been found during the last archaeological campaign in Salut.

Reading of the inscription of text:

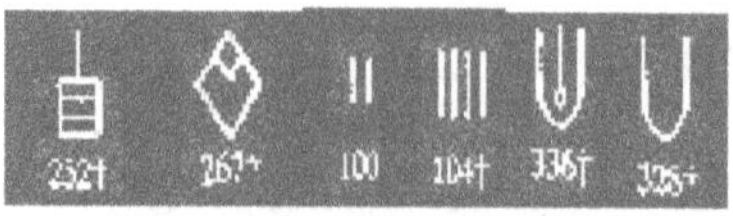

field symbol: ox with a trough (?) in front. this was a stone seal with a perforated boss and was perhaps tied to a trade load from meluhha.

glyphic elements read rebus: blacksmith guild; native metal + tin + turned metalwork from furnace.

ran:ku = liquid measure (Santali) rebus: ran:ku = tin (Santali)
kōnṭa corner (Nk.); tu. kōṇṭu angle, corner (Tu.); rebus: kõdā 'to turn in a lathe' (B.)
dāmṛa, damrā ' young bull (A.)(CDIAL 6184). glyph: *ḍaṅgara1 ' cattle 'rebus: ḍhangar 'blacksmith' (H.)
खांडा [khāṇḍā] *m* a jag, notch, or indentation (as upon the edge of a tool or weapon). khāṇḍā 'tools, pots and pans, metal-ware'.
gaṇḍa 'four' (Santali); rebus: kaṇḍ fire-altar, furnace' (Santali)
ḍabu 'an iron spoon' (Santali)
baṭhu m. 'large pot in which grain is parched, rebus; bhaṭṭhā m. 'kiln' (P.) baṭa = a kind of iron (G.)

Tablet of destiny: *Ancu*, 'iron' (Tocharian) *amśu* (Vedic)

The eagle anzu gets deified in the Ancient Near East.
Cognate ancu, *amśu* (synonym *soma*) gets deified in India.

Contact of Indus language speakers span an expansive area from Muztagh Ata to Altyn depe along the silk road, from Rakhigarhi to Haifa across the Persian Gulf, and are attested by evidences of the eagle and other glyphic narratives. In the mesopotamian epic of Anzu, the eagle steals from Enlil the tablets of destinities, a deed which causes the norms to be suspended and 'all brightness to be poured out.' Anzu flies away with his prize into his far-away mountain. He is vanquished 'cut down with weapons'. There is testimony in writing – on Indus writing glyphs and on mesopotamian cylinder seals -- for this expression of life-experience, which finds echoes in allegories, metaphors and narratives in the oral vedic-avestan traditions of soma-haoma.

Tocharian of Kyrgystan and Muztagh Ata (Mt. Mujavant of Rigveda) provides the semantic link.

Zu as a lion-headed eagle, ca. 2550–2500 bc, Louvre. Zu is also called Anzu and Imdugud (Sumerian). Anzu is explained as An 'heaven' and Zu 'to know' in Sumerian and as son of the bird divinity Siri conceived by the pure waters of the Apsu and the wide earth. "Anzu was a servant of the chief sky god Enlil, guard of the throne in Enlil's sanctuary, (possibly previously a symbol of Anu), from whom Anzu stole the Tablet of Destinies, so hoping to determine the fate of all things. In one version of the legend, the gods sent Lugalbanda to retrieve the tablets who in turn, killed Anzu. In another, Ea and Belet-Ili conceived Ninurta for the purpose of retrieving the tablets. In a third legend, found in The Hymn of Ashurbanipal, Marduk is said to have killed Anzu."[21] A variant of the legend in Akkadian mythology shows Zu as a divine storm-bird and personification of the southern wind and the thunder clouds and as half-bird, half-man, stole the 'Tablets of Destiny' from Enlil and hid them on a mountaintop.

Marduk, sun god of babylon, with his thunderbolts pursues anzu after anzu stole the tablets of destiny (*dup shimati* in Sumerian). The thunderbolts carried by Marduk are comparable to the glyph of Indus writing which is read rebus: *kolmo* 'paddy plant' rebus: *kolami* 'smithy'. This kolami would have processed anzu, ancu 'iron (metal)' to produce soma ! The mountaintop where the tablets of destiny are hidden is likely to be Muztagh Ata where Tocharian was spoken referring to Anzu, Ancu as 'iron'. Dup Shimati is a clay tablet inscribed with cuneiform (and maybe, Indus) writing sometimes impressed with cylinder seals to create a permanent legaldocument. The tablet conferred on god Enlil the title of supreme authority to rule the universe. In the Sumerian poem *Ninurta and the Turtle*[22], the tablet is shown as held by god Enki. The theft of the tablet is by the bird Imdugud (Sumerian) or Anzu (Akkadian).[23]

Anu ordered the gods to retrieve the tablets and one legend says that Marduk killed the bird, while another legend notes that Anzu was killed by the arrows of the divinity Ninurta.

Samuel Kramer[24] consecutively numbers 64 of more than100 *me*s mentioned in the myths. "A ***me*** (sumerian, conventionally pronounced [mɛ]) or ***ñe*** [ŋɛ] or ***parşu*** (Akkadian,[parsˤu]) is one of the decrees of the gods foundational to those social institutions, religious practices,technologies, behaviors, mores, and human conditions that make civilization...They are fundamental to the Sumerian understanding of the relationship between humanity and the gods. The *me*s were originally collected by Enlil and then handed over to the guardianship of Enki who was to broker them out to the various Sumerian centers beginning with his own city of Eridu and continuing with Ur, Meluhha, and Dilmun. This is described in the poem, "Enki and the world order" which also details how he parcels out responsibility for various crafts and natural phenomena to the lesser gods."[25] Inanna triumphantly delivers them to Uruk. Four items are missing between 'art

of metalworking' (numbered 42) and 'scribeship' (numbered 43) on the fragmentary tablets. After arriving in her boat, Inanna is able to display them to the people of Uruk. Some are indeed physical objects like musical instruments but include technologies like 'basket weaving' or abstractions like 'victory'. Now we know how, in Indus writing, many physical objects like musical instruments were hieroglyphic representations of the artisans' repertoire. Alongside functions such as 'heroship' and 'victory' are 'the destruction of cities', 'falsehood', 'enmity' which though evil are an inevitable part of humanity, divinely decreed.

1. Art of metalworking (42)
2. Scribeship (43)
3. Craft of the smith
4. Craft of the leatherworker
5. Craft of the builder
6. Craft of the basket weaver

Maybe, some day, the Tablet of Destiny will be discovered from Muztagh Ata, to unravel the mystery of soma processing elaborated in one of the oldest human documents: the Rigveda. A beautiful depiction of a falcon in flight (*śyena*) occurs In vedic tradition,[26] steps for constructing the falcon-shaped vedi (sacred fire-altar) are elaborated in a text.

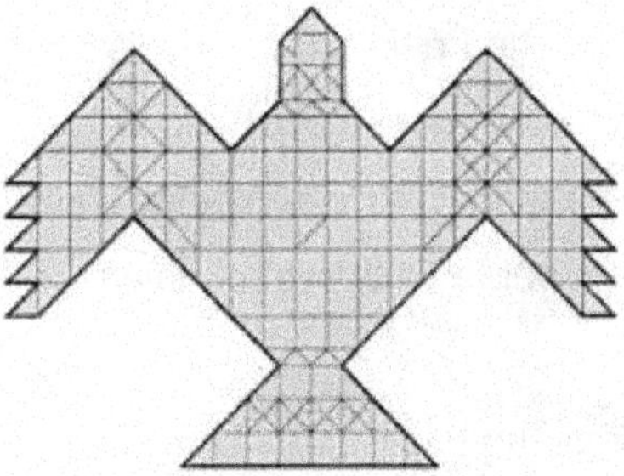

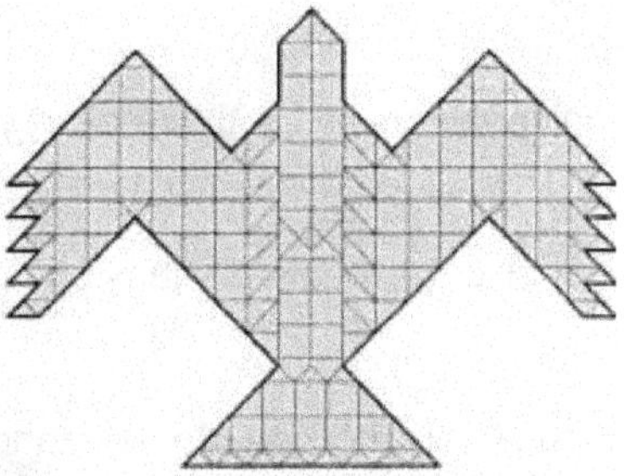

Śyena citi: layers 1,3, and 5; layers 2 and 4 of complex brick platforms. One verse connects the construction of citi to consciousness, revealing that after constructing a citi for the third time, a chandaŚciti is constructed. Chandas are mantras, sounds of the Veda, structures of pure knowledge. One interpretation is that the fourth and later constructions are carried out in consciousness, mantras

replacing the bricks used in the construction of citi-s.[27] "The Zoroastrian innovations did not change the basic vedic character of the culture in iran." śyena of

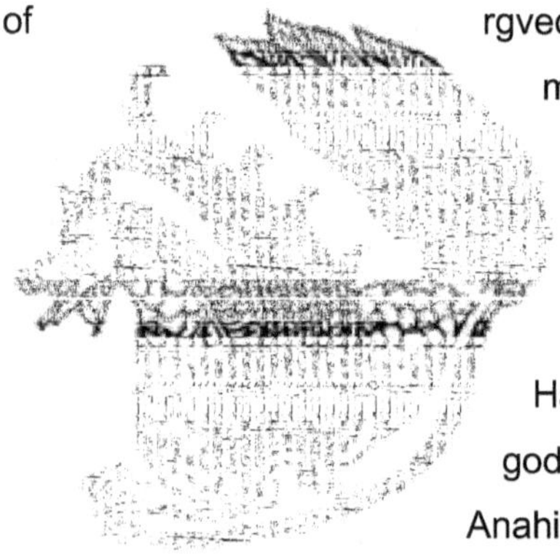

rgveda gets exemplified in ancient Iranian glyphics matching the cultural traditions. Common cultural concepts include: saena (syena): the eagle; also saena meregh (mr.ga), simurg.[28]

"Ahura Mazda, the god who created High Hara, also built palaces on it for the greatest gods: Mithra, Sraosha, Rashnu, Ardvi-sura Anahita, and Haoma, all of whom ride in special chariots. While humans could not live on the holy mountain, the greatest mythical heroes made sacrifices there. The way to the other world, a special abode of the blessed (where the largest and most choice specimens of plants and animals were found) lay through the foothills of Hara/Meru. The Chinvat bridge of Zoroastrian mythology, over which the souls of the dead had to pass was on or near High Hara. The motif of birds dwelling near the summit is shared by Iranian and Indian accounts, as is the theme of the theft of the intoxicating plant haoma/soma from the mountain's summit by a magical bird (Syena/Garuda/Simurgh); and the slaying of a multi-headed, multi-eyed dragon nearby. In the Indian tradition, Agni, the rock-born god of fire with tawny hair and iron teeth is connected with the sacred mountain. In the Iranian tradition, High Hara is also associated with metallurgy. Fire and metals were introduced to humanity after the hero Hoshang(Haoshyangha) sacrificed on the mountain. High Hara was also the locale of many of the most memorable contests in Iranian mythology."[29]

"Sênmurw (Pahlavi), Sîna-Mrû (Pâzand), a fabulous, mythical bird. The name derives from Avestan mərəγô saênô 'the bird Saêna', originally a raptor, either eagle or falcon, as can be deduced from the etymologically identical Sanskrit śyena."[30]

Lapis lazuli square stamp seal with hieroglyphs of Indus writing. Behind the man are a long-horned goat above a zebu.[31]

kandhi 'lump, piece' (Santali) Rebus: kand 'stone (ore)'

ḍumgara 'mountain' (Pkt.)(CDIAL 5423). Rebus: damgar 'merchant'.

meḍho 'ram' (G.) Rebus: 'iron' (Ho.)

ḍhol 'drum' (Gujarati.Marathi)(CDIAL 5608) Rebus: large stone; dul 'to cast in a mould'

khut ‘zebu’ (Gujarati) Rebus: kote ‘forged’ (Santali)

Ved. *amśu-* as a borrowed word from Tocharian had the cognate semantics 'metal', while **añcu-*(Tocharian) meant 'iron'. And, in the poetic metaphors which are abundant in Vedic copora, the characterisics of *soma-*as 'metal' processed in yajña, are elaborated by the *kavi-* 'smiths'. The key is in the proto-indic lexeme: kavi, semant. ‘smith, poet'. Cognate, *kayanian.*[32]

Meaning of the word, amśu used by Valmiki

Valmiki's description of how sun's rays heat the icy water of Himalaya, results in an extraordinary metaphor – related to minerals -- of ‘a great mountain of sorrow, with its deep gorge of brooding, its minerals of heaving sighs, thickets of desolation, numberless creatures of delirium, plants and rushes of misery, and peaks of grief, care and woe.’

अंशु [Monier-Williams lexicon, p. 1,1] [L=47] m. a filament (especially of the सोम plant), a kind of सोम libation S3Br., thread, end of a thread , a minute particle, a point , end, a ray , sunbeam. Cf. अग्रांशु [agrāṃśu] m S The extremity of a ray of light; the focal point. अंशुजाल [aṃśujāla] n S A collection of (sun-) beams, a pencil of rays. (Marathi). अंशुमत् aṃśumat अंशुमत् a. [अंशु-अस्त्यर्थे मतुप्] 1 Luminous, radiant; ज्योतिषां रविरंशुमान् Bg.1.21. -2 Pointed. -3 Fibrous, abounding in filaments (Ved.) -m. (˚मान्)1 The sun. aṁśú m. ‘ filament esp. of soma -- plant ’ RV., ‘ thread, minute particle, ray ’.Pa. aṁsu -- m. ‘ thread ’; Pk. aṁsu -- m. ‘ sunbeam ’; A. ãh ‘ fibre of a plant ’, OB. ãsu; B. ãs ‘ fibre of tree or stringy fruit, nap of cloth ’; Or. ãsu ‘ fibrous layer at root of coconut branches, edge or prickles of leaves ’, ãs f. ‘ fibre, pith ’; -- with -- i -- in place of -- u -- : B. ãiś ‘ fibre ’; M. ãsī̃ n. ‘ fine particles of flattened rice in winnowing fan ’; A. ãhiyā ‘ fibrous ’. (CDIAL 4) aṁśuka ‘ *fibrous ’, n. ‘ cloth, garment ’ lex. [aṁśú --] Pk. aṁsuya -- n. ‘ cloth ’; A. ãhu ‘

coloured thread '; B. ãsuyā ' fibrous, stringy ', Or. ãsuā. (CDIAL 5) áṁsya of Rigveda may refer to a metallic scythe (sickle), cognate with Ku. ãsī ' scythe '. Aŋsa [see next] point, corner, edge; freq. in combn with numerals, e. g. catur° four -- cornered, chaḷ°, aṭṭh°, soḷas° etc. (q. v.) all at Dhs 617 (cp. DhsA 317). Aŋsu [cp. Sk. aŋśu (Halāyudha) a ray of light] a thread Vin iii.224. -- mālin, sun Sāsv 1. (Pali) அம்சபூதன் amca-pūtaṉ, n. < aṃša- bhūta. One who forms part, as of a deity; அமிசமாயிருப்பவன். நம்முடைய அம்சபூத ரொருவரை (குருபரம். 166).(Tamil) அமிசை amicai, n. < aṃša. Lot; தலை யெழுத்து (destiny). ஆசை யிருக்கிறது தாசில்பண்ண, அமிசை யிருக்கிறது கழுதை மேய்க்க. Semantics of अंशुकं help identify अंशु which is a 'clothing or cover' to 'soma'. When the rṣi-s employ the poetic metaphors in the vedic allegory related to soma, the reference to अंशु is an enveloping mineral compound - 'iron' element called अंशु covering the core dhātu – soma, 'electrum'. Radiance of the 'sun' in the phrase used by Valmiki, suryāmśu samtaptah can be explained as the heating by radiant mineral अंशु In a poetic exposition, Valmiki uses the term amśu to describe the sun's heat: suryāmśu samtaptah ('heated by sunbeam') and vinihśvasita dhātunā ('minerals in the shape of groans and sighs'). In the context of the poet's metaphor, the word amśu cannot be explained as related to part of a plant (e.g. 'stalk').

The semantic component of 'clothing or cover' and Marathi compound: अंशुजाल [aṃśujāla] is consistent with the garuḍa narrative of breaking the ayah jālāni 'iron-grid or iron-net' shield of a metamorphic mineral compound, to get to the ambrosia, amṛtam -- soma.

Electrum is a natural alloy of gold with at least 20 percent silver and contains also copper, iron, palladium, bismuth and perhaps other metals. 'The colour varies from white-gold to brassy, depending on the percentages of the major constituents and copper.' (Encyclopaedia Britannica).

Greek word ἤλεκτρον (elektron) mentioned in the Odyssey meaning a metallic substance consisting of gold alloyed with silver. The same word was also used for the substance amber, probably because of the pale yellow color of certain

varieties, and it is from the electrostatic properties of amber that the modern English words "electron" and "electricity" derive. Electrum was often referred to as white gold in ancient times but could be more accurately described as "pale gold".

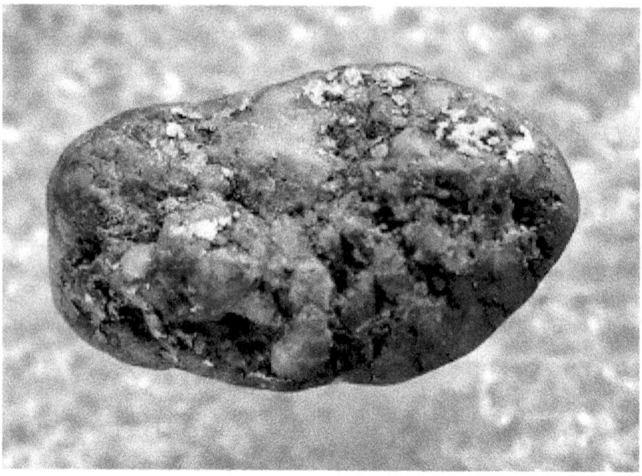

Manhattan, Manhattan District, Nye Co., Nevada, USA. 1.8 x 0.7 x 0.6 cm. Electrum is a rare natural amalgam of gold and silver (sometimes with trace amounts of copper and other minerals as well). This smooth, water-worn nugget is from Nevada. It weighs about 7.5 cts. Ex. Carl Davis Coll.

Electrum was used as early as the third millennium BC in Old Kingdom Egypt. In the Babylonian Talmud (+2nd cent.), asemon is a commonly used word referring to bullion (gold, silver of mixed). Leiden X papyrus (c. +3rd cent.) says: "no.8. It will be asem, (i.e. electrum, an alloy of gold and silver) which will deceive even the artisans (a tin-copper-gold-silver alloy); no. 1. Falsification of gold (a zinc-copper-lead-gold alloy)…"[33] Hopkins states: "The existence of this alloy (asse*m) may have been the original cause for the suggestion of transmutation since by adding silver to it, one would get a metal nearly identical with the crude silver from the mine; and by adding gold, something indistinguishable from gold. [The paucity of the Egyptian language may perhaps have been responsible for a confusion. Gold was 'the yellow metal', and the alloy produced was also a 'yellow metal'.]"[34] Metals were not fully distinguished from their alloys; all carried names such as aes, electrum etc. Ayas meant metal. Asem denoted the natural alloy of silver and gold; it also meant any bright metal made with copper, tin, lead, zinc, arsenic and mercury. Twelve or thirteen different alloys were called asem…[35]

"*ancu- is admitted by Lubotsky (2001: 304, 310) as meaning 'Soma plant', being the substratum source of Ved. ams'u- 'Soma plant' and Late Av. asu- 'Haoma plant'...This claim presupposes that the Soma/Haoma cult had been borrowed from the BMAC culture together with the name of the plant...A very useful discussion of the whole problem, with abundant bibliography, has been provided by Houben (2003), in his report of the conference held at Leiden University in July 1999..."[36]

"...The contrast between Soma as god and ams'u- as material unit is clear from the following mantra (TS 1.2.11a, etc. quoted in SB 3.4.3.19) *ams'ur-ams'us te deva somaapyaayataam indraayaikadhanavide* 'Let stalk after stlk of thine swell strong, O divine Soma, for Indra, the winner of one part of the booty!'. It is true that in Vedic literature ams'u- refers only to the twigs of the Soma plant and not of any other plant, but it is only to be expected, given the prestige of the hymns, where the word was used in hieratic language for the whole Soma plant: in this poetic usage, it can be explained by a commonplace metonymy, and by the pressure to give many names to Soma. Therefore, I shall assume that **ancu-* originally referred to the 'twig' or 'stalk', as a special term given to the 'body' of the holy plant, which was the most important part for ritual purposes. There exists in Tocharian no word of similar form referring to a plant or part of a plant. From the Tocharian vocabularies,we have Toch. A. **ancu* 'iron', the basis of the derived adjective ancwaashi 'made of iron', to which corresponds Toch. B *encuwo*, with the parallel derived adjective encuwanne 'made of iron'...The two forms go back to CToch. *oencuwoen-* non.sg. **oencuwo*, the final part of which is a regular product of IE *-on. Nasal enlargement (from: IE *-on-) of nominal stems is very common in Tocharian. This noun is deprived of any convincing IE etymology (cf. Adams 1999:80), which is not surprising, since IE did not have a common word for 'iron'. The connection with an Iranian form *as'wanya- according to Bailey (1957: 55-56), which does not fit in with the first cluster, was later abandoned (Bailey, Harold W., 1979, Dictionary of Khotan Saka. Cambridge: Cambridge University Press, pp. 32, 487). The CToch. form may reflect a term proper to the Central Asiatic region, cf. Chorasmian hnc'w 'iron'

('iron tip', see Benzing 1983: 319) < Iranian *anśuwan- (Schwartz, Martin, 1974. Irano-Tocharica. In: Philippe Gignoux & Tafazzoli (eds.), Memorial Jean de Menasce. Louvain: Imprimerie Orientaliste. p. 409): the formal shape is extremely close to the CToch. transposition, so that the Iranian and Tocharian words may have been borrowed from a common substratum language. The problem now becomes: if the original meaning of *ancu had been 'sacred plant', or the like, it would become impossible to explain the meaning of the CToch. loan-word. A simple solution to this dilemma is near at hand. Metals are not named from designations of plants, but they are often named after the colour, see for instance Ved. hiraNya- and suvarNa- 'gold', rajata- 'silver', lohita- or loha- 'copper', etc. (Rau, Wilhelm, 1974, Metalle und Metallgerate im vedischen Indien. Mainz. Akademie der Wissenschaften und der Literatur. Abhandlungen der Geistes- und Sozialwissenschaftlichen Klasse, Jg. 1973, Nr.8. Wiesbaden: Steiner, pp. 18-24). A secondary differentiation (from AV onwards) was also provided by colour adjectives, cf. lohitam ayah 'reddish metal' (for 'copper') vs. s'yaamam ayah 'dark metal' (for 'iron'). The primitive system opposed Ved. ayas- (Av. aiiah-) 'metal of utility' to hiraNya- 'noble metal': the former term originally referred to 'copper', later to 'iron'. I recall that the prominent colour of iron ore is rusty red, reddish-brown. Besides Toch. B eñcuwo (A *añcu), we know several names of metals in Tocharian: B yasa (A was) 'gold', B ñakante (A nkiñc) 'silver', B pilke 'copper', B lant* (adj. lantaṣṣe) 'lead'. Interestingly enough, the name of copper is obviously derived from the root palk- 'to shine': it originally meant 'shining like fire, gleaming', as corresponding to loha-, lohita-, which referred to copper for its red colour. It would be likely that the name of iron be derived from another colour, that is 'rusty (brown)'. Compare the designations of the colours in Tocharian: B ratre A rtar 'red', B tute 'yellow', AB tsem 'blue', B motartstse 'green', B erkent- A arkant- 'black', B kwele 'grey'. Going back to Vedic, we may assume that the borrowed word *ancu- referred to the characteristic colour of the twig or stalk of the sacred plant. The soma plant is qualified and also designated by various colour adjectives: hari-, aruṣa-, aruṇa-, babhru-. The terms hari- (cf. Av. zairi-) 'yellow, fawn' to 'green'...(p.187) "...It is all the more interesting to find an isolated reference to foreign (non-Aryan) people who also practise the Soma cult,

while using amśu-: RV VIII.53.4c (Vālakhilya hymn) śiṣṭeṣu cit te madirāso amśavah 'Among the ś. also the exciting (Soma) plants belong to you (Indra)'. The form śiṣṭa- with variants śīṣṭra-, śīrṣṭra- testifies to a non-Aryan name with 'intrusive -r-' (Kuiper 1991: 7,70). It would be one of the last echoes of the widespread practice of the cult of the sacred plant in Central Asia. To summarize my present contribution to the Soma/Haoma problem, I should like to point out the most important provisory results: (i) The term Ved. amśu-, Av. asu- goes back to a noun borrowed from some donor language of Central Asia, as confirmed by CToch. *oeñcuwoen-. (ii) Since the original meaning referred to the colour of the marrow, that is the internal part of the twigs of the plant, one may wonder whether the designation of the heart of the plant as 'the rusty red one' had already been coined by the ritualists of the donor language, or whether this denomination was conceived by the speakers of Indo-Iranian, in order to possess a supplementary secret term to designate this holy substance. The last interpretation is admittedly tentative, because it concerns one of the most discussed issues of Indo-Iranian studies, and it will certainly be refined and tested according to other parameters. I should point out that this example is not fundamentally different from others which have been discussed previously. Once it is admitted that Ved. amśu-, Av. asu- are of foreign origin, it is legitimate to look for the most similar form in other languages of Central Asia. Since one finds a corresponding noun of very close, almost identical, formal shape, but with a very different meaning, referring to 'iron', there are two possible strategies...The term Ved. *ams'u-*, Av . *asu-* goes back to a noun borrowed from some donor language of Central Asia, as confirmed by CToch. **oencuwoen-*...the BMAC language would not belong to the Indo-European family; it does not seem to be related to Dravidian either...New identifications and reconstructions will certainly help to define more precisely the contours of the BMAC vocabulary in Indo-Iranian, as well as in Tocharian."[37]

Following this insightful analysis of the Ved. amśu- cognate Toch. añcu- there is a simple strategy to deal with Ved.*soma-* as a material related to the borrowed word: *añcu-*'iron'...As the following are lexemes from Indian linguistic area attest,

Ved. *soma-* might have referred to a metallic ore from the Mount Mujavant:

சோமமணல், s. Sand containing silver, வெள்ளிமணல். (R.)சோமனுப்பு, s. Rock-salt, as இந்துப்பு.(Winslow dictionary)

samanom = an obsolete word for gold (Santali. Campbell lexicon)

sambr.o bica = gold ore (Mundarica)

hom = gold (Kannada)

somnakay = gold (Gypsy)

assem, s'm, asemon = electrum (Old Egyptian. cf. Joseph Needham)

soma man.al = sand containing silver ore (Tamil. Winslow lexicon)

Soma was a metallic ore, a compound of silver and gold called by metallurgists as: electrum. Thus, for Rgvedic kavi, description of soma in metaphoric terms comparing it to a plant should not be treated literally as a reference to a 'plant'. The reference could as well have been to a metallic ore subjected to refining process of smelting in fire which could raise upto 1500 degrees C in a yajna -- agnishthoma, for example -- which lasted continuously for 5 days and 5 nights.[38]

Expiatory prayers in Indian tradition apologize to the divinities for the use of a substitute plant (somalataa, e.g. the pūtīka --*Guilandina Bonduc*?) because Soma had become unavailable. Texts provide an extensive list of plants that can be used as substitutes and end the list by saying that any plant is acceptable, provided it is yellow.[39] Tandya Mahabrahmana 9.5.1-3 suggests the use of putika -- *basella cordifolia*? -- as a substitute for Soma. Other substitutes (e.g. Satapatha Brahmana 4.5.10; 5.3.3; 6.6.3) mentioned in many Brahmana texts were praprotha, adara, usana and prsniparni (122). Prsniparni had speckled

leaves and its wood was used to protect from the negative effects caused by evil spirits. ApSS 14.24,13 suggests the use of rice and barley as substitutes for Soma.

Jaiminiya Brahmana notes that "if they do not find Soma...they should press out Phalguna plants with tawny panicles. Indra killed Vrtra with the Vajra. The Soma which flowed out of his nose, became these Phalguna plants with tawny panicles. And what was produced on account of the drawing out of the omentum, that became Phalguna plants with red panicles. Therefore they press out Phalguna plants with tawny panicles, since these are more suitable to be used in a sacrifice. They say: 'This (pseudo-Soma) belongs to the Asuras, therefore it should not be pressed out (for a Soma sacrifice)'. (The answer should be:) 'In the beginning all here was with the Asuras. The gods placed this with themselves after their victory. Therefore it should be used for the Soma presing.' If they should not find this (substitute), they should press out Utika plants. Indra having thrown the Vajra at Vrtra but thinking 'I have not slain him' entered the Utika plants. Someone whose Soma they steal loses his help (Uti). They find help for him (in the form of the Utika). When the head of the sacrifice was cut off, the sap which streamed forth out of it became the Utika plants. Therefore also they obviously press out sacrifice itself in the form of these Utika plants. If they should not find this---355. -- they should press out light-coloured grass. When king Soma came to this world, then he stayed in the grasses. This is a trace of him. Thus they press him out (when they press out the grasses). If they should not find this, they should press out the Parna. When Suparna fetched king Soma, then the feather which fell down became the Parna (leaf). That is his trace. Thus they press him out (when they press out the Parna). If they should not find this, they may press out whatever plants there are. When Suparna fetched king Soma and broke him, then the drops which fell down, became these plants. And all plants are related to Soma. That is this trace of him. Him they thereby press out. At the morning pressing one should pour fresh milk, at the midday pressing boiled milk and at the third pressing coagulated milk to (these substitutes of Soma). It is

obvious that they also consume this Soma, when they consume milk, for that is the sap of all the plants."[40]

The sons of Kadru Nagas, the son of Vinata, the Gandharvas, the lords of the creation, and the seven great Rishis, viz, Bharadwaja, Kasyapa, Gautama, Viswamitra, Jamadagni, Vasishtha, and the illustrious Atri who illumined the world of old when the Sun was lost, all came there (Kadru's naga yajna). (MBh.1.123.6648)

Kadru told Suparni 'Verily I have won thine own self. Yonder is Soma in the heaven' she said. 'Fetch him hither for the gods and thereby redeem thyself from death'. 'So be it' (said) Suparni and created the meters. Speech indeed, is Suparni and from vaak (speech) the metre are born. From among them (the meters) Gayatri fetched soma. That soma was concealed in two golden vessels. These (vessels) were having their sharp-edged (lids) closing together at every moment (at every twinkling of the eye). These two foresooth are consecration (diksha) and penance (tapas). Him (Soma) these Gandharvas guarded. They are these hearths (dhishnyas), these Hotrs (fire-priests). The Gayatri tore off one of the two vessels and brought it. Thus was consecration (Dikshaa). By that, the gods consecrated themselves. Again she took off (to the heaven) and tore off the other vessel and brought it. That was penance (tapas). Therewith the gods underwent penance. They are 'the Upasadas'. Again she flew (to heaven). She took (consumed) soma by means of a Khadira-wood-(piece). Since she ate (achakaad) with it, it is named Khadira. Hence the yupa (sacrificial stake) is of Khadira wood. So too the wooden sword (sphya) (is of Khadira wood). She took it (soma) away when the Acchāvāka was protecting it. That is why Acchāvāka fell from grace.[41]

"Like the Revelation (śruti) itself, we must begin with the Myth (Itihāsa), the penultimate truth, of which all experience is the temporal reflection. The mythical narrative is of timeless and placeless validity, true nowever and everywhere: just as in Christianity, 'In the beginning God created' and 'Through him all things were made,' regardless of the millennia that come between the datable words, amount

to saying that the creation took place at Christ's 'eternal birth.' 'In the beginning' (agre), or rather 'at the summit,' means 'in the first cause': as as in our still told myths, 'once upon a time' does not mean 'once' alone, but once for all.' 'The Myth is not a "poetic invention" in the sense these words now bear; on the other hand, and just because of its universality, it can be told, and with equal authority, from many differnet points of view...It is in the marvels themselves that the truth inheres. 'There is no other origin of philosophy than wonder, ' Plato, Theatetus 1556. And in the same way Aristotle who adds 'therefore even a lover of fables is in a way a lover of wisdom, for fables are compounded of wonder' (Metaphysics 982B). Myth embodies the nearest approach to absolute truth that can be stated in words."[42]

Excavated site - Purola, Uttarakashi district Uttarakhand province; Geo-Coordinates-Lat. 30° 52'54" N Long. 77° 05'33" E

"The ancient site at Purola is located on the left bank of the river Kamal. The excavation yielded the remains of Painted Grey Ware (PGW) from the earliest level alongwith other associated materials including terracotta figurines, beads, potter-stamp, the dental and femur portions of domesticated horse (equus caballus linn). The most important finds from the site is a brick alter identified as syenachiti by the excavator. The structure is in the shape of a flying eagle (garuda), head facing east with outstretched wings. In the center of the structure is the chiti is a square chamber yielding remains of pottery assignable to circa first century BCE to second century CE. In addition, copper coin of Kuninda and other material i.e. ash, bone pieces etc and a thin gold leaf impressed with a human figure, tentatively identified as agni have also been recovered from the central chamber."[43] Ptolemy[44] locates Kulindrine in the mountainous region around

sources of Vipasha (Beas) and Shatadru (Sutlej), Yamuna and Ganga rivers. Manu recognizes Kulinda as vratya kshatriya.[45] Kuninda coins of copper, silver and bronze are found mostly in the Himalayan foothills between the rivers Sutlej and Yamuna.

Silver coin of the Kuninda kingdom, c. 1st century BCE.
Obv: deer standing right, crowned by two cobras, attended by lakshmi holding a lotus flower. Legend in Prakrit (brahmi script, from left to right): rajnah kunindasya amoghabhutisya maharajasya ("great king amoghabhuti, of the kunindas").
Rev: stupa surmounted by the buddhist symbol triratna, and surrounded by a swastika, a "y" symbol, and a tree in railing. Legend in kharoshti script, from righ to left: rana kunidasa amoghabhutisa maharajasa, ("great king amoghabhuti, of the kunindas"). Nb: note the svastika, tree and mountain glyphs; these are indus script hieroglyphs on the coin, attesting to the survival of the writing system in metallurgical contexts -- in this case, in the context of a mint.

Harosheth, kharoṣṭī

Kuninda copper coin. Alternative rebus readings are considered to explain the 'meaning' of varieties of antelope hieroglyphs in an archaeological and trade contexts of interaction areas of the Near East and Meluhha (commonly identified with the areas of speakers who employed Indus script). The conclusion is that antelope hieroglyphs denoted mineral (metal ore) worked on by artisans and also denoted a merchant or a

helper of a merchant. An example of antelope device on Kuninda coin with Indian hieroglyphs, kharoṣṭī brāhmī syllables is instructive to evidence the continuity of the Indus writing tradition.

Together with these syllables, other Indian hieroglyphs were used such as a woman (1. *kola*), svastika (2. *satthiya*), mountain-summit (3. *kōṭu*), tree (4. *kuṭi*), portable furnace (5. *sangada*), hole (6. *kōḍ* कोड् m. a kernel (Kashmiri). This is instructive to evidence the continuity of the Indus writing tradition. The hieroglyphs conveyed information on minerals/metal work: 1. kol 'furnace, forge' (Kuwi), *kol* working in iron, blacksmith (Tamil); 2. satthiya 'zinc', jasta 'zinc' (Kashmiri), satva, 'zinc' (Pkt.); 3. खोट [*khōṭa*] *f* 'A mass of metal (unwrought or of old metal melted down); an ingot or wedge' (Kashmiri); *khoṭā* ' alloyed' (Marathi) 4. *kuṭi* 'smelter furnace'; 5. *sangada* 'guild' ; 6. *khóṛnõ* 'to dig, scratch, engrave' (Western Pahari). This is an Indus Writing catalog of the professional competence of the mint which issued the coin.

There are intimations, as in Kanmer seals, of markings which may have been precursors of kharoṣṭhī/brāhmī syllabic scripts. From ca. 3rd century BCE, birch-bark manuscripts have been found in kharoṣṭhī script and also cast/punch-marked coins inscribing hieroglyphs combined with kharoṣṭhī/brāhmī syllabic scripts (used only to denote names, titles).

kharoṣṭī 'blacksmith lip, carving' and harosheth 'smithy' Suniti Kumar Chatterjee suggested that kharōṣṭī may be cognate with harosheth in: harosheth hagoyim 'smithy of nations'. Etymology of harosheth is variously elucidated, while it is linked to 'chariot-making in a smithy of nations'.

Harosheth Hebrew: חרשת הגויים; is pronounced khar-o-sheth? Most likely, (haroshet) a noun meaning a carving. Hence, kharoṣṭī came to represent a 'carving, engraving' art, i.e. a writing system. Harosheth-hagoyim See: Haroshet [Carving]; a forest; agriculture; workmanship;Harsha [Artifice: deviser: secret work]; workmanship; a wood http://tinyurl.com/d7be2qh Cognate with haroshet:

karṣá m. ' dragging ' Pāṇ., ' agriculture ' Āp.(CDIAL 2905).karṣaṇa n. ' tugging, ploughing, hurting ' Mn., ' cultivated land ' MBh. [kárṣati, √kr̥ṣ] Pk. karisaṇa -- n. ' pulling, ploughing '; G. karsaṇ n. ' cultivation, ploughing '; OG. karasaṇī m. ' cultivator ', G. karasṇī m. -- See *kr̥ṣaṇa -- .(CDIAL 2907). *Harosheth-hagoyim* is the home of general Sisera, who was killed by Jael during the war of Naphtali and Zebulun against Jabin, king of Hazor in Canaan (Judges 4:2). The lead players of this war are the general Barak and the judge Deborah. The name Harosheth-hagoyim obviously consists of two parts. The first part is derived from the root , which HAW Theological Wordbook of the Old Testament treats as four separate roots (harash I, II, III, & IV). The verb (harash I) means to engrave or plough. HAW Theological Wordbook of the Old Testament reads, "The basic idea is cutting into some material, e.g. engraving metal or plowing soil." Derivatives of this verb are: (harash), meaning engraver; (haroshet) a noun meaning a carving. This word is equal to the first part of the name Harosheth-hagoyim; (harish), meaning plowing or plowing time; (maharesha) meaning ploughshare; (harishi), a word which is only used in Jona 4:8 to indicate a certain characteristic of the sun - vehement (King James) or scorching (NIV). The verb (harash II) most commonly denotes refraining from speech or response, either because one is deaf or mute, or because one doesn't want to respond. None of the sources indicates a relation with the previous root, and perhaps there is none, but on the other hand, perhaps deafness was regarded in Biblical as either being marked or else cut or cut off. The noun (horesh) from root (hrsh III) occurs only in Isaiah 17:9 and has to do with a wood or forest. The noun (heresh) from root (hrsh IV) occurs only in Isaiah 3:3 and probably means magical art or expert enchanter, or something along those lines. The second part of the name, hagoyim, comes from the definite article (ha plus the common word (goy) meaning nation, people, gentile. This word comes from the assumed root (gwh), which is not translated but which seems to denote things that are surpassed or left behind. Other derivatives are: (gaw a and gew), meaning back, as in "cast behind the back," i.e. put out of mind (1 Kings 14:9, Nehemiah 9:26, Isaiah 38:17); (gewiya), meaning body, either dead or alive (Genesis 47:18, Judges 14:8, Daniel 10:6). The meaning of the name Harosheth-hagoyim can be found as any combination of

the above. NOBS Study Bible Name List reads Carving Of The Nations, but equally valid would be Silence Of The Gentiles or Engraving Of What's Abandoned. Jones' Dictionary of Old Testament Proper Names reads Manufactory for Harosheth and "of the Gentiles" for Hagoyim. http://www.abarim-publications.com/Meaning/Harosheth.html

This may suggest a fresh look at and reconsideration of the messages conveyed by thousands of cylinder seals which depict many animals, including antelopes, goats, rams, scorpions or composite animals with wings. Some of these may also be explained as hieroglyphs read rebus by literate-language communities, instead of merely explaining away some representations -- only as objects of art appreciation -- to be hunting or banquet scenes or metaphors in the context of assumed rituals in temples or communities.

Context for use of 'fish' glyph. This photograph of a fish and the 'fish' glyph on susa pot are comparable to the 'fish' glyph on an indus seal.
Kalibangan 37, 34

Two Kalibangan seals show an antelope and fish glyphs as the inscription. Mẽḍha 'antelope'; rebus: 'iron' (Ho.)

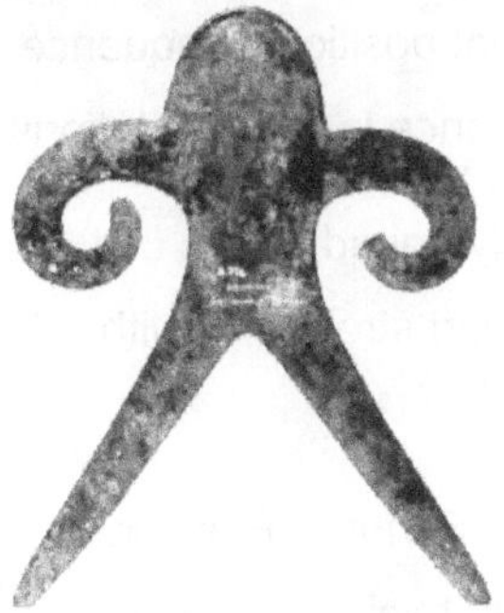

ayo 'fish'; rebs: ayo 'metal' (G.) [These are examples which clearly demonstrate that Indus script is a glyptic writing system and hence, all glyphs and glyptic elements have to be decoded.]

A copper anthropomorph had a 'fish' glyph incised. Anthropomorph with 'fish' sign incised on the chest and with curved arms like the horns of a markhor. Sheorajpur (Kanpur Dist., UP, India). State Museum, Lucknow (O.37) Typical find of Gangetic Copper Hoards. 47.7 X 39 X 2.1 cm. C. 4 kg. Early 2nd millennium BCE.

Miṇḍāl markhor (Tor.wali) meḍho a ram, a sheep (G.)(CDIAL 10120) iron (Ho.) meṛed-bica = iron stone ore, in contrast to bali-bica, iron sand ore (Mu.lex.)

Fish on an Indus seal. National Museum 135.

Fish glyph occurs on a cylinder seal together with the glyphs of 'bull', 'heifer' and also of 'bird'.

Tell Suleimeh Cylinder seal. A fish over a short-horned bull and a bird over a one-horned bull; cylinder seal

impression, (Akkadian to early Old Babylonian). Gypsum. 2.6 cm. Long 1.6 cm. Dia. Tell Suleimeh (level IV), Iraq; IM 87798; (al-Gailani Werr,1983, p. 49 No. 7). [Drawing by Larnia Al-GailaniWerr. Cf. Dominique Collon 1987, First impressions: cylinder seals in the ancient Near East, London: 143, no. 609] baṭa = quail (Santali) Rebus: baṭa = furnace (Santali) bhrāṣṭra = furnace (Skt.) baṭa = a kind of iron (G.) bhaṭa 'furnace' (G.) baṭa = kiln (Santali).

Figure 20: Positional Order of the "Fish" Signs

Fish is a frequently-used glyph on Indus script and the glyph together with ligatured glyphs has a consistent positional sequence and contextual occurrence in the inscriptions.

The glyph is frequently paired with 'circumscribed four short strokes' or with 'arrow' glyph.

Table from: The Indus Script: A Positional-statistical Approach By Michael Korvink, 2007, Gilund Press. Mahadevan notes (Para 6.5 opcit.) that 'a unique feature of the FISH signs is their tendency to form clusters, often

as pairs, and rarely as triplets also. This pattern has fascinated and baffled scholars from the days of Hunter posing problems in interpretation.' One way to resolve the problem is to interpret the glyptic elements creating ligatured fish signs and read the glyptic elements rebus to define the semantics of the message of an inscription.

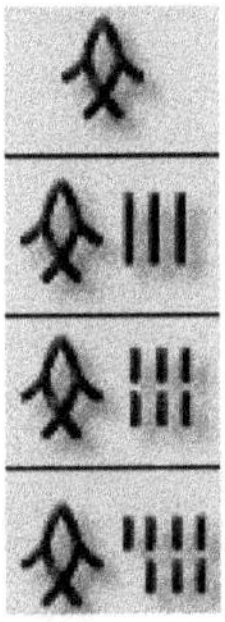

Kolmo 'three' (Mu.); rebus: kolami 'smithy' (Te.) hence, *ayo kolmo* 'iron smithy'.

Bhaṭa 'six' (G.); rebus: *bhaṭa* 'furnace' (Santali)

Four + three strokes are read (since the strokes are shown on two lines one below the other) : gaṇḍa 'four' (Santali); rebus: 'furnace, kaṇḍ fire-altar'; kolmo 'three' (Mu.) dula 'pair' (Kashmiri); rebus: dul 'cast metal' (Mu.)

<ayu?>(A) {N} ``^fish''. #1370. <yO>\\<AyO>(L) {N} ``^fish''. #3612. <kukkulEyO>,,<kukkuli-yO>(LMD) {N} ``prawn''. !Serango dialect. #32612. <sArjAjyO>,,<sArjAj>(D) {N} ``prawn''. #32622. <magur-yO>(ZL) {N} ``a kind of ^fish''. *Or.<>. #32632. <ur+Gol-Da-yO>(LL) {N} ``a kind of ^fish''. #32642.<bal.bal-yO>(DL) {N} ``smoked fish''. #15163. Vikalpa: Munda: <aDara>(L) {N} ``^scales of a fish, sharp bark of a tree''.#10171. So<aDara>(L) {N} ``^scales of a fish, sharp bark of a tree''. Indian mackerel Ta. *Ayirai, acarai, acalai* loach, sandy colour, *Cobitis thermalis*; *ayilai* a kind of fish. Ma. *Ayala* a fish, mackerel, scomber; *aila, ayila* a fish; *ayira* a kind of small fish, loach (DEDR 191) aduru native metal (Ka.); ayil iron (Ta.) ayir, ayiram any ore (Ma.); ajirda karba very hard iron (Tu.)(DEDR 192). Ta. Ayil javelin, lance, surgical knife, lancet.Ma. ayil javelin, lance; ayiri surgical knife, lancet. (DEDR 193). Aduru = gan.iyinda tegadu karagade iruva aduru = ore taken from the mine and not subjected to melting in a furnace (Ka. Siddhānti Subrahmaṇya' Śastri's new interpretation of the AmarakoŚa, Bangalore, Vicaradarpana Press, 1872, p.330); adar = fine sand (Ta.); ayir – iron dust, any ore (Ma.) Kur. Adar the waste of pounded rice, broken grains, etc. Malt. Adru broken grain (DEDR 134). Ma. Aśu

thin, slender;ayir, ayiram iron dust.Ta. ayir subtlety, fineness, fine sand, candied sugar; ? atar fine sand, dust. அய.ர³ ayir, n. 1. Subtlety, fineness; நணசம. (த_வ_.) 2. [M. ayir.] Fine sand; நணமணல. (மலசலப. 92.) ayiram, n. Candied sugar; ayil, n. cf. ayas. 1. Iron; 2. Surgical knife, lancet; Javelin, lance; ayilavaṉ, Skanda, as bearing a javelin (DEDR 341).Tu. gadarů a lump (DEDR 1196) kadara— m. 'iron goad for guiding an elephant' lex. (CDIAL 2711). अयोगू: A blacksmith; Vāj.3.5. अयस् a. [इ-गतौ-असुन्] Going, moving; nimble. N. (-यः) 1 Iron (एति चलति अयस्कान्तसंनिकर्षं इति तथात्वम्; नायसोल्लिख्यते रत्नम् Śukra 4.169. अभितप्तमयो$पि मार्दवं भजते कैव कथा शरीरिषु R.8.43. -2 Steel. -3 Gold. -4 A metal in general. Ayaskāṇḍa 1 an iron-arrow. -2 excellent iron. -3 a large quantity of iron. –क_नत_(अयसक_नत_) 1 'beloved of iron', a magnet, load-stone; 2 a precious stone; °मजण_ a loadstone; ayaskāra 1 an iron-smith, blacksmith (Skt.Apte) ayas-kāntamu. [Skt.] n. The load-stone, a magnet. Ayaskāruḍu. n. A black smith, one who works in iron. ayassu. N. ayō-mayamu. [Skt.] adj. made of iron (Te.) áyas— n. 'metal, iron' RV. Pa. ayō nom. Sg. N. and m., aya— n. 'iron', Pk. Aya— n., Si. Ya. AYAŚCŪRṆA—, AYASKĀṆḌA—, *AYASKŪṬA—. Addenda: áyas—: Md. Da 'iron', dafat 'piece of iron'. ayaskāṇḍa— m.n. 'a quantity of iron, excellent iron' Pāṇ. Gaṇ. Viii.3.48 [ÁYAS—, KAA'ṆḌA—]Si.yakaḍa 'iron'.*ayaskūṭa— 'iron hammer'. [ÁYAS—, KUU'ṬA—1] Pa. ayōkūṭa—, ayak m.; Si. Yakuḷa'sledge —hammer', yavuḷa (< ayōkūṭa) (CDIAL 590, 591, 592). Cf. Lat. Aes , aer-is for as-is ; Goth. Ais , Thema aisa; Old Germ. E7r , iron ;Goth. Eisarn ; Mod. Germ. Eisen.

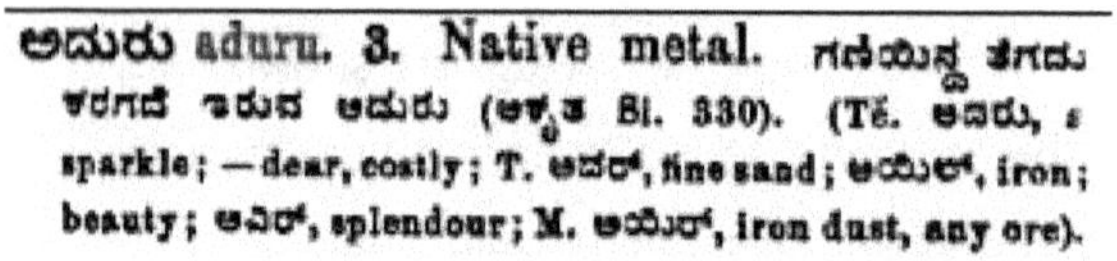

ಅದುರು aduru. 3. Native metal. ಗಣಿಯುಕ್ಕ ತೆಗದು ಕರಗದೆ ಇರುವ ಅದುರು (ಅಶ್ವ Bl. 330). (Tē. ಅದರು, to sparkle; —dear, costly; T. ಅದರ್, fine sand; ಅಯಿಲ್, iron; beauty; ಅವಿರ್, splendour; M. ಅಯಿರ್, iron dust, any ore).

 Fish + corner, *aya koṇḍa*, 'metal turned, i.e. forged).

 Fish + scales, *aya ās (amśu)* 'metallic stalks of stone ore'. Vikalpa: *badhoṛ* 'a species of fish with many bones' (Santali) Rebus: *baḍhoe* 'a carpenter, worker in wood'; *badhoria* 'expert in working in wood'(Santali)

 Fish + splinter, *aya +* खांडा [khāṇḍā] *m* A jag, notch, or indentation (as upon the edge of a tool or weapon). Rebus: khāṇḍa 'tools, pots and pans, and metal-ware'. *Ayaskāṇḍa* is a compounde word attested in Panini.

 Fish + sloping stroke, *aya ḍhāḷ* 'metal ingot'

  Fish + arrow or allograph, Fish + circumscribed four short strokes

ayakāṇḍa 'large quantity of metal' or *aya kaṇḍa,* 'metal fire-altar', aya. Khāṇḍa 'tools, pots and pans and metal-ware'.

 *ayo, hako* 'fish'; *ās* = scales of fish (Santali); rebus: *aya* 'metal, iron' (G.); *ayah, ayas* = metal (Skt.) Santali lexeme, *hako* 'fish' is concordant with a proto-Indic form which can be identified as *ayo* in many glosses, Munda, Sora glosses in particular, of the Indian linguistic area. *Beḍa hako (ayo)* 'fish' (Santali); *beḍa* 'either of the sides of a hearth' (G.)

Vikalpa: badhoṛ 'a species of fish with many bones' (Santali) Rebus: *baḍhoe* 'a carpenter, worker in wood'; *badhoria* 'expert in working in wood'(Santali) Glyph: gaḍa4 m. 'young of the fish Ophiocephalus lata or Cyprinus garra', *°aka* – m. lex. B. *gaṛ*, *gaṛai* 'species of gilt-head fish'; Or. *Gaṛiśa*, *°śā* 'the fish O. lata', *gaḷa* 'a kind of fish'.(CDIAL 3970). Rebus: stone-mould to forge: Pk. *Gaḍa* – n. 'large stone'? (CDIAL 3969). Pk. *Gaḍhaï* ' forms '; A. *gariba* ' to mould, form '; B. *gaṛā* ' to hammer into shape, form (CDIAL 3966).

Aḍaren, ḍaren lid, cover (Santali) Rebus: aduru 'native metal' (Ka.) aduru = gan.iyinda tegadu karagade iruva aduru = ore

taken from the mine and not subjected to melting in a furnace (Ka. Siddha_nti Subrahman.ya' S'astri's new interpretation of the Amarakos'a, Bangalore, Vicaradarpana Press, 1872, p. 330)

ḍhāḷ = a slope; the inclination of a plane;m ḍhāḷiyum = adj. sloping, inclining (G.) Rebus: ḍhāḷako = a large metal ingot (G.)

Vikalpa: डगर [ḍagara]A slope or ascent (as of a river's bank, of a small hill). M. ḍagar f. ' little hill, slope '.S. ṭakuru m. ' mountain ' N. ṭākuro, ri ' hill top '. P. ṭekrā m., rī f. ' rock, hill '; H. ṭekar, krā m. ' heap, hillock '; G. ṭekrɔ m., rī f. ' mountain, hillock '.6. K. ṭẽg m. ' hillock, mound '.7. G. ṭũk ' peak '.8. M. ṭũg n. ' mound, lump '. – Ext. – r -- : Or. ṭuṅguri ' hillock '; M. ṭũgar n. ' bump, mound ' (see *uṭṭungara --); -- -- l -- : M. ṭũgaḷ, gūḷ n.9. K. ḍaki f. ' hill, rising ground '. – Ext. – r -- : K. ḍakürü f. ' hill on a road '.10. Ext. – r -- : Pk. ḍaggara – m. ' upper terrace of a house '; 11. Ku. ḍāg, ḍāk ' stony land '; B. ḍāṅ ' heap ', ḍāṅgā ' hill, dry upland '; H. ḍãg f. ' mountain – ridge '; M. ḍãg m.n., ḍãgaṇ, gāṇ, ḍãgāṇ n. ' hill – tract '. – Ext. – r -- : N. ḍaṅgur ' heap '.12. M. ḍũg m. ' hill, pile ', gā m. ' eminence ', gī f. ' heap '. – Ext. – r -- : Pk. ḍuṁgara – m. ' mountain '; Ku. ḍũgar, ḍũgrī; N. ḍuṅgar ' heap '; Or. ḍuṅguri ' hillock ', H. ḍũgar m., G. ḍũgar m., ḍũgrī f. 13. S.ḍũgaru m. ' hill ', H. M. ḍõgar m. 14. Pa. tuṅga -- ' high '; Pk. Tuṁga -- ' high ', tuṁgīya – m. ' mountain '; K. tŏng, tọngu m. ' peak ', P. tuṅg f.; A. tuṅg ' importance '; Si. Tuňgu ' lofty, mountain '. – Cf. uttuṅga -- ' lofty ' MBh. 15. K. thọngu m. ' peak '. 16. H. dãg f. ' hill, precipice ', dãgī ' belonging to hill country '. Addenda: *ṭakka – 3. 12. *ḍuṅga -- : S.kcch. ḍũṅghar m. ' hillock '. (CDIAL 5423). Unc An eminence, a mount, a little hill (Marathi). ṭākuro = hill top (N.); ṭāngī = hill, stony country (Or.); ṭān:gara = rocky hilly land (Or.); ḍān:gā = hill, dry upland (B.); ḍā~g = mountain-ridge (H.)(CDIAL 5476). Marathi. डांग [ḍāṅga] m n (H Peak or summit of a hill.) Rebus: ḍhaṅgar 'blacksmith' (H.)

koṇḍa bend (Ko.); Tu. Kōḍi corner; kōṇṭu angle, corner, crook. Nk. Kōnṭa corner (DEDR 2054b) G. khũṭrī f. 'angle' Rebus: *kõdā* 'to turn in a lathe'(B.) कोंद kōnda 'engraver, lapidary setting or infixing gems' (Marathi) koḍ 'artisan's workshop' (Kuwi) koḍ = place where artisans work (G.) ācāri koṭṭya 'smithy' (Tu.) कोंडण [kōṇḍaṇa] f A fold or pen. (Marathi) B. kõdā 'to turn in a lathe'; Or.kũnda 'lathe',

kūdibā, kūd 'to turn' (→ Drav. Kur. Kūd ' lathe') (CDIAL 3295) A. kundār, B. kūdār, ri, Or. Kundāru; H. kūderā m. 'one who works a lathe, one who scrapes', rī f., kūdernā 'to scrape, plane, round on a lathe'; kundakara— m. 'turner' (Skt.)(CDIAL 3297). कोंदण [kōndaṇa] n (कोंदणें) Setting or infixing of gems.(Marathi) খোদকার [khōdakāra] n an engraver; a carver. **খোদকারি** n. engraving; carving; interference in other's work. খোদাই [khōdāi] n engraving; carving. **খোদাই করা** v. to engrave; to carve. **খোদানো** v. & n. en graving; carving. খোদিত [khōdita] a engraved. (Bengali) खोदकाम [khōdakāma] n Sculpture; carved work or work for the carver. खोदगिरी [khōdagirī] f Sculpture, carving, engraving: also sculptured or carved work. खोदणावळ [khōdaṇāvaḷa] f (खोदणें) The price or cost of sculpture or carving. खोदणी [khōdaṇī] f (Verbal of खोदणें) Digging, engraving &c. 2 fig. An exacting of money by importunity. V लाव, मांड. 3 An instrument to scoop out and cut flowers and figures from paper. 4 A goldsmith's die. खोदणें [khōdaṇēṃ] v c & i (H) To dig. 2 To engrave. खोद खोदून विचारणें or –पुसणें To question minutely and searchingly, to probe. खोदाई [khōdāī] f (H.) Price or cost of digging or of sculpture or carving. खोदींव [khōdīṃva] p of खोदणें Dug. 2 Engraved, carved, sculptured. (Marathi)

koṇḍa bend (Ko.); Tu. Kōḍi corner; kōṇṭu angle, corner, crook. Nk. Kōnṭa corner (DEDR 2054b) G. khūṭrī f. 'angle' Rebus: *kõdā* 'to turn in a lathe'(B.) कोंद kōnda 'engraver, lapidary setting or infixing gems' (Marathi) koḍ 'artisan's workshop' (Kuwi) koḍ = place where artisans work (G.) ācāri koṭṭya 'smithy' (Tu.) कोंडण [kōṇḍaṇa] f A fold or pen. (Marathi) B. kõdā 'to turn in a lathe'; Or.kūnda 'lathe', kūdibā, kūd 'to turn' (→ Drav. Kur. Kūd ' lathe') (CDIAL 3295) A. kundār, B. kūdār, ri, Or. Kundāru; H. kūderā m. 'one who works a lathe, one who scrapes', rī f., kūdernā 'to scrape, plane, round on a lathe'; kundakara— m. 'turner' (Skt.)(CDIAL 3297). कोंदण [kōndaṇa] n (कोंदणें) Setting or infixing of gems.(Marathi) খোদকার [khōdakāra] n an engraver; a carver. **খোদকারি** n. engraving; carving; interference in other's work. খোদাই [khōdāi] n engraving; carving. **খোদাই করা** v. to engrave; to carve. **খোদানো** v. & n. en graving; carving. খোদিত [khōdita] a engraved. (Bengali) खोदकाम [khōdakāma] n Sculpture; carved work or work for the carver. खोदगिरी [khōdagirī] f Sculpture, carving,

engraving: also sculptured or carved work. खोदणावळ [khōdaṇāvaḷa] f (खोदणें) The price or cost of sculpture or carving. खोदणी [khōdaṇī] f (Verbal of खोदणें) Digging, engraving &c. 2 fig. An exacting of money by importunity. V लाव, मांड. 3 An instrument to scoop out and cut flowers and figures from paper. 4 A goldsmith's die. खोदणें [khōdaṇēṃ] v c & i (H) To dig. 2 To engrave. खोद खोदून विचारणें or – पुसणें To question minutely and searchingly, to probe. खोदाई [khōdāī] f (H.) Price or cost of digging or of sculpture or carving. खोदींव [khōdīṃva] p of खोदणें Dug. 2 Engraved, carved, sculptured. (Marathi*)*

"...we have Toch. A. *ancu 'iron', the basis of the derived adjective ancwaashi 'made of iron', to which corresponds Toch. B encuwo, with the parallel derived adjective encuwanne 'made of iron'...The two forms go back to Ctoch. Oencuwoen- non.sg. *oencuwo, the final part of which is a regular product of IE *-on...This noun is deprived of any convincing IE etymology...The term Ved. Ams'u-, Av . asu- goes back to a noun borrowed from some donor language of Central Asia, as confirmed by Ctoch. *oencuwoen-...the BMAC language would not belong to the Indo-European family; it does not seem to be related to Dravidian either...New identifications and reconstructions will certainly help to define more precisely the contours of the BMAC vocabulary in Indo-Iranian, as well as in Tocharian."[46] As the term Ved. *Amśu* relatable to Tocharian *ancu* 'iron', the early meaning of *amśu* may be close to the protrusions of a mineral stone ore block explained in lexical meanings as 'stalk, ray of light'. It is possible that the Santali lexeme *ās,* 'scales of fish' may be read rebus as *amśu,* 'metallic stalks of stone ore'.[47]

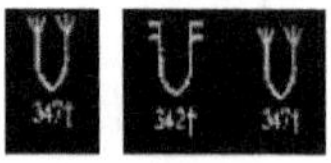

Glyph 347 is a ligature of a wide-mouthed, rimless pot and a pair of 'sprout, paddy-plant' glyphs. Kolom'sprout'; kolom = cutting, graft; to graft, engraft, prune; kolma hoṛo = a variety of the paddy plant (Desi)(Santali.) kolmo 'rice plant' (Mu.) Rebus: kolami 'furnace,smithy' (Te.) Since a pair of 'sprout.rice-plant' glyphs are used, the pair connotes : dula 'pair'; Rebus: dul 'cast (metal)(Santali) This pair is ligatured to: baṭhu m. 'large pot in which grain is parched (S.) Rebus: baṭa = a kind of iron (G.) bhaṭa 'furnace' (G.) baṭa = kiln (Santali).

Glyph 342: *kaṇḍ kanka* 'rim of jar'; Rebus: karṇaka 'scribe'; kaṇḍ 'furnace, fire-altar'. Thus

the ligatured Glyph is decoded: *kaṇḍ karṇaka* 'furnace scribe

Thus, the pair os Glyphs 347 + 342 is decoded: *dul kolmo baṭa kaṇḍ kanka* 'casting smithy (iron) furnace scribe'.

Haifa: tin ingots from a shipwreck

The Indus script inscriptions using hieroglyphs on two pure tin-ingots found in Haifa were reviewed. (Kalyanaraman, S., 2010, The Bronze Age Writing System of Sarasvati Hieroglyphics as Evidenced by Two "Rosetta Stones" – Decoding Indus script as repertoire of the mints/smithy/mine-workers of Meluhha. *Journal of Indo-Judaic Studies*. Number 11. Pp. 47–74).

The picture of these two ingots was published by J.D. Muhly [New evidence for sources of and trade in bronze age tin, in: Alan D. Franklin, Jacqueline S. Olin, and Theodore A. Wertime, The Search for Ancient Tin, 1977, Seminar organized by Theodore A. Wertime and held at the Smithsonian Institution and the National Bureau of Standards, Washington, D.C., March 14-15, 1977]. Muhly notes:"A long-distance tin trade is not only feasible and possible, it was an absolute necessity. Sources of tin stone or cassiterite were few and far between, and a common source must have served many widely scattered ontana pped centers. This means that the tin would have been brought to a metallurgical center utilizing a nearby source of copper. That is, copper is likely to be a local product; the tin was almost always an import…The ingots are made of a very pure tin, but what could they have to do with Cyprus? There is certainly no tin on Cyprus, so at best the ingots could have been ontana pped from that island… What the ingots do demonstrate is that metallic tin was in use during the Late Bronze Age…rather extensive use of metallic tin in the ancient eastern Mediterranean, which will probably come as a surprise to many people." (p.47)

m0516At m0516Bt 3398 [Copper tablet; side B perhaps is a graphemic representation of an antelope; note the ligatured tail takaram tin, white lead, metal sheet, coated with tin (Ta.); tin, tinned iron plate (Ma.); tagarm tin (Ko.); tagara, tamara, tavara id. (Ka.) tamaru, tamara, tavara id. (Ta.): tagaramu, tamaramu, tavaramu id. (Te.); ṭagromi tin metal, alloy (Kuwi); tamara id. (Skt.)(DEDR 3001). Trapu tin (AV.); tipu (Pali); tau, taua lead (Pkt.); tu~_ tin (P.); ṭau zinc, pewter (Or.); tarūaum lead (OG.); tarvu~ (G.); tumba lead (Si.)(CDIAL 5992).

takar sheep, ram, goat (Ta.); tagar ram (Ka.); tagaru (Tu.); tagaramu, tagaru (Te.); tagar (M.)(DEDR 3000).

ṭagara = tabernae   ontana (Skt.)

Heb. Tamar "palm tree, date palm." Tam(b)ra = copper (Pkt.) tabar = a broad axe (P.lex.) Rebus: tebṛa, tebor. 'three times, thrice'; tebṛage emok hoyoktama you will have to give three times that (Santali)

Chanhudaro 23 seal:

M0592 double-axe shown on a copper plate, which depicts a double-axe identical to the one unearthed in Sumer, Mesopotamia, ca. 3000 BCE.

double-axe shown in front of antelope

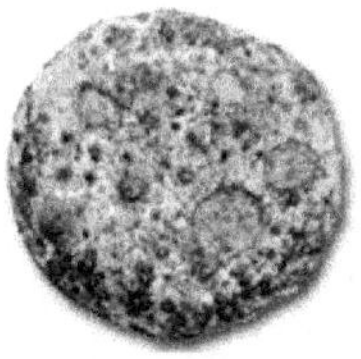

Tin bun ingot. Late Bronze Age, 10th-9th century B.C.E. Salcombe shipwreck, 300 yards off the South Devon coast, England, 2009.[48]

"The Uluburun shipwreck documents the earliest appearance of tin ingots of oxhide shape. G.F. Bass had identified white, oxhide-shaped ingots portrayed in Theban tombs as tin."[49]

 One ton of ox-hide tin ingots were found. (See N11 and N12 on the map of the wreck.)	Bun ingots (tin?) with incised markings from Uluburun shipwreck.[50] 

Archaeological context

Archaeological evidence for types of ingots comes from the Uluburun shipwreck which included ten tons of copper ingots, one ton of tin ingots, perhaps constituting one complete package. Artifacts found included:

- Three hundred and fifty-four copper ox-hide ingots (four-handled and two-handled types)
- One hundred and twenty one copper bun ingots (discoid or plano-convex)
- One ton of ox-hide tin ingots (N11 and N12 on the map grid)[51]

Ox-hide copper ingots (four handles) 	Ox-hide copper ingots (two handles) 	Copper bun ingots 
Three hundred and fifty-four copper ox-hide ingots (four-handled and two-handled types were found. The ingots are called "ox-hide" because their shape resembles the stretched skin of an ox, drying on a rack… It is speculated that the copper ingots on this ship were molded with four handles so they could be easily carried. They are called ox-hide ingots because they looked like the hide of an ox with four legs.	The ten tons of raw copper on the ship comprised the main cargo. This raw material would have been mixed with tin when the ship reached its destination to make bronze for weapons, tools etc. The hold carried enough copper and tin to make three hundred bronze helmets and breast plates. An ingot is metal that has been molded into a particular shape. The two handled variety was not as popular because it would be more difficult to carry. The ingots on this ship weighed about 60 lbs. each. (A talent in the ancient world was 60 lbs. of metal.)	One hundred and twenty-one copper bun ingots (discoid or plano-convex) were found. This was an alternative shape of copper ingot on the ship. It is interesting that many of these ingots had signs scratched onto the surface (anchor design etc.). The signs were probably the mark of the person who controlled this commodity.

Cyprus cylinder seals and bronze stand

Cylinder seal: man grasping an antelope, bull's head over ingot

Period: Late Cypriot Date: ca. 16th–12th century B.C.E. Geography: Cyprus, Ayia Paraskevi; Cyprus Culture: Cypriot Medium: Black-grey steatite

Dimensions: 0.63 in. (1.6 cm) The face of ox shown on the seal impression includes a dot between the horns. This glyphic is comparable to the face of ox shown on the Warka vase, between two large storage jars.

The dot also recurs in the middle of the oxhide iingot shown on the seal impression.

Bull's head over the ox-hide ingot is a phonetic determinant of the hieroglyphs: Hieroglyph: *kõdā* खोंड [khōṇḍa] m A young bull, a bullcalf. (Marathi) Rebus 1: kọnḍu or konḍu । कुण्डम् m. a hole dug in the ground for receiving consecrated fire (Kashmiri) Rebus 2: A. *kundār*, B. *kũdār*, *°ri*, Or. *kundāru*; H. *kũderā* m. ' one who works a lathe, one who scrapes ', *°rī* f., *kũdernā* ' to scrape, plane, round on a lathe '.(CDIAL 3297).

K. *ḍangur* m. 'bullock' (CDIAL 5526). Rebus: ḍāṅgar 'blacksmith' (H.) (CDIAL 5524). mũh 'face'; rebus: mũh 'ingot' (Mu.) The antelope on the Cypriot seal is mṛeka 'goat' (Telugu); rebus: mleccha-mukha 'copper'; *milakkhu* 'copper' (Pali). meṛh 'helper of merchant' (G.)

The 'dot' glyph is an allograph for mũhe 'face'; rebus: mũh 'ingot' (Santali) : kōḍ कोड् m. a kernel (Kashmiri) खोट [khōṭa] A lump or solid bit (as of phlegm, gore, curds, inspissated milk); any concretion or clot. (Marathi) Rebus: L. *khoṭ* f. '

alloy, impurity ', *°ṭā* ' alloyed ', awāṇ. *khoṭā* ' forged '; P. *khoṭ* m. ' base, alloy ' M.*khoṭā* ' alloyed ', (CDIAL 3931)

The depiction of the antelope is a phonetic determinant of the profession – merchant, smith -- of the person who stands beteen the antelope and the oxhide ingot shown on the seal impression: tagar 'antelope'; rebus: damgar 'merchant' Rebus: ḍāṅgar 'blacksmith' (H.) (CDIAL 5524).

Cylinder seal: lion and sphinx over an antelope[52]

Period: Late Cypriot II Date: ca. 14th century B.C.E. Geography: Cyprus Culture: Cypriot Medium: Black-grey steatite Dimensions: 0.83 in. (2.11 cm) Classification: Stone-Cylinder Seal Credit Line: The Cesnola Collection, Purchased by subscription, 1874-76
Accession Number: 74.51.4313

The depiction of a bull's head together with an antelope is significant and recalls the association of bull's head with oxhide ingots. The antelope looking backwards is flanked by a lion (with three dots at the back of the head) and a winged animal woman's face with talons on feet of tiger?) kola 'woman'; kol 'tiger'; rebus: kol 'smithy'. eṟaka 'wing' (Telugu) Rebus: eraka 'copper'. Thus, the ligatured glyph denotes: copper smithy.

At the back of the lion are depicted: three dots and face of ox. *aryeh* 'lion'. Rebus: *āra* 'brass' as in ārakūṭa (Skt.) ayir = iron dust, any ore (Ma.) The 'dot' glyph is an allograph for mũhe 'face'; rebus: mũh 'ingot' (Santali) : kōḍ कोड् m. a kernel (Kashmiri) खोट [khōṭa] alloyed ingot (Marathi). Thus, the lion ligatured with three dots behind its head denotes: *āra* 'brass *khoṭ* 'alloyed ingots.

The information transferred by the hieroglyphs on the cylinder seal impression: tagar 'antelope'; rebus: damgar 'merchant' Rebus: ḍāṅgar 'blacksmith' (H.) is thus flanked by an alloyed ingot (from) copper smithy.

Seal impression of Tell Umma with Indus writing: evidence of ANE-Meluhha minerals/metals trade

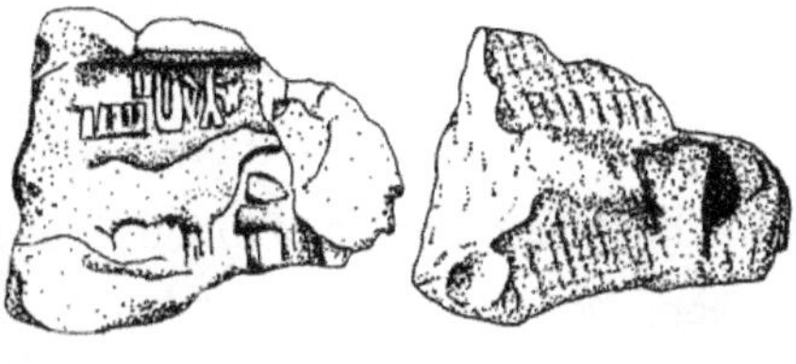

Impression of a 'unicorn' seal thought to come from Tell Umma.[53] Umma (modern Tell Jokha/Djoha) was a Sumerian city state in central southern Mesopotamia. One-horned young bull. Scheil 1925. Indicative of the receipt of goods from the Sarasvati-Sindhu and of the possible presence of Indus traders in Mesopotamia. Tell Asmar seals, together with ceramics, knobbed ware, etched beads and kidney shaped inlay of bone provide supporting evidence for this possibility.[54]

Indus seal with cuneiform inscription

Ur III texts indicate the need for interpreters to translate the Meluhha language. Alternatively, the cuneiform characters were meant to be used by a Meluhha settler in Umma for trade transactions with the Akkadian literate groups.

Seal impression and reverse of seal (with pierced lug handle) from Ur provides evidence for use of cuneiform writing together with Indus writing. "No.1. First

among the seals discovered at Ur (in 1923) is the unique object …in the British Museum…On the face stands, below, the figure of a bull with head bent down…the inscription…is in archaic cuneiform writing…of a period before 2500 B.C. There are three signs and very probably traces of a fourth, almost obliterated; the three preserved are themselves scratchy and rather worn, though not ill-formed. Hence their reading is doubtful—the choices are, for the first SAG(K) or KA, for the second KU or possibly LU, while the third is almost certainly S'I, and the fourth, it existed at all, is quite uncertain…using the commonest values of the signs, sak-ku-s'i—(with possible loss of something at the end) may be pronounced the best provisional reading…It does not, at least, seem to be any Sumerian or Akkadian name…(the seal is) probably, a product of some place under the influence both of Indus (Sarasvati-Sindhu) and of the Sumerian civilizations."[55]

Cuneiform signs may be read as (1) *sag(k)* or *ka,* (2) *ku* or *lu* or *ma*, and (3) *zi* or *ba (4)?.* SAG.KU(?).IGI.X or SAG.KU(?).P(AD)(?) The commonest value: *sag-ku-zi* A rebus reading can be hypothesized as a possible trade contact: sag (Akkadian), 'head'; कुसितः, कुसी (सि) द 1 An inhabited country. -2 One who lives on usury (Sanskrit). Cf. kù-sig 17: gold ('noble metal' + yellow') (Akkadian)

Sea-faring merchants/artisans of Meluhha

Akkadian. Cylinder seal Impression. Inscription records that it belongs to 'S'u-ilis'u, Meluhha interpreter', i.e., translator of the

Meluhha language (EME.BAL.ME.LUH.HA.KI) The Meluhha being introduced carries an goat on his arm. Musee du Louvre. Ao 22 310, Collection De Clercq 3rd millennium BCE. The Meluhha is accompanied by a lady carrying a kamaṇḍalu.

காண்டம் kāṇṭam Ewer; கமண்டலம்.(Tamil); rebus: *khaṇḍa* 'metalware, tools, pots and pans'. *kola* 'woman'; rebus: *kol* 'smithy'. *tagara* 'antelope'; rebus: *tagara* 'tin'; *damgar, tamkaru* 'merchant'; *thakur* 'smith'.

Since he needed an interpreter, it is reasonably inferred that Meluhha did not speak Akkadian.

Antelope carried by the Meluhha woman is a hieroglyph: mlekh 'goat' (Br.); mṟeka (Te.); mēṭam (Ta.); meṣam (Skt.) Thus, the goat conveys the message that the carrier is a Meluhha speaker. A phonetic determinant. Ka. mēke she-goat; mē the bleating of sheep or goats. Te. mēka, mēka goat. Kol. me·ke id. Nk. mēke id. Pa. mēva, (S.) mēya she-goat. Ga. (Oll.) mēge, (S.) mēge goat. Go. (M) mekā, (Ko.) mēka id. ? Kur. mēxnā (mīxyas) to call, call after loudly, hail. Malt. méqe to bleat. [Te. mṟēka (so correct) is of unknown meaning. Br. mēl̤h is without etymology; see MBE 1980a.] / Cf. Skt. (lex.) meka- goat (Monier-Williams lex.) (DEDR 5087) meluh.h.a !

The Meluhha is accompanied by a woman. kola 'woman' (Nahali). Rebus: *kol* 'pañcalōha, alloy of five metals' (Ta.) கொல் kol, n. 1. Iron; இரும்பு. மின் வெள்ளி பொன் கொல்லெனச் சொல்லும் (தக்கயாகப். 550). 2. Metal; உலோகம். (நாமதீப. 318.) *kola* 'blacksmith'

(Ka.); Koḍ. *kollë* blacksmith (DEDR 2133). It appears that the same hieroglyphs are used: antelope, woman in the following artifact produced during Jacques de Morgan's excavations at Susa (1905). He had also published the tokens. The tokens were used for categorizing property items.

'Based on cuneiform documents from Mesopotamia we know that there was at least one Meluhha village in Akkad at that time, with people called 'Son of Meluhha' living there. The cuneiform inscription (ca. 2020 BCE) says that the cylinder seal belonged to Shu-ilishu, who was a translator of the Meluhha language. "The presence in Akkad of a translator of the Meluhha language suggests that he may have been literate and could read the undeciphered Indus script. This in turn suggests that there may be bilingual Akkadian/Meluhha tablets somewhere in Mesopotamia. Although such documents may not exist, Shu-ilishu's cylinder seal offers a glimmer of hope for the future in unraveling the mystery of the Indus script."[56]

Figure, "nude goddess", 7000 Years of Iranian Art, no. 204.[57] On this statue, a ram is ligatured to a woman (*kola*). *meḍho* a ram, a sheep (G.)(CDIAL 10120);

Rebus: *mẽṛhẽt,* 'iron' (Mu.Ho.) Rebus: meṛha, meḍhi 'merchant's clerk; (G.) Rebus: mḗdha m. ' sacrificial oblation ' RV. mēdha -- m. ' sacrifice ' (Pa.) (CDIAL 10327).

The ram could also be denoted by *ṭagara* 'antelope'; takar, *n.* [தகர் T. *tagaru,* K. *tagar.*] 1. Sheep; ஆட்டின்பொது. (திவா.) 2. Ram; செம் மறியாட்டுக்கடா. (திவா.) பொருநகர் தாக்கற்குப் பேருந் தகைத்து (குறள், 486). Rebus: *ṭagara* 'tin'.

Two Elamites carrying animals (bull, antelope) as

phonetic determinatives -- the same way a Meluhha carried an antelope on his hands (as shown on a cylinder seal).[58]

Alik Tilmun, picture-writing Dilmunite traders

In the following account of trade transactions with Mesopotamia, the traders coming through Dilmun are referred to as '*alik tilmun*'. What did the word '*alik*' mean?

From the following etyma, the word '*alik*' can be interpreted as 'carved picture-writing'. Thus, alik tilmun refers to traders from Dilmun characterized by use of carved picture-writing.

ālēkha m. ' writing ' Apte. [Cf. *ā´likhati* ' scratches, de- lineates by scratching ' ŚBr., ' draws, paints ' MBh.: √likh] Pa. *ālēkha* -- m. ' picture ', Pk. *ālēha* -- m., Si. *alevuva.* 1394 ālēkhya n. ' writing, painting, picture ' R. [√likh]Pk. *ālekkha* -- ' painted '; Si. *älik* ' picture '. (CDIAL 1393-4). likhá m. ' writer ' Pāṇ.com., *likhitṛ* -- m. ' painter ' Viddh. [√likh] G. *lahiyɔ, laiyɔ* m. ' writer, scribe '.likháti ' scratches ' AV., ' writes ' Yājñ. [√likh] Pa. *likhati* ' scratches, carves, writes '; Aś.shah. *likhapeśami*, man. *likhapita* -- , gir. *likhāpisaṁ*, dh. *likhiyisāmi* ' will write ', NiDoc. *lihati*, Pk. *lihaï*, MB. *lihe*, Or.*lihibā*, M. *lihiṇẽ*, Ko. *liuṁk*, Si. *liyanavā*, caus. *liyavanavā*; Md. *liyāka* sb. ' writing '. *alikhant -- .WPah.poet. *līṇo* ' to draw, write ', Md. *liyanī* (absol. *lī*), *liyum* ' writing '.2. †likhyatē ' is written ' Kathās.: OP. *likhaṇu* ' to write ', P. *likhṇā*, B. *lekhā*, H. *likhnā.* likhana n. ' writing ' MārkP. [√likh] Pa. *likhana* -- n. ' writing ', Pk. *lihaṇa* -- n.; Si. *liyanuvā* ' writer ' (< **likhanaka* --). likhitá ' scraped ' AV., ' written ' Pañcat., n. ' written document ' Yājñ.com. [√likh] Pa. *likhita* -- ' carved, written '; Aś. *likhita* -- ' written ', NiDoc. *lihida, °aǵa*, Pk. *lihia* -- ; Gy. eur. *lil* (gr. also *lir*) m. ' letter, book '; Si. *liyu* ' inscribed, written ', *li* SigGr ii 460. likhitá ' scraped ' AV., ' written ' Pañcat., n. ' written document ' Yājñ.com. [√likh] Pa. *likhita* -- ' carved, written '; Aś. *likhita* -- ' written ', NiDoc. *lihida, °aǵa*, Pk. *lihia* -- ; Gy. eur. *lil* (gr. also *lir*) m. ' letter, book ';

Si. *liyu* ' inscribed, written ', //SigGr ii 460. liṅga n. ' characteristic attribute ' MaitrUp. (CDIAL 11047-11051).

Tilmun, Telmun, Dilmun, the land of the famous red stone

Note: The land of the famous red stone is a reference to the land of copper mineral stone, cassiterite.

"Documents of the Larsa period in Ur were on tablets. Volume UET V includes texts which deal with Ur as the port of entry for copper into Mesopotamia during the time of the Dynasty of Larsa. The copper was imported by boat from Telmun. (Tilmun is associated with the famous red stone, of which Gudea speaks repeatedly as being imported from Meluhha.) "This 'Telmun-trade' was in the hands of seafaring merchants--called alik Telmun-- who worked hand in hand with enterprising capitalists in Ur to take garments to the island in order to buy large quantities of copper there... In our period-- that of the fifth to seventh king of the Dynasty of Larsa-- the island exported not only copper in ingots but also copper objects, beads of precious stones, and-- most of all-- ivory... Travels to Telmun are repeatedly mentioned in a group of tablets whih come patently from the archives of the temple of the goddess Ningal and list votive offerngs, incoming tithe, etc. The contexts suggest that returning sailors were wont to offer the deity in gratitude a share of their goods. In UET V 526 we read of a small amount of gold, copper and copper utensils characterized as 'tithe of the goddess Ningal from an expedition to Telmun and (from) single persons having gone (there) on their own', during the first 3 months of the year. UET V 292... listing of merchandise is more extensie; besides 'red' gold, copper, lapiz lazuli in lumps, various stone beads, ivory-inlaid tables, et., we find also 'fish-eyes'-- perhaps pearls. (The meaing 'pearl' for IGI.HA has been proposed by R.C. Thompson (1936y: 53, n2) on the basis of UET V... The appearance of rather numerous references to IGI.HA in Ur and especialy in connection with imports from Tilmun must be considered an argument in favor of an interpretation which is not based on philological evidence. The lack of archaeological proof for the use of pearls is of course an important argument against the identification but its value is somewhat diminished when one considers that no ivory object has been found in Ur although the texts report on ivory as raw material as well

as on ivory objects.) ... UET 78, recording ivory combs, eye-paint and certain kinds of wood, not to mention designations which we fail to understand... UET V 367: '2 mina of silver (the value of): 5 gur of oil (and of) 30 garments for an expedition to Telmun to buy (there) copper, (as the) capital for a partnership, L. and N. have borrowed from U. After safe termination of the voyage, he (the creditor) will not recognize commercial losses (incurred by the debtor); they (the debtors) hae agree to satisfy U (the creditor) with 4 mina of copper for each shel of silver as a just (price(?)].'.. babtum must denote some kind of customs or dues imposed on the merchants by the city administration... all extant Old and Neo-Babylonian contracts on partnership reserve for the tamkarum not only the invested capital (plus interest) but also an equal share of the profit yielded by the business venture... The complex legal relationship between the investing and the travelling merchant has created a number of loan types of which at least two are mentioned in the Code of Hammurabi. One of them uses the characteric termtadmiqtu. We encounter this word in the paragraphs 102-103 of the Code and in a few documents of that period... UET V 428: '5 shekels of silver as a tadmiqtu-loan PN1 has borrowed from PN2. He will return the silver at a moment (yet) to be determined (?) (This) he has sworn by the life of the king.' The specific designation of the loans as tadmiqtu 'favor, kindness' (in Sumerian: KA.sa 'friendly word') should not, in spite of the obvious etymology of these terms in both languages, induce us to presume that this business transaction was not as completely under the sway of the laws of economic life as any other loan... As to the main object of the Telmun trade, the copper (termed URUDU), we obtain most of the evidence from the letters (UET V 22,29, 71 and 81) addressed to a certain Ea-na_s.ir, a travelling merchant and importer of Telmun copper. The metal came in large quantities (UET V 796 mentions more than 13,000 minaz of copper according to the weight standard of Telmun) and often in ingots termed gubarum which weighed up to 4 talents each (UET V 678). The ingots are sometimes qualified as damqu (UET V 22,81) as is also the copper itself (UET V 20 wariam la damqam, but wariam dummuqam in UET V 5 and 6). The quoted passages do not entitle us to speak of refining of copper, because Ea-na_s.ir was not a coppersmith but a merchant and because the meaning of damqum as well as dummuqum as 'good (in quality)' is borned out by such letter passages as UET V 5:28 or 22: 10-13 ('show him 15 ingots so that he may select 6 damqu ingots' ... UET V 81, lines 33-39: 'I myself gave on account of you 19 talents of copper to the palace and S'umi-abum gave (likewise) 18 talents of copper, apart from the sealed document which we both handed over to the

temple of Shamash.'... Ea-na_s.ir is supposed to have imported a large copper kettle (UET V 5:25)... UET V 428: '1 mina of...silver, 1/2 mina of... silver to buy (precious stones), 'fish-eyes' and other merchandise on an expedition to Telmun, PN2 has borrowed from PN1...'... ivory as raw material (UET V 546) as well as finished ivory objects have been imported from Telmun. Among the latter we find exactly the same objects which we know so well from the dowry inventories, etc. of the Amarna letters: ivory combs (UET V 292, 678), breast plates (UET V 279), boxes (UET V 795), inlaid pieces of furniture (UET 292) and spoons (UET V 795)... Southern Mesopotamia had to rely exclusively upon ivory imported from the East, to be exact: via Telmun... we have from Mohenjodaro actual ivory combs... UET V 82 refers to the karum as a locality in which business accounts have been settled, which in Old-Babylonian practice is normally done in the temple of Shamash... A certain Lu-En-li_l-la_ is said in UET III 1689 (Ibbi-Sin, 4th year) to have received large amounts of garments and wool from the storehouse of the temple of Nanna in order to buy copper in Makkan (nig.s'am.marudu Ma.gan ki, literally: equivalent for buying copper in M.)... When Sargon of Agade proudly proclaims (Legrain 1923: 208f., col. v-vi) that ships from or destined for Meluhha, Makkan and Telmun were moored in the harbor which was situated outside of his capital, this obviously proves the existence of flourishing commercial relations with the East... We even know the name of a person, a native of 'Great-Makkan' i.e. Ur-Nammu (UET III 1193). In the period, Makkan-- 'the country of mines' seems to have been the only importer of copper... After the collapse of the Dynasty of Ur, Telmun replaces Makkan in the Eastern trade of the city... Telmun, as against Makkan, seems never to have completely lost contact with Mesopotamia... Telmun had lost contact with the mining centers of Makkan and with those regions which supplied it with stone and timber, etc. some time between the fall of the Dynasty of Larsa and the decline of power of the Hammurabi Dynasty... It turned again into an island famous only for its agricultural products, its sweet water, etc. Copper, precious stones, and rare woods have now to come to Southern Mesopotamia either over the mountain ranges and from the West along the river routes... Sometime in the second half of the 2nd millennium B.C., Telmun seems to have come in closer contact with the rulers of Southern Babylonia (Goetze 1952)... We are fortunate indeed to have three letters at our disposal, two written by Assurbanipal's general Bel-ibni mentioning Hundaru, king of Telmun, and one written by Assurbanipal and addressed to Hundaru. The details of the dealings of the king of Telmun in his fight for survival are of little interest in the present context, far more revealing is the mention of metal (bronze), precious woods and 'kohl' i.e. eye-paint in these letters. We read of great amounts of kohl, 26 talent of bronze, numerous copper and

bronze objects, of sticks of precious wood as part of the booty taken from Telmun, while another speaks of the tribute of Telmun mentioning, at the same time, bronze, perfumes and likewise 'sticks' of precious wood offered by merchants from Bit-Naialu... a passage of the inscription KAH 122 of Sennacherib which describes the tools of the crew of corvee-workers sent from Telmun to Babylon to assist the Assyrian king to tear down the city. Their tools are characterized as follows: 'bronze spades and bronze pikes, tools which are the (characteristic) product of their (native) country.' Thus, it becomes evident that Telmun has again access to the copper mines of Makkan, to the spices, perfumes and rare woods of the East... Assurbanipal's inscription in the temple of Ishtar in Niniveh mentions another island-- beyond Telmun--: '[x-y]-i-lum, king of the [ ]-people who resides in Hazmani which is an island alongside Telmun' whose messengers had to travel a long way across the sea and overland to Assyria."[59]

Tepe Yahya, Susa

Cultural interactions of 3rd - 2nd millennium BCE between Ancient Near East and Meluhha are evidenced by what started as glyptic art to represent reality which transformed into glyptic writing systems in Mesopotamian cylinder seals or Elam tablets (and inscriptions on other artifacts) and in Indus Script (on seals and other artifacts) to establish and sustain trade contacts to announce, describe and market new products of the Bronze Age artisans emerging out of the chalcolithic era.

Lamberg-Karlovsky who excavated the Elamite site of Tepe-Yahya records a seal with Indus script:

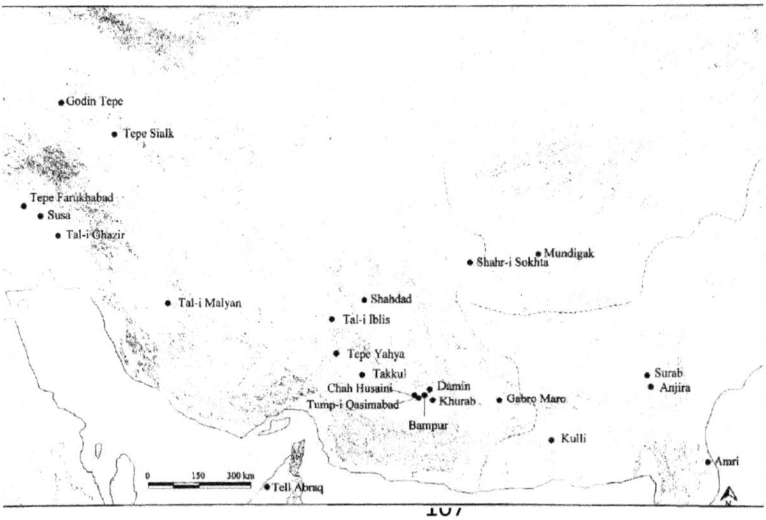

Fig Fig A.1 Map of the Indo-Iranian borders illustrating the principal sites (e.g.

Amri, Tepe Yahya, Tell Abraq, Susa).

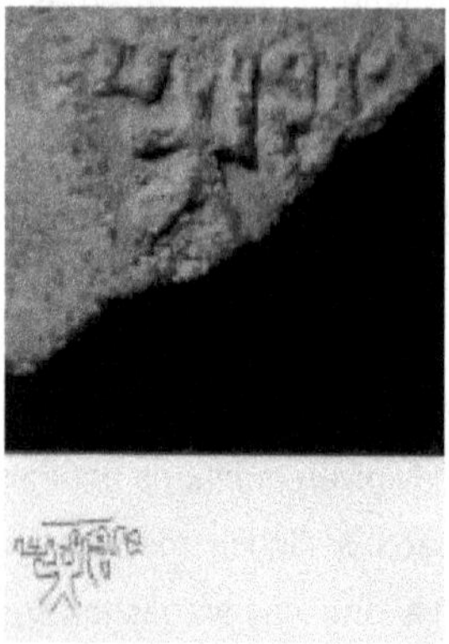

10.63 Stamp seal impression on plain red ware sherd of Tepe Yahya with Harappa inscription firmly establishing the site as the mid-point contact area in Persian Gulf sites (e.g. Tell Abraq). Objects with Indus script hieroglyphs had also been discovered in Mesopotamian civilization area (Elamite site of Susa and other sites).

Glyptic art tradition of Mesopotamia and Elam has been well-documents and the meanings/significance of glyphs explained in the writings of savants like Edith Porada, Henri Frankfort, Beatrice Teissier and Amiet. This note suggests that the glyptic art tradition evidenced on many tablets and cylinder seals of the Mesopotamian civilization area has to be re-evaluated as complementary to the writing systems which developed both in Mesopotamia (cuneiform, proto-elamite and elamite writing systems) and in Indus script (hieroglyphs). "Susa... profound affinity between the Elamite people who migrated to Anshan and Susa and the Dilmunite people... Elam proper corresponded to the plateau of Fars with its capital at Anshan. We think, however that it probably extended further north into the Bakhtiari Mountains... likely that the chlorite and serpentine vases reached Susa by sea... From the victory proclamations of the kings of Akkad we also learn that the city of Anshan had been re-established, as the capital of a revitalised political ally: Elam itself... the import by Ur and Eshnunna of inscribed objects typical of the Harappa culture provides the first reliable chronological evidence.[60] It is certainly possible that writing developed in India before this time, but we have no real proof. Now Susa had received evidence of this same civilisation, admittedly not all dating from the Akkadian period, but apparently spanning all the closing years of the third millennium...[61] The finds of object with Indus script had served the purpose of validating the chronology and dating of Indus Civilization (Meluhha).

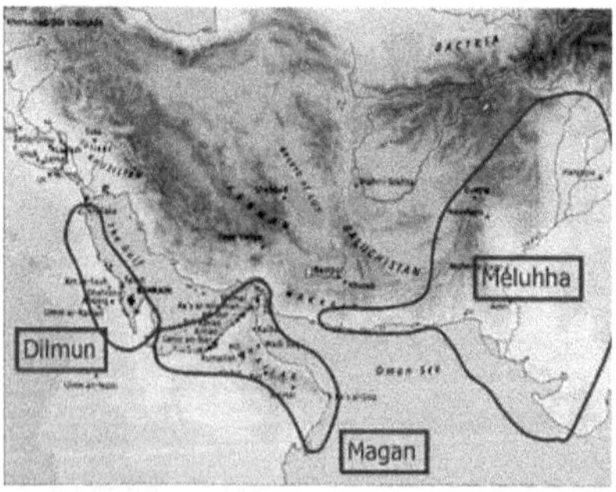

1. Indus writing in Susa is evidenced by the 'fish' glyph inscribed below the rim on a storage jar which contained metal artifacts. This pot was found in Susa (reported by Prof. Maurizio Tosi:

context of interactions between Meluhha and Susa).[62]

2. Seal of Telloh with Indus writing Text 9851.[63]

3. Cylinder Seal of Ibni-Sharrum

Agade period, reign of Sharkali-Sharri (c. 2217-2193 BC) Mesopotamia Serpentine H. 3.9 cm; Diam. 2.6 cm Formerly in the De Clercq collection; gift of H. de Boisgelin, 1967 AO 22303 Richelieu wing Ground floor Mesopotamia, c. 2350–2000 BC Room 2

Cylinder seal impression of Ibni-sharrum, a scribe of Shar-kalisharri ca. 2183–2159 BCE The inscription reads "O divine Shar-kali-sharri, Ibni-sharrum the

scribe is your servant." Cylinder seal. Chlorite. AO 22303 H. 3.9 cm. Dia. 2.6 cm.[64] *khaṇṭi* 'buffalo bull' (Tamil) kaṭā, kaṭamā 'bison' (Tamil)(DEDR 1114) (glyph). Rebus: *khaṇḍ* 'tools, pots and pans, metal-ware'; kaḍiyo [Hem. Des. kaḍa-i-o = (Skt. Sthapati, a mason) a bricklayer, mason (G.)] <lo->(B) {V} ``(pot, etc.) to ^overflow". See <lo-> `to be left over'. @B24310. #20851. Re<lo->(B) {V} ``(pot, etc.) to ^overflow". See <lo-> `to be left over'. (Munda) Rebus: loh 'copper' (Hindi) Glyph of flowing water in the second register: காண்டம் kāṇṭam , *n.* < *kāṇḍa.* 1. Water; sacred water; நீர்;

kāṇṭam 'ewer, pot' கமண்டலம். (Tamil) Thus the combined rebus reading: Ku. *lokhaṛ* 'iron tools '; H. *lokhaṇḍ* m. ' iron tools, pots and pans '; G. *lokhā̃ḍ* n. 'tools, iron, ironware'; M. *lokhā̃ḍ* n. ' iron '(CDIAL 11171). The kneeling person's hairstyle has six curls. *bhaṭa* 'six'; rebus: *bhaṭa* 'furnace'. मेढा mēḍhā A twist or tangle arising in thread or cord, a curl or snarl. (Marathi) Rebus: meḍ 'iron' (Ho.) Thus, the orthography denotes *meḍ bhaṭa* 'iron furnace'.

Hieroglyphs on Susa limestone vat

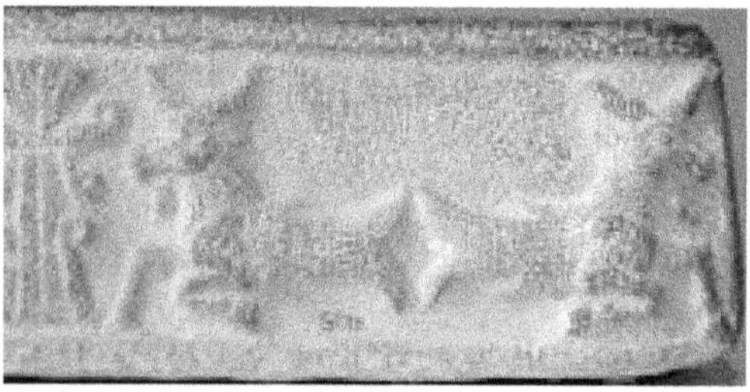

Susa limestone vat, Middle Elamite period (c. 1500 BC – 1100 BCE). Louvre Musuem. An ornate design on this limestone ritual vat from the Middle Elamite period depicts creatures with the heads of goats and the tails of fish. Goatfishes ornating a cultual tank, symbolizing the sweet water abyss, domain of the god Ea. Found in Susa, limestone, Middle Elamite period (c. 1500 BC – 1100 BC). Louvre Museum. Department of Near Eastern antiquities, Sully wing, ground floor, room 10. It may also relate to Sargonids (23rd or 22nd cent.

BCE). "Ce bas-relief ne porte aucune inscription et par suite nous ne pouvons dire à quelle époque il appartient ; toutefois, par beaucoup de détails, je crois qu'il est permis de le considérer comme contemporain des Sargonides, c'est-à-dire du temps où l'Élam, continuellement en rapports avec Ninive et se trouvant dans son déclin, subissait l'influence de ses puissants voisins du Nord." (http://www.archive.org/download/mmoires01franuoft/mmoires01franuoft.pdf Jacques de Morgan, Fouilles à Suse en 1897-1898 et 1898-1899, Mission archéologique en Iran, Mémoires I, 1990, p.160).

Susa ritual basin decorated with goatfish figures, molluscs, reeds – all these are interpretable as hieroglyphs. N" 16. Tête de bé-lier à'Ea surmontant une maison posée sur une antilope munie d'un corps de poisson (fig.459 Figurations emblematiques du koudourrou N" XX); antelope fitted with a fish body.

Ea, l'antilope à corps de poisson, surmonté d'un carré dont je ne puis expliquer la Signification. Fiti. 453. — Emblèmes du koudouukou n" xv .[65]

The pictographs on the ritual basin show: molluscs as center-piece flanked by a ligatured goat-fish. Molluscs as hieroglyphs occur in Indian artefacts of historical periods. Goat and fish are hieroglyphs used in Indus writing, though a ligatured goat-fish does not appear in the Indus script corpora, there are many other

examples of ligatured animals (e.g. ligatured heads of 3 or more animals; ligatured crocodile-fish). The mollusc design compares with śrivatsa (entwined pair of fishes) and molluscs depicted on Mathura Lion Capital.

A combination of a markhor's horns + fish occurs on a copper anthropomorph of Sheorajpur, Uttar Pradesh, India.

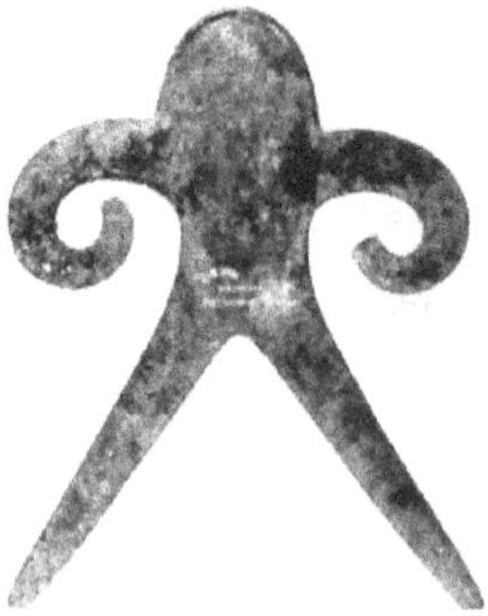

A copper anthropomorph had a 'fish' glyph incised. Anthropomorph with 'fish' sign incised on the chest and with curved arms like the horns of a markhor. Sheorajpur (Kanpur Dist., UP, India). State Museum, Lucknow (O.37) Typical find of Gangetic Copper Hoards. 47.7 X 39 X 2.1 cm. C. 4 kg. Early 2nd millennium BCE. Tagara 'ram' + ayo 'fish'; rebus: tagara 'tin', ayo 'metal' (perhaps bronze formed by alloying copper mineral with tin mineral).

If the molluscs are stylized composition of a palm tree, the rebus reading may be: *tamar* "palm tree, date palm" (Heb.) Rebus: *tam(b)ira* 'copper' (Pkt.) The glyphic composition on Susa ritual vat thus reads: tagara, 'tin'; ayo 'alloyed bronze'; tam(b)ra 'copper'.

If the composition represents a pair of reeds, the rebus reading of the pair of reeds in Sumer standard is: *khāṇḍa* 'tools, pots and pans and metal-ware', *khōṭ* 'alloyed ingots', dhatu 'mineral (ore)'.

Hieroglyphs of Uruk trough

Two views of the trough. "Two lambs exit structure identical to the present-day

mudhif on this ceremonial trough from the site of Uruk in southern Iraq...Dating to ca. 3000 BCE, the trough documents the extraordinary length of time such arched reed buildings have been in use." Sumerian mudhif[66] facade, with uncut

reed fonds and sheep entering, carved into a gypsum trough from Uruk, c. 3200 BCE (British Museum WA 120000). Maybe a sacred object in the temple of Inana (Ishtar) of Uruk.

The animals exiting the mudhif are comparable to the animals shown in procession on Warka vase.

The rebus reading of the pair of reeds in Sumer standard is: *khāṇḍa* 'tools, pots

and pans and metal-ware', *khōṭ* 'alloyed ingots', dhatu 'mineral (ore)'.

pasaramu, pasalamu = quadrupeds (Telugu); pasra 'smithy, forge' (Santali) (Third register).

Glyph: कोंडण [kōṇḍaṇa] f A fold or pen. (Marathi) goṭ = the place where cattle are collected at mid-day (Santali); goṭh (Brj.)(CDIAL 4336). Goṣṭha (Skt.); cattle-shed (Or.) koḍ = a cow-pen; a cattlepen; a byre (G.) कोठी cattle-shed (Marathi) कोंडी [kōṇḍī] A pen or fold for cattle. गोठी [gōṭhī] f C (Dim. Of गोठा) A pen or fold for calves. (Marathi) Allograph: koṭṭhaka1 (nt.) "a kind of koṭṭha," the stronghold over a gateway, used as a store — room for various things, a chamber, treasury, granary Vin ii.153, 210; for the purpose of keeping water in it Vin ii.121=142; 220; treasury J i.230; ii.168; -- store — room J ii.246; koṭṭhake pāturahosi appeared at the gateway, i. e. arrived at the mansion Vin i.291. (Pali) kuṛī, kuṛo house, building'(Ku.)(CDIAL 3232) कोठी [kōṭhī] f (कोष्ट S) A granary, garner, storehouse, warehouse, treasury, factory, bank. (Marathi) कोठी The grain and provisions (as of an army); the commissariat supplies.

Rebus: कोंदण [kōndaṇa] n (कोंदणें) Setting or infixing of gems.(Marathi) *kõdā* 'to turn in a lathe'(B.)

Text 1330 (appears with Zebu glyph) showing Glyph 39. Pictorial motif: Zebu (*Bos indicus*) This sign is comparable to the cattle byre of Southern Mesopotamia dated to c. 3000 BCE.

The hut of a Toda Tribe of Nilgiris, India. Note the decoration of the front wall, and the very small door.

The architecture of Iraqi mudhif and Toda mund — of Indian linguistic area — is comparable.[67]

Cattle Byres c.3200-3000 B.C. Late Uruk-Jemdet Nasr period. Magnesite. Cylinder seal. In the lower field of this seal appear three reed

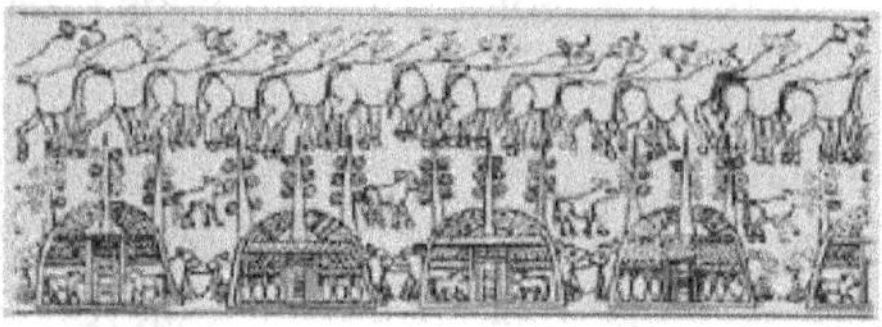

cattle byres. Each byre is surmounted by three reed pillars topped by rings, a motif that has been suggested as symbolizing a male god, perhaps Dumuzi. Within the huts calves or vessels appear alternately; from the sides come calves that drink out of a vessel between them. Above each pair of animals another small calf appears. A herd of enormous cattle moves in the upper field. Cattle and cattle byres in Southern Mesopotamia, c. 3500 BCE. Drawing of an impression from a Uruk period cylinder seal. (After Moorey, PRS, 1999, Ancient materials and industries: the archaeological evidence, Eisenbrauns.)

Stand. Bronze, Cyprus. AN258515001 Excavated/Findspot Kourion (perhaps) (Europe, Cyprus, Limassol (district), Kourion) 1250BC-1050BC Bronze four-sided

stand with figural decoration on each panel; the frame is formed of cast bronze rods, standing on four feet with flat legs; on top is a composite ring consisting of a wavy band between two parallel rods; the four panels are decorated with the figures cast separately in open moulds; all the constituent parts of the stand are hard soldered together; the four figural scenes depict a more or less identical male figure facing a highly stylized tree with voluted leaves; he wears a long, kilt-like garment extending to the ankles but is naked from the waist up; the facial features are fleshy with a prominent nose; his hair (or wig) falls to the nape of the neck; each scene shows a different gesture: approaching the tree with an oxhide ingot over shoulder; holding fish-like objects in lowered hands; carrying a long, scarf-like indeterminate object over his right shoulder, one end of which trails on the ground; seated playing a large, many-stringed lyre supported with a strap around his neck, apparently serenading the tree (possibly a sacred image of fertility). Dimensions Height: 12.5 centimetres Width: 9.5 centimetres Diameter: 8.5 centimetres (ring) http://tinyurl.com/7u7xwwe

"In the Late Bronze Age, Cyprus produced numerous bronze stands that depicted a man carrying an oxhide ingot. The stands were designed to hold vases, and they were cast through the lost-wax process." [Vassos Karageorghis and George Papasawas, "A Bronze Ingot-Bearer from Cyprus," Oxford Journal of Archaeology 20 (2001): 341, 344.]
http://en.wikipedia.org/wiki/Oxhide_ingot#cite_note-50

The cyprus bronze stand has a glyph which is comparable to the pair of reets or mollusc composition depicted on Warka vase. This glyphic composition recurs on four sides of the stand.

hāngi 'snail' *sangi* 'pilgrim, association'. sangaḍa 'association' (guild) (Marathi).

If the composition represents a pair of reeds, the rebus reading

of the pair of reeds in Sumer standard is: *khāṇḍa* 'tools, pots and pans and metal-ware', *khōṭ* 'alloyed ingots', dhatu 'mineral (ore)'.

Side 1: Glyph: tambura 'harp'; rebus: tambra 'copper' (Pkt.)

Side 2: Glyph: A male carrying a scarf on his right hand and fish on his left. ayo 'fish' ayas 'bronze'. dhatu 'scarf'. dhatu 'mineral'.

Side 3: Glyph: A male carrying an oxhide ingot. mũh '(copper) ingot' (Santali) Allograph: mũhe 'face' (Santali)

Side 4: Glyph: A female carrying a pot. kola 'woman'; rebus: kol 'smithy'. காண்டம் kāṇṭam Ewer; கமண்டலம்.(Tamil); rebus: khaṇḍa 'metalware, tools, pots and pans'. kuṇḍa 'pot; rebus: 'consecrated fire-pit'. khũṭ 'community, guild' (Munda)

The *tabernae montana* glyph shown on Warka vase has parallels in Indus script corpora shown in examples below:

In interaction areas, *tabernae montana* glyph appears: 1. on an ivory comb discovered at Oman Peninsula site of Tell Abraq, 2. on a Bactria-Margiana Archaeological Complex stone flask and, 3. on a copper alloy shaft-hole axe-head of (unverified provenance) attributed to Southeastern Iran, ca. late 3rd or early 2nd millennium BCE 6.5 in. long, 1980.307 Metropolitan Museum of Art, New York.

The ivory comb found at Tell Abraq measures 11 X 8.2 X .4 cm. Both sides of the comb bear identical, incised decoration in the form of two

long-stemmed flowers with crenate or dentate leaves, flanking three dotted circles arranged in a triangular pattern. The occurrence of wild tulip glyph on the ivory comb can be explained. The spoken word *tagaraka* connoted a hair fragrance from the flower *tagaraka.* These flowers are identified as tulips, perhaps Mountain tulip or Boeotian tulip (both of which grow in Afghanistan) which have an undulate leaf. There is a possibility that the comb is an import from Bactria, perhaps transmitted through Meluhha to the Oman Peninsula site of Tell Abraq.

Ivory comb with Mountain Tulip motif and dotted circles. TA 1649 Tell Abraq. [D.T. Potts, South and Central Asian elements at Tell Abraq (Emirate of Umm al-Qaiwain, United Arab Emirates), c. 2200 BC—AD 400, in Asko Parpola and Petteri Koskikallio, South Asian Archaeology 1993: , pp. 615-666] h337, h338 Texts 4417, 4426 (Dotted circles on leaf-shaped tablets) Tell Abraq comb and axe with epigraph After Fig. 7Holly Pittman, 1984, Art of the Bronze Age: Southeastern Iran, Western Central Asia, and the Indus Valley, New York, The Metropolitan Museum of Art, pp. 29-30].

A soft-stone flask, 6 cm. tall, from Bactria (northern Afghanistan) showing a winged female deity (?) flanked by two flowers similar to those shown on the comb from Tell Abraq.(After Pottier, M.H., 1984, *Materiel funeraire e la Bactriane meridionale de l'Age du Bronze*, Paris, Editions Recherche sur les Civilisations: plate 20.150)

Susa: sacred fire-smithy

There is a possibility that there was a Meluhha settlement of traders in Susa who could read the messages conveyed by Indus script inscriptions.

The ziggurat shown on the Sit-Shamshi bronze compares with a ziggurat which might have existed in the Stupa mound of Mohenjodaro (lit. mound of the dead), indicating the veneration of ancestors in Susa and Meluhha in contemporaneous times.Some glyphics of the bronze model have parallels in Indian hieroglyphs. Glyph: 'stump of tree': M. khũṭ m. 'stump of tree'; P. khuṇḍ, °ḍā m. 'peg, stump';

G. *khūṭ* f. 'landmark', *khūṭo* m., *°ṭī* f. ' peg ', *°ṭū* n. 'stump' (CDIAL 3893). Allograph: (Kathiawar) khūṭ m. 'Brahmani bull'(G.) Rebus: khūṭ 'community, guild' (Munda) The ceremony involved lo 'pouring (water) oblation' (Munda) for the setting sun. Rebus: loa 'copper' (Santali) The glyphic representations connote a guild of coppersmiths in front of a ziggurat, temple and is a veneration of ancestors. The authors of the bronze model seem to have interacted with the groups of artisans of Mohenjo-daro who had a ziggurat in front of the 'great bath'.

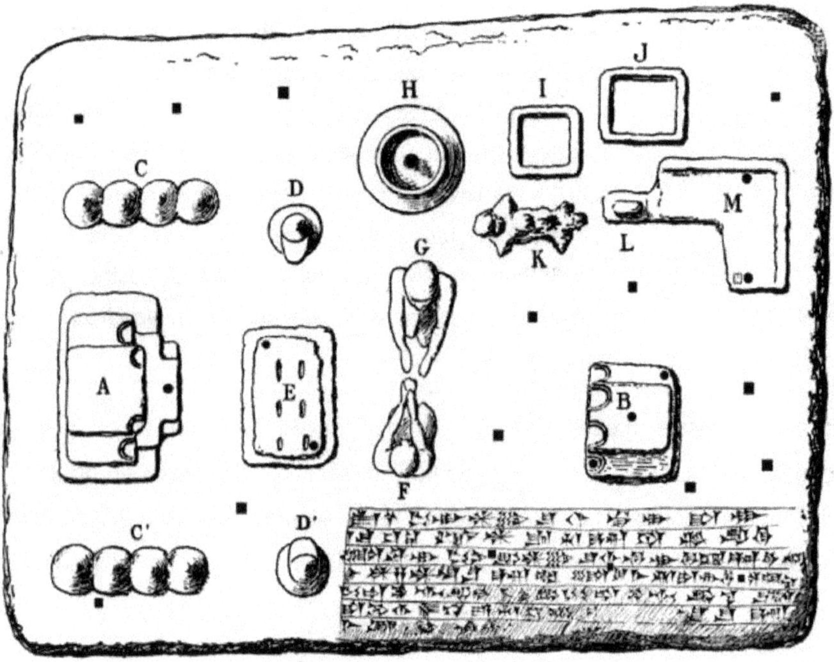

Fig. 200

Gautier 1911: 145, fig. 200 + F.W. König, *Corpus Inscriptionum Elamicarum*, no. 56, Hannover 1926 + Tallon & Hurtel 1992: 140, fig. 43. The base measures 60 x 40 cm.

After Fig. 200 in Gautier 1911:145 + FW Konig, Corpus Inscriptionum Elamicarum, no. 56, Hanover 1926 + Tallon & Hurtel 1992: 140, fig. 43. The base measures 60 X 40 cm. Sit Shamshi 'sunrise ceremony'. Discovery location: Ninhursag Temple, Acropole, Shūsh (Khuzestan, Iran); Repository: Musée du Louvre (Paris, France) ID: Sb 2743 width: 40 cm (15.75 inches); length: 60 cm (23.62 inches)

Sit Shamshi. Model of a place of worship, known as the Sit Shamshi, or "Sunrise (ceremony)" Middle-Elamite period, toward the 12th century BC Acropolis mound, Susa, Iran; Bronze; H. 60 cm; W. 40 cm Excavations led by Jacques de Morgan, 1904-5; Sb 2743; Near Eastern Antiquities, Musée du Louvre/C. Larrieu. Two nude figures squat on the bronze slab, one knee bent to the ground. One of the figures holds out open hands to his companion who prepares to pour the

contents of a lipped vase onto them.The scene takes place in a stylized urban landscape, with reduced-scale architectural features: a tiered tower or ziggurat flanked with pillars, a temple on a high terrace. There is also a large jar resembling the ceramic pithoi decorated with rope motifs that were used to store

water and liquid foodstuffs. An arched stele stands by some rectangular basins. Rows of 8 dots in relief flank the ziggurat; jagged sticks represent trees.An inscription tells us the name of the piece's royal dedicator and its meaning in part: "I Shilhak-Inshushinak, son of Shutruk-Nahhunte, beloved servant of Inshushinak, king of Anshan and Susa [...], I made a bronze sunrise."[68]

Three jagged sticks on the Sit Shamshi bronze, in front of the water tank (Great Bath replica?) If the sticks are orthographic representations of 'forked sticks' and if the underlying language is Meluhha (mleccha), the borrowed or substratum lexemes which may provide a rebus reading are:

kolmo 'three'; rebus; *kolami* 'smithy' (Telugu)

Glyph: मेंढा [mēṇḍhā] A crook or curved end (of a stick, horn &c.) and attrib. such a stick, horn, bullock. मेढा [mēḍhā] m A stake, esp. as forked. meḍ(h), meḍhī f., meḍhā m. ' post, forked stake '.(Marathi)(CDIAL 10317) Rebus: mẽṛhẽt, meḍ 'iron' (Mu.Ho.) Vikalpa: P. *khuṇḍ, °ḍā* m. ' peg, stump '; khuṇṭ 'stump'. Rebus: 1. khũṭ 'community, guild' (Mu.) 2. Skt. kuṇḍa- round hole in ground (for water or sacred fire).

Thus, three jagged sticks on the Sit Shamshi bronze may be decoded as *khũṭ kolami* 'smithy guild' or, kuṇḍa kollami 'sacred fire smithy' or, *meḍ kolami* 'iron (metal) smithy'. 'Iron' in such lexical entries may refer to 'metal'.

Sit Shamshi bronze illustrates the complex technique of casting separate elements joined together with rivets, the excavations at Susa have produced one of the largest bronze statues of Antiquity: dating from the 14th century BC, the effigy of "Napirasu, wife of Untash-Napirisha," the head of which is missing, is 1.29 m high and weighs 1,750 kg. It was made using the solid-core casting method.

Bas-relief of spinner with hieroglyphs of Indus writing

Relief of a woman being fanned by an attendant while she holds what may be a spinning device before a table with a bowl containing a whole fish. Young woman spinning and servant holding a fan. Fragment of a relief known as "The spinner". Bitumen mastic, Neo-Elamite period (8th century BCE–middle of the 6th century BCE). Found in Susa.[69]

kola 'woman' rebus: kol 'smithy'. meḍhi, miḍhī, meṇḍhī = a plait in a woman's hair; a plaited or twisted strand of hair (P.) मेढा [mēḍhā] meṇḍa A twist or tangle arising in thread or cord, a curl or snarl. (Marathi) (CDIAL 10312). [dial., cp. Prk. mĕṇṭha & miṇṭha: Pischel, Prk. Gr. § 293. The Dhtm (156) gives a root meṇḍ (meḍ) in meaning of "koṭilla," i. e. crookedness.(Pali)[70] Vikalpa: ḍhompo = knot on a string (Santali) ḍhompo = ingot (Santali) Vikalpa: cūḍa 'diadem, hairdress' (Skt.) Rebus: cūḷa 'furnace' (H.) Rebus: meḍ 'iron' (Ho.) Thus, the glyptic elements of woman, plaited hair can be decoded as: meḍ kolami 'iron smelter smithy'.

kola 'woman' (Nahali); Rebus: kolami 'smithy' (Te.)

ayo 'fish' (Mu.); rebus: aya 'metal' (G.) Glyphs of 'six dots on the back of fish': *khoṭ* 'alloyed ingots' (from) *kaṇḍ* 'furnace, fire-altar' yielding *khaṇḍa* 'tools, pots and pans and metal-ware'.

The glyphics represent *kol khũṭ khati,'* working in iron, a guild of wheelwrights '.

kola 'tiger' (Telugu); rebus: kol 'working in iron (Tamil). The legs of the two stools shows glyphic of tiger's foot. Glyph: 'foot, hoof': Glyph: 'hoof': Ku. *khuṭo* ' leg, foot ', *°ṭī* ' goat's leg '; N. *khuṭo* ' leg, foot '(CDIAL 3894). S. *khuṛī* f. ' heel '; WPah. paṅ. *khūṛ* ' foot '. khura m. ' hoof ' KātyŚr̥. 2. *khuḍa -- 1 (*khuḍaka* -- , *khula°* ' ankle -- bone ' Suśr.). [← Drav. T. Burrow BSOAS xii 376: it belongs to the word -- group ' heel <-> ankle -- knee -- wrist ', see *kuṭṭha --](CDIAL 3906).
Ta. kuracu, kuraccai horse's hoof. *Ka.* gorasu, gorase, gorise, gorusu hoof.
Te. gorija, gorise, (B. also) gorije, korije id. / Cf. Skt.khura- id. (DEDR 1770).
Allograph: (Kathiawar) *khũṭ* m. ' Brahmani bull ' (G.) Rebus: *khũṭ* 'community, guild' (Santali)

Glyph: kātī 'spinner' (G.) Rebus: khati 'wheelwright' (H.) kāṭi = fireplace in the form of a long ditch (Ta.Skt.Vedic) kāṭya = being in a hole (VS. XVI.37); kāṭ a hole, depth (RV. i. 106.6) khāḍ a ditch, a trench; khāḍ o khaiyo several pits and ditches (G.) khaṇḍrun: 'pit (furnace)' (Santali)

bhaṭa 'six' (G.) rebus: baṭa = kiln (Santali); baṭa = a kind of iron (G.) bhaṭṭhī f. 'kiln, distillery', awāṇ. bhaṭh; P. bhaṭṭh m., °ṭhī f. 'furnace', bhaṭṭhā m. 'kiln'; S. bhaṭṭhī keṇī 'distil (spirits) Glyph: 'animals': pasaramu, pasalamu = an animal, a beast, a brute, quadruped (Te.) Rebus: pasra = a smithy, place where a black-smith works, to work as a blacksmith; kamar pasra = a smithy; pasrao lagao akata se ban:? Has the blacksmith begun to work? pasraedae = the blacksmith is at his work (Santali.lex.) pasra 'smithy' (Santali) pasra meṛed, pasāra meṛed = syn. of koṭe meṛed = forged iron, in contrast to dul meṛed, cast iron (Mundari.)

Importance of a count of 'six' Elamite lady spinner. Musee du Louvre. Paris. An elegantly coiffed, exquisitely-dressed and well fanned Elamite woman sits on a feline footed stool winding thread on a spindle. The stool on which the lovely Elamite lady sits has the legs of a feline; the fish is also placed on a similar stool

in front her.This five-inch fragment is dated 8th century BCE. It was molded and carved from a mix of bitumen, ground calcite, and quartz. The Elamites used bitumen, a naturally occurring mineral pitch, or asphalt, for vessels, sculpture, glue, caulking, and waterproofing.[71]

Glyphic: 'count of six': bhaṭa 'six' (G.); rebus: bhaṭa 'furnace' (Santali) kola 'woman' (Nahali); Rebus: kolami 'smithy' (Te.) Vikalpa: goti 'woman'; rebus; goṭ 'cow-pen'; rebus: koḍ 'place where artisans work' (Kuwi) Kur. kaṇḍō a stool. Malt. kanḍo stool, seat. (DEDR 1179) Rebus: kaṇḍ 'fire-altar, furnace' (Santali) kola 'tiger, jackal' (Kon.); rebus: kolami 'smithy' (Te.) Grapheme as a phonetic determinant of the depiction of woman, kola; rebus: kolami 'smithy' (Te.) khaṇḍa 'tools, pots and pans and metal-ware'.

Lyre with Bearded Bull's Head and Inlaid Panel, Royal Cemetery, Ur, Iraq, Early Dynastic III, 2550-2450 BCE, Wood, lapis lazuli, gold, silver, shell, bitumen, H. 35.6 cm. Penn Museum Object B17694. It is possible that glyphs showing, for e.g., a fox with a dagger tucked in its waist on a lyre panel or a scorpion on a kuddurru may have underlying sounds of spoken words of language connoting a logographic writing system.

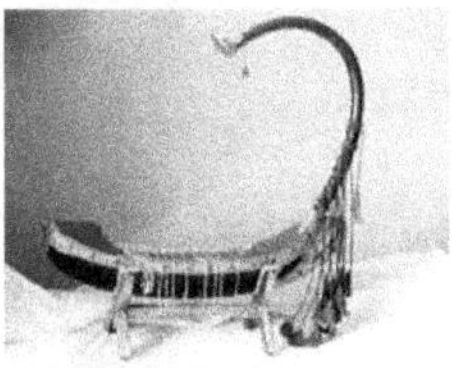

Burmese harp with 15 strings.

The Bulgarian Tambura has 8 steel strings in 4 doubled courses.

तंबुरा [tamburā] *m* (A) A Turkish guitar with four wires. (Marathi) tambūra तंबूर (=) । वाद्यविशेषः m. a kind of mandoline, or Turkish guitar, with strings of brass wire (Kashmiri) Allographs: tanbūra (Middle East) Arabic *tunbur* (طنبور) tembûr, *Tanboor* (Persian:تنبور)[72]. Rebus: Pk. *taṁbira*- - 'coppercoloured, red';

Samudragupta holding tambur on coin.[73]

The four registers depict hieroglyphs: Register 1: Smith. Bearded bull is a way of representing a profession: ḍangar 'bull' (Hindi) Rebus: ḍhangar 'blacksmith' (Hindi).

Register 2 Copper and brass ingots, copper knife: *lōī* f., *lo* m.2. Pr. *ẓūwī* 'fox' (Western Pahari)(CDIAL 11140-2). Rebus: *loh* 'copper' (Hindi). *aryeh* 'lion'. Rebus: *āra* 'brass' as in ārakūṭa (Skt.) खुंट [khuṇṭa] The square or area formed by the meeting of four roads; An end or a point of a street or road. Rebus: खोट [khōṭa] an ingot or wedge or old metal melted down (Marathi). kr̥tí2 ' knife or dagger ' RV. [√kr̥t1] Bashg. *kaṙå* ' knife ', Tor. (Biddulph) *kera* f. Rebus reading of the 'personified' fox: G lōhakāra m. ' iron -- worker ', *°rī* -- f., *°raka* -- m. lex., *lauhakāra* -- m. Hit. [lōhá -- , kāra -- 1] Pa. *lōhakāra* -- m. ' coppersmith, ironsmith '; (CDIAL 11159).

Register 3: Metal turning. loh 'fox'; rebus: loh 'copper' (Hindi) tamb(u)ra 'guitar' (Hindi) Rebus: tambira 'copper' (Pkt.) *khūṭ* m. 'Brahmani bull' (G.) Rebus: खोदणी [khōdaṇī] *f* engraving (Marathi) Rebus reading of the 'personified fox': tāmrakāra m. ' coppersmith ' lex. [tāmrá -- , kāra -- 1] Or. *tāmbarā* ' id. '.(CDIAL 5780). Register 4: Metal furnace, metalware. loh 'fox'; rebus: loh 'copper' (Hindi) Rebus: kŏnḍ कंड् 'a hole dug in the ground for receiving consecrated fire' (Kashmiri). . Skt. kuṇḍa- round hole in ground (for water or sacred fire), pit, well, spring. Ku. *lokhaṛ* ' iron tools '; H. *lokhaṇḍ* m. ' iron tools, pots and pans '; G. *lokhãḍ* n. ' tools, iron, ironware '; M. *lokhãḍ* n. ' iron ' (LM 400 < -- *khaṇḍa* --) (CDIAL 11171).

[quote]Susa… profound affinity between the Elamite people who migrated to Anshan and Susa and the Dilmunite people… Elam proper corresponded to the plateau of Fars with its capital at Anshan. We think, however that it probably extended further north into the Bakhtiari Mountains… likely that the chlorite and serpentine vases reached Susa by sea… From the victory proclamations of the

kings of Akkad we also learn that the city of Anshan had been re-established, as the capital of a impression political ally: Elam itself... the import by Ur and Eshnunna of inscribed objects typical of the Harappan culture provides the first reliable chronological evidence. [C.J. Gadd, Seals of ancient style found at Ur, *Proceedings of the British Academy, XVIII, 1932*; Henry Frankfort, Tell Asmar, Khafaje and Khorsabad, *OIC*, 16, 1933, p. 50, fig. 22). It is certainly possible that writing developed in India before this time, but we have no real proof. Now Susa had received evidence of this same civilization, admittedly not all dating from the Akkadian period, but apparently spanning all the closing years of the third millennium
(L. Delaporte, Musee du Louvre. *Catalogues des Cylindres Orientaux..., vol. I*, 1920pl. 25(15), S.29. P. Amiet, Glyptique susienne, *MDAI*, 43, 1972, vol. II, pl. 153, no. 1643).[unquote] Source: Shaika Haya Ali Al Khalifa and Michael Price, 1986, *Bahrain through the ages, the Archaeology*, Kegan Paul International, p.264.]

B. Buchanan has published a tablet dating from the reign of Gungunum of Larsa, in the twentieth century BC, which carries the impression of such a stamp seal. (B.Buchanan, Studies in honor of Benno Landsberger, Chicago, 1965, p. 204, s.).

The date so revealed has been wholly confirmed by the impression of a stamp seal from the group, fig. 85, found on a Susa tablet of the same period. (P. Amiet, Antiquites du Desert de Lut, *RA*, 68, 1974, p. 109, fig. 16. Maurice Lambert, RA, 70, 1976, p. 71-72). It is in fact, a receipt of the kind in use at the beginning of the Isin-Larsa period, and mentions a certain Milhi-El, son of Tem-Enzag, who, from the name of his god, must be a Dilmunite. In these circumstances we may wonder if this document had not been drawn up at Dilmun and sent to Susa after sealing with a local stamp seal. This seal is decorated with six tightly-packed, crouching animals, with legs under their bodies, huge heads and necks sometimes striped obliquely. The impression of another seal of similar type, fig. 86, depicts in the centre a throned figure who seems to dominate the animals,

continuing a tradition of which examples are known at the end of the Ubaid period in Assyria... Fig. 87 to 89 are Dilmun-type seals found at Susa. The boss is semi-spherical and decorated with a band across the centre and four incised circles. [Pierre Amiet, *Susa and the Dilmun Culture*, pp. 262-268].

[Figure Nos. showin in the following examples are adapted from:Shaika Haya Ali Al Khalifa and Michael Price, 1986, *Bahrain through the ages, the Archaeology*, Kegan Paul International.]

Fig.85; Susa, tablet: seal impression, Louvre Sb 11221

Fig. 86; Susa, sealing: seal impression Louvre MDAI, 43, no. 240 Six antelopes. Baṭa 'six' (G.); rebus: bhaṭa furnace (Santali)

Fig. 87; Susa, stamp seal from the Gulf, Louvre, MDAI, 43, No. 1716; depicts two goat-antelopes crouching head to tail, inside and outside an oval. Incised eyes are saucer-shaped.

Stamp seal from Susa , at Louvre Museum. "Susa is one of the oldest known settlements of the world, possibly founded about 4200 BC, although the first traces of an inhabited village have been dated to ca. 7000 BCE. The seal depicts two goat-antelopes head to tail, outside an oval."

http://arxiv.org/ftp/arxiv/papers/0809/0809.3566.pdf (Amelia Carolina Sparavigna, 2008, Symmetries in images on ancient seals.)

An early cylinder seal from Mesopotamia (Frankfort, pl.IIIb).Double snake and rosette between double goat .

Bactria: tablet depicting an animal with its head looking back; similar pictorials are seen in seals at Chanhudaro (Mackay 1943: pl. L1).

Bactria; metal pins; fig 2.10 is a pin with a head in the shape of two sitting rams;

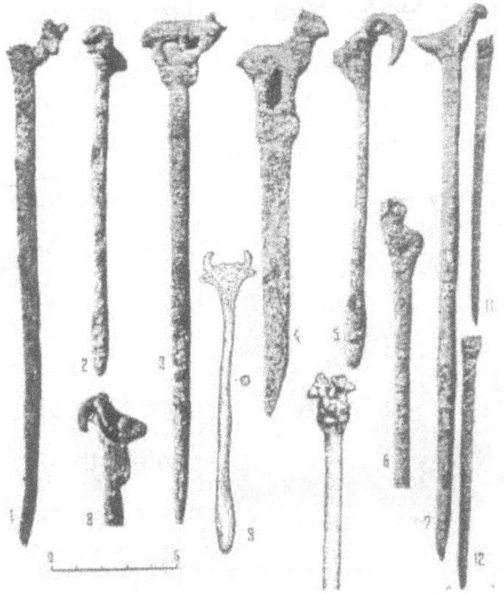

this resembles a pin was found in Mohenjodaro with a head in the form of seated goats with helically bent horns (Mackay 1937: pl. C3). Pins with zoomorphic heads is typically noticed in southwest Iran and the Near East. Fig. 2.11-12 show pins with heads in the shape of clenched fist with parallels of similar pins in Mesopotamian royal tombs of Ur (Maxwell-Hyslop 1971: 13, fig.11). Good examples of Iranian-Afghan-Indian ties.

Fig. 88; Susa, stamp sealfrom the Gulf, Teheran museum, MDAI, 43, no. 1717; an animal tamer wearing a skirt and grasping with one hand a goat-antelope with its head turned back and with its feet bound; with the other hand, the person holds a large object which looks like an architectural feature or shield or perhaps, a ladder.

Fig. 89; Susa, stamp seal from the Gulf, Teheran Museum, MDAI, 43, no. 1718; a person, naked and thin, has a stylised head shaped like a narrow arch with indentations to mark the nose and mouth. Animals have bound feet and surround a square object on which the person stands.

Fig.90; Susa, cylinder seal from the Gulf, Louvre, MDAI, 43, no. 2021; made of steatite; a person with a horned tiara, wearing an unevenly chequered robe; the person is attended by a naked man and alongside are two tamers grasping a pair ofcrossed animals.

Fig. 91; Susa, cylinder seal from the Gulf, Teheran Museum, MDAI, 43, no. 1975; steatite; three figures with stylised heads in the form of notched arches, wearing boldly chequered skirts; one is seated; the other two stand with backs turned, hold an enormous feathered arrow, and one of them extends a hand towards a stylised goat-antelope.

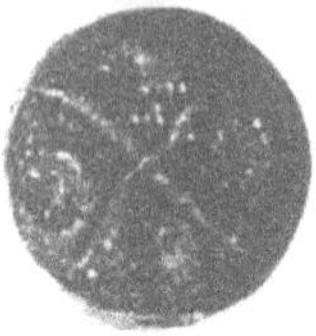

Fig. 92; Susa, stamp seal made of bitumen compound, Louvre, MDAI, 43, no. 1726; a tamer with three heavily hatched animals

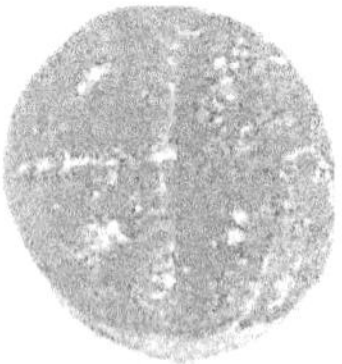

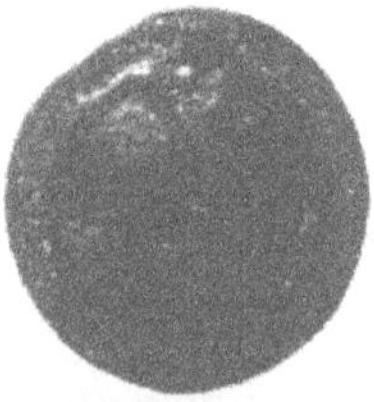

Fig. 93; Susa stamp seal made of bitumen compound, Louvre, MDAI, 43, no. 1720

Fig. 94; Susa, stamp seal from a butimen compound, Louvre, MDAI, 43, no. 1726

Fig. 95; Susa, stamp seal of bitumen compound, Louvre, MDAI, 43, no. 1725; a woman shown full-face is squatting with

legs apart, possibly on a stool. (A similar image of a woman with legs spread outoccurs on an Indus tablet).

Roach, Karen Jane, 2009, The Elamite Cylinder Seal Corpus, c.3500 - 1000 BC, University of Sydney is a landmark event in the compilation of catalogue of Elamite cylinder seals. The catalogue presents all 3597 published excavated Elamite cylinder seals and sealings from the period of the earliest manifestation of cylinder seals through to the end of the Middle Elamite period. This also presents a group of unpublished sealings from Susa held in the Tehran Museum. The material presented include administrative/accounting devices such as bullae, tablets and clay tokens. Many cylinder seals were used to seal clay tablets and envelopes and pieces of clay affixed to vessels (ceramic containers, baskets and bales) and doors (and walls). These are control functions, a type of information processing, transference or recording, in a society.

The bullae, tablets and clay tokens as classifying devices for 'numerical' accounts could be treated as a first step in the development of writing and may be discussed, together with 'proto-Elamite' texts or standard cuneiform tablets, under the category of 'writing' – a writing system which can express language, for example, authorization of integrity of goods or transference of pieces of information such as identity of goods or individuals engaged in a transaction.

Glyptic styles where 'animals acting as humans' or 'animals for transference of information' motifs get used are indicative of a method of transference of information related to the individuals engaged in the glyptic representation.

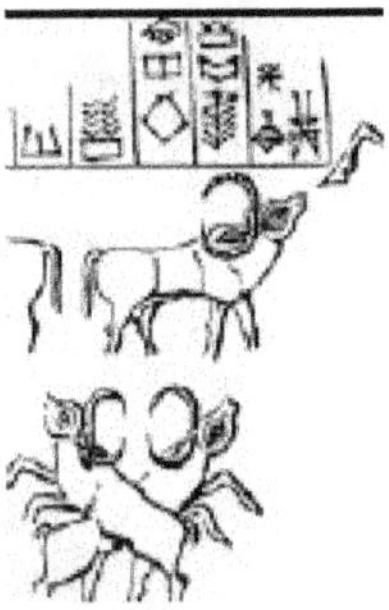

Current Number M154 Inscription: En-hedu-anna, daughter of Sargon: ….-kikudu, the scribe, (is your servant)

Current Number M178 Inscription: Kidin-Marduk, son of Ša-ilimma-damqa, the *ša reši* official of king of the world, as long as he lives

Burnaburiah,

may he be noble.

Number	**82**
Material	sealing
Site	Chogha Mish
Provenance	R17
Style	STS (4)
Orig. Class.	Protoliterate; men with cattle or other ruminants

Number	**14**
Material	door sealing
Site	Chogha Mish
Provenance	Q18
Style	STS (1)
Orig. Class.	Protoliterate; lions attacking herbivores

Number	**253**
Material	sealed tablet
Dimensions	h. c.25mm
Site	Susa
Provenance	Acropole south, Level 17.5m
Style	STS (12)
Orig. Class.	PUR

Number	**15**
Material	jar sealing
Site	Chogha Mish
Provenance	R17
Style	STS (1)
Orig. Class.	Protoliterate; lions attacking herbivores

Number	**789**
Material	faience?
Dimensions	34 x 24mm
Site	Susa
Style	CPE (1)
Orig. Class.	Agadé

Number	**163**
Material	sealed bulla
Site	Chogha Mish
Provenance	R17
Style	STS (7)
Orig. Class.	Protoliterate; lion attacking bull

Classic Proto-Elamite Style

Material	sealed tablet
Site	Susa
Style	CPE (3)
Orig. Class.	Proto-Elamite

Number	**837**
Material	sealing
Site	Susa
Style	CPE (2)
Orig. Class.	GPE

Number	**820**
Material	sealed tablet
Site	Susa
Style	CPE (1)
Orig. Class.	PEC

Number	**1042**
Material	sealed tablet
Site	Susa
Style	CPE (8)
Orig. Class.	Proto-Elamite

Number	**90**
Material	sealed tablet
Site	Susa
Style	STS (5)
Orig. Class.	PUR

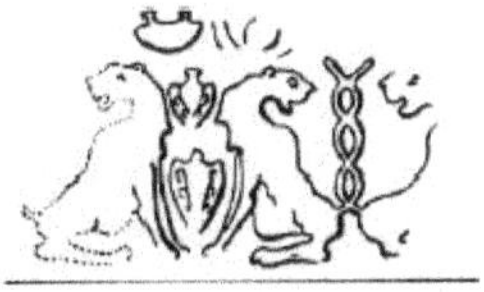

Number	**2208**
Material	black serpentine
Dimensions	42 x 29mm
Site	Susa
Provenance	"Temple of Shushinak"
Style	ARS (10)
Orig. Class.	Agadé period

Number	**2209**
Material	yellowish-green jasper
Dimensions	38 x 25mm
Site	Susa
Style	ARS (10)
Orig. Class.	Agadé period

Number	**792**
Material	sealed tablet
Site	Susa
Style	CPE (1)
Orig. Class.	Proto-Elamite period

Number	**1032**
Material	sealed tablet
Site	Susa
Style	CPE (8)
Orig. Class.	Proto-Elamite

Number	**1033**
Material	sealed tablet
Site	Susa
Style	CPE (8)
Orig. Class.	Proto-Elamite

Number	**1034**
Material	sealed tablet
Site	Susa
Style	CPE (8)
Orig. Class.	Proto-Elamite

Number	**73**
Material	jar stopper
Site	Chogha Mish
Provenance	North of R17
Style	STS (4)
Orig. Class.	Protoliterate; single species animal file

Number	**420**
Material	sealing
Site	Susa
Style	STS (17)
Orig. Class.	GPE

Number	**1061**
Material	sealed tablet
Site	Susa
Style	CPE (8)
Orig. Class.	PEC

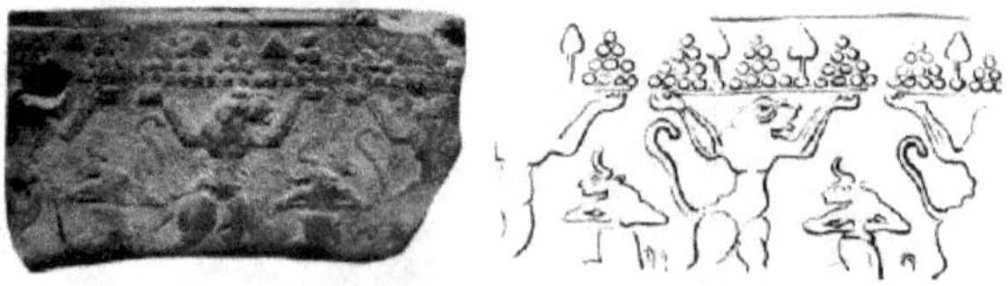

Number	**434**
Material	tablet sealed by three cylinders (cf. *134*, *440*)
Dimensions	h: 21mm
Site	Susa
Style	STS (19)
Orig. Class.	PUR

Number	**435**
Material	sealed tablet
Site	Susa
Style	STS (19)
Orig. Class.	PUR

Number 2214
Material serpentine
Dimensions 14 x 23mm
Site Susa
Style ARS (10)
Orig. Class. APA

Number 2211
Material sealings
Site Susa
Style ARS (10)
Inscription *untranslated*

Number 841
Material sealed tablet
Site Susa
Style CPE (3)
Orig. Class. Proto-Elamite period

Number 2228
Material light green serpentine
Dimensions 13 x 23mm
Site Susa
Style ARS (10)
Orig. Class. APA

Number 263
Material sealing
Site Chogha Mish
Provenance Q18
Style STS (12)
Orig. Class. Protoliterate, herbivores, plants and nets

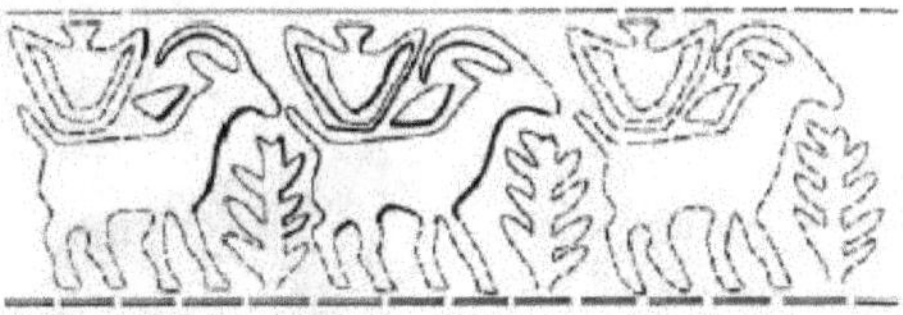

Number 65
Material sealed bulla
Site Susa
Style STS (4)
Orig. Class. PUR

Number	**2242**
Material	sealing
Dimensions	h: 19mm
Site	Susa
Style	ARS (10)
Orig. Class.	APA
Inscription	Shu-ilishu, son of Ish…

Number	**2244**
Material	serpentine
Dimensions	13 x 24mm
Site	Susa
Style	ARS (10)
Orig. Class.	APA
Inscription	Dudu, / tailor

Number	**2248**
Material	sealed bulla
Site	Susa
Style	ARS (10)
Orig. Class.	APA
Inscription	Epirmupi, the Strong, Liburbeli, cupbearer, his servant

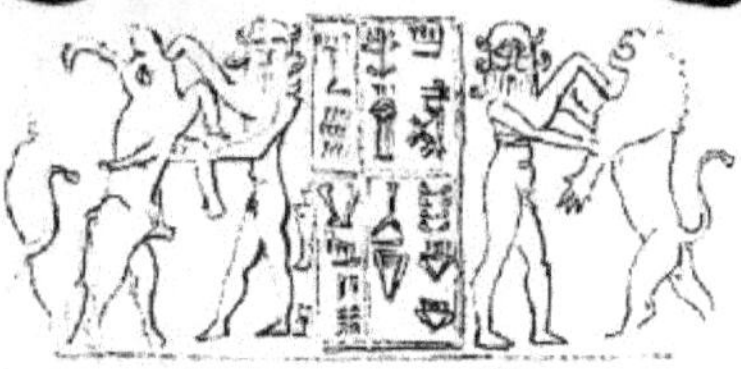

Number	**2781**
Material	sealing
Site	Haft Tepe
Style	EME (1)
Orig. Class.	NSH

[quote] The ancient region of Elam (southwestern Iran) has produced a significant assemblage of cylinder seals across a considerable chronological span. Unlike the glyptic material from the related and neighbouring region Mesopotamia, the Elamite cylinder seals have not previously been studied in detailed reference to one another, nor has there been an established paradigm of stylistic development articulated. This study addresses this lacuna by compiling all the published cylinder seals from Elam (as defined here, thus incorporating

the historical provinces of Khuzistan, Luristan and Fars), from their earliest appearance (c.3500 BC), throughout the era of their typological dominance (over stamp seals, thus this study departs c.1000 BC). This compilation is presented in the Elamite Cylinder Seal Catalogue (Volume II), and is annotated and described through the annunciation of eighteen chronologically defined developmental styles (with another two non-chronological type classifications and four miscellaneous groups). Through the further analysis of this data, including the newly formulated and articulated styles, several facets and problems of Elamite glyptic material have been addressed (and thus the reliance upon assumed similarity in type and function with the Mesopotamian glyptic material is abandoned). These problems particularly pertain to the function of cylinder seals in Elam and the type and form of the Elamite-Mesopotamian glyptic interaction. In regards to function, a standard administrative function can be discerned, though of varying types and forms across the region and the period of study. Other, non-standard, symbolic glyptic functions can also be demonstrated in the Corpus, including the apparent proliferation of a form known as the 'votive' seal, perhaps a specifically Elamite form. The analysis of the style type (whether 'Elamite', 'Mesopotamian Related' or 'Shared Elamite-Mesopotamian'), in association with their relative geographical and chronological distribution, has also enabled the discussion of the nature of Elamite-Mesopotamian glyptic interaction, and thereby the constitution of Elamite civilisation (especially in regards to Mesopotamian cultural impact and influence, and thus the testing of several previously presented paradigms [Amiet 1979a; 1979b; Miroschedji 2003]). [unquote]

01kj-roach-2008-thesis.pdf Vol. I, Part I

02kj-roach-2008-thesis.pdf Vol. I, Part II

03kj-roach-2008-thesis.pdf Vol. I, Part III

04kj-roach-2008-thesis.pdf Vol. II, Part I

05kj-roach-2008-thesis.pdf Vol. II, Part II

First bronze alloy of arsenical-copper was due to the dual occurrence of arsenic and copper in some ores. The argument is that Sumerians of ED III adopted tin bronze, that is, intentional addition of tin to copper, mainly for its fuel efficiency over copper and arsenical copper:

[quote] By 3600 BCE, people at thesite of Tepe Hissar were using a crucible that required a highdegree of pyrotechnic knowledge to produce (Thornton, C. P., and T. Rehren. 2009. A truly Refractory Crucible from Fourth Millennium Tepe Hissar, Northeast Iran. *Journal of Archaeological Science* 36:2700–2712).

By the late □ourth/early third millennium BCE, arsenical iron (speiss) was being produced at the same site, perhaps indicating an attempt to create an arsenic-rich metal tobe melted down later into a copper alloy.[74] This would represent the earliest attempt toco-smelt multiple metals. Tin bronze was adopted most thoroughly on the Iranian plateau in the early second millennium BCE, but some sites were already beginning to incorporate tinbronze in the third millennium[75]...Not only was Mesopotamia witness to the earliest fully developed urban civilization, writing, and irrigation agriculture, but the Sumerians of the EDIII period (ca. 2500 BCE) were the first to adopt tin bronze technology.[76] This was likely due in large part to a lack of timber fuel, a by-product of both natural conditions and land-clearing activities intended to create pasturelands for faunal domesticates such as goat, sheep, and cattle. In tandem, this proliferation of faunal domesticates made huge quantities of dung fuel available. As mentioned above, tin can be melted in an ordinary fire, and it is likely that access to dung fuel helped spur the adoption of tin. As discussed above, tin bronze technology was invented in the mountainous areas to the north of Mesopotamia some half-millennium earlier, but the technology and tin resources were never in demand until the time of the Sumerians, which raises some interesting questions: Why tin? Why at different times across various regions was tin bronze in demand, hundreds of years after its invention? It is unfortunate that modern geopolitical circumstances preclude scientific excavations at present in Iraq, but it may be possible to clarify these questions via application of thermo-technological principles, combined with what we already know about the mechanical and aesthetic properties of copper and its

alloys. The field of archaeology is currently witnessing a sea change in analytical capabilities, making it possible for research questions to be answered in the laboratory and not just in the field. Under the Akkadian Empire (ca 2250–2100 BCE), perhaps the world's first empire and with its famous early leaders such as Sargon and his grandson Naram-Sin, the production of tin bronze was halted in the Jezireh (northern Mesopotamia).Interestingly enough, tin bronze production continued in Sumer at Ur and was resumed by the Ur III dynasty.[77] The Sumerians likely had continual access to the Persian Gulf in this period despite their Akkadian overlords. Does this mean they were receiving tin from what they called Meluhha—the Harappan of the Indus Valley—via sea trade? The best scholarship can do currently isto pose these questions, as the answers remain elusive. The sphere of Sumerian infuence extended from India to Anatolia. Just after the Sumerians of the ED III adopted tin bronze, so did the Harappans and the Anatolians.[78] It is also likely that tin bronze was adopted at around the same time in the Khabur triangle and the Balikh, at sites such as Tell Brak, as well as at Mari, but we are still awaiting a comprehensive analysis of the metals that have been excavated from this region.[unquote][79]

Egyptian hieroglyphs

The extensive use of hieroglyphs in Indus writing is comparable to the ones used on Narmer palette which is rebus method of writing. The name of the king ca. 31st

century BCE was depicted by two glyphs (on top of the palette between two ox-heads). The same set of hieroglyphs is repeated on the second register which shows Narmer in a procession with some carrying banners. A person following Narmer is shown with a 'rosette' hieroglyph. The 'rosette' hieroglyph is also shown together with 'scorpion' hieroglyph on what has been referred to as a 'Scorpion macehead'. (Ashmolean museum).

kunda m. 'Jasminum multiflorum or pubescens' MBh. (' olibanum or resin of Boswellia thurifera ' lex., see kunduru -), n. 'its flower'. Pa. *kunda* -- n. 'jasmine'; Pk. *kuṁda* -- m. 'a flowering tree', n. 'a kind of flowe '; B. *kũd* 'J. multiflorum',

M. *kũd* m. ' id. ', *kũdā* m. 'a partic. kind of flowering shrub'; Si. *kon̆da* 'jasmine'. (CDIAL 3296)

meṭ sole of foot, footstep, footprint (Ko.); meṭṭu step, stair, treading, slipper (Te.)(DEDR 1557). Rebus: मेढ 'merchant's helper' (Pkt.); *m.* an elephant-keeper Gal. (cf. मेठ). *Ta.* mēṭṭi haughtiness, excellence, chief, head, land granted free of tax to the headman of a village; *mēṭṭimai* haughtiness; leadership, excellence. *Ka.* mēṭi loftiness, greatness, excellence, a big man, a chief, a head, head servant. *mēti.* n. Lit: a helper. A servant, a cook, a menial who cleans plates, dishes, lamps and shoes, &c. (Eng. 'mate') మే టి[mēṭi] or మే టరి *mēṭi* [Tel.] n. A chief, leader, head man, lord (Telugu) மேட்டி mēṭṭi, *n.* Assistant house-servant; waiting-boy (Tamil)

He also carries a pot. కుండ kuṇḍa] *kuṇḍa.* [Tel.] n. An earthern pot. A pot. కుంచుకుంట a bell metal pot. కుండము [kuṇḍamu] *kuṇḍamu.* [Skt.] n. An earthen pot. A pit or pot for receiving and preserving consecrated fire. A fire pit (Telugu) T*a.* kuṭam waterpot, hub of a wheel (DEDR 1651). Thus the three hieroglyphs of 'rosette', 'feet', 'pot' may denote that the person was a chief metal-turner: *meḍ* 'iron' *kundār* 'turner'.

Ia. 18

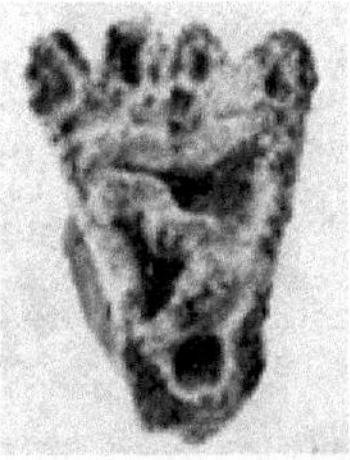

Tepe Yahya. Seal impressions of two sides of a seal. Six-legged lizard and opposing footprints shown on opposing sides of a double-sided steatite stamp seal perforated along the lateral axis. Lamberg- Karlovsky 1971: fig. 2C Shahr-i-Soktha Stamp seal shaped like a foot. Shahdad seal (Grave 78)

Tepe Yahya. Two sides of Tepe Yahya ('weight'?) fragment apparently reused as door socket during IVB times. One side depicts palms, and the other has a representation of a humped bull with a scorpion set above its back.

Tepe Yahya. Steatite stamp seal made from four-sided perforated bead with images of a scorpion, palm tree, fish, and two stars. Lamberg-Karlovsky, C. C., 1979, Excavations at Tepe Yahya, Iran 1967-1969: progress report 1, Bulletin (American School of Prehistoric Research) ; no. 27, Cambridge, Mass.: Peabody Museam, (Jointly with The Asia Institute of Pahlavi University).

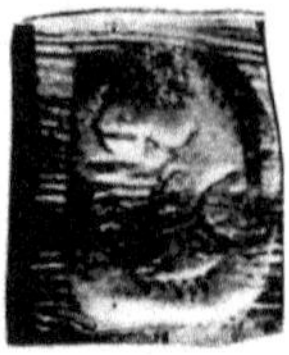

Rectangular stamp seal of dark steatite; U. 11181; B.IM. 7854; ht. 1.4, width 1.1 cm.; Woolley, Ur Excavations, IV (1956), p. 50, n.3. Scorpion.

Obverse of steatite Dilmun stamp seal from Failaka Island (c. 2000 BCE). A human figure and a variety of animals – two antelopes one with its head looking backward; possibly a scorpion at the feet of the human figure. A dotted circle is seen above one antelope and a vase in between the antelope and the human figure. Kuwait National Museum. French Archaeological Expedition in Kuwait. Several inscriptions at Failaka mention the Dilmunite god Enzak and his temple or Mesopotamian deities. [Remi Boucharlat, Archaeology and Artifacts of the Arabian Peninsula, in: Jack M. Sasson (ed.), Civilizations of the Ancient Near East, pp. 1335-1353].

Glyph: *meṭṭu* 'foot'. Rebus: *meḍ* 'iron' (Ho.Mu.) dula 'pair' (Kashmiri); dul 'cast (metal)(Santali). Six legs of a lizard is an enumeration of six 'portable furnaces' ; rebus: kakra. 'lizard'; kan:gra 'portable furnace'. bhaṭa 'six' (G.) rebus: baṭa = kiln (Santali); baṭa = a kind of iron (G.) bhaṭṭhī f. 'kiln, distillery', awāṇ. bhaṭh; P. bhaṭṭh m., °ṭhī f. 'furnace', bhaṭṭhā m. 'kiln'; S. bhaṭṭhī keṇī 'distil (spirits)'. Read rebus as : *dul (pair) meḍ* 'cast iron'; *kan:gra bhaṭa* 'portable furnace'.

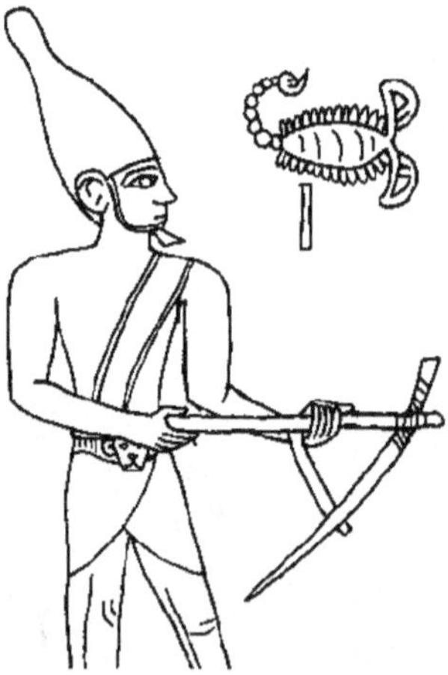

kundau to turn on a lathe, to carve, to chase;

kundau dhiri = a hewn stone; kundau murhut = a graven image (Santali)

kunda1 m. ' a turner's lathe ' lex. [Cf. *cunda -- 1] N. *kũdnu* ' to shape smoothly, smoothe, carve, hew ', *kũduwā* ' smoothly shaped '; A. *kund* ' lathe ', *kundiba* ' to

turn and smooth in a lathe ', *kundowā* ' smoothed and rounded '; B. *kũd* ' lathe ', *kũdā, kõdā* ' to turn in a lathe '; Or. *kū̆nda* ' lathe ', *kũdibā, kũd°* ' to turn ' (→ Drav. Kur. *kũd* ' lathe '); Bi. *kund* ' brassfounder's lathe '; H.*kunnā* ' to shape on a lathe ', *kuniyā* m. ' turner ', *kunwā* m. (CDIAL 3295) kundakara m. ' turner ' W. [Cf. *cundakāra -- : kunda -- 1, kará -- 1] A. *kundār*, B. *kũdār, °ri*, Or. *kundāru*; H. *kũderā* m. ' one who works a lathe, one who scrapes ', *°rī* f., *kũdernā* ' to scrape, plane, round on a lathe '.(CDIAL 3297). कोंदण [kōndaṇa] n (कोंदणें) Setting or infixing of gems.(Marathi) খোদকার [khōdakāra] n an engraver; a carver (Bengali) kundan कुंदन् । निर्मलं हेम m. pure gold, the finest gold (Śiv. 531, 1293). -- char hyuhu -- छर् हिहु । अतिनिर्मलम् भूषणम् adj. (f. -- hishü), like a drop of pure gold; hence, very flawless and brilliant (Kashmiri). Possible parallel with Egyptian hieroglyphs? The readings of the Egyptian hieroglyphs on the 'scorpion macehead' are unclear.[80] However, the hoe carried by the person yields a hieroglyphic clue: Gaw. *kundā́l* ' hoe '; Wg. *koṇḍāl, kondāl* ' mattock, hoe '. (CDIAL 3286) *Ta.* kuntāli, kuntāḷi pickaxe. *Ma.* kuntāli, kūntāli id. *Kurub. (LSB* 1.11) kidli a spade. *Ko.* kuda·y hoe. *Ka.* guddali, gudli a kind of pickaxe, hoe. *Koḍ.* guddalihoe with spade-like blade. *Tu.* guddali, guddoli, (B-K.) guddoḷi a kind of pickaxe; guddolipuni to dig with a pickaxe. *Te.* guddali, (*VPK*) guddili, guddela, guddēli, guddēlu a hoe; guddalincu to hoe. *Nk.* kudaḷ spade. *Go.* (G. Mu.) kudaṛ spade, axe; (Ma. M. Ko.) guddaṛ spade, hoe (*Voc.* 749); (LuS.) goodar hoe. *Konḍa* gudelihoe-like instrument for digging. *Malt.* qodali a spade. (DEDR 1722). The combination of hieroglyphs of 'rosette' + 'scorpion' may denote: *kundan,* 'gold carver' (with kundā 'hoe' as a phonetic determinant).

Seal impession from Ur showing a squatting female. L. Legrain, 1936, *Ur excavations, Vol. 3, Archaic Seal Impressions.* [cf. Nausharo seal with two scorpions flanking a similar glyph with legs apart – also looks like a frog]. kuṭhi 'pudendum muliebre' (Mu.) khoḍu m. 'vulva' (CDIAL 3947). Rebus: kuṭhi 'smelter furnace' (Mu.) khŏḍ m. 'pit', khŏḍü f. 'small pit'

(Kashmiri. CDIAL 3947),

Rahman-dheri seal. Obverse: Two scorpions. Two holes. One T glyph. One frog in the middle. Reverse: two rams.

1. mūxā 'frog'. Rebus: mũh '(copper) ingot' (Santali) Allograph: mũhe 'face' (Santali)
2. bicha 'scorpion' (Assamese) Rebus: bica 'stone ore' (Mu.)
3. tagaru 'ram' (Tulu) Rebus: tagarm 'tin' (Kota). damgar 'merchant' (Akk.)
4. T-glyph may denote a fire altar like the two fire-altars shown on Warrka vase below two animals: antelope and tiger. kand 'fire-altar' (Santali)
5. Two holes may denote ingots. dula 'pair' Rebus: dul 'cast' (Santali)

urseal11Seal; UPenn; a scorpion and an elipse [an eye (?)]; U. 16397; Gadd, PBA 18

(1932), pp. 10-11, pl. II, no. 11 [Note: Is the 'eye' an oval representation of a bun ingot.) Glyph: *bichā 'scorpion'* (As+samese) Rebus: *bica* 'stone ore' (Munda)

Glyph shown together with stong of scorpion on Urseal 1. Rebus: खोट [*khōṭa*] 'ingot, wedge'; A mass of metal (unwrought or of old metal melted down)(Maratthi) *khoṭf* 'alloy (Lahnda) Hence खोटसाळ [khōṭasāḷa] *a* (खोट & साळ from शाला) Alloyed--a metal. (Marathi) Bshk. *khoṭ* ' embers ', Phal. *khūṭo* ' ashes, burning coal '; L. *khoṭā* ' alloyed ', awāṇ. *khoṭā* ' forged '; P. *khoṭ* m. ' base, alloy ' M.*khoṭā* ' alloyed ', (CDIAL 3931) *Kor.* (O.) The seal thus depicts an ingot made of *bica*, 'stone ore'.

khōṭ 'alloyed ingots' Susa, stamp seal from the Gulf, Louvre, MDAI, 43, No. 1716[81]; depicts two goat-antelopes crouching head to tail, inside and outside an oval. Incised eyes are saucer-shaped. Stamp seal from Susa , at Louvre Museum. "Susa is one of the oldest known settlements of the world, possibly founded about 4200 BC, although the first traces of an

inhabited village have been dated to ca. 7000 BCE. The seal depicts two goat-antelopes head to tail, outside an oval."[82] Glyph: tagaru 'ram' (Tulu) Rebus: tagarm 'tin' (Kota). damgar 'merchant' (Akk.) Thus, the seal depicts a tin, alloyed ingots merchant.

khōṭ 'alloyed ingots' An early cylinder seal from Mesopotamia (Frankfort, pl.IIIb).Double snake and rosette between double goat .

Chanhu-daro Seal obverse and reverse. The oval sign of this Jhukar culture seal is comparable to other inscriptions. Fig. 1 and 1a of Plate L. After Mackay, 1943. The hieroglyphs of the seal relate representations of bun ingots to two orthographic representations of 'antelopes': one is shown walking, the other is shown with head turned backwards. A flower is shown, perhaps, a representation of *tabernae Montana.* Hieroglyph of 'looking back': క్రమ్మరు [krammaru] *krammaru.* [Tel.] v. n. To turn, return, go back. మరలు. క్రమ్మరించు or క్రమ్మరుచు *krammarinṭsu.* V. a. To turn, send back, recall. To revoke, annul, rescind. క్రమ్మరజేయు. క్రమ్మర *krammara.* Adv. Again. క్రమ్మరిల్లు or క్రమరబడు Same as క్రమ్మరు. krəm back'(Kho.)(CDIAL 3145) Kho. Krəm ' back ' NTS ii 262 with (?) (CDIAL 3145)[Cf. Ir. *kamaka – or *kamraka -- ' back ' in Shgh. Čůmč ' back ', Sar. Čomǰ EVSh 26] (CDIAL 2776) cf. Sang. kamak ' back ', Shgh. Čomǰ (< *kamak G.M.) ' back of an animal ', Yghn. Kama ' neck ' (CDIAL 14356). Kár, kãr 'neck' (Kashmiri) Kal. Gřä ' neck '; Kho. Goḷ ' front of neck, throat '. Gala m. ' throat, neck ' MBh. (CDIAL 4070) Rebus: karmāra 'smith, artisan' (Skt.) kamar 'smith' (Santali)

Glyph: tagaru 'ram' (Tulu) Rebus: tagarm 'tin' (Kota). damgar 'merchant' (Akk.) Thus, the seal depicts a tin ingot merchant. క్రమ్మరు [krammaru] v. n. To turn, return, go back (Telugu) Rebus: kamar 'smith, artisan' (Santali). Mth. *kamarsārī* 'smithy' (CDIAL 2899). An alternative reading is: tagar + khar 'tin smith' using the

word khar 'blacksmith' (Kashmiri). Thus, the side of the seal denotes a tin ingot smith.

Seal impression; UPenn; steatite; bull below a scorpion; dia. 2.4cm.; Gadd, PBA 18 (1932), p. 13, Pl. III, no. 15; Legrain, MJ (1929), p. 306, pl. XLI, no. 119; found at Ur in the cemetery area, in a ruined grave .9 metres from the surface, together with a pair of gold ear-rings of the double-crescent type and long beads of steatite and carnelian, two of gilt copper, and others of lapis-lazuli, carnelian, and banded sard. The first sign to the left has the form of a flower or perhaps an animal's skin with curly tail; there is a round spot upon the bull's back. The round spot is an indicator of an ingot made of stone ore (*bica*).

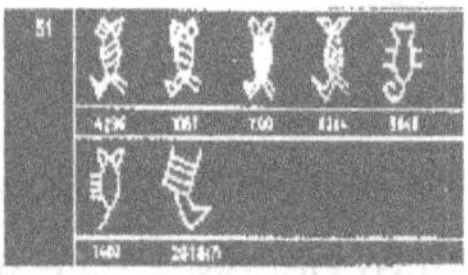

One cylinder-seal impression which includes an antelope hieroglyph may be cited: Cylinder-seal impression; a griffin and a tiger attack an antelope with its head turned back. The upper register shows two scorpions and a frog; the lower register shows a scorpion and two fishes. Syro-Mitannian, fifteenth to fourteenth centuries BCE, Pierpont Morgan Library, New York. [After Fig. 9 in: Jack M. Sasson (ed.), 1995, *Civilizations of the Ancient Near East*, Gale Cengage, Independence, KY, p.2705].

The following rebus readings of the hieroglyphs are suggested:

1. mūxā 'frog'. Rebus: mũh '(copper) ingot' (Santali) Allograph: mũhe 'face' (Santali)
2. bicha 'scorpion' (Assamese) Rebus: bica 'stone ore' (Mu.)
3. tagaru 'ram' (Tulu) Rebus: tagarm 'tin' (Kota). damgar 'merchant' (Akk.)
4. kola 'tiger, jackal' (Kon.) Rebus: kol working in iron, blacksmith (Tamil) kol 'furnace, forge' (Kuwi) Note: Smithy was designated by cognate words which also meant 'temple'. Allograph: kolom 'cob'; kolmo 'seedling, rice (paddy) plant' (Munda.)

5. ayo 'fish' (Mu.) Rebus: aya 'cast metal' (G.); ayah, ayas = metal (Skt.) ayaskāṇḍa 'a quantity of iron, excellent iron' (Pāṇ.gaṇ)

Glyph *Ka. koṇḍi* the sting of a scorpion. *Tu. koṇḍi* a sting. *Te. koṇḍi* the sting of a scorpion.(DEDR 2080).

Rebus: kuṇḍī = chief of village. kuṇḍi-a = village headman; leader of a village (Pkt.lex.) i.e. śreṇi jeṭṭha chief of metal-worker guild. khŏḍ m. 'pit', khŏḍü f. 'small pit' (Kashmiri. CDIAL 3947), kuṭhi 'smelter furnace' (Mu.)

The Narmer Palette (Great Hierakonpolis Palette) Cairo J.E. 14716, C.G. 32169 Hierakonpolis (Horus Temple 'Main Deposit') At the top of both sides of the Palette are the central serekhs bearing the rebus symbols n'r (catfish) and m'r (chisel) inside, being the phonetic representation of Narmer's name. The Narmer Palette is a 63-centimetre tall (2.07 ft), shield-shaped, ceremonial palette, carved from a single piece of flat, soft dark gray-green siltstone.[83]

Impression from a cylinder seal. urseal6 Cylinder seal; BM 122947; U. 16220 (cut down into Ur III mausolea from Larsa level; U. 16220), enstatite; Legrain, 1951, No. 632; Collon, 1987, Fig. 611. Humped bull stands before a plant, feeding from a round manger or a bundle of fodder (or, probably, a cactus); behind the bull is a scorpion and two snakes; above the whole a human figure, placed horizontally, with fantastically long arms and legs, and rays about his head.

Six hieroglyphs of the cylinder seal denote: 1. tin (tagara, tabernae Montana) 2. Pewter, alloy of tin and antimony (ranga, thorny) 3. Alloyed metal (*khoṭā* 'alloyed'; khũṭ 'zebu bull') 4. stone ore (bica, scorpion) 5. Copper (tampur 'longlegged', tambira 'copper' 6. Smithy, mine (*koḍ* 'where artisans work' khondu 'small ditch or moat') khāḍ 'creek'; khaḍḍā 'mine' .

Six hieroglyphs:

1.tagara 'tabernae montana' (Skt.) Rebus: tagara 'tin' (Ka.) tagromi 'tin, metal alloy' (Kuwi) takaram tin, white lead, metal sheet, coated with tin (Ta.); tin, tinned iron plate (Ma.); tagarm tin (Ko.); tagara, tamara, tavara id. (Ka.) tamaru, tamara, tavara id. (Ta.): tagaramu, tamaramu, tavaramu id. (Te.); ṭagromi tin metal, alloy (Kuwi); tamara id. (Skt.)(DEDR 3001). trapu tin (AV.); tipu (Pali); tau, taua lead (Pkt.); tū_ tin (P.); ṭau zinc, pewter (Or.); tarūaum lead (OG.); tarvu~ (G.); tumba lead (Si.)(CDIAL 5992).

2. ran:ga ron:ga, ran:ga con:ga = thorny, spikey, armed with thorns; (Santali) Rebus: ran:ga, ran: pewter is an alloy of tin lead and antimony (añjana) (Santali). Glyph: 'bush, thorn': Pk. *kaṁṭiya* -- ' thorny '; S. *kaṇḍī* f. ' thorn bush '; N. *kāṛe* ' thorny '; A. *kāṭi* ' point of an oxgoad ', *kāiṭīyā* ' thorny '; H. *kāṭī* f. ' thorn bush '; G.*kāṭī* f. ' a kind of fish '; M. *kāṭī, kāṭī* f. ' thorn bush '. -- Ext. with -- *la* -- : S. *kaṇḍiru* ' thorny, bony '; -- with -- *lla* -- : Gy. pal. *ḳăndī́la* ' prickly pear '; H. *kāṭīlā, kaṭ°* ' thorny '.(CDIAL 2679). kāṇṭaka -- ĀpŚr.1. Paš. *kāṛ* ' porcupine ' (cf. *kaṇṭakaśrēṇi* -- , *kaṇṭakāgāra* --). 2. S. *kāḍo* ' thorny ', Si. *kaṭu.* -- Deriv.: S. *kāḍero* m. ' camel -- thorn ', *°rī* f. ' a kind of thistle '(CDIAL 3022). Rebus: *Tu.* kandůka, kandaka ditch, trench. *Te.* kandakamu id. *Konḍa* kanda trench made as a fireplace during weddings. *Pe.* Kanda fire trench. *Kui* kanda small trench for fireplace. *Malt.* kandri a pit.(DEDR 1214). Rebus: *kaṇḍ* 'tools, pots and pans and metal-ware'.

3. adar ḍangra 'zebu or humped bull'; rebus: aduru 'native metal' (Ka.); ḍhangar 'blacksmith' (H.) khūṭro = entire bull; khūṭ= brāhmaṇi bull (G.) khūṭ 'guild, community' (Santali) Rebus: L. *khoṭ* f. ' alloy, impurity ', *°ṭā* ' alloyed ', awāṇ. *khoṭā* ' forged '; P. *khoṭ* m. ' base, alloy ' M.*khoṭā* ' alloyed ', (CDIAL 3931)

4.koṇḍi 'the sting of a scorpion'. Rebus: kŏnḍ क्रंड् 'a hole dug in the ground for receiving consecrated fire' (Kashmiri) *bichā 'scorpion'* (Assamese) *vicchī* m. ' scorpion '.; Pa. *vicchika* -- m. ' scorpion ', Pk. *vicchia* -- , *viṁchia* -- m., Sh.koh. *bič̣h* m. (< **vr̥ści* -- ?), Ku. *bichī,* A. *bisā* (also ' hairy caterpillar ': -- *ī* replaced by m. ending --*ā*), B. Or. *bichā,* Mth. *bīch,* Bhoj. Aw.lakh. *bīchī,* H. poet. *bīchī* f., *bīchā* m., G. *vīchī, vīchī* m.; -- **vicchuma* -- : Paš.lauṛ. *ućúm,* dar. *učum,* S. *vichū* m., (with greater deformation) L.mult. *vaṭhūhā,*

khet. *vaṭṭhūha*; -- Pk. *vicchua* -- , *viṁchua* -- m., L. *vichū* m., awāṇ. *vicchū*, P. *bicchū* m., Or. (Sambhalpur) *bichu*, Mth. *bīchu*, H.*bicchū*, *bīchū* m., G. *vīchu* m.; -- Pk. *viccu* -- , *°ua* -- , *viṁcua* -- m., K. *byucu* m. (← Ind.), P.bhaṭ. *biccū*, WPah.bhal. *biċċū* m., cur. *biccū*, bhiḍ. *biċċoṭū* n. ' young scorpion ', M. *vīċū*, *vĩċū* m. (*vĩċḍā* m. ' large scorpion '), *vĩċvī*, *°ċvīṇ*, *°ċīṇ* f., Ko. *viccu*, *viṁcu*, *iṁcu*. -- N. *bacchiũ* ' large hornet '? (Scarcely < **vapsi* -- ~ *vaspi --).vṛ́ścika -- : Garh. *bicchū*, *°chī* ' scorpion ', A. also *bichā* (phonet. -- *s* --) (CDIAL 12081) Rebus: meṛed-bica = iron stone ore, in contrast to bali-bica, iron sand ore (Munda) *bica meṛed* iron extracted from stone ore; *bali meṛed* iron extracted from sand ore (Munda) kuṭire bica duljaḍko talkena, they were feeding the furnace with ore (Santali) samr.obica, stones containing gold (Mundari.lex.)

AllographA viciṟi fan; vicukk-eṉal onom. expr. of quick movement; vicai (-pp-, -tt-) to hasten, cause to move swiftly, swing, leap, hop, burst, split, be forceful; *n.* haste, speed, impetus, elasticity, spring, force, contrivance as a trap, lever. *Ma.* vīcuka to fan, cast (nets); vīcci fan (DEDR 5450). vyajana -- n. ' fan ' Mn. (CDIAL 12043). Rebus: bica 'stone ore' (Munda)

5. Glyph: tampur 'long-legged' (Santali) Rebus: Pa. Pkt. *tamba* -- ' red ', n. 'copper', Pk. *taṁbira* -- 'coppercoloured, red'; S.kcch. *trāmo*, *tām(b)o* m. 'copper'; G.*tābaṛ* n., *trābṛī*, *tābṛī* f. ' copper pot '; Pa. Pkt. *tamba* -- 'red ', n. 'copper' (CDIAL 5779). Allograph: tebṛa, tebor. 'three times, thrice'; tebṛage emok hoyoktama you will have to give three times that (Santali) Allograph: ṭakkarā f. ' blow on the head ' Rājat. [Cf. *ṭakk -- 2] Pk. ṭakkara -- m. ' collision ', K. ṭakara m.; S. ṭakaru m. ' knocking the head against anything, butting ', ṭakiraṇu ' to knock against, encounter, be compared with '; L. ṭakkaraṇ ' to meet, agree '; P. ṭakkar f. ' pushing, knocking ', ṭakkarṇā ' to collide, meet '; Ku. ṭakkar ' shock, jerk, loss '; N. ṭakar ' obstacle, collision '; B. ṭakkar ' blow ', Or. ṭakkara, ṭākara, H. G. M. ṭakkar f. (CDIAL 6701)

6. Glyph:khondu 'small ditch or moat' (Kashmiri) gaḍa m. ' ditch ' lex. Pk. *gaḍa* -- n. ' hole '; Paš. *gaṛu* ' dike '; Kho. (Lor.) *gōḷ* ' hole, small dry ravine '; A. *garā* ' high bank '; B. *gaṛ* ' ditch, hole in a husking machine '; Or. *gaṛa* '

ditch, moat'; M. *gaḷ* f. ' hole in the game of marbles '.Wpah. khaḍḍā 'stream'; gaḍōṛ 'river, stream'; N. gaṛ—tir 'bank of a river'; S. khāṛī f. 'gulf, creek'; P. khāṛ 'level country at the foot of a mountain', ṛī f. 'deep watercourse, creek'; Bi. khārī 'creek, inlet'; M. khāḍ f. 'hole, creek', ḍā m. 'hole', ḍī f. 'creek, inlet' (CDIAL 3863, 3947) rebus: khāḍ 'trench, firepit' (G.) Te. kōḍu rivulet, branch of a river. koḍ = the place where artisans work (G.) Mine: Pk. khaḍḍā 'mine' *khaḍḍaga* -- m. ' one who digs a hole ' (CDIAL 3790).

Allograph: gaḍa4 m. ' young of the fish Ophiocephalus lata or Cyprinus garra ', *°aka* -- m. lex. B. *gaṛ, gaṛai* ' species of gilt -- head fish '; Or. *gaṛiśa, °śā* ' the fish O. lata ', *gaḷa* ' a kind of fish '.(CDIAL 3970-1)

Allograph: 1. S. *gaḏo* m. ' bundle of grass &c. ', *°ḏī* f. ' small do. '; L. *gaḍḍā* m. ' armful of straw ', *°ḍī* f. ' sheaf '; P. *gaḍḍā* m. ' handful of sticks ', *°ḍī* f. ' load of rice in straw ', WPah. bhal. *gaḍḍi* f. (CDIAL 3982).

Uruk boat model, Mohenjo-daro boat on Indus writing

Model of a bitumen-covered wooden boat from Ur. "The shape of its upswung prow mirrors that of the tarada...propelled through the water with long poles."[84] The boat is comparable to the boat shown on a Mohenjo-daro prism tablet, m1429C.

Text 2937. Reading: *dul ḍhālako* 'cast metal ingot'. *kaṇḍa kanka*, 'fire-altar

account'

Seal impression on pot. Glyphs: Pair of dotted ovals; rim-of-jar. The glyphs are part of the three glyphs used on copper tablet with raised script.

Text 3246 on m1429A. The same sequence of three signs (Glyphs of a

pair of dotted ovals + rim-of-jar) occurs on one side of a prism tablet: m1429 (The other two sides show a boat and a crocodile holding fish glyph on its jaw).

The 'notch' glyph ligatured within the pair of ovals: खांडा [*khāṇḍā*] *m* a jag, notch, or indentation (as upon the edge of a tool or weapon). Rebus: *khāṇḍā* '(alloyed metal) tools, pots and pans'. The three part message is read rebus: 1. *ayo khaṇḍ khōṭ kolmo* cast alloyed metal tools of smithy furnace account; 2. dul *khāṇḍā kan-ka* cast metal tools furnace account; 3. *dhatu kāḍ* mineral (ore) stones:

Part 1:

khaṇḍ khōṭ 'alloyed ingots, tools, pots and pans, metal-ware'.

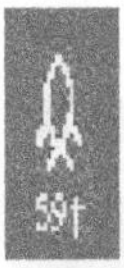

kolmo 'three'; rebus: kolami 'smithy'.

ayo 'fish' (Mu.) Rebus: aya 'cast metal' (G.); ayah, ayas = metal (Skt.)

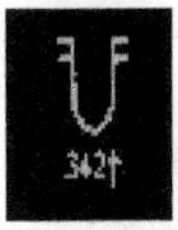

kaṇḍ kan-ka 'furnace account'

Part 2:

() The first sign from right on line 1 of Inscribed text 4251 and connotes खोट [khōṭa] alloyed ingot (Marathi). The alloy is 'cast bronze'; it is a glyptic formed of a pair of brackets (): kuṭila 'bent'; rebus: kuṭila, katthīl = bronze (8 parts copper and 2 parts tin) [cf. āra-kūṭa, 'brass' (Skt.) (CDIAL 3230) kuṭi— in cmpd. 'curve' (Skt.)(CDIAL 3231).

dul and

'pair'; rebus: dula 'cast'; *kuṭila* 'bronze' (8 parts copper 2 parts tin) Rebus 2: kuṭhi 'smelting furnace' (Santali)

koṭe ‘forged (metal) (Santali) खांडा [khāṇḍā] *m* a jag, notch, or indentation (as upon the edge of a tool or weapon). *kuṭila khāṇḍā* ‘bronze tools, pots and pans’. *kaṇḍ kan-ka* ‘funace account’

Part 3:

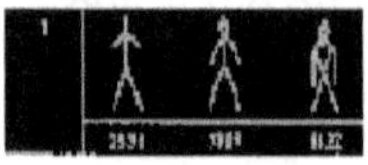

dhaṛu ‘body’ (Sindhi) rebus: *dhatu* ‘ore’ (Santali) kāḍ 2 काड् a man's length, the stature of a man (as a measure of length) Rebus: *kāḍ* ‘stone’. Ga. (Oll.) kanḍ, (S.) kanḍu (pl. kanḍkil) stone

m1429C. Glyph: Boat. bagalo = an Arabian merchant vessel (G.) bagala = an Arab boat of a particular description (Ka.); bagalā (M.); bagarige, bagarage = a kind of vessel (Ka.)(Ka.lex.); rebus: *bangala* = kumpaṭi = an:gāra śakaṭī = a chafing dish a portable stove a goldsmith’s portable furnace (Telugu) cf. *bangaru bangaramu* = gold (Te.)

Glyphs: 1. కోడి [kōḍi] *kōḍi.* [Tel.] n. A fowl, a bird. (Telugu) Rebus: *khōṭ* ‘alloyed ingots’ 2. Heb. *tamar* "palm tree, date palm." Rebus: *tam(b)ra* = copper (Pkt.) 3. *tagara* ‘tin’ ingots 4. *ban:gala* ‘Chafing dish’. The glyphic composition on m1429C thus reads: tin, copper alloyed furnace ingots.

m1429B. Glyphs: crocodile + fish ayakāra ‘blacksmith’ (Pali)

kāru a wild crocodile or alligator (Te.) కారు mosale ‘wild crocodile or alligator. S. ghaṛyālu m. long — snouted porpoise ’; N. ghaṛiyāl ‘ crocodile’ (Telugu)’; A. B. ghāṛiyāl ‘ alligator ’, Or. Ghaṛiāḷa, H. ghaṛyāl, ghariār m. (CDIAL 4422) கரவு² karavu, n. < கரா. Cf. grāha. Alligator; முதலை. கரவார்தடம் (திவ். திருவாய். 8, 9, 9). கரா karā, n. prob. Grāha.

1. A species of alligator; முதலை. கராவதன் காலினைக்கதுவ (திவ். பெரியதி. 2, 3, 9). 2. Male alligator; ஆண்முதலை. (பிங்.) கராம் karām n. prob. Grāha. 1. A species of alligator ; முதலைவகை. முதலையு மிடங்கருங் கராமும் (குறிஞ்சிப். 257). 2. Male alligator; ஆண் முதலை. (திவா.)

kāruvu = mechanic, artisan, Viśvakarma, the celestial artisan (Te.)Pali: ayakāra 'iron-smith'.] Both ayaskāma and ayaskāra are attested in Panini (Pan. Viii.3.46; ii.4.10). Wpah. Bhal. Kamīṇ m.f. labourer (man or woman) ; MB. Kāmiṇā labourer (CDIAL 2902) N. kāmi blacksmith (CDIAL 2900). Khār 1 खार् । लोहकारः m. (sg. Abl. Khāra 1 खार; the pl. dat. Of this word is khāran 1 खारन्, which is to be distinguished from khāran 2, q.v., s.v.), a blacksmith, an iron worker (cf. bandūka-khār, p. 111b, l. 46; K.Pr. 46; H. xi, 17); a farrier (El.). This word is often a part of a name, and in such case comes at the end (W. 118) as in Wahab khār, Wahab the smith (H. ii, 12; vi, 17). Khāra-basta खार-बस्ॅत । चर्मप्रसेविका f. the skin bellows of a blacksmith. —büṭhü —ब&above;ठ्&below; । लोहकारभित्तिः f. the wall of a blacksmith's furnace or hearth. —bāy —बाय् । लोहकारपत्नी f. a blacksmith's wife (Gr.Gr. 34). —dŏkuru; । लोहकारायोघनः m. a blacksmith's hammer, a sledge-hammer.-gȧji —ग&above;जि&below; or —güjü; । लोहकारचुल्लिः f. a blacksmith's furnace or hearth. —hāl —हाल् । लोहकारकन्दुः f. (sg. Dat. —höjü —हा&above;जू&below;), a blacksmith's smelting furnace; cf. hāl 5. —kūrü; । लोहकारकन्या f. a blacksmith's daughter. —koṭu; । लोहकारपुत्रः m. the son of a blacksmith, esp. a skilful son, who can work at the same profession. —küṭü; । लोहकारकन्या f. a blacksmith's daughter, esp. one who has the virtues and qualities properly belonging to her father's profession or caste. —mëˇtsü लोहकारमृत्तिका f. (for 2, see [khāra 3]), 'blacksmith's earth,' i.e. iron-ore. —nĕcyuwu —न्यचिवु&below; । लोहकारात्मजः m. a blacksmith's son. —nay —नय् । लोहकारनालिका f. (for khāranay 2, see [khārun]), the trough into which the blacksmith allows melted iron to flow after smelting. -tsañĕ लोहकारशान्ताङ्गाराः f.pl. charcoal used by blacksmiths in their furnaces. —wān लोहकारापणः m. a blacksmith's shop, a forge, smithy (K.Pr. 3). —waṭh —वठ् । आघाताधारशिला m. (sg. Dat. —waṭas —वटि), the large stone used by a blacksmith as an anvil. (Kashmiri) kāruvu = mechanic, artisan, Viśvakarma, the celestial artisan (Te.); కారువు [kāruvu] kāruvu. [Skt.] n.

An artist, artificer. An agent; gāre = affix of noun denoting one who does it, e.g. samagāre = cobbler (Tu.); garuva (Ka.); gar_uva = an important man (Te.) cf. –ka_ra suffix. 'worker' (Skt.) kāri— m. 'artisan, worker' Pāṇ. 2. F. 'action, work' Bhaṭṭ. [√KR̥ 1] 1. P.kārī m. 'worker'. 2. Kt. Kår 'work', Wg.kō̤, Pr. Kā̃; S. kāri f. 'work, occupation, use'; L. kār f. 'work'; P. kārī f. 'remedy'; Or. Kāri 'work'. (CDIAL 3064) karuvu n. Melting: what is melted (Te.)कारु [kāru] m (S) An artificer or artisan. 2 A common term for the twelve बलुतेदार q. v. Also कारुनारु m pl q. v. in नारुकारु. (Marathi) कारिगर, कारिगार, कारागीर, कारेगार, कारागार [kārigara, kārigāra, kārāgīra, kārēgāra, kārāgāra] m (P) A good workman, a clever artificer or artisan. 2 Affixed as an honorary designation to the names of Barbers, and sometimes of सुतार, गवंडी, & चितारी. 3 Used laxly as adj and in the sense of Effectual, availing, effective of the end. बलुतें [balutēṃ] n A share of the corn and garden-produce assigned for the subsistence of the twelve public servants of a village, for whom see below. 2 In some districts. A share of the dues of the hereditary officers of a village, such as पाटील, कुळकरणी &c. बलुतेदार or बलुता [balutēdāra or balutā] or त्या m (बलुतें &c.) A public servant of a village entitled to बलुतें. There are twelve distinct from the regular Governmentofficers पाटील, कुळकरणी &c.; viz. सुतार, लोहार, महार, मांग (These four constitute पहिली or थोरली कास or वळ the first division. Of three of them each is entitled to चार पाचुंदे, twenty bundles of Holcus or the thrashed corn, and the महार to आठ पाचुंदे); कुंभार, चाम्हार, परीट, न्हावी constitute दुसरी orमधली कास or वळ, and are entitled, each, to तीन पाचुंदे; भट, मुलाणा, गुरव, कोळी form तिसरी or धाकटी कास or वळ, and have, each, दोन पाचुंदे. Likewise there are twelve अलुते or supernumerary public claimants, viz. तेली, तांबोळी, साळी, माळी, जंगम, कळवांत, डवऱ्या, ठाकर, घडशी, तराळ, सोनार, चौगुला. Of these the allowance of corn is not settled. The learner must be prepared to meet with other enumerations of the बलुतेदार (e. g. पाटील, कुळ- करणी, चौधरी, पोतदार, देशपांड्या, न्हावी, परीट, गुरव, सुतार, कुंभार, वेसकर, जोशी; also सुतार, लोहार, चाम्हार, कुंभार as constituting the first-class and claiming the largest division of बलुतें; next न्हावी, परीट, कोळी, गुरव as constituting the middle class and claiming a subdivision of बलुतें; lastly, भट, मुलाणा, सोनार, मांग; and, in the Konkaṇ, yet another list); and with other accounts of the assignments of corn; for this and many similar matters, originally determined diversely, have undergone the usual influence of time,

place, and ignorance. Of the बलुतेदार in the Indápúr pergunnah the list and description stands thus:--First class, सुतार, लोहार, चाम्हार, महार; Second, परीट, कुंभार, न्हावी, मांग; Third, सोनार, मुलाणा, गुरव, जोशी, कोळी, रामोशी; in all fourteen, but in no one village are the whole fourteen to be found or traced. In the Panḍharpúr districts the order is:--पहिली or थोरली वळ (1st class); महार, सुतार, लोहार, चाम्हार, दुसरी or मधली वळ(2nd class); परीट, कुंभार, न्हावी, मांग, तिसरी or धाकटी वळ (3rd class); कुळकरणी, जोशी, गुरव, पोतदार; twelve बलुते and of अलुते there are eighteen. According to Grant Duff, the बलतेदार are सुतार, लोहार, चाम्हार, मांग, कुंभार, न्हावी, परीट, गुरव, जोशी, भाट, मुलाणा; and the अलुते are सोनार, जंगम, शिंपी, कोळी, तराळ or वेसकर, माळी, डवऱ्यागोसावी, घडशी, रामोशी, तेली, तांबोळी, गोंधळी. In many villages of Northern Dakhaṉ the महार receives the बलुतें of the first, second, and third classes; and, consequently, besidesthe महार, there are but nine बलुतेदार. The following are the only अलुतेदार or नारू now to be found;--सोनार, मांग, शिंपी, भट गोंधळी, कोर- गू, कोतवाल, तराळ, but of the अलुतेदार & बलुते- दार there is much confused intermixture, the अलुतेदार of one district being the बलुतेदार of another, and vice versâ. (The word कास used above, in पहिली कास, मध्यम कास, तिसरी कास requires explanation. It means Udder; and, as the बलुतेदार are, in the phraseology of endearment or fondling, termed वासरें (calves), their allotments or divisions are figured by successive bodies of calves drawing at the कास or under of the गांवunder the figure of a गाय or cow.) (Marathi)

बलुतें [balutēṃ] *n* A share of the corn and garden-produce assigned for the subsistence of the twelve public servants of a village, for whom see below. (Marathi)

Metals trade catalog on a seal

The glyphic composition denotes a *sodagor*, trader of mineral ores, metal-ware, ingots of bronze, brass, tin and iron.

Broken seal m0304 Mohenjo-daro. Reconstructed as a seal impression using seal m0304 creating a pair of antelopes and a pair of hayricks below the platform (stool) base (After J. Huntington).

The platform glyphs read rebus: *kāṛ* 'stack of stalks of large millet'(Maithili) Rebus: *kaṇḍ* 'furnace, fire-altar, consecrated fire'. *khaṇḍ* 'tools, pots and pans and metal-ware' (Gujarati) *tagar kamar* 'tin artisan'. The artisan is *kũderā* m. 'one who works a lathe, one who scrapes' (CDIAL 3297).His horns denote that he is a brass worker, brass turner: *ṭhaṭera* 'buffalo horns'. *ṭhaṭerā* 'brass worker' (Punjabi) with *kuṇḍa* n. ' clump ' e.g. *darbha-kuṇḍa* — Pāṇ.(CDIAL 3236).

The first set of three glyphs are read rebus: *dhatu kuṭi* 'mineral (ore) smelter furnace' (Santali) kuṭila, katthīl = bronze (8 parts copper and 2 parts tin)

 A खांडा *khāṇḍā* 'jag' infixed inside *kanka* 'rim of jar' glyph is read as the phrase: *kaṇḍa kanka*, 'fire-altar account': *kul -- karṇī* m. 'village accountant' (Marathi); *karṇikan* id. (Tamil) கணக்கு kaṇakku, n. cf. gaṇaka. [M. kaṇakku] 1. Number, account, reckoning, calculation, computation (Tamil) kaṇḍ 'fire-altar' (Santali)

aya 'fish' (Mu.); rebus: aya 'metal' (G.) ayo kanka 'fish rim-of-jar' rebus: metal (alloy) account (*kaṇakku*) scribe.

The five glyphs on either side of the seated person read rebus:

- ib, 'elephant', dhaṛu 'body', kol 'tiger', gaṇḍá 'rhinoceros', kāṛā 'buffalo' கண்டி kaṇṭi buffalo bull (Tamil)

- ib 'iron' dhatu 'ore'; kol 'iron'; kaṇḍ 'fire-altar, furnace' *khaṇḍ* 'tools, pots and pans and metal-ware'; khar 'smith' *gaḍa* 'large stone mould'.
- Elephant: ibha (glyph). Rebus: ibbo (merchant of ib 'iron')
- Tiger: kola (glyph). Rebus: kol (working in iron, kolami 'smithy/forge')

- Rhinoceros: gaṇḍá4 m. ' rhinoceros ' lex., *°aka* -- m. lex. 2. *ga- yaṇḍa -- . [Prob. of same non -- Aryan origin as khaḍgá --1: cf. *gaṇōtsāha* -- m. lex. as a Sanskritized form ← Mu. PMWS 138]1. Pa. *gaṇḍaka* -- m., Pk. *gaṁḍaya* -- m., A. *gā̃r*, Or. *gaṇḍā*. 2. K. *gōḍ* m., S. *geṇḍo* m. (lw. with *g* --), P. *gaĩḍā* m., *°ḍī* f., N. *gaĩṛo*, H. *gaĩṛā* m., G. *gẽḍɔ* m., *°ḍī* f., M. *gẽḍā* m. WPah.ktg. *geṇḍɔ mirg* m. ' rhinoceros ', Md. *genḍā* ← H. (CDIAL 4000). காண்டாமிருகம் kāṇṭā-mirukam , *n.* [M. *kāṇṭāmṛgam*.] Rhinoceros; கல்யானை. (Tamil)

- Buffalo: கண்டி kaṇṭi , *n.* 1. Buffalo bull; எருமைக் கடா. (தொல். பொ. 623.) kāṛā young buffalo (Go.) kaṭā, kaṭamā 'bison' (Ta.)(DEDR 1114) (glyph). Rebus: *kaṇḍ* 'furnace, fire-altar, consecrated fire'. kaḍiyo [Hem. Des. kaḍa-i-o = (Skt. Sthapati, a mason) a bricklayer, mason (G.)] Pk. *gaḍa* -- n. 'large stone'? (CDIAL 3969) K. *garun*, vill. *gaḍun* ' to hammer into shape, forge, put together '. (CDIAL 3966). khār 1 खार् । लोहकारः m. (sg. abl. khāra 1 खार; the pl. dat. of this word is khāran 1 खारन्, which is to be distinguished from khāran 2, q.v., s.v.), a blacksmith, an iron worker. Or. *gaṛhibā* 'to mould, build', *gaṛhaṇa* 'building'; ghaṭ 'mould, form' (CDIAL 4407). Pk. *khaḍḍā*-- f. 'hole, mine, cave'(CDIAL 3970).

- Thus, *gaṇḍá* 'rhinoceros', *kaṇṭi* 'buffalo' read rebus: *kāṇḍa* 'tools, pots and pans and metal-ware'; *kaṇḍ* 'furnace, fire-altar, consecrated fire'.

Glyphs constituting the seated person composition: Villa+ge chief brass-worker, metals turner (*kundār*).

Shoggy hair; face. *Sodo bodo, sodro bodro* adj. adv. Rough, hairy, shoggy, hirsute, uneven; *sodo* [Persian. *Sodā*, dealing] trade; traffic; merchandise; marketing; a bargain; the purchase or sale of goods; buying and selling; mercantile dealings (G.lex.) sodagor = a merchant, trader; *sodāgor* (P.B.) (Santali.lex.) The face is depicted with bristles of hair, representing a tiger's mane. *mũh* 'face; *mũhe* 'ingot' (Santali) So, this seal is an ingot trade catalog: *mũhe sodo* 'ingot trade'.

G.*karā* n. pl. 'wristlets, bangles'; S. *karāī* f. 'wrist' (CDIAL 2779). Rebus: khār खार् 'blacksmith' (Kashmiri)

ṭhaṭera 'buffalo horns'. *ṭhaṭerā* 'brass worker' (Punjabi)(CDIAL 5493). *Ta.* tuttāri a kind of bugle-horn. *Ma.* tuttāri horn, trumpet. *Ka.* tutūri, tuttāri, tuttūri a long trumpet. *Tu.* tuttāri, tuttūri trumpet, horn, pipe. *Te.* tutārā a kind of trumpet. / Cf. Mar. tutārī a wind instrument, a sort of horn. (DEDR 3316). *ḍabe, ḍabea* 'large horns, with a sweeping upward curve, applied to buffaloes' (Santali) Rebus: *ḍab*, ḍhimba, ḍhompo 'lump (ingot?)', clot, make a lump or clot, coagulate, fuse, melt together (Santali)

Glyph: clump between the two horns: kuṇḍa n. ' clump ' e.g. darbha—kuṇḍa— Pāṇ.(CDIAL 3236). kundār turner (A.)(CDIAL 3295). kuṇḍī 'crooked buffalo horns' (Lahnda.) Rebus: kuṇḍī = chief of village (Prakrit). The artisan is kundakara— m. 'turner' (Skt.); H. kũderā m. 'one who works a lathe, one who scrapes' (CDIAL 3297).

Glyphs in composition of the platform: stool of a pair of hayricks flanking a pair of antelopes: kanḍo 'seat'; rebus: kaṇḍ 'furnace, fire-altar' *khaṇḍ* 'tools, pots and pans and metal-ware' (Gujarati); *kāṛ* 'stack of stalks of large millet'(Maithili) Rebus: *kaṇḍ* 'furnace, fire-altar, consecrated fire'. mēṭa 'stack of hay '; rebus: meḍ 'iron'; takar 'sheep, ram'; rebus: tagara 'tin'. Thus, the platform denotes furnaces, tools, pots and pans and metal-ware of tin and iron.

Kur. kaṇḍō a stool. Malt. kanḍo stool, seat. (DEDR 1179) Rebus: kaṇḍ, 'a furnace, fire-altar' (Santali.lex.) mēṭu, mēṭa, mēṭi stack of hay (Te.)(DEDR 5058). Rebus: meḍ 'iron' (Ho.) Vikalpa: kuntam 'haystack' (Te.)(DEDR 1236) Rebus: kuṇḍamu 'a pit for receiving and preserving consecrated fire' (Te.) *khaṇḍ* 'tools, pots and pans and metal-ware' (Gujarati).

In the following lexemes related to product derivatives of copper, H. *lokhaṇḍ* m. 'iron tools, pots and pans'; G. *lokhāḍ* n. 'tools, iron, ironware', the word *khaṇḍ* denotes 'tools, pots and pans and metal-ware'.

Ta. takar sheep, ram, goat, male of certain other animals (yāḷi, elephant, shark). பொருநகர் தாக்கற்குப் பேருந் தகைத்து (குறள், 486).Ma. takaran huge, powerful as a man,

bear, etc. Ka. tagar, ṭagaru, ṭagara, ṭegaru ram. Tu. tagaru, ṭagarů id. Te. tagaramu, tagaru id. / Cf. Mar. tagar id. (DEDR 3000). Rebus: tagromi 'tin, metal alloy' (Kuwi) ran:ga, ran: pewter is an alloy of tin lead and antimony (añjana) (Santali). takaram tin, white lead, metal sheet, coated with tin (Ta.); tin, tinned iron plate (Ma.); tagarm tin (Ko.); tagara, tamara, tavara id. (Ka.) tamaru, tamara, tavara id. (Ta.): tagaramu, tamaramu, tavaramu id. (Te.); ṭagromi tin metal, alloy (Kuwi); tamara id. (Skt.)(DEDR 3001). trapu tin (AV.); tipu (Pali); tau, taua lead (Pkt.); tũ_ tin (P.); ṭau zinc, pewter (Or.); tarūaum lead (OG.); tarvu~ (G.); tumba lead (Si.)(CDIAL 5992).

The pair of antelopes have their heads turned backwards. క్రమ్మర *krammara.* adv. Again. క్రమ్మరిల్లు or క్రమరబడు Same as క్రమ్మరు. krəm back'(Kho.) karmāra 'smith, artisan' (Skt.) kamar 'smith' (Santali) The two antithetical antelopes thus denote: *tagar kamar* 'tin artisan'; *meḍ kamar* 'iron artisan'.

kamaḍha 'penance' (Pkt.) Rebus: kampaṭṭam 'coiner, mint' (Tamil)

daṭṭi 'waistband' (Kannada)(DED 2465) Ku. dhaṛo 'piece of cloth', N. dharo, B. dhaṛā; Or. dhaṛā 'rag, loincloth', dhaṛi ' rag '; Mth. dhariā 'child's narrow loincloth'.(CDIAL 6707). Rebus: dhatu '(ore) mineral' (Skt.)

Ta. koṭiṟu pincers. Ma. koṭil tongs. Ko. koṛ hook of tongs. / Cf. Skt. (P. 4.4.18) kuṭilikā- smith's tongs.(DEDR 2052). Rebus: kuṭi 'smelter furnace' (Santali) kuṭila, katthīl = bronze (8 parts copper and 2 parts tin)(CDIAL 3230).

'Body' glyph ligatured to 'pincers' glyph is a phonetic determinant of the nature of ore - *kanḍ* 'stone': dhaṛu 'body' (Sindhi), ḍato 'claws or pincers of crab' (Santali) rebus: dhatu 'ore' (Santali) kāḍ 2 काड् । पौरुषम् m. a man's length, the stature of a man (as a measure of length) (Rām. 632, zangan kaḍun kāḍ, to stretch oneself the whole length of one's body. So K. 119). Rebus: kāḍ 'stone'. Ga. (Oll.) kanḍ, (S.) kanḍu (pl. kanḍkil) stone (DEDR 1298).

ḍato 'claws or pincers (chelae) of crabs'; ḍaṭom, ḍiṭom to seize with the claws or pincers, as crabs, scorpions; ḍaṭkop = to pinch, nip (only of crabs) (Santali) Vikalpa: erā 'claws'; Rebus: era 'copper'.

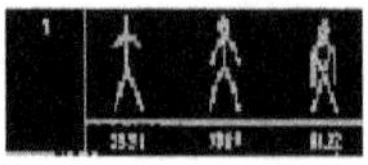

Pk. dhaḍa -- n. ' trunk of body ', S. dhaṛu m., P. dhaṛ f.; Ku. dhaṛ m. ' trunk of body or tree, middle part of anything '; B. dhaṛ 'trunk of body', Or. dhaṛa ' trunk of body or tree '; Mth. dhar ' headless body '; OAw. dhara m. ' body, heart '; H. dhaṛ m. ' trunk of body ' (→ Mth. N. dhaṛ), OMarw. dhaṛa m., G. dhaṛ n.; M. dhaḍ n. ' headless body '. (CDIAL 6712). Rebus: dhātu 'mineral' (Vedic); dhatu 'a mineral, metal' (Santali) meḍ 'body', 'dance' (Santali) meḍ 'iron' + dhatu 'mineral' (Santali) Glyph: kāḍ 2 काड् । पौरुषम् m. a man's length, the stature of a man (as a measure of length) (Rām. 632, zangan kaḍun kāḍ, to stretch oneself the whole length of one's body. So K. 119). Rebus: kāḍ 'stone'. Ga. (Oll.) kanḍ, (S.) kanḍu (pl. kanḍkil) stone (DEDR 1298).

Ligature, a technique used by scribes/artisans of the civilization

Ligatured sculpture: three-faced: tiger, bovine, elephant, Nausharo NS

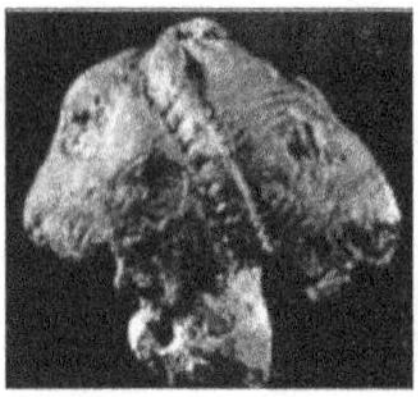

92.02.70.04 6.76 cm (h); three-headed: elephant, buffalo, bottom jaw of a feline. NS 91.02.32.01.LXXXII. Dept. of Archaeology, Karachi. EBK 7712. These glyphs of elephant, buffalo and tiger occur on Mohenjo-daro Seal m0304.

अष्टधातु [aṣṭadhātu] *m pl* (S) The eight metals, viz. सोनें, रूपें, तांबें, कथील, शिसें, पितळ, लोखंड, तिखें, Gold, silver, copper, tin, lead, brass, iron, steel. (Marathi) लोखंडकाम [lōkhaṇḍakāma] *n* Iron work; that portion (of a building, machine &c.) which consists of iron. 2 The business of an ironsmith. lōhá 'red, copper -- coloured' ŚrS. (CDIAL 11158) Ku. *lokhaṛ* 'iron tools'; H. *lokhaṇḍ* m. 'iron tools, pots and pans'; G. *lokhãḍ* n. 'tools, iron, ironware'; M. *lokhãḍ* n. 'iron'(CDIAL 11171).

கண்டி kaṇṭi , *n.* 1. Buffalo bull; எருமைக் கடா. (தொல். பொ. 623.)

காண்டம் kāṇṭam , *n.* < *kāṇḍa.* 1. Water; sacred water; நீர். துருத்திவா யதுக்கிய குங்குமக் காண் டமும் (கல்லா. 49, 16). 2. Staff, rod; கோல். (சூடா.) 3. Stem, stalk; அடித்தண்டு. (யாழ். அக.) 4. Arrow; அம்பு. (சூடா.) 5. Weapon; ஆயுதம். (சூடா.) Collection, multitude, assemblage; திரள். (அக. நி.)
கண்டானுமுண்டானும் kaṇṭāṉumuṇṭ- āṉum, *n.* Redupl. of கண்டானும். Household utensils, great and small, useful and useless; வீட்டுத் தட்டுமுட்டுகள். கண்டானு முண்டானும் இத் தனை எதற்கு? *Loc.*

காண்டம் kāṇṭam , *n.* < *karaṇḍaka.* (சூடா.) 1. Jewel-box; ஆபரணச் செப்பு. (Tamil)

காண்டம் kāṇṭam Ewer; கமண்டலம்.(Tamil)

கண்டம்[3] kaṇṭam , *n.* < *khaṇḍa.* 1. Piece, cut or broken off; fragment, slice, cutting, chop, parcel, portion, slip; துண்டம். செந்தயிர்க் கண்டம் (கம்பரா. நாட்டுப். 19).

Pa. *kaṇḍa* -- m.n. joint of stalk, lump. काठः A rock, stone. kāṭha m. ' rock ' lex. [Cf. *kānta* -- 2 m. ' stone ' lex.]Bshk. *kōr* ' large stone ' AO xviii 239.(CDIAL 3018).

కండె [kaṇḍe] *kaṇḍe.* [Tel.] n. A head or ear of millet or maize. జొన్నకండె.

लोखंडी [lōkhaṇḍī] *a* (लोखंड) Composed of iron; relating to iron.

काढतें [kāḍhatēṃ] n Among gamesters. An ivory counter &c. placed to represent a sum of money.

खांडा [khāṇḍā] *m* A jag, notch, or indentation (as upon the edge of a tool or weapon). A gap in the teeth.

खांडा [khāṇḍā] A flock (of sheep or goats) (Marathi) கண்டி[1] kaṇṭi Flock, herd (Tamil)

खांडा [khāṇḍā] A chump or division of a tree (Marathi)

खांडा [khāṇḍā] A division of a field. (Marathi)

M. *kāḍ* n. f. ' straw ',*kāḍī* f. ' little stick, blade of grass '(CDIAL 3017)

Glyph: 'full stretch of one's arms': kāḍ 2 काड् । पौरुषम् m. a man's length, the stature of a man (as a measure of length) (Rām. 632, zangan kaḍun kāḍ, to stretch oneself the whole length of one's body. So K. 119).

Rebus: kāḍ 'stone'. Ga. (Oll.) kanḍ, (S.) kanḍu (pl. kanḍkil) stone (DEDR 1298).

L. *kaṇḍ* f., *kaṇḍā* m. 'backbone', awāṇ. *kaṇḍ,* *°ḍī* ' back '; P. *kaṇḍ* f. ' back, pubes '; WPah. bhal. *kaṇṭ* f. ' syphilis '; N. *kaṇḍo* ' buttock, rump, anus ',*kaṇḍeulo* ' small of the back '; B. *kāṭ* ' clitoris '; Or. *kaṇṭi* ' handle of a plough '; H. *kāṭā* m. ' spine ', G. *kāṭɔ* m., M. *kāṭā* m.; Si. *äṭa -- kaṭuva* ' bone ', *piṭa -- k°* ' backbone '. 2. Pk. *kaṁḍa --* m. ' backbone '. 3. Pk. *karaṁḍa --* m.n. ' bone shaped like a bamboo ', *karaṁḍuya --* n. ' backbone '. (CDIAL 2670).

Kur. kaṇḍō a stool. *Malt.* kanḍo stool, seat. (DEDR 1179).

Steatite ornament of a smith, courier

The steatite ornament transfers the following hieroglyphs and related information of metallurgical repertoire and trade:

1. Short-necked jar and rim of jar *kaṇḍa kanka* rebus: furnace account

2. Water *kāṇḍa*.rebus: tools, pots and pans and metal-ware

3. Overflow of jar *lo* rebus: *lo* 'copper'

4. Young bull ligatured with one-horn and pannier on shoulder *kōnda* 'bull' *kōṭ* 'horn' *gōta* 'sack' rebus: *kũdār* 'turner, brass-worker' *khoṭa* 'ingot forged, alloy'

5. Lathe ligatured to portable furnace with dotted circles *sangaḍa* 'lathe, furnace' *khāṇḍā* 'dotted circles' rebus: *jangaḍ* 'entrustment articles' *jangaḍiyo* 'military guard who accompanies treasure into the treasury' *sanghāḍiyo*, a worker on a lathe *khāṇḍā* 'tools, pots and pans and metal-ware'

The most frequently occurring glyph among Sarasvati hieroglyphs is *kaṇḍ kan-ka* 'rim of jar' (the emphasis is on the rim). This denotes rebus: scribe accounting tools, pots and pans and metalware, *khaṇḍ*. This becomes the only glyph on a Daimabad seal dated circa 14th century BCE.

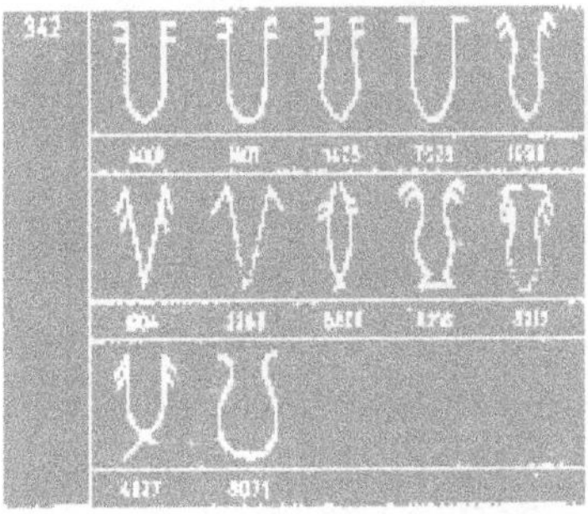

Daimabad seal (Glyph 342 and allographs or glyph variants) . *kaṇḍa kanka* 'Rim of jar' (Santali); *karṇaka* rim of jar'(Skt.) Rebus: *karṇaka* 'scribe' (Telugu); *gaṇaka* id. (Skt.) (Santali) The orthography of 'jar' glyph (Glyph 342) clearly emphasizes the 'rim' of a jar. The glyph has a frequency of 1395 occurrences in the corpus of inscriptions (Mahadevan)

The rim of a jar is kaṇḍ kan-ka (Santali). kaṇḍ denotes a brass pot; Rebus: kaṇḍ karṇaka 'furnace scribe' (Skt.)

kaṇḍa 'pot' (Santali) kāṇṭam , *n.* < *kāṇḍa.* 1. Water; sacred water; நீர்; kāṇṭam 'ewer, pot' கமண்டலம். (Tamil) kŏnḍ क्रंड् or kŏnḍa क्रंड । कुण्ड m. a kind of large bowl or basin made of metal or earthenware (Gr.Gr. 145)(Kashmiri) Kan. *guṇḍi*, Pk. *kōḍaya* -- , *°ḍia* -- n. 'small earthen pot'; Dm. *kōṟí* 'milking pail'; G. *koṛiyũ* n. ' earthen cup for oil and wick '; M. *koḍẽ* n. 'earthen saucer for a lamp'. (CDIAL 3227). Rebus: kaṇḍ = altar, furnace (Santali) लोहकारकन्दुः f. a blacksmith's smelting furnace (Kashmiri) payĕn-kōda पयन्-कौं द । परिपाककन्दुः f. a kiln (a potter's,

a lime-kiln, and brick-kiln, or the like); a furnace (for smelting) kuṇḍa round hole in ground (for water or sacred fire), as in *agni kuṇḍa* (Skt.) *khaṇḍ* 'tools, pots and pans, metal-ware'.

m0478A On this tablet, 'lid' glyph is ligatued to a 'rim-of-jar' glyph.

ḍaren, aḍaren cover, lid (Santali); rebus: aduru 'native metal' (Ka.) Other glyphs of the tablet have been decoded: kola 'tiger, jackal' (Kon.); rebus: kol working in iron, blacksmith, 'alloy of five metals, panchaloha' (Tamil) kol 'furnace, forge' (Kuwi) kolami 'smithy' (Te.) erg a = act of clearing jungle (Kui) [Note image showing two men carrying uprooted trees]. This glyptic composition depicting the act of clearing jungle may be a phonetic determinant for the person seated on the tree branch and the glyph of a woman pushing them apart: eraka, hero = a messenger; a spy (G.lex.) heraka = spy (Skt.); er to look at or for (Pkt.); er uk- to play 'peeping tom' (Ko.) Rebus: eraka 'copper' (Ka.)

kol 'working in iron, blacksmith (Ta.); kollan- blacksmith (Ta.); kollan blacksmith, artificer (Ma.)(DEDR 2133) kolme = furnace (Ka.) kole.l 'temple, smithy' (Ko.); kolme smithy' (Ka.) kol = pañcaloha (five metals); kol metal (Ta.lex.) pan~caloha = a metallic alloy containing five metals: copper, brass, tin, lead and iron (Skt.); an alternative list of five metals: gold, silver, copper, tin (lead), and iron (dhātu;Nānārtharatnākara 82; Mangarāja's Nighaṇṭu. 498)(Ka.) kol, kolhe, 'the koles, an aboriginal tribe if iron smelters speaking a language akin to that of Santals' (Santali)

The next most frequently-occurring glyph is the one-horned young bull (seen on 1159 epigraphs). The identifying feature of this glyph is the pannier which adorns it. See m1656 Steatite ornament of Mohenjo-daro . It is possible that the depressions on the neck, shoulder, stomach and thigh regions of the heifer were filled with 'red pigment' emphasizing that each of these glyphic elements had a semantic determinative role in rebus readings: koḍiyum 'rings on neck'. kāru-kōḍe. [Tel.] n. A bull in its prime. खोंड [khōṇḍa] m A young bull, a bullcalf. (Marathi) గోడ [gōda] gōda. [Tel.] n. An ox. A beast. kine, cattle.(Telugu)

Rebus : B. kõdā 'to turn in a lathe'; Or. kūnda 'lathe', kūdibā, kūd 'to turn' (→ Drav. Kur. kūd 'lathe') (CDIAL 3295). koḍ 'workshop' (Kuwi.G.)The standard device has been read rebus: *sangaḍa* 'lathe, portable furnace'. Rebus: *jaṅgaḍ* 'entrusment articles'. *jangaḍiyo* 'military guard who accompanies treasure into the treasury' (G.) *sangaḍa* 'association, guild'.

The glyphics of 'water-overflow' from the 'rim' of the 'short-necked jar' completes the semantic rendering by the *lo* 'overflow'. Rebus readings: <lo->(B) {V} ``(pot, etc.) to ^overflow''. See <lo-> `to be left over'. @B24310. #20851. Re<lo->(B) {V} ``(pot, etc.) to ^overflow''. See <lo-> `to be left over'. (Munda) Rebus: loh 'copper' (Hindi) Glyph of flowing water in the second register: காண்டம் kāṇṭam , *n.* < *kāṇḍa.* 1. Water; sacred water; நீர்; kāṇṭam 'ewer, pot' கமண்டலம். (Tamil) Thus the combined rebus reading: Ku. *lokhaṛ* 'iron tools '; H. *lokhaṇḍ* m. ' iron tools, pots and pans '; G. *lokhā̃ḍ* n. 'tools, iron, ironware'; M. *lokhā̃ḍ* n. ' iron '(CDIAL 11171).

Thus, the functions assigned to the pectoral owner in the guild are clearly, semantically explained by the hieroglyphic composition of this extraordinary Indus script inscription on the steatite ornament. He is a military guard entrusted by the guild with the function of delivering copper/metal goods made by the artisans of workshops into the treasury on *jaṅgaḍ*-basis, that is, as 'entrustment articles' subject to approval. These are accounted for using the short-inscription tablets delivered with the goods by the artisans.

Dotted circle glyph: context, vedi glyph, ivory artifacts

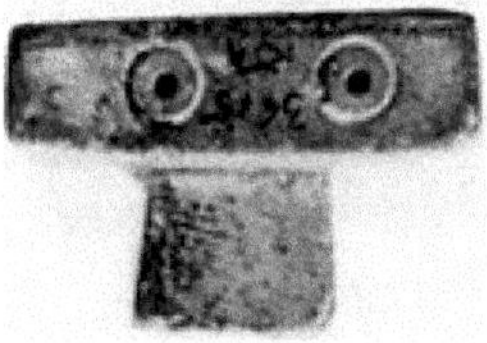

There are three distinct glyphs in this composition:

1. Round dot like a blob -- .  raised large-sized dot -- (*gōṭī* 'round pebble);

2. Dotted circle *khaṇḍa* 'A piece, bit, fragment, portion'; kandi 'bead';

3. A + shaped structure where the glyphs 1 and 2 are infixed. The + shaped structure is *kaṇḍ* 'a fire-altar' (which is associated with glyphs 1 and 2)..

Rebus readings are: 1. *khoṭ* m. 'alloy'; 2. *khaṇḍā* 'tools, pots and pans and metal-ware'; 3. *kaṇḍ* 'furnace, fire-altar, consecrated fire'.

Four 'round spot'; glyphs around the 'dotted circle' in the center of the composition: gōṭī 'round pebble; Rebus 1: L. *khoṭ* 'alloy, impurity', *°ṭā* 'alloyed', awāṇ. *khoṭā* 'forged'; P. *khoṭ* m. 'base, alloy' M.*khoṭā* 'alloyed' (CDIAL 3931) Rebus 2: kōṭhī] f (कोष्ट S) A granary, garner, storehouse, warehouse, treasury, factory, bank. *khoṭā* 'alloyed' metal is produced from *kaṇḍ* 'furnace, fire-altar' yielding *khaṇḍā* 'tools, pots and pans and metal-ware'. This word *khaṇḍā* is denoted by the dotted circles.

Tin ingots, forged alloys of smithy guild furnace account

dolio 'spotted antelope' (deśi. Hemachandra); *dolo* 'the eye' (deśi. Hemachandra). Rebus: dul 'to cast metal in a mould' (Santali) It is possible that 'fish-eyes' or 'eye stones' referred to in ancient Mesopotamian texts as imports from Dilmun (Akkadian IGI-HA, IGI-KU6) mentioned in Mesopotamian texts., refer to the hieroglyph of dotted circle (hieroglyph: fish-eye or antelope-eye) connotes *dol* 'eye'; rebus: *dul* 'cast metal'.

M1909. Pict-49 Uncertain animal (perhaps antelope) with dotted circles on its body.

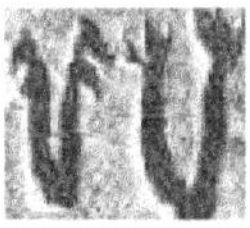

This seal has Glyph 347, 342 sequence, which is a terminal pair with 110 occurrences. An additional glyph shown in front of the animal is: a sloped stroke.

sangaḍa khaṇḍ kuṇḍa 'smithy guild (with) furnace -- consecrated fire (pit)'. *kaṇḍ kanka* 'furnace account'.

ṭagara 'antelope'; தகர் takar, *n.* [T. *tagaru*, K. *tagar.*] 1. Sheep; ஆட்டின்பொது. (திவா.) 2. Ram; செம் மறியாட்டுக்கடா. (திவா.) பொருநகர் தாக்கற்குப் பேருந் தகைத்து (குறள், 486). Rebus: tagara 'tin'.

kōṭu (in cmpds. *kōṭṭu-*) horn (Tamil);(DEDR 2200). Rebus: *khōṭ* 'alloyed' (Punjabi) koṭe 'forged (metal) (Santali)

The hieroglyph of a slanted stroke in front of the animal on m1909 is: *dhāḷ* 'a slope'; 'inclination of a plane' (G.); ḍhāḷiyum = adj. sloping, inclining (G.) Rebus: ḍhālako = a large metal ingot (G.) ḍhālakī = a metal heated and poured into a mould; a solid piece of metal; an ingot (Gujarati) Antelope: miṇḍāl 'markhor' (Tōrwālī) meḍho a ram, a sheep (G.)(CDIAL 10120); rebus: mẽṛhẽt, meḍ 'iron' (Mu.Ho.)

The ligatured animal can be read as a set of allographs:

piserā 'small deer' ; rebus: pasra 'smithy'; kãg 'boar's tusk'; rebus: kãgar 'portable brazier'; kandi 'hole, opening' (Ka.); kan 'eye' (Ka.); rebus: kandi (pl. –l) necklace, beads (Pa.) Thus, the entire ligatured animal is decoded rebus: meḍ pasra kãgar kandil 'iron smithy, forge, portable furnace, beads'. Pa.kandi (pl. –l) necklace, beads. Ga. (P.) kandi (pl. –l) bead, (pl.) necklace; (S.2) kandiṭ bead (DEDR 1215). Kandil, kandīl = a globe of glass, a lantern (Ka.lex.)

A gloss in Telugu explains such a group, lexeme clusters which can, semantically, be interpreted as an 'animal specie'. Pasaramu, pasalamu = an animal, a beast, a brute, quadruped (Te.lex.)

Phonetic determinant of kandi 'beads' and kaṇḍ 'furnace' is the tusk glyph, which is read khaṇḍ 'ivory'; rebus: kaṇḍ = altar, furnace (Santali) kaṇḍ = altar, furnace (Santali) लोहकारकन्दुः f. a blacksmith's smelting furnace (Grierson Kashmiri lex.) payĕn-kōda पयन्-कौँद। परिपाककन्दुः f. a kiln (a potter's, a lime-kiln, and brick-kiln, or the like); a furnace (for

smelting)]. Kāndavika = a baker; kandu = an iron plate or pan for baking cakes etc. (Ka.lex.) jaṇḍ khaṇḍ = ivory (Jat.ki) khaṇḍi_ = ivory in rough (Jat.ki_); gaṭī = piece of elephant's tusk (S.)

Ka. kaṇḍi, kiṇḍi, gaṇḍi chink, hole, opening. Tu. Kaṇḍi, khaṇḍi, gaṇḍi hole, opening, window; kaṇḍeriyuni to make a cut. Te. Gaṇḍi, gaṇḍika hole, orifice, breach, gap, lane (DEDR 1176). Kandhi = a lump, a piece (Santali.lex.) Rebus: *kaṇḍ* 'stone (ore)'.

Ta. Kaṇ eye, aperture, orifice, star of a peacock's tail. Ma. Kaṇ, kaṇṇu eye, nipple, star in peacock's tail, bud. Ko. Kaṇ eye. To. Koṇ eye, loop in string. Ka. Kaṇ eye, small hole, orifice. Koḍ. Kaṇṇï id. Te. Kanu, kannu eye, small hole, orifice, mesh of net, eye in peacock's feather. Kol. Kan (pl. kanḍl) eye, small hole in ground, cave. Ga. (Oll.) kaṇa (pl. Kaṇul) hole; (S.) kanu (pl. Kankul)eye. Go. (Tr.) kan (pl. Kank) id.; (A.) kaṟ (pl. Kaṟk) id. Konḍa kaṇ id. Pe. Kaṇga (pl. –ŋ, kaṇku) id. Manḍ. Kan (pl. –ke) id. Kui kanu (pl. Kan-ga), (K.) kanu (pl. Kaṟka) id. Kuwi (F.) kannū (pl. Kar&nangle;ka), (S.) kannu (pl. Kanka), (Su. P. Isr.) kanu (pl. Kaṇka) id. (DEDR 1159a). Pa. kanḍp- (kanḍt-) to look for, seek. Ga. (Oll.) kanḍp- (kanḍt-) to search. Ta. Kāṇ (kāṇp-, kaṇṭ-) to see, consider, investigate, appear, become visible; n. sight, beauty Te. Kanu (allomorph kān-), kāncu to see (DEDR 1443)

B. kan ' eye of corn, particle ', kanā ' piece of dust, onta seed ', kanī ' atom, particle '; Or.kaṇa, ṇā ' particle of dust, eye of seed, atom ', kaṇi ' particle of grain '; Oaw. Kana ' drop (of dew) ' M. kaṇ m. ' grain, atom, corn ', kaṇī f. ' hard core of grain, pupil of eye, broken bit ', kaṇẽ n. ' very small particle ' (CDIAL 2661)

Glyph: dotted circles. Rebus: *khāṇḍa* 'tools, pots and pans and metal-ware'.

Dotted circle: pāso 'die' (orthography: dotted circle). Rebus: pāśo = a silver ingot; pāśātāṇiyo = one who draws silver into a wire (G.) pāslo = a nugget of gold or silver having the form of a die (G.) Rebus: pasra 'smithy' (Santali) kandhi = a lump, a piece (Santali.lex.) [The dotted circle thus connotes metalware taken out of a kaṇḍ, furnace]. kāndavika = a baker; kandu = an iron plate or pan for baking cakes etc.

(Ka.lex.)

Mohenjo-daro. Dotted circle decoration on a steatite bowl (DK 3178), DK-B, house 3, room VIII (Jansen and Urban, 1985, RTWH, Aachen).9

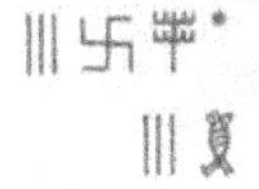

Altyn-tepe seals compare with an inscription on a miniature tablet, Text 4500 (Harappa. Incised miniature tablet; not illustrated). Line 2 of inscription: A pair of 'harrows' glyph: dula 'pair'; rebus dul 'cast (metal)'; aḍar 'harrow'; rebus: aduru 'native metal'. Thus, the duplicated 'harrow' glyph read rebus: cast native metal. Glyph: svastika; rebus: jasta 'zinc' (Kashmiri). Glyph 'three liner strokes': kolmo 'three'; rebus: kolami 'smithy'. Line 1 of inscription: Ligatured glyph: cunda 'musk-rat'; rebus: cundakāra 'ivory turner'; kolmo 'three'; rebus: kolami 'smithy'. Thus the Text 4500 on an incised miniature tablet read rebus: ivory turner smithy'; cast native metal, tin, smithy.

Finds at Altyn-depe: ivory sticks and gaming pieces (?) obtained from Meluhha; similar objects with dotted circles found in Mohenjodaro and Harappa.

Vessel fragments with dot-in-circle design from Susa. Louvre Museum. At the Royal Cemetery of Ur, Woolley 1934: 558-59 found a small container with a narrow neck and sides decorated with three dot-incircle designs.

Bhagawanpura is a site located on the right bank of the River Sarasvati_ in Dist. Kuruṣetra. Remains of semi-circular huts leaving behind only post-holes and rammed floors have been found. From Period IB levels bones of true domesticatd horse, equus caballus have been found. Intersecting dotted circle

designs are found on pottery of Painted Grey Ware which overlap the Late Harappan ware.

Terracotta female adorned with 'dotted circles'; Period Namazga II; Yalangach Tepe, Geoksyur (Weiner, 1984, Fig. 183) kola 'woman'; rebus: kolami 'smithy, forge'.

Ko. kaṇṭ-po·t flesh of hind thigh of animal; kaṇṭ-ka·l calf of leg. *Ka.* kaṇḍa flesh, meat. *Koḍ.* kaṇḍa piece or lump of meat. *Te.* kaṇḍa id., flesh. *Nk.* khaṇḍepiece, piece of flesh. *Ga.* (S.3) kaṇḍa muscle (< Te.). *Go.* (Tr.) khānḍum (*pl.* khānḍk), (Ch.) khānḍ, khānḍum, (Ph.) khānḍk flesh; (SR.) khānḍum id., mutton (*Voc.*1001). *Konḍa* kaṇḍa meat, flesh, muscle. *Kuwi* (Isr.) kaṇḍa piece. / Probably < Skt. khaṇḍa- (Turner, *CDIAL*, no. 3792) with development of meaning: piece > piece of flesh > flesh (DEDR 1175). khaṇḍi = a saṛi, a full dress for a woman, a piece of cloth twelve cubits long by two in width; khaṇḍa = a piece of cloth suitable for the dress of a woman's sar.i; khaṇḍi bande, bande = to dress, of women binding round waist (Santali) khand 'ivory' kandhi 'a lump, a piece' (Santali) kandi 'beads' (Pa.)(DEDR 1215). khaṇḍ 'ivory' (H.) kandi (pl. –l) beads, necklace (Pa.); kanti (pl. –l) bead, (pl.) necklace; kandiṭ 'bead' (Ga.)(DEDR 1215). काढतें [kāḍhatēṃ] n Among gamesters. An ivory counter &c. placed to represent a sum of money. (Marathi) The dotted circles also adorn the standard device which is a drill-lathe, sangaḍa खंड [khaṇḍa] A piece, bit, fragment, portion.(Marathi)

Rebus: *khānḍa* 'tools, pots and pans and metal-ware'. Thus, the glyph which denotes this lexeme is a set of 'dotted circles'. Hence, the depiction of 'dotted circles' (like perforated beads) surrounding a fire-altar and also on ivory objects.

Vedi as fire-altar denoted by vēdha ‘hole’

vēdha m. ‘ hitting the mark ’ MBh., ‘ penetration, hole ’ VarBr̥S. [√vyadh] Pa. vēdha -- m. ‘ prick, wound ’; Pk. vēha -- m. ‘ boring, hole ’, P. veh, beh m., H. beh m., G. veh m. karṇavēdha -- .(CDIAL 12108) வேதிதம் vētitam , n. < vēdhita. (யாழ். அக.) 1. Perforating, drilling; துளைக்கை. 2. Tube; துளையுடைப்பொருள். வேதை[3] vētai , n. < vēdha. 1. Drilling, boring; துளைக்கை. (Tamil) Vedhin (adj.) [fr. vidh=vyadh] piercing, shooting, hitting (Pali) Rebus: vḗdi f. ‘ raised piece of ground serving as an altar and usu. strewed with kuśa grass ’ RV., ‘ stand, bench ’ MBh., ‘ platform for wedding ceremony ’ Kāv., vēdika<-> m. ‘ bench ’ R., °kā -- f. MBh. [Cf. vēdá -- m. ‘ bunch of kuśa grass used as broom ’ AV.] Pa. vēdi -- , °dī -- , °dikā -- f. ‘ cornice, ledge, rail ’; Pk. vēi -- , vēiā -- f. ‘ platform ’; A. bei ‘ quadrangular frame of greenery forming platform on which ceremonial bathing of bride and bridegroom is performed ’.(CDIAL 12107).

There are three glyptic elements in the composition:1. + shape denoting: kaṇḍ = a furnace, altar (Santali.lex.); khaṇḍaran, khaṇḍrun ‘pit furnace’ (Santali) 2. (.dot) infixed circle (dotted circle): khaṇḍa ‘tools, pots and pans and metal-ware’; 3.  raised large-sized dot: गोटी [gōṭī] f (Dim. Of गोटा) A roundish stone or pebble. Rebus: *khoṭ* m. ‘alloy’ (Punjabi)

Ta. katu a scar. *Ka.* gadu, gaduvu a swelling (as from a blow), a tumour; gaddarisu to swell (as the face or limbs); gādari weal. *Tu.* gadarů a lump. *Te.* kadumu a swelling, bump; kanti excrescence, lump, wen, swelling. (DEDR 1196).

गोदा [gōdā] m A circular brand or mark made by actual cautery (Marathi)गोटा [gōṭā] m A roundish stone or pebble. 2 A marble (of stone, lac, wood &c.) 2 A marble. 3 A large lifting stone. Used in trials of strength among the Athletæ. 4 A

stone in temples described at length underउचला 5 fig. A term for a round, fleshy, well-filled body. 6 A lump of silver: as obtained by melting down lace or fringe. गोटुळा or गोटोळा [gōṭuḷā or gōṭōḷā] a (गोटा) Spherical or spheroidal, pebble-form. (Marathi) Rebus 1: खोट [khōṭa] *f* A mass of metal (unwrought or of old metal melted down); an ingot or wedge. Hence खोटसाळ [khōṭasāḷa

] *a* (खोट & साळ from शाला) Alloyed--a metal. (Marathi) Bshk. *khoṭ* 'embers', Phal. *khūṭo* 'ashes, burning coal'; L. *khoṭ* 'alloy, impurity', *°ṭā* 'alloyed', awāṇ. *khoṭā* 'forged'; P. *khoṭ* m. 'base, alloy' M.*khoṭā* 'alloyed', (CDIAL 3931) Rebus 2: krvṛi f. 'granary (Wpah.); kuṛī, kuṛo house, building'(Ku.)(CDIAL 3232) कोठी [kōṭhī] f (कोष्ट S) A granary, garner, storehouse, warehouse, treasury, factory, bank. (Marathi) कोठी The grain and provisions (as of an army); the commissariat supplies. Ex. लशकराची कोठी चालली-उतरली- आली-लुटली. कोठ्या [kōṭhyā] कोठा [kōṭhā] m (कोष्ट S) A large granary, store-room, warehouse, water-reservoir &c. 2 The stomach. 3 The chamber of a gun, of water-pipes &c. 4 A bird's nest. 5 A cattle-shed. 6 The chamber or cell of a hunḍí in which is set down in figures the amount. कोठारें [kōṭhārēṃ] n A storehouse gen (Marathi)

Ropar 1,Text 9021 h128

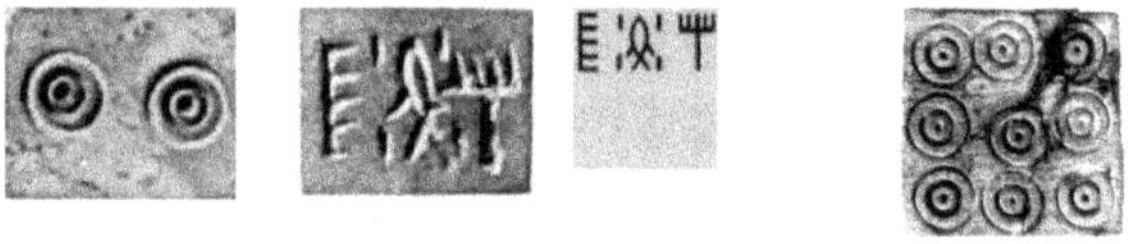

h342A h342B 4413 m1259 m1260

m0352A m0352C m0352D m0352E

m0352F m1654A ivory cube m1654B ivory cube

m1654D ivory cube m1254 m1255 Nausharo10 Slide 187 A faience button seal with geometric motif (H2000-4491/9999-34) was found on the surface of Mound AB at Harappa by one of the workmen. [Harappa 2000 find] m1256 m1257 m1258

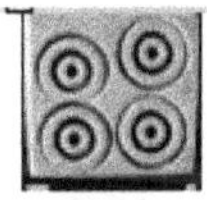

Slide 203 (Kenoyer, 2002). Steatite button seal Fired steatite button seal with four concentric circle designs from the Trench 54 area (H2000-4432/2174-3)

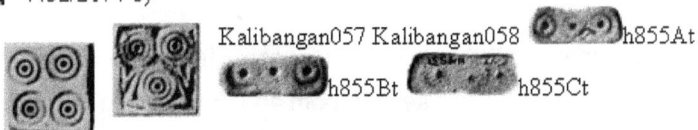

  Kalibangan057 Kalibangan058  h855At  h855Bt  h855Ct

 m1259  m1260  h974Ait  h974Bit  h974Cit

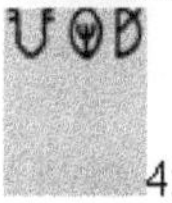 4592  h978Ait  h978Bit  h978Cit 

5412   h888Abit 4466   h889Abit 5477

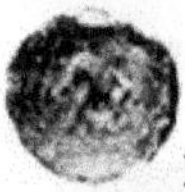 h832At  h832Bt Tablet in bas-relief  h638 

h352A  h352B  h352C  4575 Pict-120: One or more dotted circles. [54 out of 67 objects on which this glyph occurs, are miniature tablets]
The text on top line occurs mainly on miniature tablets of Harappa over 46 times.

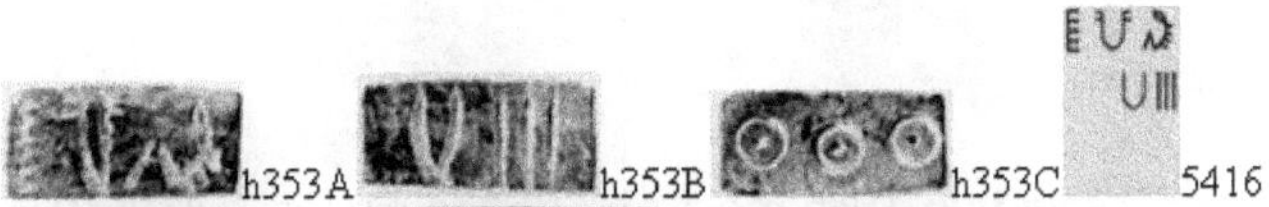
h353A h353B h353C 5416

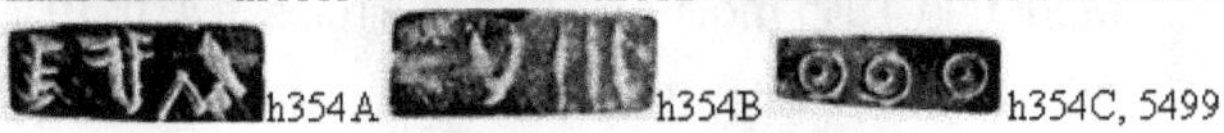
h354A h354B h354C, 5499

h359a h359B h359C

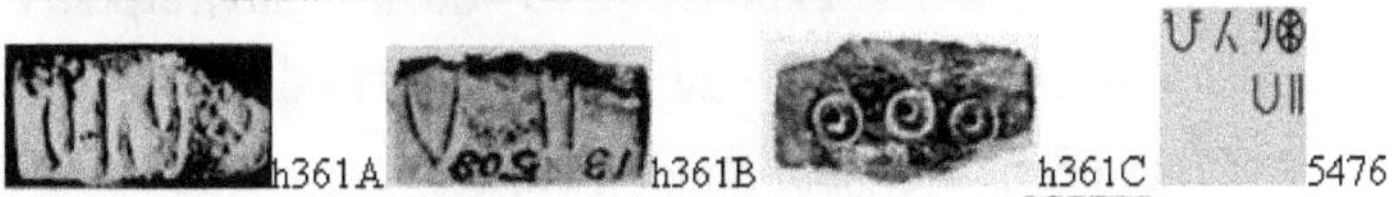
h361A h361B h361C 5476

h362A h362B h362C 5466

h365A h365B h365C h365E

h367A h367B h367C h367E

After Vats, Pl.CXIX,.No.6 An ivory comb fragment with one preserved tooth and ornamented with double incised circles (3.8 in. long).

Kalibangan, Ivory comb with three dotted circles; Kalibangan, Period II; Thapar 1979, Pl.XXVII, in: Ancient Cities of the Indus.

Ivory rod, ivory plaque with dotted circles.

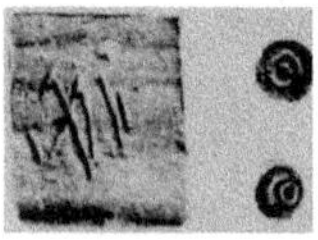

Mohenjodaro. [Musee National De Arts Asiatiques Guimet, 1988-1989, Les cites oubliees de l'Indus Archeologie du Pakistan.] h1017ivorystick

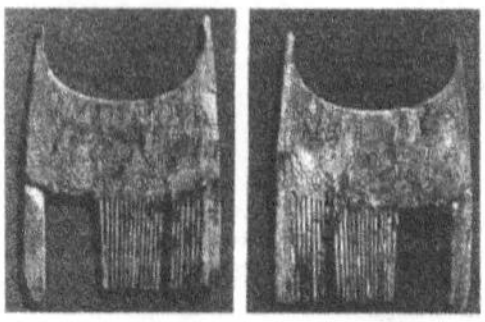

Ivory comb with Mountain Tulip motif and dotted circles. TA 1649 Tell Abraq. [D.T. Potts, South and Central Asian elements at Tell Abraq (Emirate of Umm al-Qaiwain, United Arab Emirates), c. 2200 BC—AD 400, in Asko Parpola and Petteri Koskikallio, South Asian Archaeology 1993: , pp. 615-666] h337, h338 Texts 4417, 4426 (Dotted circles on leaf-shaped tablets) Tell Abraq comb and axe with epigraph After Fig. 7Holly Pittman, 1984, Art of the Bronze Age: Southeastern Iran, Western Central Asia, and the Indus Valley, New York, The Metropolitan Museum of Art, pp. 29-30].

Wild tulip motif. A motif that occurs on southeast Iranian cylinder seals and on Persian Gulf seals. 1st row: Bactrian artifacts; 2nd row: a comb from the Gulf

area and late trans-Elamite seals [After Marie-Helene Pottier, 1984, Materiel funeraire de la Bactriane meridionale de l'age du bronze, Recherche sur les Civilizations, Memoire 36, Paris, fig. 21; Sarianidi, V.I., 1986, Le complexe culturel de Togolok 21 en Margiane, Arts Asiatiques 41: fig. 6,21; Potts, 1994, fig. 53,8; Amiet, 1986, fig. 132].

The ivory comb found at Tell Abraq measures 11 X 8.2 X .4 cm. Both sides of the comb bear identical, incised decoration in the form of two long-stemmed flowers with crenate or dentate leaves, flanking three dotted circles arranged in a triangular pattern. Bone and ivory combs with dotted-circle decoration are well-known in the Harappan area (e.g. at Chanhu-daro and Mohenjo-daro), but none of the Harappan combs bear the distinctive floral motif of the Tell Abraq comb. These flowers are identified as tulips, perhaps Mountain tulip or Boeotian tulip (both of which grow in Afghanistan) which have an undulate leaf. There is a possibility that the comb is an import from Bactria, perhaps transmitted through Meluhha to the Oman Peninsula site of Tell Abraq.

Orthographically, the dotted circle is also a fish-eye or eye of an antelope. The eye is *kāṇ* rebus: *kāṇḍ* 'tools, pots and pans, metal-ware' as in *ayaskāṇḍa* 'excellent iron' (Pan.). It may also be rebus for *kaṇḍ* 'fire-altar'. *kaṇḍ* also denotes 'ivory'.

The gloss related to the dotted circle is thus, decoded rebus as *kāṇ*.

- kandhi = a lump, a piece (Santali.lex.) [The dotted circle thus connotes an ingot taken out of a kaṇḍ, furnace; *kāṇḍ* 'tools, pots and pans, metal-ware']. kāndavika = a baker; kandu = an iron plate or pan for baking cakes etc. (Ka.lex.)

- kaṇḍ = altar, furnace (Santali) लोहकारकन्दुः f. a blacksmith's smelting furnace (Grierson Kashmiri lex.) payĕn-kōda पयन्-कौंद। परिपाककन्दुः f. a kiln (a potter's, a lime-kiln, and brick-kiln, or the like); a furnace (for smelting) This yajn~a kuṇḍam can be denoted rebus, by perforated beads (kandi) or on ivory (khaṇḍ):

- kandi (pl. -l) beads, necklace (Pa.); kanti (pl. -l) bead, (pl.) necklace; kandit. bead (Ga.)(DEDR 1215). The three stringed beads depicted on the pictograph may perhaps be treated as a phonetic determinant of the substantive, the rimmed jar, the khaṇḍa kanka. khaṇḍa, xanro, sword or large sacrificial knife. kandil, kandi_l = a globe of glass, a lantern (Ka.lex.)

khaṇḍ 'ivory' (H.) jaṇḍ khaṇḍ = ivory (Jaṭkī) khaṇḍ ī = ivory in rough (Jaṭkī); gaṭī = piece of elephant's tusk (S.) [This semant. may explain why the dotted circle -- i.e., kandi, 'beads' -- is often depicted on ivory objects, such as ivory combs]. See also: khaṇḍiyo [cf. khaṇḍaṇī a tribute] tributary; paying a tribute to a superior king (G.lex.) [Note glyph of a kneeling adorant]. kandi (pl. -l) beads, necklace (Pa.); kanti (pl. -l) bead, (pl.) necklace; kandit. bead (Ga.)(DEDR 1215). The three stringed beads depicted on the pictograph may perhaps be treated as a phonetic determinant of the substantive, the rimmed jar, the khaṇḍa kanka. khaṇḍa, xanro, sword or large sacrificial knife. kandil, kandīl = a globe of glass, a lantern (Ka.lex.) kandhi 'a lump, a piece' (Santali) काढतें [kāḍhatēṃ] n Among gamesters. An ivory counter &c. placed to represent a sum of money. (Marathi) The dotted circles also adorn the standard device which is a drill-lathe, sangaḍa खंड [khaṇḍa] A piece, bit, fragment, portion.(Marathi) Rebus: khaṇḍaran, khaṇḍrun 'pit furnace' (Santali)

- Rebus: kaṇḍ 'tools, pots and pans, metal-ware'. kaṇḍ = altar, furnace (Santali) लोहकारकन्दु: f. a blacksmith's smelting furnace (Grierson Kashmiri lex.) payĕn-kōda पयन्-कोँद। परिपाककन्दु: f. a kiln (a potter's, a lime-kiln, and brick-kiln, or the like); a furnace (for smelting) This yajn~a kuṇḍam can be denoted rebus, by perforated beads (kandi) or on ivory (khaṇḍ):

- aya = iron (G.); ayah, ayas = metal (Skt.) *ayaskāṇḍa* 'excellent iron (metal) tools, pots and pans, metal-ware'. Allograph: Glyph: 'eye'.

m0008, m0021, h228B

Carved Ivory Standard in the middle

har501 Harappa 1990 and 1993.

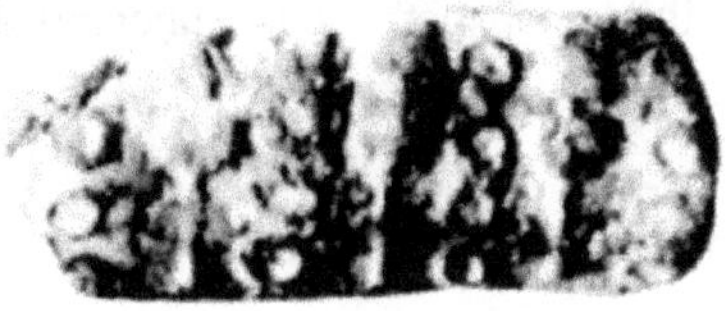

Standard device, model reconstructed

after Mahadevan

? The dotted circles on the bottom portion of the device connote ghangar ghongor; rebus: kangar 'portable furnace'.

The standard device thus connotes: *khāṇḍa* 'tools, pots and pans and metal-ware' of . *sangaḍa* 'lathe, furnace'.

Smithy

Glyph 162. Glyph or symbol of spoken word: *kolmo* 'seedling, paddy (rice) plant' (Munda); rebus, similar sounding word connoting mental experience: *kolmi* 'smithy' (Go.) కండె [kaṇḍe] *kaṇḍe*. [Tel.] n. A head or ear of millet or maize. జొన్న కంకి. *kāṛ* 'stack of stalks of large millet'(Maithili) Rebus: *kaṇḍ* 'furnace, fire-altar, consecrated fire'. *khaṇḍ* 'tools, pots and pans and metal-ware.'

The Glyhph 162 which reads *khaṇḍ* is infixed in 'oval' glyph which is read rebus: *khōṭ*

'alloyed' (Punjabi) Thus, the ligatured glyph is read as: *khaṇḍ khōṭ* 'alloyed tools, pots and pans, metal-ware'.

Glyph shown together with stong of scorpion on Urseal 1. Rebus: खोट [*khōṭa*]

'ingot, wedge'; A mass of metal (unwrought or of old metal melted down)(Maratthi) kōḍ कोड् m. a kernel (Kashmiri) खोट [khōṭa] A

lump or solid bit (as of phlegm, gore, curds, inspissated milk); any concretion or clot. (Marathi)

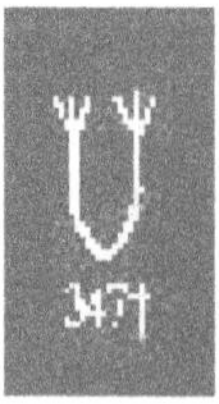

A pair of glyphs 162 are joined to form a pot. The combined glyph 347: *sangaḍi.* n. A couple, pair (Telugu). Rebus: *sangaḍa.'* associattion (guild)' (Marathi) kuṇḍa 'pot'; rebus: kuṇḍamu 'a pit for receiving and preserving consecrated fire' (Te.)

Thus, a combined reading for the joined or ligatured glyphs is: *sangaḍa khaṇḍ kuṇḍa* 'smithy guild (with) furnace -- consecrated fire (pit)'.

Seal impression from Harappa.[85] *Ka.* koṇḍe, goṇḍe tuft, tassel, cluster (DEDR 2081) Rebus: kŏnḍ क्वंड् or kŏnḍa क्वंड । कुण्ड m a deep still spring (El., Gr.Gr. 145); (amongst Hindūs) a hole dug in the ground for receiving consecrated fire (Kashmiri) The tuft is a phonetic determinant of *kaṇḍ* 'furnace, fire-altar'; *kuṇḍa* id. As in: *agni-kuṇḍa* 'consecrated fire-pit' (Sanskrit).

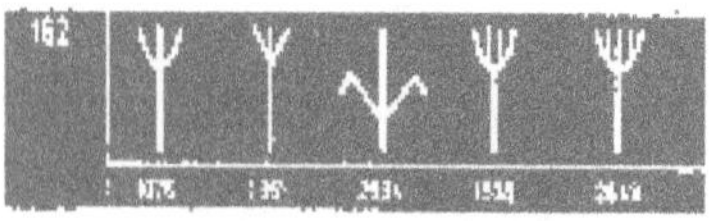

Allographs of Glyph 162 with three prongs.

Allographs of Glyph 165 with five prongs. *tagaraka* 'wild tulip *taberna montana*' (Sanskrit).

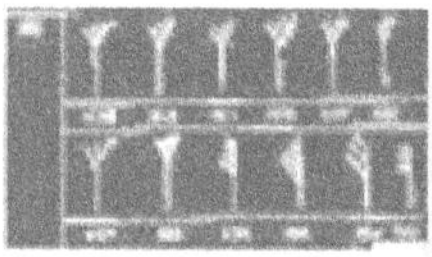

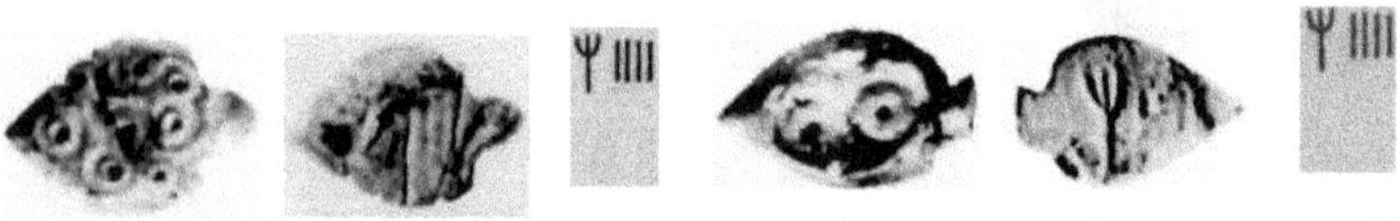

h337, h338 Texts 4417, 4426 with two glyphs each on leaf-shaped, miniature Harappa tablets.

Glyph; *goḍe* a rat's hole (DEDR 1660). Pk. *kōḍara* -- , *kōla°*, *kōṭa°*, *koṭṭa°* n. ' hole, hollow '; Or. *koraṛa* ' hollow in a tree, cave, hole '; H. (X *khōla --

2) *khoḍar* m. ' pit, hollow in a tree ', *khoṛrā* m.; Si.*kovuḷa* ' rotten tree ' (< **kōḷalla* -- with H. Smith JA 1950, 197, but not < Pa. *kōḷāpa* --). (CDIAL 3496).

Rebus: खोट [*khōṭa*] 'ingot, wedge'; A mass of metal (unwrought or of old metal melted down). (Maratthi) *khoṭ* 'alloy (Lahnda) Hence खोटसाळ [khōṭasāḷa] *a* (खोट & साळ from शाला) Alloyed--a metal. (Marathi) Bshk. *khoṭ* ' embers ', Phal. *khūṭo* ' ashes, burning coal '; L. *khoṭā* ' alloyed ', awāṇ. *khoṭā* ' forged '; P. *khoṭ* m. ' base, alloy ' M.*khoṭā* ' alloyed ', (CDIAL 3931) *Kor.* (O.)

gaṇḍa 'four' (Santali); rebus: 'furnace, *kaṇḍ* fire-altar'

Glyph: *kolom* 'cob'; rebus: *kolmo* 'seedling, rice (paddy) plant' (Munda.)

Photograph of paddy plant.

Photograph of millet, buckwheat, maize, taro.

కండె [kaṇḍe] *kaṇḍe*. [Tel.] n. A head or ear of millet or maize. జొన్నకండె. Mth. *kāṛ* 'stack of stalks of large millet'(CDIAL 3023). Rebus: *kaṇḍ* 'furnace, fire-altar, consecrated fire'. Rebus: *khāṇḍā* 'tools, pots and pans, and metal-ware'.

Smithy was designated by a term which also meant 'temple'. *kole.l* 'smithy, temple' (Kota): Ta. *kol* working in iron, blacksmith; kollaṉ blacksmith. Ma. *kollan* blacksmith, artificer. Ko. *kole·l* smithy, temple in Kota village. To. *kwala·l* Kota smithy. Ka. *kolime, kolume, kulame, kulime, kulume, kulme* fire-pit, furnace; (Bell.; U.P.U.) *konimi* blacksmith; (Gowda) *kolla* id. Koḍ. *kollë* blacksmith. Te. *kolimi* furnace. Go. (SR.) *kollusānā* to mend implements; (Ph.) *kolstānā, kulsānā* to forge; (Tr.) *kōlstānā* to repair (of ploughshares); (SR.) *kolmi* smithy (Voc. 948). Kuwi (F.) *kolhali* to forge. (DEDR 2133).

Indus writing on Mitathal seal

Two clearly visible glyphs on the broken seal constitute the (partial) inscription[86].

Glyph1 This is a ligatured glyph comprising: four numeral strokes and three numeral strokes. Each glyph denotes a lexeme and is read rebus.

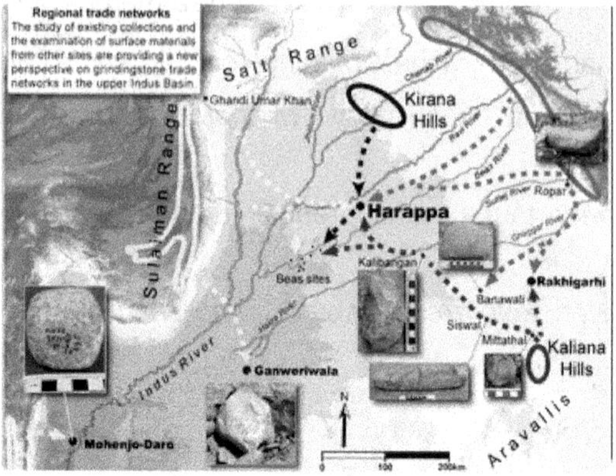

gaṇḍa 'four' (Santali); rebus: *kaṇḍ* fire-altar, furnace' (Santali)

kolmo 'three' (Mu.); *kolami* 'smithy, forge' (Te.)

Thus, the glyph reads: *kolmo gaṇḍa* 'smithy with fire-altar'.

Glyph 2 This is a ligatured glyph comprising: 'plant' infixed within a 'hole'.

dulo 'hole' (N.); rebus: *dul* 'to cast metal in a mould' (Santali)

కండె [kaṇḍe] *kaṇḍe*. [Tel.] n. A head or ear of millet or maize. జొన్నకండె. Rebus: *kaṇḍ* 'furnace, fire-altar, consecrated fire'. Rebus: *kaṇḍ* 'furnace, fire-altar, consecrated fire'.

Thus, the glyph reads: *dul kaṇḍ* 'casting (metal) furnace.'

The entire inscription thus connotes the repertoire of the artisan: casting metal workshop with smithy (forge) and fire-altar (furnace).

Indian *sprachbund*, meluhha (mleccha) words

Ancient India is often associated in cuneiform texts as meluhha (cognate: mleccha), and *mlecchitavikalpa* as a language art mentioned in Vatsyayana's list of 64 arts means 'cryptography '. This may refer to mleccha picture-writing which was also evidenced by alik tilmun. Other to language-related arts mentioned are: *akṣara muṣṭika kathanam* (messaging through wrist-finger gestures); *deśa bhāṣā jñānam* (knowledge of dialects). *Nāṭyaśāstra* XVII.29-30 attests mleccha as a common (spoken) language or *lingua franca* used on the stage: *dvividhā jātibhāṣāca prayoge samudāhṛtā mlecchaśabdopacārā ca bhāratam varṣam aśritā* 'The jātibhāṣā (common language), prescribed for use (on the stage) has various forms. It contains words of mleccha origin and is spoken in Bhāratavarṣa only…'

According to Matsya Purāṇa (10.7), King Veṇa was the ancestor of the mleccha; according to Mahābhārata (MB. 12.59, 101-3), King Veṇa was a progenitor of the Niṣāda dwelling in the Vindhya mountains. Nirukta 3.8 includes Niṣāda among the five peoples mentioned in the ṛgveda 10.53.4, citing Aupamanyava; the five peoples are: brāhmaṇa, kṣatriya, vaiśya, śūdra and Niṣāda. Niṣāda gotra is mentioned in the gaṇapāṭha of Pāṇini (Aṣṭādhyāyī 4.1.100). Niṣāda were mleccha. It should be noted that Pāṇini associated yavana with the Kāmboja (Pāṇini, *Gaṇapāṭha*, 178 on 2.1.72).

Ancient text of Panini also refers to two languages in *śikṣā*: Sanskrit and Prākṛt. Prof Avinash Sathaye provides a textual reference on the earliest occurrence of the word, 'Sanskrit' :

triṣaṣṭiścatuh ṣaṣṭirvā varṇāh ṣambhumate matāh |

prākṛite samskṛte cāpi svayam proktā svayambhuvā || (pāṇini's śikṣā)

Trans. There are considered to be 63 or 64 varṇā-s in the school (mata) of

shambhu. In Prakrit and Sanskrit by swayambhu (manu, Brahma), himself, these varṇā-s were stated.

This demonstrates that pāṇini knew both samskṛta and prākṛita as established languages. (Personal communication, 27 June 2010 with Prof. Shrinivas Tilak.) Manusmṛti refers to two languages, both of dasyu (daha): ārya vācas, mleccha vācas. *mukhabāhū rupajjānām yā loke jātayo bahih mlecchavācas'cāryav ācas te sarve dasyuvah smṛtāh* Trans. 'All those people in this world who are excluded from those born from the mouth, the arms, the thighs and the feet (of Brahma) are called Dasyus, whether they speak the language of the mleccha-s or that of the ārya-s.' (Manu 10.45)] This distinction between *lingua franca* and literary version of the language, is elaborated by Patañjali as a reference to 1) grammatically correct literary language and 2) ungrammatical, colloquial speech (*deśī*). Nandana, another commentator of *Mānava Dharma śāstra*. X.45, defines *āryavāc as samskṛtavāc.*

The reality of mleccha (cognate meluhha) is attested in linguistic studies by referring to the ancient Indian language region as Indian *sprachbund*, linguistic area. *Mahābhārata* also attests to mleccha used in a conversation with Vidura. Mahābhārata speaks of the Yavanas, Kambojas, Darunas etc as the fierce mleccha from Uttarapatha : *uttaraścāpare mlechchha jana bharatasattama. || 63 || Yavanashcha sa Kamboja Daruna mlechchha jatayah. | — (MBH 6.11.63-64) They are referred to as papakritah (sinful): uttara pathajanmanah kirtayishyami tanapi. | Yauna Kamboja Gandharah Kirata barbaraih saha. || 43 || ete pāpakṛtāstatra caranti prṛthivīmimām. | śvakakabalagridhraṇān sadharmaṇo narādhipa. || 44 ||* — (MBh 12/207/43-44) There are references to Mleccha (that is, *śaka, Yavana, Kamboja, Pahlava*) in Bāla Kāṇḍa of the *Valmiki Rāmāyaṇa* (1.54.21-23; 1.55.2-3). *Śatapatha Brāhmaṇa* refers to mleccha as language (with pronunciation variants) and also provides an example of such mleccha pronunciation by asuras. A Pali text, *Uttarādhyayana Sūtra* 10.16 notes: *ladhdhaṇa vimānusattaṇṇam āriattam puṇrāvi dullaham bahave dasyū milakkhuyā*; trans. 'though one be born as a man, it is rare chance to be an ārya, for many are the dasyu and milakkhu'. Milakkhu and dasyu constitute the

majority, they are the many. Dasyu are milakkhu (mleccha speakers). Dasyu are also ārya vācas (Manu 10.45), that is, speakers of Sanskrit. Both ārya vācas and mleccha vācas are dasyu [cognate *dahyu, daŋ́ha, daha* (Khotanese)], people, in general. Such people are referred to in Rgveda by Viśvāmitra as 'Bhāratam janam.'[87] Mahābhārata alludes to 'thousands of mlecchas', a numerical superiority equaled by their valour and courage in battle which enhances the invincibility of Pandava (MBh. 7.69.30; 95.36).

Dasyu is cognate with *dahyu* country (often with reference to the people inhabiting it): "DAHYU (OIr. *dahyu-*), attested in Avestan *daxíiu-, daŋ́hu-* "country" (often with reference to the people inhabiting it; cf. *AirWb.*, cot. 706; Hoffmann, pp. 599-600 n. 14; idem and Narten, pp. 54-55) and in Old Persian *dahyu-* "country, province" (pl. "nations"; Gershevitch, p. 160). The term is likely to be connected with Old Indian *dásyu* "enemy" (of the Aryans), which acquired the meaning of "demon, enemy of the gods" (Mayrhofer, *Dictionary* II, pp. 28-29). Because of the Indo-Iranian parallel, the word may be traced back to the root *das-*, from which a term denoting a large collectivity of men and women could have been derived. Such traces can be found in Iranian languages: for instance, in the ethnonym Dahae (q.v., i) "men" (cf. Av. ethnic name [fem. adj.] *dāhī,* from *dåŋ́ha-*; *AirWb.*, col. 744; Gk. Dáai, etc.), in Old Persian *dahā* "the Daha people" (Brandenstein and Mayrhofer, pp. 113-14), and in Khotanese *daha* "man, male" (Bailey, *Dictionary*, p. 155)... The connection *daxíiu, dańhu-* and *arya-* "Aryans" is very common to indicate the Aryan lands and peoples, in some instances in the plural: *airiiå daŋ́hāuuō,airiianąm daxíiunąm, airiiābiiō daŋ́hubiiō...* the loanword *da-a-yau-iš* in Elamite."[88]

Excerpt from a translation of the text of ŚB 3.2.1.22-28 refers to mleccha speech: *upajijñāsyāṃ sa mlecastasmānna brāhmaṇo mlecedasuryā haiṣā vā natevaiṣa dviṣatāṃ sapatnānāmādatte vācaṃ te 'syāttavacasaḥ parābhavanti ya evam etadveda o 'yaṃ yajño vācamabhidadhyau* "Asuras being deprived of speech, were undone, crying, 'He 'lavah! He 'lavah!' (79) 24. Such was the unintelligible speech which they then uttered, -- and he (who speaks thus) is a Mleccha (barbarian). Hence let no Brahman speak barbarous language, since such is the

speech of the Asuras."[89]

Many rearchers[90] have reached a consensus that ancient India constituted a linguistic area that is, an area wherein specific language-speakers absorbed features from other languages and made the features their own. To delineate such a linguistic area and the glosses that might have been used in that area, the glosses are chosen from all Indian languages. Indian language glosses are compared because there is evidence for cultural continuum of the civilization which produced the objects inscribed with Indus script. The glosses are semantically-phonetically clustered together in the *Indian lexicon* which is a veritable substrate dictionary of the linguistic area. The assumption is that one or more languages of this lexicon could hold the legacy of the words used by the authors of the civilization who also invented the writing system. Readings of inscriptions with Indus Writing confirm this Indian linguistic area which may also be termed mleccha (meluhha).

In places north of Lamgham district, i.e. north bank of river Kabul, near Peshawar were regions known as Mi-li-ku, the frontier of the mleccha lands.[91]

That the mleccha were also adored as ṛṣi-s is clear from the verse of *Bṛhatsamhitā* 2.15: *mlecchā hi yavanās teṣu samyak śāstram kadam sthitam ṛṣivat te 'pi pūjyante kim punar daivavid dvijāh* (The yavana are mleccha, among them this science is duly established; therefore, even they (although mleccha) are honoured as ṛṣi; how much more (praise is due to an) astrologer who is a brāhmaṇa').

Meluhha referred to in Sumerian and old Akkadian texts refers to an area in Sarasvati Civilization; Asko and Simo Parpola add: '...probably, including NW India with Gujarat as well as eastern Baluchistan'.[92]

Imports from Meluhha into Mesopotamia included the following commodities which were found in north-western and western Bhāratavarṣa: copper, silver, gold, carnelian, ivory, uśu wood (ebony), and another wood which is translated as 'sea wood' – perhaps mangrove wood on the coasts of Sind ad Baluchistan. [J. Hansman, 'A Periplus of Magan and Meluhha', Bulletin of the School of

Oriental and African Studies, vol. 36, pt. III, 1973, pp. 560.] The Ur texts specifically refer to 'seafaring country of Meluhha" and hence, Leemans' thesis that Meluhha was the west coast (modern state of Gujarat) of Bhārata. The Lothal dockyard had fallen into disuse by c.1800 BCE, a date when the trade between Mesopotamia and Meluhha also ended. [WF Leemans, 'Old Babylonian Letters and Economic History', Journal of Economic and Social History of the Orient, vol. XI, 1968, pp. 215-26. P. Aalto, 1971, 'Marginal Notes on the Meluhha Problem,' Professor KA Nilakanta Sastri Felicitation Volume, Madras, pp. 222-23.] In Leemans' view, Gujarat was the last bulwark of the (Indus or Sarasvati) Civilization. Records refer to Meluhhan ships docking at Sumer. There were Meluhhans in various Sumerian cities; there was also a Meluhhan town or district at one city. The Sumerian records indicate a large volume of trade; according to a Sumerian tablet, one shipment from Meluhha contained 5,900 kg of copper (13,000 lbs, or 6 ½ tons)! The bulk of this trade was done through Dilmun, not directly with Meluhha. In our view, the formative stages of the Civilization also had their locus in the coastal areas – in particular, the Gulf of Khambat, Gulf of Kutch and Makran coast, as evidenced by the wide conchshell-bangle, dated to c. 6500 BCE, made of *turbinella pyrum* or *śankha*, found in Mehergarh, 300 miles north of the Makran coast.

Like Nahali (Nahari > Nagari) on banks of River Tapati, mleccha is a language-composite of Indo-Aryan, Dravidian and Munda linguistic area circa 5000 years Before Present on Sarasvati-Indus River Basins; all proto-versions of present-day languages of Bharat are a dialectical continuum from this linguistic area (Further researches and identification of isoglosses are called for).

Mould, to forge in copper smithy guild

Glyph 391 is ligatured on the neck of young bull with one horn:

m0712 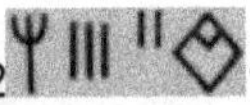 1091

This could be an orthographic style of representing the use of mould (large stone) in a forge for copper, *eraka* 'molten cast

(metal)(Tulu). The reading of inscription on seal m0712 can thus be: *khũṭ* 'corner'; rebus: *khũṭ* 'community, guild'; *tebra* 'three'; rebus: *tambra* 'copper'; *kolmo* 'seedling, plant'; rebus: *kolami* 'smithy'. *gaḍa* 'mould' for eraka 'knave of wheel'; rebus: *eraka* 'molten cast metal).

Glyph corner: *khũṭ* m. 'corner, direction' (→ P. *khũṭ* f. ' corner, side '); G. *khũṭṛī* f. 'angle '.

Glyph excrescence on neck: gaḍu m. ' excrescence on neck, goitre, hump on back ' Pāṇ. Vārtt. (CDIAL 3977).

Pk. *gaḍa* -- n. 'large stone'? (CDIAL 3969). Pk. *gaḍhaï* ' forms '; A. *gariba* ' to mould, form '; B. *gaṛā* ' to hammer into shape, form ' (CDIAL 3966).

aṭar 'a splinter' (Ma.) *aṭaruka* 'to burst, crack, sli off,fly open; *aṭarcca* ' splitting, a crack'; *aṭarttuka* 'to split, tear off, open (an oyster) (Ma.); *aḍaruni* 'to crack' (Tu.) (DEDR 66) Rebus: *aduru* 'native, unsmelted metal' (Kannada) *aduru* '*gan.iyinda tegadu karagade iruva aduru*', that is, ore taken from the mine and not subjected to melting in a furnace (Kannada).[93] Vikalpa: *sal* 'splinter'; rebus: *sal* 'workshop' (Santali)

A pair of glyphs 391 shown on Dholavira sign board may thus denote: *eraka sangaḍa* 'lathe' (G.), that is, copper (delivered) as entrustment articles -- *jangaḍ.*

Dholavira signboard

The signboard measuring 3 metres long, must have been placed above the north gate of the citadel that existed at the Harappan city of Dholavira. All the signs in white gypsum may have made the board visible from afar.[94]

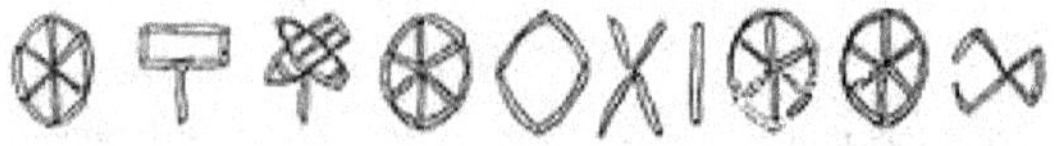

[The fourth glyph from right may also be read as ^]

Each glyph is 35 cm to 37 cm tall and 25 cm to 27 cm wide, made of baked gypsum and inlaid on a wooden board. The 10 signs constitute an exquisite work of artisans. Each sign is made of several pieces.

Rebus readings indicate this as perhaps the first advertisement hoarding atop the gateway of a citadel visible to navigators on ships and boats traversing the Persian Gulf reaching Kotda (Dholavira) port.

Three types of metallurgical services are announced.
Segment 1: Mint, gold turner-carver entrustment articles

Claws of crab 'kamaṭha'; rebus: kampaṭṭam 'mint'; Vikalpa: ḍato = claws of crab (Santali); dhātu = mineral (Skt.)

Glyph knave of wheel: erako nave; era = knave of wheel ; rebus: eraka, (copper) 'metal infusion'; kund opening in the nave or hub of a wheel to admit the axle (Santali) erka = ekke (Tbh. of arka) aka (Tbh. of arka) copper (metal); crystal (Ka.lex.) cf. eruvai = copper (Tamil) Rebus: kunda a turner's lathe (Skt.)(CDIAL 3295). Rebus: kundan 'pure gold'. kuṇḍamu 'a pit for receiving and preserving consecrated fire' (Te.)

Glyph: pair. sangaḍa 'pair'.

Thus, the pair of 'knave' glyphs is read: kundan sangaḍa 'that is, (delivered) as kundan 'gold' entrustment articles (on approval basis) -- jangaḍ.

Segment 2: Silver, iron native metal, turner-carver

[The second glyph from right may also be read as Λ]

Glyph: long linear stroke. met 'one' (Santali); rebus: meḍ 'iron'; vikalpa: goṭ = one

(Santali); goṭi = silver (G.)

aḍaren, ḍaren lid, cover (Santali) Rebus: aduru 'native metal' (Ka.)

Glyph: H. khū̃ṭ m. ' corner, direction ' (→ P. khū̃ṭ f. ' corner, side ') (CDIAL 3898) Rebus: kuṇḍamu 'a pit for receiving and preserving consecrated fire' (Te.) kundam, *kund* a sacrificial fire-pit (Skt.) *kunda* 'arsenic' (to produce the alloy bell-metal) (Skt.) Tamil lexicon points to *kuntam* as the synonym of tāla-pāṣāṇam (lit. bell metal stone) or śilā 'stone, red arsenic' (Skt.) Allograph: khū̃ṭ 'zebu'.

eraka 'knave of wheel'; rebus: eraka 'copper'

Segment 3: Copper mint, workshop, turner-carver

Fig leaf 'loa'; rebus: loh '(copper) metal' kamaḍha = ficus religiosa (Skt.); kamaṭa = portable furnace for melting precious metals (Te.); kampaṭṭam = mint (Ta.)

Peg 'khuṇṭa'; khū̃ṭi = pin (M.) rebus: kuṭi= furnace (Santali) kūṭa 'workshop' kuṇḍamu 'a pit for receiving and preserving consecrated fire' (Te.) kundār turner (A.); kū̃dār, kū̃dāri (B.);

eraka 'knave of wheel'; rebus: eraka 'copper'

Two unique ligatured glyphs: professionals

Some ligatures of Indus writing are orthographic abstractions. That one ligature set is

unique is clear from the fact tht it occurs only on two glyphs [Glyphs 52 and 327 of inscription texts: One is a *loha-kāra* (metalsmith); *kāruvu* [Skt.] n. An artist, artificer. An agent (Telugu). The other is a *cunda-kāra*

(ivory turner) or *kundār* turner]. The ligaturing glyptic elements may be read as: *kāra* or- *khar* 'smith' (Kashmiri). The lexeme *kāruvu* may explain one of Kubera's navanidhi (nine treasures): *kharva* which may mean 'artifice'.

Glyph: *loa* = a species of fig tree, ficus glomerata, the fruit of ficus glomerata (Santali) Rebus: *lo* 'iron' (Assamese, Bengali); *loa* 'iron' (Gypsy) *lauha* = made of copper or iron (Gr.S'r.); metal, iron (Skt.) *loha-kāra* a metal worker, coppersmith, blacksmith Miln 331 (Pali)

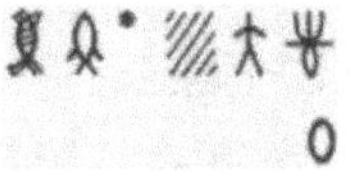

urseal159845 Ur [The first sign looks like an animal with a long tail – as seen from the back and may have been the model for the orthography of Sign 51 as noted in Mahadevan corpus].

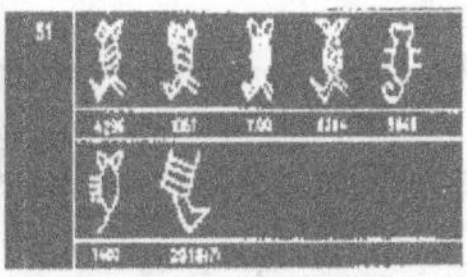

Variants of Glyph 51. Many allographs of glyph 51 seek to emhasise the 'sting' of the scorpion. Seal impression; UPenn; steatite; bull below a scorpion; dia. 2.4cm.; Gadd, PBA 18 (1932), p. 13, Pl. III, no. 15; Legrain, MJ (1929), p. 306, pl. XLI, no. 119; found at Ur in the cemetery area, in a ruined grave .9 metres from the surface, together with a pair of gold ear-rings of the double-crescent type and long beads of steatite and carnelian, two of gilt copper, and others of lapis-lazuli, carnelian, and banded sard. The first sign to the left has the form of a flower or perhaps an animal's skin with curly tail; there is a round spot upon the bull's back.

Glyph of musk-rat. Or, is it glyph of scorpion? If it denotes a scorpion, some rebus readings are: *koṇḍi* 'sting of scorpion'; rebus: kundār turner (Assamese)

Glyph *Ka. koṇḍi* the sting of a scorpion. *Tu. koṇḍi* a sting. *Te. koṇḍi* the sting of a scorpion.(DEDR 2080).

Rebus: kuṇḍī = chief of village. kuṇḍi-a = village headman; leader of a village (Pkt.lex.) i.e. śreṇi jeṭṭha chief of metal-worker guild. khōḍ m. 'pit', khōḍü f. 'small pit' (Kashmiri. CDIAL 3947), kuṭhi 'smelter furnace' (Mu.) kuṇḍamu 'a pit for receiving and preserving consecrated fire' (Te.) kundār turner (A.); kũdār, kũdāri (B.); kundāru

(Or.); kundau to turn on a lathe, to carve, to chase; kundau dhiri = a hewn stone; kundau murhut = a graven image (Santali)

If the orthography denotes a mouse, the rebus readings are:

Ta. cuṇṭaṉ grey musk shrew; cuṇṭ-eli, (Koll.) *cuṇṭān* mouse, *Mus urbanus*; cūṟaṉ grey musk shrew; mūñ-cūṟu musk-rat, *Sorex indicus. Ma.* Cuṇṭ-eli mouse, musk-rat. *Ka.* Suṇḍa, suṇḍ-ili, suṇḍil-ili, soṇḍ-ili, soṇḍil-ili, cuñc-ili musk-rat. *Koḍ.* Ciṇḍ-elihouse-mouse, field-mouse. *Tu.* Suṇḍ-eli musk-rat. *Te.* cuncu mouse, musk-rat; cunc-eluka, cuṇḍ-eluka mouse; cūr-eluka species of mouse *Kol* (Kin.) cinḍrag musk-rat. *Go.* (Mu. Ma.) cūci musk-rat (*Voc.* 1353); (Ma.) cuṭṭi-eli, (Mu.) cuṭi, cuṭiyal small rat (*Voc.*1344); (Ph.) coṭe mouse (*Voc* 1368). *Konḍa* (BB) susuki musk-rat. *Kur.* coṭṭō mouse. For eli, etc., see 833 Ta. Eli. Cf. 2664 Ta. cuṇṭu; the shrews seem to be differentiated from rats and mice by the length of the snout. / Cf. Skt. *śuṇḍi-mūṣikā-*, gandha-śuṇḍinī-(Burrow, *Kratylos* 15.56), cuñcu-mūṣikā-, chucchūndura-, cucundarī-; Turner, *CDIAL*, no. 5053. Cf. also Skt. Tuṭuma- mouse, rat. For similar words in Munda languages, see Pinnow, p. 95 (Santali cũnd musk-rat, etc.), and Emeneau, *JAOS* 82.109.(DEDR 2661) cunda an artist who works in ivory J vi.261 (Com: dantakāra); Miln 331. *cundakāra* a turner J vi.339 (Pali)

The superscript ligatures can also be read as suffixes: - *kāra* 'artisan'. *kāruvu* = mechanic, artisan, Viśvakarma, the celestial artisan (Te.); kāruvu [Skt.] n. An artist, artificer. An agent . One is a *loha-kāra* (metalsmith). The other is a *cunda-kāra* (ivory turner).

Copper furnace account

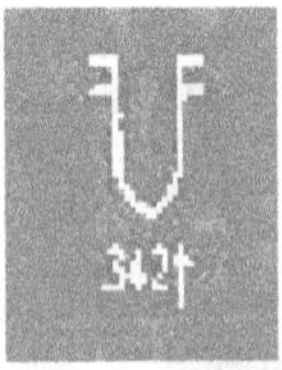

kan- 'copper' (Ta.)

Ga. (Oll.) kanḍ, stone, (S.) kanḍu (*pl.* kanḍkil) id. (DEDR 1298). kanḍ 'furnace' (Santali)

Rebus: The rim of a jar is kaṇḍ kan-ka (Santali).Thus, the combined words *ayaskāṇḍa* connoted 'metal stone (ore)' with the word *kaṇḍ* meaning: '(smelted) stone (ore) metal'.

Daimabad seal (c. 1400 BCE). Frequency of occurrence of sign: 1395. kaṇḍ is pot; kan-ka in Sanskrit is karṇaka 'ear or rim of jar'. kaṇḍ also means 'fire-altar'. Rebus1: kaṇḍ kan-ka lit. 'engraved account in stone. 'furnace account (scribe, engraver)' or 'stone (ore) metal account (scribe, engraver)'. Pk. *kaṁḍa* -- m. ' piece, fragment '; -- Deriv. Pk. *kaṁḍārēi* ' scrapes, engraves '; M. *kā̃ḍārṇē̃, karā̃ḍṇē̃* ' to gnaw ', *kā̃ḍārṇē̃* n. ' jeweller's hammer, barber's nail -- parer '. (CDIAL 2683) कंडारणें [kaṇḍāraṇēṃ] *n* An instrument of goldsmiths,--the iron spike which is hammered upon plates in reducing them to shape (Marathi) khanun खनुन् to engrave (Śiv. 414, 671, 176; Rām. 1583). (Kashmiri) *Ta.* karaṇṭu (karaṇṭi-) to paw (as a dog), gnaw (as a rat), scrape. *Ma.* karaṇṭuka to scrape the inside of metal vessels with a grating noise. (DEDR 1268).khanaka m. one who digs , digger , excavator MBh. iii , 640 R. ; a miner L. ; a house-breaker , thief L. ; a rat L. ; N. of a friend of Vidura MBh. i , 5798 f. ; (%{I}) f. a female digger or excavator Pāṇ. 3-1 , 145 Pat. ; iv , 1 , 41 Ka1s3. kanka 'rim (of jar, kaṇḍ)' (Santali) kárṇa— m. 'ear, handle of a vessel' RV., 'end, tip (?)' RV. ii 34, 3. [Cf. *kāra—6] Pa. kaṇṇa— m. 'ear, angle, tip'; Pk. kaṇṇa—, °aḍaya- m. 'ear', Gy. as. pal. eur. kan m., Ash. (Trumpp) karna NTS ii 261, Niṅg. kõmacr;, Woṭ. kanΘ, Tir. kana; Paš. kan, kaṇ(ḍ)— 'orifice of ear' IIFL iii 3, 93; Shum. kõmacr;ṛ 'ear', Woṭ. kan m., Kal. (LSI) kuṛõmacr;, rumb. kuŕũ, urt. kŕã (< *kaṇ), Bshk. kan, Tor. k *l ṇ, Kand. kōṇi, Mai. kaṇa, ky. kān, Phal. kāṇ, Sh. gil. ko̜n pl. ko̜ṇí m. (→ Ḍ kon pl. k *l ṇa), koh. kuṇ, pales. kuāṇΘ, K. kan m., kash. pog. ḍoḍ. kann, S. kanu m., L. kann m., awāṇ. khet. kan, P. WPah. bhad. bhal. cam. kann m., Ku. gng. N. kān; A. kāṇ 'ear, rim of vessel, edge of river'; B. kāṇ 'ear', Or. kāna, Mth. Bhoj. Aw. lakh. H. kān m., OMarw. kāna m., G. M. kān m., Ko. kānu m., Si. kaṇa, kana. — As adverb and postposition (ápi kárṇē 'from behind' RV., karṇē 'aside' Kālid.): Pa. kaṇṇē 'at one's ear, in a whisper'; Wg. ken 'to' NTS ii 279; Tir. kõ; 'on' AO xii 181 with (?); Paš. kan 'to'; K. kȧni with abl. 'at, near, through', kani with abl. or dat. 'on', kun with dat. 'toward'; S. kani 'near', kanā 'from'; L. kan 'toward', kannũ

'from', kanne 'with', khet. kan, P. ḍog. kanē 'with, near'; WPah. bhal. k *l ṇ, °ṇi, k e ṇ, °ṇi with obl. 'with, near', kiṇ, °ṇiā, k *l ṇiā, k e ṇ° with obl. 'from'; Ku. kan 'to, for'; N. kana 'for, to, with'; H. kane, °ni, kan with ke 'near'; OMarw. kanai 'near', kanā sā 'from near', kā̃nı̄ 'towards'; G. kan e 'beside'. Addenda: kárṇa—: S.kcch. kann m. 'ear', WPah.kṭg. (kc.) kān, poet. kanṛu m. 'ear', kṭg. kanni f. 'pounding—hole in barn floor'; J. kā'n m. 'ear', Garh. kān; Md. kan— in kan—fat 'ear' (CDIAL 2830).

The Sohgaura copper plate (4th cent. BCE) refers to a pair of koṣṭhāgāra (dvāra koṭṭhaka); the two storehouses described as tri-garbha (i.e. having three rooms) are illustrated on line 1. (Fleet, JRAS, 1907). The illustrations indicate that the three rooms are in three storeys, with supporting pillars clearly seen. The inscription refers to the junction of three highways named Manavati, in two villages called Dasilimita and Usagama. The storehouses were made at this junction for the goods of people using the highways, which are indicated in line 3 by mentioning the three places to and from which they led. One of the names give is recognized by Fleet as Chanchu. (Fleet, JRAS, 63, 1894 proceedings, 86, plate, IA 25. 262; cf. Sohgaura copper plate/B.M. Barua. The Indian Historical Quarterly, ed. Narendra Nath Law. Reprint. 41)

Punchmarked coin. Fifth glyph from left is a rimmed, short-necked jar (Sign 342, Daimabad seal, which has the most-frequent, 1,395 occurrences on epigraphs).

Other glyphs on the coin/Sohgaura copper plate:

kandhi = a lump, a piece (Santali.lex.)

kaṇḍ = altar, furnace (Santali) लोहकारकन्दुः f. a blacksmith's smelting furnace (Grierson Kashmiri lex.) payĕn-kōda पयन्-कौँद। परिपाककन्दुः f. a kiln (a potter's, a lime-kiln, and brick-kiln, or the like); a furnace (for smelting) This yajn~a kuṇḍam can be denoted rebus, by perforated beads (kandi) or on ivory (khaṇḍ):

kandi (pl. -l) beads, necklace (Pa.); kanti (pl. -l) bead, (pl.) necklace; kandit. bead (Ga.)(DEDR 1215). The three stringed beads depicted on the pictograph may perhaps be treated as a phonetic determinant of the substantive, the rimmed jar, the khaṇḍa kanka. khaṇḍa, xanro, sword or large sacrificial knife. kandil, kandi_l = a globe of glass, a lantern (Ka.lex.)

jaṇḍ khaṇḍ = ivory (Jat.ki) khaṇḍī = ivory in rough (Jat.ki_); gaṭī = piece of elephant's tusk (S.) [This semant. may explain why the dotted circle -- i.e., kandi, 'beads' -- is often depicted on ivory objects, such as ivory combs]. See also: khaṇḍiyo [cf. khaṇḍaṇī a tribute] tributary; paying a tribute to a superior king (G.lex.)

Rim of jar as a hieroglyph

Glyph: kaṇḍ kanka, kaṇḍ karṇaka 'rim of jar' (Santali. Sanskrit). Rebus: furnace account (scribe). This hieroglyph announces a professional, an expert carver who can keep accounts of the industrial goods produced in guild mineral/metal workshops – such as those tallied, sorted out or displayed on circular working platforms or warehouses.

This hieroglyph is often the terminal signature tune of many inscriptions conveying the message that goods tallied using tablets have been consolidated together to create seal impressions as bills of lading for multi-commodity trade loads. The invention of writing has created a new professional: (accountant) scribe.

kaṇḍa kanka 'rim of jar' (Santali); rebus: furnace scribe (account). *Kaṇḍa kanka* may be a dimunitive form of *kan-khār 'copper smith' comparable to the cognate gloss: kaṉṉār 'coppersmiths, blacksmiths' (Tamil) If so, kaṇḍa kan-khār connotes: 'copper-smith furnace.'kaṇḍa 'fire-altar (Santali); kan 'copper' (Ta.)

kárṇaka m. ' projection on the side of a vessel, handle ' ŚBr. [kárṇa --] Pa. kaṇṇaka -- ' having ears or corners '; Wg. Kaṇə ' ear — ring ' NTS xvii 266; S. kano m. ' rim, border '; P. kannā m. ' obtuse angle of a kite ' (→ H. kannā m. ' edge, rim, handle '); N. kānu ' end of a rope for supporting a burden '; B. kāṇā ' brim of a cup ', G. kānɔ m.; M. kānā m. ' touch — hole of a gun '.(CDIAL 2831).

Rebus: கணக்கு kaṇakku , n. cf. gaṇaka. [M. kaṇakku.] 1. Number, account, reckoning, calculation, computation; எண். (திவா.) 2. The four simple rules of arithmetic, viz., கூட்டல், கழித்தல், பெருக்கல், வகுத்தல். 3. Account book, ledger; வரவுசெலவுக்கணக்குக் குறிப்பு. காவலர் கணக் காய் வகையின் வருந்தி (குறுந். 261). 4. Science of arithmetic; கணிதசாஸ்திரம். (Tamil)gaṇáyati ' counts ' MBh. [Prob. Like guṇáyati1 < gr̥ṇ- (MIA. Gaṇ -- , giṇ -- , guṇ --) in gr̥ṇā´ti, ' addresses, praises ' RV., cf. gārayatē ' teaches ' Dhātup., *girati3, *gr̥ta<-> (J. C. Wright). -- √g&rcirclemacr;3. See Add. S.v. gr̥ṇā´ti] Pa. gaṇēti ' counts, takes notice of '; Aś. Ganīyati ' is counted '; Pk. Gaṇēi, °ṇaï ' counts '; Ash. Gäṇ -- ' to count, read ', Wg. Gaṇ -- NTS xvii 255; Dm. gaṇ -- ' to say '; Paš. Gaṇ -- ' to count ', Bshk. Gän -- , K. ḍoḍ. gaṇṇo, S. gaṇaṇu, L. gaṇaṇ, (Ju.) g°, Wpah. Jaun. Gaṇnō, Ku. Gaṇṇo, N. gannu, A. gaṇiba, B. gaṇā, Or. Gaṇibā, Mth. Ganab, Bhoj. Ganal, Aw. Lakh. Ganab, G. gaṇvũ, M. gaṇṇẽ, Si. Gaṇinavā. — Gy. As. Gen -- , eur. Gin -- , Bashg. Gĩr -- , L. giṇaṇ, P. giṇṇā, Bi. Ginab, H. ginnā. (CDIAL 3993)

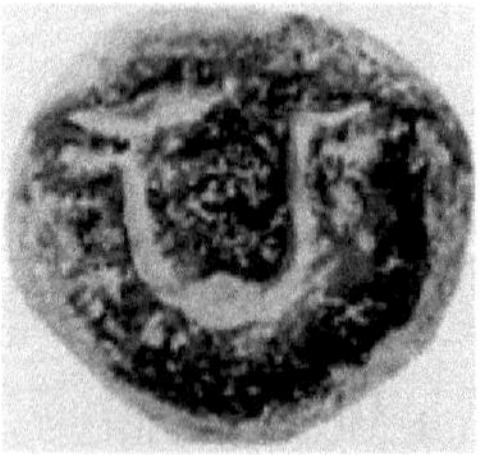

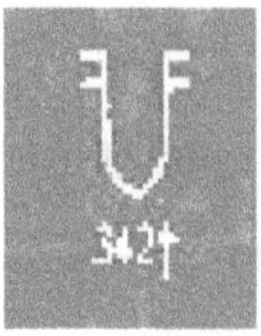

Daimabad seal. 'Rim of jar' hieroglyph is shown on a circular seal.

Daimabad seal (c. 1400 BCE). Frequency of occurrence of sign: 1395. kaṇḍ is pot; kan-ka in Sanskrit is karṇaka 'ear or rim of jar'. kaṇḍ also means 'fire-altar'. Rebus1: kaṇḍ kan-ka lit. 'engraved account in stone. 'furnace account (scribe, engraver)' or 'stone (ore) metal account (scribe, engraver)'. Pk. *kaṁḍa* -- m. ' piece, fragment '; -- Deriv. Pk. *kaṁḍārēi* ' scrapes, engraves '; M. *kā̃ḍārṇẽ, karā̃ḍṇẽ* ' to gnaw ', *kā̃ḍārṇẽ* n. ' jeweller's hammer, barber's nail -- parer '. (CDIAL 2683) कंडारणें [kaṇḍāraṇēṃ] *n* An instrument of goldsmiths,--the iron spike which is hammered upon plates in reducing them to shape (Marathi)

khanun खनुन् to engrave (Śiv. 414, 671, 176; Rām. 1583). (Kashmiri) *Ta.* karaṇṭu (karaṇṭi-) to paw (as a dog), gnaw (as a rat), scrape. *Ma.* karaṇṭuka to scrape the inside of metal vessels with a grating noise. (DEDR 1268).khanaka m. one who digs , digger , excavator MBh. iii , 640 R. ; a miner L. ; a house-breaker , thief L. ; a rat L. ; N. of a friend of Vidura MBh. i , 5798 f. ; (%{I}) f. a female digger or excavator Pāṇ. 3-1 , 145 Pat. ; iv , 1 , 41 Ka1s3. kanka 'rim (of jar, kaṇḍ)' (Santali) kárṇa— m. 'ear, handle of a vessel' RV., 'end, tip (?)' RV. ii 34, 3. [Cf. *kāra—6] Pa. kaṇṇa— m. 'ear, angle, tip'; Pk. kaṇṇa—, °aḍaya- m. 'ear', Gy. as. pal. eur. kan m., Ash. (Trumpp) karna NTS ii 261, Niṅg. kõmacr;, Woṭ. kanΘ, Tir. kana; Paš. kan, kaṇ(ḍ)— 'orifice of ear' IIFL iii 3, 93; Shum. kõmacr;ṛ 'ear', Woṭ. kan m., Kal. (LSI) kuṛõmacr;, rumb. kuŕũ, urt. kŕã (< *kaṇ), Bshk. kan, Tor. k *l ṇ, Kand. kōṇi, Mai. kaṇa, ky. kān, Phal. kāṇ, Sh. gil. kọ̈n pl. kọ̈ṇí m. (→ Ḍ kon pl. k *l ṇa), koh. kuṇ, pales. kuāṇΘ, K. kan m., kash. pog. ḍoḍ. kann, S. kanu m., L. kann m., awāṇ. khet. kan, P. WPah. bhad. bhal. cam. kann m., Ku. gng. N. kān; A. kāṇ 'ear, rim of vessel, edge of river'; B. kāṇ 'ear', Or. kāna, Mth. Bhoj. Aw. lakh. H. kān m., OMarw. kāna m., G. M. kān m., Ko. kānu m., Si. kaṇa, kana. — As adverb and postposition (ápi kárṇē 'from behind' RV., karṇē 'aside' Kālid.): Pa. kaṇṇē 'at one's ear, in a whisper'; Wg. ken 'to' NTS ii 279; Tir. kõ; 'on' AO xii 181 with (?); Paš. kan 'to'; K. kấni with abl. 'at, near, through', kani with abl. or dat. 'on', kun with dat. 'toward'; S. kani 'near', kanã 'from'; L. kan 'toward', kannũ 'from', kanne 'with', khet. kan, P. ḍog. kanē 'with, near'; WPah. bhal. k *l ṇ, °ṇi, k e ṇ, °ṇi with obl. 'with, near', kiṇ, °ṇiã, k *l ṇiã, k e ṇ° with obl. 'from'; Ku. kan 'to, for'; N. kana 'for, to, with'; H. kane, °ni, kan with ke 'near'; OMarw. kanai 'near', kanã sā 'from near', kãñı 'towards'; G. kan e 'beside'. Addenda: kárṇa—: S.kcch. kann m. 'ear', WPah.kṭg. (kc.) kān, poet. kanṛu m. 'ear', kṭg. kanni f. 'pounding—hole in barn floor'; J. kā'n m. 'ear', Garh. kān; Md. kan— in kan—fat 'ear' (CDIAL 2830).

Antelope as a hieroglyph, Akk. *tamkāru*, Skt. *thākur* 'smith, merchant'

damgar [MERCHANT] (914x: ED IIIb, Old Akkadian, Lagash II, Ur III, Old Babylonian) wr. dam-gar$_3$ "merchant, trader" Akk. *tamkāru* [Note: cf. *makaarum* 'to do business'] Source: *The Pennsylvania Sumerian Dictionary* http://psd.museum.upenn.edu/epsd/epsd/e878.html

Could tāmrakam 'copper' (Skt.) be a metathesis of *tamkārum* ?

There is a language group which explains *damgar* as Sumerian substrate. That language group is the Indian *sprachbund* which included glosses from 'Language X + Munda = Meluhha (mleccha)'.

If there is one set of hieroglyphs which occurs with high frequency on Ancient Near East artifacts and on cylinder seals and other objects and on Indus script corpora of inscriptions, it is the 'antelope' set. Antelope occurs in 91 even-toed ungulate species indigenous to various regions in Africa, Eurasia including India. According to the present classification, antelopes within the family bovidae include species which are not cattle, sheep, buffalo, bison or goats. Greek antholops (anthos, 'flower' + ops 'eye') were considered fabulous animals 'haunting the banks of Euphrates, very savage, hard to catch and having saw-like horns capable of cutting down trees.' ("Antelope". *Dictionary.com. Online Etymology Dictionary.* Douglas Harper, Historian.) The antelope species which have differences in appearance, sizes and shapes of horns, include: Arabian oryx, dorcas, gazelle, ibex, nilgai, chinkara, blackbuck, nyala, elands, kudus, Tibetan and Saiga antelopes. http://en.wikipedia.org/wiki/Antelope#cite_ref-1

While there is a variety of orthographic representations of the bovidae in Near East and Indus writing artifacts, it is possible to identify some etyma which could possibly have identified the animals, ca. 3500 BCE in the archaeological context and in the context of messages conveyed through hieroglyphs and other script signs. Desinamamala of Hemacandra ed. R. Pischel (1938) includes a gloss *ibbho* 'merchant' (Deśi substrate), which may be a semantic cognate of *ibira* which occurs on Near East texts. Sumerian King List notes Bad-tibira as the second city to 'exercise kingship' in Sumer before the flood, following Eridu. "...the earliest lexically attested term for merchant is *ibira* or *tibira*, equated with Akkadian *tamkāru* in the basic lexical series *ea=A=Naqu.* [B. Landsberger, JAOS 88 (=Speiser AV, 1968) 133-147, esp. p. 139 line 126 and Landsberger's comments *ad loc.,* p. 146; cf. now MSL 14 (1979) 308:126.]The alternation

between a vocalic onset and an initial t- marks the term as a substrate word. But the same term is also equated with *gurgurru,* (MSL 12:103:231 and CAD G *s.v.*) 'craftsman', and this may be its earlier meaning. What the nature of the craft may have been is suggested by the fact that it is occasionally written with the logogram for metal-worker, URUDU.NAGAR. [Landsberger, JAOS 88 (=Speiser AV, 1968) 146 and 126; elsewhere KA X KIB: Ea III 126 and MSL 12:137:263; 16:87:270.

For *tibira* in the meaning 'm with itinerant metal-workers, a situation familiar, for example, from the Irish tin-metal-worker' see also idem 1974: 11.] This implies an early association of tradingsmiths or tinkers of later European history. Another term for trader with a possible substrate origin may be dam-gar, here presumed to be the source of Akkadian *tamkāru.* [Landsberger 1974: 12.]" (William W. Hallo, 1996, *Origins: the ancient near eastern background of some modern western institutions,* EJ Brill., p. 69.) Noting the semantics 'merchant' and 'metallurgist', Forbes notes: "...like the mercatores of the Middle Ages who were often both artisans and merchants at the same time. Hence the trade was only partly a State-affair and dam-gar (tamkaru) was allowed a certain latitude to do some business of his own. Hence the lots of 6-12 talents of metal sometimes go to the e-DUB-ba, the State storehouse, also called 'house of the silver and the lapis lazuli, the great storehouse'. Several tons of copper were consumed yearly in each Sumerian town and the gold-smith's shops seem to have worked some 6K of red gold, 8K of refined gold and nearly 6K of silver in one year." (RJ Forbes, 1964, *Studies in ancient technology,* Volume I, EJ Brill., p.86).

MS 4551
Account of grain products, bread, beer, butter oil, Sumer, 32nd c. BC

Inscribed tablet as an evolution from Sumer token/bulla envelope system

The three perforated tablets (seal impressions) of Kanmer might have been strung together and the account compiled by the guild scribe to prepare a bill of lading. It is also possible that a seal impression on a bulla might have authenticated the bill of lading together with the three tablets (seal impressions) of Kanmer.

This is an example of bulla in clay. MS 4523 Schoyen collection. Bulla for holding a string of complex counting tokens concerning a transaction.

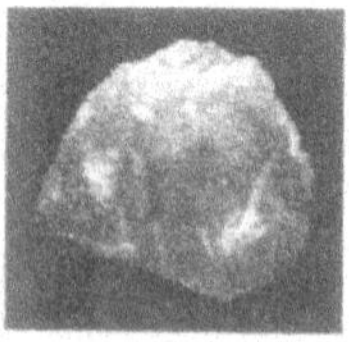

M-2131 A

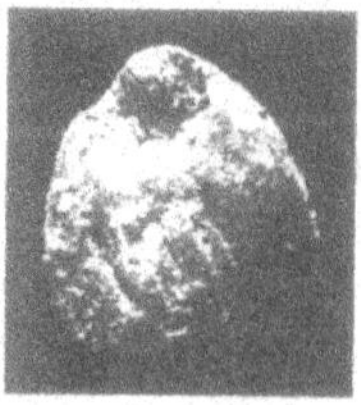

M-2131 B

Bulla for holding a string of complex counting tokens concerning a transaction

Bulla in clay, Syria/Sumer/Highland Iran, ca. 3500-3200 BC, 1 oblong bulla, diam. 2,5x6,5 cm, rollsealed with a line of animals walking left or 2 men standing with arms raised, pierced for holding a string of counting tokens.

Commentary: The bulla originally locked the ends of a string with a number of complex counting tokens attached to it, representing 1 transaction. The string with the tokens was hanging outside the bulla like a necklace. If the string had, say, 5 disk type tokens representing types of textiles, this number could not be tampered with without breaking the seal. The tokens could also be entirely enclosed in the center of the bulla, see MSS 4631, 4632 and 4638. Tokens were used for accounting purposes in the Near East from the Neolithic period ca. 8000 BC until ca. 3200 BC, when they were superseded by counting tablets and

pictographic tablets. Some of the earliest tablets have actual tokens impressed into the clay to form numbers and pictographs, and some of the pictographs were illustrations of tokens.

MS in Old Sumerian on clay, Sumer, Uruk IV, 32nd c. BC, 1 tablet, 5,0x5,7x2,1 cm, 17+14 compartments of pictographic script

Context: For disk type tokens, see MS 4522/2-8.

Commentary: 6 different disk type tokens, actually drawn to represent real counting tokens. This represents the second stage in the development from counting tokens to actual pictographic writing on tablets. The first stage was to depress actual tokens into the wet clay on a bulla or tablet. Apart from the sheep token (cross within the circle, group 3:51), none of these tokens have been found so far, cf. Denise Schmandt-Besserat. How writing came about, group 3 disks, listing about 80 different types. MS 2963 that might be even older.

Exhibited: The Norwegian Institute of Palaeography and Historical Philology (PHI), Oslo, 13.10.2003-06.2005

Only one object from Mohenjo-daro comes close to being a bulla. Photograph from ASI: Sindh series Photo archive of ASI, Janpath, New Delhi. Si. 5:6639, 5:6640. Recorded in the corpora as m-2131 (Parpola et al. Corpus, Vol. 3, Part 1, p. 131). Rattle? Bulla? There are no records recording the provenance of this object and if the glyph inscribed on the bulla (rattle?) can in anyway be related to any glyph of Indus script.

Cylinder seal impression. British Museum (Reg. No. OA 1960.7-18.1). Found in Seistan. Called the MacMahon cylinder seal. The end of the cylinder shows a combination of triangles (like a range of mountains) reminiscent of a Mohenjo-daro seal (M-443B). The inscription has six signs: a human figures ligatured to three rows of four vertical lines (total count of 12).. Next is a human figure holding

in his left hand a rectangular device filled with single hatching (see Marshall 1931, II: 446, no. 196b).

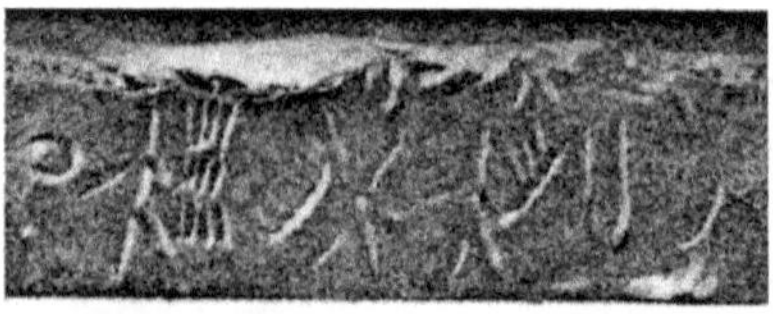

"...the four examples of round seals found in Mohenjodaro show well-supported sequences, whereas the three from Mesopotamia show sequences of signs not paralleled elsewhere in the Indus Script. But the ordinary square seals found in Mesopotamia show the normal Mohenjodaro sequences. In other words, the square seals are in the Indian language, and were probably imported in the course of trade; while the circular seals, although in the Indus script, are in a different language, and were probably manufactured in Mesopotamia for a Sumerian- or Semitic-speaking person of Indian descent..." [G.R. Hunter,1932. Mohenjodaro--Indus Epigraphy, *JRAS*: 466-503]

Texts related to West Asian inscriptions (either not illustrated or not linked):

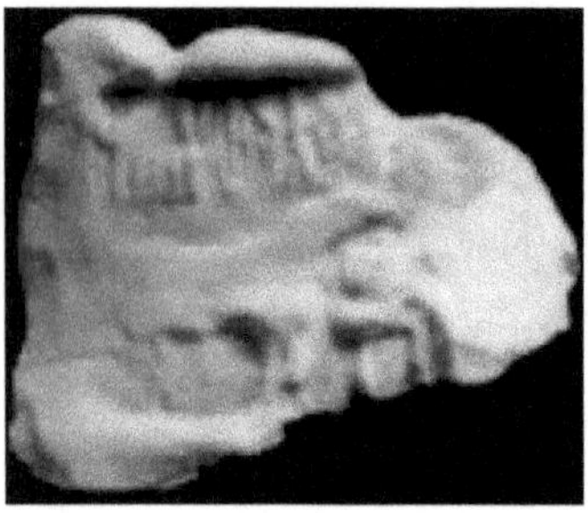

9811Djoka (Umma) Seal impression. "...an imprint of (Indus (Sarasvati-Sindhu)) seal upon the fragment of a clay label from a bale of cloth had also been published by Father Scheil (Revue d'Assyriologie, Vol. 22: 56), and this was said to come from the site of Umma, the neighbor city of Lagash...(Gadd, 1932, pp.3-32.)

9821 Kish A good example of contact between Kish and Meluhha (Indus script corpora area) is provided by two seals with almost identical texts from (a) Kish (IM 1822); cf. Mackay 1925 and (b) Mohenjodaro (M-228); cf.

(a)

(b)

Parpola, 1994, p. 132.

9822 Kish

9834 Ur

9842 Ur

9903 Prob. West Asian find

9904 Prob. West Asian find

M0592 double-axe shown on a copper plate, which depicts a double-axe identical to the one unearthed in Sumer, Mesopotamia, ca. 3000 BCE.

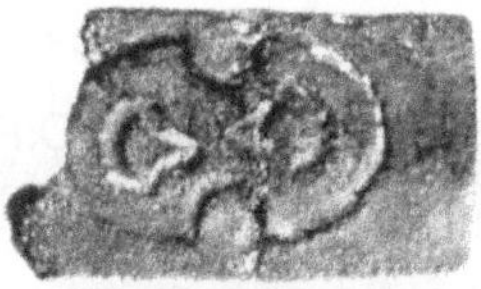

Chanhudaro 23 seal: double-axe shown in front of antelope

Dagger and axes found in an Ur grave. Sumerian double-bladed axe, Ur.[95]

Chanhudaro is named the 'Sheffield' of ancient India by the excavator, Ernest Mackay.

Tablets as bullae

In the Elam-Susa-Mesopotamia interaction area of Ancient Near East and Meluhha, tokens designed to count goods evolved into hieroglyphs to represent words which constitution information transferred on the bronze-age goods and processes. This stage of rebus representation of sounds of words of meluhha (mleccha language) was the stage penultimate to the culminating stage which used representation of syllables graphically in kharoṣṭī and brāhmī scripts. This culmination of the process for literacy and civilization was the contribution made

by artisans of the bronze-age of Indus-Sarasvati civilization (also called Harappan or Indus civilization).

An evidence comes from Kanmer, for the use of tablets created with duplicate seal impressions. These tablets may have been used as category tallies of lapidary workshops. (Source: http://www.antiquity.ac.uk/projgall/agrawal323/Antiquity, D.P. Agrawal et al, Redefining the Harappan hinterland, *Anquity*, Vol. 84, Issue 323, March 2010)

It is a category mistake to call these as 'seals'. These are three duplicate tablets

created with seal impressions (glyphs: one-horned heifer, standard device, PLUS two text inscription glyphs (or 'signs' as written characters): one long linear stroke, ligatured glyph of body + 'harrow' glyph. There are perforations in the center of these duplicate seal impressions which are tablets and which contained identical inscriptions. It appears that three duplicates of seal impressions -- as tablets -- were created using the same seal.

Obverse of these tiny 2 cm. dia. tablets show some incised markings. It is unclear from the markings if they can be compared with any glyphs of the Indus script corpora. They may be 'personal' markings like 'potter's marks' – designating a particular artisan's workshop (working platform) or considering the short numerical strokes used, the glyphs may be counters (numbers or liquid or weight measures). More precise determination may be made if more evidences of such glyphs are discovered. Excavators surmise that the three tablets with different motifs on the obverse of the three tablets suggest different users/uses. They may be from different workshops of the same guild but as the other side of the tables showed, the product taken from three workshops is the same.

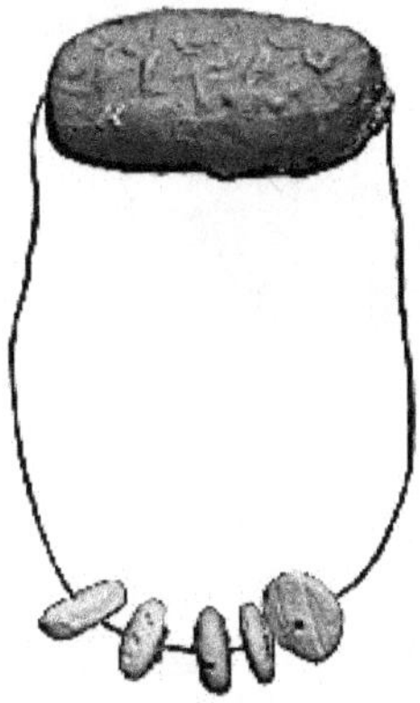

Decoding of the identical inscription on the three tablets of Kanmer.

Glyph: One long linear stroke. koḍa 'one' (Santali) Rebus: koḍ 'artisan's workshop' (Kuwi) Glyph: meḍ 'body' (Mu.) Rebus: meḍ 'iron' (Ho.) Ligatured glyph : aḍar 'harrow' Rebus: aduru 'native metal' (Kannada). Thus the glyphs can be read rebus. Glyph: koḍiyum 'heifer' (G.) Rebus: koḍ 'workshop (Kuwi) Glyph: sangaḍa 'lathe' (Marathi) Rebus 1: Rebus 2: sangaḍa 'association' (guild). Rebus 2: sangatarāsu 'stone cutter' (Telugu). The output of the lapidaries is thus described by the three tablets: *aduru meḍ sangaḍa koḍ* 'iron, native metal guild workshop'.

Functions of tablets and seals: an archeological context

Examples of 22 duplicates steatite triangular tablets h-2218 to h-2239 were excavated in an archaeological context by HARP Project[96]. Tablets were tallies of products from workers' platforms. Seals were consolidated data from tablets to

prepre bills of lading or 'entrustment notes', *jangaḍa*, for approval.

h2219A First side of three-sided tablet

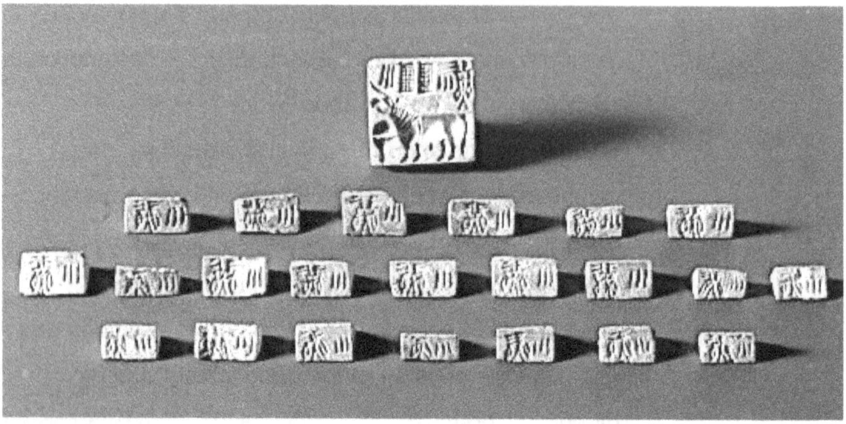

h2219B Second side of three-sided tablet

h2219C Third side of three-sided tablet

The two glyphs which appear on the h2219A example also appear on a seal. "In a street deposit of similar age just inside the wall, a seal was found with two of the same characters as seen on one side of the tablets."

h1682A. The seal which contained the two glyphs used on the 'tally' three-sided tablets. The seal showed a one-horned heifer + standard device and two segments of inscriptions: one segment showing the two glyphs shown on one side of the 'tally' tablet; the other segment showing glyphs of a pair of 'rectangle with divisions' + 'three long linear strokes'.

Treating each side of a tablet as a token information presented from the workers' platforms to the storehouse. The seal h1682 can be taken as a bulla prepared in a storehouse, consolidating information on two sides of the tablet. With the bossed reverse which has a hole, the seals can be strung together to constitute a bill of lading consolidated information for a consignment from the storehouse.

The first set of glyphs may connote furnace output (accounted smelted metal) delivered to smithy.

The second set of glyphs may connote ingots (cast metal) delivered to smithy.

These duplicated inscriptions on tablets found indicates that there was a differentiation among professions, say between workers working on working platforms and using tablets to document delivery of products for 'approval' as entrustment notes -- *jangaḍ* and the scribes documenting the furnace accounts. Such tablets delivered by the artisans will be compiled into seals by scribes to describe the consolidated consignment. The seal impressions could then be used as tallies or accompaniments to bills of lading of a consignment entrusted to a courier, *jangaḍiyo*. Such seal impressions constituted enrustment notes of the package: *jangaḍ*.]

Guild, entrustment account-book, courier, worker on a lathe

Guild

सांगडणी [sāṅgaḍaṇī] *f* (Verbal of सांगडणें) Linking or joining together (Marathi). संगति [saṅgati] *f* (S) pop. संगत *f* Union, junction, connection, association. संगति [saṅgati] *c* (S) pop. संगती *c* or संगत *c* A companion, associate, comrade, fellow.

संगतीसोबती [saṅgatīsōbatī] *m* (संगती & सोबती) A comprehensive or general term for Companions or associates. संग [saṅga] *m* (S) Union, junction, connection, association, companionship, society. संगें [saṅgēṃ] *prep* (संग S) With, together with, in company or connection with. संघात [saṅghāta] *m* S Assembly or assemblage; multitude or heap; a collection together (of things animate or inanimate). संघट्टणें [saṅghaṭṭaṇēṃ] *v i* (Poetry. संघट्टन) To come into contact or meeting; to meet or encounter. (Marathi)

Entrustment account-book

जांगड [jāṅgaḍa] *f* (H) Goods taken from a shop, to be retained or returned as may suit: also articles of apparel taken from a tailor or clothier to sell for him. 2 or जांगड वही The account or account-book of goods so taken. जांगड [jāṅgaḍa] *ad* Without definitive settlement of purchase--goods taken from a shop. jākaṛ A deposit or pledge left with a vendor for goods brought away for inspection or approval; goods taken from a shop for approval, a deposit orr pledge being left, a conditional purchase; articles taken on commission sale (Hindi) The meaning of jāṅgaḍ is well-settled in Indian legal system as 'goods sent on approval or 'on sale or return'. http://www.indiankanoon.org/doc/39008

Armed courier

jangaḍiyo 'military guard who accompanies treasure into the treasury' (G.) జాంఘికుడు [jāṅghikuḍu] *jānghikuḍu.* [Skt.] n. A courier, an express. (Telugu)

Is this a depiction of a *jangaḍiyo* in an Indus interaction area?

Deutsch: Barren-Gott, 12. Jh. v. Chr., Fundort Enkomi, Zypern-Museum Nikosia. Protector of the ingot, bronze, Enkomi, Cyprus[97]

This process related to *jangaḍiyo* yields a clue to the rebus reading of the 'standard device' in front of the young bull with one-horn. The 'standard device' was a ligature of a 'lathe' and a 'portable furnace', both meanings are represented by the lexeme *sangaḍa*.

Worker on a lathe

sãghāḍiyo a worker a lathe (G.)

Rebus glyphs, allographs

Allographs are alternative glyphs which can represent the same sound of a word or phoneme: For example, *m and M are allographs.*

जांगड [jāṅgaḍa] Linking together (of beasts): joining or attaching (as a scholar to a superior one, in order to learn). *v* घाल, कर. Also the state, linkedness, co-yokedness, attachment, association. (Marathi). saṁghaṭayati ' strikes (a musical instrument) ' R., ' joins together ' Kathās. [√ghaṭ]Pa. *saṅghaṭita* -- ' pegged together '; Pk. *saṁghaḍia*<-> ' joined ', caus. *saṁghaḍāvēi*, M. *sāgaḍṇẽ* ' to link together '. (CDIAL 12855).

Allograph 1: M. *sãgaḍ* f. ' a body formed of two or more fruits or animals or men &c. linked together (CDIAL 12859). Oriya. *saṅghāṛibā* ' to mix up many materials, stir boiling curry, tie two cattle together and leave to graze ' (CDIAL 12860). A body formed of two or more animals is a 'composite animal' glyphic ligature.

Allograph 2: *sãgāḍā* m. ' frame of a building ' (M.)(CDIAL 12859)

Mohenjo-daro guild standard tablet

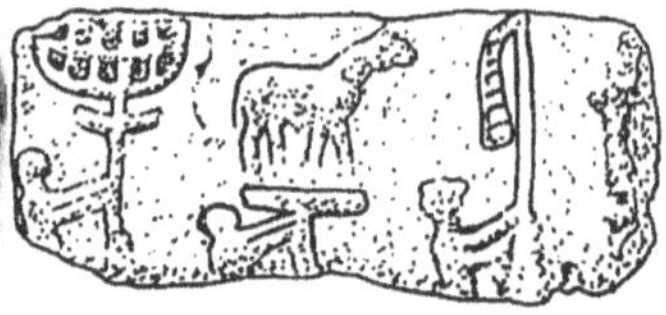

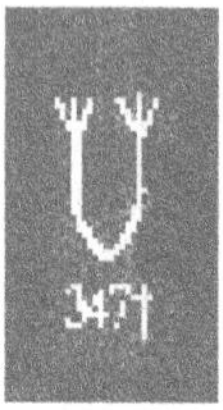

m0491 Tablet. Line drawing (right)

Ccombined reading for the joined or ligatured glyphs is: *sangaḍa kolmo*'smithy guild'.

Dawn of the bronze age is best exemplified by this Mohenjo-daro tablet which shows a procession of three hieroglyphs carried on the shoulders of three persons. The hieroglyphs are: 1. Scarf carried on a pole; 2. A young bull carried on a stand; 3. Portable standard device (Top part: lathe-gimlet; Bottom part: portable furnace).

The procession is a celebration of the graduation of a stone-cutter as a metal-turner in a smithy/forge.

A san:gatarāśū 'stone-cutter' or lapidary of neolithic/chalolithic age had graduated into a metal turner's workshop (koḍ), working with metallic minerals (dhatu) of the bronze age.

Three professions are described by the three hieroglyphs: scarf, young bull, standard device *dhatu kõdā sāgāḍī* Rebus words denote: ' mineral worker; metals turner-joiner (forge); worker on a lathe' – associates (guild).

The rebus readings are:

1. WPah.kṭg. dhàṭṭu m. ' woman's headgear, kerchief ', kc. dhaṭu m. (also dhaṭhu m. ' scarf ', J. dhāṭ(h)u m. Him.I 105). dhaṭu m. (also dhaṭhu) m. 'scarf' (WPah.) (CDIAL 6707) Rebus: dhatu = mineral (Santali) dhātu 'mineral (Pali) dhātu 'mineral' (Vedic); a mineral, metal (Santali); dhāta id. (G.) H. dhāṛnā 'to send out, pour out, cast (metal)' (CDIAL 6771).

2. koḍiyum ‘heifer’ (G.) [kōḍiya] kōḍe, kōḍiya. [Tel.] n. A bullcalf. . k* దూడA young bull. Plumpness, prime. తరుణము. జోడు కోడయలు a pair of bullocks. kōḍe adj. Young. kōḍe-kāḍu. n. A young man.పడుచు వాడు. [kārukōḍe] kāru-kōḍe. [Tel.] n. A bull in its prime. खोंड [khōṇḍa] m A young bull, a bullcalf. (Marathi) గోద [gōda] gōda. [Tel.] n. An ox. A beast. kine, cattle.(Telugu) koḍiyum (G.) Rebus: koḍ artisan’s workshop (Kuwi).

3. sangāḍo a lathe (G.); śaghaḍi = a pot for holding fire (G.)

Alograph 3: sangāḍo a lathe (G.); on sãgaḍ part of a turner's apparatus (M.); sãgāḍī part of a turner's apparatus by which the piece to be turned is confined (Tu.)(CDIAL 12859). sāṅgaḍa That member and steadied. सांगडीस धरणें To take into linkedness or close connection with, lit. fig. (Marathi) सांगाडी [sāṅgāḍī] f The machine within which a turner confines and steadies the piece he has to turn. (Marathi)

Allograph 4: stone-cutting. sanghāḍo (G.) cutting stone, gilding (G.); san:gatarāśū = stone cutter; san:gatarāśi = stone-cutting; san:gsāru karan.u = to stone (S.) san:ghāḍiyo, a worker on a lathe (G.)

Orthography of Standard device (often shown in front of young bull) to depict stone-cutting or stone-drilling

The device is an orthographic ligature of a lathe and a portable furnace.

m1203A m1203B1018 Note the gimlet precisely indicated on the standard

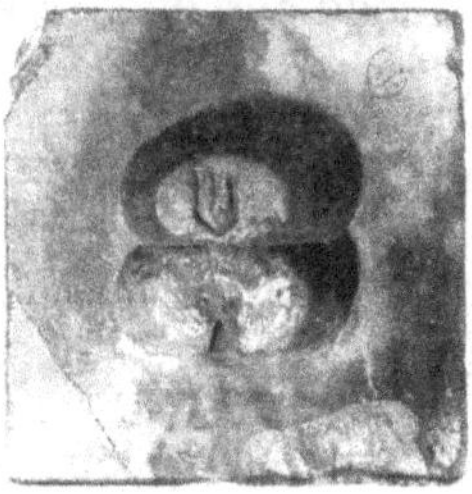

device on m1203A, the sharp point is drilling into a disc-shaped bead].

The bottom portion of the 'standard device' is sometimes depicted with

'dotted circles'. khan:ghar, ghan:ghar, ghan:ghar gon:ghor 'full of holes' (Santali) Rebus: kangar 'portable furnace' (Kashmiri). This device also occurs by itself and as variants on 19 additional epigraphs, in one case held aloft like a banner in a procession which also includes the glyph of the one-horned heifer as one of the banners carried.

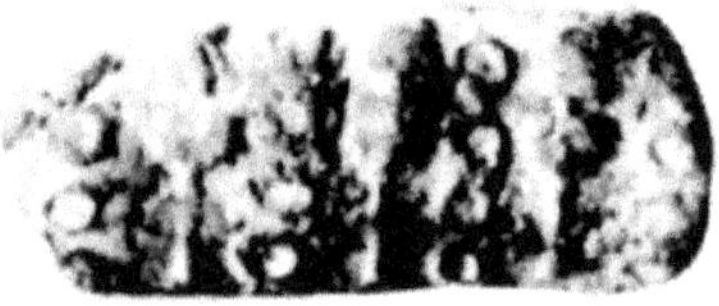

m0008,

m0021, h228B

Carved Ivory Standard in the middle

har501 Harappa 1990 and 1993. Standard device, model reconstructed after Mahadevan

Allograph 5: *sangaḍi.* n. A couple, pair (Telugu)

Allograph 6: *சங்கடம் caṅkaṭam, n. < Port. jangada.* Ferry-boat of two canoes with a platform thereon; இரட்டைத்தோணி. (J.)

Allograph 7: सगडी [sagaḍī] f (Commonly शेगडी) A pan of live coals or embers. (Marathi) sanghāḍo, saghaḍī (G.) = firepan; saghaḍī, śaghaḍi = a pot for holding fire (G.)[culā sagaḍī portable hearth (G.)] Note the smoke emanating from the bottom pot of the device.

Banawali 23 Seal impression. This uses an assemblage of glyphs: a person standing with raised arm, a ram, a one-horned heifer, two glyphs: fish and arrow. Eache of these glyphs can be read rebus to complete the reading of the message conveyed by the inscription, as a bill of lading on a consignment, a trade package. Decoding: meḍ 'body'(Mu.); rebus: 'iron' (Ho.) eṛaka 'upraised arm' (Ta.); rebus: eraka = copper (Ka.) Glyph: kaṇḍa 'arrow' (Skt.) rebus: *kaṇḍa* 'fire-altar, furnace'. Glyph: aya 'fish'; rebus: aya 'metal' (G.) ayaskāṇḍa 'excellent quantity of iron' (Pāṇ.)koḍiyum 'heifer'(G.) koḍe 'heifer' (Telugu) खोंड [khōṇḍa] m A young bull, a bullcalf. Rebus: कोंडण [kōṇḍaṇa] f A fold or pen. (Marathi) koḍ 'workshop' (G.) Glyph: miṇḍāl markhor (Tor.wali) meḍho a ram, a sheep (G.)(CDIAL 10120) kunda 'turner' kundār turner (A.); kũdār, kũdāri (B.); kundāru (Or.); kundau to turn on a lathe, to carve, to chase; kundau dhiri = a hewn stone; kundau murhut = a graven image (Santali) kunda a turner's lathe (Skt.)(CDIAL 3295) Rebus: meḍ iron (Ho.) meṛed-bica = iron stone ore, in contrast to bali-bica, iron sand ore (Mu.lex.)

Thus, the Banawali seal impression connotes an assemblage of categories of copper (smelted metal); iron (native metal); iron (smelted metal); (turner's) workshop.

The load prepared in package decribes these categories of products.

Impression and line-drawing of a steatite stamp seal with a water-buffalo and leapers. Buffalo attack or bull-leaping scene, Banawali (after UMESAO 2000:88, cat. no. 335). A figure is impaled on the horns of the buffalo; a woman acrobat wearing bangles on both arms and a long braid flowing from the head, leaps over the buffalo bull. Two Indus script glyphs in front of the buffalo.

Glyphs: '1. arrow, 2. jag/notch':

1. kaṇḍa 'arrow' (Skt.) H. kā̃ḍerā m. ' a caste of bow -- and arrow -- makers (CDIAL 3024). Or. kāṇḍa, kāṛ 'stalk, arrow '(CDIAL 3023). *ayaskāṇḍa* 'a quantity of iron, excellent iron' (Pāṇ.gaṇ)

2. खांडा [khāṇḍā] *m* A jag, notch, or indentation (as upon the edge of a tool or weapon). (Marathi) Rebus: *khāṇḍā* 'tools, pots and pans, metal-ware'.

The message of stone ore is reinforced by the glyphics of buffalo and overthrow of an acrobat woman (*kola* 'woman'; rebus: *kol* 'smithy'):

கண்டி kaṇṭi buffalo bull (Tamil) kaṇḍ 'buffalo'; rebus: kaṇḍ 'stone (ore)'. *kiḍāvu.* He-buffalo; எருமைக்கடா(Malayalam) *Colloq.* கடவு[3] kaṭavu , *n.* < கடா. 1. Male buffalo; எருமைக்கடா. முதுகடவு கடவி (அழகர்கல. 33). *kaḍawan hoṛ* 'a man who has buffaloes'. (George L. Campbell, Compendium of the World's Languages, Routledge, London, 1991, p. 1199).Rebus: khāḍ 'trench, firepit' (G.) khāṛo 'pit, bog' (Nepali) "In Santali, any word may (in theory at least) be used as a verb simply by adding *a*, which is the verbal sign, and other signs to signify tense, mood etc. The *a* alone signifies the general or future tense in the active voice — used to make general statements, or statements referring to the future… The verb generally comes at the end of a sentence or phrase… (Santali language) consists of root-words and various infixes, suffixes and particles, joined together or agglutinated in such a way as to form phrases and sentences… dalgot' kedeae… dal the root word, meaning to strike or striking; got' an adverbial

particle giving the sense of quickly or suddenly; ked the sign ket', denoting the past tense of the active voice, modified to ked… e … signifying an animate object — him, or her… a the verbal sign, showing that the idea of striking is used verbally; e the short form of the 3rd personal pronoun, singular… denoting the subject — he, or she." (R.M. Macphail, An Introduction to Santali, 1953, p.2).

m0312 Persons vaulting over a water-buffalo.

Humped bull or water buffalo attack scene, circular button seal, Mehrgarh. An abstract form of a human body seems to be shown on the space around the animal (after SHAH – PARPOLA 1991:MR-17)

Glyph: 'full stretch of one's arms': kāḍ 2 काड् । पौरुषम् m. a man's length, the stature of a man (as a measure of length) (Rām. 632, zangan kaḍun kāḍ, to stretch oneself the whole length of one's body. So K. 119).

Rebus: kāḍ 'stone'. Ga. (Oll.) kanḍ, (S.) kanḍu (pl. kanḍkil) stone (DEDR 1298). mayponḍi kanḍ whetstone; (Ga.)(DEDR 4628). (खडा) Pebbles or small stones: also stones broken up (as for a road), metal. खडा [khaḍā] *m* A small stone, a pebble. 2 A nodule (of lime &c.): a lump or bit (as of gum, assafœtida, catechu, sugar-candy): the gem or stone of a ring or trinket: a lump of hardened fæces or scybala: a nodule or lump gen. CDIAL 3018 kāṭha m. ' rock ' lex. [Cf. *kānta* -- 2 m. ' stone ' lex.] Bshk. *kōr* ' large stone ' AO xviii 239. கண்டு[3] kaṇṭu , *n.* < *gaṇḍa.* 1. Clod, lump; கட்டி. (தைலவ. தைல. 99.) 2. Wen; கழலைக்கட்டி. 3. Bead or something like a pendant in an ornament for the neck; ஓர் ஆபரணவுரு. புல்லிகைக்கண்ட நாண் ஒன்றிற் கட்டின கண்டு ஒன்றும் (S.I.I. ii, 429). (CDIAL 3023) kāṇḍa cluster, heap ' (in *tṛṇa -- kāṇḍa* -- Pāṇ. Kāś.). [Poss. connexion with gaṇḍa -- 2 makes prob. non -- Aryan origin (not with P. Tedesco Language 22, 190 < *kṛntáti*). Pa. *kaṇḍa* -- m.n. joint of stalk, lump. काठः A rock, stone. kāṭha m. ' rock ' lex. [Cf. *kānta* -- 2 m. ' stone ' lex.]Bshk. *kōr* ' large stone ' AO

xviii 239.(CDIAL 3018). অয়সঠিন [aẏaskaṭhina] as hard as iron; extremely hard (Bengali)

baṭi trs. To overturn, to overset or ovethrow; to turn or throw from a foundation or foothold (Santali) baṭi to turn on the ground to any extent, or roll; uaurbaṭi, to upset or overthrow by shoving or pushing; mabaṭi to overturn by cutting, to fell trees; baṭi-n rflx. v., to lay oneself down; ba-p-aṭi repr. V., to throw each other; baṭi-o to be overturned, overthrown; ba-n-at.i vrb.n., the extent of the overturning, falling down or rolling; baṭi-n rlfx.v., to lie down; baṭi-aṛagu to bring or send down a slope by rolling; baṭi bar.a to roll again and again or here and there; baṭi-bur to turn over by rolling (Mundari) Rebus: baṭi, bhaṭi 'furnace' (H.) Rebus: baṭa = a kind of iron (G.) bhaṭa 'furnace' (G.) baṭa = kiln (Santali). bhaṭa = an oven, kiln, furnace (Santali) baṭhi furnace for smelting ore (the same as kuṭhi) (Santali) bhaṭa = an oven, kiln, furnace; make an oven, a furnace; iṭa bhaṭa = a brick kiln; kun:kal bhaṭa a potter's kiln; cun bhaṭa = a lime kiln; cun tehen dobon bhaṭaea = we shall prepare the lime kiln today (Santali); bhaṭṭhā (H.) bhart = a mixed metal of copper and lead; bhart-īyā = a barzier, worker in metal; bhaṭ, bhrāṣṭra = oven, furnace (Skt.) me~r.he~t bat.i = iron (Ore) furnaces. [Synonyms are: mẽt = the eye, rebus for: the dotted circle (Santali.lex) baṭha [H. baṭṭhī (Sad.)] any kiln, except a potter's kiln, which is called coa; there are four kinds of kiln: cunabat.ha, a lime-kin, iṭabaṭha, a brick-kiln, ērēbaṭha, a lac kiln, kuilabaṭha, a charcoal kiln; trs. Or intrs., to make a kiln; cuna rapamente ciminaupe baṭhakeda? How many limekilns did you make? Baṭha-sen:gel = the fire of a kiln; baṭi [H. Sad. Baṭṭhi, a furnace for distilling) used alone or in the cmpds. Arkibut.i and bat.iora, all meaning a grog-shop; occurs also in ilibaṭi, a (licensed) rice-beer shop (Mundari.lex.) bhaṭi = liquor from mohwa flowers (Santali)

Rebus: dul 'to cast in a mould'; dul *mẽṛhẽt, dul meṛeḍ, dul; koṭe meṛeḍ* 'forged iron' (Santali) WPah.kṭg. (kc.) ***ḍhō`ḷ*** m. 'stone', kṭg. *ḍhòḷṭɔ* m. 'big stone or boulder', *ḍhòḷṭu* 'small id.' Him.I 87.(CDIAL 5536).

Allographs: ḍollu. [Tel.] v. n. To fall, to roll over. పడు, పొరలు డొలుచు [ḍolucu] or ḍoluṭsu. [Tel.] v. n. To tumble head over heels as dancing girls do (Telugu) Mth.

Bhoj. Aw. lakh. Marw. G. M. *ḍhol* m. ***ḍhōlayati** 'makes fall'(CDIAL 5608).

Glyph: *ḍhol* 'a drum beaten on one end by a stick and on the other by the hand' (Santali); *ḍhol* 'drum' (Nahali); *dhol* (Kurku); *ḍhol* (Hi.) *dhol* a drum (G.)(CDIAL 5608) డోలు [ḍōlu] [Tel.] n. A drum.

The association of the 'endless-knot' glyph with the 'svastika' glyph points to both the glyphs as related to the description of a metal artifact.

Svastika: sathiyā (H.), sāthiyo (G.); satthia, sotthia (Pkt.) Rebus: svastika pewter (Kannada)

 h182A  h182B

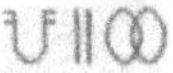

4306Tablet in bas-relief

h182a Pict-107: Drummer and a tiger. h182b Five svastika signs alternating right- and left-handed.  har609 terracotta tablet, bas-relief [The drummer is also shown on h182B tablet with a comparable epigraph and five svastika glyphs alternating right- and left-handed arms. [Lexeme : *mõṛẽ* = five (Santali. lex.)]

m1180 Mohenjo-daro seal. Human-faced markhor.

m0301 Mohenjo-daro seal.

m0302 Mohenjo-daro seal.

m0303 Mohenjo-daro seal.

m0299. Mohenjo-daro seal.

m0300. Mohenjo-daro seal.

m1179. Mohenjo-daro seal. Markhor or ram with human face in composite hieroglyph.

h594. Harappa seal. Composite animal (with elephant trunk and rings (scarves) on shoulder visible).koṭiyum = a wooden circle put round the neck of an animal; koṭ = neck (G.)

m1175 Composite animal with a two-glyph inscription (water-carrier, rebus: kuti 'furnace'; road, bata; rebus: bata 'furnace'). M1186A Composite animal hieroglyph. Text of inscription (3 lines).

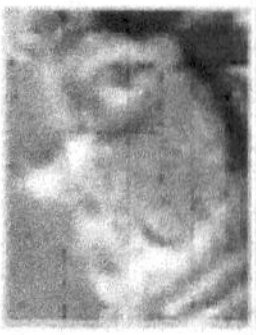

There are many examples of the depiction of 'human face' ligatured to animals:

Ligatured faces: some close-up images.

The animal is a quadruped: pasaramu, pasalamu = an animal, a beast, a brute, quadruped (Te.)Rebus: pasra 'smithy' (Santali) Allograph: panǰãr 'ladder, stairs'(Bshk.)(CDIAL 7760) Thus the composite animal connotes a smithy. Details of the smithy are described orthographically by the glyphic elements of the composition.

Rebus reading of the 'face' glyph: mũhe 'face' (Santali) mũh opening or hole (in a stove for stoking (Bi.); ingot (Santali) mũh metal ingot (Santali) mũhã = the quantity of iron produced at one time in a native smelting furnace of the Kolhes; iron produced by the Kolhes and formed like a four-cornered piece a little pointed at each end; mūhā mẽṛhẽt = iron smelted by the Kolhes and formed into an equilateral lump a little pointed at each of four ends; kolhe tehen mẽṛhẽt ko mūhā akata = the Kolhes have to-day produced pig iron (Santali.lex.) kaula mengro 'blacksmith' (Gypsy) mleccha-mukha (Skt.) = milakkhu 'copper' (Pali) The Sanskrit loss mleccha-mukha should literally mean: copper-ingot absorbing the Santali gloss, mũh, as a suffix.

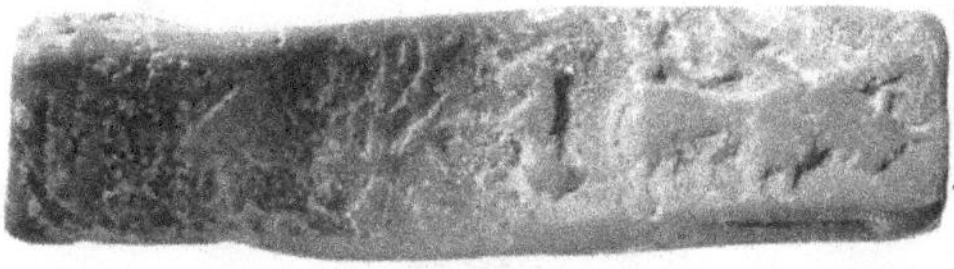

m1430C, body of bison, three heads: bison, antelope, bull; a pair of goat(s), tree branch

खोंड [khōṇḍa] *m* A young bull, a bullcalf (Marathi). kōḍiya, kōḍe young bull (Telugu) Rebus: kọ̆nḍu or konḍu । कुण्डम् m. a hole dug in the ground for receiving consecrated fire (Kashmiri) koḍ 'workshop' (Kuwi) mēḍha 'antelope'; rebus: meḍ 'iron' (Ho.) ḍangar 'bull' Rebus: ḍangar 'blacksmith'.

Ur. Shell plaque. Shell plaque From Ur, Southern Iraq (c. 2,600-2,400 B.C.) Entwined in the branches of a flowering tree, two goats appear to be nibbling on its leaves. This decorative plaque, which was carved from shell and highlighted with bitumen, was also excavated from the Royal Tombs of Ur. The glyphics on this plaque are comparable to the glyphics on Tablet 1431E showing two goat glyphs flanking a tree glyph.

Orthography of the two goats on the prism tablet is comparable to the glyph on a shell plaque from Ur. Mlekh, mṛeka 'goat' (Br.Telugu); rebus: milakkhu 'copper'. डगर [ḍagara] A slope or ascent (as of a river's bank, of a small hill). A pair is dula; rebus: dul 'cast (metal)'(Santali)Rebus: ḍāṅgar 'blacksmith' (H.) Thus, the glyptic composition is read rebus: dul mlekh ḍāṅgar 'cast copper-smith'.

Glyph: tagara 'ram'; rebus: tagara 'tin'

Glyph: Ta. kōṭu branch of tree, cluster, bunch, coil of hair, line, diagram kuvaṭu branch of a tree; Go. (Tr.) kōr (obl. kōt-, pl. kōhk)horn of cattle or wild animals, branch of a tree; Ka. kōḍu horn, tusk, branch of a tree (DEDR 2200).

Glyph: *Ta.* kōṭu summit of a hill, peak, mountain; kōṭai mountain; kōṭar peak, summit of a tower; kuvaṭu mountain, hill, peak; kuṭumi summit of a mountain, top of a building, crown of the head, bird's crest, tuft of hair (esp. of men), crown, projecting corners on which a door swings. (DEDR 2049).

Rebus: खोट [khōṭa] *f* A mass of metal (unwrought or of old metal melted down); an ingot or wedge. Hence खोटसाळ [khōṭasāḷa] *a* (खोट & साळ from शाला) Alloyed--a metal. (Marathi) Bshk. *khoṭ* 'embers', Phal. *khūṭo* 'ashes, burning coal'; L. *khoṭf.* 'alloy, impurity', *°ṭā* 'alloyed', awāṇ. *khoṭā* 'forged'; P. *khoṭ* m. 'base, alloy' M.*khoṭā* 'alloyed' (CDIAL 3931)

After Amiet, P., 1961, *La glyptique mesopotamienne archaique*, Paris: 497; Mundigak IV.3; 3.

Sumerian cylinder seal showing flanking goats with hooves on tree and/or mountain. Uruk period. (After Joyce Burstein in: Katherine Anne Harper, Robert L. Brown, 2002, The roots of tantra, SUNY Press, p.100)

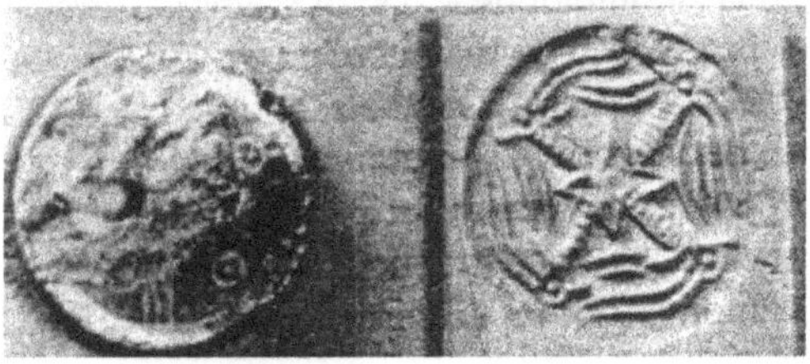

Bahrain seal: four antelope heads emanating from a star. Four antelopes. Dotted circles on reverse.

meḍha 'polar star' (Marathi). meḍ 'iron' (Ho.Mu.) Allograph: meḍh 'ram'.

meḍha 'polar star' (Marathi). Rebus: meḍ 'iron' (Ho.) tagara 'ram'; rebus: tagara 'tin'. Rebus: damgar 'merchant'.

gaṇḍa 'four'; khaṇḍ 'dotted circles'. Rebus: khaṇḍ 'tools, pots and pans and metal-ware'; kaṇḍ = a furnace, altar (Santali.lex.)

Hence, two goats + mountain glyph reads rebus: Leaf on mountain: kamaṛkom 'petiole of leaf'; rebus: kampaṭṭam 'mint'.

loa = a species of fig tree, ficus glomerata, the fruit of ficus glomerata (Santali) Rebus: lo 'iron' (Assamese, Bengali); loa 'iron' (Gypsy). rebus: loh 'metal' (Skt.) Rebus: lo 'copper'. meḍha 'polar star' (Marathi). Rebus: meḍ 'iron' (Ho.)

Glyph: *Ta.* kōṭu summit of a hill. Rebus: *khoṭf*. 'alloy, impurity', *°ṭā* 'alloyed'.

tagara 'ram'; rebus: tagara 'tin'

soḍu fireplace, stones set up as a fireplace (Mand.); ule furnace (Tu.)(DEDR 2857).

mlekh 'goat' (Br.); rebus: milakku 'copper' (Pali); mleccha 'copper' (Skt.) Thus, the composition of glyphs on the platform: pair of antelopes + pair of hayricks read rebus: milakku kundār 'copper turner'. Thus the seal is a framework of glyphic compositions to describe the repertoire of a brazier-mint, 'one who works in brass or makes brass articles' and 'a mint'.

m1431E. From R.—a person holding a vessel; a woman with a platter (?); a kneeling person with a staff in his hands facing the woman; a goat with its forelegs on a platform under a tree. [Or, two antelopes flanking a tree on a platform, with one antelope looking backwards?]

Line drawing of Indus script seal impression on one side of a prism tablet M1431E. Mohenjodaro. Symmetrically flanking goats with feet on central tree and mountain (ASI).

The turner on a lathe is depicted on this glyphic narrative. kõdā 'to turn in a lathe' (Bengali)

Glyph: 'broken tree branch': khōṇḍa A tree of which the head and branches are broken off, a stock or stump: also the lower portion of the trunk—that below the branches. (Marathi) Rebus 1: koḍ 'workshop' (G.)

Allograph glyph: खोंड [khōṇḍa] m A young bull, a bullcalf. (Marathi) గోద [gōda] gōda. [Tel.] n. An ox. A beast. kine, cattle.(Telugu) koḍiyum 'heifer' (G.) [kōḍiya] kōḍe, kōḍiya. [Tel.] n. A bullcalf. . k* దూడA young bull. Plumpness, prime. రుణముత. జోడుకోడయలు a pair of bullocks. kōḍe adj. Young. kōḍe-kāḍu. n. A young man.పడుచువాడు. [kārukōḍe] kāru-kōḍe. [Tel.] n. A bull in its prime. koḍiyum (G.) Rebus : B. kõdā 'to turn in a lathe'; Or. kũnda 'lathe', kũdibā, kũd 'to turn' (→ Drav. Kur. kũd 'lathe') (CDIAL 3295).

M1431E shows a turner at work, assisted by a person bending on all fours. kunda 'turner' kundār turner (A.); kũdār, kũdāri (B.); kundāru (Or.); kundau to turn on a lathe, to carve, to chase; kundau dhiri = a hewn stone; kundau murhut = a graven image (Santali) kunda a turner's lathe (Skt.)(CDIAL 3295) Glyph: Br. Kōṇḍō on all fours, bent double. (DEDR 204a) The seated person is shown wearing knot of hair at back. Sūnd gaṭ (Go.) cundī the hairtail as worn by men (Kur.)(DEDR 2670). Rebus: cundakāra a turner J vi.339 (Pali) cundakāra cognate kundār.

Three identical catalogs of two-sided tablets of Harappa

A ligatured glyph wad used to connote the professional competence of an artisan who performed the roles of merchant, smith and mason.

h1973B h1974B Two tablets. One side shows a person seated on a tree branch, a tiger looking up, a crocodile on the top register and other animals in procession in the bottom register. Obverse side (comparable to h1970, h1971 and h1972) shows an elephant, a person strangling two tigers (jackals or foxes) and a six-spoked wheel.

The glyphic which is common to both set 1 (h1970B, h1971B and h1972B) and set 2: (h1973B and h1974B) is: crocodile on the top register. karā 'crocodile' (Telugu). Rebus: khara 'blacksmith' (Kashmiri)

Set 1: crocodile + person with foot on head of animal + spearing + bison + horned (with twig) seated person in penance

Set 2: crocodile + person seated on branch of tree + tiger looking back and up + rhinoceros + tiger in procession.

h1971B Harappa. Three tablets with identical glyphic compositions on both sides: h1970, h1971 and h1972. Seated figure or deity with reed house or shrine at one side. Left: H95-2524; Right: H95-2487.

Harappa. Planoconvex molded tablet found on Mound ET. A. Reverse. a female deity battling two tigers and standing above an elephant and below a six-spoked wheel; b. Obverse. A person spearing with a barbed spear a buffalo in front of a seated horned deity wearing bangles and with a plumed headdress. The person presses his foot down the buffalo's head. An alligator with a narrow snout is on the top register. "We have found two other broken tablets at Harappa that appear to have been made from the same mold that was used to create the scene of a deity battling two tigers and standing above an elephant. One was found in a room located on the southern slope of Mount ET in 1996 and another example comes from excavations on Mound F in the 1930s. However, the flat obverse of both of these broken tablets does not show the spearing of a buffalo, rather it depicts the more well-known scene showing a tiger looking back over its shoulder at a person sitting on the branch of a tree. Several other flat or twisted rectangular terracotta tablets found at Harappa combine these two narrative scenes of a figure strangling two tigers on one side of a tablet, and the tiger looking back over its shoulder at a figure in a tree on the other side."[98]

The following glyphics of m1431 prism tablet show the association between the tiger + person on tree glyphic set and crocile + 3 animal glyphic set.

Glyph: Animals in procession: खांडा [*khāṇḍā*] A flock (of sheep or goats) (Marathi) கண்டி[1] kaṇṭi Flock, herd (Tamil) Rebus: *khāṇḍā* 'tools, pots and pans, and metal-ware'.

m0489A One side of a prism tablet shows: crocodile + fish glyphic above:

elephant, rhinoceros, tiger, tiger looking back and up.

m1431A m1431B Crocodile+ three animal glyphs: rhinoceros, elephant, tiger

It is possible that the broken portions of set 2 (h1973B and h1974B) showed three and up

animals in procession: tiger looking back + rhinoceros + tiger.

Reverse side glyphs:

eraka 'nave of wheel'. Rebus: era 'copper'.

Animal glyph: elephant 'ibha'. Rebus ibbo, 'merchant' (Gujarati).

Composition of glyphics: Woman with six locks of hair + one eye + thwarting + two pouncing tigers (jackals)+ nave with six spokes. Rebus: *kola* 'woman' + kaṇga 'eye' (Pego.), *bhaṭa* 'six'+ *dul* 'casting (metal)' + *kũdā kol* (tiger jumping) or *lo* 'fox' (WPah.) *rebus: lōha* 'metal' (Pali) + *era āra* (nave of wheel, six spokes), *ibha* (elephant). Rebus: *era* 'copper'; *kũdār dul kol* 'turner, casting, working in iron'; *kan* 'brazier, bell-metal worker'; *ibbo* 'merchant'.

The glyphic composition read rebus: copper, iron merchant with *taṭu kanḍ kol bhaṭa* 'iron stone (ore) mineral furnace'.

lōpāka m. 'a kind of jackal' Suśr., *lōpākikā* -- f. lex. 1. H. *lowā* m. 'fox'.2. Ash. *ẓōki*, *žōkī* 'fox', Kt. *ŕwēki*, Bashg. *wrikī*, Kal.rumb. *lawák*: < **raupākya* -- NTS ii 228; -- Dm. *rõpak* ← Ir.? lōpāśá m. 'fox, jackal' RV., *lōpāśikā* -- f. lex. [Cf. *lōpāka* -- . -- *lōpi --] Wg. *liwášä, laúša* 'fox', Paš.kch. *lowóċ*, ar. *lṓeč* 'jackal' (→ Shum. *lṓeč* NTS xiii 269), kuṛ. *lwāinč*, K. *lośu, lōh, lohu, lôhu* 'porcupine, fox'.1. Kho. *lōw* 'fox', Sh.gil. *lótilde;i* f., pales. *lṓi* f., *lṓo* m., WPah.bhal. *lōī* f., *lo* m.2. Pr. *ẓūwī* 'fox'.(CDIAL 11140-2).Rebus: lōhá 'red, copper -- coloured' ŚrS., 'made of copper' ŚBr., m.n. 'copper' VS., 'iron' MBh. [*rudh --] Pa. *lōha* -- m. 'metal, esp. copper or bronze'; Pk. *lōha* -- m. 'iron', Gy. pal. *li°*, *lihi*, obl. *elhás*, as. *loa* JGLS new ser. ii 258; Wg. (Lumsden) "*loa*" 'steel'; Kho. *loh* 'copper'; S. *lohu* m. 'iron',

L. *lohā* m., awāṇ. *lō`ā*, P. *lohā* m. (→ K.rām. ḍoḍ. *lohā*), WPah.bhad. *lɔ̃u* n., bhal. *lòtilde;* n., pāḍ. jaun. *lōh*, paṅ. *luhā*, cur. cam. *lohā*, Ku. *luwā*, N. *lohu*, *°hā*, A. *lo*, B. *lo*, *no*, Or. *lohā*, *luhā*, Mth. *loh*, Bhoj. *lohā*, Aw.lakh. *lōh*, H. *loh*, *lohā* m., G. M. *loh* n.; Si. *loho*, *lō* ' metal, ore, iron '; Md. *ratu -- lō* ' copper lōhá -- : WPah.kṭg. (kc.) *lóɔ* 'iron', J. *lohā* m., Garh. *loho*; Md. *lō* 'metal'. (CDIAL 11158). Glypg: 'woman': kola 'woman' (Nahali). Rebus kol 'working in iron' (Tamil)

Glyph: 'impeding, hindering': taṭu (Ta.) Rebus: dhatu 'mineral' (Santali) Ta. taṭu (-pp-, -tt) to hinder, stop, obstruct, forbid, prohibit, resist, dam, block up, partition off, curb, check, restrain, control, ward off, avert; n. hindering, checking, resisting; taṭuppu hindering, obstructing, resisting, restraint; Kur. ṭaṇḍnā to prevent, hinder, impede. Br. taḍ power to resist. (DEDR 3031)

Allograph: 'notch': Marathi: खांडा [khāṇḍā] *m* A jag, notch, or indentation (as upon the edge of a tool or weapon).

Glyph: 'full stretch of one's arms': kāḍ 2 काड् । पौरुषम् m. a man's length, the stature of a man (as a measure of length) (Rām. 632, zangan kaḍun kāḍ, to stretch oneself the whole length of one's body. So K. 119). Rebus: kāḍ 'stone'. Ga. (Oll.) kanḍ, (S.) kanḍu (pl. kanḍkil) stone (DEDR 1298). maypony kanḍ whetstone; (Ga.)(DEDR 4628). (खडा) Pebbles or small stones: also stones broken up (as for a road), metal. खडा [khaḍā] *m* A small stone, a pebble. 2 A nodule (of lime &c.): a lump or bit (as of gum, assafœtida, catechu, sugar-candy): the gem or stone of a ring or trinket: a lump of hardened fæces or scybala: a nodule or lump gen. CDIAL 3018 kāṭha m. ' rock ' lex. [Cf. *kānta* -- 2 m. ' stone ' lex.] Bshk. *kōr* ' large stone ' AO xviii 239. கண்டு[3] kaṇṭu , *n.* < *gaṇḍa*. 1. Clod, lump; கட்டி. (தைலவ. தைல. 99.) 2. Wen; கழலைக்கட்டி. 3. Bead or something like a pendant in an ornament for the neck; ஓர் ஆபரணவுரு. புல்லிகைக்கண்ட நாண் ஒன்றிற் கட்டின கண்டு ஒன்றும் (S.I.I. ii, 429). (CDIAL 3023) kāṇḍa cluster, heap ' (in *tṛṇa -- kāṇḍa* -- Pāṇ. Kāś.). [Poss. connexion with gaṇḍa -- 2 makes prob. non -- Aryan origin (not with P. Tedesco Language 22, 190 < *kṛntáti*). Pa. *kaṇḍa* -- m.n. joint of stalk, lump. काठ: A rock, stone. kāṭha m. ' rock ' lex.

[Cf. *kānta* -- 2 m. ' stone ' lex.]Bshk. *kōr* ' large stone ' AO xviii 239.(CDIAL 3018). অয়স্কঠিন [aẏaskaṭhina] as hard as iron; extremely hard (Bengali)

Glyph: 'one-eyed': काण *a.* [कण् निमीलने कर्तरि घञ् Tv.] 1 One-eyed; अक्ष्णा काणः Sk; काणेन चक्षुषा किं वा H. Pr.12; Ms.3.155. -2 Perforated, broken (as a cowrie) <kaNa>(Z) {ADJ} ``^one-^eyed, ^blind''. Ju<kaNa>(DP),,<kana>(K) {ADJ} ``^blind, blind in one eye''. (Munda) Go. (Ma.) kaṇḍ reppa eyebrow (Voc. 3047(a))(DEDR 5169). *Ka.* kāṇ (kaṇḍ-) to see; *Ko.* kaṇ-/ka·ṇ- (kaḍ-) to see;

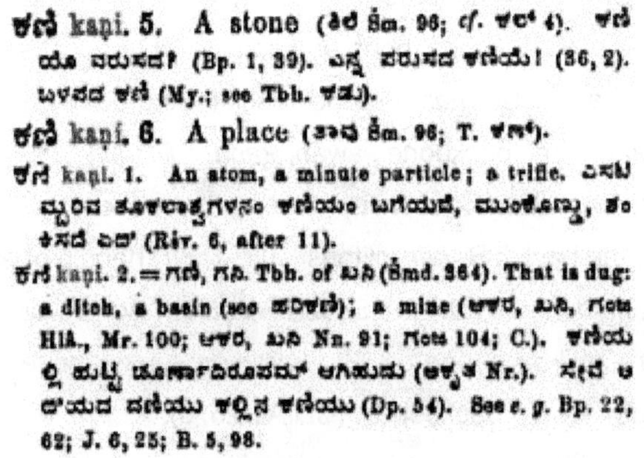
ಕಣಿ kaṇi. 5. A stone ([illegible] Śm. 96; *cf.* [illegible] 4). [illegible] (Bp. 1, 39). [illegible] (36, 2). [illegible] (My.; see Tbh. [illegible]).
ಕಣಿ kaṇi. 6. A place ([illegible] Śm. 96; T. [illegible]).
ಕಣಿ kaṇi. 1. An atom, a minute particle; a trifle. [illegible] (Rév. 6, after 11).
ಕಣಿ kaṇi. 2. = [illegible], [illegible]. Tbh. of [illegible] (Śmd. 364). That is dug: a ditch, a basin (see [illegible]); a mine ([illegible], [illegible], [illegible] Hlā., Mr. 100; [illegible], [illegible] Nr. 91; [illegible] 104; C.). [illegible] (Nr.). [illegible] (Dp. 54). See *e. g.* Bp. 22, 62; J. 6, 25; B. 5, 98.

Koḍ. ka·ṇ- (ka·mb-, kaṇḍ-) to see; *Ta.* kāṇ (kāṇp-, kaṇṭ-) to see; *Kol.*kanḍt, kanḍakt seen, visible. (DEDR 1443). *Ta.* kaṇ eye, aperture, orifice, star of a peacock's tail. (DEDR 1159a) Rebus 'brazier, bell-metal worker': கன்னான் kaṉṉāṉ , *n.* < கன்[1]. [M. *kannān.*] Brazier, bell-metal worker, one of the divisions of the Kammāḷa caste; செம்புகொட்டி. (திவா.) *Ta.* kaṉ copper work, copper, workmanship; kaṉṉāṉ brazier. *Ma.* kannān id. (DEDR 1402). கன்[1] kaṉ , *n.* perh. கன்மம். 1. Workmanship; வேலைப்பாடு. கன்னார் மதில்சூழ் குடந்தை (திவ். திருவாய். 5, 8, 3). 2. Copper work; கன்னார் தொழில். (W.) 3. Copper; செம்பு. (ஈடு, 5, 8, 3.) 4. See கன்னத்தட்டு. (நன். 217, விருத்.) கன்[2] kaṉ , *n.* < கல். 1. Stone; கல். (சூடா.) 2. Firmness; உறுதிப்பாடு. (ஈடு, 5, 8, 3.)

kāḍ 2 काँड् m. a section, part in general; a cluster, bundle, multitude (Śiv. 32). kāḍ 1 काँड् । काण्डः m. the stalk or stem of a reed, grass, or the like, straw. In the compound with dan 5 (p. 221*a,* l. 13) the word is spelt kāḍ.

kōda कोँद । कुलालादिकन्दुः f. a kiln; a potter's kiln (Rām. 1446; H. xi, 11); a brick-kiln (Śiv. 133); a lime-kiln. -bal -बल् । कुलालादिकन्दुस्थानम् m. the place where a kiln is erected, a brick or potter's kiln (Gr.Gr. 165). -- । कुलालादिकन्दुयथावद्भावः f.inf. a kiln to arise; met. to become like such a kiln (which contains no imperfectly baked

articles, but only well-made perfectly baked ones), hence, a collection of good ('pucka') articles or qualities to exist.

కండె [kaṇḍe] *kaṇḍe*. [Tel.] n. A head or ear of millet or maize. జొన్న కండి.

Khânaka, mfn. ifc. one who digs or digs out, Mn. viii, 260; (cf. *kapa-*); m. a house-breaker, thief, VarBṛS. lxxxix, 9; (*ikā*), f. a ditch, Gal.
Khânam, ind. p. so as to dig, HParis. ii, 376.
Khâni, *is*, f. a mine, Śatr. x, 112 (ifc.)
Khânika, n. an opening in a wall, breach, L.
Khânina, mfn., v.l. for °*nila*, L.
Khânila, mfn. a house-breaker, L.
Khânya, mfn. (Pāṇ. iii, 1, 123) anything that is being digged out, Lāṭy. viii, 2, 4 f.

*kaṇṭa ' backbone, podex, penis '. 2. *kaṇḍa -- . 3. *karaṇḍa -- 4. (Cf. *kāṭa -- 2, *ḍākka -- 2: poss. same as káṇṭa -- 1] 1. Pa. *piṭṭhi -- kaṇṭaka* -- m. ' bone of the spine '; Gy. eur. *kanro* m. ' penis ' (or < káṇṭaka --); Tir. *mar -- kaṇḍḗ* ' back (of the body) '; S.*kaṇḍo* m. ' back ', L. *kaṇḍ* f., *kaṇḍā* m. 'backbone', awāṇ. *kaṇḍ*, *°ḍī* ' back '; P. *kaṇḍ* f. ' back, pubes '; WPah. bhal. *kaṇṭ* f. ' syphilis '; N. *kaṇḍo* ' buttock, rump, anus ',*kaṇḍeulo* ' small of the back '; B. *kāṭ* ' clitoris '; Or. *kaṇṭi* ' handle of a plough '; H. *kāṭā* m. ' spine ', G. *kāṭɔ* m., M. *kāṭā* m.; Si. *äṭa -- kaṭuva* ' bone ', *piṭa -- k°* ' backbone '. 2. Pk. *kaṁḍa* -- m. ' backbone '. 3. Pk. *karaṁḍa* -- m.n. ' bone shaped like a bamboo ', *karaṁḍuya* -- n. ' backbone '. (CDIAL 2670).

<kana.kana>(A) {ADJ} ``^perforated''. #15890. <kaNa>>: *De.<kana>(GM) `a hole; perforated'. ??hole, to make a hole? #10761. <kaNa-gu-nu> {ADJ} ``^perforated''. |<gu> `?perfect/past', <nu> `adjective'. *De.<kana>(GM) `a hole; perforated'. (Munda) Pk. *kāṇa* -- ' full of holes ', G. *kāṇũ* ' full of holes ', n. ' hole ' (CDIAL 3019) Marathi: खड्डा [khaḍḍā] *m* A rough hole or pit. M. *khāḍ* f. ' hole, creek ', *°ḍā* m. 'hole' (CDIAL, no. 3874).

Pk. khāṇī -- f. ' mine '; Gy. as. xani, eur. sp. xaní f., boh. xaníg f., gr. xaníng f. ' well '; K. khān f. ' mine '; S. khāṇi f. ' mine, quarry, water in a pit '; L. khāṇ f. ' mine ' (CDIAL 3873)

Rebus: 'to engrave, write; lapidary': <kana-lekhe>(P) {??} ``??''. |. Cf. <kana->. %16123. #16013. <lekhe->(P),,<leke->(KM) {VTC} ``to ^write''. Cf. <kana-lekhe>. *Kh.<likhae>, H.<lIkhAna>, O.<lekhIba>, B.<lekha>; Kh.<likha>(P), Mu.<lika>. %20701. #20541. Kashmiri: khanun खनुन् । खननम् conj. 1 (1 p.p. khonu for 1, see s.v.; f. khüñü to dig (K.Pr. 155, 247; L. 459; Śiv. 59, 746,

994, 143, 1197, 1214, 1373, 1754; Rām. 343, 958, 1147, 1724; H. xii, 6); to engrave (Śiv. 414, 671, 176; Rām. 1583). khonu-motu खनुमतु; । खातः perf. part. (f. khüñümütsü) dug (e.g. a field, or a well); engraved. mŏhara-khonu म्वहर-खनु; or (Gr.M.) mŏhar-kan । मुद्राखननकारः m. a seal-engraver, a lapidary (El. *mohar-kand*). -wöjü । *अङ्गुलिमुद्रा f. a signet-ring.

DEDR 1170 *Ta.* kaṇṭam iron style for writing on palmyra leaves. *Te.* gaṇṭamu id.

DEDR 1179 *Kur.* kaṇḍō a stool. *Malt.* kanḍo stool, seat. గడమంచె *gaḍa-manche.* n. A wooden frame like a bench to keep things on. గంపలు మొదలగునవాటిని ఉంచు మంచె.

3986 *gaḍha ' fort '. [Poss. with ODBL 500 < **gr̥dha-* (> gr̥há --), Av. *gərəda* --] Pk. *gaḍha* -- m., *°ḍhā* -- f. ' fort '; K. *gaḍ* m. (= vill. **gaṛ*?) ' small masonry fort built in the hills by a local chieftain '; S. *gaṛhu*m. ' fort ', P. *gaṛh* m., Ku. *gaṛ*, A. *gar*, B. *gaṛ*, Or. *gaṛ(h)a*, Mth. Bhoj. *gaṛh*, OAw. *gaḍha* m., H. *gaṛhī* f. (→ N. *gaṛi*), OMarw. OG. *gaḍha* m., G. *gaḍh*, *ghaṛ* m. (whence *gaḍhī* m. ' inhabitant of a hill fort '), M. *gaḍhī*, *gaḍḍī* f. *gaḍhapati -- ; saṁgaḍha -- .Addenda: *gaḍha -- : S.kcch. *gaḍḍh* m. ' fort '.

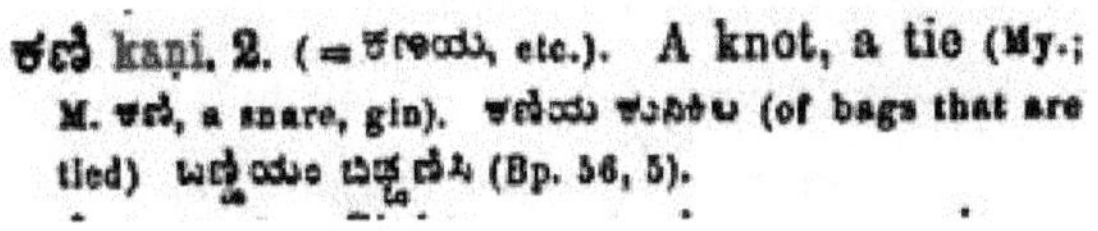
ಕಣಿ kaṇi. 2. (= ಕಣ್ಣಿ, etc.). A knot, a tie (My.; M. ಕಣಿ, a snare, gin). ಕಣಿಯು ... (of bags that are tied) ... (Bp. 56, 5).

Allograph: 'rhinoceros': gaṇḍá4 m. ' rhinoceros ' lex., *°aka* -- m. lex. 2. *ga- yaṇḍa -- . [Prob. of same non -- Aryan origin as khaḍgá --1: cf. *gaṇōtsāha* -- m. lex. as a Sanskritized form ← Mu. PMWS 138]1. Pa. *gaṇḍaka* -- m., Pk. *gaṁḍaya* -- m., A. *gãr*, Or. *gaṇḍā*. 2. K. *gõḍ* m., S. *geṇḍo* m. (lw. with *g* --), P. *gaĩḍā* m., *°ḍī* f., N. *gaĩṛo*, H. *gaĩṛā* m., G. *gẽḍɔ* m., *°ḍī* f., M. *gẽḍā* m.Addenda: gaṇḍa -- 4. 2. *gayaṇḍa -- : WPah.kṭg. *geṇḍɔ mirg* m. ' rhinoceros ', Md. *genḍā* ← H. (CDIAL 4000).

1. Pk. *kaṁkaya* -- m. ' comb ', *kaṁkaya* -- , *°kaï* -- m. ' name of a tree '; Gy. eur. *kangli* f.; Wg. *kuṇi -- prũ* ' man's comb ' (for *kuṇi* -- cf. *kuṇälík* beside *kuṅälík* s.v. kr̥muka -- ; -- *prũ* see prapavaṇa --); Bshk. *kēṅg* ' comb ', Gaw. *khēṅgī́*, Sv. *khḗṅgiā*, Phal. *khyḗṅgia*, *kēṅgī* f., *kāṅga* ' combing ' in *ṣiṣ k°*

dūm ' I comb my hair '; Tor. *kyäṅg* ' comb ' (Dard. forms, esp. Gaw., Sv., Phal. but not Sh., prob. ← L. P. type < *kaṅgahiā -- , see 3 below); Sh. kōṅyi f. (→ Ḍ. k*lṅi f.), gil. (Lor.) kōĩ f. ' man's comb ', kōũ m. ' woman's comb ', pales. kōgōm. ' comb '; K. kanguwu m. ' man's comb ', kangañ f. ' woman's '; WPah. bhad. kã´kei ' a comb -- like fern ', bhal. kãkei f. ' comb, plant with comb -- like leaves '; N. kãṅiyo, kãĩyo ' comb ', A. kãkai, . kãkui; Or. kaṅkāi, kaṅkuā ' comb ', kakuā ' ladder -- like bier for carrying corpse to the burning -- ghat '; Bi. kakwā ' comb ', kakahā, °hī, Mth. kakwā, Aw. lakh. kakawā, Bhoj. kakahī f.; H. kakaiyā ' shaped like a comb (of a brick) '; G. (non -- Aryan tribes of Dharampur) kãkhāī f. ' comb '; M. kaṅkvā m. ' comb ', kãkaī f. ' a partic. shell fish and its shell '; -- S. kaṅgu m. ' a partic. kind of small fish ' < *kaṅkuta -- ? -- Ext. with -- l -- in Ku. kãgilo, kãĩlo ' comb '.2. G. (Soraṭh) kãgaṛ m. ' a weaver's instrument '?3. L. kaṅghī f. ' comb, a fish of the perch family ', awāṇ. kaghī ' comb '; P. kaṅghā m. ' large comb ', °ghī f. ' small comb for men, large one for women ' (→ H.kaṅghā m. ' man's comb ', °gahī, °ghī f. ' woman's ', kaṅghuā m. ' rake or harrow '; Bi. kãgahī ' comb ', Or. kaṅgei, M. kaṅgvā); -- G. kãgsī f. ' comb ', with metath. kãsko m., °kī f.; WPah. khaś. kãgśī, śeu. kãśkī ' a comblike fern ' or < *kaṅkataśikha -- .*kaṅkatakara -- , *kaṅkataśikha -- .Addenda: káṅkata -- : WPah.kṭg. kaṅgi f. ' comb '; J. kãṅgṛu m. ' small comb .kaṅkatakara CDIAL 2599 *kaṅkatakara ' comb -- maker '. [káṅkata -- , kará -- 1]H. *kãgherā* m. ' caste of comb -- makers ', *°rī* f. ' a woman of this caste '.

1161 *Ta.* kaṇ place, site. *Ka.* kaṇi a place.

Kashmiri: khān 2 खान् m. a table (not used by Hindūs) (El., K.Pr. 13, YZ. 29).

Glyph: 'hare': N. *kharāyo* ' hare ', Or. *kharā*, *°riā*, *kherihā*, Mth. *kharehā*, H. *kharahā* m. (CDIAL 3823). Glyph: 'thicket': khāra 2 खार (=) or khār 4 खार् (L.V. 96, K.Pr. 47, Śiv. 827) । द्वेषः m. (for 1, see khār 1), a thorn, prickle, spine (K.Pr. 47; Śiv. 827, 153)(Kashmiri) Rebus: khār 'blacksmith' (Kashmiri). Thus, 'hare' glyph is an allograph for 'crocodile' which reads rebus: *kara.* khār 1 खार् । लोहकारः m. (sg. abl. khāra 1 खार; the pl. dat. of this word is khāran 1 खारन्, which is to be distinguished from khāran 2, q.v., s.v.), a blacksmith, an iron worker

(cf. bandūka-khār, p. 111*b,* l. 46; K.Pr. 46; H. xi, 17); a farrier (El.). This word is often a part of a name, and in such case comes at the end (W. 118) as in Wahab khār, Wahab the smith (H. ii, 12; vi, 17). khāra-basta

Pict-123 Standard device which is normally in front of a one-horned bull. The device is flanked by columns of dotted circles.

Glyphs and rebus readings: kolami 'smithy, forge' + *kanka, karṇaka 'account' + bhaṭa* furnace' *+ kūdā* 'turner' + kol 'working in iron' + era 'copper' + āra 'brass' as in ārakūṭa (Skt.)

Thus side 1 glyphs refer to: merchant (of) furnace (outputs) account (from) smithy/forge of turner, working in copper and brass.

Obverse side glyphs are of two sets:

Set 1: crocodile + person with foot on head of animal + spearing + bison + horned (with twig) seated person in penance

ayakāra 'ironsmith' (fish, *aya* + crocodile, *karā*) + kolami 'smithy/forge' (kolsa 'kicking') + sal 'workshop' (sal 'bison') + kol 'working in iron' (kol 'killing') + kammaṭi 'coiner'; kammaṭa 'mint' (kamaḍha 'penance) + kuṭhi 'smelter' (kūdī 'twig') + koḍ 'artisan's workshop' (koḍ 'horns')

Set 2: crocodile + person seated on branch of tree + tiger looking back and up + rhinoceros + tiger in procession.

ayakāra 'ironsmith' (fish, *aya* + crocodile, *karā*) + era 'copper' (eraka 'spy') + ḍhālako, 'large metal ingot' (ḍāḷ, 'branch of a tree') + three animals in procession: badhoe 'worker in wood and iron' [badhi 'castrated boar'] + kol 'smith working in iron with smithy/forge' [kol + kammara 'tiger looking up'] + kolami 'smithy/forge' [kola 'tiger']

Details of the tiger + spy + leafless tree glyphics are clearly seen on a Mohenjodaro seal m0309.

m0309  2522

Ko. er uk- (uky-) to play 'peeping tom'. *Kui* ēra (ēri-) to spy, scout; *n.* spying, scouting; *pl action* ērka (ērki). ? *Kuwi* (S.) hēnai to scout; hēri kiyali to see; (Su. P.) hēnḍ- (hēṭ-) id. *Kur.* ērnā (īryas) to see, look, look at, look after, look for, wait for, examine, try; ērta'ānā to let see, show; ērānakhrnā to look at one another. *Malt.*ére to see, behold, observe; érye to peep, spy. Kur. ēthrnā. / Cf. Skt. heraka- spy, Pkt. her- to look at or for, and many NIA verbs (DEDR 903). *hērati 'looks for or at'. 2. hēraka -- , *°rika* -- m. 'spy' lex., *hairika* -- m. 'spy' Hcar., 'thief' lex. [J. Bloch FestschrWackernagel 149 ← Drav., Kui *ēra* 'to spy', Malt. *ére* 'to see']1. Pk. *hēraï* 'looks for or at' (*vihīraï* 'watches for'); K.ḍoḍ. *hērūō* 'was seen'; WPah.bhad. bhal. *he_rnū* 'to look at' (bhal. *hirāṇū* 'to show'), pāḍ. *hēraṇ*, paṅ.*hēṇā*, cur. *hērnā*, Ku. *herṇo*, N. *hernu*, A. *heriba*, B. *herā*, Or. *heribā* (caus. *herāibā*), Mth. *herab*, OAw. *heraï*, H. *hernā*; G. *hervũ* 'to spy', M. *herṇẽ*.2. Pk. *hēria* -- m. 'spy'; Kal. (Leitner) "*hériu*" 'spy'; G. *herɔ* m. 'spy', *herũ* n. 'spying'. WPah.kṭg. (Wkc.) *hèrnõ*, kc. *erno* 'observe'; Garh. *hernu* 'to look'.(CDIAL 14165).

> Glyphics read rebus: *kol kammara* 'iron smith' [*kola* 'tiger' (Telugu); *krammaru* 'head turned back' (Telugu)]; *eraka* 'copper' [*heraka* 'spy']; *kõdār* 'turner' (Bengali) [*khōṇḍa* 'leafless tree' (Marathi).]

Glyphs on text inscription

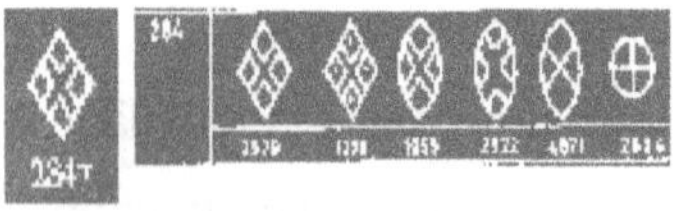

V284 Glyph: *kōṇṭa* 'corner' (Nk.); Tu. *kōṇṭu* 'angle, corner' (Tu.). Rebus: *kõdā* 'to turn in a lathe' (B.) Four corners marked may denote a worker guild working with 4 types of pure metal and alloyed ingots (copper + arsenic/tin/zinc).

Glyph: 'splinter' sal 'splinter'. Rebus: sal 'artisan's workshop'. खांडा [khāṇḍā] *m* A jag, notch, or indentation (as upon the edge of a tool or

weapon. Rebus: *kāṇḍa* 'tools, pots and pans and metal-ware'.

Glyph: taṭṭai 'mechanism made of split bamboo for scaring away parrots from grain fields (Ta.); taṭṭe 'a thick bamboo or an areca-palm stem, split in two' (Ka.) (DEDR 3042) Rebus: toṭxin, toṭ.xn goldsmith (To.); taṭṭāṉ 'gold- or silver-smith' (Ta.); taṭṭaravāḍu 'gold- or silver-smith' (Te.); *ṭhaṭṭakāra 'brass-worker' (Skt.)(CDIAL 5493). Thus, the glyph is decoded: taṭṭara 'worker in gold, brass'.

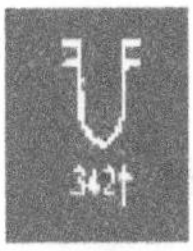

Glyph: *kaṇḍa kanka* 'rim of jar'. Rebus: furnace (stone ore) account (scribe).

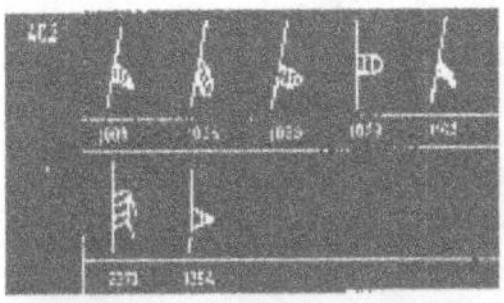

Allographs of Glyph 402 Glyph: *koḍi* 'flag' (Ta.)(DEDR 2049). Rebus: *koḍ* 'workshop' (Kuwi)

Glyph: *ayo, hako* 'fish'; a~s = scales of fish (Santali). Rebus: aya = iron (G.); ayah, ayas = metal (Skt.)

koṛa 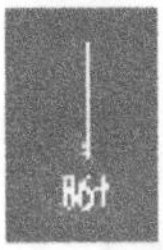

Glyph: one long linear stroke. koḍa, koṛa = in arithmetic one; 4 or koḍa = 1 gaṇḍa = 4 (Santali) Rebus: koḍ, 'artisan's workshop' (Kuwi.)

The text inscription reads rebus: Lathe-turner metal-ware workshop; brass-worker, furnace (stone ore) account (scribe); metal artisan's workshop.

kõdā 'lathe-turner'; *kāṇḍa* 'tools, pots and pans and metal-ware'. *sal* 'artisan's workshop'. taṭṭara 'worker in gold, brass'; *kaṇḍa kanka* furnace (stone ore) account (scribe); *koḍ* 'workshop'; *aya* 'metal'; *koḍ* 'artisan's workshop'

Thus set 2 is distinctively a different set of trade loads compared to set 1.

Set 2 has copper ingots of ironsmith, worker in wood and iron, smith working in iron with smithy/forge.

Set 1 has the trade loads of ironsmith with smithy/forge workshop, smith working as coiner in mint, with a smelter and artisan's workshop.

Thus, two specialist guilds of workers' bronze age products are being collected together to further compile the bills of lading for the two trade loads.

Indus writing "fish-eyes" traded with Ur

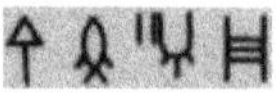

m0308 sāṅgāḍā सांगाडा frame of a building' (Marathi); saṅgaḍ 'portable furnace'; खांडा [khāṇḍā] *m* A jag, notch, or indentation (as upon the edge of a tool or weapon); *ayaskāṇḍa* is a compounded word attested in Panini. Rebus: aya 'iron' (G.) khāṇḍa 'tools, pots and pans, and metal-ware'. One-eyed glyph: *kāṇa* 'one-eyed'; rebus: *kāṇḍa* 'tools, pots and pans and metal-ware'; Glyph 'eyelashes': *Kol.* (SR.) kaṇlā mindī, (Kin.) kandl mindig (*pl.*) eyelash. *Go.* (A. Ch. Ma.) mindi, (Tr. W. Ph.) mindī id.; (M.) konḍā-mindī eyebrow; (Ko.) konḍa-minḍi eyelid, eyelash (*Voc.* 2831). / Cf. Halbi mendī eyelashes. (DEDR 4864). मेढा mēḍhā A twist or tangle arising in thread or cord, a curl or snarl. (Marathi) Rebus: meḍ 'iron' (Ho.)

bhaṭa 'six (hair-knots)'; rebus: *bhaṭa* 'furnace'. kola 'woman'; kol 'tiger'; rebus: kol 'iron'. Slide 90 harappa.com (one-eye glyph) kāṇá 'one -- eyed' RV. Pa. Pk. *kāṇa* -- 'blind of one eye, blind'; Ash. *kāṛa, °ṛī* f. 'blind', Kt. *kāŕ*, Wg. *kŕãmacrdotdot;*, Pr. *k&schwatildemacr;*, Tir. *kāˊna*, Kho. *kāṇu* NTS ii 260, *kánu* BelvalkarVol 91; K. *kônu* 'one -- eyed', S. *kāṇo*, L. P. *kāṇā*; WPah. rudh. śeu. *kāṇā* 'blind'; Ku. *kāṇo*, gng. *kã&rtodtilde;* 'blind of one eye', N. *kānu;* A. *kanā*ˋ 'blind'; B. *kāṇā* 'one -- eyed, blind'; Or. *kaṇā*, f. *kāṇī* 'one -- eyed', Mth. *kān, °nā, kanahā*, Bhoj. *kān*, f. *°ni, kanwā* m. 'one -- eyed man', H. *kān, °nā*, G. *kāṇũ*; M. *kāṇā* 'one -- eyed, squint -- eyed'; Si. *kaṇa* 'one -- eyed, blind'. -- Pk. *kāṇa* -- 'full of holes', G. *kāṇũ* 'full of holes', n. 'hole' (< ' empty eyehole '? Cf.*ādhḷũ* n. 'hole' < andhala --). kāṇá -- : S.kcch. *kāṇī* f.adj. 'one -- eyed'; WPah.kṭg. *kaṇɔ* 'blind in one eye', J. *kāṇā*; Md. *kanu* 'blind'.(CDIAL 3019).

Glyph: 'pair of tigers': kola 'tiger'. dula 'pair'. Rebus: dula kol 'casting working in iron'. Rebus: kol , *n.* < கொல்-. Working in iron; கொற்றொழில். 4. Blacksmith; கொல்லன். *கொல்லன் kollan̲ , n. < கொல்². [M. kollan.] Blacksmith; கருமான். மென்றோன் மிதியுலைக் கொல்லன் (பெரும்பாண். 207).* கொற்றுறை kor̲r̲ur̲ai , *n.* < கொல்² + துறை. Blacksmith's workshop, smithy; கொல்லன் பட் டடை. கொற்றுறைக் குற்றில (புறநா. 95). கொற்று[1] kor̲r̲u , *n.* prob. கொல்-. 1. Masonry, brickwork; கொற்றுவேலை. கொற்றுள விவரில் (திரு வாலவா. 30, 23). 2. Mason, bricklayer; கொத் தன். *Colloq.* 3. The measure of work turned out by a mason; ஒரு கொத்தன் செய்யும் வேலை யளவு. இந்தச் சுவர் கட்ட எத்தனை கொற்றுச் செல்லும்?

A count of six locks of hair on the bearded person in the middle, flanked by – holding apart -- two one-horned young bulls. Personified as bull-man (bearded person ligatured to the back of a bovine) battles with lions.

Ka. koṇḍe, goṇḍe tuft, tassel, cluster (DEDR 2081) Rebus: kŏnḍ क्ंड् or kŏnḍa क्ंड । कुण्ड m a deep still spring (El., Gr.Gr. 145); (amongst Hindūs) a hole dug in the ground for receiving consecrated fire (Kashmiri) *bhaṭa* 'six (hair-knots)'; rebus: *bhaṭa* 'furnace'. *kõdā* खोंड [khōṇḍa] m A young bull, a bullcalf. (Marathi) Rebus: A. *kundār*, B. *kũdār*, *°ri*, Or. *kundāru*; H. *kũderā* m. 'one who works a lathe, one who scrapes', *°rī* f., *kũdernā* ' to scrape, plane, round on a lathe '.(CDIAL 3297). Thus, *kũdār kŏnḍ* 'turner furnace (consecrated fire). మేడము mēḍamu] *mēḍamu.* [Tel.] n. Joining,union, కూడిక. A fight, battle, యుద్ధము (Telugu)

Rebus: *meḍ* 'iron' (Ho.) *aryeh* 'lion'. Rebus: *āra* 'brass' as in ārakūṭa (Skt.) ayir = iron dust, any ore (Ma.) Thus, *kũdār āra meḍ* 'iron, brass turner'.

The glyphics are repeated on a circular seal of Mohenjo-daro. It shows a warrior. Mohenjo-daro seal m417 six heads from a core.

The core is a glyphic 'chain' or 'ladder'. Glyph: kaḍī a chain; a hook; a link (G.); kaḍum a bracelet, a ring (G.) Rebus: kaḍiyo [Hem. Des. kaḍaio = Skt. sthapati a mason] a bricklayer; a mason; kaḍiyaṇa, kaḍiyeṇa a woman of the bricklayer caste; a wife of a bricklayer (G.)

The glyphics are:

1. Glyph: 'one-horned young bull': *kondh* 'heifer'. *kũdār* 'turner, brass-worker'.
2. Glyph: 'bull': *ḍhangra* 'bull'. *Rebus: ḍhangar* 'blacksmith'.
3. Glyph: 'ram': *meḍh* 'ram'. Rebus: *meḍ* 'iron'
4. Glyph: 'antelope': *mṛeka* 'goat'. Rebus: *milakkhu* 'copper'. Vikalpa 1: *meluhha* '*mleccha*' 'copper worker'. Vikalpa 2: *meṛh* 'helper of merchant'.
5. Glyph: 'zebu': *khũṭ* 'zebu'. Rebus: *khũṭ* 'guild, community' (Semantic determinant of the 'jointed animals' glyphic composition). *kūṭa* joining, connexion, assembly, crowd, fellowship (DEDR 1882) Pa. *gotta* 'clan'; Pk. *gotta, gōya* id. (CDIAL 4279) Semantics of Pkt. lexeme *gōya* is concordant with Hebrew *'goy'* in *ha-goy-im* (lit. the-nation-s). Pa. *gotta* -- n. ' clan ', Pk. *gotta* -- , *gutta* -- , amg. *gōya* -- n.; Gau. *gū* ' house ' (in Kaf. and Dard. several other words for ' cowpen ' > ' house ': gōṣṭhá -- , Pr. *gū´ṭu* ' cow '; S. *goṭru* m. ' parentage ', L. *got* f. ' clan ', P. *gotar, got* f.; Ku. N. *got* ' family '; A. *got -- nāti* ' relatives '; B. *got* ' clan '; Or. *gota* ' family, relative '; Bhoj. H. *got* m. ' family, clan ', G. *got* n.; M. *got* ' clan, relatives '; -- Si. *gota* ' clan, family ' ← Pa. (CDIAL 4279).

6. The sixth animal can only be guessed. Perhaps, a tiger (A reasonable inference, because the glyph 'tiger' appears in a procession on some Indus script

inscriptions. Glyph: 'tiger?': *kol* 'tiger'. Rebus: *kol* 'worker in iron'. Vikalpa (alternative): perhaps, rhinoceros. gaṇḍa 'rhinoceros'; rebus: khaṇḍ 'tools, pots and pans and metal-ware'. Thus, the entire glyphic composition of six animals on the Mohenjodaro seal m417 is semantically a representation of a *śrēṇi*, 'guild', a *khũṭ*, 'community' of smiths and masons.

This guild, community of smiths and masons evolves into Harosheth Hagoyim, 'a smithy of nations'.

A bas-relief in a fragment of a vessel has been reported from Salut, Oman. It has an Indian hieroglyph: A pair of hoods of snakes.

Hooded snake is shown on some Indus script inscriptions (e.g., tail of composite animal glyph on a Mohenjodaro seal).

Rebus reading: 'cast, sharp (tempered) alloy (metal, iron?)'

"Tempering is a heat treatment technique for metals, alloys and glass…The temperatures used in tempering are often too low to be gauged by the color of the workpiece. In this case, the blacksmith will heat the work piece for a known amount of time. Doing this ensures a certain degree of consistency in the tempering process from work piece to work piece. The cumulative effects of time and temperature can also be gauged by monitoring the color of the oxide film formed while tempering a well-polished blade."

Glyph: 'pair': dula 'pair'. Rebus: dul 'cast (metal)

Glyph: Glyph: 'cobra's hood': *paṭam* , *n.* < *phaṭa.* 1. Cobra's hood (CDIAL 9040). Rebus: 'sharpness of iron': *padm* (obl.*padt-*) temper of iron (Ko.)(DEDR 3907). *patam* 'sharpness, as of the edge of a knife' (Ta.)

Wing and eagle as hieroglyphs

eṟaka 'wing' (Telugu) Rebus: erako 'molten cast' (Tulu) loa 'ficus'; rebus: loh 'copper'. Pajhar 'eagle'; rebus: pasra 'smithy'. Thus the information conveyed by the glyphs on the Nal pot is thus related to: copper molten cast (metal) smithy.

Griffin, Baluchistan (Provenance unknown); ficus leaves, tiger, with a wing,

ligatured to an eagle. The ligature on the Nal pot ca 2800 BCE (Baluchisan: first settlement in southeastern Baluchistan was in the 4th millennium BCE) is extraordinary: an eagle's head is ligatured to the body of a tiger. In BMAC area, the 'eagle' is a recurrent motif on seals. Ute Franke-Vogt: "Different pottery styles link this area also to central and

northern Balochistan, and after about 2900/2800 BCE to southern Sindh where, at this time, the Indus Civilization took shape. The Nal pottery with its particular geometric and figurative patterns painted in blue, yellow, red and turquoise after firing is among the earliest and most dominanstyles in the south."

Lentoid seal with a griffin, ca. 1450–1400 B.C.;Late Minoan II Minoan; Greece, Crete Agate; H. 1 1/16 in. (2.7 cm), W. 1 1/16 (2.7 cm), Diam. ½ in. (1.2 cm) It is engraved with an image of a crouching griffin, a powerful mythical creature with the head and wings of a bird and the body of a lion. "This Minoan seal is lentoid, which describes its shape when viewed in profile. It is engraved with an image of a crouching griffin, a powerful mythical creature with the head and wings of a bird and the body of a lion. Before literacy became widespread, such seals served for identification or to mark ownership. While the first seals may have been made of organic materials that have perished, the earliest surviving examples are of clay. Later, in the Early Minoan period, various easily worked materials such as ivory,

bone, shell, and soft stones, including serpentine and steatite, were adopted. In the Middle and Late Minoan periods, harder stones such as rock crystal, hematite, jasper, agate, and chalcedony gained favor. The general dating of seals is correlated with that of the palaces that were the centers of culture on Crete. The apogee of Minoan gem engraving occurred during the time of the second palaces, between about 1600 and 1450 B.C., when semiprecious stones such as agate were engraved with consummately rendered figural subjects, particularly animals."

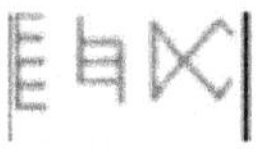

m1390Bt Text 2868 Pict-74: Bird in flight.m0451A,B Text3235 h166A,B Harappa Seal; Vats 1940, II: Pl. XCI.255.http://www.metmuseum.org

Bird-in-flight Mohenjodaro tablet (m1390) with Indus script inscription (Text 2868)

Sign 216 and variants. ḍato = claws of crab (Santali) ḍato 'claws or pincers (chelae) of crabs'; ḍaṭom, ḍiṭom to seize with the claws or pincers, as crabs, scorpions; ḍaṭkop = to pinch, nip (only of crabs) (Santali) Rebus: dhātu = mineral (Skt.)

Vikalpa: Ta. koṭiṟu pincers. Ma. koṭil tongs. Ko. koṛ hook of tongs. / Cf. Skt. (P. 4.4.18) kuṭilikā- smith's tongs.(DEDR 2052). ulai-k-kuṟaṭu smith's tongs (Ta.)

Vikalpa: erā 'claws'; Rebus: era 'copper'. Vikalpa: kamaṭha crab (Skt.) Rebus: kammaṭa = portable furnace (Te.) kampaṭṭam coiner, mint (Ta.) Vikalpa: sannī, sannhī = pincers, smith's vice (P.) Rebus: sāna 'grindstone' (Te.)

Peg 'khuṇṭa'; rebus: kūṭa 'workshop' khũṭi = pin (M.) kuṭi= smelter furnace (Santali) konḍu मूलिकादिघर्षणवस्तु m. a washerman's dressing iron (El. kunḍh); a scraper or grater for grating radishes, or the like; usually ° -- , the second member being the article to be grated, as in the following: -- kȧnḍi-mujü घर्षिता मूलिका f. grated radish, but mujĕ-konḍu, a radish-grater (cf. mujü). (Kashmiri) *khuṭṭa1 ' peg, post '. 2. *khuṇṭa -- 1. [Same as *khuṭṭa -- 2? -- See also kṣōḍa -- .]1. Ku. khuṭī ' peg '; N. khuṭnu ' to stitch ' (der. *khuṭ ' pin ' as khilnu

from khil s.v. khī́la --); Mth. khuṭā ' peg, post '; H. khūṭā m. ' peg, stump '; Marw. khuṭī f. ' peg '; M. khuṭā m. ' post '.2. Pk. khuṁṭa -- , khoṁṭaya -- m. ' peg, post '; Dm. kuṇḍa ' peg for fastening yoke to plough -- pole '; L. khū̃ḍī f. ' drum -- stick '; P. khuṇḍ, ḍā m. ' peg, stump '; WPah. rudh. khuṇḍ ' tethering peg or post '; A. khũṭā ' post ', ṭi ' peg '; B. khũṭā, ṭi ' wooden post, stake, pin, wedge '; Or. khuṇṭa, ṭā' pillar, post '; Bi. (with -- ḍa --) khũṭrā, rī ' posts about one foot high rising from body of cart '; H. khũṭā m. ' stump, log ', ṭī f. ' small peg ' (→ P.khũṭā m., ṭī f. ' stake, peg '); G. khũṭ f. ' landmark ', khũṭɔ m., ṭī f. ' peg ', ṭũ n. ' stump ', ṭiyũ n. ' upright support in frame of wagon ', khũṭṛũn. ' half -- burnt piece of fuel '; M. khũṭ m. ' stump of tree, pile in river, grume on teat ' (semant. cf. kīla -- 1 s.v. *khila -- 2), khũṭā m. ' stake ', ṭī f. ' wooden pin ', khũṭaḷṇẽ ' to dibble '.Addenda: *khuṭṭa -- 1. 2. *khuṇṭa -- 1: WPah.kṭg. khv́ndɔ ' pole for fencing or piling grass round ' (Him.I 35 nd poss. wrong for ṇḍ); J. khuṇḍā m. ' peg to fasten cattle to '. (CDIAL 3893) Vikalpa: pacar = a wedge driven ino a wooden pin, wedge etc. to tighten it (Santali.lex.) pasra = a smithy, place where a black-smith works, to work as a blacksmith; kamar pasra = a smithy; pasrao lagao akata se ban:? Has the blacksmith begun to work? pasraedae = the blacksmith is at his work (Santali.lex.)

The ligatured Glyph 382 is decoded as: dul mũhã kharādī 'cast bronze ingot turner'. kharedo = a currycomb (G.) Rebus: kharādī ' turner' (G.)

The following pair terminates 184 inscriptions:

    (10) (Variant sign pair, sign sequence reversed).

The following pairs of signs terminate 8 and 26 sequences, respectively:

Glyph 12: kuṭi 'water-carrier' (Te.); Rebus: kuṭhi 'smelter' (Santali) kharedo = a currycomb (G.) Rebus: kharādī ' turner' (G.) Vikalpa: kāmsako, kāmsiyo = a large sized comb (G.); Rebus: kãsāri 'pewterer' (Bengali) The ligature of 'rim of jar' glyph is denoted by the ligatured Glyph 15; this ligaturing glyptic element has been decoded as 'furnace scribe'. Thus, the pair of Glyph 176 together with either Glyph 342 or Glyhph 15 can be read, respectively

as: kuṭhi kan-ka kharādī 'smelter-furnace-scribe, turner' or kan-ka kharādī 'scribe, turner'.

Vikalpa: kāmsako, kāmsiyo = a large sized comb (G.) Rebus: kaṁsa= bronze (Te.) kāsāri 'pewterer' (Bengali) kãsārī; H. kasārī m. ' maker of brass pots' (Or.) Rebus: kaṁsá1 m. ' metal cup ' AV., m.n. ' bell -- metal ' Pat. as in S., but would in Pa. Pk. and most NIA. lggs. collide with kā´ṁsya -- to which L. P. testify and under which the remaining forms for the metal are listed. 2. *kaṁsikā -- .1. Pa. kaṁsa -- m. ' bronze dish '; S. kañjho m. ' bellmetal '; A. kāh ' gong '; Or. kãsā ' big pot of bell -- metal '; OMarw. kāso (= kā -- ?) m. ' bell -- metal tray for food, food '; G. kāsā m. pl. ' cymbals '; -- perh. Woṭ. kasṓṭ m. ' metal pot ' Buddruss Woṭ 109. 2. Pk. kaṁsiā -- f. ' a kind of musical instrument '; A. kāhi ' bell -- metal dish '; G. kāśī f. ' bell -- metal cymbal ',kāśiyɔ m. 'open bellmetal pan' kā´ṁsya -- ; -- *kaṁsāvatī -- ? Addenda: kaṁsá -- 1: A. kāh also ' gong ' or < kā´ṁsya – (CDIAL 2576). kāṁsya ' made of bell -- metal ' KātyŚr., n. ' bell -- metal ' Yājñ., ' cup of bell -- metal ' MBh., aka -- n. ' bell -- metal '. 2. *kāṁsiya -- .[kaṁsá -- 1] 1. Pa. kaṁsa -- m. (?) ' bronze ', Pk. kaṁsa -- , kāsa -- n. ' bell -- metal, drinking vessel, cymbal '; L. (Jukes) kājā adj. ' of metal ', awāṇ. kāsā ' jar ' (← E with -- s-- , not ñj); N. kāso ' bronze, pewter, white metal ', kas -- kuṭ ' metal alloy '; A. kāh ' bell -- metal ', B. kāsā, Or. kāsā, Bi. kāsā; Bhoj. kās ' bell -- metal ',kāsā ' base metal '; H. kās, kāsā m. ' bell -- metal ', G. kāsũ n., M. kāsẽ n.; Ko. kāśẽ n. ' bronze '; Si. kasa ' bell -- metal '. 2. L. kāihā m. ' bell -- metal ', P. kāssī, kāsī f., H. kāsī f.*kāṁsyakara -- , kāṁsyakāra -- , *kāṁsyakuṇḍikā -- , kāṁsyatāla -- , *kāṁsyabhāṇḍa -- .Addenda: kāṁsya -- : A. kāh also ' gong ', or < kaṁsá -- . (CDIAL 2987).*kāṁsyakara ' worker in bell -- metal '. [See next: kāṁsya -- , kará -- 1] L. awāṇ. kasērā ' metal worker ', P. kaserā m. ' worker in pewter ' (both ← E with -- s --); N. kasero ' maker of brass pots '; Bi. H. kaserā m. ' worker in pewter '. (CDIAL 2988). kāṁsyakāra m. ' worker in bell -- metal or brass ' Yājñ. com., kaṁsakāra -- m. BrahmavP. [kā´ṁsya -- , kāra -- 1] N. kasār ' maker of brass pots '; A. kāhār ' worker in bell -- metal '; B. kāsāri ' pewterer, brazier, coppersmith ', Or. kãsārī; H. kasārī m. ' maker of brass pots '; G.kāsārɔ, kas m. ' coppersmith '; M. kāsār, kās m. ' worker in white metal ', kāsārḍā m. ' contemptuous term for the same '. (CDIAL 2989).

The eagle on Mohenjodaro tablet reads: pajhar, which connotes (rebus): pasra 'smithy, forge'. The inscription on Mohenjodaro tablet m1390 reads: dhatu kuta 'mineral workshop'; the comb, kharedo is read rebus: kharadi, 'maker of brass pots'. These are rebus readings based on the Indian linguistic area.

It would thus appear that the user of Indus script hieroglyphs on the Gonur Tepe inscriptions – showing eagle hieroglyphs, wings of falcon (seals/seal impressions) is describing the nature of metalworking he or she is engaged in. It would also appear that the explanations of the narratives in Rigveda and in Mesopotamian hieroglyphs (cf. Apkallu) are echoes of these metalworking activities of Indus artisans (smiths and mine-workers).

Electrum is believed to have been used in coins circa 600 BC in Lydia under the reign of Alyattes II.

Early 6th century BC Lydian electrum coin (one-third stater denomination). KINGS of Lydia. Uncertain King. Early 6th century BC. EL Third Stater - Trite (4.71 gm). Head of roaring lion right, sun with multiple rays on forehead / Double incuse punch. In Lydia, electrum was minted into 4.7-gram coins, each valued at 1/3 stater (meaning "standard"). Three of these coins (with a weight of about 14.1 grams, almost half an ounce) totaled one stater, about one month's pay for a soldier. To complement the stater, fractions were made: the trite (third), the hekte (sixth), and so forth, including 1/24 of a stater, and even down to 1/48th and 1/96th of a stater. The 1/96 stater was only about 0.14 to 0.15 grams. Larger denominations, such as a one stater coin, were minted as well.

An image of the obverse of a Lydian coin made of electrum

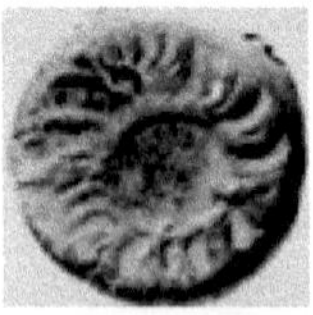

The 'wart' on the nose of the tiger.

Is it intended to depict rays of the sun?

M428b The 'rays of the sun' glyph of this Mohenjodaro seal also recurs on early punch-marked coins of India. Rebus reading:

arka 'sun'; agasāle 'goldsmithy' (Ka.) erka = ekke (Tbh. of arka) aka (Tbh. of arka) copper (metal); crystal (Ka.lex.) cf. eruvai = copper (Ta.lex.) eraka, er-aka = any metal infusion (Ka.Tu.); erako molten cast (Tulu) Rebus: eraka = copper (Ka.) eruvai = copper (Ta.); ere - a dark-red colour (Ka.)(DEDR 817). eraka, era, er-a = syn. erka, copper, weapons (Ka.)

Or, does the 'wart' glyph connote a polar star? If so, the lexeme could be: mēḍha 'The polar star' (Marathi). Does it make a rebus reading of Medes? "The original source for different words used to call the Median people, their language and homeland is a directly transmitted Old Iranian geographical name which is attested as the Old Persian "Māda-" (sing. masc.).The meaning of this word is not precisely established. The linguist W. Skalmowski proposes a relation with the proto-Indoeuropean word "med(h)-" meaning "central, suited in the middle" by referring to Old Indic "madhya-" and Old Iranic "maidiia-" both carrying the same meaning."[99]

med(h) 'central, middle'; rebus: *meḍ* 'iron' (Ho.)

It is remarkable that the Indian linguistic area attests the following lexeme for sun: aru m. ' sun ' lex. Kho. yor Morgenstierne NTS ii 276 with ? <-> Whence y -- ? (CDIAL 612)

Some glyphs used in the writing were combined to form words which sounded like the glyphs. For example, the glyph 'arrow' sounded like the word kāṇḍa which also expressed meaning in a similar sounding word: Pa. *khaṇḍa* -- ' broken (usu. of teeth) ', m.n. ' piece ', *°ḍikā* -- f. ' broken bit, stick '; Pk. *khaṁḍa* -- m.n., *°ḍiā* -- f. ' piece '; P. *khannā* adj. ' half ', *°nī* f. ' piece '; Ku. *dwī* -- *khan* ' two halves ', *khānuṛo* ' piece '; B. *khān, °nā, °ni* ' piece, article (as a determinative) ' ; Bhoj. *khāṛā* ' piece '; K. *khaṇḍarun* ' to break in pieces '; H. *khaṇḍar* ' broken ', m. ' hole, pit ', *khāṛar* ' dilapidated ', m. ' broken ground, chasm, hole ' (CDIAL 3792). *gaṇḍa*-- m. ' piece, part ' (Buddhist Hybrid Sanskrrit), which also meant

'four' to be represented by four short linear strokes. The 'arrow' glyph was combined with another 'fish' glyph which was pronounced *ayo*, 'fish' to create the text *ayaskāṇḍa* 'metal piece, part'.

A miniature, incised tablet from Harappa h329A has a fish-shaped tablet with two signs: fish + arrow (which combination was also pronounced as *ayaskāṇḍa* on a *bos indicus* seal Kalibangan032).

The dotted circle (eye) is decoded rebus as *kaṇ* 'aperture' (Tamil); kāṇũ hole (Gujarati) (i.e. glyph showing dotted-circle); kāṇa 'one eye' and these glyphs may have been interpreted as the 'fish-eyes' or 'eye stones' (Akkadian IGI-HA, IGI-KU6) mentioned in Mesopotamian texts. ayo 'fish' 9Mu.); rebus: aya = iron (G.); ayah, ayas = metal (Skt.) kaṇi 'stone' (Kannada) கன்[1] kaṉ Copper (Tamil) கன்[2] kaṉ , n. < கல். stone (Tamil) खडा (Marathi) is 'metal, nodule, stone, lump'. *kaṇi* 'stone' (Kannada) with Tadbhava *khaḍu*. *khaḍu, kaṇ* 'stone/nodule (metal)'. . Ga. (Oll.) kanḍ, (S.) kanḍu (pl. kanḍkil) stone (DEDR 1298). These could be the substratum glosses for *kāṇḍa* in ayas *kāṇḍa* 'excellent iron' (Pan.) 'metal tools, pots and pans and metal-ware'. h329A has a fish-shaped tablet with two signs: fish + arrow (which has been decoded as *ayaskāṇḍa* on a *bos indicus* seal). The 'fish-eye' is a reinforcement of the gloss *kāṇḍ* stone/nodule (metal)'. The dotted circle (eye) is decoded rebus as *kaṇ* 'aperture' (Tamil); kāṇũ hole (Gujarati) (i.e. glyph showing dotted-circle); kāṇa 'one eye' and these glyphs may have been interpreted as the 'fish-eyes' or 'eye stones' (Akkadian IGI-HA, IGI-KU6) mentioned in Mesopotamian texts. The commodities denoted may be nodules of mined stones/nodules of chalcopyrite. See Annex. 'Eye stones' elucidating, based on textual and archaeological contexts, that 'fish-eyes' do NOT refer to pearls. While one surmises that they refer to agate stones, it can be evidenced that the glyphs of 'dotted circles' denoting 'fish-eyes' or 'antelope-eyes', refer to

'stone/nodules of mineral (perhaps, chalcopyrite)' or 'tools, pots and pans and metal-ware', decoded rebus as *kāṇḍ* as in *ayaskāṇḍa* 'excellent iron'.

Combination of 'fish' glyph and 'four-short-linear-strokes' circumgraph also pronounced the same text *ayaskāṇḍa* on another *bos indicus* seal m1118. This

seal uses circumgraph of four short linear strokes which included a morpheme which was pronounced variantly as *gaṇḍa* 'four' (Santali).

Thus, the circumgraph of four linear strokes used on m1118 Mohenjo-daro seal was an allograph for 'arrow' glyph used on h329A Harappa tablet.

The hieroglyphic use of 'fish' glyph on Indus writing resolves the transactions related 'fish-eyes' traded between Ur and Meluhha mentioned in cuneiform texts as related to ayas 'fish' and *khoṭ* 'alloyed metal':

A 'hole' or a 'diotted-circle' glyph may denote a word which was pronounced *khoṭ* 'alloyed metal':

खोट [khōṭa] *f* A mass of metal (unwrought or of old metal melted down); an ingot or wedge. Hence खोटसाळ [khōṭasāḷa] *a* (खोट & साळ from शाला) Alloyed--a metal. (Marathi) Bshk. *khoṭ* 'embers', Phal. *khūṭo* 'ashes, burning coal'; L. *khoṭ* 'alloy, impurity', *°ṭā* 'alloyed', awāṇ. *khoṭā* 'forged'; P. *khoṭ* m. 'base, alloy' M.*khoṭā* 'alloyed' (CDIAL 3931)

Kor. (O.) goḍe a rat's hole (DEDR 1660). Pk. *kōḍara* -- , *kōla°*, *kōṭa°*, *koṭṭa°* n. ' hole, hollow '; Or. *koraṛa* ' hollow in a tree, cave, hole '; H. (X *khōla -- 2) *khoḍar* m. ' pit, hollow in a tree ', *khoṛrā* m.; Si.*kovuḷa* ' rotten tree ' (< **kōḷalla* -- with H. Smith JA 1950, 197, but not < Pa. *kōḷāpa* --). (CDIAL 3496).

Thus, the 'dotted circle' glyph may be distinguished from a 'wort' glyph (which is a blob or small lump). The dotted circle denotes: *khaṇḍa* 'tools, pots and pans and metal-ware'

[quote] The suggestion that 'fish-eyes' (IGI.HA, IGI-KU6), imported through Ur, may have been pearls has been advanced by a number of scholars. 'Fish-eyes' were among a number of valuable commodities (gold, copper, lapis lazuli, stone beads) offered in thanksgiving at the temple of the Sumerian goddess Ningal at Ur by seafaring merchants who had returned safely from Dilmun and perhaps further afield. Elsewhere they are said to have been bought in Dilmun. Whether 'fish-eyes' differed from 'fish-eye stones' (NA4 IGI.HA, NA4 IGI-KU6) and from simply 'eye-stones' is not entirely clear. The latter are included among goods imported from Meluhha (NA4 IGI-ME-LUH-HA) ca. 1816-1810 BCE and ca. 1600-1570 BCE. Any pearls from Meluhha – probably coastal Baluchistan-Sind – would have been generally inferior to those from Dilmun itself. It has been strongly argued that 'fish-eyes', 'fish-eye stones' and 'eye-stones' in Old Babylonian and Akkadian texts were not in fact pearls, but rather (a) etched cornelian beads, imported from India and/or (b) pebbles of banded agate, cut to resemble closely a black/brown pupil and white cornea. The nearest source of good agate is in northwest India, which would accord with supplies obtained from Meluhha. 'Eye-stones' of agate were undoubtedly treasured: some were inscribed and used as amulets, others have been found in votive deposits. Perhaps pearls were at times included among 'fish-eyes,' if not 'fish-eye stones'. More likely, however, the word for 'pearl' is among the 'more than 800 terms in the lexical lists of stones and gems [that] remain to be identified.[unquote][100]

Circular working platform as a workshop (anvil, smithy, forge)

Example of a worker's platforfm at Harappa.

Many such circular working platforms were discovered. A lexeme of indian linguistic area which described a circular working platform of the type found at harappa: ku. Pathrauṭī f. '

pavement of slates and stones '(cdial 8858) ta. Paṭṭaṭai, paṭṭarai anvil, smithy, forge. Ka. Paṭṭaḍe, paṭṭaḍi anvil, workshop. Te. Paṭṭika, paṭṭeḍa anvil; paṭṭaḍa

workshop.(dedr 3865). கடைசற்பட்டறை kaṭaicar-paṭṭarai , n. < id. +. turner's shop; கடைசல்வேலைசெய்யுஞ் சாலை. pathürü f. ' level piece of ground, plateau, small village '; s. patharu m. ' rug, mat '; or. athuripathuri ' bag and baggage '; m. pāthar f. ' flat stone '; omarw. pātharī ' precious stone '.(CDIAL 8857) allograph indus script glyph: pātra 'trough' in front of wild/domesticated/composite animals. pattar 'trough' (dedr 4079) 4080 ta. cavity, hollow, deep hole; pattar (dedr 4080) rebus: பத்தர்² pattar , n. < t. battuḍu. a caste title of goldsmiths. it was a smiths' guild at work on circular platforms of harappa using tablets as category 'tallies' for the final shipment of package with a seal impression.

Trough as a hieroglyph

ಪಟ್ಟಲೆ paṭṭalĕ. A district, a community. (R.).

See examples of 'trough' glyph are shown in front of wild, domesticated and composite animals — an evidence for the use of 'trough' glyph as a hieroglyph, together with the 'animal' glyph. Maybe, the 19 circular working platforms of Harappa were used for assembling 19 'types' of products — the 'trough' glyph denoting the working platform and the 'animal' glyph denoting the product type (e.g. copper, gold, metal alloy, output of furnaces (of various types), minerals).

ಪಟ್ಟಡಿ paṭṭu 2-aḍi 4. = ಪಟ್ಟಡೆ, q. v. (My.; Sk. 390). 2, = ಪಟ್ಟಡಿಮನೆ (My.). — ಪಟ್ಟಡಸಾಲೆ. A workshop (ಅಕ್ಕಸಾಲೆ, ಕಮ್ಮಾರಸಾಲೆ Sl. 108; My.).

Identical glyphs on 8

tablets which flank the 'backbone' glyph on these tablets is an oval (variant 'rhombus') sign — like a metal ingot — and is ligatured with an infixed sloping stroke: ḍhāḷiyum = adj. sloping, inclining (G.). This example of a uniquely scripted tablet with raised Indus writing glyphs shows that copper tablets were also used in Harappa, while hundreds of copper tablets with incised script inscriptions were found in Mohenjo-daro. *dul mũh khāṇḍā* 'cast ingot tools, pots and pans and metal-ware'. The ligatured glyph (oval with infixed jag) is read rebus as: ḍhālako = a large metal ingot (G.) ḍhālakī = a metal heated and poured into a mould; a solid piece of metal; an ingot (G.) ḍhāḷiyum = adj. sloping, inclining (G.) खांडा [*khāṇḍā*] *m* a jag, notch, or indentation (as upon the edge of a tool or weapon).

Rebus: *kaṇḍa* 'stone (ore)(Gadba)'. . Ga. (Oll.) kanḍ, (S.) kanḍu (pl. kanḍkil) stone (DEDR 1298).

kaṇḍ 'backbone' (Lahnda); rebus: *kaṇḍ* 'furnace, fire-altar' (Santali)

h1931A

h1931B

h1931C

h1827A

h1827B

h1302A

h1302B

h1303A

h1303B

h1932A

h1932B

h1932C These examples show a thre-glyph sequence including an 'E-shaped' glyph, like the teeth of a currycomb.

kharedo = a currycomb (G.) Rebus: *kharādī* ' turner' (G.)

Pa. *piṭṭhi -- kaṇṭaka* -- m. 'bone of the spine'; Tir. *mar -- kaṇḍḗ* 'back (of the body)'; S. *kaṇḍo* m. 'back', L. *kaṇḍ kaṇḍā* m. 'backbone', awāṇ. *kaṇḍ, °ḍī* 'back'; P. *kaṇḍ* f. 'back, pubes'; N. *kaṇḍo* 'buttock, rump, anus', *kaṇḍeulo* 'small of the back'; Or. *kaṇṭi* 'handle of a plough'; H. *kā̃ṭā* m. 'spine', G. *kā̃ṭɔ* m., M. *kā̃ṭā* m.; *piṭa -- k°* 'backbone'.2. Pk. *kaṁḍa* -- m. 'backbone'.3. Pk. *karaṁḍa* -- m.n. 'bone shaped like a bamboo', *karaṁḍuya* -- n. 'backbone'. (CDIAL 2670).

kaśēru 'the backbone' (Bengali. Skt.); kaśēruka id. (Skt.) Rebus: kasērā' metal worker ' (Lahnda)(CDIAL 2988, 2989) L. awāṇ. Kasērā ' metal worker ', P. kaserā m. ' worker in pewter ' (both ← E with — s --); N. kasero ' maker of brass pots '; Bi. H. kaserā m. ' worker in pewter '. (CDIAL 2988) கசம்¹ kacam , n. cf. ayas. (அக. நி.) 1. Iron; இரும்பு. 2. Mineral fossil; தாதுப்பொருள் (Tamil) N. kasār ' maker of brass pots '; A. kāhār ' worker in bell — metal '; B. kāsāri ' pewterer, brazier, coppersmith ', Or. Kāsārī; H. kasārī m. ' maker of brass pots '; G.kāsārɔ, kas m. ' coppersmith '; M. kāsār, kās m. ' worker in white metal ', kāsārḍā m. ' contemptuous term for the same '. (CDIAL 2989)

These eight copper tablets with raised writing were found on circular platforms. The circular platforms functioned as sorting, marketing platforms if, in the center of the circle, a storage pot containing metal artefacts, beads, ivory products etc. were kept for display, marketing, trade. [The center of the circle may also have held a drill-lathe as guild trade platforms for artisans of forge/smithy and lapidaries.] "During excavations of the circular platform area on Mound F numerous Cemetery H-type sherds and some complete vessels were recovered in association with pointed base goblets and large storage vessels that are usually associated with Harappa Period 3C." South fo the platforms was a furnace. "A large kiln was also found just below the surface of the mound to the south of the circular platforms."[101] The circular platforms are used in conjunction with the products taken out of the kiln (furnace) and large storage vessels which could have been plced in the center of any of the street platforms, constituting the main market street of early times of Harappa settlement. Circular platforms

(with a dia. of 1.5 m) found within rooms (of a coppersmith) as in Padri might have served as working platforms for the brass-workers, lapidaries, artisans of the civilization or as a display counter if the room was used as a shop for sales.

Pattharika [fr. Patthara] a merchant Vin ii.135 (kaŋsa˚). (Pali) [An allograph pattara 'trough' is a glyph used in front of many types of animals including wild animals and composite animal glyphs. Pātra 'trough'; pattar 'merchant'. The lexeme also connotes a 'guild'.]

Glyph: पात्र pātra, (l.) s. Vessel, cup, plate; receptacle. [lw. Sk. Id.] (Nepali) pātramu A utensil, ఉపకరణము. Hardware. Metal vessels. (Telugu) பத்தல் pattal, n. பத்தர்[1] pattar 1. A wooden bucket; மரத்தாலான நீரிறைக்குங் கருவி. தீம்பிழி யெந்திரம் பத்தல் வருந்த (பதிற்றுப். 19, 23).

Rebus: பத்தர்[2] pattar , n. < T. battuḍu. A caste title of goldsmiths; தட்டார் பட்டப்பெயருள் ஒன்று. பட்டடை[1] paṭṭaṭai , n. prob. படு[1]- + அடை[1]-. 1. [T. paṭṭika, K. paṭṭaḍe.] Anvil; அடைகல். (பிங்.) சீரிடங்காணி னெறிதற்குப் பட்ட டை (குறள், 821). 2. [K. paṭṭaḍi.] Smithy, forge; கொல்லன் களரி பத்தல் pattal , n. 1. A wooden bucket; மரத்தாலான நீரிறைக்குங் கருவி. தீம்பிழி யெந்திரம் பத்தல் வருந்த (பதிற்றுப். 19, 23). பத்தர்[1] pattar , n. 1. See பத்தல், 1, 4, 5. 2. Wooden trough for feeding animals; தொட்டி. பன்றிக் கூழ்ப்பத்தரில் (நாலடி, 257).

WPah. páttʰər m. ' stone, rock '; pəthreuṇõ ' to stone '; J. pāthar m. ' stone '; Omarw. Pātharī ' precious stone '. (CDIAL 8857) paṭṭarai 'workshop' (Ta.)

Paṭṭar-ai community; guild as of workmen (Ta.); pattar merchants; perh. Vartaka (Skt.) వడ్లబత్తుడు *vaḍrangi.* [Tel.] n. A carpenter. బత్తుడు *battuḍu.* n. A worshipper. భక్తుడు The caste title of all the five castes of artificers as వడ్లబత్తుడు a carpenter. కడుపుబత్తుడు one who makes a god of his belly. L. xvi. 230.(Telugu) The merchant, *battuḍu, pattar is shown in a worshipful state kneeling in adoration on many inscriptions.*

Entrustment articles जांगड jāṅgaḍa of metal (copper alloys, *khoṭā* alloyed forged ingots, turner)'

m1405 Tablet. Person standing at the center points with his right hand at a bison facing a trough, and with his left hand points to the ligatured glyph. This tablet is a clear and unambiguous example of the fundamental orthographic style of Indus Script inscriptions that: both signs and pictorial motifs are integral components of the message conveyed by the inscriptions. The inscription on the tablet juxtaposes – through the hand gestures of a person - a 'trough' gestured with the right hand; a ligatured glyph composed of 'rim-of-jar' glyph and 'water-carrier' glyph (Sign 15) gestured with the left hand.

The inscription of this tablet is composed of four glyphs: bison, trough, shoulder (person), ligatured glyph -- Glyph 15 (rim-of-jar glyph ligatured to water-carrier glyph).

Variants for Glyph 15 (Mahadevan)

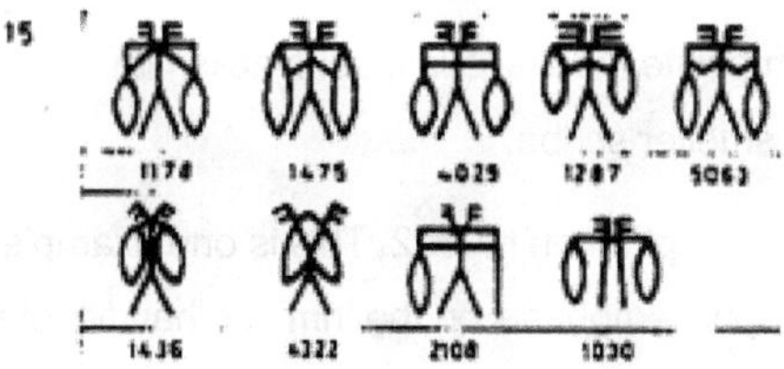

Variants (Parpola)

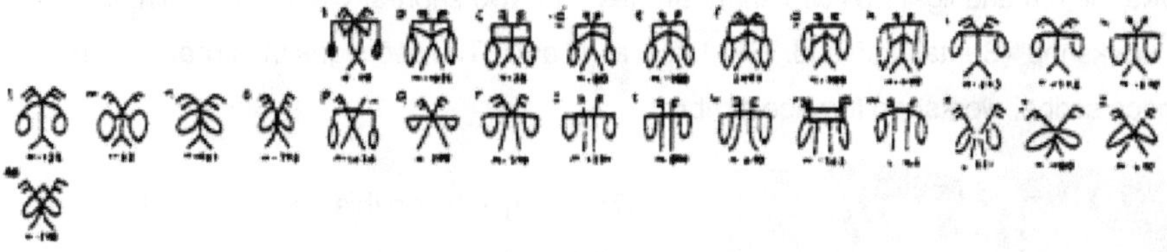

ḍangur m. 'bullock', rebus: ḍāṅro 'blacksmith' (Nepali)

pattar 'trough' (Ta.), rebus paṭṭar-ai community; guild as of workmen (Ta.); pattar merchants (Ta.); perh. vartaka (Skt.) pātharī 'precious stone' (OMarw.) (CDIAL 8857)

meḍ 'body' (Mu.); rebus: meḍ 'iron' (Ho.); *eṛaka* 'upraised arm' (Ta.); rebus: *eraka* 'copper' (Kannada)

Ligature in composite glyph: kan-ka 'rim of jar' (Santali), rebus karṇaka 'scribe, accountant' (Pa.); vikalpa: 1. kāraṇika -- m. 'arrow-maker' (Pa.) 2. khanaka 'miner, digger,

excavator' (Skt.). Ligature 2 in composite glyph: kuṭi 'water-carrier' (Telugu), rebus: kuṭhi 'smelter furnace' (Santali)

Water-carrier glyph kuṭi 'water-carrier' (Telugu); Rebus: kuṭhi 'smelter furnace' (Santali) kuṛī f. 'fireplace' (H.); krvṛı f. 'granary (WPah.); kuṛī, kuṛo house, building'(Ku.)(CDIAL 3232) kuṭi 'hut made of boughs' (Skt.) guḍi temple (Telugu) [The bull is shown in front of the trough for drinking; hence the semantics of 'drinking'.]

The most frequently occurring glyph is thus explained as a 'furnace scribe' and is consistent with the readings of glyphs which occur together with this glyph. Kan-ka may denote an artisan working with copper, kaṉ (Ta.) kaṉṉār 'coppersmiths, blacksmiths' (Ta.) Thus, the phrase kaṇḍ karṇaka may be decoded rebus as a brassworker, scribe. karṇaka 'scribe, accountant'.

A splinter glyph – two short strokes -- is ligatured within the rim of jar glyph. sal stake, spike, splinter, thorn, difficulty (H.); Rebus: sal 'workshop' (Santali)

The composite message is thus: blacksmith, merchant, copper smelter scribe.

Text of inscription on m0892. This is one example of the orthographic emphasis on the 'rim' or 'handle' of the short-necked jar on two glyphs: one shows the rim and the other shows the rim and ligatures two short-strokes. The two short-strokes are a splinter; rebus: sal 'workshop' (Santali); śāla id. (Skt.). ālai id. (Tamil) The two signs thus read, rebus: furnace scribe, workshop furnace scribe.

m1179 The glyphs on this seal are: markhor, scarf, wavy (curved) lines, rim-of-jar.

miṇḍāl 'markhor' (Tōrwālī) meḍho a ram, a sheep (G.)(CDIAL 10120); rebus: mẽṛhet, meḍ 'iron' (Mu.Ho.) ['scarf' glyph is ligatured on the neck of markhor. Scarf [read rebus as dhaṭu m. (also dhaṭhu) m. 'scarf' (WPah.) (CDIAL 6707) Rebus: dhatu 'minerals' (Santali); dhātu 'mineral' (Pali)].

Wavy(curved) lines glyph is relatable to: *kuṭi*— in cmpd. 'curve' (Skt.)(CDIAL 3231). Rebus: *khoṭ e* 'alloyed' (Marathi). *koṭe* 'forging (metal)(Mu.)

kuṭika— 'bent' MBh. [√kuṭ 1] Ext. in H. kuṛuk f. 'coil of string or rope'; M. kuḍcā m.

'palm contracted and hollowed', kuḍapṇẽ 'to curl over, crisp, contract'. CDIAL 3231 Ta. koṭu curved, bent, crooked; koṭumai crookedness, obliquity; koṭukki hooked bar for fastening doors, clasp of an ornament. A pair of curved lines: dol 'likeness, picture, form' [e.g., two tigers, two bulls, sign-pair.] Kashmiri. dula दुल । युग्मम् m. a pair, a couple, esp. of two similar things (Rām. 966)

Glyph 'leaf, petal': A 'leaf' glyph has to be distinguished from a 'petals' glyph because the leaf orthography is clearly representative of the *ficus* genus which attains sacredness in later historical periods in the Indian linguistic area.

Glyptic elements of m296 seal impression: 1. Two heads of one-horned young bulls; 2. ligatured to a pair of rings and a standard device; 3. ligatured to a precise count of nine leaves. Read rebus: koḍiyum 'heifer, rings on neck'; खोंड [khōṇḍa] m A young bull, a bullcalf. (Marathi) గోద [gōda] gōda. [Tel.] n. An ox. A beast. kine, cattle.(Telugu) koḍiyum (G.) Rebus : B. kõdā 'to turn in a lathe'; Or. kũnda 'lathe', kũdibā, kũd 'to turn' (→ Drav. Kur. kũd 'lathe') (CDIAL 3295). Rebus: koḍ 'workshop' (Kuwi.G.); dula 'pair' (Kashmiri); rebus: dul 'cast metal' (Mu.) lo, no 'nine' (B.); loa 'ficus religiosa' (Santali); rebus: loh 'metal' (Skt.); loa 'copper' (Santali) sangaḍa 'jointed animals' (Marathi); sangaḍa 'lathe' (G.) Rebus: jaṅgaḍ 'entrusment articles'. Part of the pictorial motif is thus decoded rebus: loh dul koḍ 'metal cast(ing) smithy turner (lathe) workshop'. Part of the inscription is read rebus: *ayaskāṇḍa kole.l* 'smithy, excellent quantity of iron'.

The stem in the orthographic composition relates to *sangaḍa* 'lathe/furnace' (yielding crucible stone ore nodules), the standard device which is depicted frequently in front of 'one-horned heifer'. Rebus: *sangāta* 'association, guild' or, *sangatarāsu* 'stone-cutter' (Telugu). The 'globules' glyphic joining the two ringed necks of a pair of one-horned heifers may connote: goṭi. It may connote a forge.

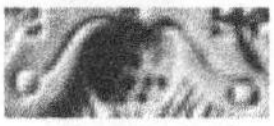

Glyph: 'piece'; the two rings emanating from the top of the portable

furnace denote *khoṭā* 'forged'; *khoṭa* 'alloy': guḍá—1. — In sense 'fruit, kernel' cert. ← Drav., cf. Tam. koṭṭai 'nut, kernel'; A. goṭ 'a fruit, whole piece', °ṭā 'globular, solid', guṭi 'small ball, seed, kernel'; B. goṭā 'seed, bean, whole'; Or. goṭā 'whole, undivided', goṭi 'small ball, cocoon', goṭāli 'small round piece of chalk'; Bi. goṭā 'seed'; Mth. goṭa 'numerative particle' (CDIAL 4271) Rebus: *khoṭ* m. 'base, alloy' (Punjabi) Rebus: koṭe 'forging (metal)(Mu.) Rebus: goṭī f. 'lump of silver' (G.) goṭi = silver (G.) koḍ 'workshop' (G.). Glyph: 'two links in a chain': kaḍī a chain; a hook; a link (G.); kaḍum a bracelet, a ring (G.) Rebus: kaḍiyo [Hem. Des. kaḍaio = Skt. sthapati a mason] a bricklayer; a mason; kaḍiyaṇa, kaḍiyeṇa a woman of the bricklayer caste; a wife of a bricklayer (G.) The stone-cutter is also a mason.

kamaḍha = *ficus religiosa* (Skt.); kamar.kom 'ficus' (Santali) rebus: kamaṭa = portable furnace for melting precious metals (Te.); kampaṭṭam = mint (Ta.) Vikalpa: Fig leaf 'loa'; rebus: loh '(copper) metal'. loha-kāra 'metalsmith' (Skt.).

Text on m296 seal.

Glyphs: ayas 'fish'. Rebus: aya 'metal'. Glyph: *kaṇḍa* 'arrow' Rebus: 'stone (ore)metal'; kaṇḍa 'fire-altar'. *ayaskāṇḍa* is explained in Panini as 'excellent quantity of iron' or 'tools, pots and pans and metal-ware'.

The last sign on epigraph 5477 and 1554 (m296 seal) is read as: kole.l = smithy, temple in Kota village (Ko.) *sāgāḍā* m. ' frame of a building ' (M.)(CDIAL 12859) Rebus: जांगड jāṅgaḍa *f* (H) Goods taken from a shop, to be retained or returned as may suit: also articles of apparel taken from a tailor or clothier to sell for him or जांगड वही The account or account-book of goods so taken.

Thus, the three text sign sequence can be explained rebus as smithy for metal of stone (ore) iron.

There are two glyphs preceding the 'fish' glyph on Text of m296 seal: *ḍhāḷako* 'a large metal ingot' and *khāṇḍā* 'tools, pots and pans, metal-

ware'.खांडा khāṇḍā *m* A jag, notch, or indentation (as upon the edge of a tool or weapon). A gap in the teeth. Rebus: *khāṇḍā* 'tools, pots and pans, metal-ware'. ḍhāḷ = a slope; the inclination of a plane; m ḍhāḷiyum = adj. sloping, inclining (G.) Rebus: *ḍhāḷako* 'a large metal ingot' (Gujarati)

This is a complex, ligatured glyph with a number of glyphic elements. May denote a cast metal (copper) worker guild working with 4 types of pure metal and alloyed ingots (copper + arsenic/tin/zinc). *kūṭ* f. 'corner, side' (Punjabi) Rebus: *khoṭa* 'alloy'. Allograph: *khũṭ* 'zebu'.

Glyphic element: erako nave; era = knave of wheel. Glyphic element: āra 'spokes'. Rebus: āra 'brass' as in ārakūṭa (Skt.) Rebus: Tu. eraka molten, cast (as metal); eraguni to melt (DEDR 866) erka = ekke (Tbh. of arka) aka (Tbh. of arka) copper (metal); crystal (Ka.lex.) cf. eruvai = copper (Ta.lex.) eraka, er-aka = any metal infusion (Ka.Tu.); erako molten cast (Tu.lex.) Glyphic element: kund opening in the nave or hub of a wheel to admit the axle (Santali) Rebus: kunda 'turner' kundār turner (A.); kũdār, kũdāri (B.); kundāru (Or.); kundau to turn on a lathe, to carve, to chase; kundau dhiri = a hewn stone; kundau murhut = a graven image (Santali) kunda a turner's lathe (Skt.)(CDIAL 3295). kundan 'pure gold'. Allograph: wing: *Ta.* ciṟai, ciṟaku, ciṟakar wing; iṟai, iṟaku, iṟakar, iṟakkai wing, feather. *Ma.* iṟaku, ciṟaku wing. *Ko.* rek wing, feather. *Ka.* eṟake, eṟaṅke, ṟakke, ṟekke wing; ṟaṭṭe, ṟeṭṭe wing, upper arm. *Koḍ.* rekke wing; raṭṭe upper arm. *Tu.* ediṅke, reṅkè ing. *Te.* eṟaka, ṟekka, rekka, neṟaka, neṟi id. *Kol.* reḍapa, (SR.) reppā id.; (P.) reṛapa id., feather. *Nk.* rekka, reppa wing. *Pa.* (S.) rekka id. *Go.* (S.) rekka wing-feather; reka (M.) feather, (Ko.) wing (*Voc.* 3045). *Konḍa* ṟeka wing, upper arm. *Kuwi* (Su.) rekka wing. (DEDR 2591). *Ko.* kerŋgl, kergl feather, wing. (DEDR 1983).

Glyphic element: 'corner': khuṇṭa 'corner'. Phal. khun ' corner '; H. khũṭ m. ' corner, direction ' (→ P. khũṭ f. ' corner, side '); G. khũṭṛī f. ' angle '. <-> X kōṇa -- : G. khuṇ f., khũˇṇɔ m. ' corner '.2. S. kuṇḍa f. ' corner '; P. kũṭ f. 'corner, side' (← H.). (CDIAL 3898). Rebus: khũṭ 'community, guild' (Mu.); kunḍa 'consecrated fire-pit'.

The 'U' glyphic on this variant of Sign 243 could be to denote the sounds of words: 1. baṭi and 2. kuṇḍa: 1. baṭi 'broad-mouthed, rimless metal vessel'; rebus: baṭi 'smelting furnace'; 2. kuṇḍa 'pot; rebus: 'consecrated fire-pit'. The 'U' glyphic is a semantic determinant to emphasise that this is a temple with a smithy furnace and a consecrated fire-pit. The structural form within which this 'U' glyphic is enclosed may represent a temple: kole.l 'temple, smithy' (Ko.); kolme smithy' (Ka.) The structural form (*sangaḍa* frame of a building') within which this sign is enclosed may represent a temple: kole.l 'temple, smithy' (Ko.); kolme smithy' (Ka.) The ligatured sign may thus be read: *sangaḍa kuṇḍ* to mean 'entrustment articles (of) consecrated fire-altar or furnace (of) temple'.

Copper

K. *lŏy* f. ' white copper, bell -- metal '. (CDIAL 11166) lōhakāra m. ' iron -- worker ', *°rī* -- f., *°raka* -- m. lex., *lauhakāra* -- m. Hit. [lōhá -- , kāra -- 1] Pa. *lōhakāra* -- m. ' coppersmith, ironsmith '; Pk. *lōhāra* -- m. ' blacksmith ', S. *luhāru* m., L. *lohār* m., *°rī* f., awāṇ. *luhār*, P. WPah.khaś. bhal. *luhār* m., Ku. *lwār*, N. B. *lohār*, Or. *lohaḷa*, Bi.Bhoj. Aw.lakh. *lohār*, H. *lohār*, *luh°* m., G. *lavār* m., M. *lohār* m.; Si. *lōvaru* ' coppersmith '.lōhakāra -- : WPah.kṭg. (kc.) *lhwā`r* m. ' blacksmith ', *lhwàri* f. ' his wife ', Garh. *lwār* m.lōhá ' red, copper -- coloured ' ŚrS., ' made of copper ' ŚBr., m.n. ' copper ' VS., ' iron ' MBh. [*rudh --]Pa. *lōha* -- m. ' metal, esp. copper or bronze '; Pk. *lōha* -- m. ' iron ', Gy. pal. *li°*, *lihi*, obl. *elhás*, as. *loa* JGLS new ser. ii 258; Wg. (Lumsden) "*loa*" ' steel '; Kho. *loh* ' copper '; S. *lohu* m. ' iron ', L. *lohā* m., awāṇ. *lō`ā*, P. *lohā* m. (→ K.rām. ḍoḍ. *lohā*), WPah.bhad. *lōu* n., bhal. *lòtilde;* n., pāḍ. jaun. *lōh*, paṅ. *luhā*, cur. cam. *lohā*, Ku. *luwā*, N. *lohu*, *°hā*, A. *lo*, B. *lo*, *no*, Or. *lohā*, *luhā*, Mth. *loh*, Bhoj. *lohā*, Aw.lakh. *lōh*, H. *loh*, *lohā* m., G. M. *loh* n.; Si. *loho*, *lō* ' metal, ore, iron'; Md. *ratu* -- *lō* ' copper '.lōhá -- : WPah.kṭg. (kc.) *lóɔ* ' iron ', J. *lohā* m., Garh. *loho*; Md. *lō* ' metal (CDIAL 11158-9). N. *lokhar* ' bag in which a barber keeps his tools '; H. *lokhar* m. ' iron tools, pots and pans '; -- X lauhabhāṇḍa -- : Ku. *lokhaṛ* ' iron tools '; H. *lokhaṇḍ* m. ' iron tools, pots and pans '; G. *lokhāḍ* n. ' tools, iron, ironware '; M. *lokhāḍ* n. ' iron ' (LM 400 < -- *khaṇḍa* --).laúha -- ' made

of copper or iron ' GṛŚr., ' red ' MBh., n. ' iron, metal ' Bhaṭṭ. [lōhá --]Pk. *lōha* -- ' made of iron '; L. *lohā* ' iron -- coloured, reddish '; P. *lohā* ' reddish -- brown (of cattle) '.lauhabhāṇḍa n. ' iron pot, iron mortar ' lex. [laúha -- , bhāṇḍa -- 1]Pa. *lōhabhaṇḍa* -- n. ' copper or brass ware '; S. *luhāḍiṛī* f. ' iron pot ', L.awāṇ. *luhāḍā*; P. *luhāḍā, lohṇḍā*, ludh. *lōhḍā* m. ' frying pan '; N. *luhũṛe* ' iron cooking pot '; A. *lohorā* ' iron pan '; Bi. *lohãṛā* ' iron vessel for drawing water for irrigation '; H. *lohaṇḍā, luh°* m. ' iron pot '; G. *loḍhũ* n. ' iron, razor ', pl. ' car<-> penter's tools ', *loḍhī* f. ' iron pan '.(CDIAL 11171-3)

Rebus glyphs, allographs

Bronze coin of Taxila, single die (Fig. 1, W. W. Tarn., 1902, Notes on Hellenic Studies *Journal of Hellenic Studies*, Vol. 22 (1902), pages 268–293).

Nine ingots (next to the mound) on Fig. 1: Rebus: *khoṭ* m. 'base, alloy' (Punjabi) made of: lo, no 'nine'; rebus: *loa* 'copper' (Santali); loha 'copper' (Skt.) L. *nõ*ᵛ, khet. *naũ*, awāṇ. *naɔ̃*, Ku. *nau*, gng. *nɔ*, náva2 ' nine ' RV. Kal.rumb. *nō*, Kho. *nyoh* (whence *y*? -- *h* from Pers.? BelvalkarVol 94), Pa. *nava*, Pk. *ṇava*, Ḍ. *nau*, Ash. *no*, *nū*, Wg. *nū*, Pr. *nū*, Dm. *nõ*, Tir. *nāb*, Paš.lauṛ. *nā'wa*, ar. *nāu*, dar. *nõ*, Shum. *nū*, Niṅg. *nū*, Woṭ. *nau*, Gaw. *nū*, Bshk. *nab*, *num*, Tor. *nom*, Kand. *nāū*, Mai. *naū*, Sv. *nōu*, Phal. *nau*, *nū*, *nū*, Sh.gil. *náŭ*, pales. *nāū*, K. *nav,nau*, *nam*, pog. *nāu*, rām. kash. ḍoḍ. *nau*, S. *nãvã*, P. *naũ*, bhaṭ. *nau*, WPah.bhal. paṅ. cur. *nao*, N. *nau*, A. B. *na*, Or.*na*, *naa*, Bi. Mth. Aw.lakh. *nau*, H. *nau*, *nam*, OMarw. *nova*, G. *nav*, M. *nav*, *naū*, Ko. *nav*, OSi. *nava*, Si. *namaya*, Md. *nuva*.(CDIAL 6984).

Glyph of shawl, a gaudy dress for an idol; rebus: potti 'priest'

The glyphs decorating the shawl are trefoils, that is, three hollow circles. Read rebus, the shawl is potti. potti, pottika n. Same as. Doll's clothes, a gaudy dress for an idol or for a little girl. (Telugu) S. potī f. ' shawl ' Pk. potta -- , °taga -- , °tia -- n. ' cotton cloth ', pottī -- , °tiā -- , °tullayā -- , puttī -- f. ' piece of cloth, man's dhotī, woman's sāṛī ', pottia -- ' wearing clothes ' (CDIAL 8400) pōtramu ' a cloth'

(Telugu) போத்து² pōttu , n. < பொத்து. 1. Hole, hollow (Tamil) buḍhi mala 'a bead with wide hole' (Santali) peaṭa 'three' (Santali)

posta 'red thread employed to make borders of cloth' (Santali) pōta2 m. ' cloth ', pōtikā -- f. lex. 2. *pōtta -- 2 (sanskrit- ized as pōtra -- 2 n. ' cloth ' lex.). 3. *pōttha -- 2 ~ pavásta<-> n. ' covering (?) ' RV., ' rough hempen cloth ' AV. T. Chowdhury JBORS xvii 83. 4. pōntī -- f. ' cloth ' Divyāv. 5. *pōcca -- 2 < *pōtya -- ? (Cf. pōtyā = pōtānāṁ samūhaḥ Pāṇ.gaṇa. -- pṓta -- 1?). [Relationship with prōta -- n. ' woven cloth ' lex., plōta -- ' bandage, cloth ' Suśr. or with pavásta -- is obscure: EWA ii 347 with lit. Forms meaning ' cloth to smear with, smearing ' poss. conn. with or infl. by pusta -- 2 n. ' working in clay ' (prob. ← Drav., Tam. pūcu &c. DED 3569, EWA ii 319)] 1. Pk. pōa -- n. ' cloth '; Paš.ar. pōwok ' cloth ', pōg ' net, web ' (but lauṛ. dar. pāwāk ' cotton cloth ', Gaw. pāk IIFL iii 3, 150). 2. Pk. potta -- , °taga -- , °tia -- n. ' cotton cloth ', pottī -- , °tiā -- , °tullayā -- , puttī -- f. ' piece of cloth, man's dhotī, woman's sāṛī ', pottia -- ' wearing clothes '; S. potī f. ' shawl ', potyo m. ' loincloth '; L. pot, pl. °tā̃ f. ' width of cloth '; P. potṛā m. ' child's clout ', potṇā ' to smear a wall with a rag '; N. poto ' rag to lay on lime -- wash ', potnu ' to smear '; Or. potā ' gunny bag '; OAw. potaï ' smears, plasters '; H. potā m. ' whitewashing brush ', potī f. ' red cotton ', potiyā m. ' loincloth ', potṛā m. ' baby clothes '; G. potn. ' fine cloth, texture ', potũ n. ' rag ', potī f., °tiyũ n. ' loincloth ', potṛī f. ' small do. '; M. pot m. ' roll of coarse cloth ', n. ' weftage or texture of cloth ', potrẽ n. ' rag for smearing cowdung '.3. Pa. potthaka -- n. ' cheap rough hemp cloth ', potthakamma -- n. ' plastering '; Pk. pottha -- , °aya -- n.m. ' cloth '; S. potho m. ' lump of rag for smearing, smearing, cloth soaked in opium '. 4. Pa. ponti -- ' rags '. 5. Wg. pōč ' cotton cloth, muslin ', Kt. puč; Pr. puč ' duster, cloth ', pū´čuk ' clothes '; S. poco m. ' rag for plastering, plastering '; P. poccā m. ' cloth or brush for smearing ',pocṇā ' to smear with earth '; Or. pucāra, pucurā ' wisp of rag or jute for whitewashing with, smearing with such a rag '. (CDIAL 8400) போத்தி pōtti போற்றி pōṟṟi , < id. n. 1. Praise, applause, commendation; புகழ்மொழி. (W.) 2. Brahman temple-priest of Malabar; கோயிற்

பூசைசெய்யும் மலையாளநாட்டுப் பிராமணன். (W.) 3. See போத்தி, 1.--int. Exclamation of praise; துதிச்சொல்வகை. பொய்தீர் காட்சிப் புரையோய் போற்றி (சிலப். 13, 92) (Tamil) potR `" Purifier "'N. of one of the 16 officiating priests at a sacrifice (the assistant of the Brahman (RV. Br. ŚrS. Hariv.)

trika, a group of three (Skt.) The occurrence of a three-fold depiction on a trefoil may thus be a phonetic determinant, a suffix to potṛ as in potṛka

Rebus reading of the hieroglyph: potti 'temple-priest' (Ma.) போத்தி pōtti போற்றி pōr̲r̲i , < id. n. 1. Praise, applause, commendation; புகழ்மொழி. (W.) 2. Brahman temple-priest of Malabar; கோயிற் பூசைசெய்யும் மலையாளநாட்டுப் பிராமணன். (W.) 3. See போத்தி, 1.--int. Exclamation of praise; துதிச்சொல்வகை. பொய்தீர் காட்சிப் புரையோய் போற்றி (சிலப். 13, 92) (Tamil) potR `" Purifier "'N. of one of the 16 officiating priests at a sacrifice (the assistant of the Brahman (RV. Br. ŚrS. Hariv.)

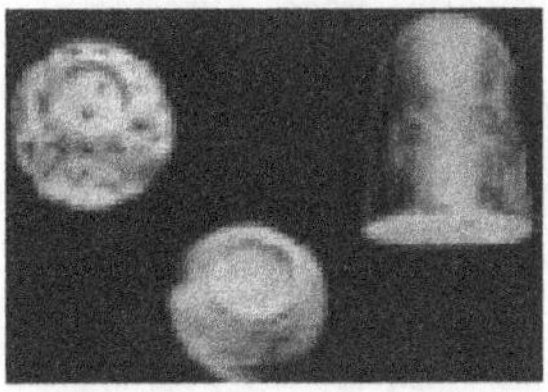

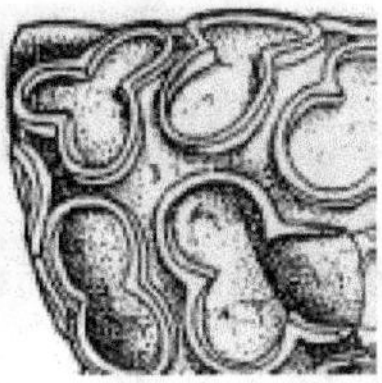

Rebus: Bi. *pot* ' jeweller's polishing stone ' (CDIAL 8403). [The 'dotted circle' may denote a polished bead; hence, Pk. *pottī* -- f. 'glass ' (CDIAL 8403).]

Sacredness connoted by the temple-priest explains the occurrence of the trefoil glyph on the base for holding a śivalinga. Two bases decorated with trefoil and a lingam. Smoothed, polished pedestal of dark red stone. National Museum of Pakistan, Karachi. After Mackay 1938: 1,411; II, pl. 107:35; cf. Parpola, 1994, p. 218.

pheṭār a heifer (Santali) Heifer with trefoil inlays, Uruk (W.16017) c. 3000 BCE; shell mass with inlays of lapis lazuli, 5.3 cm long. Vorderasiatisches Museum, Berlin; cf. Parpola, 1994, p. 213.

Trefoil decorated bull; traces of red pigment remain inside the trefoils. Steatite statue fragment. Mohenjodaro (Sd 767). After Ardeleanu-Jansen, 1989: 196, fig. 1; cf. Parpola, 1994, p. 213. pōtu 'male of animals' (Telugu) A phonetic determinative of the trefoil motif.

Trefoils painted on steatite beads. Harappa (After Vats. Pl. CXXXIII, Fig. 2)

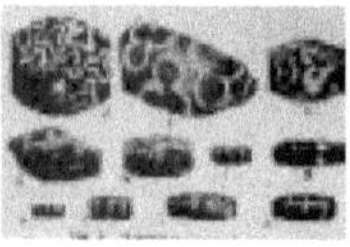

Glyph: pottar, பொத்தல் pottal, n. < id. [Ka.poṭṭare, Ma. pottu, Tu.potre.]

Fillet on the fore-head of the priest statuette, 2700 BCE. Stone. Mohenjo-daro. Karachi Museum. The priest wears a fillet similar to the two fillets of gold which bears the standard device embossed on them. The fillets of gold were discovered

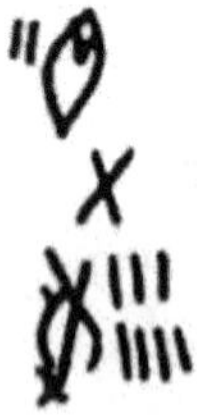

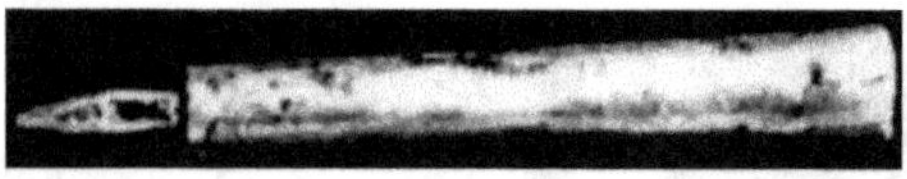

at Mohenjo-daro. Similar gold ornaments with embossed standard devices were also reported from an Akkadian burial site in West Asia. [Source: Page 22, Fig. 12 in: Deo Prakash Sharma, 2000, *Harappan seals, sealings and copper tablets*, Delhi, National Museum].

The central ornament worn on the forehead of the famous "priest-king" sculpture from Mohenjo-daro appears to represent an eye bead, possibly made of gold with steatite inlay in the center.

Golden pendant with inscription from jewelry hoard at Mohenjo-daro. Drawing of inscription that encircles the gold ornament. Needle-like pendant with cylindrical body. Two other examples, one with a different series of incised signs were found together. The pendant is made from a hollow cylinder with soldered ends and perforated point. Museum No. MM 1374.50.271; Marshall 1931:

521, pl. CLI, B3. [After Fig. 4.17a, b in: JM Kenoyer, 1998, p. 196].

Gold fillet depicting the standard device, Mohenjo-daro, 2600 BCE. [Source: Page 32 in: Deo Prakash Sharma, 2000, *Harappan seals, sealings and copper tablets*, Delhi, National Museum]. At *a* Marshall, *MIC*, Pl. CLI are specimens of fillets consisting of thin bands of beaten gold with holes for cords at their ends.

Harappa. Standard device shown on faience tablets (left: H90-1687, right, H93-2051) and carved in ivory (center, H93-2092). [After Fig. 5.12 in JM Kenoyer, 1998]. The miniature replica object has been recovered in 1993 from excavations at Harappa. This may be an ivory replica of a device made of basketry and wood. This replica shows a hemispherical lower basin with dotted circles and a cylindrical top portion with cross-hatching. The shaft extending from the base seems to be broken on this replica.

'Dotted circle' is a sacred glyph. It is a hieroglyph.

Comparble to m0304 showing a seated person in penance, is a seal showing a person in penance:

He also has scarf as a pigtail, is horned with two stars shown within the horn-curves.

Glyph of 'a pair of stars' also on the 'water-carrier' glyph of Gadd seal (PBA18).

Other glyphic elements are: twig, horns.

The text of the inscription shows two types of 'fish' glyphs: one fish + fish with scales circumscribed by four short-strokes: aya 'fish' (Mu.); rebus: aya 'metal' (Skt.)
gaṇḍa set of four (Santali) Rebus: kaṇḍ 'fire-altar, furnace' (Santali) kaṇḍa 'fire-

altar' cf. ayaskāṇḍa a quantity of iron, excellent iron (Pāṇ.gaṇ) The reading is consistent with the entire glyphic composition related to the mineral, mint forge to create alloyed metal.

meḍha 'polar star' (Marathi). Rebus: meḍ 'iron' (Ho.) mēḍha dula 'pair' (Kashmiri); Rebus: dul 'cast (metal)'(Santali)
kamaḍha 'penance' (Pkt.) Rebus: kammaṭi a coiner (Ka.) kampaṭṭam 'mint' (Ta.) Kur. kaṇḍō a stool. Malt. kanḍo stool, seat. (DEDR 1179) Rebus: kaṇḍ = a furnace, altar (Santali.lex.)

dhaṭu m. (also *dhaṭhu*) m. 'scarf' (WPah.) (CDIAL 6707) Allograph: ḍato = claws of crab (Santali); dhātu = mineral (Skt.), dhatu id. (Santali)

ṭhaṭera 'buffalo horns'. *ṭhaṭerā* 'brass worker' (Punjabi)(CDIAL 5493).
Ta. tuttāri a kind of bugle-horn. *Ma.* tuttāri horn, trumpet. *Ka.* tutūri, tuttāri, tuttūri a long trumpet. *Tu.* tuttāri, tuttūri trumpet, horn, pipe. *Te.* tutārā a kind of trumpet. / Cf. Mar. tutārī a wind instrument, a sort of horn. (DEDR 3316). *ḍabe, ḍabea* 'large horns, with a sweeping upward curve, applied to buffaloes' (Santali) Rebus: *ḍab*, ḍhimba, ḍhompo 'lump (ingot?)', clot, make a lump or clot, coagulate, fuse, melt together (Santali)

kūdī, kūṭī bunch of twigs (Skt.lex.) kūdī (also written as kūṭī in manuscripts) occurs in the Atharvaveda (AV 5.19.12) and Kauśika Sūtra (Bloomsfield's ed.n, xliv. Cf. Bloomsfield, American Journal of Philology, 11, 355; 12,416; Roth, Festgruss an Bohtlingk, 98) denotes it as a twig. This is identified as that of Badarī, the jujube tied to the body of the dead to efface their traces. (See Vedic Index, I, p. 177). Rebus 1: kuṭila, katthīl = bronze (8 parts copper and 2 parts tin) [cf. āra-kūṭa, 'brass' (Skt.) (CDIAL 3230) Rebus 2: kuṭhi 'smelting furnace' (Santali) koṭe 'forged (metal) (Santali) Vikalpa: మండ [manḍa] *manḍa*. [Tel.] n. A twig with leaves on it. చెట్టుకొమ్మ. A small branch, ఉపశాఖ. the back of the hand. మీజేయి. A frying brush,వేపుడుకుంచె.

ḍabe, ḍabea 'large horns, with a sweeping upward curve, applied to buffaloes' (Santali) Rebus: ḍab, ḍhimba, ḍhompo 'lump (ingot?)', clot, make a lump or clot, coagulate, fuse, melt together (Santali)

The glyphic composition of the seal read rebus: *dul meḍ ḍab dhatu kammaṭi* 'cast metal ingot, metallic minerals coiner.'

Another comparable glyphic composition is provided by seal m1181.

m1181. Seal. Mohenjo-daro. Three-faced, horned person (with a three-leaved branch on the crown), wearing bangles and armlets and seated on a hoofed platform.

m1181 Text of inscription.

Glyph 323. Together with a 'pannier' glyphic on the shoulder of the heifer, a remarkable glyph appears on the back (stomach) of the heifer: a bag. K. kŏthul, lu m. ' large bag or parcel ' (CDIAL 3511) 3545 kṓṣṭha1 m. ' any one of the large viscera ' MBh. [Same as kṓṣṭha -- 2? Cf. *kōttha --] Pa. *koṭṭha* -- m. ' stomach ', Pk. *koṭṭha* -- , *kuṭ°* m.; L. (Shahpur) *koṭhī* f. ' heart, breast '; P. *koṭṭhā, koṭhā* m. ' belly ', G. *koṭhɔ* m., M. *koṭhā* m. (CDIAL 3545).Rebus: S. *koṭāru* m. ' district officer who watches crops, police officer ' (CDIAL 3501). Cf. *kṓṣṭhaka* 'treasury' (Skt.); *kóṭṭhi* 'temple treasury' (WPah.); *koṭho* 'warehouse' (G.)(CDIAL 3546).

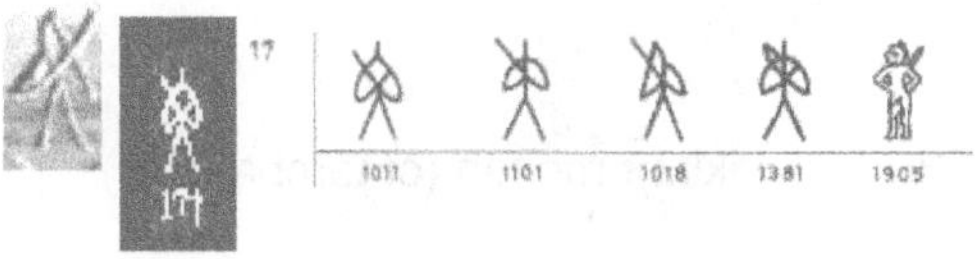

Glyph which appears on the inscription on a large Mohenjodaro seal, m1203. This lends added emphasis on the possible use of 'standard device' glyphic composition to denote: *jangaḍiyo* 'military guard who accompanies treasure into the treasury'; *sanghāḍiyo*, a worker on a lathe (G.) With the ligature of glyphic element of Sign 323 ('bag'), as a semantic determinant , the glyphic composition of Sign 17 reads: *koṭha jangaḍiyo* 'treasury military guard'.

damya ' tameable ', m. ' young bullock to be tamed ' Mn. [~ *dāmiya -- . -- √dam] Pa. *damma* -- ' to be tamed (esp. of a young bullock) '; Pk. *damma* -- ' to be tamed '; S. *ḏamu* ' tamed '; -- ext. -- *ḍa* -- : A. *damrā* ' young bull ', *dāmuri* ' calf '; B.*dāmṛā* ' castrated bullock '; Or. *dāmaṛī* ' heifer ', *dāmaṛiā* ' bullcalf, young castrated bullock ', *dāmuṛ, °ṛi* ' young bullock '.WPah.kṭg. *dām* m. ' young ungelt ox '. (CDIAL 6184).

tāmrakuṭṭa m. ' coppersmith ' R. [tāmrá -- , kuṭṭa --] N. *tamauṭe, tamoṭe* ' id. '.Garh. *ṭamoṭu* ' coppersmith '; Ko. *tāmṭi.* (CDIAL 5781).

5786 tāmrapaṭṭa m. ' copper plate (for inscribing) ' Yājñ. [Cf. tāmrapattra -- . -- tāmrá -- , paṭṭa -- 1]
M. *tāboṭī* f. ' piece of copper of shape and size of a brick '

तांबट or तांबटकर [tāmbaṭa or tāmbaṭakara] *m* A caste or an individual of it. They are coppersmiths.

तांबड [tāmbaḍa] *f* (तांबडा) Red soil. तांबडा [tāmbaḍā] *a* (ताम्र S) Red.

तांबें [tāmbēṃ] *n* (ताम्र S) Copper.

तांबोटी [tāmbōṭī] *f* A piece of copper of the shape and size of a brick. 2 The metal water-holder of barbers

తామ్రము [tāmramu] *tāmramu.* [Skt.] n. Copper. రాగి. Red color ఎరుపు. adj. Red ఎర్రని. తామ్రకుట్టకుడు *tāmra-kuṭṭakuḍu.* n. A coppersmith. రాగిపనివాడు.

Kuṭṭhita hot, sweltering (of uṇha) S iv.289 (v. l. kikita); molten (of tamba (Pali)

Tamba (nt.) [Sk. tāmra, orig. adj.=dark coloured, leaden; cp. Sk. adj. taŋsra id., to tama] copper ("the dark metal"); usually in combinations, signifying colour of or made of (cp. loha bronze), e. g. lākhātamba (adj.) Th 2, 440 (colour of an ox); ˚akkhin Vv 323 (timira˚) Sdhp 286; ˚nakhin J vi.290; ˚nettā (f.) ibid.; ˚bhājana DhA i.395;˚mattika DhA iv.106; ˚vammika DhA iii.208; ˚loha PvA 95 (=loha).

தாம்பரம் tāmparam

, *n.* < *tāmra.* See தாமிரம். (பதார்த்த. 1170.)

தாம்பிரகம் tāmpirakam

, *n.* < *tāmraka.* See தாமிரம். (யாழ். அக.)

தாம்பிரகாரன் tāmpira-kāraṉ

, *n.* < id. + *kāra.* Coppersmith; செம்புகொட்டி. (யாழ். அக.)

தாம்பிரம் tāmpiram

, *n.* < *tāmra.* 1. Copper. See தாமிரம். (சூடா.) 2. Red; சிவப்பு. (இலக். அக.)

ताम्र *a.* [तम्-रक् दीर्घः Uṇ.2.16.] 1 Made of copper. -2 Of a coppery red colour, red; ततो$नुकुर्याद्विशदस्य तस्यास्ताम्रौष्ठपर्यस्तरुचः स्मितस्य Ku.1.44; उदेति सविता ताम्रस्ताम्र एवास्तमेति च Subhāṣ. -म्रः A kind of leprosy with red spots. -म्रम् 1 Copper. -2 A dark or coppery red. -3 A coppery receptacle; ताम्रलोहैः परिवृता निधयो ये चतुः- शताः Mb.2.61.29. -म्री A copper pot having a small hole at the botton used in measuring time by placing it in a water-vessel. -Comp. -अक्षः 1 a crow. -2 the (Indian) cuckoo. -अर्धः bell-metal. -अश्मन् *m.* a kind of jewel (पद्मराग); ताम्राश्मरश्मिच्छुरितैर्नखाग्रैः Śi.3.7. -आभम् red sandal (रक्तचन्दन). -उपजीविन् *m.* a coppersmith. -ओष्ठः(forming ताम्रोष्ठ or ताम्रौष्ठ) a red or cherry lip; Ku.1.44. -कारः, -कुट्टः a brazier, coppersmith. -कृमिः 1 a kind of red insect (इन्द्रगोप). -2 the lady bird. -3 cochineal. -गर्भम् sulphate of copper. -चूडः a cock; संध्याचूडैर- निबिडतमस्ताम्रचूडैरुडूनि । प्रासूयन्त स्फुटमधिवियद्भ्राण्डमण्डानि यानि ॥ Rām. Ch.6.96;7.56. -चडकः a particular position of the hand. -त्रपुजम् brass. -द्रुः the red sandalwood. -द्वीपः the island of Ceylon; Divyāvadāna.36. -धातुः 1 red chalk. -2 Copper; Rām.3. -पट्टः, -पत्रम् a cop- per-plate on which grants of land were frequently inscribed; पटे वा ताम्रपट्टे वा स्वमुद्रोपरिचिह्नितम् । अभिलेख्यात्मनो वंश्यानात्मानं च महीपतिः ॥ Y.1.319. -पर्णी N. of a river rising in Malaya, celebrated for its pearls; R.4.5. Hence ताम्रपर्णिक (= obtained

in the same river); Kau. A.2.11. -पलः Alangium Hexapetalum; दद्यात्ताम्रपलं वापि अभावे सर्वकर्मणः Yuktikalpataru. -पल्लवः the Aśoka tree. -पाकिन् Thespesia Populneoides (Mar. लाखी-पारासा पिंपळ). -पुष्पः Kæmpferia Rotunda (Mar. बाहवा). -ष्पी Bignonia Suaveolens (Mar. धायरी, भुईपाडळ) -फलकम्a copper-plate. -मुख *a.* copper-faced. (-खः) 1 a Frank or European; -2 the Moghals. -वदनः (see ताम्रमुख); योत्स्यन्ति ताम्रवदनैरनेकैः सैनिका इमे Śiva. B.26.23. -वर्णीthe blossom of sesamum. -लिप्तः N. of a country. -प्ताः (pl.) its people or rulers. -वृक्षः a species of sandal. -शिखिन् *m.* a cook. -सारकः a sort of Khadira. (-कम्) red sandal-wood.

ताम्रकम् tāmrakam

ताम्रकम् Copper.

దమ్మిడి [dammiḍi] *dammiḍi.* [H.] n. A pie, one twelfth part of an anna. అరదుడ్డు. డబ్బు [ḍabbu] *ḍabbu.* [Tel.] n. A copper coin worth either three or four copper pies చిన్నమొత్తురాగిముద్ర. Cash, money దుడ్డు, Wealth ధనము.

1676 *Ma.* kuṭṭa a knotty log. *Ko.* guṭḷ stake to which animal is tied, any large wooden peg. *To.* kuṭy a stump. *Ka.* (Coorg) kuṭṭu stem of a tree which remains after cutting it. *Koḍ.* kuṭṭe log. *Tu.* kuṭṭi stake, peg, stump. *Go.* (Mu.) kuṭṭa, guṭṭa, (G. Ma.) guṭṭa, (Ko.) guṭa stump of tree; (S.) kuṭṭa id., stubble; (FH.) kuta jowari stubble (*Voc.* 731). *Pe.* kuṭa stump of tree. *Kui* gūṭa, (K.) guṭa id. *Kuwi* (Su.) guṭṭu

*khuṭṭa1 ' peg, post '. 2. *khuṇṭa -- 1. [Same as *khuṭṭa -- 2? -- See also kṣōḍa -- .]
1. Ku. *khuṭī* ' peg '; N. *khuṭnu* ' to stitch ' (der. **khuṭ* ' pin ' as *khilnu* from *khil* s.v. khī́la --); Mth. *khuṭā* ' peg, post '; H. *khūṭā* m. ' peg, stump '; Marw. *khuṭī* f. ' peg '; M. *khuṭā* m. ' post '.
2. Pk. *khuṁṭa* -- , *khoṁṭaya* -- m. ' peg, post '; Dm. *kuṇḍa* ' peg for fastening yoke to plough -- pole '; L. *khū̃ḍī* f. ' drum -- stick '; P. *khuṇḍ, °ḍā* m. ' peg, stump '; WPah. rudh. *khuṇḍ* ' tethering peg or post '; A. *khū̃ṭā* ' post ', *°ṭi* ' peg '; B. *khū̃ṭā, °ṭi* ' wooden post, stake, pin, wedge '; Or. *khuṇṭa, °ṭā* ' pillar, post '; Bi.

(with --*ḍa* --) *khū̃ṭrā, °rī* ' posts about one foot high rising from body of cart '; H. *khū̃ṭā* m. ' stump, log ', *°ṭī* f. ' small peg ' (→ P. *khū̃ṭā* m., *°ṭī* f. ' stake, peg '); G. *khū̃ṭ* f. ' landmark ', *khū̃ṭɔ* m., *°ṭī* f. ' peg ', *°ṭū̃* n. ' stump ', *°ṭiyū̃* n. ' upright support in frame of wagon ', *khū̃ṭrū̃* n. ' half -- burnt piece of fuel '; M. *khū̃ṭ* m. ' stump of tree, pile in river, grume on teat ' (semant. cf. kīla -- 1 s.v. *khila -- 2), *khū̃ṭā* m. ' stake ', *°ṭī* f. ' wooden pin ', *khū̃ṭalṇẽ* ' to dibble '.WPah.kṭg. *khv́ndɔ* ' pole for fencing or piling grass round ' (Him.I 35 *nd* poss. wrong for *ṇḍ*); J. *khuṇḍā* m. ' peg to fasten cattle to '. (CDIAL 3893).

3894 *khuṭṭa2 ' leg '. [Perh. same as *khuṭṭa -- 1 ' peg ', but see word -- group s.v. *kuṭṭha --]
Ku. *khuṭo* ' leg, foot ', *°ṭī* ' goat's leg '; N. *khuṭo* ' leg, foot ', *khuṛkilo* ' ladder ' (< **khuṭ+kilo* ' peg ' < kīla -- 1). WPah.poet. *khvṭe* f. ' leg (of a domestic animal) '; J. *khuṭi* f.pl. ' legs '; Garh. *khuṭu* ' foot '.(CDIAL 3894).

3236 kuṭṭa1 in cmpd. ' breaking, cutting ', *°aka* -- ' id. ', m. ' cutter, breaker, grinder '. 2. *kōṭṭa -- 2. [√kuṭṭ]
1. S. *kāṭha -- kuṭo* m. ' woodpecker '; WPah. bhal. *kuṭṭū* m. ' wooden bar serving as pivot of door, wooden peg in socket of flour mill, hip, buttock ';
Ku. *kuṭo, °ṭī, °ṭlo* ' hoe ', N. *kuṭo, °ṭi*; A. *kuṭ* ' mark of punctuation '; Or. *kuṭa* ' small hammer for breaking stones ', *°ṭā* ' act of beating or pounding or husking ';
M. *kuṭā -- kuṭī* f. ' fighting '.2. Pa. *koṭṭa* -- in cmpd. ' breaking '; Pk. *koṭṭaga* -- m. ' carpenter ', *koṭṭila* -- , *°illa* -- m. ' mallet '.

1171 *Ta.* kaṇṭal mangrove, *Rhizophora mucronata*; dichotomous mangrove, *Kandelia rheedii. Ma.* kaṇṭa bulbous root as of lotus, plantain; point where branches and bunches grow out of the stem of a palm; kaṇṭal what is bulb-like, half-ripe jackfruit and other green fruits; *R. candel. Ka.* gaḍḍe, geḍḍe any bulbous root, esp. that of the lotus; (Gowda) gEṇḍE bulbous root. *Koḍ.* kaṇḍe root-stock from which small roots grow; ila·ti kaṇḍe sweet potato (ila·ti England). *Tu.* kaṇḍe, gaḍḍè a bulbous root; kāṇḍelů a kind of tree growing near salt water. *Te.* gaḍḍa, geḍḍa a bulbous root,

bulb. *Kol.* (Wagh.) gaḍḍa tuber. *Kuwi* (S.) gidda, in: ulli gidda onion. / Cf. Sgh.kaḍol mangrove. DED(S) 984.

One-horned young bull

Glyptic elements read rebus include the following:

The zebu (brāhmaṇi bull) is: aḍar ḍangra (Santali); ḍhangar 'bull'; rebus: dhan:gar 'blacksmith' (Mth.) ḍangar 'blacksmith' (H.)

koḍiyum koḍiyum 'heifer' (G.) [kōḍiya] kōḍe, kōḍiya. [Tel.] n. A bullcalf. . k* దూడA young bull. Plumpness, prime. తరుణము. జోడుకోడయలు a pair of bullocks. kōḍe adj. Young. kōḍe-kāḍu. n. A young man.పడుచువాడు. [kārukōḍe] kāru-kōḍe. [Tel.] n. A bull in its prime. खोंड [khōṇḍa] m A young bull, a bullcalf. (Marathi) గోద [gōda] gōda. [Tel.] n. An ox. A beast. kine, cattle.(Telugu) koḍiyum (G.) koḍiyum 'heifer' (G.) koḍiyum; खोंड [khōṇḍa] m A young bull, a bullcalf. (Marathi) [kōḍe] kōḍe. [Tel.] n. A bullcalf. *-దూడ. A young bull. kāru-kōḍe. [Tel.] n. A bull in its prime. [kōḍiya] G. godhɔ m. ' bull ', dhũ n. ' young bull ', OG. godhalu m. ' entire bull ', G. godhliyũ n. ' young bull ' (CDIAL 4315). Te. kōḍiya, kōḍe young bull; adj. male (e.g. kōḍe dūḍa bull calf), young, youthful; kōḍek;ḍu a young man. Kol. (Haig) kōḍē bull. Nk. khoṛe male calf. Konḍa kōḍi cow; kōṛe young bullock. Pe.kōḍi cow. Manḍ. kūḍi id. Kui kōḍi id., ox. Kuwi (F.) kōdi cow; (S.) kajja kōḍi bull ; (Su. P.) kōḍi cow (DEDR 2199) cf. koṛa 'a boy, a young man' (Santali)

- A young bull is kōḍe, khōṇḍa
- One horn is koḍ, kōṇḍa Pa. kōḍ (pl. kōḍul) horn; Ka. kōḍu horn, tusk, branch of a tree; kōṟ horn Tu. kōḍů, kōḍu horn Ko. kṛ (obl. kṭ-)((DEDR 2200) Paš. kōṇḍā'bald', Kal. rumb. kōṇḍa 'hornless'.(CDIAL 3508). Kal. rumb.khōṇḍ a' half' (CDIAL 3792).
- Rings on neck are: koṭiyum (G.) koṭiyum = a wooden circle put round the neck of an animal; koṭ = neck (G.) Vikalpa: kaḍum 'neck-band, ring'; rebus: khāḍ 'trench, firepit' (G.) Vikalpa: khaḍḍā f. hole, mine, cave (CDIAL 3790) kanduka, kandaka ditch, trench (Tu.); kandakamu id. (Te.); kanda trench

made as a fireplace during weddings (Konda); kanda small trench for fireplace (Kui); kandri a pit (Malt)(DEDR 1214) khaḍḍa— 'hole, pit'. [Cf. *gaḍḍa— and list s.v. kartá—1] Pk. khaḍḍā— f. 'hole, mine, cave', ḍaga— m. 'one who digs a hole', ḍōlaya— m. 'hole'; Bshk. (Biddulph) "kād" (= khaḍ?) 'valley'; K. khŏḍ m. 'pit', khŏḍü f. 'small pit', khoḍu m. 'vulva'; S. khaḏa f. 'pit'; L. khaḍḍ f. 'pit, cavern, ravine'; P. khaḍḍ f. 'pit, ravine', ḍī f. 'hole for a weaver's feet' (→ Ku. khaḍḍ, N. khaḍ; H. khaḍ, khaḍḍā m. 'pit, low ground, notch'; Or. khā̃ḍi 'edge of a deep pit'; M. khaḍḍā m. 'rough hole, pit'); WPah. khaś. khaḍḍā 'stream'; N. khāṛo 'pit, bog', khāṛi 'creek', khāṛal 'hole (in ground or stone)'. — Altern. < *khāḍa—: Gy. gr. xar f. 'hole'; Ku. khāṛ 'pit'; B. khāṛī 'creek, inlet', khāṛal 'pit, ditch'; H. khāṛī f. 'creek, inlet', khaṛ—har, al m. 'hole'; Marw. khāṛo m. 'hole'; M. khā̃ḍ f. 'hole, creek', ḍā m. 'hole', ḍī f. 'creek, inlet'. 3863 khātra— n. 'hole' HPariś., 'pond, spade' Uṇ. [√khan] Pk. khatta— n. 'hole, manure', aya— m. 'one who digs in a field'; S. khāṭru m. 'mine made by burglars', ṭro m. 'fissure, pit, gutter made by rain'; P. khāt m. 'pit, manure', khāttā m. 'grain pit', ludh. khattā m. (→ H. khattā m., khatiyā f.); N. khāt 'heap (of stones, wood or corn)'; B. khāt, khāṭṛū 'pit, pond'; Or. khāta 'pit', tā 'artificial pond'; Bi. khātā 'hole, gutter, grain pit, notch (on beam and yoke of plough)', khattā 'grain pit, boundary ditch'; Mth. khātā, khattā 'hole, ditch'; H. khāt m. 'ditch, well', f. 'manure', khātā m. 'grain pit'; G. khātar n. 'housebreaking, house sweeping, manure', khātriyũ n. 'tool used in housebreaking' (→ M. khātar f. 'hole in a wall', khātrā m. 'hole, manure', khātryā m. 'housebreaker'); M. khāt n.m. 'manure' (deriv. khatāviṇẽ 'to manure', khāterẽ n. 'muck pit'). — Un- expl. ṭ in L. khāṭvā m. 'excavated pond', khāṭī f. 'digging to clear or excavate a canal' (~ S. khātī f. 'id.', but khāṭyāro m. 'one employed to measure canal work') and khaṭṭaṇ 'to dig'. (CDIAL 3790) •gaḍa— 1 m. 'ditch' lex. [Cf. *gaḍḍa—1 and list s.v. kartá—1] Pk. gaḍa— n. 'hole'; Paš. gaṛu 'dike'; Kho. (Lor.) gōḷ 'hole, small dry ravine'; A. garā 'high bank'; B. gaṛ 'ditch, hole in a husking machine'; Or. gaṛa 'ditch, moat'; M. gaḷ f. 'hole in the game of marbles'. 3981 *gaḍḍa— 1 'hole, pit'. [G. < *garda—? — Cf. *gaḍḍ—1 and list s.v. kartá—1] Pk. gaḍḍa— m. 'hole'; WPah. bhal. cur. gaḍḍ f., paṅ. gaḍḍrī, pāḍ. gaḍōṛ 'river, stream'; N. gaṛ—tir

'bank of a river'; A. gārā 'deep hole'; B. gāṛ, ṛā 'hollow, pit'; Or. gāṛa 'hole, cave', gāṛiā 'pond'; Mth. gāṛi 'piercing'; H. gāṛā m. 'hole'; G. garāḍ, ḍɔ m. 'pit, ditch' (< *graḍḍa— < *garda—?); Si. gaḍaya 'ditch'. — Cf. S. giḏi f. 'hole in the ground for fire during Muharram'. — X khānī́—: K. gān m. 'underground room'; S. (LM 323) gāṇ f. 'mine, hole for keeping water'; L. gāṇ m. 'small embanked field within a field to keep water in'; G. gāṇ f. 'mine, cellar'; M. gāṇ f. 'cavity containing water on a raised piece of land' WPah.kṭg. gāṛ 'hole (e.g. after a knot in wood)'. (CDIAL 3947) 3860 *khāḍa— 'a hollow'. [Cf. *khaḍḍa— and list s.v. kartá—1] S. khāṛī f. 'gulf, creek'; P. khāṛ 'level country at the foot of a mountain', ṛī f. 'deep watercourse, creek'; Bi. khārī 'creek, inlet'; G. khāṛi , ṛī f., ṛɔ m. 'hole'. — Altern. < *khaḍḍa—: Gy. gr. xar f. 'hole'; Ku. khāṛ 'pit'; B. khāṛī 'creek, inlet', khāṛal 'pit, ditch'; H. khāṛī 'creek, inlet', khaṛ—har, al m. 'hole'; Marw. khāṛo m. 'hole'; M. khāḍ f. 'hole, creek', ḍā m. 'hole', ḍī f. 'creek, inlet'.

1. A sack slung on the front shoulder of the young bull is khōṇḍā, khōṇḍī , kothḷɔ

खोंडा [khōṇḍā] m A कांबळा of which one end is formed into a cowl or hood. खोंडी [khōṇḍī] f An outspread shovelform sack (as formed temporarily out of a कांबळा, to hold or fend off grain, chaff &c. (Marathi) khŏdrang, khudrang ख्वद्ॗरंग adj. c.g. self-coloured; as subst. m. N. of a kind of blanket having the natural colour of the wool (L. 37). khudürü और्णशाटकविशेषः f. a kind of coarse woollen blanket. (Kashmiri) Pa. kotthalī -- f. ' sack (?) '; Pk. kotthala -- m. ' bag, grainstore ' (kōha -- m. ' bag ' < *kōtha?); K. kŏthul, lu m. ' large bag or parcel ', kothüjü f. ' small do. '; S. kothirī f. ' bag '; Ku. kuthlo ' large bag, sack '; B. kūthlī ' satchel, wallet '; Or. kuthaḷi, thuḷi, kothaḷi, thiḷi ' wallet, pouch '; H. kothlā m. ' bag, sack, stomach (see *kōttha --) ', lī f. ' purse '; G.kothḷɔ m. ' large bag ', ḷī f. ' purse, scrotum '; M. kothḷā m. ' large sack, chamber of stomach (= peṭā ċā k) ', ḷẽ n. ' sack ', ḷī f. ' small sack '; -- X gōṇī́ -- : S. gothirī f. ' bag ', L. gutthlā m.(CDIAL 3511) Ta. kaṇṭāḷam travelling sack placed on a bullock, pack-saddle. Ka. kaṇṭale, kaṇṭāḷa, kaṇṭāḷe, kaṇṭle double bag carried across a beast. Te. kaṇṭalamu, kaṇṭlamubullock-load consisting of two bags filled with goods. / Cf. Mar. kaṇṭhāḷī

a bag having opening in the middle (DEDR 1174) gōṇī́ f. ' sack ' Pāṇ., gōṇikā -- f. ' blanket ' BHS ii 215. [← Drav. EWA i 345 with lit.]Pa. gōṇa -- saṁthata -- ' covered with a woollen rug ', gōṇaka -- m. ' woollen rug with a long fleece '; NiDoc. goni ' sack '; Gy. pal. gṓni ' bag, purse ', eur. gono m. ' sack '; Ash.gō̃ ' carpet ', Wg. gř̥ōĩ, gř̥ẽ, Dm. gūni; Paš. gōnī ' saddlebag '; K. guna f. ' pair of large saddlebags usu. of goat's hair for carrying grain '; S. guṇī f. ' coarse sackcloth '; L. ```gūṇī f. ' sack '; P. gūṇ f. ' hair cloth, hempen sacking ', gūṇī f. ' sack '; B. gun ' sacking '; Or. goṇī ' sackcloth, sack, corn measure, ragged garment '; Bi. gon ' grain sack '; H. gon f. ' sack '; G. gū̆ṇi f. ' sacking, sack '; M. goṇ f. ' sack ', ṇī f. ' sackcloth ', ṇā m. ' large grain sack '.Addenda: gōṇī́ -- : WPah.kṭg. gv̄ṇ f. (obl. -- i) ' sack for corn '; <-> Md. (RTMV1) gōni ' sack ' ← Ind. (CDIAL 4275) gōṇamu. [Tel. of Tam. కోణము.] n. A waist cloth or modesty piece. [gōṇi] gōṇi. [Skt.] n. A sack, sackcloth. a sackful. [Tel.] gōtamu. [Tel.] n. A sack, a bag. (Telugu)

Rebus: B. kõdā 'to turn in a lathe'; Or. kũnda 'lathe', kũdibā, kũd 'to turn' (→ Drav. Kur. kũd 'lathe') (CDIAL 3295)

Rebus: koṭṭil 'workshop' (Ma.)(DEDR 2058). koṭe 'forged metal' (Santali) koḍ 'artisan's workshop' (Kuwi) koḍ = place where artisans work (G.) कोंडण [kōṇḍaṇa] f A fold or pen. (Marathi) koṭṭil cowhouse, shed, workshop, house; Malt. koṭa hamlet. / Influenced by Skt. goṣṭha-. (DEDR 2059). kūṭam = workshop (Tamil); கோட்டம் kōṭṭam,n. <kōṣṭha. 1. Room, enclosure; அறை. சுடும ணோங்கிய நெடு நிலைக் கோட்டமும் (மணி. 6, 59). 2. Temple; கோயில். கோழிச் சேவற் கொடியோன் கோட்டமும் (சிலப். 14, 10). koṭe meṛed = forged iron (Mu.) meḍ 'iron' (Ho.) dul meṛed, cast iron (Mu.) koṭe 'forged metal' (Santali) கொட்டுக்கன்னார் koṭṭu-k-kaṉṉār , n. < கொட்டு² +. Braziers who work by beating plates into shape and not by casting; செம் படிக்குங் கன்னார். (W.)

dāmṛa, damrā ' young bull (A.)(CDIAL 6184). Glyph: *ḍaṅgara1 ' cattle '. 2. *daṅgara -- . [Same as ḍaṅ- gara -- 2 s.v. *ḍagga -- 2 as a pejorative term for cattle] 1. K. ḍangur m. ' bullock ', L. ḍaṅgur, (Ju.) ḏãgar m. ' horned cattle '; P. ḍaṅgar m. ' cattle ', Or. ḍaṅgara; Bi. ḍãgar ' old worn -- out beast, dead cattle ', dhūr ḍãgar ' cattle in general '; Bhoj. ḍā̃ngar ' cattle '; H. ḍãgar, ḍãgrā m. ' horned cattle '.2. H. dãgar m. = prec. (CDIAL 5526) Rebus: ḍaṅgar 'blacksmith'. ḍāṅgar

'blacksmith' (H.); ḍhā~gar., dhā~gar blacksmith; digger of wells (H.) Nepali. डाड़े ḍāṅre , or ḍāgre, adj. Large; lazy; working with- out thoroughness or seriousness; -- s. A partic. kind of bird, the mainā; -- a contemptuous term for a blacksmith डाङ्रो ḍāṅro , or ḍāgro, s. A term of contempt used for a blacksmith (kāmi). [v.s.v. ḍāṅre.] ḍān:ro = a term of contempt for a blacksmith (N.)(CDIAL 5524). ṭhākur = blacksmith (Mth.) (CDIAL 5488). ठाकूर [ṭhākūra] m (ठक्कुर S through H) A tribe or an individual of t. They inhabit woods and wilds (esp. of N. Konkaṇ). 2 A chief among certain castes of Rájpúts, Bhíls &c., a title or compellation of respect. 3 The Supreme God: also an idol or a god. 4 A family priest among certain tribes of Shúdras. ठाकूरजी [ṭhākūrajī] m (ठक्कुर S) A name for the Deity. Among Byrágís. ठाकूरद्वार [ṭhākūradvāra] n sometimes ठाकूरदारा m (ठाकूर The Deity, द्वार A door.) Among Byrágís. A temple or idol-house: also the adytum or penetralia.ठकूरदारा मांडून बसणें To make an outlay or great display (of sanctity or piety). ṭhakkaru, ṭhakkaruḍu = a deity; an idol; an honorific title same as ṭhākūru = a father; a religious preceptor (Te.lex.) ṭhākur blacksmith (Mth.)(CDIAL 5488).

damya ' tameable ', m. ' young bullock to be tamed ' Mn. [~ *dāmiya -- . -- √dam] Pa. damma -- ' to be tamed (esp. of a young bullock) '; Pk. damma -- ' to be tamed '; S. ḍamu ' tamed '; -- ext. -- ḍa -- : A. damrā ' young bull ', dāmuri ' calf '; B. dāmṛā ' castrated bullock '; Or. dāmaṛī ' heifer ', dāmaṛiā ' bullcalf, young castrated bullock ', dāmuṛ, ṛi ' young bullock '. Addenda: damya -- : WPah.kṭg. dām m. 'young ungelt ox'.(CDIAL 6184).

kamarasāla = waist-zone, waist-band, belt (Te.) kammaru = the loins, the waist

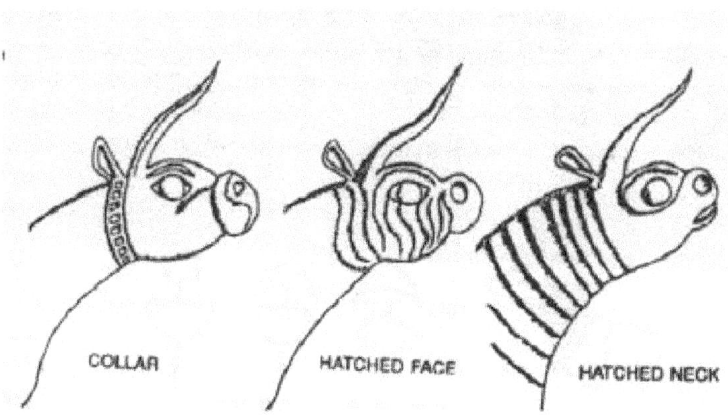

(Ka.Te.M.); kamara (H.); kammarubanda = a leather waist band, belt (Ka.H.) kammaru = a waistband, belt (Te.) kammariñcu = to cover (Te.) kamari = a woman's girdle (Te.) komor = the loins; komor kat.hi = an ornament made of shells, resembling the tail of a tortoise, tied round the waist and sticking out behind worn by men sometimes when dancing (Santali) kambra = a blanket (Santali) [Note the pannier tied as a waist band to the one-horned heifer.] [Bartleby.com notes that the English word 'shawl' meaning 'a square or oblong piece of cloth worn as a covering for the head, neck, and shoulders' has th eymology: Persian *shāl*, ultimately from Sanskrit śāṭī, cloth, sari. Hence, kamarsaala in Telugu to refer to the pannier taken through the kamar 'loins'.]

damṛa m. a steer; a young bull; damkom = a bull calf (Santali)

Rebus: damṛi = copper; tamb(r)a = copper (Skt.); tamba = copper (Santali) *damṛi, dambṛi, daṭi* 'one-eighth of a pice (copper)'; dammid.i id. (Telugu) damr.i, dambr.i one eighth of a pice (Santali) damḍ ī, damḍo lowest copper coin (G.) tāmbaḍa copper plate; tāmbaḍī, tāmbaḍo a copper pot; tāmbum copper (G.)

The imagery on the pectoral m1656 shows overflowing (liquid) from the rim of the jar. The words which evoke this imagery are: eṟe = to pour any liquids; to pour (Ka.); iṟu (Ta.Ma.); ira- ī (Ta.); eṟe = to cast, as metal; to overflow, to cover with

water, to bathe (Ka.); e_re, ele = pouring; fitness for being poured(Ka.lex.) erako molten cast (Tu.lex.)

Rebus: eraka, e_raka = any metal infusion (Ka.Tu.); urukku (Ta.); urukka melting; urukku what is melted; fused metal (Ma.); urukku (Ta.Ma.); eragu = to melt; molten state, fusion; erakaddu = any cast thng; erake hoyi = to pour meltted metal into a mould, to cast (Ka.)

The owner of the pectoral is a coppersmith with a workshop and professional in working with metal infusion or fused metal or cast metal.

Rings on neck of one-horned heifer. One horn is kod. Rings on neck are: kot.iyum.

Rebus: kot. 'artisan's workshop'.(Kuwi)

kūṭa 'horn'; rebus: kūṭam 'workshop' (Ta.) kūṭam is also connoted by a glyph: a 'summit of a mountain'.

koṭiyum [*koṭ, koṭī* neck] a wooden circle put round the neck of an animal (G.) [cf. the orthography of rings on the neck of one-horned young bull]. kōd.iya, kōḍe = young bull; kōḍelu = plump young bull; *kōḍe* = a. male as in: *kōḍe dūḍa* = bull calf; young, youthful (Te.lex.) *kōḍiya, kōḍe* young bull; adj. male (e.g., *kōḍe dūḍa* bull calf), young, youthful; *kōḍekāḍu* a young man (Te.); *kōḍē* bull (Kol.); *khoṛe* male calf (Nk.); *kōḍi* cow; *kōṛe* young bullock (Konḍa); *kōḍi* cow (Pe.); *kūḍi* id. (Mand.); *kōḍi* id., ox (Kui); *kajja kōḍi* bull; *kōḍi* cow (Kuwi)(DEDR 2199). *koṛa* a boy, a young man (Santali) *gōnde* bull, ox (Ka.); *gōda* ox (Te.); *kondā* bull (Kol.); *kōnda* bullock (Kol.Nk.); bison (Pa.); *kōnde* cow (Ga.); *kōndē* bullock (Ga.); *kondā , konda* bullock, ox (Go.)(DEDR 2216).

ācāri koṭṭya = forge, kammārasāle (Tu.) kod. = place where artisans work (G.) *koṭḍī* a room (G.)

koḍ = place where artisans work (G.lex.) *koḍ* = a cow-pen; a cattlepen; a byre (G.lex.) goṛa = a cow-shed; a cattleshed; goṛa orak = byre (Santali.lex.) got.ho [Skt. koṣṭha the inner part] a warehouse; an earthen vessel in wich indigo is stored (G.lex.) koṭṭamu = a stable (Te.lex.)

koḍ = artisan's workshop (Kuwi)

kōḍ (pl. *kōḍul*) horn (Pa.); *kōṭu* (in cmpds. *kōṭṭu-*) horn (Ta.); ko.r. (obl. *koṭ-*) horns (one horn is kob), half of hair on each side of parting, side in game, line marked out (Ko.); kwiṛ (obl. *kwiṭ.-*) horn (To.); *kōḍ* horn (Ka.); *kōṟ* horn (Ka.); *kōḍu* horn (Tu.); *kōḍu* rivulet (Te.); *kōr* (pl. *kōrgul*) id. (Ga.); *kōr* (obl. *kōt-*, pl. *kōhk*) horn of cattle or wild animals (Go.); *kōr* (pl. *kōhk*), *kōṛu* (pl. *kōhku*) horn (Go.); kogoo a horn (Go.); kōju (pl. kōska) horn, antler (Kui)(DEDR 2200). Tailless he-buffalo; ox with blunt horns: kūṟai that which is short; dwarf snake, calamaridae; kūṟai-k-kiṭā, kūṟai-k-kaṭā tailless he-buffalo (Ta.)(DEDR 1914). Image: horn: kūṭa any prominence: a horn (Ka.); *kōḍu, kōṟ* a horn of animals; a tusk (Ka.)(Ka.lex.) *kōṟ, kōḍu* a horn; *kōṟke, kōṟkil., kōṟkiḷim, kōṟge* id. (Ka.); *kōḍu* kut.t.u to strike or gore with the horn or with the tusk (Ka.); *kōḍu* a horn of animals; a tusk (Ka.); *kōḍu* -v ī sa the allowance of a vis of corn etc. for every bullock-load that comes into town etc.; *kuḍu* the state of being crooked, bent (Ka.); *koḍu* (Ma.)(Ka.lex.) kūṭa horn, bone of the forehead, prominence (Vedic); prominence, top (Pali.lex.) kūṭa a horn; an ox whose horns are broken; kūṇikā the horn of any animal (Skt.lex.) sin:ghin horn projecting in front (Santali.lex.); kūṭa bone of the forehead with its projections, the crown of the head; end, corner (Skt.lex.)

kūṭa = horn (RV 10.102.4; AV 8.8.16; AitBr. 6.24; S'Br. 3.8.1.15; JBr.1.49.9; 50.1 (JAOS, 19, 114). Rebus: *khũṭ* 'community, guild' (Mu.)

The entire composition of the heifer with a panier and a horn can be read rebus: Glyphic composition: *kōḍē* (heifer) *koḍiyum* (rings on neck) *kūṭa* (horn) Rebus: *kõda koḍ khũṭ kammarsāla* 'pannier' (Telugu); rebus: *karmāraśāla* 'workshop of smith' (Skt.) 'turner, smithy workshop, guild'. The composition animal is often shown in front of the 'standard' device which reads: *sãgaḍa* (lathe/portable furnace) Rebus: *sãngatarāsu* 'stone-cutter, stone-carver'. The two glyphic compositions together thus semantically read: *kõda koḍ kammarsāla khũṭ sãngāta* 'association and guild of smithy workshop turner, stone-carver'. That a lapidary, carver, engraver,scribe is involved becomes emphatically denoted with a semantic determinant using a glyphic composition of 'rim of jar'. This

composition of 'rim of short-necked jar' is used as frequently as the 'heifer-standard-device' composition glyph. This rim of jar glyphic composition connotes: *kaṇḍa kanka* 'furnace, stone (ore) metal account (scribe)'.

Ingots

Glyph: mũh 'face'. Rebus: mũh metal ingot (Santali) mũhã = the quantity of iron produced at one time in a native smelting furnace

múkha n. 'mouth, face' RV., 'entrance' MBh.Pa. *mukha* -- m.; Aś.shah. man. gir. *mukhato,* kāl. dh. jau. *°te* 'by word of mouth'; Pk. *muha* -- n. 'mouth, face', Gy. gr. hung. *muy* m., boh. *muy,* span. *muí,* wel. *mūī̃f.*, arm. *muç,* pal. *mu',* *mi',* pers. *mu;* Tir. *mū* 'face'; Woṭ. *mū* m. 'face, sight'; Kho. *mux* 'face'; Tor. *mū* 'mouth', Mai. *mū̃;* K. in cmpds. *mu* -- *ganḍ* m. 'cheek, upper jaw', *mū* -- *kāla* 'having one's face blackened', rām. *mūī̃,* pog. *mūī̃,* ḍoḍ. ***mū̃h*** 'mouth'; S. *mū̃hū̃* m. 'face, mouth, opening'; L. *mū̃h* m. 'face', awāṇ. *mū̃* with descending tone, mult. *mū̃hā̃* m. 'head of a canal'; P. *mū̃h* m. 'face, mouth', *mū̃hā̃* m. 'head of a canal'; WPah.śeu. *mùtilde;* 'mouth' cur. *mū̃h;* A. *muh* 'face', in cmpds. -- *muwā* 'facing'; B. *mu* 'face'; Or. *muhã* 'face, mouth, head, person'; Bi. *mū̃h* 'opening or hole (in a stove for stoking, in a handmill for filling, in a grainstore for withdrawing)'; Mth. Bhoj. *mū̃h* 'mouth, face', Aw.lakh. *muh,* H. *muh, mū̃h* m.; OG. *muha,* G. *mɔ̃h* n. 'mouth', Si. *muya, muva.* -- Ext. -- *k->* or -- *ll* -- : Pk.*muhala* -- , *muhulla* -- n. 'mouth, face'; S. *muhuro* m. 'face' (or < mukhará --); Ku. *do -- maulo* 'confluence of two streams'; Si. *muhul, muhuna, mūṇa* 'face' H. Smith JA 1950, 179.; -- -- *ḍ* -- : S. *muhaṛo* m. 'front, van'; Bi. (Shahabad) *mohṛā* 'feeding channel of handmill'. WPah.kṭg. (kc.) *mū̃* (with high level tone) m. (obl. -- *a*) 'mouth, face'; OMarw. *muhaṛaü* 'face'.(CDIAL 10158).

Rebus: mũh 'ingot' (Mu.) *kolhe tehen me~ṛhe~tko mūhā akata* = the Kolhes have to-day produced pig iron (Santali.lex.)

Rebus: **múkhya** ' pertaining to face or mouth ' AV., ' chief ' TS. [múkha --] Kt. *myuk,mīk*, Pr. *mikh*, Dm. *muk*, Paš. *mūkh* m., Gaw. Bshk. *muk*, Sv. *mukhá*,

Sh. *mŭkh* m. 'face' (koh. ' cheek '), K. *mŏkh* m. -- Pa. *mukkhaka* -- 'foremost, chief'; Aś.kāl.*mukha* -- 'important', kb. rdh. *mukhya* -- , top. *mukha* -- m. 'chief official'; Pk. *mukkha* -- 'chief'; N. *mukhiyā* 'village headman'; H. *mukhyā* 'chief'. WPah.kṭg. *múkkhiɔ* 'chief'.(CDIAL 10174).

Glyph 'composite (animals)' or ligatured glyphs: మే డము[mēḍamu] *mēḍamu.* [Telugu] n. Joining,union, కూడిక.

Glyph 'oppositon': *mētha ' opposing, quarrelling with '. [√mith] Pa. *mēdhaka* -- , *°aga* -- m. ' quarrel, abuse '; L. *mī̆hā̃* m. ' accusation, reproach '. (CDIAL 10314) *mēḍamu.* A fight, battle, యుద్ధము. మే డముపొడుచు *mēdamu-poḍuṭsu.* v. n. To fight a battle.యుద్ధముచేయు, కోడిమే డముa cock fight. మే ండ్రించు[mēṇḍriñcu] *mēṇḍrinṭsu.* [Tel.] v. a. To divide, cut, sever; భేదించు. (Telugu)

Glyph 'curl of hair': *mēṇḍhī ' lock of hair, curl '. [Cf. **mēṇḍha* -- 1 s.v. *miḍḍa --] S. *mī̆ḍhī* f., *°ḍho* m. ' braid in a woman's hair ', L. *mẽḍhī* f.; G. *mī̃ḍlɔ, miḍ°* m. 'braid of hair on a girl's forehead'(CDIAL 10312)

Glyph 'tangled cord': M. *meḍhā* m. ' curl, snarl, twist or tangle in cord or thread ' (CDIAL 10312)

Glyph 'spear': మే డెము[mēḍemu] or మే డియము*mēḍemu.* [Tel.] n. A spear or dagger. ఈటె, బాకు. The rim of a bell-shaped earring, set with ems.రాళ్లు చెక్కిన□మికీ అంచు యొక్క పనితరము. "క ఓడితినన్నన్ వారక మే డెముపొడుతురొ BD. vi. 116.

Glyph: 'neck-band': kaḍum 'neck-band, ring' kaḍī a chain; a hook; a link (G.); kaḍum a bracelet, a ring (G.) Rebus: kaḍiyo [Hem. Des. kaḍaio = Skt. sthapati a mason] a bricklayer; a mason; kaḍiyaṇa, kaḍiyeṇa a woman of the bricklayer caste; a wife of a bricklayer (G.) *kadumu* a swelling, bump; *kanti* excrescence, lump, wen, swelling (Telugu)(DEDR 1196) Rebus: *kaṇḍ* 'furnace, fire-altar, consecrated fire'

[The decoration on the neck of the 'ram' glyph is comparable to the rings on the neck of a young bull or flowing scarves on the neck of a composite animal.]

m0302

miṇḍāl 'markhor' (Tōrwālī) meḍho a ram, a sheep (G.)(CDIAL 10120); rebus: mẽṛhet, meḍ 'iron' (Mu.Ho.)

- Glyph: mEḍi plait (Kannada). *Ta.* miṭai (-v-, -nt-) to weave as a mat, etc. *Ma.* miṭayuka to plait, braid, twist, wattle; miṭaccal plaiting, etc.; miṭappu tuft of hair; miṭala screen or wicket, ōlas plaited together. *Ka.* meḍaṟu to plait as screens, etc. (Hav.) maḍe to knit, weave (as a basket); (Gowda) mEḍi plait. *Ga.* (S.3) miṭṭe a female hair-style. *Go.* (Mu.) mihc-to plait (hair) (DEDR 4853) Rebus: meḍ 'iron' (Ho.)
- Glyph: six: bhaṭa 'six'; rebus: bhaṭa 'furnace'
- Glyph: seven: eae 'seven' (Santali); rebus: eh-ku 'steel' (Ta.)

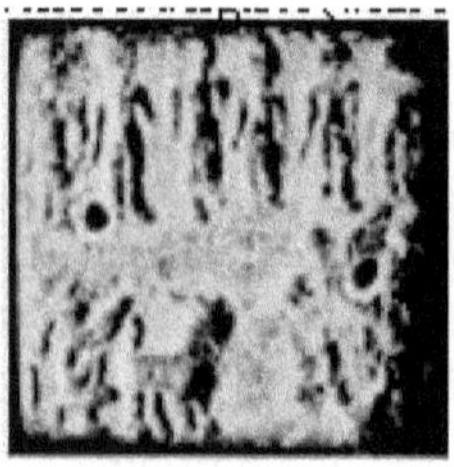

m0442At m0442Bt

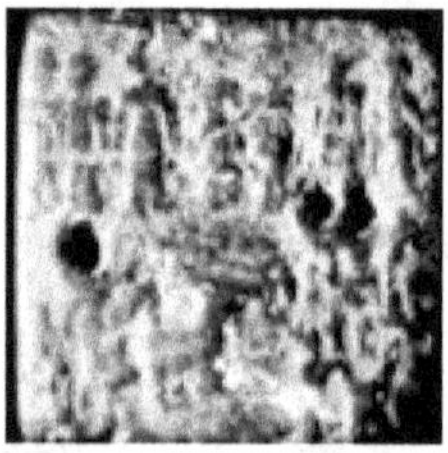

Mohenjo-daro, excavation number HR 4161, now in the National Museum of India, New Delhi. A seal from Mohenjo-daro, excavation number DK 6847 (m1186A), now in the National Museum of Pakistan, Karachi. Department of Archaeology and Museums, Government of Pakistan.

?Pleiades clustered in the context of other Indus script glyphs

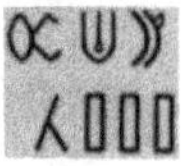

Text 4251 h097 Pict-95: Seven robed figures (with stylized twigs on their head and pig-tails) standing in a row. bagaḷā 'pleiades'; rebus: *bagala bangaru* 'gold, chafing dish'

Rebus reading of Top line of inscription: Alloyed bronze ingot, iron mineral

- 1. kuṭila, katthīl = bronze (8 parts copper and 2 parts tin) *khōṭ* 'alloyed' (Punjabi) koṭe 'forged (metal) (Santali)
- 2. ḍabu 'an iron spoon' (Santali) Rebus: ḍab, ḍhimba, ḍhompo 'lump (ingot?)' (Mu.) Rebus: baṭa = a kind of iron (G.) bhaṭa 'furnace' (G.)
- 3. ḍato = claws of crab (Santali) ḍato 'claws or pincers (chelae) of crabs'; ḍaṭom, ḍiṭom to seize with the claws or pincers, as crabs, scorpions; ḍaṭkop = to pinch, nip (only of crabs) (Santali) Rebus: dhātu = mineral (Skt.)

Rebus reading of Bottom line of inscription: ingots, metal-ware entrustment articles

- ḍhāḷ = a slope; the inclination of a plane;m ḍhāḷiyum = adj. sloping, inclining (G.) Rebus: ḍhāḷako = a large metal ingot (G.) खांडा [khāṇḍā] *m* A jag, notch, or indentation (as upon the edge of a tool or weapon).khāṇḍā 'tools, pots and pans and metal-ware'.
- kolmo 'three'; rebus: kolami 'smithy'. *sāgāḍā* m. ' frame of a building ' (Marathi) Rebus: jaṅgaḍ 'entrusment articles'.

A group of six or seven women wearing twigs may not represent Pleiades, bagaḷā). The groups of such glyphs occur on four inscribed objects of Indus writing. (See four pictorial compositions on: m1186A, h097, m0442At m0442Bt).

Glyph (seven women): bahulā = Pleiades (Skt.) bagaḷā = name of a certain godess (Te.) bagaḷā ,bagaḷe, vagalā (Ka.); baka , bagaḷḷā , vagaḷā (Te.)

Rebus 1: bagalo = an Arabian merchant vessel (G.) bagala = an Arab boat of a particular description (Ka.); bagalā (M.); bagarige, bagarage = a kind of vessel (Ka.)(Ka.lex.);

Reebus 2: *bangala* = kumpaṭi = an:gāra śakaṭī = a chafing dish a portable stove a goldsmith's portable furnace (Telugu) cf. *bangaru bangaramu* = gold (Te.)

Rebus 3: bhāgaḷiyo = a bazaar shopkeeper (G.lex) bakāḷa (Ka.); baāla = a shopkeeper with contemptuous implications (M.)(Ka.lex.) bakāl = [Ar. bakkāl, a greengrocer fr. bakcū, vegetable] a petty shopkeeper; bānia (so called in contempt); bakālu = fresh vegetables (Gujarati)

kūdī, kūṭī bunch of twigs (Skt.lex.) kūdī (also written as kūṭī in manuscripts) occurs in the Atharvaveda (AV 5.19.12) and Kauśika Sūtra (Bloomsfield's ed.n, xliv. Cf. Bloomsfield, American Journal of Philology, 11, 355; 12,416; Roth, Festgruss an Bohtlingk, 98) denotes it as a twig. This is identified as that of Badarī, the jujube tied to the body of the dead to efface their traces. (See Vedic Index, I, p. 177). Rebus 1: kuṭila, katthīl = bronze (8 parts copper and 2 parts tin) [cf. āra-kūṭa, 'brass' (Skt.) (CDIAL 3230) Rebus 2: kuṭhi 'smelting furnace' (Santali) koṭe 'forged (metal) (Santali)

Slide 142. Moulded tablets from Trench 11 Harappa (Kenoyer); m1186; m488C adorant with 'scarf'; markhor in front, with rings (or neck-bands, scarves) on neck.

Glyph 'fig, ficus glomerata': మేడి [mēḍi] *mēḍi.* [Tel.] అత్తి, ఉదుంబరము. మేడిపండు the fruit of this tree.

Ka. mēḍi glomerous fig tree, *Ficus racemosa*; opposite-leaved fig tree, *F. oppositifolia. Te.* mēḍi *F. glomerata.* *Kol.* (Kin.) mēṛi id. [*F. glomerata* Roxb. = *F. racemosa* Wall.](DEDR 5090).

Glyph: kuṇḍī = chief of village. kuṇḍi-a = village headman; leader of a village (Pkt.lex.) i.e. śreṇi jeṭṭha chief of metal-worker guild. Rebus: khōḍ m. 'pit', khōḍü f. 'small pit' (Kashmiri. CDIAL 3947), kuṭhi 'smelter furnace'

(Mu.) kuṇḍamu 'a pit for receiving and preserving consecrated fire' (Te.) kundār turner (A.); kũdār, kũdāri (B.); kundāru (Or.); kundau to turn on a lathe, to carve, to chase; kundau dhiri = a hewn stone; kundau murhut = a graven image (Santali)

m1186A, Text 2430 Composition: horned person with a pigtail standing between the branches of a pipal on a creeper; a low pedestal with offerings (? Bowl with two ladles?);a horned person kneeling in adoration;a ram with short tail and curling horns; a row of seven robed figures, with twigs on their pigtails.

khaḍaka ' *erect ', m. ' bolt, post ' KātyŚr; stand '. [Cf. *khadáti* ' is firm ' Dhātup.] and 1. K. *khoru* ' standing ', ḍoḍ. *khaṛo* ' up ', pog. *khaṛkhuṛ* ' erect '; S. *khaṛo* ' standing erect ', P. *khaṛā*, WPah. paṅ. *khaṛā*, bhad. *khaṛo*, Or. B. *khāṛā*, H. *khaṛā* (→ N. *khaṛā*), Marw. *khaṛo*, G. *khaṛũ*; M. *khaḍā* ' standing, constant '.2. K. pog. *khaṛnu* ' to stand ', rām. *khaṛōnu*, ḍoḍ. *khaṛōnō*; WPah. bhal. caus. *khaṛēṇu* ' to fix '; -- G. *khaṛakvũ* ' to make a heap '.3. K. *khārun* ' to make ascend, lift up '.WPah.kṭg. *khɔ́ṛɔ* ' erect, upright '; *khɔ́ṛhnõ*, kc. *khɔṛiṇo* ' to stand, rise ', J. *khaṛuwṇu.*(CDIAL 3784).

- bhaṭa 'six'; rebus: bhaṭa 'furnace'; bhaṭa 'iron' (G.)
- eae 'seven' (Santali); rebus: eh-ku 'steel' (Ta.)

adaru 'twig'; rebus: aduru 'native, unsmelted metal'. kola 'woman'; rebus: kol 'working in iron' (Ta.) Thus the group of women (six or seven) may connote: pl. kole.l rebus: 'smithy, temple' (Ko.)(DEDR 2133). Six women with twigs: adaru kol bhaṭa 'native metal, iron furnace'; seven women with twigs: adaru kol eh-ku 'native metal, iron, steel'.

A group of six or seven persons constitute unique glyphs. Each of the six or seven glyphs is ligatured with a twig on the head and a scarf as a hair-dress. The other glyphs associated with the Pleiades, in the four pictorial compositions are:

- Human face ligatured to a ram with neck-bands
- Kneeling adorant with horns and scarf as pigtail
- Standing person (horns, twig as head-dress, scarf as pigtail) within a pot ligatured with leaves
- Temple (smithy?) glyph (third line of signs)
- Dotted fish, rim of jar, body (person)
- Pincers, claws (ligatured to ingots) ḍhālako Sign 274; rebus: 'a large metal ingot (G.)'
- Spoon in a rimless pot (Second sign on line 1, text 4251)

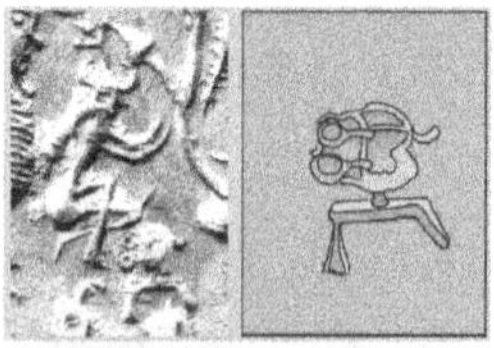

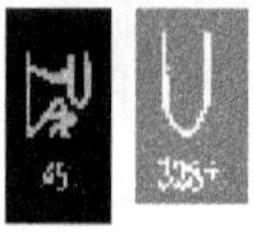

- meṛgo = rimless vessels (Santali) Rebus: meḍ 'iron' (Ho.)
- bārṇe, bāraṇe = an offering of food to a demon; a meal after fasting, a breakfast (Tu.) barada, barda, birada = a vow (G.lex.) Rebus: baran, bharat (5 copper, 4 zinc and 1 tin)(P.B.) karadamu present to a superior (Te.) kareṭum = an annual offering and present to a godess or to an evil spirit (G.) karavṛtti (Skt.) Rebus; kharādī 'turner' (G.) saman: = to offer an offering, to place in front of; front, to front or face (Santali) Rebus: samr.obica, stones containing gold (Mundari.lex.) cf. soma (ṛgveda) samanom = an obsolete name for gold (Santali). kharādī 'turner' (G.) कातारी or कांतारी [kātārī or kāntārī] m (कातणें) A turner. (Marathi) karaḍo, karāḍī 'a goldsmith's tool' (G.)

- S. baṭhu m. 'large pot in which grain is parched, Rebus; bhaṭṭhā m. 'kiln' (P.)

baṭa = a kind of iron (G.)

- bhaṭa 'furnace' (G.) baṭa = kiln (Santali); baṭa = a kind of iron (G.) bhaṭṭha -- m.n. ' gridiron (Pkt.) baṭhu large cooking fire' baṭhī f. 'distilling furnace'; L. bhaṭṭh m. 'grain—parcher's oven', bhaṭṭhī f. 'kiln, distillery', awāṇ. bhaṭh; P. bhaṭṭh m., ṭhī f. 'furnace', bhaṭṭhā m. 'kiln'; S. bhaṭṭhī keṇī 'distil (spirits)'. (CDIAL 9656)

- Kur. kaṇḍō a stool. Malt. kanḍo stool, seat. (DEDR 1179) Rebus: kaṇḍ = a furnace, altar (Santali.lex.) khaṇḍa 'tools, pots and pans and metal-ware'. kāṇṭam 'ewer, pot' கமண்டலம். (Tamil) prob. *karaṇḍa- ka* 'Pot with a spout, ewer'; करङ्कः karaṅkḥ1 A skeleton. -2 The skull; प्रेतरङ्कः करङ्का- दङ्कस्थादस्थिसंस्थं स्थपुटगतमपि क्रव्यमव्यग्रमत्ति Māl.5.16; also 5.19; प्रेतरङ्को$ङ्कमारोप्य करङ्कमकुतोभयः Śiva. B.14.79. -3 A small pot (of cocoa-nut) karaka m. ' water vessel ' MBh. Pa. *karaka* -- m., Pk. *karaya* -- m., *kariā* -- f. 'cup for serving spirituous liquor'; Paš. *karā* 'a well' IIFL iii 3, 96; Bi. *karaī* 'spouted water vessel'; H. *karaī* f. 'small earthen pipkin'. -- With -- *uka* -- (cf. gaḍḍuka --): P. Ku. *karuā* 'spouted water vessel '; N. *karuwā* 'small brass waterpot with a spout'; Bi. *karwā* 'pot for pouring water on plaster'; Mth. *karwā* 'waterpot with a spout', H. *karuā.* -- Bi. Mth. *karnā* 'earthen vessel for milk or curds'; -- M. *karhā* m. 'waterpot (esp. that used in the marriage ceremony)'.(CDIAL 2781). G. *ghāḍvɔ* m. 'earthen pot for ghee' M. *gaḍū, °ḍuvā* m. 'drinking cup' (CDIAL 3984). Rebus: *khaṇḍa* 'tools, pots and pans and metal-ware'.

- ḍabu 'an iron spoon' (Santali) Rebus: ḍab, ḍhimba, ḍhompo 'lump (ingot?)' (Mu.)

- Rebus: baṭa = a kind of iron (G.) bhaṭa 'furnace' (G.)

- pattar 'trough' (Ta.) पात्र pātra, (I.) s. Vessel, cup, plate; receptacle. [lw. Sk. Id.] (Nepali) pātramu A utensil, ఉపకరణము. Hardware. Metal vessels. (Telugu) Rebus paṭṭar-ai community; guild as of workmen (Tamil)

() The glyph is an oval with a handle, like a spoon in a U-shaped pot and connotes 'cast bronze'; it is a glyptic formed of a pair of brackets (): kuṭila 'bent'; rebus: kuṭila, katthīl = bronze (8 parts copper and 2

parts tin) [cf. āra-kūṭa, 'brass' (Skt.) (CDIAL 3230) kuṭi— in cmpd. 'curve' (Skt.)(CDIAL 3231).

kuṭika— 'bent' MBh. [√kuṭ 1] Ext. in H. kuṛuk f. 'coil of string or rope'; M. kuḍċā m. 'palm contracted and hollowed', kuḍapṇẽ 'to curl over, crisp, contract'. CDIAL 3231 kuṭilá— 'bent, crooked' KātyŚr., aka— Pañcat., n. 'a partic. plant' lex. [√kuṭ 1] Pa. kuṭila— 'bent', n. 'bend'; Pk. kuḍila— 'crooked', illa— 'humpbacked', illaya— 'bent' DEDR 2054 Ta. koṭu curved, bent, crooked; koṭumai crookedness, obliquity; koṭukki hooked bar for fastening doors, clasp of an ornament. A pair of curved lines: dol 'likeness, picture, form' [e.g., two tigers, two bulls, sign-pair.] Kashmiri. dula दुल । युग्मम् m. a pair, a couple, esp. of two similar things (Rām. 966). Rebus: dul meṛeḍ cast iron (Mundari. Santali) dul 'to cast metal in a mould' (Santali) pasra meṛed, pasāra meṛed = syn. of koṭe meṛed = forged iron, in contrast to dul meṛed, cast iron (Mundari.lex.)

Thus, dul kuṭila 'cast bronze'.

Allograph: 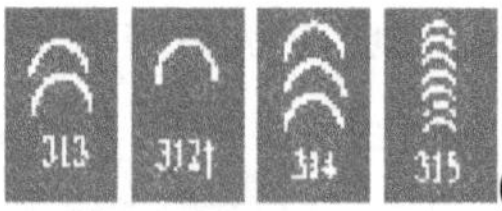 ( ) kuṭila = bent, crooked. The number of such 'arched' glyphs connote the proportions of tin alloyed with copper. kuṭila, katthīl = bronze (8 parts copper and 2 parts tin)(CDIAL 3230). kuṭi— in cmpd. 'curve', kuṭika— 'bent' MBh. (CDIAL 3231); rebus: kuṭhi 'smelter' (Santali)

Allograph

Shape of oval is consistent with the traditiojn of Koles to form equilateral lumps  pointed at each end of ingots: mũh metal ingot (Santali) mũhā = the quantity of iron produced at one time in a native smelting furnace of the Kolhes; iron produced by the Kolhes and formed like a four-cornered piece a little pointed at each end; mũhā me~r.he~t = iron smelted by the Kolhes and formed into an equilateral lump a little pointed at each end; kolhe tehen me~r.he~tko mũhā akata = the Kolhes have to-day produced pig iron (Santali.lex.)

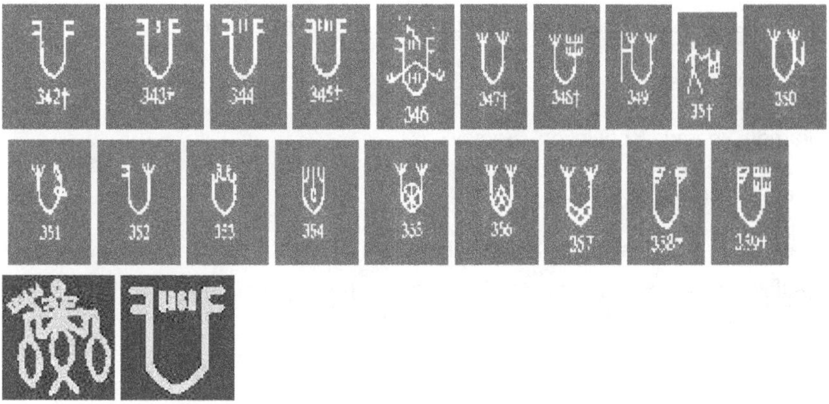

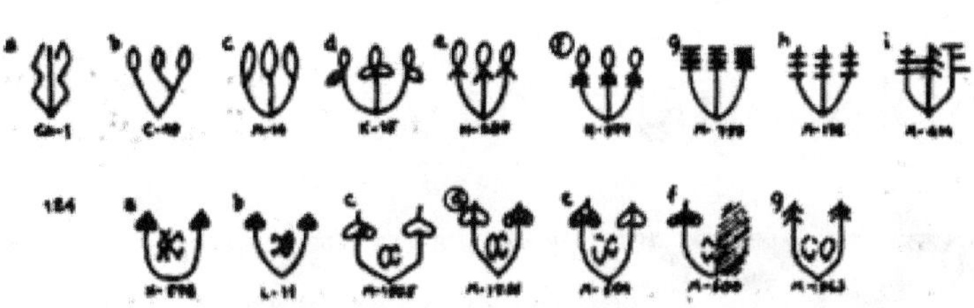

Allographs of a duplicated 'leaf' glyph, ligatured with 'crab-claws' glyph and U ('rimless pot') glyph – shown on one copper tablet [After Parpola, 1994, fig. 13.15] seems to be a comparable rebus reading of the archer shown on another copper tablet. The archer shown on one copper tablet seems to be a synonym of a ligatured complex glyph -- the 'leave's ligatured with crab and 'U' glyph on another copper tablet since the inscription on the obverse of each of the tablets is identical. [cf. Parpola, 1994, fig. 13.13] This ligatured complex glyph appears on two seals- one from Harappa and another from Lothal. Leaves ligatured with crab is a sign which occurs on these seals and with similar sign sequences. [cf. Parpola, 1994, fig. 13.12]

Glyph: 'archer': kamāṭhiyo = archer; kāmaṭhum = a bow; kāmaḍ, kāmaḍum = a chip of bamboo (G.) kāmaṭhiyo a bowman; an archer (Skt.lex.) Rebus: kammaṭi a coiner (Ka.);

kampaṭṭam coinage, coin, mint (Ta.) kammaṭa = mint, gold furnace (Te.)

Allographs (graphemes):

kamḍa, khamḍa 'copulation' (Santali)

kamaṭha crab (Skt.)

kamaṛkom = fig leaf (Santali.lex.) kamarmaṛā (Has.), kamaṛkom (Nag.); the petiole or stalk of a leaf (Mundari.lex.) kamat.ha = fig leaf, religiosa (Skt.)

Gold

kundan कुंदन् । निर्मलं हेम m. pure gold, the finest gold (Śiv. 531, 1293). -- char hyuhu -- छर् हिहु । अतिनिर्मलम् भूषणम् adj. (f. -- hishü -- हिशू&below;), like a drop of pure gold; hence, very flawless and brilliant.

B. kõdā 'to turn in a lathe'; Or. kũnda 'lathe', kũdibā, kũd 'to turn' (→ Drav. Kur. kũd 'lathe') (CDIAL 3295)

Rebus glyphs, allographs

kunda कुंद । स्थाणुः m. a billet, a log; a trunk or stump of a tree; a kind of clog or wooden fetter (for prisoners).

kundau to turn on a lathe, to carve, to chase; kundau dhiri = a hewn stone; kundau murhut = a graven image (Santali) kunda1 m. ' a turner's lathe ' lex. [Cf. *cunda -- 1] N. *kũdnu* ' to shape smoothly, smoothe, carve, hew ', *kũduwā* ' smoothly shaped '; A. *kund* ' lathe ', *kundiba* ' to turn and

smooth in a lathe ', *kundowā* ' smoothed and rounded '; B. *kũd* ' lathe ', *kũdā, kõdā* ' to turn in a lathe '; Or. *kũ˘nda* ' lathe ', *kũdibā, kũd°* ' to turn ' (→ Drav. Kur. *kũd* ' lathe '); Bi. *kund* ' brassfounder's lathe '; H.*kunnā* ' to shape on a lathe ', *kuniyā* m. ' turner ', *kunwā* m. (CDIAL 3295) kundakara m. ' turner ' W. [Cf. *cundakāra -- : kunda -- 1, kará -- 1] A. *kundār*, B. *kũdār*, *°ri*, Or. *kundāru*; H. *kũderā* m. ' one who works a lathe, one who scrapes ', *°rī* f., *kũdernā* ' to scrape, plane, round on a lathe '.(CDIAL 3297).

kunda m. ' Jasminum multiflorum or pubescens ' MBh. (' olibanum or resin of Boswellia thurifera ' lex., see kunduru -), n. ' its flower '. Pa. *kunda* -- n. ' jasmine '; Pk. *kuṁda* -- m. ' a flowering tree ', n. ' a kind of flower '; B. *kũd* ' J. multiflorum ', M. *kũd* m. ' id. ', *kũdā* m. ' a partic. kind of flowering shrub '; Si. *kon̆da* ' jasmine '. (CDIAL 3296)

Fortified place

கோடு kōṭu [M. *kōṭṭa.*] Stronghold, fortified place; அரணிருக்கை. (a) *Ta.* kōṭṭai fort, castle; kōṭu stronghold. *Ma.* kōṭṭa fort, residence ; kōṭu fort. *Ko.* ko·ṭ castle, palatial mansion. *To.* kwa·ṭ bungalow. *Ka.* kōṭe fort, rampart; (PBh.) kōṇṭe fort. *Koḍ.* ko·ṭe palace. *Tu.* kōṭè fort. *Te.* kōṭa, (Inscr.) koṭṭamu id. *Kuwi* (S.) kōṭa palace, fort. / Cf. Skt. koṭṭa-, koṭa- fort, stronghold. *(b) Ko.* go·ṛ (*obl.* go·ṭ-) wall. *Ka.* gōḍe id. *Tu.* gōḍè id. *Te.* gōḍa id. *Kol.* (SR.) goḍā id. *Kuwi* (S.) kōḍa wall, prison; (Isr.) kōḍa wall. (DEDR 2207). kōṭṭa1 m. (n. lex.) ' fort ' Kathās., *kōṭa* -- 1 m. Vāstuv.Aś. sn. *koṭa* -- ' fort, fortified town ', Pk. *koṭṭa* --, *kuṭ°* n.; Kt. *kuṭ* ' tower (?) ' NTS xii 174; Dm. *kōṭ* ' tower ',Kal. *kōṭ*; Sh. gil. *kōṭ* m. ' fort ' (→ Ḍ. *kōṭ* m.), koh. pales. *kōṭ* m. ' village '; K. *kūṭh*, dat. *kūṭas* m. ' fort ', S. *koṭu* m., L. *koṭ* m.; P. *koṭ* m. ' fort, mud bank round a village or field '; A. *kōṭh* ' stockade, palisade '; B. *koṭ, kuṭ* ' fort ', Or. *koṭa, kuṭa*, H. Marw. *koṭ* m.; G. *koṭ* m. ' fort, rampart '; M. *koṭ, koṭh* m. ' fort ', Si. *koṭuva* (CDIAL 3500).

Rebus glyph

கோடு kōṭu Horn; விலங்கின் கொம்பு. கோட்டிடை யாடினை கூத்து (திவ். இயற். திருவிருத். 21). Ka. kōḍu horn, tusk, branch of a tree; kōṟ horn. Tu. kōḍů, kōḍu horn. Te. kōḍu rivulet, branch of a river. Pa. kōḍ (pl. kōḍul) horn. Ga. (Oll.) kōr (pl. kōrgul) id. Go. (Tr.) kōr (obl. kōt-, pl.kōhk) horn of cattle or wild animals, branch of a tree; (W. Ph. A. Ch.) kōr (pl. kōhk), (S.) kōr (pl. kōhku), (Ma.) kōṛu (pl. kōẖku) horn; (M.) kohk branch (Voc.980); (LuS.) kogoo a horn. Kui kōju (pl. kōska) horn, antler. (DEDR 2200)

Alloyed metal, to engrave

WPah.kṭg. *khóṛnõ* ' to dig, scratch, engrave '(CDIAL 3892). 1. G. *kotarvũ* ' to dig, carve ', *kotar* n. ' cave, -- N. *kotranu* ' to scratch ' < **kōtraḍ* -- ?2. S. *khoṭranu* ' to dig, carve '; L. poṭh. *khotarṇā* ' to poke about ' (X khánati in *khanotarṇā* ' to poke, dig up with any small instrument '), awāṇ. *khōtruṇ* ' to scratch, dig ', G. *khotarvũ* ' to dig, scratch ', *khotarṇā* n. pl. ' old errors raked up '; -- N. *khotar* ' burnt sediment of milk ' < **khotraḍ* den '; - S.kcch. *khotarṇū* ' to scatch (for itching) ', P. *khoṭnā* ' to dig, scratch, poke '.(CDIAL 3512)

Rebus glyphs, allographs

kōḍ कोड् m. a kernel (Kashmiri) खोट [khōṭa] A lump or solid bit (as of phlegm, gore, curds, inspissated milk); any concretion or clot. (Marathi)

Ka. koḍe to hollow, excavate, scoop, scrape out, remove with the finger or a pick (as ear-wax); koḍacu, koḍasu to remove the ear-wax with the finger or with a pick, remove the impurities from out of a vessel by rubbing its inside with the hand; kuḍite, kuḍate, kuḍute palm of the hand, esp. hollowed or held as a cup; goḍagu, goḍugu hollow, hole; goṭ(a)ru hole, hollow in a wall, tree, etc. *Tu.* kuḍè, guḍè a rat's hole. *Kor.* (O.) goḍe id. *Kur.* khoḍrā, khoḍrō, khoḍor hollow (of a tree-trunk), full of holes; cavity inside a tree, hole. *Ta.* kuṭai (-v-, -nt-) to work through as bees gathering honey, scoop, hollow out, bore, perforate,

penetrate; *n.* anything hollow, ola basket for eating and drinking from;kuṭaivu hollow, cavity; kuṭā cavity, cavern; kuṭavu cave. *To.* kuḏy pit, mortar; kuḏy- (kuḏs-) to have a shallow hollow (as back of thumb by pressure of index finger); (kuḏc-) to make into a shallow hollow (e.g. pile of rice, back of thumb by pressure of index finger); (for ḏ, MBE 1974b, p. 44, n. 20). / Cf. Skt. koṭara- hollow of a tree; Turner, *CDIAL*, no. 3496, including H. khoḍar, khoṛrā (whence the Kur. items). (DEDR 1660). kōṭará n. ' hollow of a tree ' MBh., ' cave, cavity ' BhP. [← Drav. T. Burrow BSOAS xii 376: supported by variety of initial (*k* -- , *kh* --) and medial consonants (-- *ṭ* -- , -- *ṭṭ* -- , -- *l* --) in NIA.] Pk. *kōḍara* -- , *kōla°*, *kōṭa°*, *koṭṭa°* n. ' hole, hollow '; Or. *koraṛa* ' hollow in a tree, cave, hole '; H. (X *khōla -- 2) *khoḍar* m. ' pit, hollow in a tree ', *khoṛrā* m.; Si.*kovuḷa* ' rotten tree ' (< **kōḷalla* -- with H. Smith JA 1950, 197, but not < Pa. *kōḷāpa* --). (CDIAL 3496).

Ta. kōṭaram monkey. *Ir.* kōḍa (small) monkey; kūḍag monkey. *Ko.* ko·ṛṇ small monkey. *To.* kwṛṇ monkey. *Ka.* kōḍaga monkey, ape. *Koḍ.* ko·ḍë monkey. *Tu.* koḍañji, koḍañja, koḍaṅgů baboon. (DEDR 2196).

Te. kōḍu rivulet, branch of a river; Ta. kōṭu bank of stream or pool (DEDR 2200).

Ta. kōṭi weir of a tank, outlet for surplus water. *Ka.* kōḍi a passage to carry off excess of water, outlet of a tank. *Te.(VPK)* kōḍi outlet of tank. (DEDR 2197).

కోటి [kōṭi] *kōṭi.* [Tel.] n. Espionage. వేగు. కోటికాడు or కొట్టికాడు *kōṭi-kāḍu.* n. A spy. Amuk. iii. (Telugu)

కోడు [kōḍu] A leg of a bed, table, or chair. కాలు. (Telugu)

Ta. koṭi banner, flag, streamer; *Ma.* koṭi top, extremity, flag, banner, sprout; kōṭu end; kuvaṭu hill, mountain-top; kuṭuma, kuṭumma narrow point, bird's crest, pivot of door used as hinge, lock of hair worn as caste distinction; koṭṭu head of a bone. *Ko.* koṛy flag on temple; koṭ top tuft of hair (of Kota boy, brahman), crest of bird; kuṭ clitoris. *To.* kwïṭ tip, nipple, child's back lock of

hair. *Ka.*kuḍi pointed end, point, extreme tip of a creeper, sprout, end, top, flag, banner; guḍi point, flag, banner; kuḍilu sprout, shoot; kōḍu a point, the peak or top of a hill; koṭṭua point, nipple, crest, gold ornament worn by women in their plaited hair; koṭṭa state of being extreme; koṭṭa-kone the extreme point; (Hav.) koḍi sprout; *Koḍ.* koḍi top (of mountain, tree, rock, table), rim of pit or tank, flag. *Tu.* koḍi point, end, extremity, sprout, flag; koḍipuni to bud, germinate; (B-K.) koḍipu, koḍipelů a sprout; koḍirèthe top-leaf; koṭṭu cock's comb, peacock's tuft. *Te.* koḍi tip, top, end or point of a flame; koṭṭa-kona the very end or extremity. *Kol.* (Kin.) koṛi point. *Pa.* kūṭor cock's comb. *Go.* (Tr.) koḍḍī tender tip or shoot of a plant or tree; koḍḍi (S.) end, tip, (Mu.) tip of bow; (A.) koḍi point (*Voc.* 891). *Malt.* qoṛgo comb of a cock; ? qóru the end, the top (as of a tree). (DEDR 2049).

Consecrated fire, kiln

kŏnḍ क्रंड् or kŏnḍa क्रंड । कुण्ड m a deep still spring (El., Gr.Gr. 145); (amongst Hindūs) a hole dug in the ground for receiving consecrated fire; cf. ạgana-kŏnḍ (p. 16*b,* l. 34) (Rām. 631). kọ̆nḍu or konḍu । कुण्डम् m. a hole dug in the ground for receiving consecrated fire (Kashmiri) kōda कौंद। कुलालादिकन्दुः f. a kiln; a potter's kiln (Rām. 1446; H. xi, 11); a brick-kiln (Śiv. 133); a lime-kiln. -bal -बल् । कुलालादिकन्दुस्थानम् m. the place where a kiln is erected, a brick or potter's kiln (Gr.Gr. 165). -- khasüñü -- कुलालादिकन्दुयथावद्भावः f.inf. a kiln to arise; met. to become like such a kiln (which contains no imperfectly baked articles, but only well-made perfectly baked ones), hence, a collection of good ('pucka') articles or qualities to exist. Cf. Śiv. 133, where the causal form of the verb is used. (Kashmiri)(CDIAL 2726) WPah.kṭg. *kv́ṇḍh* m. ' pit or vessel used for an oblation with fire into which barley etc. is thrown '; H. *gõṛā* m. 'reservoir used in irrigatio '. (CDIAL 3264). अग्निकुण्डम्. A pool, well; especially one consecrated to some deity or holy purpose. (Sanskrit) *Kur.* xoṇḍxā, xōṛxā deep; a pit, abyss. *Malt.* qonḍe deep, low lands. (DEDR 2082). *Ta.* kuṭṭam depth, pond; kuṭṭai pool, small pond; kuṇṭam deep cavity, pit, pool; kuṇṭu depth, hollow, pond, manure-

pit. *Ma.* kuṇṭam, kuṇṭu what is hollow and deep, hole, pit. *Ka.* kuṇḍa, koṇḍa, kuṇṭe pit, pool, pond; guṇḍa hollowness and deepness; guṇḍi hole, pit, hollow, pit of the stomach; guṇḍige pit of the stomach; guṇḍitu, guṇḍittu that is deep; guṇpu, gumpu, gumbu depth, profundity, solemnity, secrecy. *Koḍ.* kuṇḍï pit; kuṇḍitere manure-pit. *Tu.* kuṇḍa a pit; koṇḍa pit, hole;guṇḍi abyss, gulf, great depth; gumpu secret, concealed. *Te.* kuṇṭa, guṇṭa pond, pit; kuṇḍu cistern; guṇḍamu fire-pit; (Inscr.) a hollow or pit in the dry bed of a stream;gunta pit, hollow, depression. *Kol.* (Pat., p.115) gunḍi deep. *Nk.* ghuṇḍik id. *Pa.* guṭṭa pool. *Go.* (A.) kunṭa id. (*Voc.* 737). *Konḍa* guṭa pit, hollow in the ground. *Kui*kuṭṭ a large pit (Chandrasekhar, *Trans. Linguistic Circle Delhi* 1958, p. 2). *Kuwi* (S.) guntomi pit; (Isr.) kuṇḍi pond. / Cf. Skt. kuṇḍa- round hole in ground (for water or sacred fire), pit, well, spring (DEDR 1669).

Rebus glyphs, allographs

खोंड [khōṇḍa] *m* A young bull, a bullcalf (Marathi). *Ka.* gōnde bull, ox. *Te.* gōda ox. *Kol.* (SR.) kondā bull; (Kin.) kōnda bullock. *Nk.* *(Ch.)* kōnda id. *Pa.* kōnda bison. *Ga.* (Oll.) kōnde cow; (S.) kōndē bullock. *Go.*(Tr.) kōnḍā, (other dialects) kōnda bullock, ox (DEDR 2216). *Te.* kōḍiya, kōḍe young bull; *adj.* male (e.g. kōḍe dūḍa bull calf), young, youthful; kōḍekāḍu a young man. *Kol.* (Haig) kōḍē bull. *Nk.* khoṛe male calf. *Konḍa* kōḍi cow; kōṛe young bullock. *Pe.* kōḍi cow. *Manḍ.* kūḍi id. *Kui* kōḍi id., ox. *Kuwi* (F.) kōdi cow; (S.) kajja kōḍi bull (DEDR 2199).

khonḍu 'divided into parts' (Kashmiri)

kŏnḍal 1 क्वंडल् or (Gr.Gr. 69) kunḍal कुंडल् । काष्ठाङ्गारिकामृण्मयो भागः, निन्दावाक्यघोषः f. (sg. dat. kŏnḍali क्वंडलि or kŏnḍüjü क्वंड;, Gr.Gr. 69), the earthenware bowl of a kāgürü, *kāngrī* or portable brazier, which holds the burning coals (K.Pr. 25, 129, 21) kŏnḍ क्वंड् or kŏnḍa क्वंड । कुण्ड m. a kind of large bowl or basin made of metal or earthenware (Gr.Gr. 145)(Kashmiri) Kan. *gunḍi*, Pk. *kōḍaya* -- , *°ḍia* -- n. '

small earthen pot '; Dm. *kōṛí* ' milking pail '; G. *koṛiyũ* n. ' earthen cup for oil and wick '; M. *koḍẽ* n. ' earthen saucer for a lamp '. (CDIAL 3227). *Ta.* kuṭam waterpot, hub of a wheel; kuṭaṅkar waterpot; kuṭantam pot; kuṭantai Kumbakonam (old name); kuṭukkai coconut or other hard shell used as vessel, pitcher; kuṭikai ascetic's pitcher; kuṭuvai vessel with a small narrow mouth, pitcher of an asectic. *Ma.* kuṭam waterpot; kuṭukka shells (as of gourds) used as vessels, small cooking vessel with narrow mouth; kuṭuka, kuṭuva small vessel. *Ko.* koṛm (*obl.* koṛt-) waterpot with small mouth; ? kuck small clay pot used to drink from (? <*kuṭikkay). *To.* kuṛky small pot. *Ka.* koḍa earthen pitcher or pot; kuḍike small earthen, metal, or wood vessel; guḍuvana, guḍāṇa large water-vessel, used also for storing grain; earthen pot used for churning. *Koḍ.* kuḍike pot in which food (esp. rice) is cooked. *Tu.* kuḍki, kuḍkè, guḍke small earthen vessel. *Te.* kuḍaka, kuḍukacup, bowl, scoop, any cup-like thing; guḍaka a coconut or other similar shell; (B) guḍaka, kuḍaka shell of a fruit prepared to serve as a snuff-box, etc., small metal box; (Inscr.) kuḍalu small earthen vessels. *Kuwi* (Su.) ḍōka, (S.) ḍoka, (F.) dōkka pot (Te. kuḍaka > *kḍōka > ḍōka). / Cf. Skt. kūṭa- waterpot (DEDR 1651). kuṇḍá1 n. (RV. in cmpd.) ' bowl, waterpot ' KātyŚr., ' basin of water, pit ' MBh. (semant. cf. kumbhá -- 1), *°ḍaka* -- m.n. ' pot ' Kathās., *°ḍī* -- f. Pāṇ., *°ḍikā* -- f. Up. 2. *gōṇḍa -- . [← Drav., e.g. Tam. *kuṭam*, Kan. *guṇḍi*, EWA i 226 with other ' pot ' words s.v. kuṭa -- 1]1. Pa. *kuṇḍi* -- , *°ḍikā* -- f. ' pot '; Pk. *kuṁḍa* -- , *koṁ°* n. ' pot, pool ', *kuṁḍī* -- , *°ḍiyā* -- f. ' pot '; Kt. *kuṇi* ' pot ', Wg. *kuṇḍä´ŕ*, Pr. *künǰút;* ' water jar '; Paš. weg. *kuṛā* ' clay pot ' < **kūṛā* IIFL iii 3, 98 (or poss. < kuṭa -- 1), lauṛ. *kuṇḍalī´* ' bucket '; Gaw. *kuṇḍuṛī´* ' milk bowl, bucket '; Kal. *kuṇḍṓk* ' wooden milk bowl '; Kho. *kúṇḍuk*, *°ug* ' milk bowl ', (Lor.) ' a kind of platter '; Bshk. *kūnḗċ* ' jar ' (+?); K. *kŏnḍ* m. ' metal or earthenware vessel, deep still spring ', *kọ̆nḍu* m. ' large cooking pot ', *kunāla* m. ' earthenware vessel with wide top and narrow base '; S. *kunu* m. ' whirlpool ', *°no* m. ' earthen churning pot ', *°nī* f. ' earthen cooking pot ', *°niṛo* m.; L.*kunnā* m. ' tub, well ', *°nī* f. ' wide -- mouthed earthen cooking pot ', *kunāl* m. ' large shallow earthen vessel '; P. *kūḍā* m. ' cooking pot ' (← H.), *kunāl*, *°lā* m., *°lī* f.,*kuṇḍālā* m. ' dish '; WPah. cam. *kuṇḍ* ' pool ', bhal. *kunnu* n. ' cistern for washing clothes in '; Ku. *kuno* ' cooking pot ', *kuni*, *°nelo* ' copper

vessel '; B. *kũṛ* ' small morass, low plot of riceland ', *kũṛi* ' earthen pot, pipe -- bowl '; Or. *kuṇḍa* ' earthen vessel ', *°ḍā* ' large do. ', *°ḍi* ' stone pot '; Bi. *kũṛ* ' iron or earthen vessel, cavity in sugar mill ', *kūṛā* ' earthen vessel for grain '; Mth. *kũṛ* ' pot ', *kūṛā* ' churn '; Bhoj. *kũṛī* ' vessel to draw water in '; H. *kũḍ* f. ' tub ', *kūṛā* m. ' small tub ', *kũḍā* m. ' earthen vessel to knead bread in ', *kũṛī* f. ' stone cup '; G. *kũḍ* m. ' basin ', *kũḍī* f. ' water jar '; M. *kũḍ* n. ' pool, well ', *kũḍā* m. ' large openmouthed jar ', *°ḍī* f. ' small do. '; Si. *keňḍiya, keḍ°* ' pot, drinking vessel '. S.kcch. *kūṇḍho* m. ' flower -- pot ',Brj. *kũṛo* m., *°ṛī* f. ' pot '. (CDIAL 3264).

Ko. ko·ṇṭḷ pocket in outside edge of cloak.(DEDR 2201). खोंडा [khōṇḍā] *m* A कांबळा of which one end is formed into a cowl or hood. खोंडी [khōṇḍī] *f* An outspread shovelform sack (as formed temporarily out of a कांबळा, to hold or fend off grain, chaff &c.) खुंडी [khuṇḍī] *f* A cloth doubled over and sewn at one end, forming a घोंगता, खोपा, or खोळ (an open or outspread shovel-form sack). Used in exposing grain in the market. 2 A species or variety of जोंधळा. (Marathi)

कोंडण [kōṇḍaṇa] f A fold or pen. (Marathi) खुडी [khuḍī] *f* A shed or thatching over a laid-up ship or boat. 2 A cow-shed, a fowl-house, a dove-cot &c.; esp. a pen or fold for calves. (Marathi).

kuṇḍa n. ' clump ' e.g. *darbha -- kuṇḍa* -- Pāṇ. Kan. *goṇḍe* ' cluster ' Pk. *kuṁḍa* -- n. ' heap of crushed sugarcane stalks '; WPah. bhal. *kunnū* m. ' large heap of a mown crop '; N. *kunyũ* ' large heap of grain or straw ', *baṛ -- kũṛo* ' cluster of berries '.(CDIAL 3236). Mar. gōḍā cluster, tuft. *Ta.* koṇtai tuft, dressing of hair in large coil on the head, crest of a bird, head (as of a nail), knob (as of a cane), round top. *Ma.* koṇṭa tuft of hair. *Ko.* goṇḍ knob on end of walking-stick, head of pin; koṇḍ knot of hair at back of head. *To.* kwïḍy Badaga woman's knot of hair at back of head (< Badaga koṇḍe). *Ka.* koṇḍe, goṇḍe tuft, tassel, cluster. *Koḍ.* koṇḍe tassels of sash, knob-like foot of cane-stem. *Tu.* goṇḍè topknot, tassel, cluster. *Te.* koṇḍe, (K. also) koṇḍi knot of hair on the crown of the head. Cf. 2049 Ta. koṭi. / Cf. Skt. kuṇḍa- clump (e.g. darbha-kuṇḍa), Pkt. (*DNM*) goṇḍī- = mañjarī-(DEDR 2081).

Ka. koṇḍi the sting of a scorpion. *Tu.* koṇḍi a sting. *Te.* koṇḍi the sting of a scorpion. (DEDR 2080).

Dm. *kuṇḍa* ' peg for fastening yoke to plough -- pole '; L. *khūḍī* f. ' drum -- stick '; P. *khuṇḍ, °ḍā* m. ' peg, stump '; WPah. rudh. *khuṇḍ* ' tethering peg or post '; A. *khũṭā* ' post ', *°ṭi* ' peg '; B. *khũṭā, °ṭi* ' wooden post, stake, pin, wedge '; Or. *khuṇṭa, °ṭā* ' pillar, post '; Bi. (with -- *ḍa* --) *khũṭrā, °rī* ' posts about one foot high rising from body of cart '; H. *khũṭā* m. ' stump, log ', *°ṭī* f. ' small peg ' (→ P. *khũṭā* m., *°ṭī* f. ' stake, peg '); G. *khũṭ* f. ' landmark ', *khũṭɔ* m., *°ṭī* f. ' peg ', *°ṭũ* n. ' stump ', *°ṭiyũ* n. ' upright support in frame of wagon ', *khũṭrũ* n. ' half -- burnt piece of fuel '; M. *khũṭ* m. ' stump of tree, pile in river, grume on teat ' (semant. cf. kīla -- 1 s.v. *khila -- 2), *khũṭā* m. ' stake ', *°ṭī* f. ' wooden pin ', *khũṭaḷṇẽ* ' to dibble '.1. Ku. *khuṭī* ' peg '; N. *khuṭnu* ' to stitch ' (der. **khuṭ* ' pin ' as *khilnu* from *khil* s.v. khī́la --); Mth. *khuṭā* ' peg, post '; H. *khũṭā* m. ' peg, stump '; Marw.*khuṭī* f. ' peg '; M. *khuṭā* m. ' post '. 2. Pk. *khuṁṭa* -- , *khoṁṭaya* -- m. ' peg, post ';WPah.kṭg. *khv́ndɔ* ' pole for fencing or piling grass round ' (Him.I 35 *nd* poss. wrong for *ṇḍ*); J. *khuṇḍā* m. ' peg to fasten cattle to '.(CDIAL 3893).konḍu spine (Kashmiri)

Cauldron

Ta. kūṉ cauldron; kūṉai large earthen boiler, baling bucket. *Ma. (DCV)* kūna earthen vessel. *Ka.* kūni earthen basin used by oilmen. *Te.* gūna large earthen pot. *Kuwi* (Isr.) gūna a large pot.(DEDR 1928).

Rebus glyphs, allographs

khũṭro = entire bull; khũṭ= brāhmaṇi bull (G.) khuṇṭiyo = an uncastrated bull (Kathiawad. G.lex.) khũṭaḍum a bullock (used in Jhālwāḍ)(G.) kuṇṭai = bull (Ta.lex.) cf. khūdhi hump on the back; khuĩdhũ hump-backed (G.)(CDIAL 3902).

G. khuṇ f., khũ˘ṇɔ m. ' corner '.2. S. kuṇḍa f. ' corner '; P. kũṭ f. ' corner, side ' (← H.). (CDIAL 3898) Phal. Khun ' corner '; H. khũṭ m. ' corner, direction ' (→ P. khũṭ f. ' corner, side '); G. khũṭṛī f. ' angle '. *Ta.* kūṉ bend, curve, hump on the back, humpback, snail; kūṉu (kūṉi-) to curve, become crooked, bend down, become hunchbacked; kūṉal bend, curve, hump; kūṉaṉ humpback; *fem.* kūṉi; kuṉi (-v-, -nt-) to bend (as a bow), bow, stoop; (-pp-, -tt-) to bend (*tr.*), curve; *n.* curvature, bow (weapon); kuṉippu bending. *Ma.* kūnuka to stoop, be crookbacked; kūn a humpback; kūnal, kūntal bending; kūnan humpbacked; *fem.* kūni, kūnicci; kuni semicircle, curve;kuniyuka to bow, stoop, bend; kunikka to make a curve, cause to stand stooping. *Ko.* ku·n- (ku·nḏ-) to be in bowed position (looking down, bent with pain, tiger crouching), become bent with
age. *To.* ku·n hunchback. *Ka.* kūn (kūnt-), kūnu to be bent or bowed, bend, stoop; *n.* a hump; kūna, gūna a humpbacked man; *fem.*kūni, gūni; kūntu bending, bent state; gūnu a hump; kuni to bend, bow, stoop, shrink; *n.* a bent or curved ground; kunuṅgu to bend, stoop, crouch, contract oneself, shrivel up. *Koḍ.* (Shanmugam) kūn hunchback; gūne hunchbacked man; gūni hunchbacked woman. *Tu.* gūnu a hump; gūnè a hunchback. *Te.* gūnu a hump, a crooked back; gūni humpbacked; gūnivāḍu a humpback; *fem.* gūnidi; (B.) kuni angle, bit of land. *Go.* (S.) gun- to bend (*Voc.* 1128). *Kuwi* (Su.) gu'u hump of cow.(DEDR 1927). kōṇa m. ' corner, angle ' MBh. [Cf. kuṇi -- , *khuṇṭa -- 2: ← Drav. T. Burrow BSOAS xi 341]Pa. *kōṇa* -- m., Pk. *kōṇa* -- , *°aga* -- , m.n. ' corner, part of a house '; Sh. (Lor.) *kunī´* ' corner ', K. *kūn* m., P. *koṇ*, *°ṇā*, *kūṇ*, *°ṇā* m., WPah. bhal. *kōṇi* f., cam. *kūṇā* m., Ku. *kuṇo*, pl. *kwāṇā*, gng. *kũ&rtodtilde;*, N. *kunu*, A. *koṇ*, B. *koṇ*, *°ṇā*, Or. *koṇa*, *kuṇa*; Bi. *kon*, *°nī*, *konā* -- *konī* ' ploughing from corner to corner '; Mth. *koniyā* ' low wall round three sides of winnowing basket '; Bhoj. *kōn* ' corner ', H. *kon*, *°nā* m., G. *kɔṇ* m. (X **khuṇṭa* -- 2 in *kāṭ* -- *khuṇ* = -- *koṇ*m. ' right angle '), M. *koṇ* m., Si. *kona*; -- Pk. *koṇṇa* -- m. ' corner of a house ' (< *kōṇa* -- as *tella* -- < tailá -- ?); M. *kon* m. ' corner ', *°nā*, *°nyā* m. ' cornerstone ' (prob., despite LM 139, *koṇ*, not *kon*, is borrowed). S.kcch. *khūṇo* m. ' corner ', WPah.kṭg. *kvṇɔ* m., kc. *kvṇe* f., J. *koṇā* m., Garh. *kōṇū*.(CDIAL 3504).

Ta. kuṉi (-pp-, -tt-) to dance; kuṉippu dance. *Ma.* kunikka to dance, jump. *Ko.* koṇy- (koṇc-), koṇc-(koṇc-) (calf or other animal) frisks. *To.*kwïḍ&ztail;- (kwïḍj-) (calf) frisks. *Ka.* kuṇi to move in a hopping, skipping, or jumping manner, dance; *n.* dancing; kuṇiyuvike, kuṇiha dancing; (K.2) koṇaku to jump, leap; *n.* a leap, jump; (Hav.) koṇi to dance; koṇippe dancing child (small girl). *Kor.* (T.) koṇi to dance. *Te.* guniyu, gunucu to dangle, dance; gunupu a dance. (DEDR 1863).

Mould, to forge, iron worker, mine

Pk. *gaḍa* -- n. 'large stone'? (CDIAL 3969). Pk. *gaḍhaï*' forms '; A. *gariba* ' to mould, form '; B. *gaṛā* ' to hammer into shape, form '; Or. *gaṛhibā* ' to mould, build ', *gaṛhaṇa* ' building '; Mth. *gaṛhāī* ' wages for making gold or silver ornaments '; OAw. *gaḍhāi* ' makes '; H. *gaṛhnā* ' to form by hammering ', G. *gaḍhvũ*. -- Altern. < gháṭatē: Wg. *gaṛawun* ' to form, produce '; K. *garun*, vill. *gaḍun* ' to hammer into shape, forge, put together '. (CDIAL 3966).

khār 1 खार् । लोहकारः m. (sg. abl. khāra 1 खार; the pl. dat. of this word is khāran 1 खारन्, which is to be distinguished from khāran 2, q.v., s.v.), a blacksmith, an iron worker

gaḍḍa -- m. ' hole ' (Pkt.) *gāṇ* f. ' mine (G.Kashmiri)(3981)

Rebus glyphs, allographs

kaḍa, kaḍru, kaṛa 'a buffalo bull' (Santali) Or. kaṛā ' castrated male buffalo ', Bi. kāṛā m., ṛī f. ' buffalo calf ', H. kāṛā m. (CDIAL 2658)

S. *khaṛo* ' standing erect ', P. *khaṛā*, WPah. paṅ. *khaṛā*, bhad. *khaṛo*, Or. B. *khāṛā*, H. *khaṛā* (→ N. *khaṛā*), Marw. *khaṛo*, G. *khaṛũ*; CDIAL 3784).

L. *gaṛhāvaṇ* 'to bring buffalo cow to bull'; P. *gaṛhṇā* 'to copulate with (of bull or buffalo)'(CDIAL 3966).

gaḍa4 m. 'young of the fish Ophiocephalus lata or Cyprinus garra', *°aka* -- m. lex. B. *gaṛ*, *gaṛai* 'species of gilt-head fish'; Or. *gaṛiśa*, *°śā* 'the fish O. lata', *gaḷa* 'a kind of fish'.(CDIAL 3970).

3971 *gaḍa5 ' hook '. Pa. *gaḷa* -- m. 'hook, fish-hook '; Pk. *gala* -- m. 'hook'; N. *gal* 'lever'; H. *gal* m. 'hook, drag hook'; G. *gaḷ* m. 'hook'; M. *gaḷ* m. 'hook, drag hook, hangman's hook'. (CDIAL 3971).

Pa. *gaḷa* -- m. 'a drop', *gaḷāgalaṁ gacchati* ' goes from fall to fall '; S. *gaṛo* m. 'hail', L. (Ju.) *gaṛā* m., P. *gaṛā* m.(CDIAL 3969).

S. *gaṭī* f. 'piece of elephant's tusk &c'; S. *gaṭu* m. 'piece of stick in a dog's (CDIAL 3965).

WPah.kṭg. *gɔṭṭɔ* m. 'small stone, pebble', J. *gaṭi* f. 'collar', S. *gaṭo* m. 'piece of wall, piece of canal left undug', P. *gaṭṭ* m. 'c luster, stopper', *gaṭṭā* m. 'stopper' (→ H. *gaṭṭā* m.)(CDIAL 3965).

Pk. *gaḍa* -- n. ' hole '; Paš. *gaṛu* 'dike'; Kho. (Lor.) *gōḷ* ' hole, small dry ravine '; A. *garā* 'high bank'; B. *gaṛ* 'ditch, hole in a husking machine'; Or. *gaṛa* 'ditch, moat'; M. *gaḷ* f. 'hole in the game of marbles'.(CDIAL 3967).

gaḍu1 m. ' excrescence on neck, goitre, hump on back ' Pāṇ. Värtt. (CDIAL 3977).gala2 m. ' throat, neck ' MBh., *°aka* -- m. VarBṛS. 1. Pa. *gala* -- m. ' throat, dewlap ', *°aka* -- n. ' throat '; Pk. *gala* -- , *°aa* -- m. ' throat, neck '; Wg. *gal* ' throat '; Gaw. *gala -- šūṭi* ' back of the tongue ' (+?); K.*golu* m. ' mouth, entrance ', ḍoḍ. *galo* ' neck '; S. *garo* m. ' neck ' (*galo* m. ' throat ' is lw.); L. *gaḷ*, (Ju.) *gal* m. ' neck '; P. *gal* m. ' neck ', *galā* m. ' throat, neck '; WPah. bhad. bhal. *gal* n. ' throat ', paṅ. *gaḷ*, Ku. *galo*, gng. *gaw*, N. *galo*; A. *gal* ' throat ', *galā -- gali* ' falling on each other's neck '; B. *gal* ' prow of boat ', *galā* ' throat '; Or. *gaḷa*, *°ḷā* ' throat, neck '; Mth. *gar*, *garā* ' neck '; Bhoj. *gar* ' throat '; H. *gal*, *galā* m. ' throat, neck ' (→ Bhoj. *galā*, OAw. *gala*), Marw.*gaḷo* m. ' throat ', G. *gaḷũ* n., M. *gaḷā* m., Ko. *gaḷo* m.; Si. *gala* ' throat, neck '.2. Kal. *gřä* ' neck '; Kho. *goḷ* ' front of neck, throat '. WPah.kṭg. *gōḷ* m. ' throat, neck ', *gɔḷɔ*, kc. *°ḷo* m., J. *gaḷā* m., Garh. *gaḷu* ' throat, neck '. (CDIAL 4070).

*gaḍḍa1 ' hole, pit '. Pk. *gaḍḍa* -- m. ' hole '; WPah. bhal. cur. *gaḍḍ* f., paṅ. *gaḍḍṛī*, pāḍ. *gaḍōṛ* ' river, stream '; N. *gaṛ -- tir* ' bank of a river '; A. *gārā* ' deep hole '; B. *gāṛ*, *°ṛā* ' hollow, pit '; Or. *gāṛa* ' hole, cave ', *gāṛiā* ' pond '; Mth. *gāṛi* ' piercing '; H. *gāṛā* m. ' hole '; G. *garāḍ*, *°ḍɔ* m. ' pit, ditch ' (< **graḍḍa* -- < **garda* -- ?); Si.*gaḍaya* ' ditch '. -- Cf. S. *giḍi* f. ' hole in the ground for fire during

Muharram '. -- X khānī -- : K. *gān* m. ' underground room '; S. (LM 323) *gāṇ* f. ' mine, hole for keeping water '; L. *gāṇ* m. ' small embanked field within a field to keep water in '; G. *gāṇ* f. ' mine, cellar ';WPah.kṭg. *gāṛ* ' hole (e.g. after a knot in wood) '.(CDIAL 3981).

1. S. *gaḏo* m. ' bundle of grass &c. ', *°ḏī* f. ' small do. '; L. *gaḍḍā* m. ' armful of straw ', *°ḍī* f. ' sheaf '; P. *gaḍḍā* m. ' handful of sticks ', *°ḍī* f. ' load of rice in straw ', WPah. bhal. *gaḍḍi* f. (CDIAL 3982).

gaḍḍuka m. ' waterpot, vessel for boiled rice ' lex., *gaḍḍūka* -- m. lex. 1. Sh. (Lor.) *gaḍubī́* ' iron vessel '; K. *güḍüwa* m. ' small metal pot ', S. *gaḏū* m., L. *gaḍvī* f., P. *gaḍvā* m.; WPah. bhal. *guḍḍū* m. ' inkpot ', *guḍri* f. ' earthen pot for boiling rice '; B. *gāṛu* ' pitcher '; Si. *kaḷa -- geḍiya* ' waterpot '; -- G. *ghāḍvɔ* m. ' earthen pot for ghee ' X ghaṭa -- .2. P. *gaṛvā* m. ' brass jug '; B. *gaṛu* ' waterpot with spout ', Or. *gaṛu, °uā*; OAw. *gaḍuvana* obl. pl. ' waterpot ', H. *gaṛuā* m. ' narrow -- mouthed waterpot ' (→ Ku. N. *gaṛuwā* ' earthen pot '); G. *gaṛvɔ* m. ' metal waterpot '; M. *gaḍū, °ḍuvā* m. ' drinking cup '. -- Paš. shut. *garū́* ' belly ', gul. *gaṛém* ' my belly ' (semant. cf. Kt. *kṭol* ' belly ' ← Eng. *kettle*, and Eng. *pot = belly*). -- N. *gariyo* ' wooden oil vessel ', *karuwā* ' spouted brass pot ' X karaka –(CDIAL 3984).

L. *gaḍ* m. ' wild sheep '. S.kcch. *gāḍar* m. ' sheep '.*gaḍḍa4 ' sheep '. 2. gaḍḍara -- , *°ḍala* -- m. Apte. [Cf. *gaḍḍārikā* -- f. ' ewe in front of a flock ' lex., *gaḍḍālikā*<-> f. ' sheep ' → Psht.*gaḍūrai* ' lamb ' NTS ii 256] 1. Ash. *gaḍewä* m. ' sheep ', *°wī* f.; Wg. *gáḍawā, goḍṓ* ' ram ', *guḍsok* ' lamb '; Paš. *giḍī́* f. ' sheep '; 2. Pk. *gaḍḍarī* -- f. ' goat, ewe ', *°riyā* -- f. ' ewe '; Woṭ. *gaḍūre* ' lamb '; B. *gāṛal, °ṛar* ' the long -- legged sheep '; Or. *gāraṛa, gaṛera, °ṛarā* ' ram ', *gāraṛi* ' ewe ', *garaṛa* ' sheep '; H. *gāḍar* f. ' ewe '; G. *gāḍar, °ḍrũ* n. ' sheep '. -- Deriv. B. *gāṛle* ' shepherd ', H. *gaḍariyā* m. (CDIAL 3983).

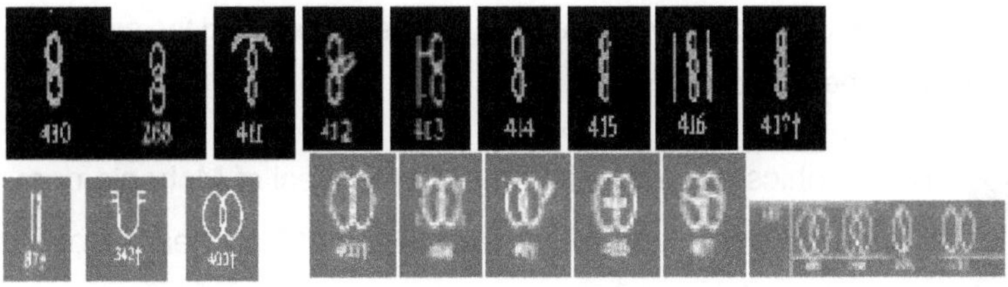

m1406B  Rebus message: alloying (mixing) zinc (sattiya). Casting (metal, iron, bronze, bell-metal); big stone mason

kaḍī a chain; a hook; a link (G.); kaḍum a bracelet, a ring (G.) Rebus: kaḍiyo [Hem. Des. kaḍaio = Skt. sthapati a mason] a bricklayer; a mason; kaḍiyaṇa, kaḍiyeṇa a woman of the bricklayer caste; a wife of a bricklayer (G.) A pair of chain-links may be read rebus: *dul* *kaḍī* 'cast stone (ore)'.

Kalibangan seal. k020 Glyphs: threaded beads + water-carrier. goṭā 'seed' (Bi.); goṭa 'numerative particle' (Mth.Hindi)(CDIAL 4271) Rebus: koṭe 'forging (metal)(Mu.) kuṭi 'water-carrier' (Telugu); Rebus: kuṭhi 'smelter furnace' (Santali)

Continuum of Indus script sign sequence on punch-marked coins

gotao to thread, to string; saire sutamko gotaca they thread needles (Santali) Rebus: goṭ, goṭh The place where cattle are collected at mid-day; got.ao, got.hao to collect cattle together for their mid-day rest (Santali) Rebus: kottaṉ a mason (Ta.) kotti pick-axe, stone-digger, carver (Ma.) (DEDR 2091) koḍ Artisans' workplace (G.) gotga.rn treasurer of the village (Ko.)(DEDR 2093) This sequence of chain of beads + rim-of-jar glyph survives on punch-marked coins.

kottukkāran- head of a company of labourers (Ta.); gottugār-a headman (Ka.)(DEDR 2093). goṭ Another name for the Sohrae festival; goṭ gai on the first day of the got. Puja or

Sohrae in the evening all the cattle of the village are driven over an egg and the animal which treads on it is called the goṭ gai (Santali).

The glyphics are repeated on a circular seal of Mohenjo-daro. It shows a warrior. Mohenjo-daro seal m417 six heads from a core.

kaḍum 'neck-band, ring'; rebus: khāḍ 'trench, firepit' (G.) Vikalpa: khaḍḍā f. Hole, mine, cave (CDIAL 3790). kanduka, kandaka ditch, trench (Tu.); kandakamu id. (Te.); kanda trench made as a fireplace during weddings (Konda); kanda small trench for fireplace (Kui); kandri a pit (Malt)(DEDR 1214) WPah. Khaś. Khaḍḍā 'stream'; khaḍḍa— 'hole, pit'. [Cf. *gaḍḍa— and list s.v. kartá—1] Pk. Khaḍḍā— f. 'hole, mine, cave', ḍaga— m. 'one who digs a hole', ḍōlaya— m. 'hole'; Bshk. (Biddulph) "kād" (= khaḍ?) 'valley'; K. khŏḍ m. 'pit', khŏḍü f. 'small pit', khoḍu m. 'vulva'; S. khaḏa f. 'pit'; L. khaḍḍ f. 'pit, cavern, ravine'; P. khaḍḍ f. har, al m. 'hole'; Marw. Khāṛo m. 'hole'; M. khāḍ f. 'hole, creek', ḍā m. 'hole', ḍī f. 'creek, inlet'. 3863 khātra— n. 'hole' Hpariś., 'pond, spade' Uṇ. [√khan] Pk. Khatta— n. 'hole, manure', aya— m. 'one who digs in a field'; S. khāṭru m. 'mine made by burglars', ṭro m. 'fissure, pit, gutter made by rain'; P. khāt m. 'pit, manure', khāttā m. 'grain pit', ludh. Khattā m. (→ H. khattā m., khatiyā f.); N. khāt 'heap (of stones, wood or corn)'; B. khāt, khāṭrū 'pit, pond'; Or. Khāta 'pit', tā 'artificial pond'; Bi. Khātā 'hole, gutter, grain pit, notch (on beam and yoke of plough)', khattā 'grain pit, boundary ditch'; Mth. Khātā, khattā 'hole, ditch'; H. khāt m. 'ditch, well', f. 'manure', khātā m. 'grain pit'; G. khātar n. 'housebreaking, house sweeping, manure', khātriyũ n. 'tool used in housebreaking' (→ M. khātar f. 'hole in a wall', khātrā m. 'hole, manure', khātryā m. 'housebreaker'); M. khāt n.m. 'manure' (lls d. khatāviṇẽ 'to manure', khāterẽ n. 'muck pit'). — Un- expl. ṭ in L. khāṭvā m. 'excavated pond', khāṭī f. 'digging to clear or excavate a canal' (~ S. khātī f. 'id.', but khāṭyāro m. 'one employed to measure canal work') and khaṭṭaṇ 'to dig'. (CDIAL 3790) •gaḍa— 1 m. 'ditch' lex. [Cf. *gaḍḍa—1 and list s.v. kartá—1] Pk. Gaḍa— n. 'hole'; Paš. Gaṛu 'dike'; Kho. (Lor.) gōḷ 'hole, small dry ravine'; A. garā 'high bank'; B. gaṛ 'ditch, hole in a husking machine'; Or. Gaṛa 'ditch, moat'; M. gaḷ f. 'hole in the

game of marbles'. 3981 *gaḍḍa— 1 'hole, pit'. [G. < *garda—? — Cf. *gaḍḍ—1 and list s.v. kartá—1] Pk. Gaḍḍa— m. 'hole'; Wpah. Bhal. Cur. Gaḍḍ f., paṅ. gaḍḍṛī, pāḍ. Gaḍōṛ 'river, stream'; N. gaṛ—tir 'bank of a river'; A. gārā 'deep hole'; B. gāṛ, ṛā 'hollow, pit'; Or. Gāṛa 'hole, cave', gāṛiā 'pond'; Mth. Gāṛi 'piercing'; H. gāṛā m. 'hole'; G. garāḍ, ḍɔ m. 'pit, ditch' (< *graḍḍa— < *garda—?); Si. Gaḍaya 'ditch'. — Cf. S. giḏi f. 'hole in the ground for fire during Muharram'. — X khāṅ̆ī—: K. gān m. 'underground room'; S. (LM 323) gāṇ f. 'mine, hole for keeping water'; L. gāṇ m. 'small embanked field within a field to keep water in'; G. gāṇ f. 'mine, cellar'; M. gāṇ f. 'cavity containing water on a raised piece of land' Wpah.kṭg. gāṛ 'hole (e.g. after a knot in wood)'. (CDIAL 3947) 3860 *khāḍa— 'a hollow'. [Cf. *khaḍḍa— and list s.v. kartá—1] S. khāṛī f. 'gulf, creek'; P. khāṛ 'level country at the foot of a mountain', ṛī f. 'deep watercourse, creek'; Bi. Khārī 'creek, inlet'; G. khāṛi , ṛī f., ṛɔ m. 'hole'. — Altern. < *khaḍḍa—: Gy. Gr. Xar f. 'hole'; Ku. Khāṛ 'pit'; B. khāṛī 'creek, inlet', khāṛal 'pit, ditch'; H. khāṛī 'creek, inlet', khaṛ—har, al m. 'hole'; Marw. Khāṛo m. 'hole'; M. khāḍ f. 'hole, creek', ḍā m. 'hole', ḍī f. 'creek, inlet'. The neck-bands hung above the shoulder of the composite animal may thus read rebus: trench or fire-pit (i.e. furnace) for the minerals/metals described by the glyphic elements connoting animals: elephant, ram (or zebu, bos indicus).

Übersichtskarte über die austroasiatischen Sprachen

Pinnow's map of Austro-AsiaticLanguage speakers correlates with bronze age sites.[102] The areal map of Austric (Austro-Asiatic languages) showing regions marked by Pinnow correlates with the bronze age settlements in Bharatam or what came to be known during the British colonial regime as 'Greater India'. The bronze age sites extend from Mehrgarh-Harappa (Meluhha) on the west to Kayatha-Navdatoli (Nahali) close to River Narmada to Koldihwa- Khairdih-Chirand on Ganga river basin to Mahisadal – Pandu Rajar Dhibi in Jharia mines

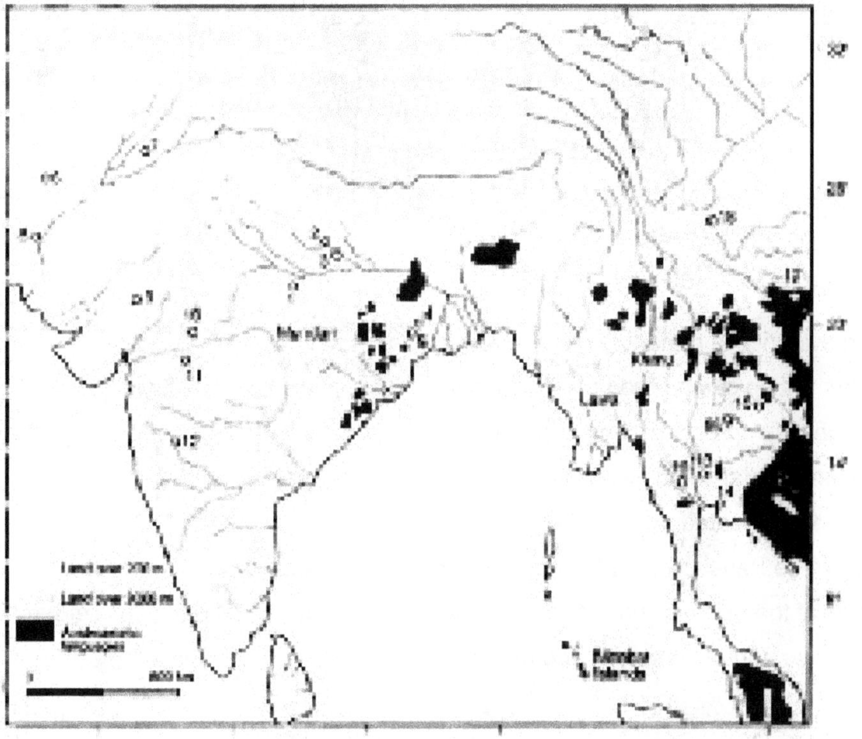

close to Mundari area and into the east extending into Burma, Indonesia, Malaysia, Laos, Cambodia, Vietnam, Nicobar islands. A settlement of Inamgaon is shown on the banks of River Godavari.

Bronze Age sites of eastern India and neighbouring areas: 1. Koldihwa; 2.Khairdih; 3. Chirand; 4. Mahisadal; 5. Pandu Rajar Dhibi; 6.Mehrgarh; 7. Harappa;8. Mohenjo-daro; 9.Ahar; 10. Kayatha; 11.Navdatoli; 12.Inamgaon; 13. Non PaWai; 14. Nong Nor;15. Ban Na Di andBan Chiang; 16. NonNok Tha; 17.

Thanh Den; 18. Shizhaishan; 19. Ban Don Ta Phet [After Fig. 8.1 in: Charles Higham, 1996, The Bronze Age of Southeast Asia, Cambridge University Press].

Conclusion

Seafaring meluhhan merchants used Indus Writing in trade transactions; artisans created metal artifacts, lapidary artificats of terracotta, ivory for trade. Glosses of the proto-Indic or Indus language are used to read rebus the Indus script inscriptions.

The glyphs of the Indus script or Indus Writing include both pictorial motifs and signs and both categories of glyphs are read rebus. As a first step in delineating the Indus language, an *Indian lexicon*[103] provides a resource, compiled semantically cluster over 1240 groups of glosses from ancient Indian languages as a proto-Indic substrate dictionary.

The evidence is remarkable that many single glyphs or glyptic elements of the Indus writing can be read rebus using the repertoire of artisans (lapidaries working with precious shell, ivory, stones and terracotta, mine-workers, stone-masons, metal-smiths working with a variety of minerals, furnaces and other tools) who created the inscribed objects and used many of them to authenticate their trade transactions. Many of the inscribed objects are seen to be calling cards of the professional artisans, listing their professional skills and repertoire. Many are veritable mining- and metal-work catalogs.

Continuing legacies of glyptic art noted by Huntington: "There is a continuity of composite creatures demonstrable in Indic culture since Kot Diji ca. 4000 BCE."[104]

The identification of glosses from the present-day languages of India on Sarasvati river basin is justified by the continuation of culture evidenced by many artifacts evidencing civilization continuum from the Vedic Sarasvati River basin, since language and culture are intertwined, resulting in a unique, logo-semantic writing system. .

Indus writing in Ancient Near East is a tribute to the Meluhhan artisans who have established an expansive contact area in Eurasia and left for posterity the bronze-age *harosheth hagoyim*, 'the smithy of nations.'

Concordance lists for epigraphs

Abbreviations and references to heiroglyphs and text transcripts

m-Mohenjodaro

h-Harappa

ABCDE at the end of a reference number indicate side numbers of an inscribed object. Multiple seal impressions on the same object are numbered 1 to 4.

At the end of the reference number:

'a' sealing; 'bangle' inscription on bangle or bangle fragment; other objects: shell, ivory stick, ivory plaque, ivory cube, faience ornament, steatite ornament; 'ct' copper tablet; 'Pict-' Pictorial motifs (0 to 145) described as illustrations of field-symbols in Appendix III of Mahadevan corpus (pp. 793 to 813); 'it' inscribed tablet; 'si' seal impression; 't' tablet.

Illegible inscribed objects are excluded in the following tabulations. Many potsherds Rahmandheri and Nausharo are excluded since the 'signs' are considered to be potters' marks; only those inscriptions which appear to have parallels of field symbols or 'signs' in the corpora are included.

Based on a number of resources and from the collections of inscribed objects held in many museums of the world, such as the Metropolitan Museum of Art, the Indus Writing Corpora include Sarasvati heiroglyphs, representing many facets of glyptic art of Sarasvati Civilization. The corporas also includes many texts of inscriptions, corresponding to the epigraphs inscribed on objects. The compilation is based mostly on published photographs in archaeological reports

right from the days of Alexander Cunningham who discovered a seal at Harappa in 1875, of Langdon at Mohenjodaro (1931) and of Madhu Swarup Vats at Harappa (1940). The corpus includes objects collected in India, Pakistan, other countries and the finds of the excavations at Harappa by Kenoyer and Meadow during the seasons 1994-1995 and 1999-2000.

Framework for decoding epigraphs of Sarasvati Sindhu Civilization

This is also intended to serve as a pictorial and text index to Mahadevan Concordance and to the three volumes published so far of pictorial corpus of Parpola et al.

Many texts are indexed to the text numbers of Mahadevan concordance. The choice of this concordance is based on four factors: (a) the concordance is priced at a reasonable cost; (b) it is a true concordance for every sign of the corpus to facilitate an analysis of the frequency of occurrence of a sign and the context of other sign clusters/ sequences in relation to a sign and for researchers to cross-check on the basic references for the inscribed objects; (c) the exquisite nature of orthography is notable and 'readings' are authentic, even for very difficult to read inscriptions; and (d) signs and variants of signs have been delineated with cross-references to selected text readings.

Mahadevan concordance excludes inscribed objects which do not contain 'texts'; for example, this concordance excludes about 50 seals inscribed with the 'svastikā' pictorial motif and a pectoral which contains the pictorial motif of a one-horned bull with a device in front and an over-flowing pot. Parpola concordance has been used to present such objects which also contain valuable orthographic data which may assist in decoding the inscriptions. Many broken objects are also contained in Parpola concordance which are useful, in many cases, to count the number of objects with specific 'field symbols', a count which also provides some

valuable clues to support the decoding of the messages conveyed by the 'field symbols' which dominate the object space.

Cross-references to excavation numbers, publications, photographs and the museum numbers based on which these texts have been compiled are provided in Appendix V: List of Inscribed Objects (pages 818 to 829) in Iravatham Mahadevan, 1977, *The Indus Script: Texts, Concordance and Tables*, Memoirs of the Archaeological Survey of India No. 77, New Delhi, Archaeological Survey of India, Rs. 250. In most cases, these text numbers are matched with the inscribed objects after Asko Parpola concordance [Two volumes: Rs. 21,000: 1. Jagat Pati Joshi and Asko Parpola, eds., 1987, *Corpus of Indus Seals and Inscriptions: 1. Collections in India*, Memoirs of the Archaeological Survey of India No. 86, Helsinki, Suomalainen Tiedeakatemia; 2. Sayid Ghulam Mustafa Shah and Asko Parpola, eds., 1991, *Corpus of Indus Seals and Inscriptions: 2. Collections in Pakistan*, Memoirs of the Department of Archaeology and Museums, Govt. of Pakistan, Vol. 5, Helsinki, Suomalainen Tiedeakatemia]. *Memoir of ASI No. 96 Corpus of Indus Seals and Inscriptions, Vol. II* by Asko Parpola, B.M. Pande and Petterikoskikallio (containing copper tablets) is in press (December 2001).

The debt owed to Iravatham Mahadevan, Asko Parpola, Archaeological Survey of India, Department of Archaeology and Museums, Govt. of Pakistan and Finnish Academy for making this presentation possible is gratefully acknowledged. I am grateful to Iravatham Mahadevan who made available to me his annotated personal copy of a document which helped in collating the texts with the pictures of inscribed objects. [Kimmo Koskenniemi and Asko Parpola, 1980, Cross references to Mahadevan 1977 in: *Documentation and Duplicates of the Texts in the Indus Script, Helsinki*, pp. 26-32].

Four epigraphs from Bhirrana from ASI website http://asi.nic.in and five epigraphs from Bagasra (Gola Dhoro) reported by VH Sonawane in *Puratattva*, Number 41, 2011 have also been included.

Pitfalls of normalising orthography of some glyphs

Parpola (1994) identifies 386 (+12?) signs (or graphemes) and their variant forms. Mahadevan (1977) identifies 419 graphemes; out of these 179 graphemes have variants totalling 641 forms.

Parpola observes: "...the grapheme count might be as low as 350...The total range of signs once present in the Indus script is certain to have been greater than is observable now, for new signs have kept turning up in new inscriptions. The rate of discovery has been fairly low, though, and the new signs have more often been ligatures of two or more signs already known as separate graphemes than entirely new signs." (Parpola, 1994, p. 79)

Many 'signs' are ligatures of two or more 'signs'.

In the process of normalizing the orthography of some glyphs to identify the core 'signs' of the script, some information is lost and at times, the process itself impedes the possibility of decoding the writing system. This can be demonstrated by (1) the 'identification' of a 'squirrel' glyph and (2) the failure to identify 'dotted circle' or 'stars' as glyphs.

It is, therefore, necessary to view the inscribed object as a composite message composed of glyphs: pictorial motifs and signs alike. Many scholars have noted the contacts between the Mesopotamian and Sarasvati Sindhu (Indus) Civilizations, in terms of cultural history, chronology, artefacts (beads, jewellery), pottery and seals found from archaeological sites in the two areas.

An outstanding contribution to the study of the script problem is the publication of the Corpus of Indus Seals and Inscriptions (CISI) Three volumes have been published so far:

> *Corpus of Indus Seals and Inscriptions, 1. Collections in India, Helsinki, 1987 (eds. Jagat Pati Joshi and Asko Parpola)*

Corpus of Indus Seals and Inscriptions, 2. Collections in Pakistan, Helsinki, 1991 (eds. Sayid Ghulam Mustafa Shah and Asko Parpola)

Corpus of Indus Seals and Inscriptions, 3. 1 Supplement to Mohenjo-daro and Harappa, 2010 (eds. Asko Parpola, B.M. Pande and Petteri Koskikallio) in collaboration with Richard H. Meadow and Jonathan Mark Kenoyer. (Annales Academiae Scientiarum Fennicae, B. 239-241.) Helsinki: Suomalainen Tiedeakatemia.

These volumes in which Asko Parpola is the co-author constitute the photographic corpus. The CISI contains all the seals including those without any inscriptions, for e.g. those with the geometrical motif called the 'svastika'. Parpola's initial corpus (1973) included a total number of 3204 texts. After compiling the pictorial corpus, Parpola notes that there are approximately 3700 legible inscriptions (including 1400 duplicate inscriptions, i.e. with repeated texts). Both the concordances of Parpola and Mahadevan complement each other because of the sort sequence adopted. Parpola's concordance was sorted according to the sign following the indexed sign. Mahadevan's concordance was sorted according to the sign preceding the indexed sign. The latter sort ordering helps in delineating signs which occur in final position. With the publication of CISI Vol. 3, Part 1, the total number of inscriptions from Mohenjo-daro totals 2134 and from Harappa totals 2589; thus, these two sites alone accounting for 4,723 bring the overall total number of inscriptions to over 6,000 from all sites (even after excluding comparable inscriptions on 'Persian Gulf type' circular seals from the total count).

Compendia of the efforts made since the discovery by Gen. Alexander Cunningham, in 1875, of the first known Indus seal (British Museum 1892-12-10, 1), to decipher the script appear in the following references:

A number of concordances and sign lists have been compiled, by many scholars, for the 'Indus' script:

Dani, A.H., *Indian Palaeography*, 1963, Pls. I-II

Gadd and Smith, *Mohenjodaro and the Indus Civilization*, London,1931,, vol. III, Pls. CXIX-CXXIX

Hunter, G.R., *JRAS*, 1932, pp. 491-503

Hunter, G.R., *Scripts of Harappa and Mohenjodaro*, 1934, pp. 203-10

Langdon, Mohenjodaro and the Indus Civilization*, London, 1931, vol. II, pp. 434-55*

Koskenniemi, Kimmo and Asko Parpola, *Corpus of texts in the Indus script,* Helsinki, 1979; *A concordance to the texts in the Indus script*, Helsinki, 1982

Mahadevan, I., *The Indus Script: Texts, concordance and tables*, Delhi, 1977, pp. 32-35

Parpola et al., *Materials for the study of the Indus script, I: A concordance to the Indus Inscriptions*, 1973, pp. xxii-xxvi

Vats, *Excavations at Harappa*, Calcutta, 1940, vol. II, Pls. CV-CXVI

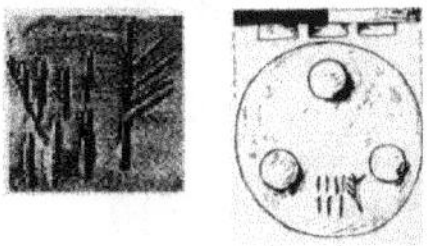

Alamgirpur Late Harappan pottery, a three-legged chakala_(After YD Sharma)

Alamgirpur Agr-1 a(2) graffiti

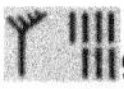9062

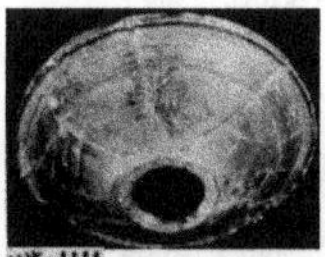

9063

Alamgirpur: Late Harappan pottery (After YD Sharma)

Alamgirpur2

Allahdino (Nel Bazaar)01

Allahdino (Nel Bazaar)02

Allahdino (Nel Bazaar)03

Allahdino (Nel Bazaar)04

Allahdino (Nel Bazaar)05

Allahdino (Nel Bazaar)06

Allahdino (Nel Bazaar)07

Allahdino (Nel Bazaar)08

Allahdino (Nel Bazaar)09

Allahdino (Nel Bazaar)11

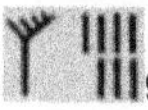9061

Amri

9084

Amri

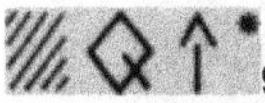9085

Amri06

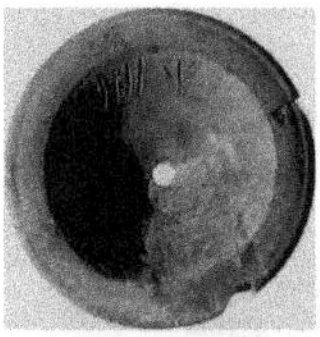

Amri07

Bagasra1 (Gola Dhoro)

Bagasra2 (Gola Dhoro)

Bagasra3 (Gola Dhoro)

Bagasra4 (Gola Dhoro)

Bagasra5 (Gola Dhoro)

Balakot01

Balakot 02

Balakot 03

Balakot 04

Balakot 05

Balakot 06 bangle

Balakot 06bangle

Balakot 06C

Banawali1

Banawali10

9204

Banawali11

Banawali12

Banawali13a

Banawali14

Banawali15

9203

Banawali16

Banawali 17

9201

Banawali 18a

Banawali19

Banawali2

Banawali 20

Banawali 21a

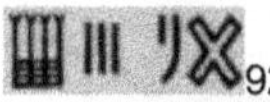
9205

Banawali 23A

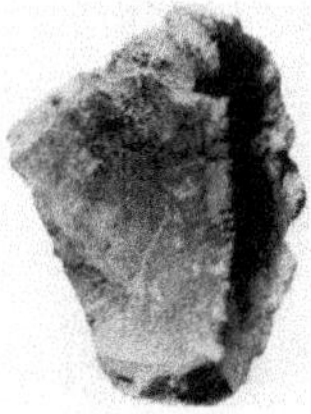

Banawali 23B

Banawali 24t

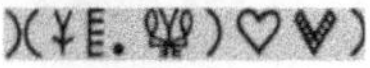
9211

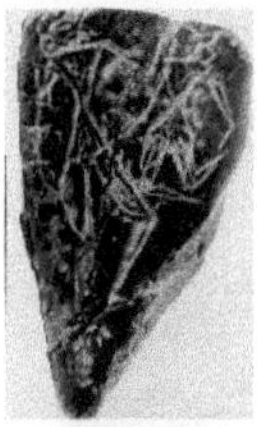

Banawali 26A

Banawali0026a

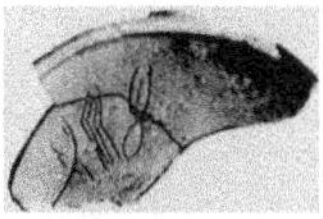

Banawali 28A

9221

Banawali 3

Banawali30

Banawali 4

Banawali 5

9203

Banawali 6

Banawali 7

Banawali 8

Banawali 9C

Bet Dwaraka 1

S'ankha seal. One-horned bull, short-horned bull looking down and an antelope looking backward.

Bhirrana1

Bhirrana2

Bhirrana3

Bhirrana4

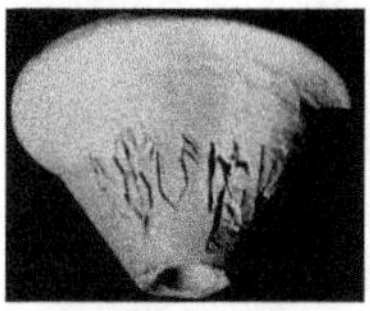

Chandigarh01

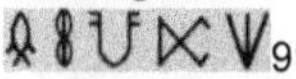
9101

Chandigarh02

9102

Chandigarh

9103

Chandigarh

9104

Chanhudaro10

6129

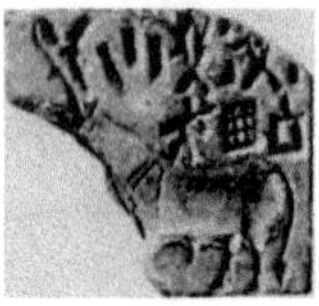

Chanhudaro 11

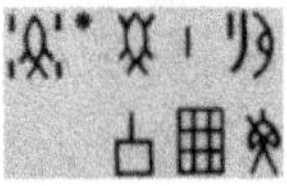

6220

Chanhudaro12a

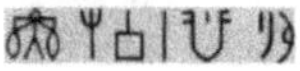

6231

Chanhudaro13

6221

Chanhudaro14a

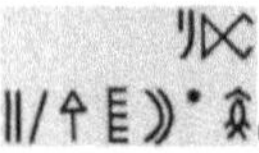
6108

Chanhudaro15a

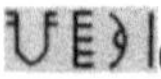
6213

Chanhudaro16a

6222

Chanhudaro17a

6122

Chanhudaro18a

621

6

Chanhudaro1a

6125

Chanhudaro2

6128

Chanhudaro20

6210

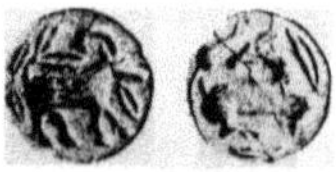

Chanhudaro Seal obverse and reverse. The oval sign of this Jhukar culture seal is comparable to other inscriptions. Fig. 1 and 1a of Plate L. After Mackay, 1943.

Chanhudaro21a

6209

Chanhudaro22a

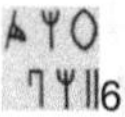
6115

Chanhudaro23

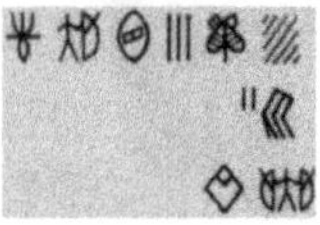

6402 Goat-antelope with a short tail.

The object in front of the goat-antelope is a double-axe.

Chanhudaro24a

6116

Chanhudaro25

Chanhudaro26

6405

Chanhudaro27

Chanhudaro28

Chanhudaro29

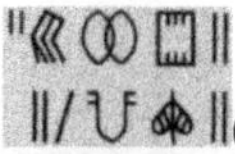6403

Chanhudaro3

6230

Chanhudaro30

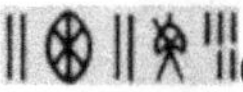6111

Chanhudaro32a

6123

Chanhudaro33a

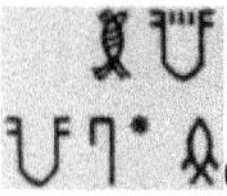6104

Chanhudaro. Tablet. Obverse and reverse. Alligator and Fish. Fig. 33 and 33a. of Plate LII. After Mackay, 1943.

6233 Pict-67: Gharial, sometimes with a fish held in its jaw and/or surrounded by a school of fish.

6303

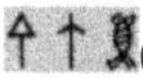6304

6301

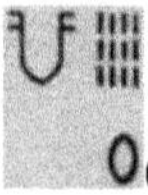6305 

6109 

6112

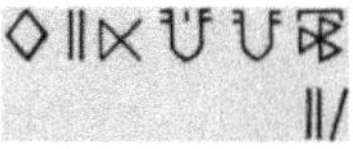

6113 Pict-98

It is seen from an enlargement of the bottom portion of the seal impression that the 'prostrate person' may not be a person but a ligature of the neck of an antelope with rings on its necks or of a post with ring-stones. The head of the 'person' is not shown. So, I would surmise that this is an artist's representation of an act of copulation (by an animal) + a ligatured neck of another bovine or alternatively, a pillar with ring-stones ligatured to the bottom portion of a body. It is not uncommon in the artistic tradition to ligature bodies to the rump of, for example, a bull's posterior ligatured to a horned woman (Pict. 103 Mahadevan) or standing person with horns and bovine features (hoofed legs and/or tail) -- Pict. 86-88 Mahadevan.

Bison (gaur) trampling a prostrate person (?) underneath. Impression of a seal from Chanhujodaro (Mackay 1943: pl. 51: 13). The prostrate 'person' is seen to have a very long neck, possibly with neck-rings, reminiscent of the rings depicted on the neck of the one-horned bull normally depicted in front of a standard device.

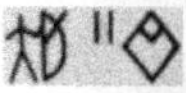 6114 Pict-108

Person kneeling under a tree facing a tiger. [*Chanhudaro Excavations*, Pl. LI, 18]  6118

Chanhudaro Seal obverse and reverse. The 'water-carrier' and X signs of this so-called Jhukar culture seal are comparable to other inscriptions. Fig. 3 and 3a of Plate L. After Mackay, 1943.

 6120

Pict-40

Ox-antelope with a long tail; a trough in front. 

6121

Chanhudaro. Seal impression. Fig. 35 of Plate LII. After Mackay, 1943.

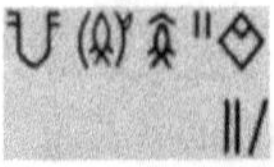 6124

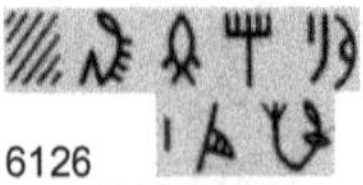

6126

6130  6131

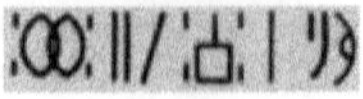

6133

6201

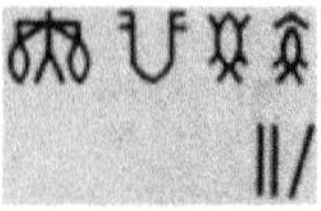

6202

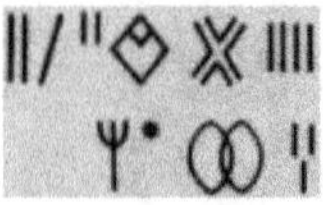

6203

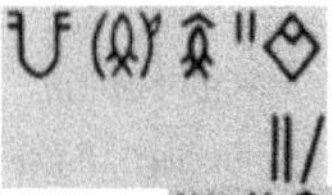

6204 

6208 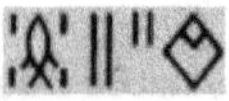

6211 

6214

6215

6217

6218

6219

6223

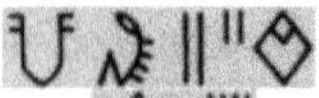

6224 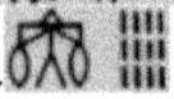 6225

6226

6228

6229

6232

Chanhudaro. Tablet. Fig. 34 of Plate LII. After Mackay, 1943.

6234

Chanhudaro. Seal impression. Fig. 35 of Plate LII. After Mackay, 1943.

 6235

Chanhudaro38A

Chanhujodaro

39A1

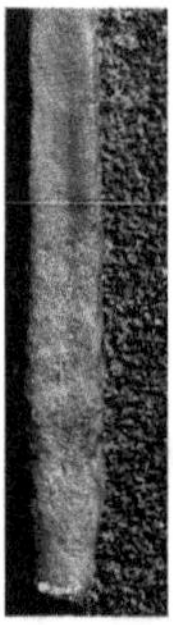

Chanhudaro

39A2

Chanhudaro4

 6206

Chanhudaro40A

6306

Chanhudaro40B

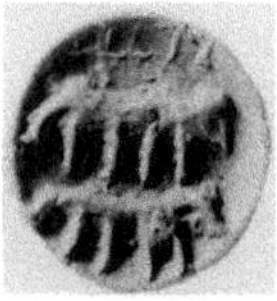
Chanhudaro41a

Chanhudaro42

Chanhudaro43

Chanhudaro46a

Chanhudaro46b

Chanhudaro47

Chanhudaro 48

Chanhudaro49A

Chanhudaro49B

Chanhudaro 5

6132

Chanhudaro50A

Chanhudaro50B

Chanhudaro 6

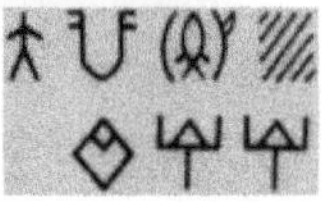

6205

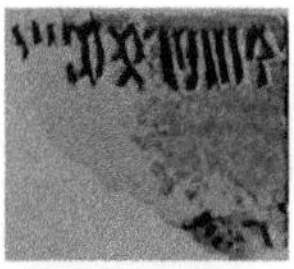
Chanhudaro 7

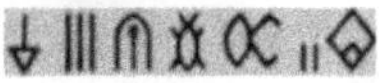
6207

Chanhudaro 8

6227

Chanhudaro 9

6127

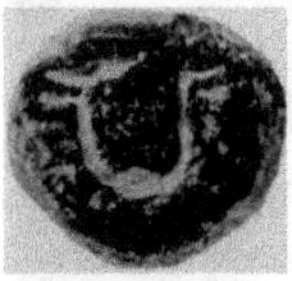
Daimabad1

Sign342

Daimabad 2a

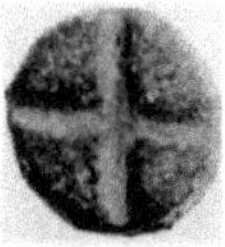
Daimabad 3A

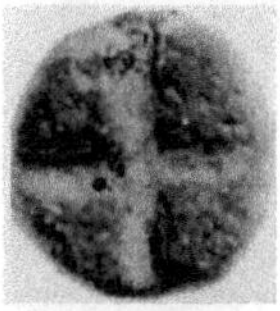
Daimabad 3B

Daimabad 4

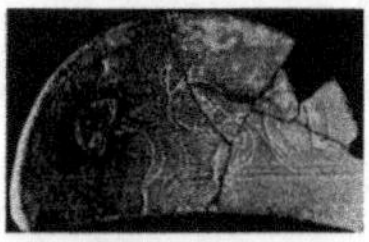
Daimabad 5A

Daimabad 5B

Desalpur1a

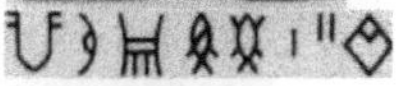

9071Desalpur2

esalpur3

9073

Dholavira Sign-board mounted on a gateway.

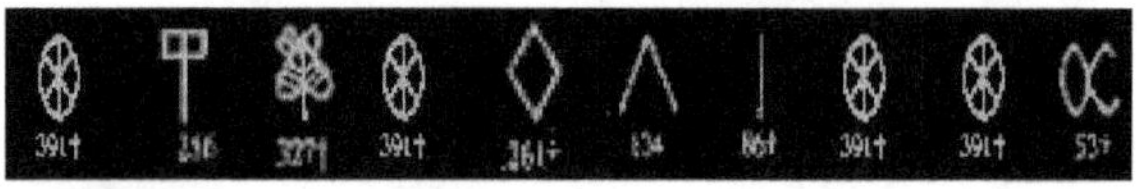

Dholavira (Kotda) on Kadir island, Kutch, Gujarat; 10 signs inscription found near the western chamber of the northern gate of the citadel high mound (Bisht, 1991: 81, Pl. IX).

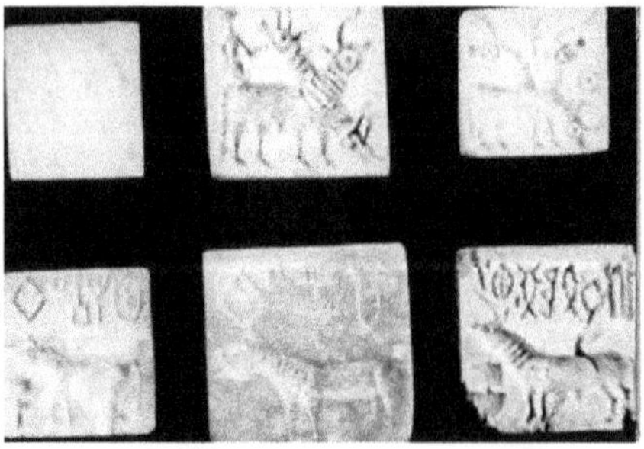

Dholavira: Seals (Courtesy ASI)

Dholavira1a

9121

Dholavira 2a

Gharo Bhiro
(Nuhato) 01

Gumla10a

Gumla8a

h001a

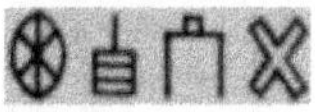

4010

h002

4012

h003

4002

h004

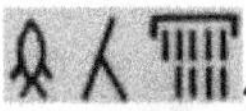

469
3

h005

4004

h006a

4006

h007

4008

h008

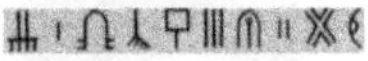

4001

h009

4009

h010a

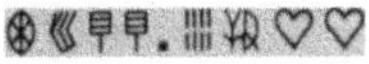

4003

h011a

4038

h012

4005

h013

5055

h014

4106

h015

4053

h017

4052

h018

4071

h019

4694

h020

4019

h021

4022

h022

4023

h023

4047

h024

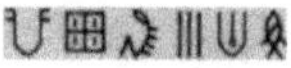

4013

h025

4081

h026

4016

h027

4017

h028

4040

h029

4042

h030

4049

h031

4103

h032

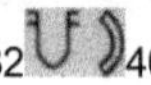

4018

h033

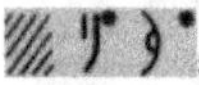

5059

h035

5083

h036

4113

h037

4031

h038

4029

h039

h040

4072

h041

4178

h042

4057

h043

4077

h044

4028

h045

4043

h046

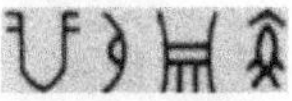

4076

h047

4030

h048 4091

h049

4133

h050

4131

h051

4090

h052

4109

h053

5089

h054

4085

h055

4107

h056

4110

h057

4086

h058

4105

h059

5120

h060

5119

h061

4118

h0

62

4128

h063

4142

h064

h065

4094

h066

4130

h067

4115

h068

4141

h069

4146

h0

70

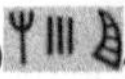

4122

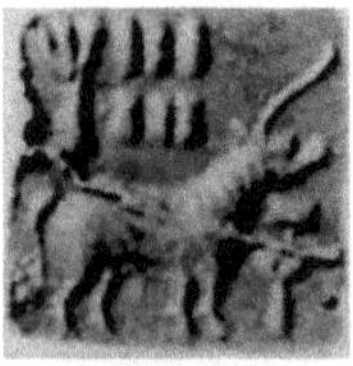

h071

5054

h072

412

0

h073

4617 [An orthographic representation of a water-carrier].

h074

4135

h075

4161

h076

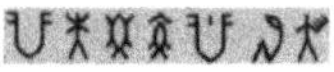

4241

h077

h078

4244

h079

5060

h08

0

4245

h081

5063

h082

a Text 4238

h0

83

4236

h084

h085

4232

h0

86

4233

h087

4240

h088

4253

h089

090

227

h091

4230

h092

4229

h093a

4231

h094

4246

h095

h096

4249

h097 Pict-95: Seven robed figures (with pigtails, twigs)

4251

h098

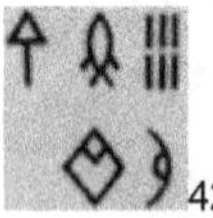
4256

Pict-122 Standard device which is normally in front of a one-horned bull.

h099

4223

h100

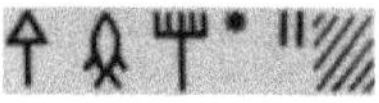
4258 One-horned bull.

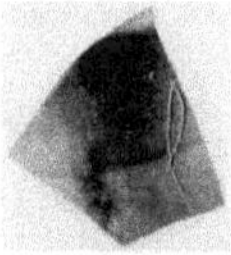
h10
02

h1007

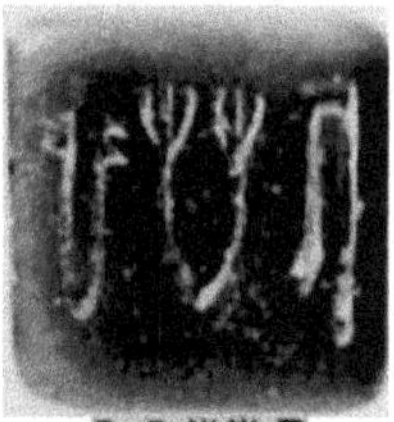
h101

5069

h1010bangle

h1011cone

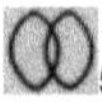
5103

h1012cone

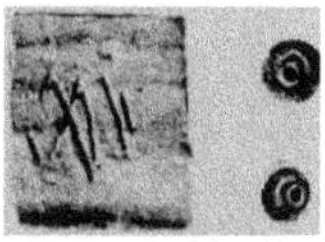
h1017ivorystick

4561

h1018copperobje ct Head of one-horned bull ligatured with a four-pointed star-fish (Gangetic octopus?)

h102A

h102B

h102D

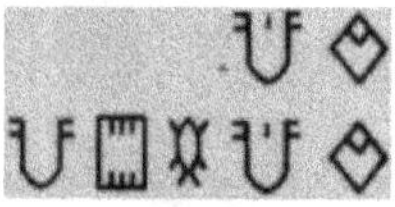
5056

h103

4254

h104

h105

h106

h107

h108

h109

h110

h111

h112

h113

h114

h115

h116

h117

h118

h119

h120

h121

h122

h123

h124

h125

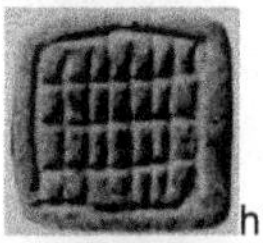

h12

6  h127

h130

5096

h131 4271

h12

8

h129A

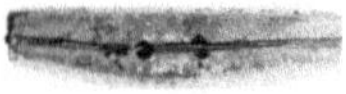

h129E

4269

h132

5052

h133

4261

h134

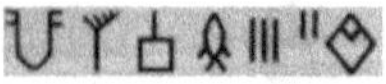

4264

h135

4270

h136

4288

h137a

5058

h138a

5072

h139

426

7

h1

40

4268

h141

4274

h142

4272

h143a

5101

h144

4280

h145

5067

h146

462

8

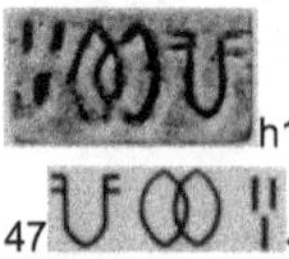

h1

47

4

629

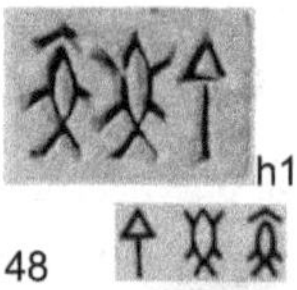

h1

48

4285

h149

4275

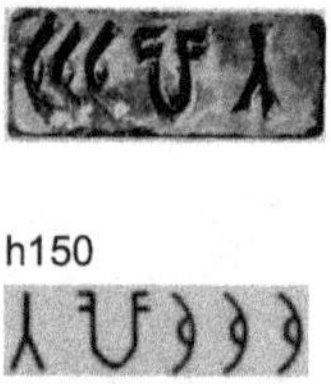

h150

4283

h151

5057

h152

5016

h153

4627

h154

4282

h155

4630

h15
6

5051

h
157

4284

h158
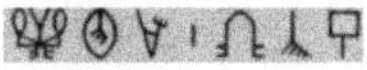
4297

h159

4633

h160A

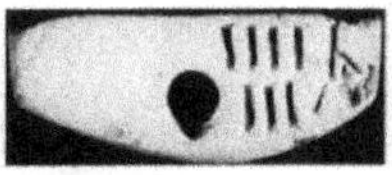
h160C
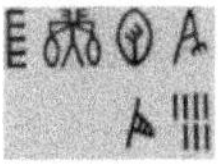

4276

h161

4262

h162

4294

h163

h164

50
46

h165

h166A

h166B

h167A

h167A2

5225

h168

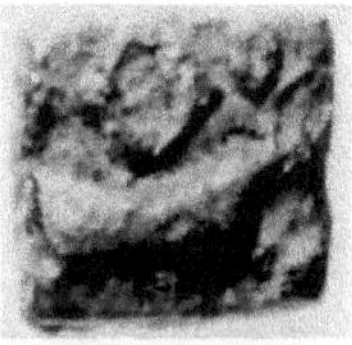
h169A

h169B

5298

h170A

h170B

47
01

h171A
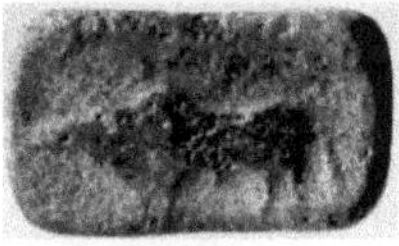
h171B tablet

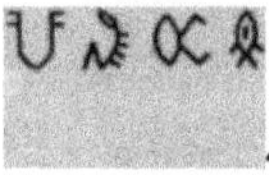
43
12 Buffalo.

h172A

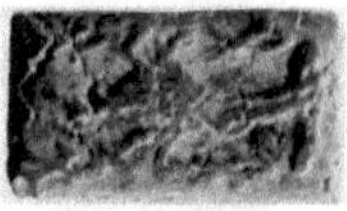

h172B

53

05 Pict-66: Gharial, sometimes with a fish held in its jaw and/or surrounded by a school of fish.

h173A

h173B

4333

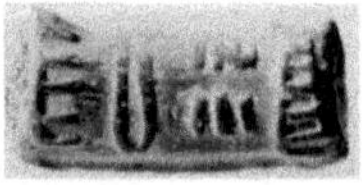

h174A

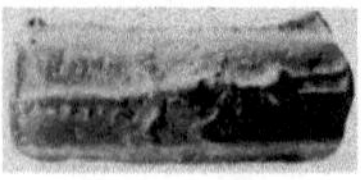

h174B

4338

h175A

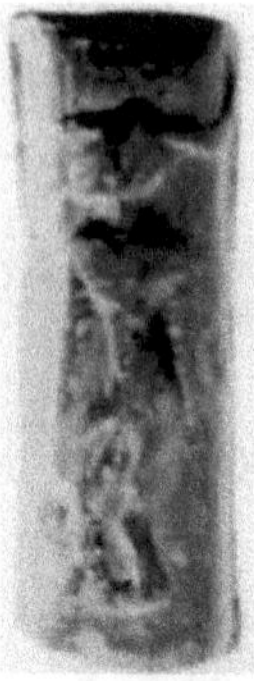

h1

75B Pict-

87

4319 Standing person with horns and bovine features (hoofed legs and/or tail).

h176A

h176B

h176bb

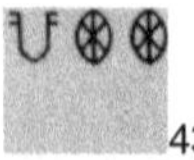

4303

Tablet in bas-relief h176a Person standing at the centerbetween a two-tiered structure at R., and a short-horned bull (bison) standing near a trident-headed post at L. h176b From R.—a tiger (?); a seated, pig-tailed person on a platform; flanked on either side by a person seated on a tree with a tiger, below, looking back. A hare (or goat?) is seen near the platform.

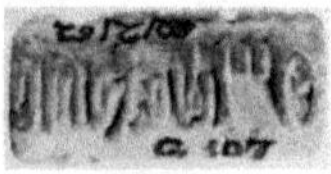

h177A

h177B

4316 Pict-115: From R.—a person standing under an ornamental arch; a kneeling adorant; a ram with long curving horns.

h178A

h178B

4318 Pict-84: Person wearing a diadem or tall head-dress (with twig?) standing within an arch or two pillars?

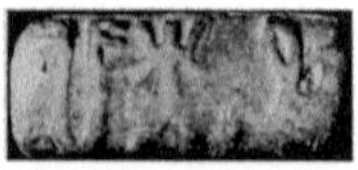

h179A

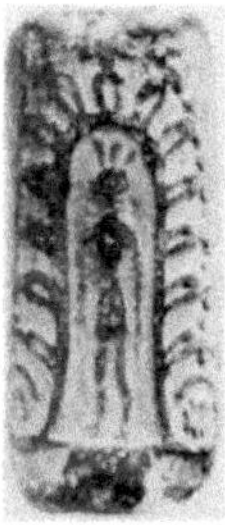

h179B

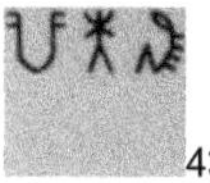
4307

Pict-83: Person wearing a diadem or tall head-dress standing within an ornamented arch; there are two stars on either side, at the bottom of the arch.

h180A

h180B

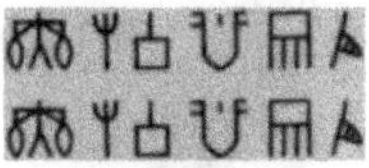

4304 Tablet in bas-relief h180a Pict-106: Nude female figure upside down with thighs drawn apart and crab (?) issuing from her womb; two tigers standing face to face rearing on their hindlegs at L.

h180b

Pict-92: Man armed with a sickle-shaped weapon on his right hand and a cakra (?) on his left hand, facing a seated woman with disheveled hair and upraised arms.

h181A

h181B

h182A

h182B 4

306Tablet in bas-relief

h182a Pict-107: Drummer and a tiger.

h182b Five svastika signs alternating right- and left-handed.

h183A

h183B

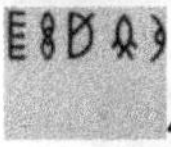
4327

h184A

h184B

h185A

h185

B

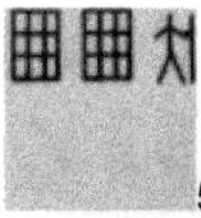
5279

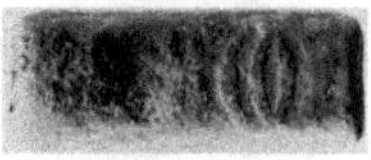

h186A

h186B

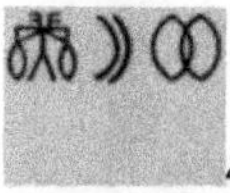
4329

h187A

h187B

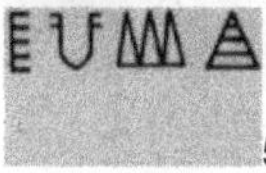
52

82 Pict-75: Tree, generally within a railing or on a platform.

h188A

h188B

4325

h189A

h189

B 4

341 Pict-126: Anchor?

h190A

h190B

4323

h191A

h191B

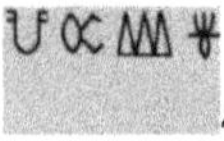

4332

h192A

h192B

53

40

h193A

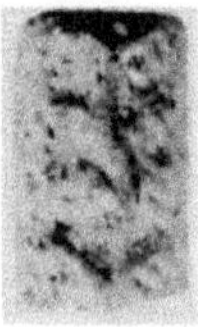

h193B

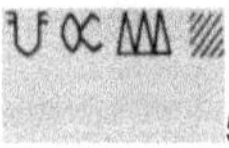

5332

h194A

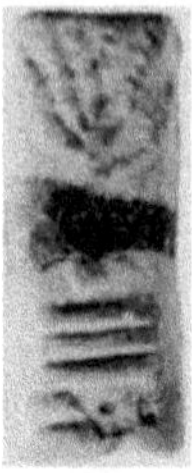

h194B

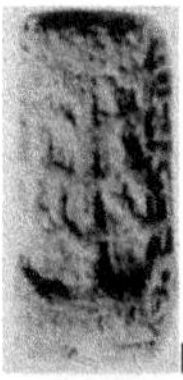

h195A

h195B

h196

A h19

6B

4309

Tablet in bas-relief h196b

Pict-91: Person carrying the standard. h196a The standard.

h197A

h197B

5333

h198A

h198B

5331

h199A

h199B

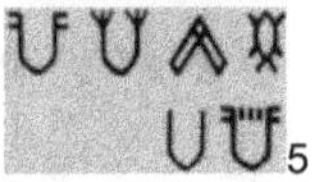

5

252

h200A

h200B

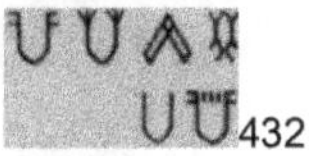

432

1

h201A

h201B

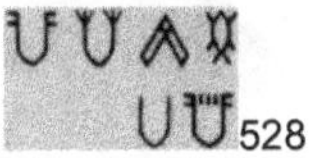

528

9

h202A

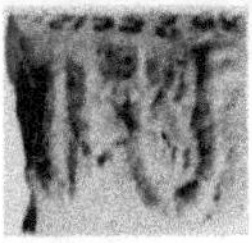

h202B

5334

h203A

5

226

5236

h204A

h204B

5211

h205A

h205B

5254

h206A

h206B

4345

h207A

5297

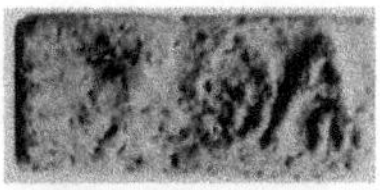

h208A

h208B

529

6

h209A

h209B

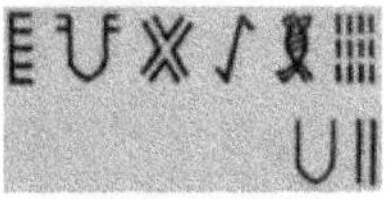

4348

h210A

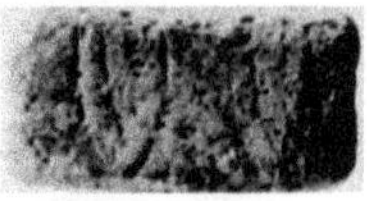

h210B

4

355

h211A

h211B

5

274

h212A

h212B

4357

h213A

h213B

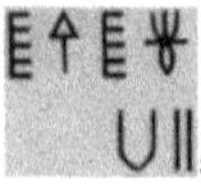
5270

h214A

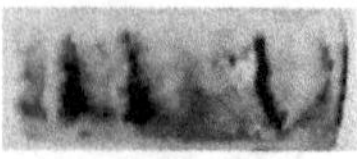

h214B

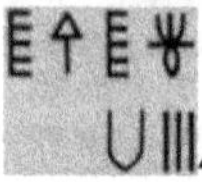
4684

h215A

h215B

5271

h216A

h216B

5335

h217A

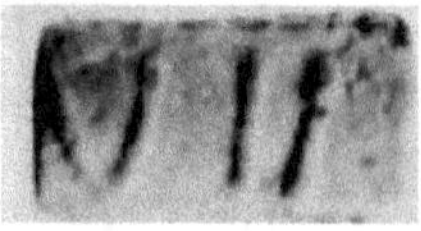

h217B

533

6

h218A

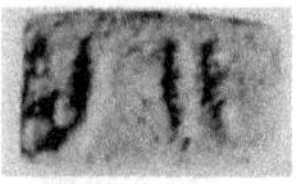

h218B

5293

h219A

h219B

5269

h220A

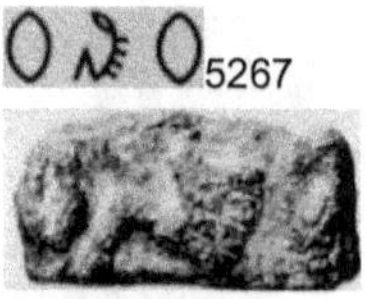
5267

h221A

h221B

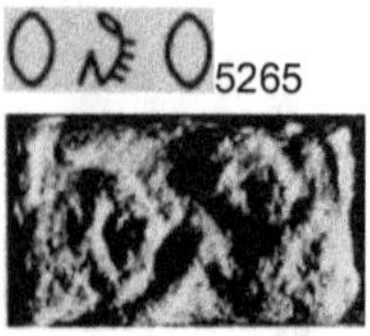
5265

h222A

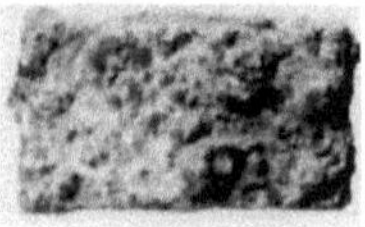

h222B

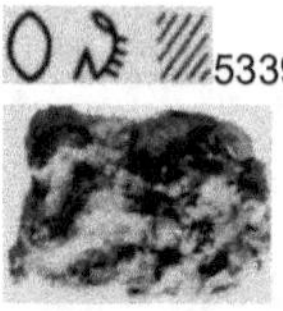
5339

h223A

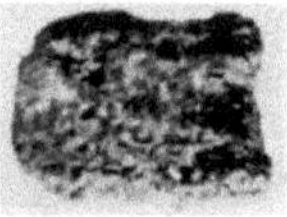

h223B

522

1

h225A

h226A

h226B

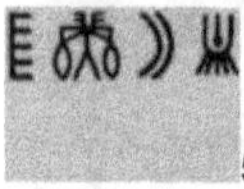
524

3 Standard.

h227A

h227B

432

2 Standard. Pict-123

Standard device which is normally in front of a one-horned bull. The device is flanked by columns of dotted circles.

h228A

h228B

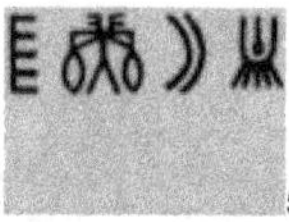
5

244 Standard.

h229A

h229B

4674

h230A

h230B

h231A

h231B

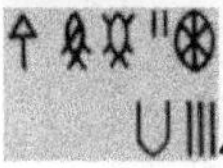4673

h232A

h232B tablet in bas relief

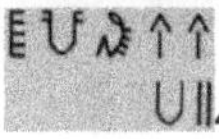4368

Inscribed object in the shape of a double-axe.

h233A

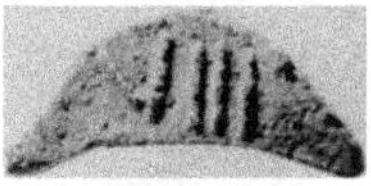

h233B

4387

Tablet in bas-relief. Sickle-shaped. Pict-131: Inscribed object in the shape of a crescent?

h234A

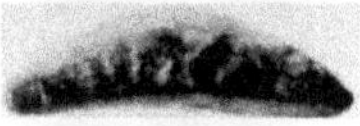

h234B

4717

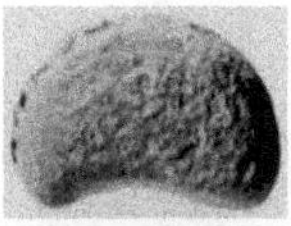

h235A

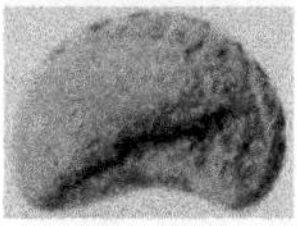

h235B

h236A

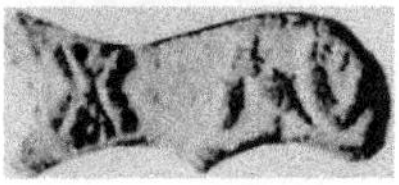

h236B

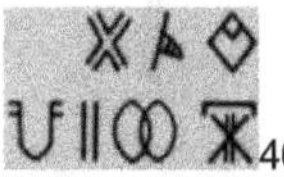46

58 Incised miniature tablet. Object shaped like fish or sickle?

h825A h825B

h237A

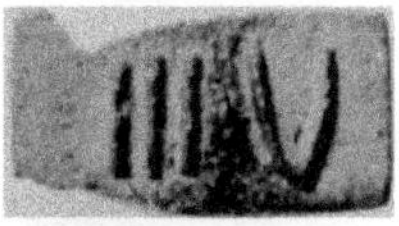

h237B

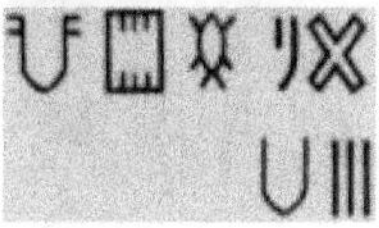

5337

h238A

h239A

h239B Tablet in bas relief

438

6

h240

4657

h241A

h241B

4663

Pict-69: Tortoise.

h242A

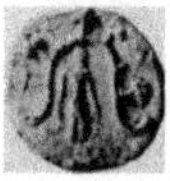

h242B

Pict-84

4317

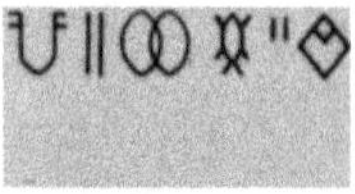

2863

h243A

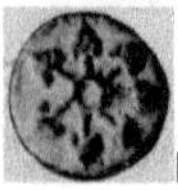
h243B

Tablet in bas-relief

Pict-78: Rosette of seven pipal (?) leaves.

4664

For See inscription: 4466

h244A

h244B

4665

h245A

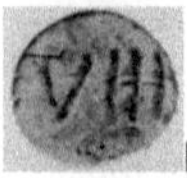
h245B

4702

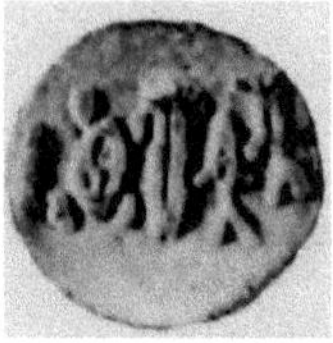

h246A

h246B

5283

h247A

h247B Tablet in bas-relief

4372

h248A

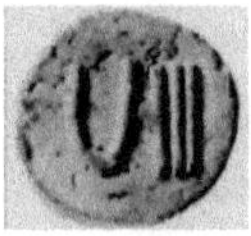

h248B Tablet in bas-relief

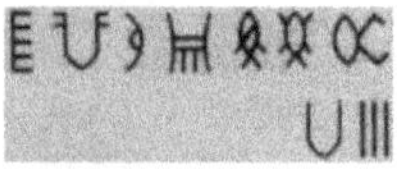

4371

See 3354.

h249A

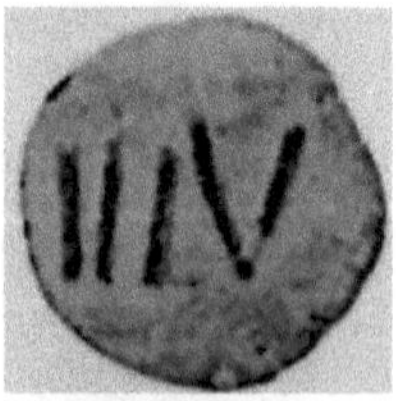

h249B Tablet in bas-relief

4374

h250A

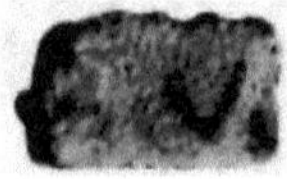

h250B

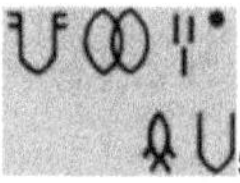
5250

h251A

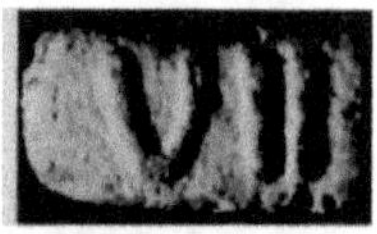

h251B

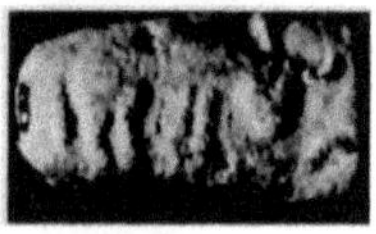

h251C

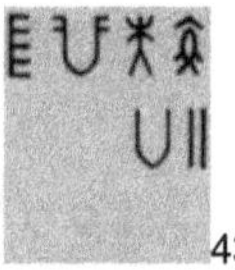
4342

Tablet in bas-relief. Prism. Bison (short-horned bull).

h252A

h252B

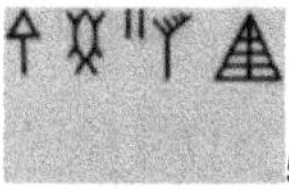

5

215

h253A

h253B

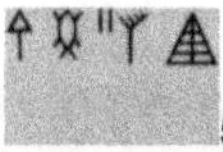

5219

h254A

h254B

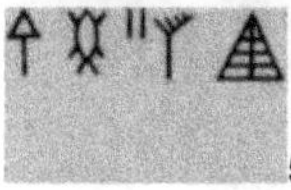

5

214

h255A

h255B

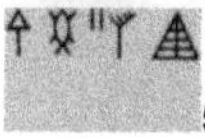

5208

h256A

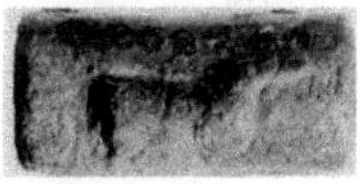

h256B

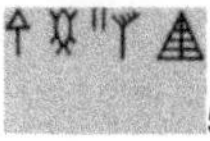

5213

h257A

h257B

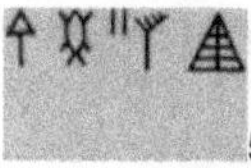

521

6

h258A

h258B

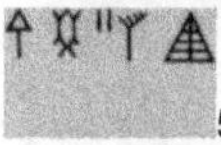

5217

h259A

h259B

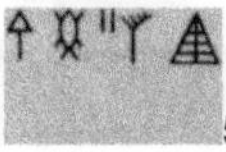

5218

h260A

h260B

h261

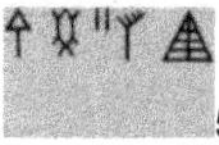

5212

h262

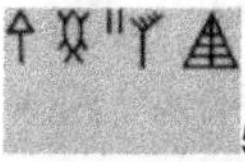

522

0

h263

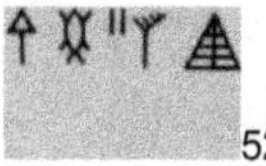

526

2

h264

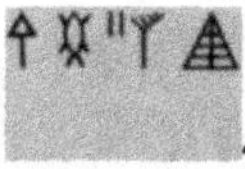

431

5

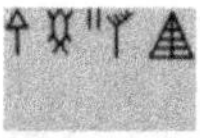

5207, 5208, 5209, 5210, 5212, 5213, 5214,5215, 5216, 5217, 5218,5219, 5220, 5262

Tablets in bas relief. The first sign looks like an arch around a pillar with ring-stones.

One-horned bull.

h252, h253, h255, h256, h257, h258, h259, h260,h261, h262, h263, h264, h265, h276, h277, h859, h860, h861, h862,h863, h864, h865, h866,h867, h868, 869, 870

h266

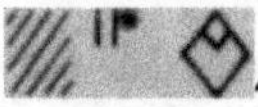

40

11

h2

67

4007

h268

4020

h269

h270
4014

h271

4069

h272

4619

h273
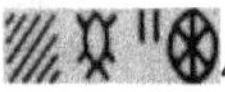
4176

h274
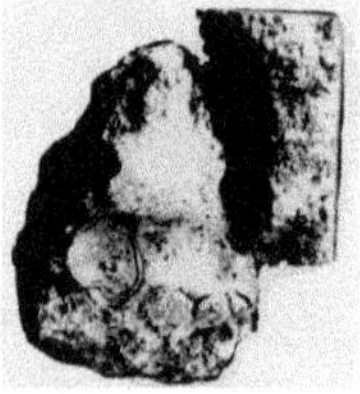
h275

h276A
h276B

h277A
h277B

5207

h278A
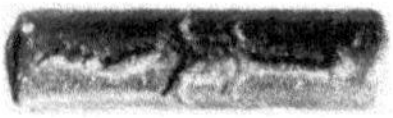
h278B

h278C
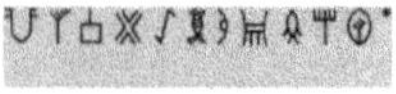
5205

h279A
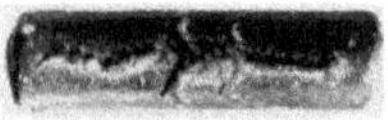
h279B
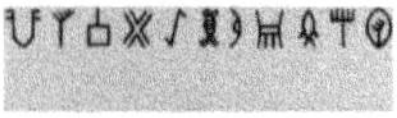
5256

h280A
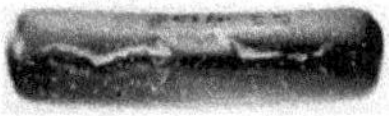
h280B
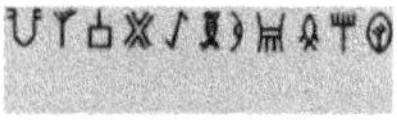
4335

h281A
h281B

4336
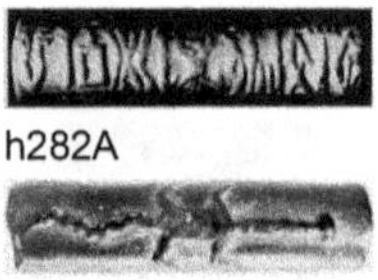
h282A
h282B

h283A

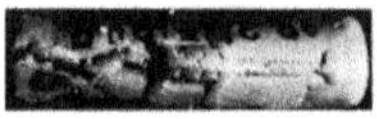
h283B

5253
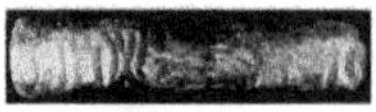
h284A
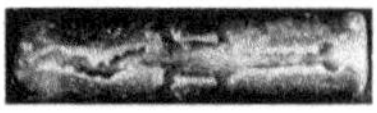
h284B

5229

h285A
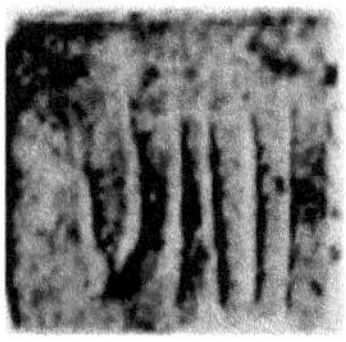
h285B

h286A

h286B

4429
Incised miniature

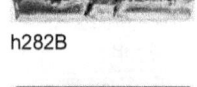

tablet
Goat-antelope
with a short tail

h287A

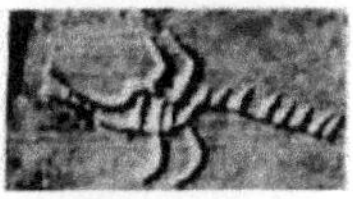
h287B

4430

h288A

h288B

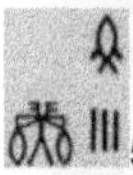
5463

h289A

h289B

5467

h290A

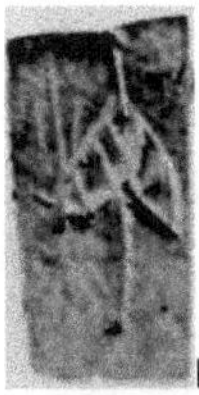
h290B

5462

h291A

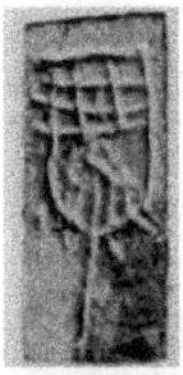
h291B

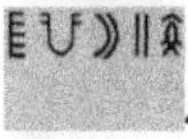
4440

Standard.

h292A

h292B

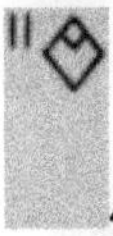
4443

Standard.

h293A

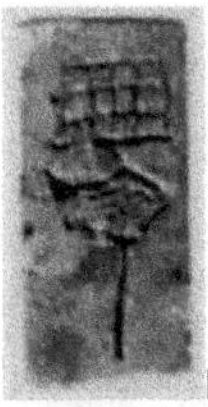
h293B

4441

Standard.

h294A

h294B

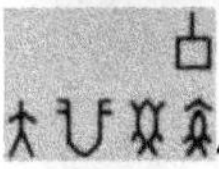
4442

h295

A 
h295

B 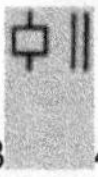
4505

h296A

h296B

445

7

h297A

h297B

5

497

h298A

h298B

5473

h299A

h299B

4478

h300A

h300B

4454

h301A

h301B

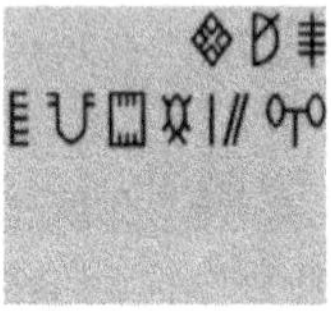

4450

h302A

h302B

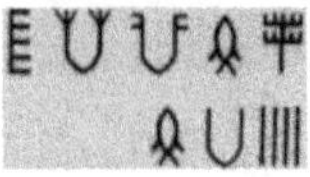

5460

h303A

h303B

4444

h304A

h304B

5401

h305A

h305B Text 5460

h306A

h306B

5474

h307A

h307B

h308A

h308B

5427

h309A

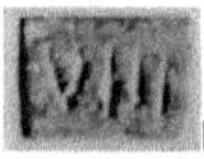

h309B

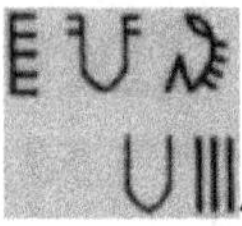

440

3

4405, 4509,

4543, 5419,

5421, 5422,

5423, 5425,

5442, 5449

Incised miniature tablets

h309, h311,

h317, h932,

h959, h935, h960

h310A

h310B

5475

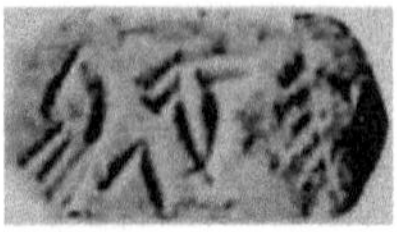

h311A

h311B

5421

h312B

h312Ac

5426

h313A

h313B

5432

5433

h314A

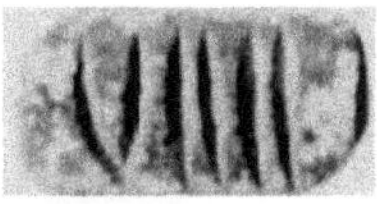

h314B

5447

h315A

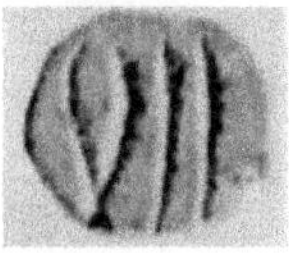

h315B

5464

h316A

h316B

h317A

h317B

5442

h318A

h318B

5451

h319A

h319B

4544

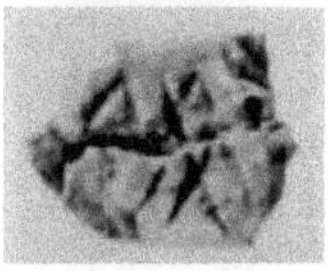

h320A

h320B

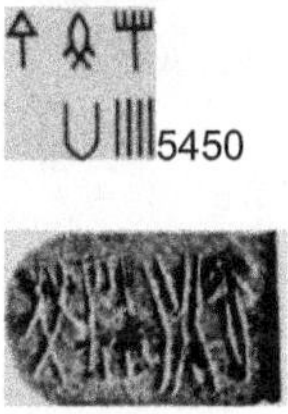

5450

h321A

h321B

5402

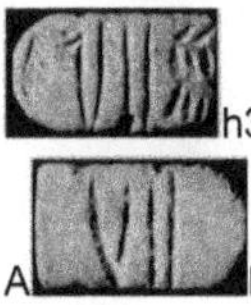

h322

A

h32

2B

5498

h323A

h323B

4497

h324A

h324B

4484

h325A

h325B

4416

Pict-130: Inscribed object in the shape of a writing tablet (?)

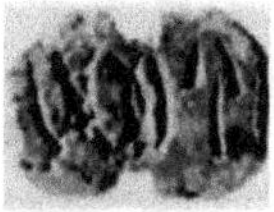

h326A

h326B

4564

Double-axe?

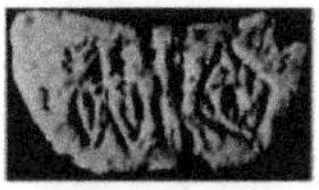

h327A

h327B

5472

5483 Shape

of object: Blade of a weapon?

h328a

h328B

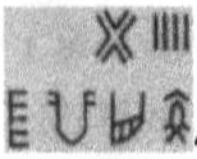4415

Shape of object: Bladeof weapon?

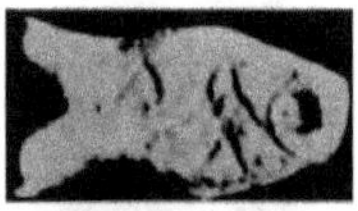

h329A

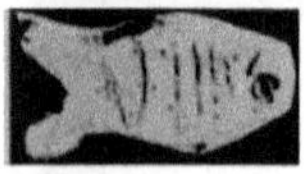

h329B

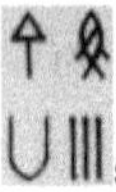5496 Pict-68: Inscribed object in the shape of a fish.

h330A

h330B 4560

h331A Incised miniature tablet.

4421, 4 422, 4423

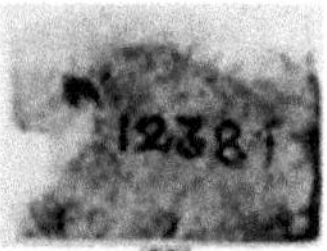

h332C 4885

h333A

h333B

 4421

h334A

h334B

4423

h335a

h335B

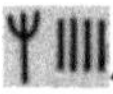4425

h336A

h336B

4424

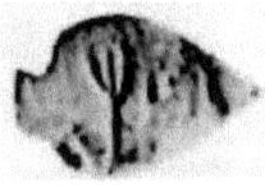

h337A

h337B

4417 Pict-79: shape of a leaf. Dotted circle on obverse.

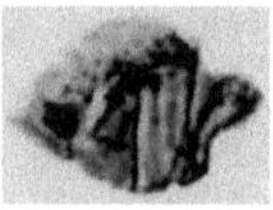

h338A

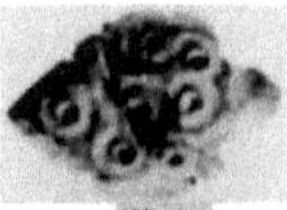

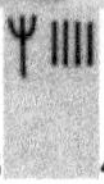

h338B 4426 Pict-39: Inscribed object in the shape of a tortoise (?) or leaf (?). Dotted circles on obverse.

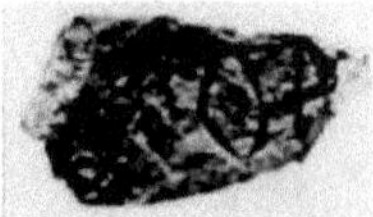

h339A

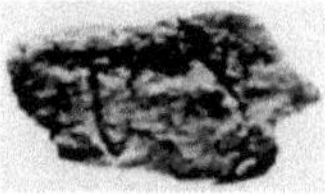

h339B

455

9

h340A

h340B

4420

h341A

h341B

4419

h342

A

h342B

4413

h343A

h343B

4549

h344A

h344B

4410

h345A

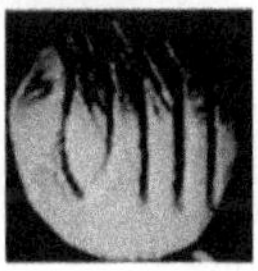

h345B

4550

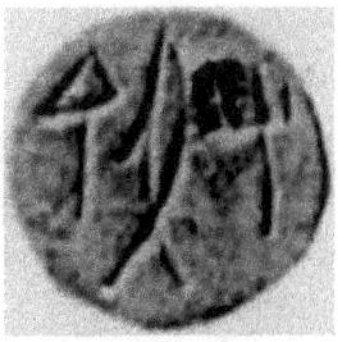

h346A

h346B Incised miniature tablet.

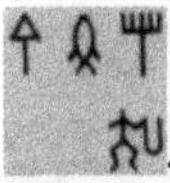

4412

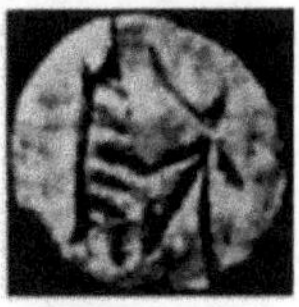

h347A  4414

h348A

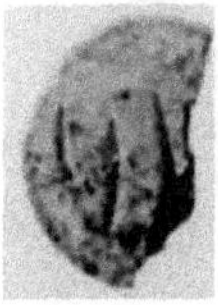

h348B

4552

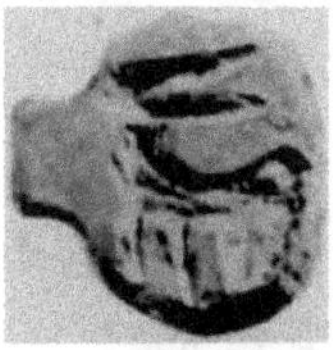

h349A

h349B

h350A

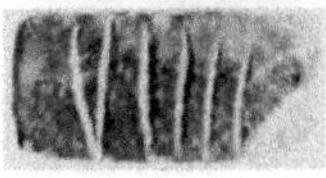

h350B

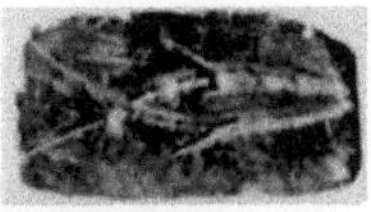

h350C

4576

h351A

h351B

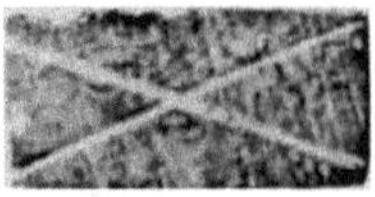

h351C

458

1

h352A

h352B

h352C

4575

Pict-120: One or more dotted circles.

h353A

h353B

h353C

5416

h354A

h354B

h354C

5499

h355A

h355B

h355C

5413

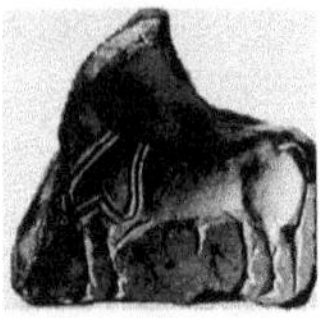

h356

h3

57

h358A

h358B

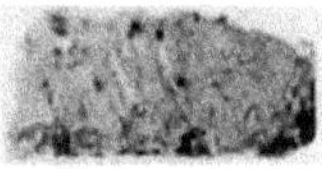

h358C

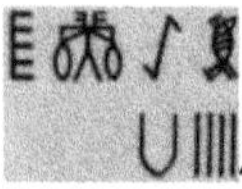

457

9

h359a

h359B

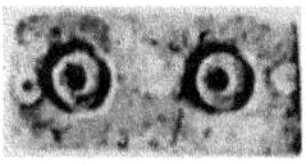

h359C

h360A

h360B

h360C

4584

h361A

h361B

h361C

5476

h362A

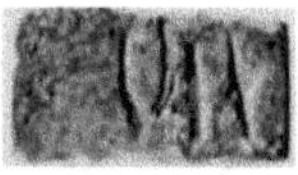

h362B

h362C

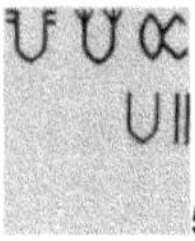

5466

h363A

h363B

h363C

h363E Pict-

86

Pict-85

Standing person with horns and bovine features (hoofed legs and/or tail).

5471

h364A

h364B

h364C

h364E

4635

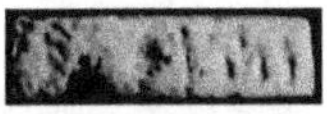

h365A

h365B

h365C

h365E

h366C

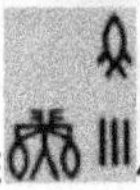

h366E 459
0

h367A

h367B

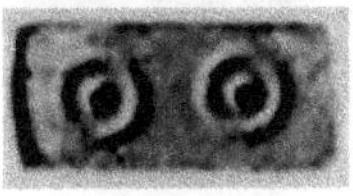

h367C

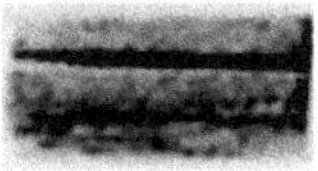

h367E 4401

h368a

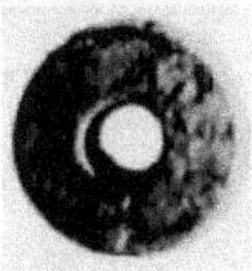

h368E

44
09

h369a

h369C

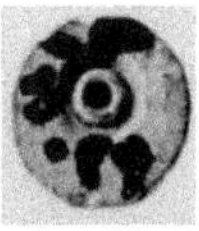

h369E

47
18

h370A

h370A2

h371

A

h371A2

h372A

h372A2

h374  4815

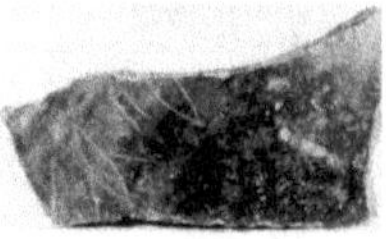

h375

4812

h377

h378

h380

 490

2 Bronze dagger

h381

 4901

Bronze dagger

h382

 481

8

h383 (Not shown).

4021

h384

h385

4045

h386

4025

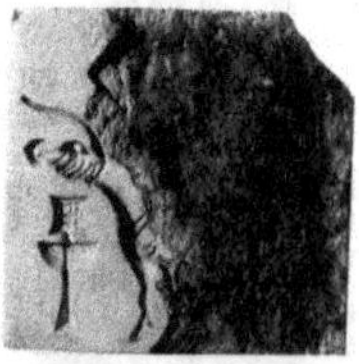

h387

h388

5062

h389

5090

h390

 40

24 [The second sign from right appears like a weaver's loom with three looped strings].

h391

5064

h392a 4207

h3

93

h394a

5003

h395a

h396

4027

h397

h398

h399

h400

h401

4168

h402

h403

h404

h405

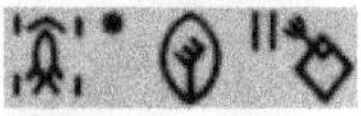

5091

h4065034

h407

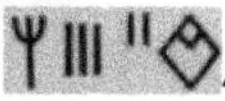4126

h408

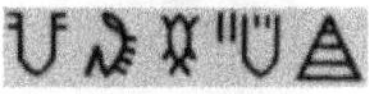

4079

h409

h410

4080

h411

407

8

h412

4036

h41

3  4032

h414

h415

420

4

h416

4059

h4

17

4051

h41

8

h419

50

92

[ The first sign may be a squirrel as in Nindowaridamb 01 Seal].

h420

4614

h421

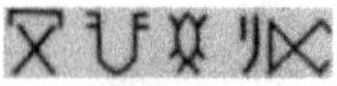
4026

h42

2 

4185

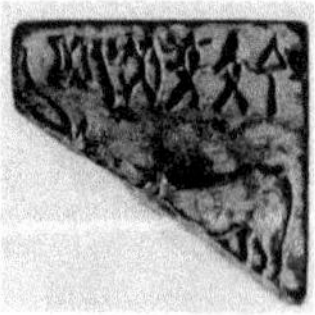
h423

4056

h424

h425

h426

4153

h427

 4217

h42

8

h429

h430

h431

5068

h432

4616

h43

3

h434

h435

h436

h437

h438

h439

h440

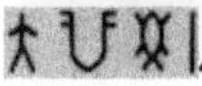

4615

h441

407

4

h442

4095

h443

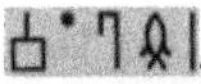

4121

h444

h445

511

0

h446

4034

h447

4089

h448

4054

h449

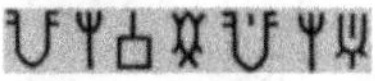

4082

h450

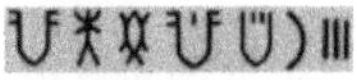

4084

h451

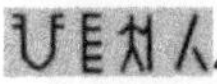

4137

h452a

4124

h453

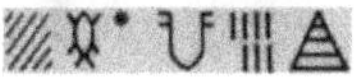

4061

h454

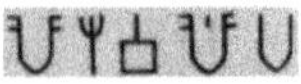

4132

h455

4

055

h456

4083

h457

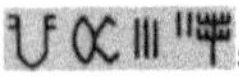508

0

h45840

50

h459

4092

h460

h461

4037

h46

24

620

h46

3 h464a

4100

h4654181

h466

4111

h4

674

624

h46

84

087

h469

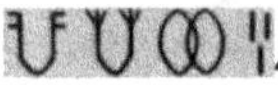41

38

h470

4186

h47

1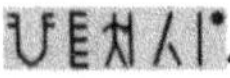414

5

h472

4152

h473

4

096

h47

4

4188

h475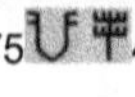4093

h476

41

02

h477

h478

4088

h479

4

099

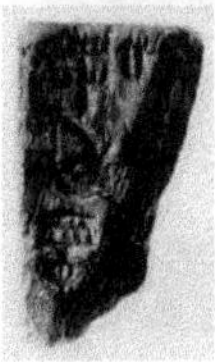

h4804180

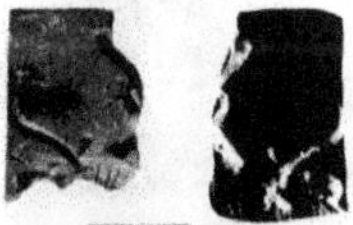

h4824208

h483

h484

415

4

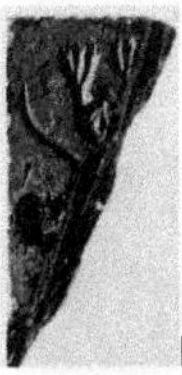h485

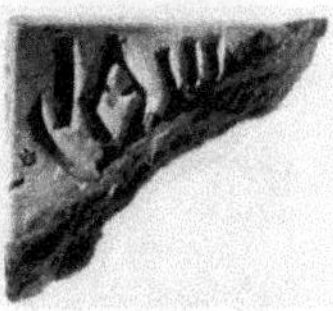

h486

h488

41

98

h4

89

4189

h490

h492

h493

h494

h4

95

h497

h498

h49

95093

h500

h501

41

12

h502

4143

h5

034129

h504

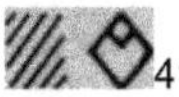4183

h505 5094

h506

4097

h507 4159

h508

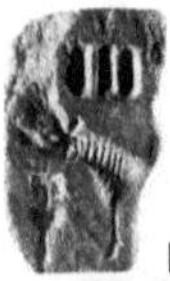

h509

 42

06

h510

 41

39

h51

1  4165

h512

a 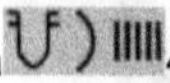 4618

h51

3  416

3

h514

4116

h515

4162

Text  4166

h516a

h517

h518  4160

h519

 4

147

h520  4127

h521  4155

h522

h523

 5

071

h5

24  41

50

h525  41

49

h526

h527

h528

h529

h530

4148

[May have to be arranged from right to left?]

h53

1

4172

h532

h53

3 462

5

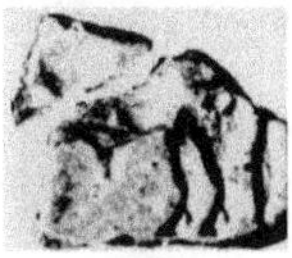

h534

h535

h536

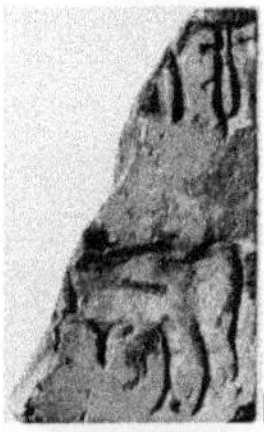

h5

37

4170

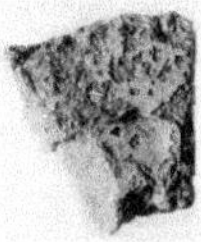

h538

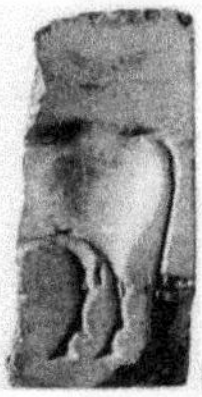

h539

h541

h542

h543

41

77

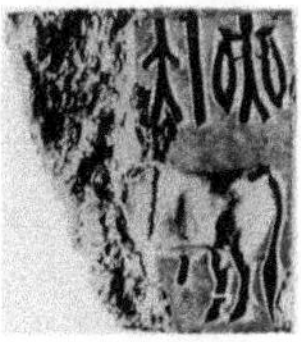

h544

41

44

h545

4622

h54

6 4697

h547

h548

h5

49

h550

4211

h551

4197

h552

h55

3

h554

h555

h556

h557

h558

4220

h559

4290

h561

h562

506

6

h563

5065

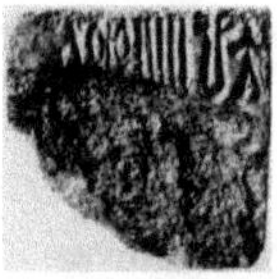

h565

4621

h566

4277

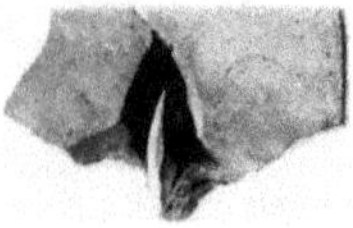

h567

h568

h569

4263

h5

70

4212

h571

h572

4695

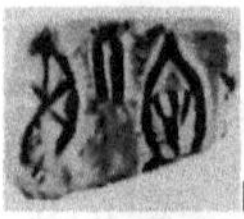

h57

4

469

6

h575

h576

h57

7

4243

h578

h579

5109

h580

h581

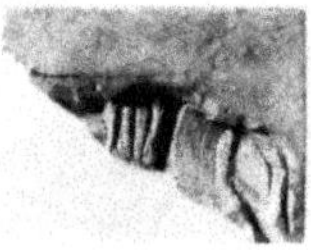

h582

h583

h584  4235

Bison.

h585

h586

 4237

h587

h588

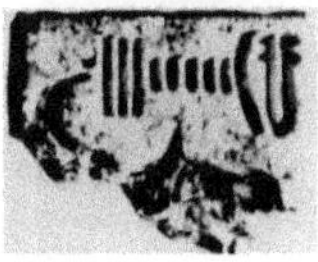

h589

 4239

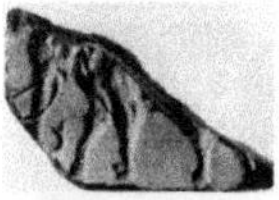

h590

h591

 4228

 h592

5081

h593

4250 [Composite animal].

h594 [Composite animal].

 h595

4623

 h596a

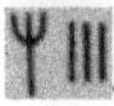 4382 [One-horned bull].

h597A

h597D

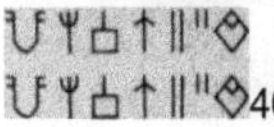 4075

h598A

h598D

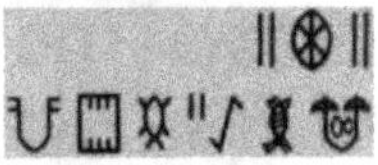

5073 [The ligature in-fixed on the last sign of the second line may be Sign

54]

h599A

h599D

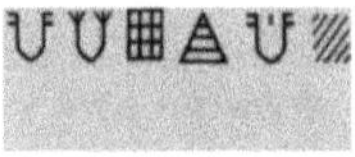

5076

h600 

4156 [The last sign may be a variant of Sign 51 ]

h60

1

4044

h602a

4169

h603

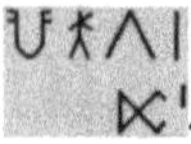

4224

h604

h605

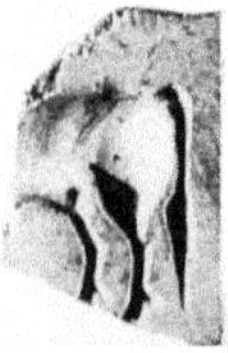

h606

4167

h608  4225

h609

4060

h61

0

4098

h611

4260 One-horned bull.

h612A 

h612B

h612D

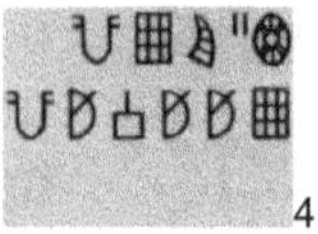

4

123

h613A

h613C

425

9 Endless-knot motif?

h614

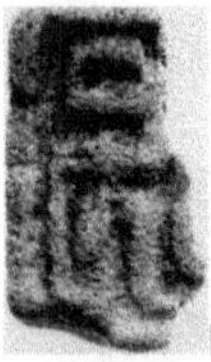

h616

h617

h618

h619

h620

h621

h62

2

h62

3

h624

h625

h626

h627

h628

h629

h630

h631

h632

h633

h634

h63

5

h636

h63

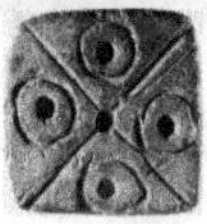
7

h638

h639

5061

h640

h641A

h641C

4698

h642

4266

h643

4

273

h644

4299

h645

4265

h646

51

08

h647

42

91

h648

h649

4281

h650A

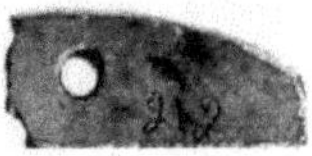
h650C

h651 4295

h65

2

h653 4301

h654

5035

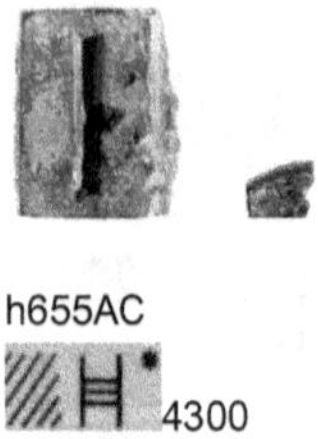

h655AC

4300

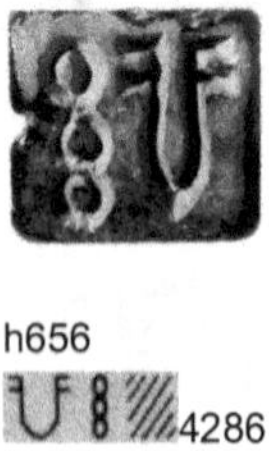

h656 4286

h657

4287

h658

4

293

h659

5074

h660

5114

h661

427

9

h662

a

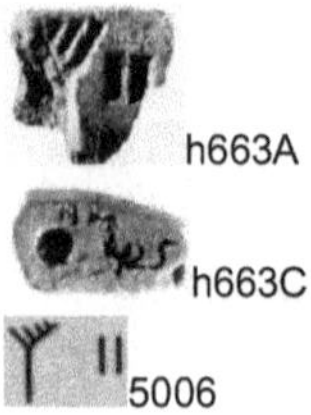

h663A

h663C

5006

h664A

h664E

5010

h665

5100

h666

4631

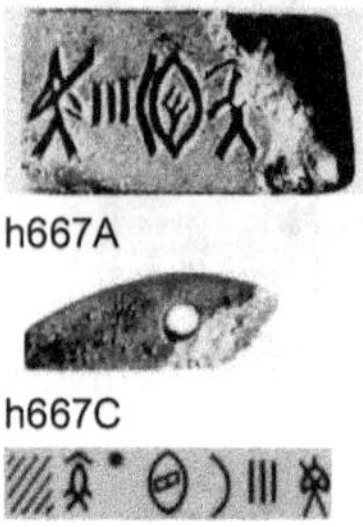

h667A

h667C

4634

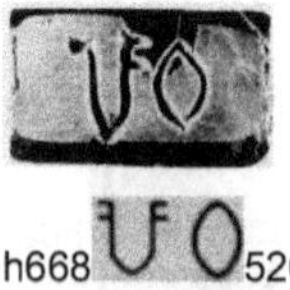

h668 526

6

h669

4289

h670

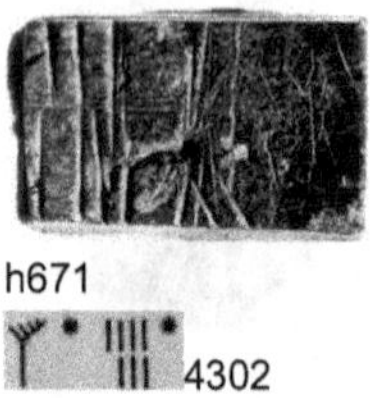

h671

4302

h679

4298

h680

5099

h681a

51

05

h682

5078

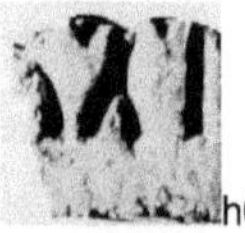

h683

h684

 4632

h685

h686

h688A

h688F

h689A

h689B

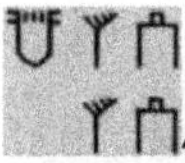 4222

h690si  5304

h691A1si

h691A2si

h692A1si

h692A2si

h693t

 4707

h694t

h695t

h696At

h696Bt

 4677

h697At

h697Bt

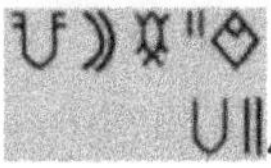 4314

h698At

h698Bt

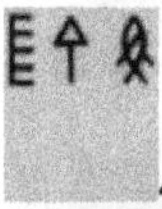 4659

h699At

h699Bt

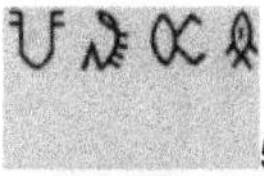 5288

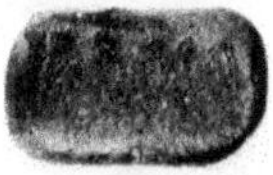

h700At

h700Bt

h701At

h701Bt

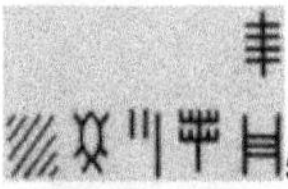 5329

h702At

h702Bt

4601

h703At

h703Bt

4595

h704At

h704Bt

h705At

h705Bt

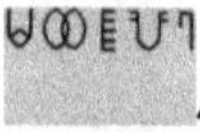4337

h706At

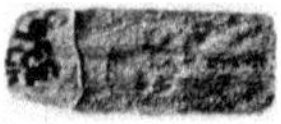

h706Bt

4340

h707At

h707

433

9

h708At

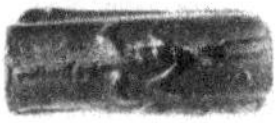

h708Bt

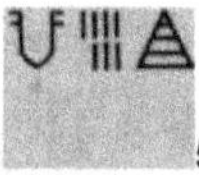5280

h709

Text 5260

h710

Text 5249

h711

Text 4

715

h713At

h713Bt

h714At

h714Bt

Standing person with horns and bovine features (hoofed legs and/or a tail) Icon of a person has bull's legs and a raised club.

h715At

h715Bt

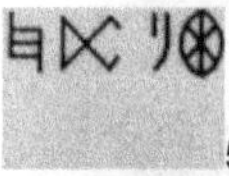5299

h716At

h716Bt

h717At

h717Bt

h718At

h718Bt

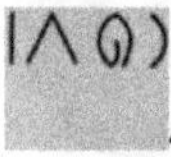4328

h719At

h719B

t 4326

h720At

h720Bt

h722At

h722Bt

h723At

h723Bt

h724At

h724Bt

5255

h725At

h725Bt

h726At

h726Bt

h727At

h727Bt

h728At

h728Bt

h729At

h729Bt

43

31
h730At

h730Bt

h731At

h731Bt

h732At

h732Bt

h733At

h733Bt
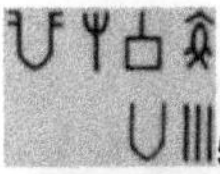
5222

h734At

h734Bt

5286

h735At

h735Bt
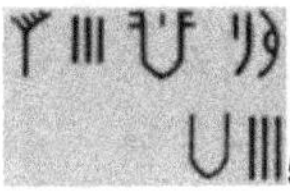
5
310

h736At

h736Bt

h737At

h737Bt

h738At

h738Bt

h739At

h739Bt

h740At

h740Bt

h741At

h741Bt

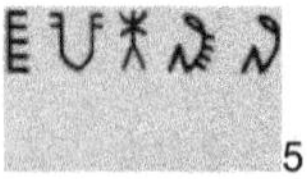

5

263

h742At

h742Bt

43

20

h743At

h743Bt

h744At

h744Bt

h745At

h745Bt

5257

h746At

h746Bt

h747At

h747Bt

4656

h748At

4654

h749At

h750At

h751At

h752At

5275

h753At

5231

h754At

4716

h755A

t

5287

h756At

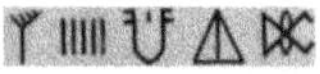

4669

h757At

4655

h758At

h759A

t

h760At

h760Bt

h761At

h761Bt

h762At

h762Bt Tablet in bas-relief.

435
4

h763At

h763Bt

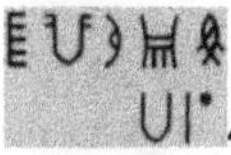

4661

h764At

h764Bt

h765At

h765Bt

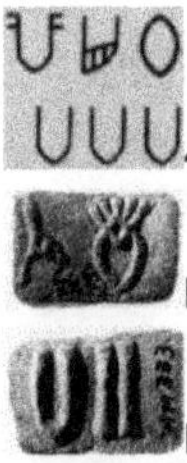

4653

h766At

h766Bt

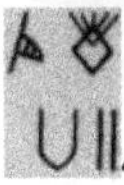

4359

h767At

h767Bt

4352

h768At

h768Bt

4
358

h769At

h769Bt

46
67

h770At

h770Bt

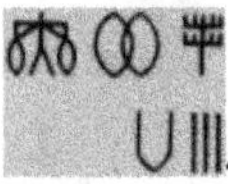

4353

h771At

h771Bt

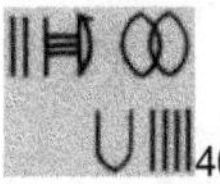

4678

[The second sign on line 1 is a squirrel ].

h772At

h772Bt

4660

h773At

h773Bt

4351

h774At

h774Bt

4
672

h775At

h776At

h776Bt

4350

h777At

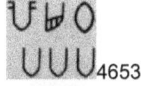

h777Bt

h778At

h778Bt

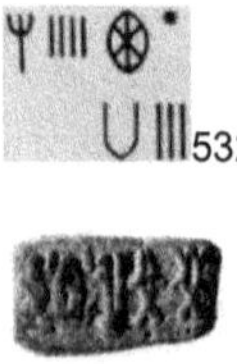

5322

h779At

h779Bt

h780At

h780Bt

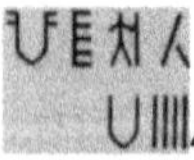

4361

h781At

h781Bt

4670

h782A

t h782Bt

53

28

h783At

h783Bt

h784At

h784Bt

4364

h785At

h785Bt

4681

h786At

h786Bt

5320

h787At

h787Bt

h788At

h788Bt

4683

h789At

h789Bt

4604

h790At

h790Bt

4605

h791At

h791Bt

4676

h792At

h792Bt

4692

h793At

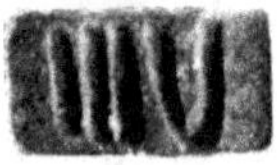

h793Bt

4680

h794At

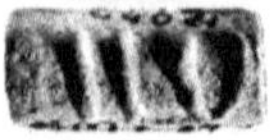

h794Bt

5323

h795At

h795Bt

 h796At

 h796Bt

5327

 h797At

 h797Bt

5281

 h798At

 h798Bt

4607

 h799At

 h799Bt

4603

h800At

h800Bt

468
9

h801At

h801Bt

h802At

h802Bt

4679

h804At

5233

h806At

h806Bt

523
7

h807At

h807Bt

434
3 One-horned bull.

h808At

h808Bt

52
38

h810At

4366

h811At

h811Bt

4349

h812At

h812Bt

4686

h813At

h813Bt

4682

h814At

h814Bt

4606

h815At

h815Bt

h816At

h816Bt

4602

h817At

h817Bt Inscribed object in the shape of a double-axe.One or more dotted circles.

h818At

h818Bt Inscribed object in the shape of a double-axe.

4376

h819At

h819Bt Shape of object: Blade of a weapon?

5302

h820At

h820Bt

h821At

h821Bt Shape of object: axe.

h822At

h822Bt Shape of object: axe.

5319

h823At

h823Bt

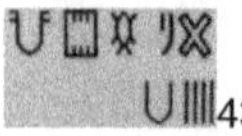4346

h824At

h824Bt

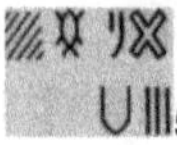5278

h825At

h825Bt Shape of object: sickle?

5324

h827At

h827Bt Shape of object: axe?

h829At

h829Bt

5303

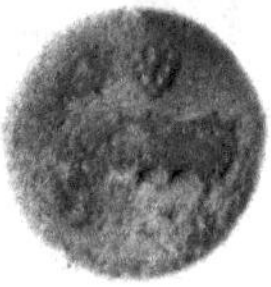

h830At

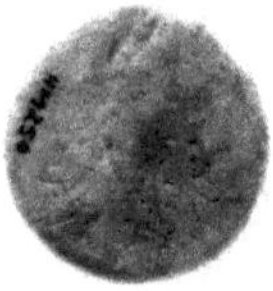

h830Bt Tablet in bas-relief. Bovid.

4311

h832At

h832Bt Tablet in bas-relief

Pict-121:

Lozenge within a circle with a dot in the center.

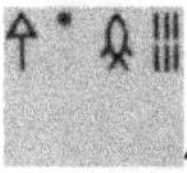
4377

h833At

h833Bt

4370

h834At

h834Bt

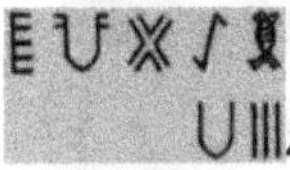
4666

h835Bt

h836At

h837At

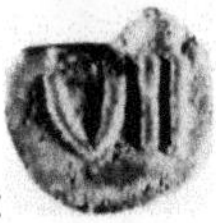
h837Bt

4381

h838At

h838Bt

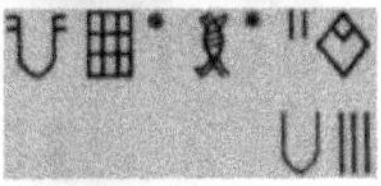
4375

h839At

h839Bt

4378

h840At

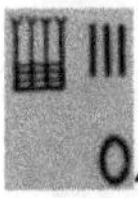
4380

h841At

4379

h842At

h843At

h843Ct

5326

h844At

h844Bt

h845At

h845Bt

h845Ct

h846At

h846Bt

h846Ct

4641

h847At

h847Bt

h847Ct

h848At

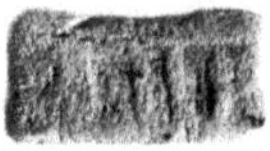

h848Bt

h848Ct

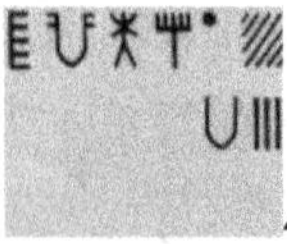

4

597

h849At

h849Bt

h849Ct

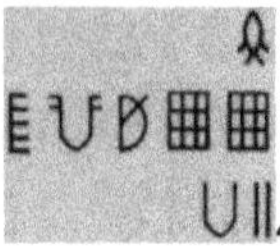

4

645

h850At

h850Bt

h850Ct

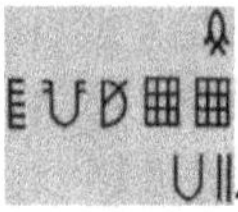

464

2

h851A

t h851Bt

h851C

t

h852At

h852Bt

h852Ct

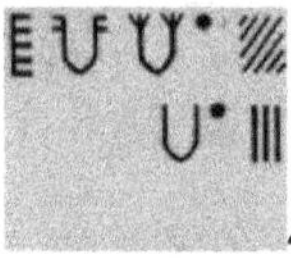

4

596

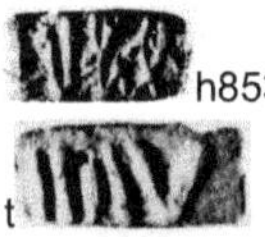

h853A

t

h853Bt

h853Ct

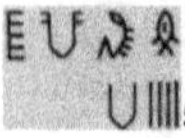

5277

h854At

h854Bt

h854Ct

4647

h855At

h855Bt

h855Ct

h856At

h856Bt

h856Ct

h857At

h857Bt

h857Ct

5276

h858At

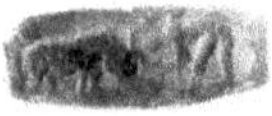

h858Bt

h858Ct

h859At

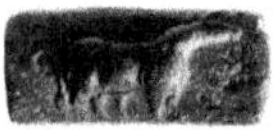

h859Bt

h859Ct

h860At

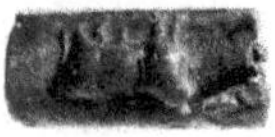

h860Bt

h861At

h861Bt

h862At

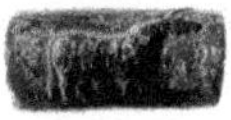

h862Bt

h863ABt

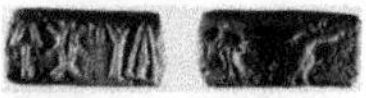

h864ABt

h865ABt

h866ABt

h867ABt

h868ABt

h869ABt

h870ABt

h871Bt

5234

h872Bt

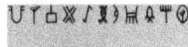

5230

h873At

h873Bt

5227

h874At

h874Bt

4362

h875At

h875Bt

4651

h876At

h876Bt

4675

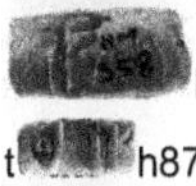

h877A

t h877Bt

4594

h878At

h878Bt

4687

h879Abit

h880ABit

4433

h881Abit

4434

h882Abit

443

6

h883Ait

h883Bit

h884Abit

4437

h885Ait

h885Bit

4530 Fish.

h887Ait

h887Bit

h888Abit

4466

h889Abit

5477

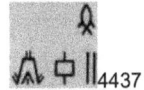

h890ABit
4446

h891ABit

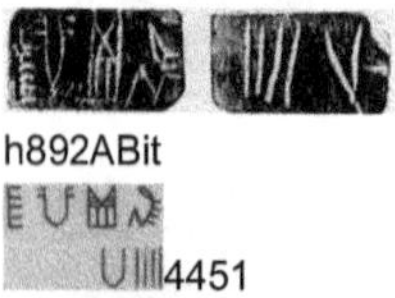
h892ABit
4451

h893Ait
h893Bit

4522

h894ABit
4487

h895Ait

h895Bit

h896ABit
4480

h897ABit

h898ABit
4506

h899Ait

h899Bit

4471

h900Ait

h900Bit

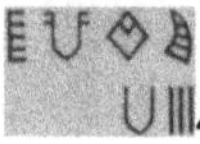
4455

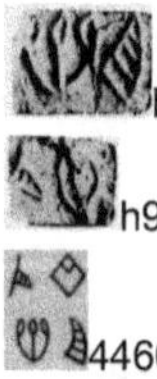
h901Ait
h901Bit
4460

h902Ait
h902Bit
4535

h903Ait

h903Bit
4485

h904Ait

h904Bit

4477

h905ABit
4
449

h906Ait

h906Bit

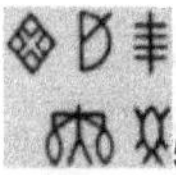
5494

h907Ait

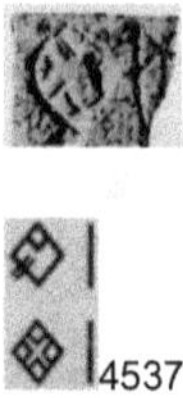
h907Bit

4537 The second sign on h907Ait may be a ligatured fish?

h908Abit

4488

h909ABit

5325

h910ABit

4470

h911Ait

h911Bit

4486

h912Abit

5

461

h913Ait

h913Bit

h914Ait

h914Bit

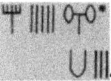

4483

h916Ait

h916Bit

4456

h917Ait

h917Bit

4472

h918Ait

h918Bit

4481

h919Ait

h919Bit

h920Ait

h920Bit

4527

h921ABit

4514

h922Abit

4518

h923Abit

4474

h924ABit

h925Abit

4512

h926Abit

4519

h927Ait

h927Bit 4502

h928Ait

h928Bit

h929Ait

h929Bit

h930Ait

h930Bit

4520

h931Ait

h931Bit

4511

h932Ait

h932Bit

4403

h933Ait

h933Bit

4516

h934Ait

h934Bit

h935Ait

h935Bit

4509

h936Ait

h936Bit

5405

h937Ait

h937Bit

5458

h938Ait

h938Bit

h939Ait

h939Bit

h940Ait

h940Bit

4453

h941Ait

h941Bit

4464

h942Ait

h942Bit

4490

h943Ait

h943Bit

4461

h944Ait

h944Bit

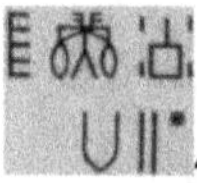
4475

h945Ait

h945Bit

4503

h946Ait

h946Bit

4501

h947Ait

h947Bit

4493

h948Abit

4489

h949Abit

4479

h950ABit

4463

h951Ait

h951Bit

4498

h952Ait

h952Bit

4469

h953Ait

h953Bit

h954Ait

4467

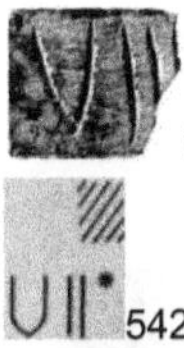

h955Bit

5429

h959Ait

h959Bit

4405

h960Ait

h960Bit

4543

h961Ait

h961Bit

5449

h962Ait

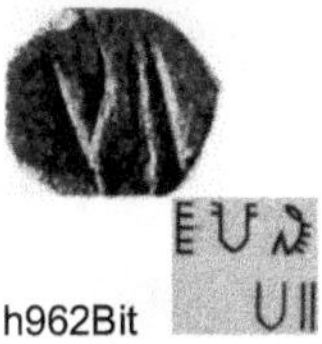

h962Bit

4548

h963Ait

h963Bit

5420

h964Ait

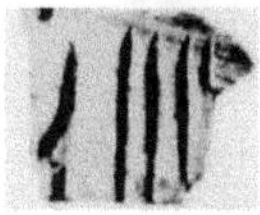

h964Bit

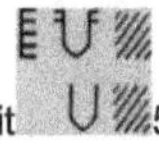

5456

h965Ait

h965Bit

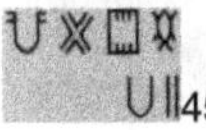

4562

h966Ait

h966Bit

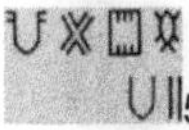

5479

h967Ait

4563

h968Ait

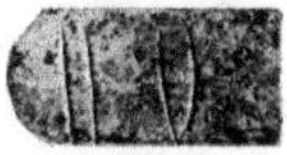

h968Bit

h969Ait

h969Bit

4555

h970Ait

h970Bit

4553

h971Ait

h971Bit

4557 Shape of object: double-axe?

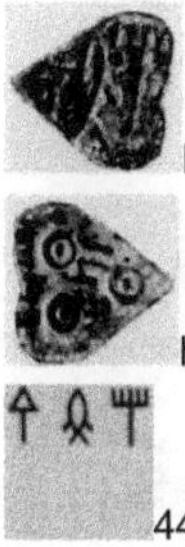

h972Ait

h972Bit

4418

Pict-128: Inscribed object in the shape of a leaf? Dotted

circles on obverse.

h973Ait

h973Bit

4411

h974Ait

h974Bit

h974Cit

4592

h975Ait

h975Bit

h975Cit

4402

h976Ait

h976Bit

h976Cit

4588

h977Ait

h977Bit

h977Cit

4591

h978Ait

h978Bit

h978Cit

5412

h979Ait

h979Bit

h979Cit

h980Ait

h980Bit

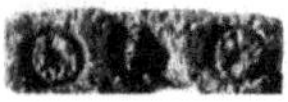

h980Cit

h981Ait

h981Bit

h981Cit

5415

h982Ait

h982Bit

h982Cit

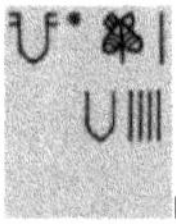

m4574

h983Ait

h983Bit

h983Cit

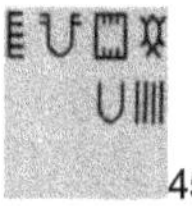

4582

h984Ait

h984Bit

h984Cit

4587

h985Ait

h985Bit

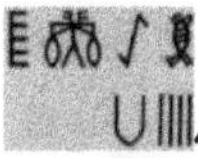

4577

h987Ait

h987Bit

h987Cit

4586

h988Ait

h988Bit

h988B2it

h988Cit

h988Eit

4

573

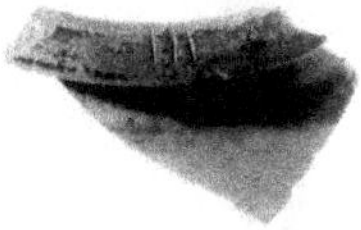

h990

h992

h994

h1020

h1021

h1022

h1023

h1024

h1025a

h1027a

h1028

h1029a

h1030a

h1031

h1032a

h1033a

h1035

h1036

h1037

h1038

h1042a

h1043a

h1044a

h1045a

h1046

h1047a

h1048

h1049a

h1050

h1051

h1052

h1053a

h1056a

h1058a

h1059

h1064

h1065

h1066a

h1067a

h1068

h1071

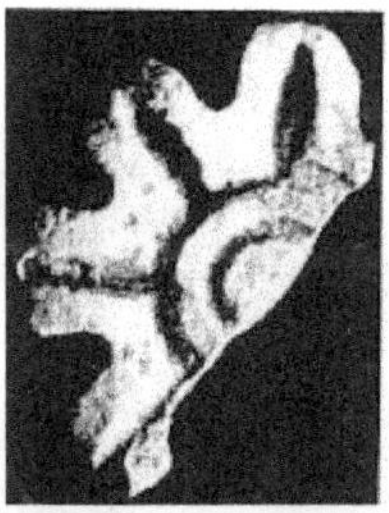
h1072

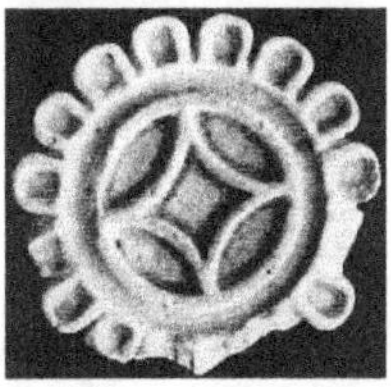
h1073

h1075

h1076

h1077

h1079a

h1080a

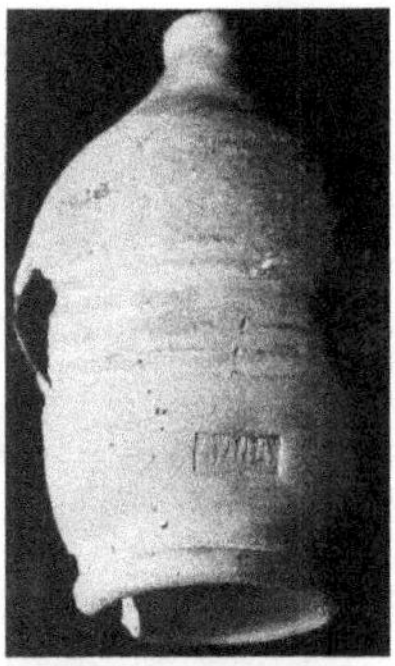
h1081

h1082

h1083

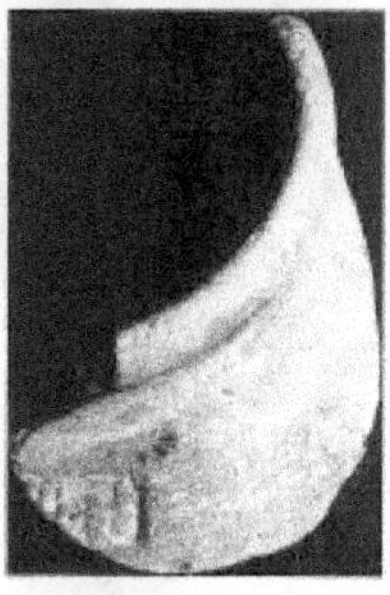
h1084

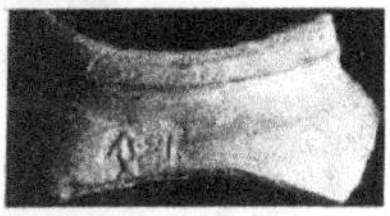
h1085

h1086

h1087

h1091

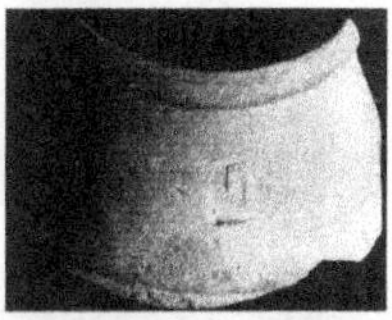
h1092

h1093

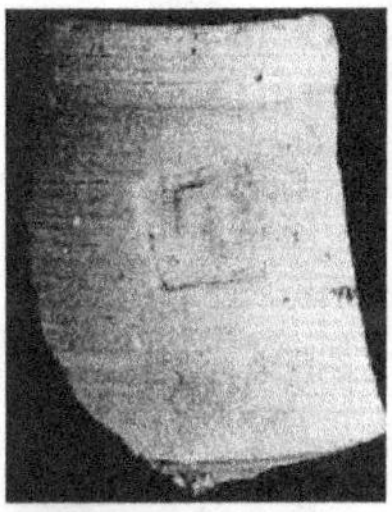
h1094

h1097

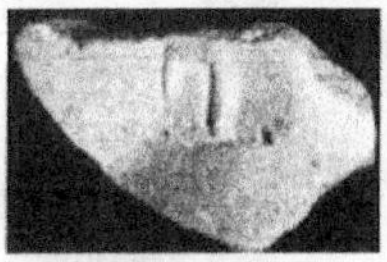
h1098

h1100A

h1100B

h1101A

h1101B

h1102A

h1102B

h1103A

h1103B

h1104A

h1104B

h1105A

h1105B

h1107A

h1107B

h1108A

h1108B

h1109A

h1109B

h1113A

h1113B

h1114B

h1115A

h1116A

h1116B

h1117A

h1121A

h1121B

h1122A

h1122B

h1123A

h1123B

h1124A

h1124B

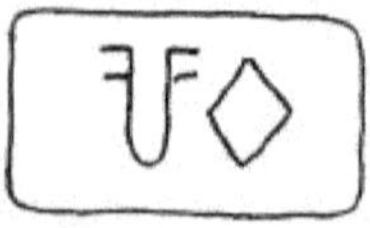

h1126A

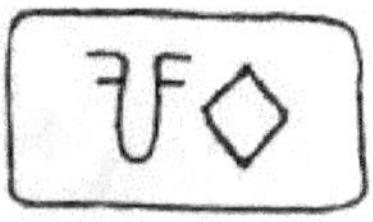

h1126B

h1130A

h1130B

h1131A

h1131B

h1133A

h1133B

h1134A

h1134B

h1137A

h1138A

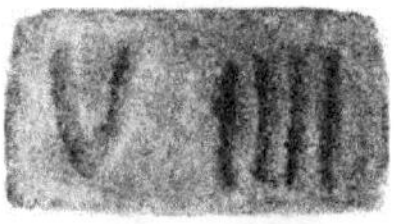

h1138B

h1139A

h1139B

h1140A

h1140B

h1141A

h1141B

h1142A

h1142B

h1144A

h1144B

h1146A

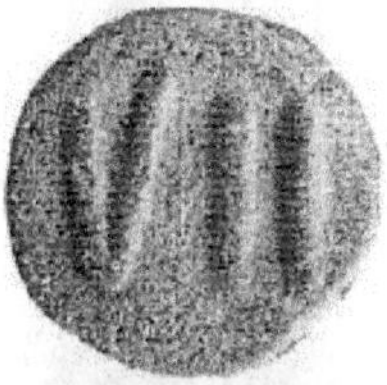

h1146B

h1148A

h1149A

h1150ABC

h1151A

h1151C

h1152A

h1152B

h1155A

h1155B

h1158A

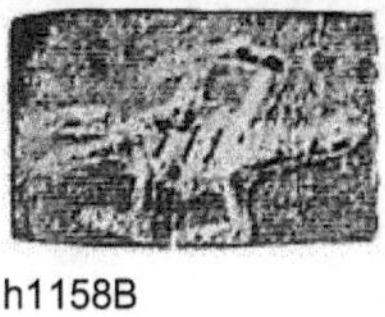

h1158B

h1159A

h1159B

h1160A

h1160B

h1165A

h1165B

h1166A

h1166B

h1178a

h1178b

h1181A

h1182A

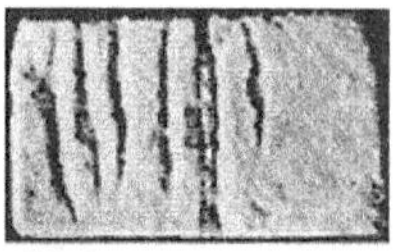
h1182B

h1184A

h1184B

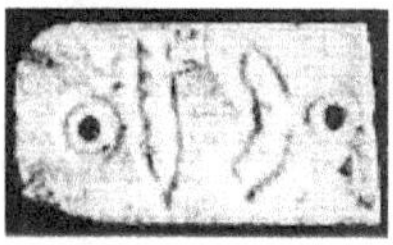
h1187a

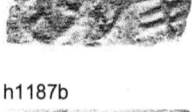

h1187b

h1188A

h1188B

h1189A

h1189B

h1190A

h1190B

h1191A

h1191B

h1192A

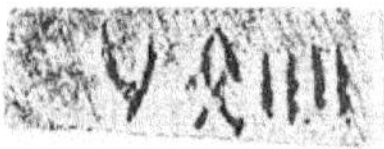
h1192B

h1198A

h1198B

h1200-
1258

h1261A

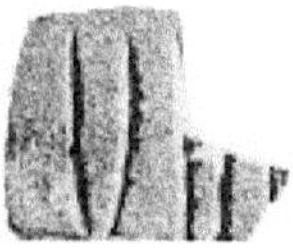
h1261B

h1272A

h1272B

h1273A

h1273B

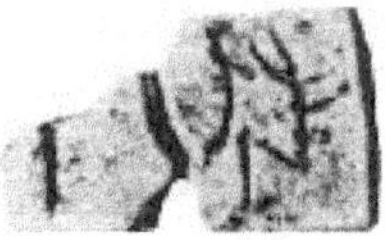
h1274A

h1274B

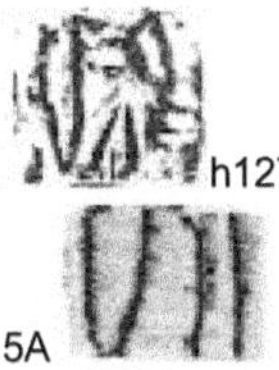
h127
5A

h1275B

h1284A

h1284B

h1287A

h1287B

h1289A

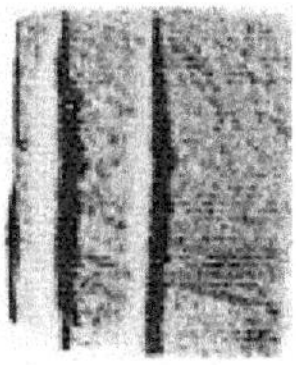
h1289B

h1293A

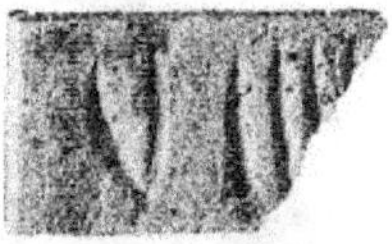
h1293B

h1294A

h1294B

h1302A

h1302B

h1303A

h1303B

h1304A

h1304B

h1308a

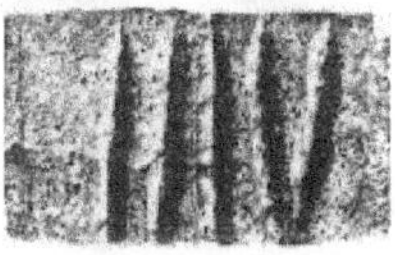
h1308b

h1309A

h1309B

h1313A

h1313B

h1319A

h1319B

h1320A

h1320B

h1321A

h1321B

h1325A

h1325b

h1326A

h1326B

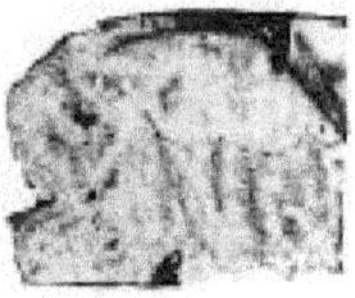
h1329A

h1329B

h1330A

h1330B

h1331A

h1331B
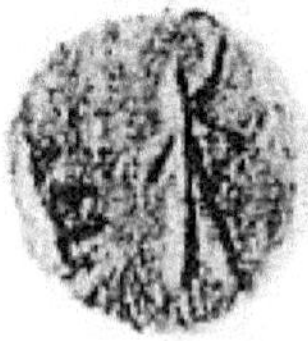
h1332A

h1332B

h1342A

h1342B

h1342C

h1344A

h1344B

h1345A

h1345B

h1345C

h1347A

h1347B

h1347C

h1348A

h1348B

h1348C

h1350A

h1350B

h1350C

h1353a

h1353b

h1353c

h1354A

h1354B

h1354C

h1354D

h1355a

h1355B

h1355c

h1355d

h1344C

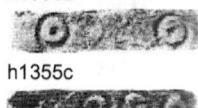

h1357

A

h1357b

h1366a

h1388A

h1392A

h1393A

h1394A

h1397A

h1403A

h1404A

h1406A

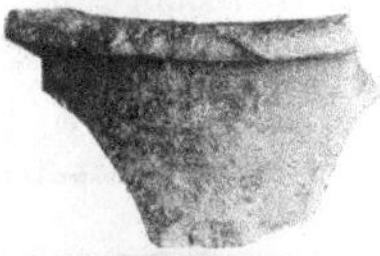

h1407A

h1408A

h1410A

h1411A

h1412A

h1421A

h1422A

h1444A

h1424A

h1431A

h1433A

h1434A

h1441A

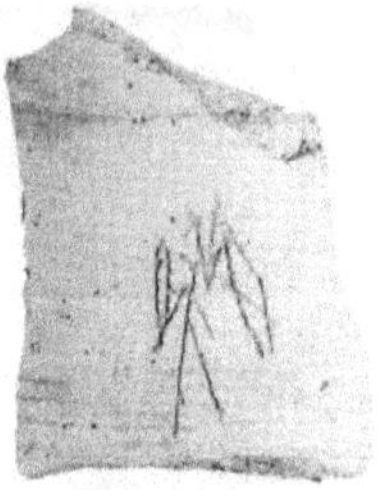
h1461A
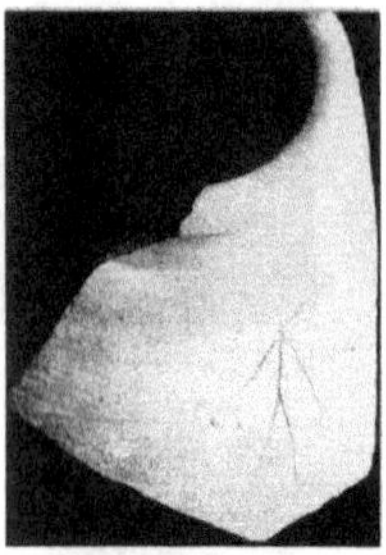
h1462A

h1464A

h1467A

h1468A

h1471A

h1481A

h1487A
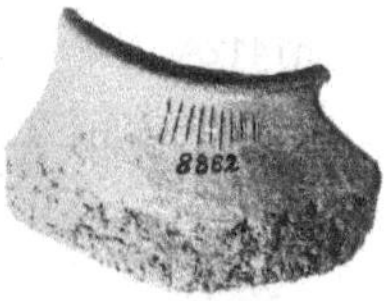
h1491A

h1501A

h1506A

h1507A

h1513A

h1516A

h1517A

h1518copperaxe
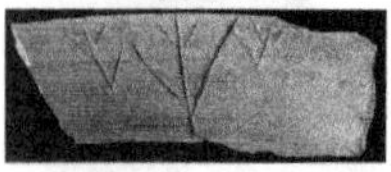
h1522A

h15533A

h1534A

h1535A

h1536A

h1537A

h1537B
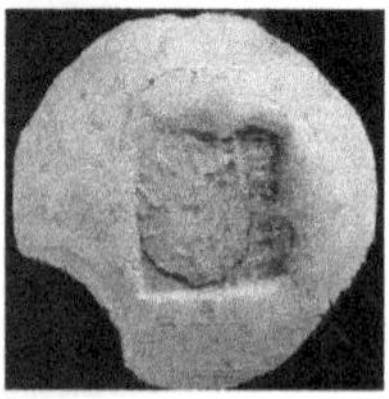
h1538A

h1541A

h1544A

h1545A

h1547A

h1559A

h1586A

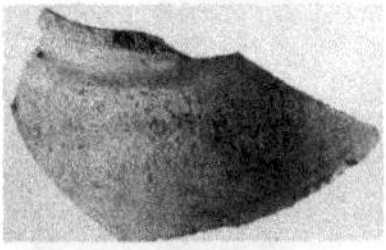

h1587A

h1657A

h1662A

h1663A

h1664A

h1666A

h1667A

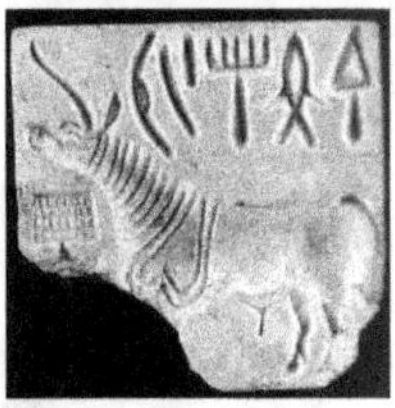

h1669A

h1670A

h1671A

h1672A

h1673A

h1676A

h1677A

h1678A

h1679A

h1680A

h1681A

h1682A

h1684A

h1685A

h1687A

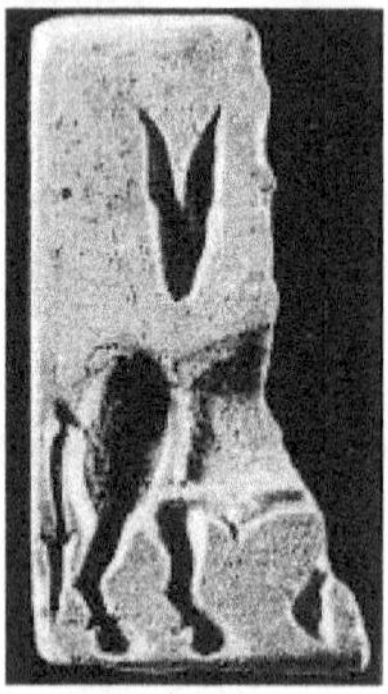

h1688A

h1690A

h1691A

h1692A

h1694A

h1695

h1696

h1697

h1698

h1699

h1700

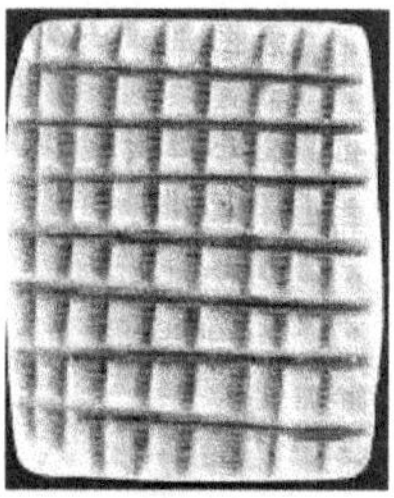

h1701

h1702

h1703

h1704

h1705

h1706

h1707

h1708

h1709

h1710

h1711

h1712

h1713

h1714

h1715

h1716

h1719A

h1719B

h1720A

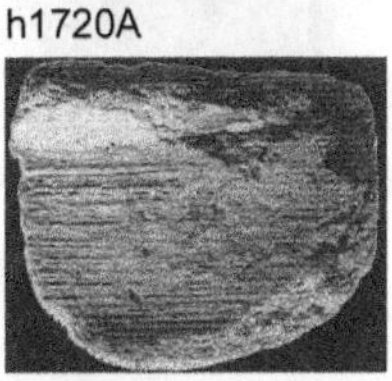
h1720B

h1721A

h1721B

h1722A

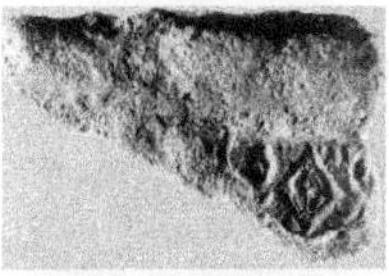
h1723

h1724

h1725A

h1726

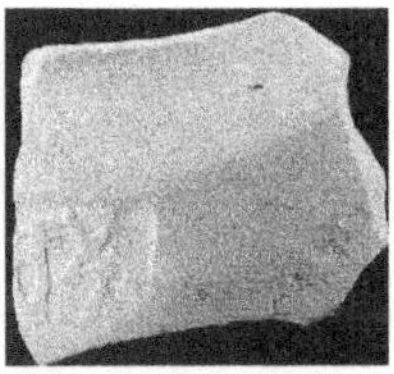
h1727

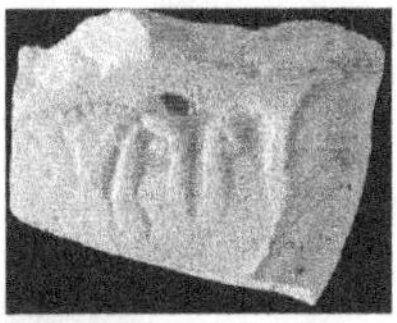
h1728

h1729

h1731

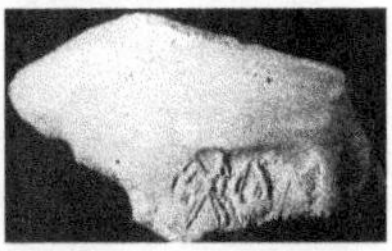
h1732

h1733

h1734

h1735

h1736

h1737

h1739

h1740

h1742

h1743

h1744

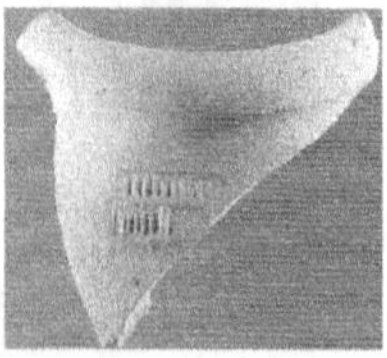

h1751

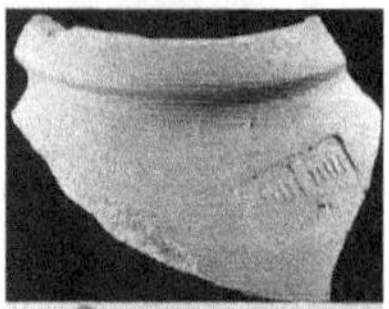

h1753

h1756

h1757

h1758

h1759

h1760

h1761

h1762

h1767A

h1767B

h1768A

h1768B

h1770A

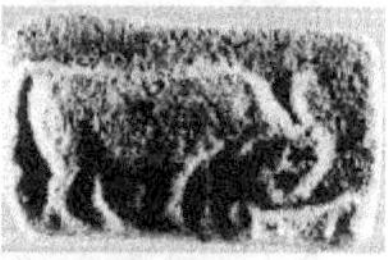

h1770B

h1771A

h1771B

h1772A

h1772B

h1773A

h1773B

h1774A

h1774B

h1775A

h1775B

h1776A

h1776B

h1777A

h1777B

h1778A

h1778B

h1779A

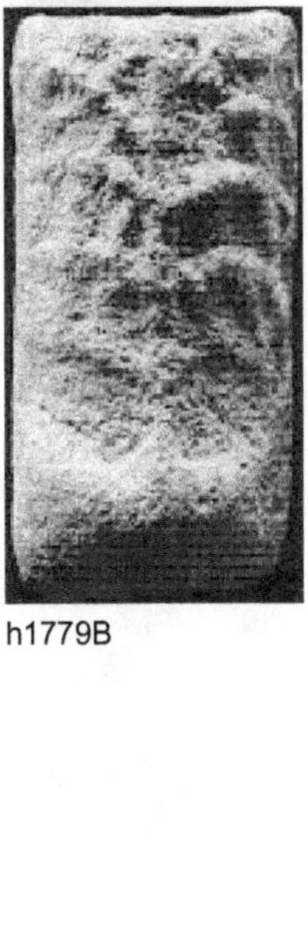
h1779B

h1780A

h1780B

h1781A

h1781B

h1782A

h1783A

h1783B

h1785A

h1785B

h1786A

h1786B

h1787A

h1787B

h1788A

h1788B

h1791A

h1791B

h1792A
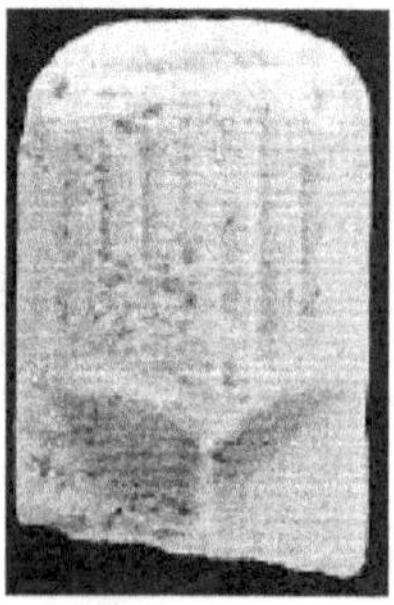
h1792B

h1793A

h1793B

h1796A

h1796B

h1797A

h1797B

h1799A

h1800A

h1800B

h1801A

h1801B

h1802A

h1802B

h1803A

h1803B

h1804A

h1804B

h1805A

h1805B

h1806A

h1806B

h1807A

h1807B
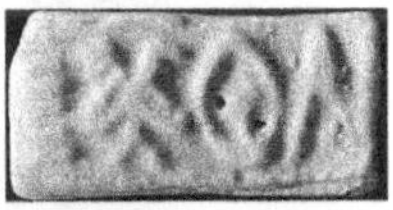
h1808A

h1809A

h1810A

h1810B

h1811A

h1811B

h1812A

h1812B

h1813A

h1813B

h1815A

h1815B

h1816A

h1816B

h1817A
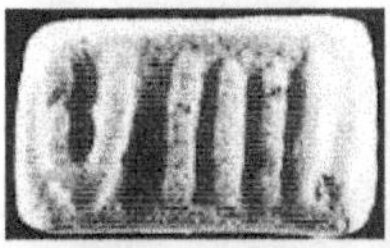
h1817B

h1818A

h1818B

h1819A

h1819B

h1820A

h1820B

h1821A

h1821B

h1822A
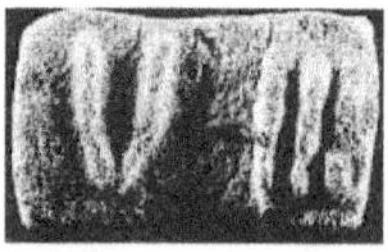
h1822B

h1823A

h1823B

h1824A

h1824B

h1825A

h1825B

h1826A

h1826B

h1827A

h1827B

h1829A

h1829B

h1830A

h1830B

h1831A

h1831B

h1832A

h1832B

h1833A

h1833B

h1834A

h1834B

h1835A
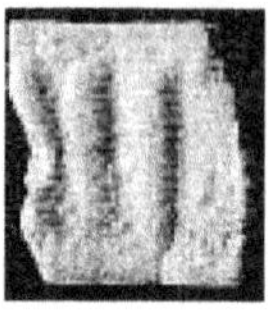
h1835B

h1836A

h1836B

h1837A

h1837B

h1839A

h1839B

h1840A

h1840B

h1841A

h1841B

h1842A

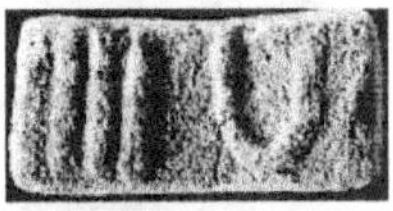
h1842B

h1843A

h1843B

h1844A

h1844B

h1845A

h1845B

h1846A

h1846B

h1848A

h1848B

h1849A

h1849B

h1850A

h1850B

h1851A

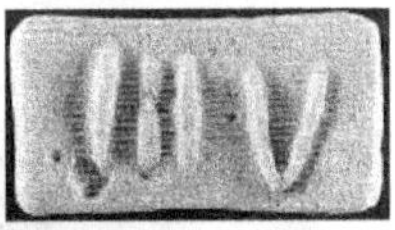
h1851B

h1853A

h1853B

h1854A

h1854B

h1856A

h1856B

h1857A

h1857B

h1858A

h1858B

h1859A

h1859B

h1860A

h1860B

h1861A

h1861B

h1862A

h1862B

h1863A

h1863B

h1864A

h1864B

h1865A

h1865B

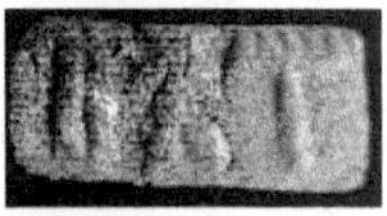

h1866A

h1866B

h1867A

h1867B

h1868A

h1868B

h1869A

h1869B

h1870A

h1870B

h1871A

h1871B

h1872A

h1872B

h1873A

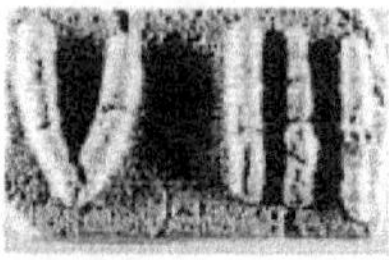

h1873B

h1874A

h1874B

h1875A

h1875B

h1876A

h1876B

h1877A

h1877B

h1878A

h1878B

h1879A

h1879B

h1880A

h1880B

h1881A

h1881B

h1882A

h1882B

h1883A

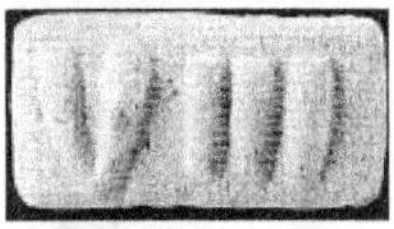

h1883B

h1886A

h1886B

h1887A

h1887B

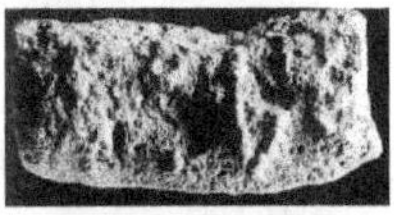

h1892A

h1892B

h1893A

h1893B

h1895A

h1895B

h1896A

h1896B

h1897A

h1897B

h1898A

h1898B

h1899A

h1899B

h1900A

h1900B

h1901A

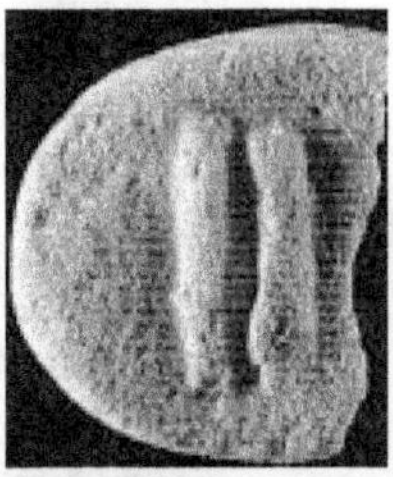

h1901B

h1902A

h1902B

h1903A

h1903B

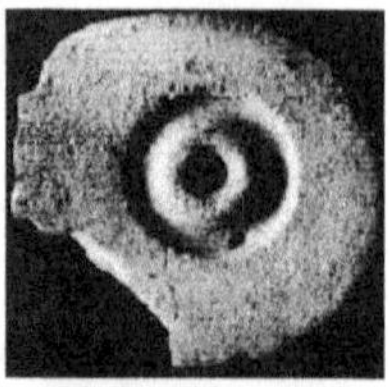
h1904A

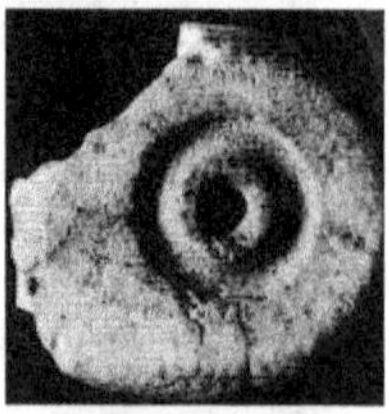
h1904B

h1905A

h1905B

h1906A

h1907A

h1907B

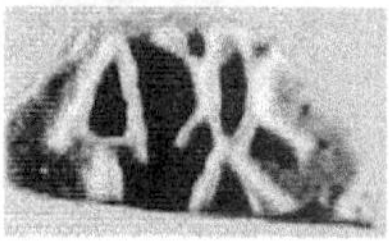
h1908A

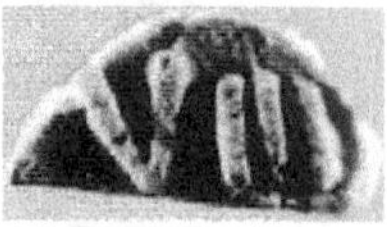
h1908B

h1909A

h1909B

h1910A

h1910B

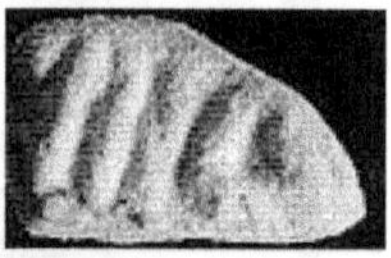
h1911A

h1911B

h1912A

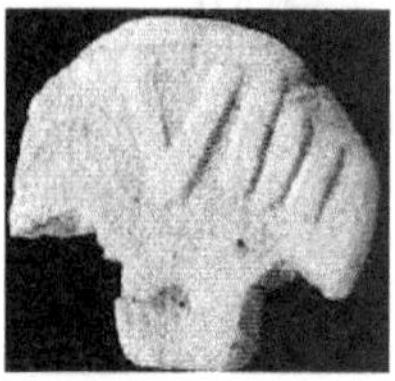
h1912B

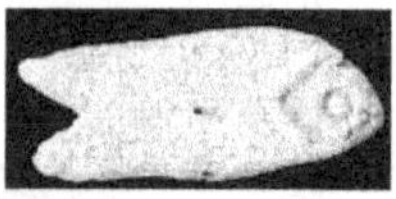
h1913A

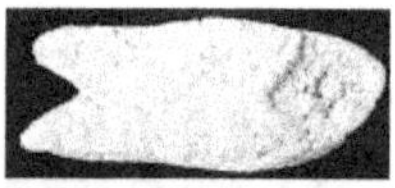
h1913B

h1914A

h1914B

h1915A

h1915B

h1916A

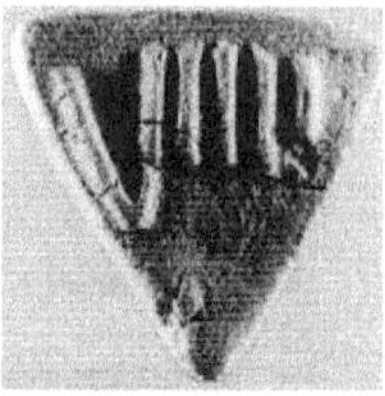
h1916B

h1917A

h1917B

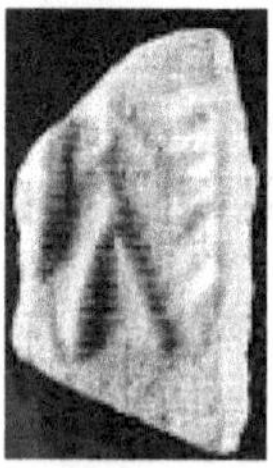
h1918A

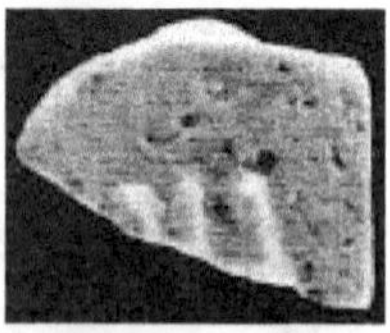
h1918B

h1920A
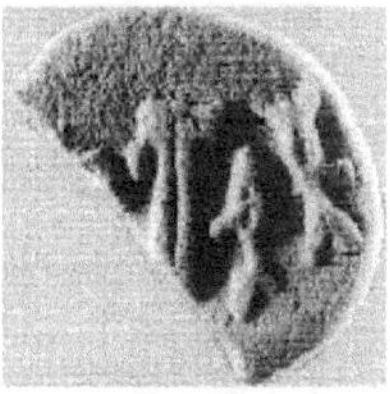
h1921A
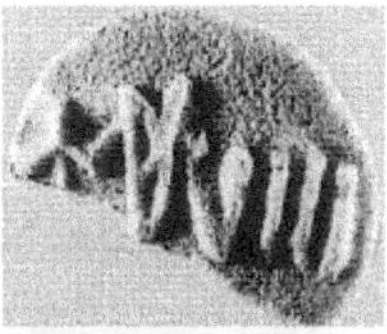
h1921B

h1922A

h1922B

h1923A

h1923B

h1924A

h1924B

h1925A

h1925B

h1926A

h1927A

h1929A

h1929B

h1929C

h1930A

h1930B
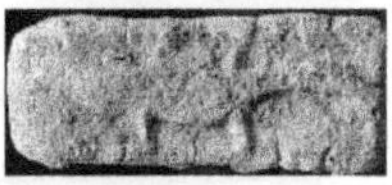
h1930C

h1931A
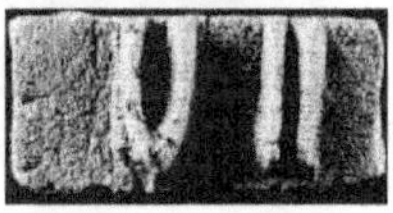
h1931B

h1931C

h1932A

h1932B
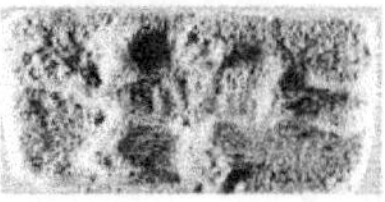
h1932C

h1933A
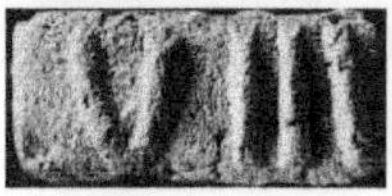
h1933B

h1933C

h1934A

h1934B

h1934C

h1935A

h1935B

h1935C

h1936A

h1936B

h1936C

h1937A

h1937B

h1937C

h1938A

h1938B

h1938C

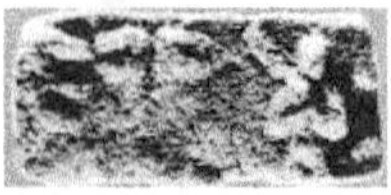
h1939A

h1939B

h1939C

h1940A

h1940B

h1940C

h1941A

h1941B

h1941c

H1942A

h1942B

h1942C

h1943A

h1943B

h1943C

h1944A

h1944B

h1944C

h1945A

h1945B

h1945C

h1946A

h1946B

h1946C

h1947A

h1947B

h1947C

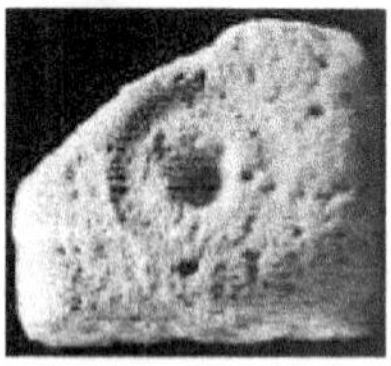
h1950A

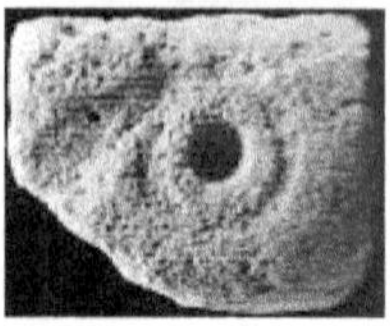
h1950B

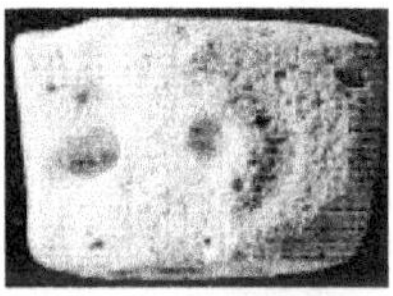

h1950C

h1950E

h1951A

h1951B

h1953A

h1953B

h1955A

(bird+fish)

h1955B

h1958A

h1958B

h1959

h1961A

h1961B

h1962A

h1962B

h1963A

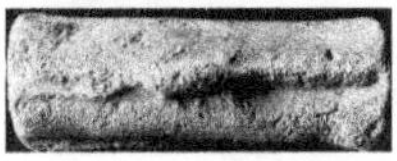

h1963B

h1964A

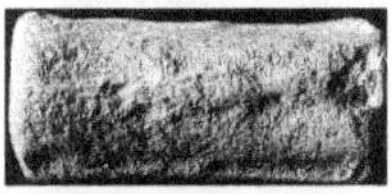

h1964B

h1966A

h1966B

h1967A

h1967B

h1968A

h1968B

h1969A

h1969B

h1970A

h1970B

h1971A

h1971B

h1972A

h1972B

h1973A

h1973B

h1974A

h1974B

h1975A

h1975B

h1976A

h1976B

h1977A

h1977B

h1978A

h1978B

h1979A

h1979B

h1980A

h1981B

h1981A

h1981B

h1985A

h1985B

h1987A

H1987B

h1988A, h1989A,

h1990A

h1988B, h1989B,

h1990B

h1991A

h1991B

h1992B

h1993A

h1993B

h1994A

h1994B

h1995A

h1995B

h1997A

h1997B

h1999A

h1999B

h2002A

h2003Ah

h2003B

h2005A

h2005B

h2006A

h2006B

h2010A

h2010B

h2012A

h2012B

h2013A

h2014A

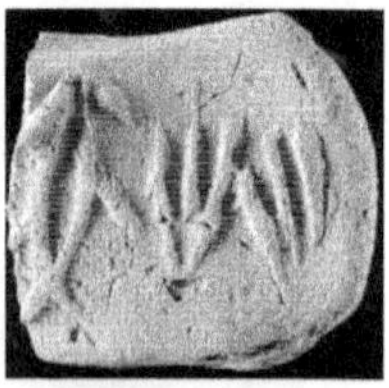

h2014B

h2015A

h2015B

h2016A

h2018A

h2018B

h2019A

h2019B

h2019C

h2020A

h2020C

h2021A

h2021B

h2021C

h2022A

h2022B

h2022C

h2023A

h2023B

h2023C

h2024A

h2024B

h2024C

h2025C

h2026A

h2026B

h2026C

h2026D

h2027A

h2027B

h2027C

h2027D

h2028A

h2028B

h2028C

h2028A

h2029A

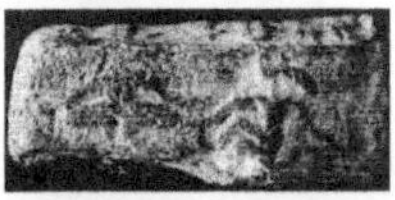

h2029B

h2029C

h2029D

h2030A

h2030C

h2030D

h2031A

h2031B

h2031C

h2031D

h2032B

h2032D

h2033A

h2033B

h2034A

h2034B

h2035A

h2035B

h2036A

h2036B

h2308A

h2038iB

h2039A

h2039B

h2040A

h2040B

h2041A

h2041B

h2043A

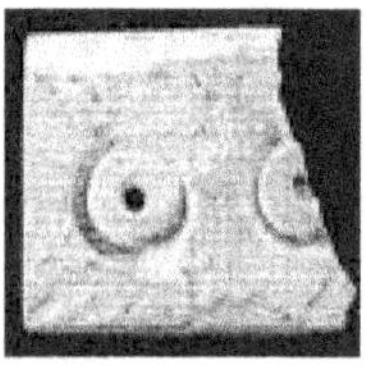

h2043B

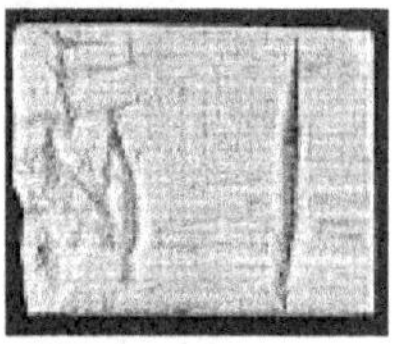

h2044A

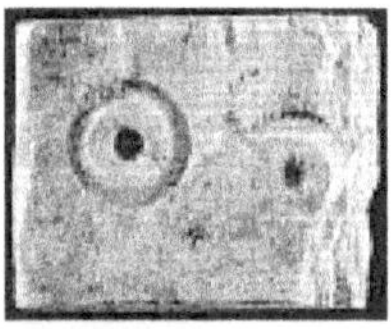

h2044B

h2045A

h2045B

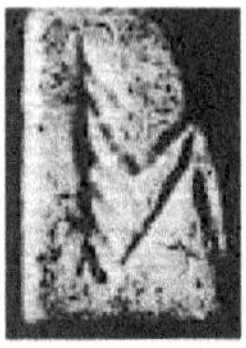

h2046A

h2046B

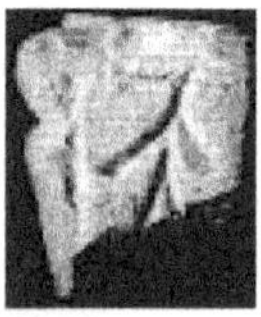

h2047A

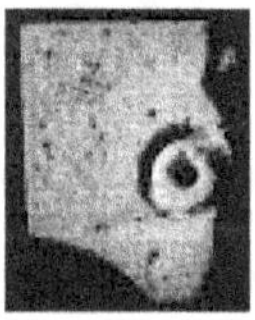

h2047B

h2048A

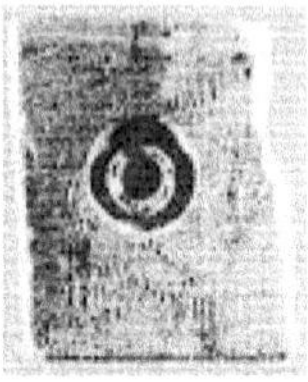

h2048B

h2049A

h2049B

h2050A

h2050B

h2051A

h2052A

h2053A

h2054B

h2055A

h2055B

h2056A

h2056B

h2057A

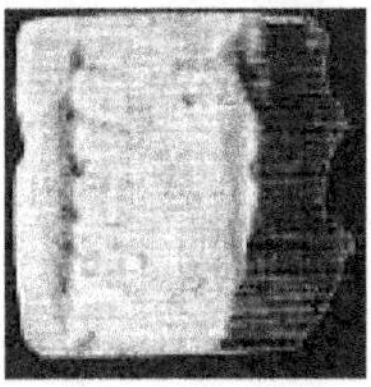

h2057B

h2058A

h2058B

h2059A

h2059B

h2062A

h2062B

h2063A

h2063B

h2064A

h2064B

h2065A

h2065B

h2066A

h2066B

h2067A

h2067B

h2068A

h2068B

h2069A

h2069B

h2070A

h2070B

h2071A

h2071B

h2072A

h2072B

h2073A

h2073B

h2074A

h2074B

h2076A

h2082A

h2082B

h2083A

h2083B

h2084A

h2084B

h2085A

h2085B

h2086A

h2086B

h2089A

h2089B

h2090A

h2090B

h2091A

h2091B

h2092A

h2092B

h2093A

h2093B

h2094A

h2094B

h2095A

h2095B

h2096A

h2096B

h2097A

h2097B

h2098A

h2098B

h2099A

h2099B

h2102A

h2102B

h2104A

h2104B

h2105A

h2105B

h2106A

h2106B

h2107A

h2107B

h2108A

h2108B

h2109A1B2

h2109B1A2

h2110A

h2110B

h2111B

h2112A

h2112B

h2113A

h2113B

h2114A

h2114B

h2115A

h2115B

h2119A

h2119b

h2120A

h2120B

h2121A

h2121B

h2123A

h2123B

h2125A

h2125B

h2127A

h2127B

h2128A

h2128B

h2129A

h2129B

h2130A

h2130B

h2131A

h2131B

h2132A

h2132B

h2133A

h2133B

h2134A

h2134B

h2135A

h2136A

h2137A

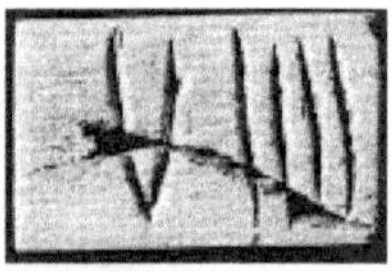
h2137B

h2138A

h2138B

h2139A

h2139B

h2140A

h2140B

h2141A

h2141B

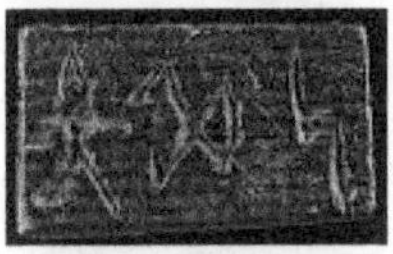

h2142A

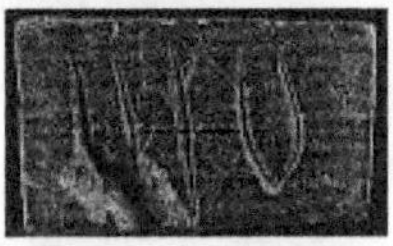

h2142B

h2143A

h2143B

h2144A

h2144 B

h2145A

h2145B

h2146A

h2146B

h2147A

h2147B

h2148A

h2148B

h2149A

h2149B

h2150A

h2150B

h2151A

h2151B

h2152A

h2152B

h2153A

h2153B

h2154A

h2154B

h2155A

h2155B

h2156A

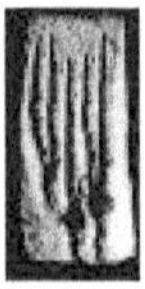

h2156B

h2158A

h2158B

h2159A

h2159B

h2160A

h2160B

h2173A

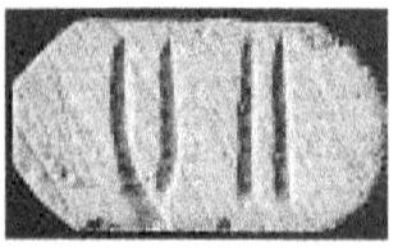

h2173B

h2174A

h2174B

h2175A

h2175B

h2176A

h2176B

h2177A

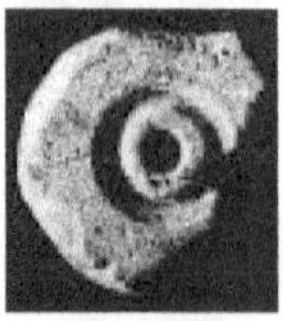

h2177B

h2178A

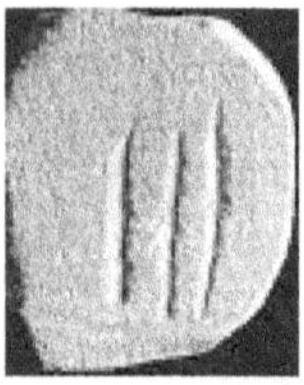

h2178B

h2180A

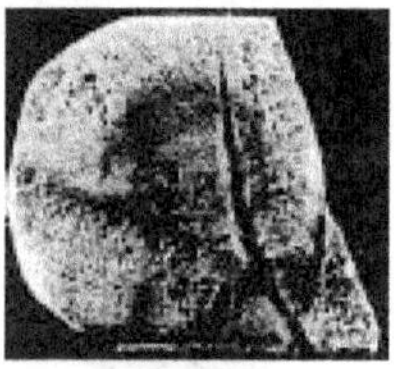

h2180B

h2181A

h2181B

h2182A

h2182B

h2183A

h2183B

h2184A

h2184B

h2185A

h2185B

h2186A

h2186B

h2187A

h2187B

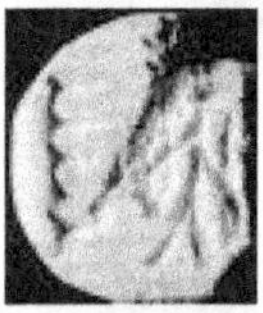

h2188A

h2188B

h2189A

h2189B

h2190A

h2190B

h2192A

h2192B

h2193A

h2193B

h2194A

h2194B

h2195A

H2195B

h2197A

h2197B

h2198A

h2198B

h2200A

h2200B

h2200C

h2201A

h2201B

h2201C

h2204A

h2204B

h2204c

h2205A

h2205B

h2205C

h2207A

h2207B

h2207C

h2208A

h2208B

h2208C

h2209A

h2209B

h2209C

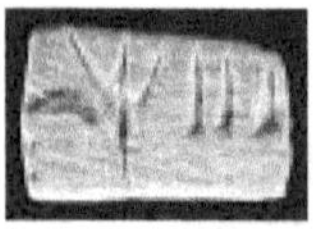

h2210A

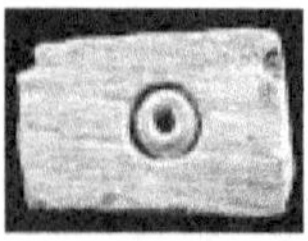

h2210B

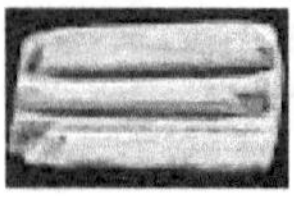

h2210C

h2211A

h2211B

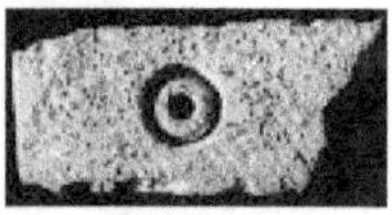

h2211C

h2212A

h2212B

h2212C

h2213A

h2213B

h2213C

h2214A

h2214N

h2214C

h2215B

h2215C

h2217A

h2217B

h2217C

h2218A

h2218B

h2218C

h2219A

h2219B

h2219C

h2220A

h2220B

h2220C

h2221A

h2221B

h2221C

h2222A

h2222B

h2222C

h2223A

h2223B

h2223C

h2224A

h2224B

h2224C

h2225A

h2225B

h2225C

h2226A

h2226B

h2226C

h2227A

h2227B

h2227C

h2228A

h2228B

h2228C

h2229A

h2229B

h2229C

h2230A

h2230B

h2230C

h2231A

h2231B

h2231C

h2232A

h2232B

h2232C

h2233A

h2233B

h2233C

h2234A

h2234B

h2234C

h2235A

h2235B

h2235C

h2236A

h2236B

h2236C

h2237A

h2237B

h2237C

h2238A

h2238B

h2238C

h2240A

h2240B

h2240C

h2240E

h2241A

h2241B

h2241C

h2241E

h2243A

h2243B

h2244A

h2244B

h2244E

h2245A

h2245B

h2245E

h2246A

h2246B

h2246C

h2246E

h2247A

h2247B

h2249Acopper

h2250Acopper

h2251Acopper

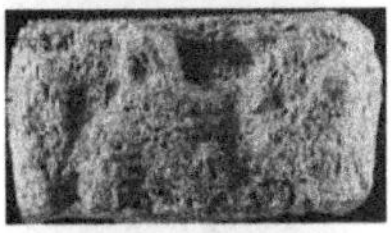
h2252Acopper

h2253Acopper

h2254Acopper

h2255Acopper

h2256Acopper

h2257Acopper

h2264A

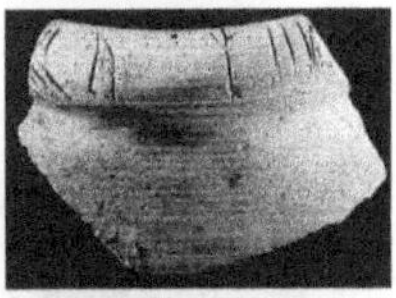
h2265A

h2270A

h2334A

h2339A

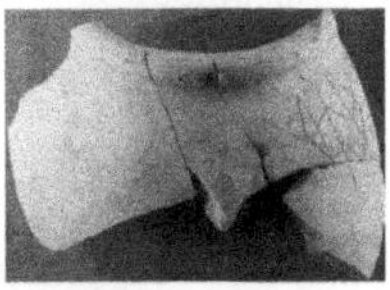
h2340A

h2341A

h2345A

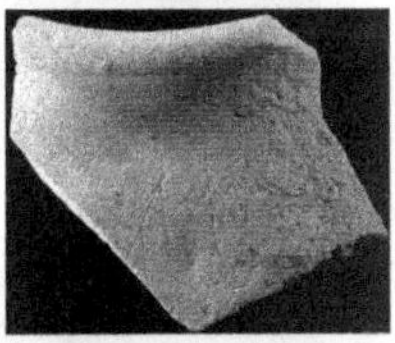
h2353A

h2354A

h2357A

h2358A

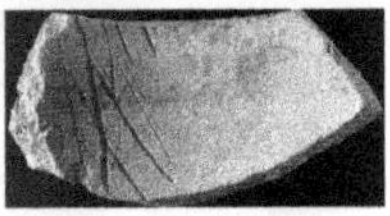
h2360A

h2367A

h2368A

h2373A

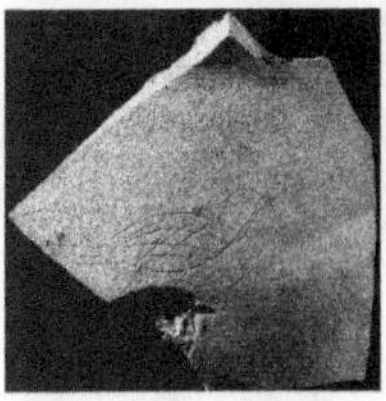
h2377A

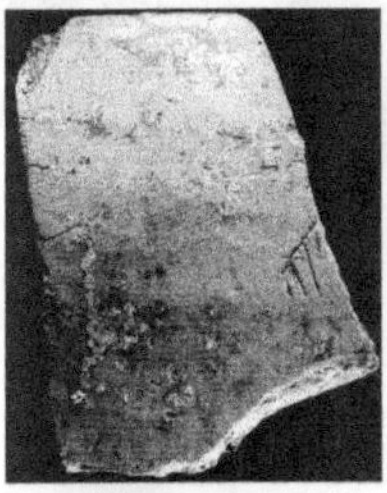
h2380A

h2383A

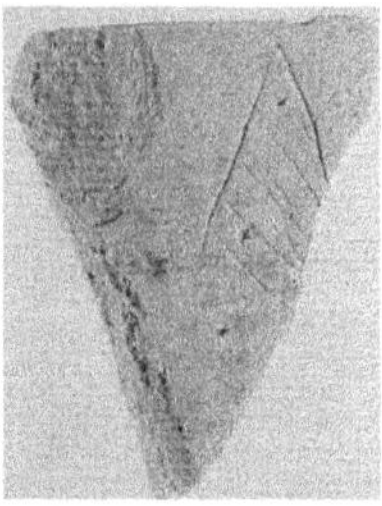

h2384A

h2390A

h2397A

j2398A

h2399A

h2400A

h2403A

h2405A

h2548A

h2549A

h2586A

h2569Alead

h2570Abone

h2576Abangle

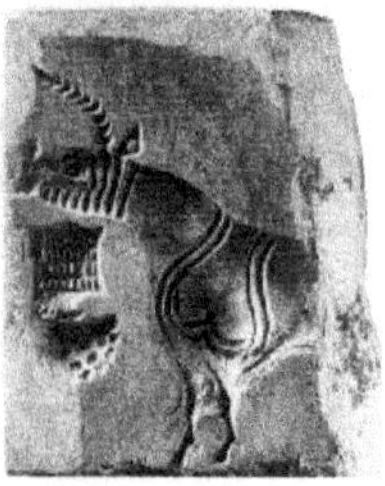

h2590

Harappa Texts (Either unmatched with inscribed objects or objects not illustrated)

4015

 40

33

4035

4046

4067

4073

 4

101

 410

8

 411

4

 4

117

4119

 4

134

 413

6

 4140

4158

4

164

42

92

4296

4305

Pict-90: Standing person with horns and bovine features holding a staff or mace on his shoulder.

4324

4330

4334

Pict-63: Gharial, sometimes with a fish held in its jaw and/or surrounded by a school of fish.

4343 Tablet in bas-relief One-horned bull

4344

4347

4356

4360

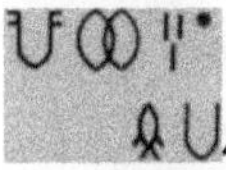
4363

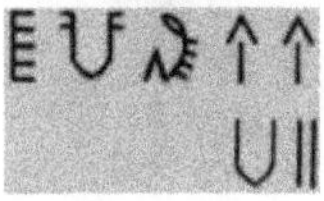

4369

4373

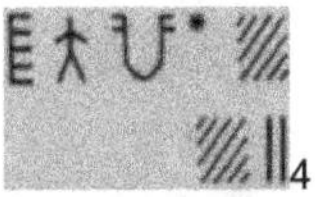
4

384

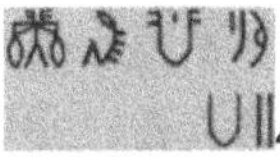
44

04

4406

4407

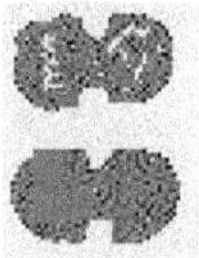
Pict-129: Inscribed object in the shape of a double-axe or double-shield?

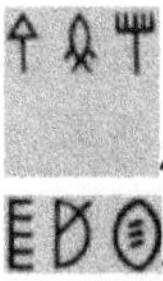
4408

4422

4427

4428

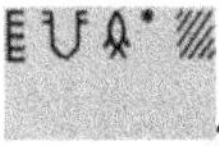
4432

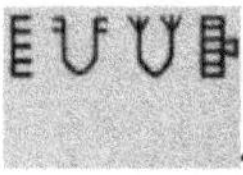
443

5

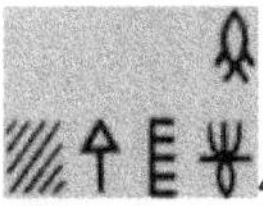
44

38

4439

444

7

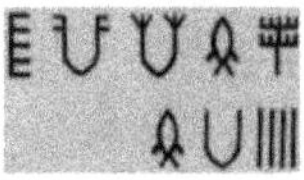

4448

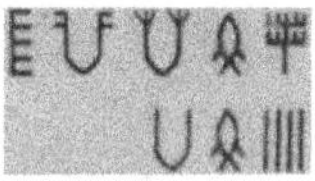

4452

4458

4459

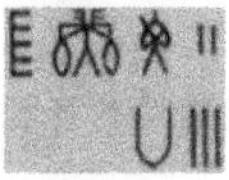

4462

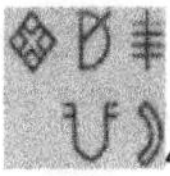
4465

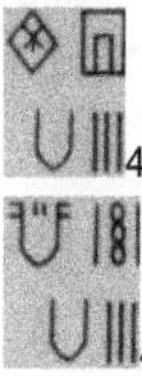
4468

4473

4476

Incised miniature tablet.

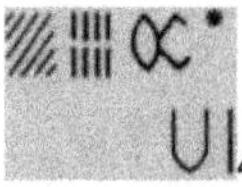
449

1

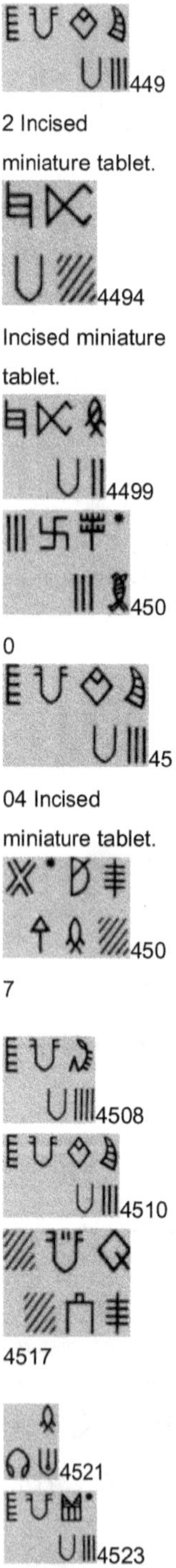

449
2 Incised
miniature tablet.
4494
Incised miniature
tablet.
4499
450
0
45
04 Incised
miniature tablet.
450
7
4508
4510
4517
4521
4523

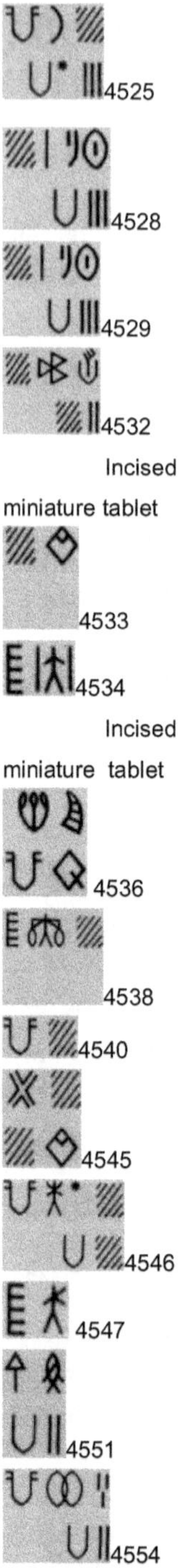

4525
4528
4529
4532
Incised
miniature tablet
4533
4534
Incised
miniature tablet
4536
4538
4540
4545
4546
4547
4551
4554

4556
4566
4571
4572
4578
4580
4583
4585
4589
4593
4599
4610
4613
4633

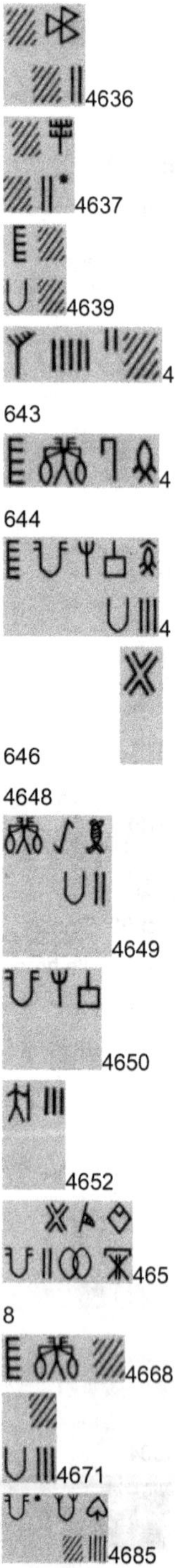

4636
4637
4639
4
643
4
644
4
646
4648
4649
4650
4652
465
8
4668
4671
4685

4690

4691

4699

4700

4703

4704

4709

4710

4712

47
13

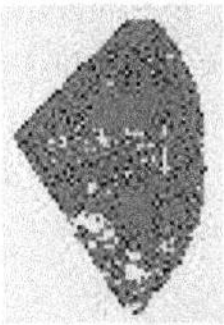

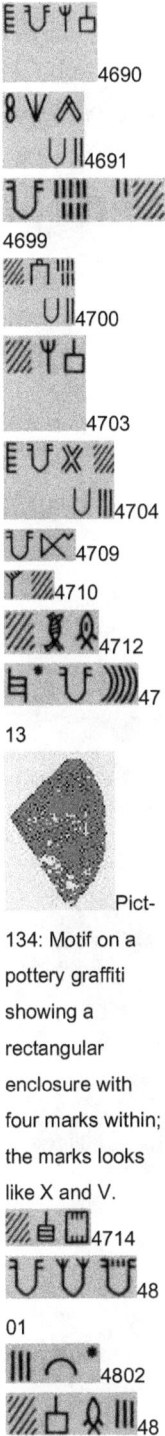

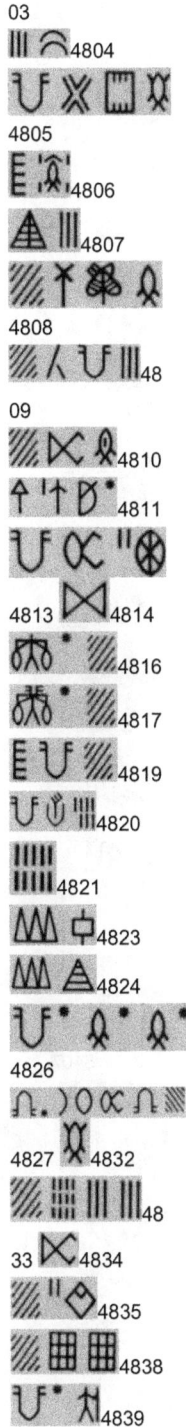

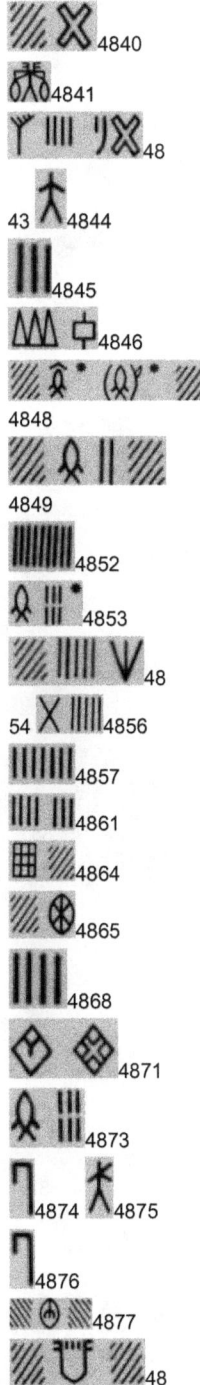

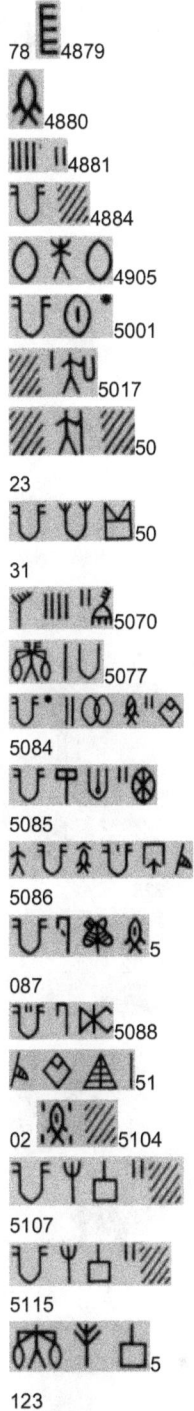

Pict-134: Motif on a pottery graffiti showing a rectangular enclosure with four marks within; the marks looks like X and V.

4714

48
01

4802

48
03

4804

4805

4806

4807

4808

48
09

4810

4811

4813 4814

4816

4817

4819

4820

4821

4823

4824

4826

4827 4832

48
33 4834

4835

4838

4839

4840

4841

48
43 4844

4845

4846

4848

4849

4852

4853

48
54 4856

4857

4861

4864

4865

4868

4871

4873

4874 4875

4876

4877

48
78 4879

4880

4881

4884

4905

5001

5017

50
23

50
31

5070

5077

5084

5085

5086

5
087

5088

51
02 5104

5107

5115

5
123

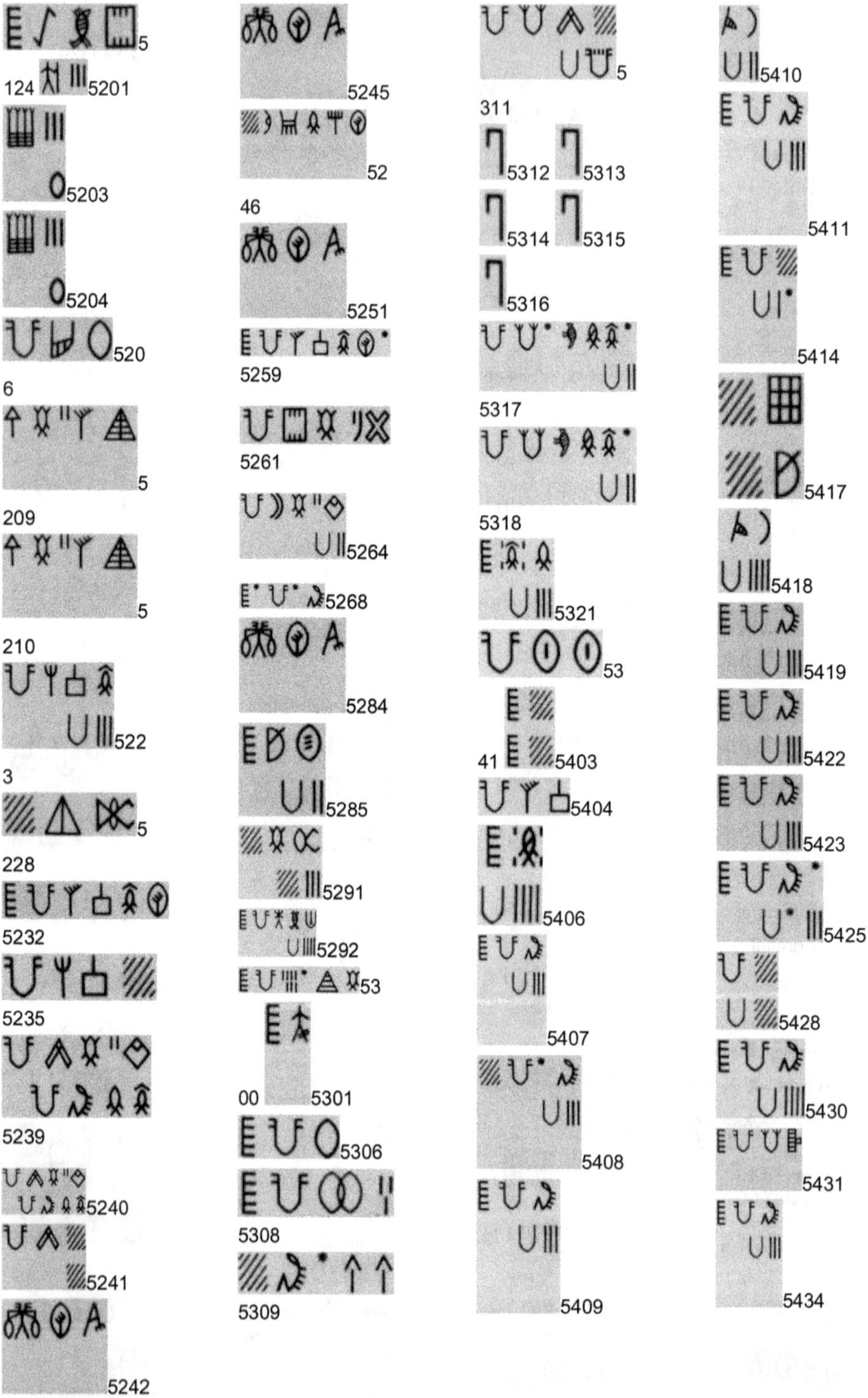
5
124
5201
5203
5204
520
6
5
209
5
210
522
3
5
228
5232
5235
5239
5240
5241
5242
5245
52
46
5251
5259
5261
5264
5268
5284
5285
5291
5292
53
00
5301
5306
5308
5309
5
311
5312
5313
5314
5315
5316
5317
5318
5321
53
41
5403
5404
5406
5407
5408
5409
5410
5411
5414
5417
5418
5419
5422
5423
5425
5428
5430
5431
5434

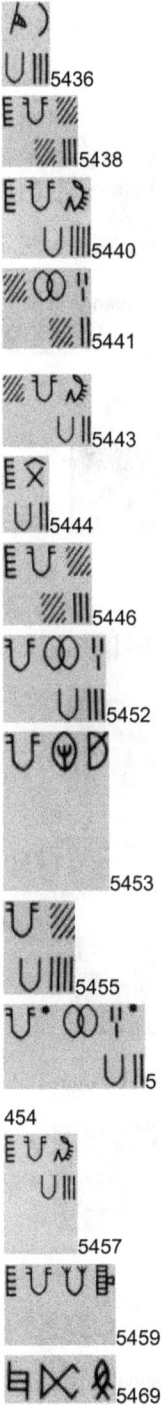

5436

5438

5440

5441

5443

5444

5446

5452

5453

5455

5
454

5457

5459

5469

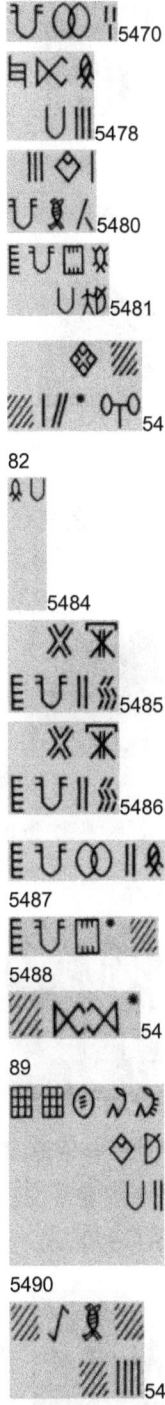

5470

5478

5480

5481

54
82

5484

5485

5486

5487

5488

54
89

5490

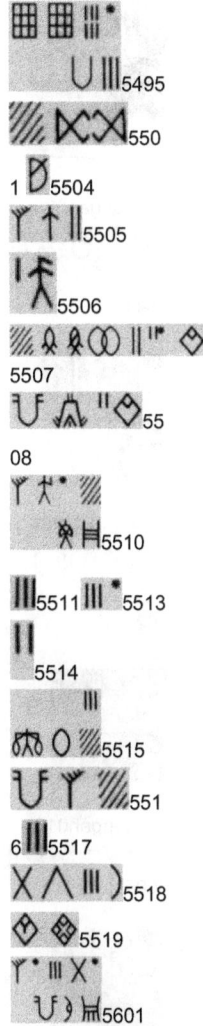

54
92

5495

550
1

5504

5505

5506

5507

55
08

5510

5511 5513

5514

5515

551
6

5517

5518

5519

5601

hd06

hulas

jhukar1

jhukar2

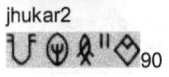

90
01

jhukar3

8009

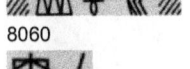

8036

8048

8060

8061

8062

8202

8214

8215

8217

Kalibangan002

8019

Kalibangan003

8030

Kalibangan004

8026

Kalibangan005

8017

Kalibangan006

8020

Kalibangan007

8043

Kalibangan008

8041

Kalibangan009

8021

Kalibangan010

8006

Kalibangan011

8034

Kalibangan012

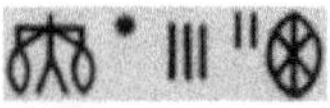

Kalibangan013

8051

Kalibangan014

8012

Kalibangan015

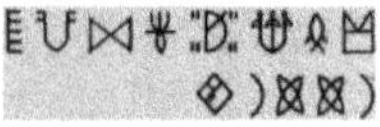

8056

Kalibangan016

8044

Kalibangan017

8027

Kalibangan018

8040

Kalibangan019

8058

Kalibangan020

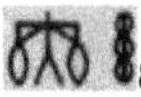

8047

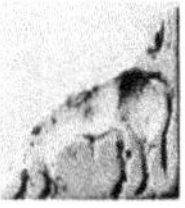

Kalibangan021

Kalibangan022

8008

Kalibangan023

8029

Kalibangan024

Kalibangan025

8037

Kalibangan026

8071

Kalibangan027

8022

'Unicorn' with two horns! "Bull with two long horns (otherwise resembling the 'unicorn')", generally facing the standard. That it is the typical 'one-horned bull' is surmised from two ligatures: the pannier on the shoulder and the ring on the neck.

Kalibangan028

8038

Kalibangan029

8018

Kalibangan030

8002

Kalibangan031a

800
7

Kalibangan032a

Kalibangan033

8025

Kalibangan034

8052

Kalibangan035

Kalibangan036

Kalibangan037

8042

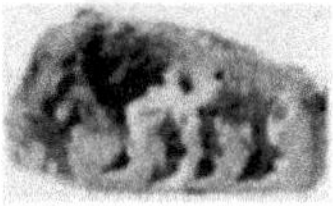

Kalibangan038

Kalibangan039

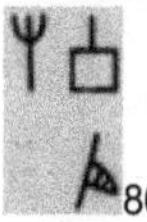8011

Kalibangan040

8072

Kalibangan041

Kalibangan042a

Kalibangan043

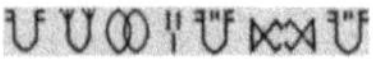

8039 Pict-59:Composite motif: body of an ox and three heads: of a one-horned bull (looking forward), of antelope (looking backward), and of short-horned bull (bison) (looking downward).

Kalibangan044

8045

Kalibangan045

8054

Kalibangan046

 8053

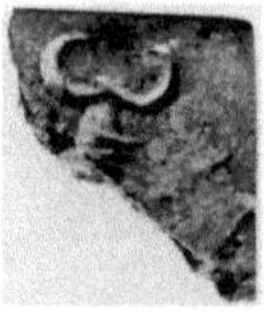

Kalibangan047

Kalibangan048

Kalibangan049

 8013

Kalibangan050c

 8031 Pict-53: Composition: body of a tiger, a human body with bangles on arm, a pig-tail, horns of an antelope crowned by a twig.

Kalibangan051

 8003

Kalibangan052

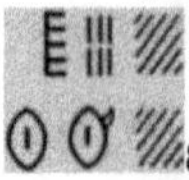 8015

Kalibangan053

Kalibangan054

 8033

Kalibangan055a

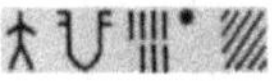

8035

Kalibangan056

8004

Kalibangan057

Kalibangan058

Kalibangan059

 8016

Kalibangan060

 8059

Kalibangan061

8001

Kalibangan062

8023

Kalibangan063

8055

Kalibangan064

Kalibangan065a

Kalibangan065A6

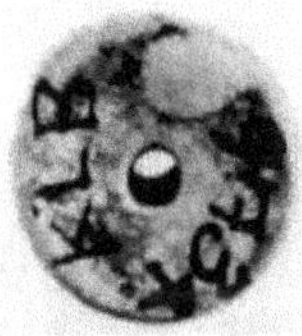

Kalibangan065E

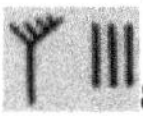8024 Pict-104: Composition: A tree; a person with a composite body of a human (female?) in the upper half and body of a tiger in the lower half, having horns, and a trident-like head-dress, facing a group of three persons consisting of a woman (?) in the middle flanked by two men on either side throwing a spear at each other (fencing?) over her head.

Kalibangan066

8102

Kalibangan067

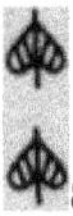8121 Ox-antelope with a long tail; sometimes with a trough in front.

Kalibangan068A

Kalibangan068B

8117 [Is it a bird or an India River Otter? Could be a scorpion, a model for Signs 51 and 52 ?  See variant in Text 9845 West Asia find]

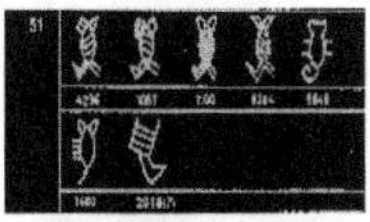

Kalibangan069A

8109

Kalibangan070A

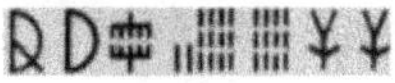

8108

Kalibangan071

8110

Kalibangan072

8111

Kalibangan073

8112

Kalibangan074

8115

Kalibangan075

8113

Kalibangan076A

Kalibangan076B

Kalibangan077A

Kalibangan077B

8118

Kalibangan078A

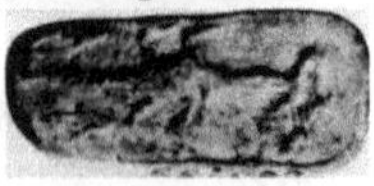
Kalibangan078B

8104

Kalibangan

079AB

Kalibangan080A

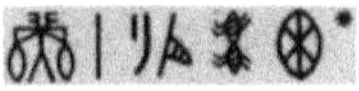
8120

Kalibangan081A

8105

Kalibangan082A

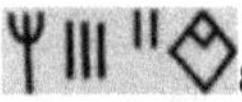
812

2

Kalibangan

083A12

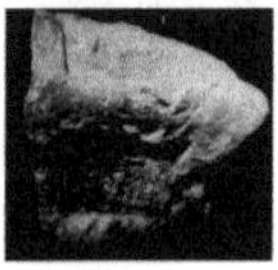
Kalibangan

084A12

Kalibangan

084A2

8103

Kalibangan

085A12

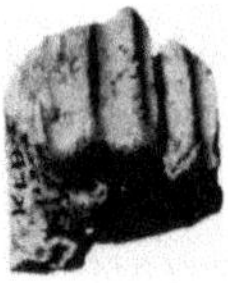
Kalibangan085B

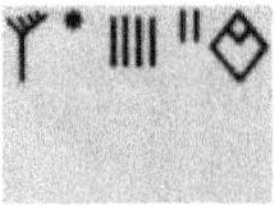

8106

Kalibangan086A1

4
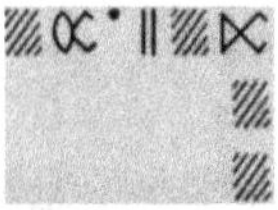

8114

Kalibangan087A1

2

8116

Kalibangan

088A14

Kalibangan088B

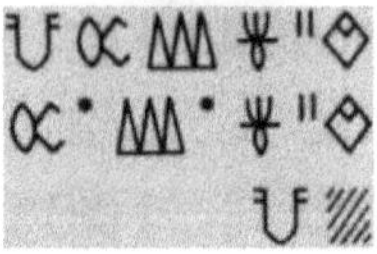
8119

Kalibangan089A1

4c

8101

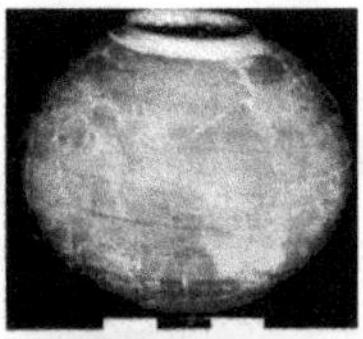

Kalibangan090A

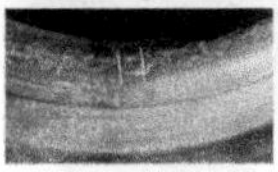

Kalibangan

090A1

Kalibangan

090A2

8202

Kalibangan091A

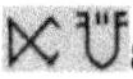8212

Kalibangan092A

8210

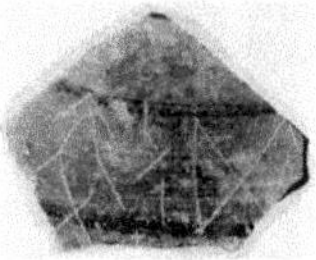

Kalibangan093A

82

19

Kalibangan094A

Kalibangan095A

Kalibangan096c

8221

Kalibangan097A

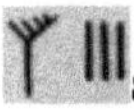8213

Kalibangan098A

8201

Kalibangan099A

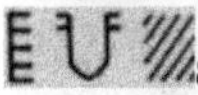8208

Kalibangan100A

Kalibangan101A

820

5

Kalibangan102A

8207

Kalibangan103A

8209

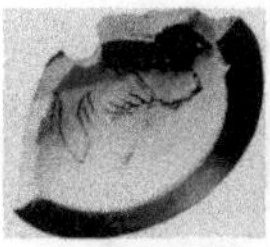

Kalibangan104A

8218

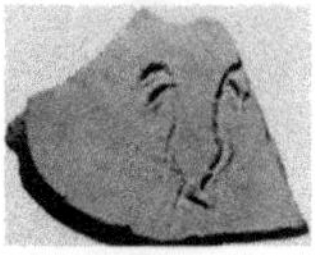

Kalibangan105A

8216

Kalibangan106A

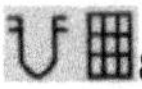8204

Kalibangan107A

Kalibangan108A

8206

Kalibangan109A

Kalibangan110A

8211

Kalibangan111A

Kalibangan112A

Kalibangan118

Kalibangan119A

Kalibangan119B

Kalibangan120A

8220

Kalibangan122B

Kalibangan

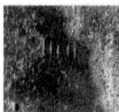

122B2

Kalibangan

121A, B

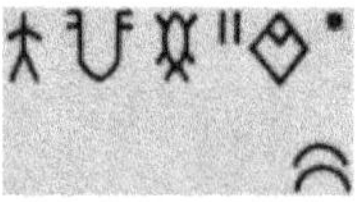

8302

Kalibangan122A

Kalibangan

122A2

8301

Kalako-deray 01

Kalako-deray 05

Kalako-deray 06

Kalako-deray 07

Kalako-deray 08

Kalakoderay10

Khirsara1a

Khirsara2a

9051 Kot-diji

Lewandheri01

Loebanr01

Lohumjodaro1a

9011

Lothal001

7015

Lothal002

7031

Lothal003

Lothal004a

7080

Lothal005

7044

Lothal006a

7

038

Lothal007a

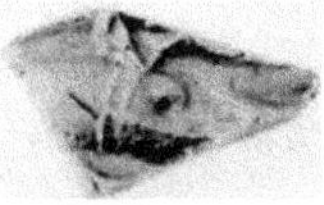

Lothal008a

Lothal009

7

022

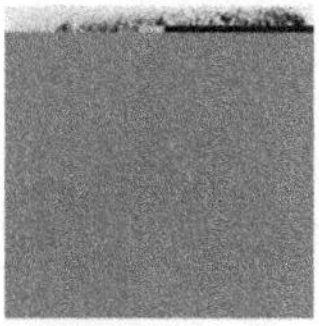

Lothal010

7009

Lothal011

7026

Lothal012a

7089

Lothal013

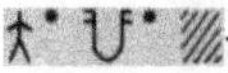
7050

Lothal014a

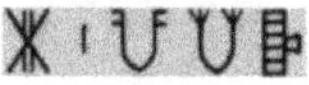

7094

Lothal015

7086

Lothal016

7002

Lothal017

7008

Lothal018

7096

Lothal019a

7092

Lothal020

7078

Lothal021

7047

Lothal022a

7035

Lothal023a

7043

Lothal024

Lothal025

7104

Lothal026

7024

Lothal027

7036

Lothal028

7045

Lothal029

7005

Lothal030a

Lothal031

7076

Lothal032a

Lothal033a

Lothal035

7101

Lothal036a

7081

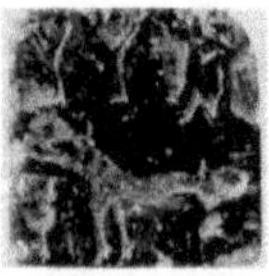

Lothal037

7034

Lothal038a

7053

Lothal039

7102

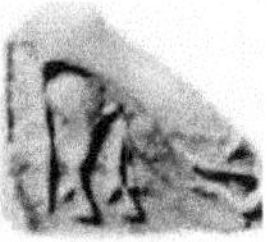

Lothal040a

Lothal041

7066

Lothal042

Lothal043

7049

Lothal044

Lothal045

7028

Lothal046

7107

Lothal047a

7074

Lothal048

7025

Lothal049

Lothal050

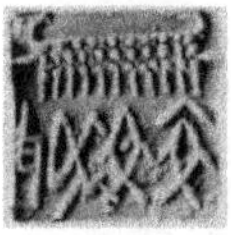

Lothal051a

70

57 Pict-127: Upper register: a large device with a number of small circles in three rows with another row of short vertical lines below; the device is horned. A seed-drill? [Is this an orthographic model for

Sign 176?]

Lothal052

7011

Lothal054a

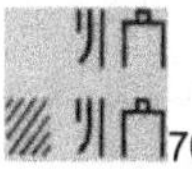7099

Lothal055

710

6

Lothal056

7100

Lothal057

7095

Lothal058a

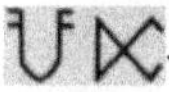7029

Lothal059

7097

Lothal060

7039

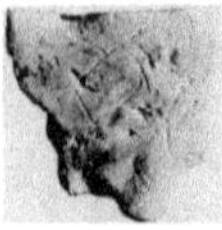

Lothal061

Lothal062

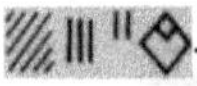7054

Lothal063

Lothal064

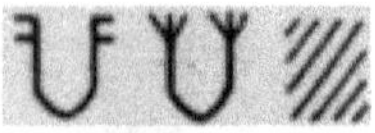

7030

Lothal065

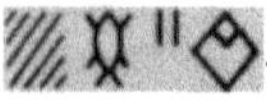71
03

Lothal066acdef

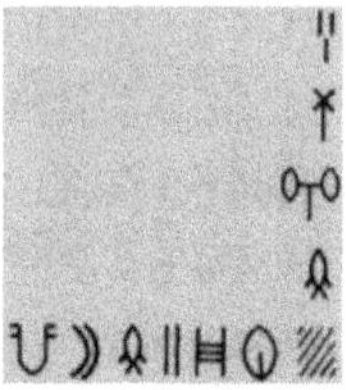

7048

Lothal068

7070

Lothal069

Lothal070

Lothal071

Lothal072

Lothal075

Lothal076a

Lothal077

Lothal078

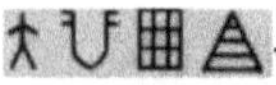70
77

Lothal079

7063

Lothal080a

Lothal081

7093

Lothal082

7
105

Lothal083

7068

Lothal084

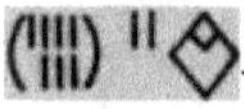711
2

Lothal085

Lothal086

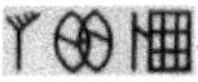

7007

Lothal087

7021

Lothal088

7017

Lothal089

7090

Lothal090

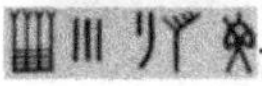

70

32

Lothal091

7111

Lothal092

7062

Lothal093

70

64

Lothal094a

7073

Lothal095

7042

Lothal096

7023

Lothal097

7072

Lothal098

708

2

Lothal099

Lothal100a

Lothal100B

7

055

Lothal101

70

01

Lothal102

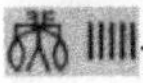

7040

Lothal103

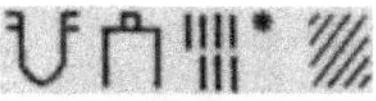

7018

Lothal104

7085

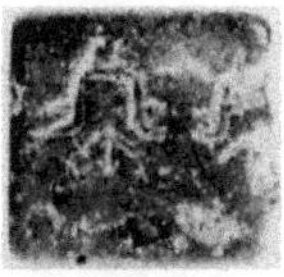

Lothal105

701

6

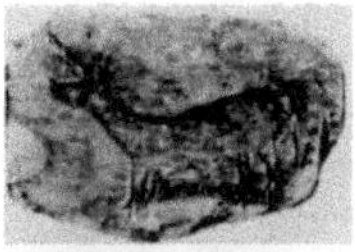

Lothal107

Lothal108

Lothal109a

70

46

Lothal110

700

6

Lothal111

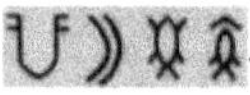
705

6

Lothal112

7020

Lothal113a

7004

Lothal114a

7013

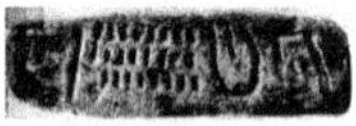

Lothal115

7065

Lothal116

7027

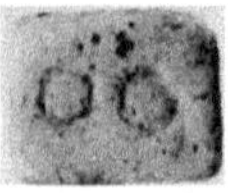

Lothal117

7075

Lothal118

7019

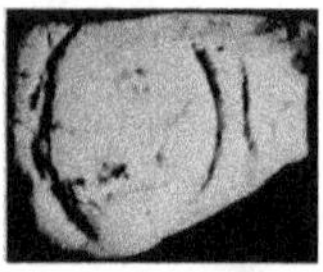

Lothal119

Lothal120

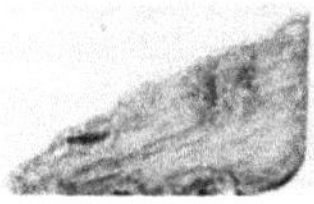

Lothal121

Lothal122

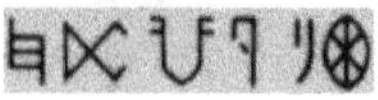

7069

Lothal123A

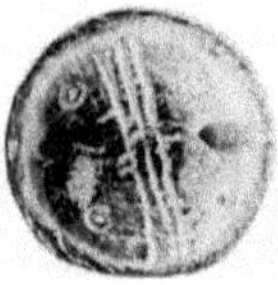

Lothal123B

Lothal124A

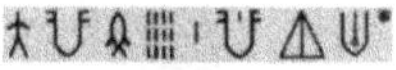

7224

Lothal125A

7241

Lothal126A

7242

Lothal127A

7221

Lothal128A

7239

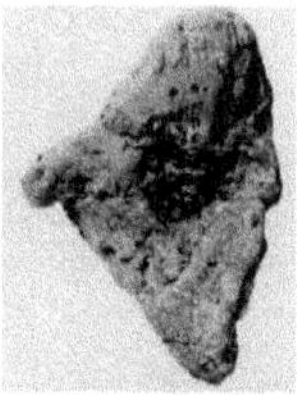

Lothal129A

Lothal130A

Lothal131A

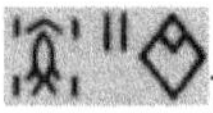
7255

Lothal132A

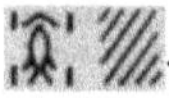
7213

Lothal133A

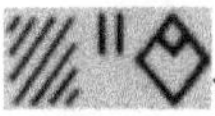

7245

Lothal134A

7252

Lothal135A

7220

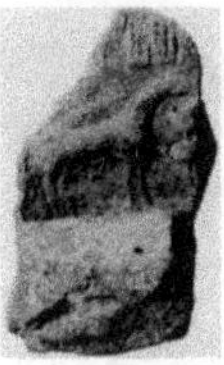

Lothal136A

722

5

Lothal137A

72

57

Lothal138A

Lothal138B

72

14

Lothal139A

7223

Lothal140A

7244

Lothal141A1

Lothal141A2

7280

Lothal142A

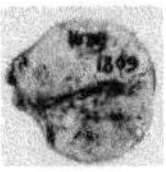

Lothal142B

7

204

Lothal143A

Lothal143B

7243

Lothal144A

7274

Lothal145A

Lothal146AB

7279

Lothal147A

72

60

Lothal148A

727

0

Lothal149A

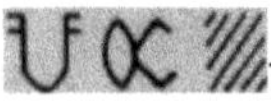72

72

Lothal150A

7268

Lothal151A

7266

Lothal152A

7222

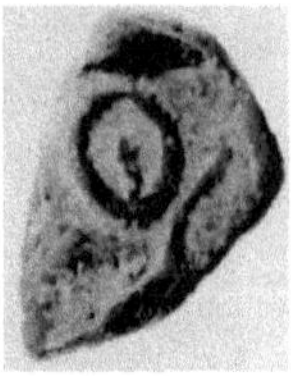

Lothal153A

7271

Lothal154A

Lothal155A

Lothal156A

Lothal157A

Lothal158A

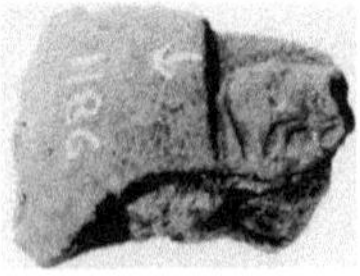

Lothal159A

Lothal160A

Lothal161A

72

05

Lothal162A

Lothal162B

Lothal163A

Lothal163C

7228

Lothal164A

7230

Lothal165A

7203

Lothal166A

72

06

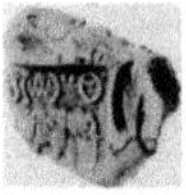

Lothal167A

723

1

Lothal168A

72

34

Lothal169A

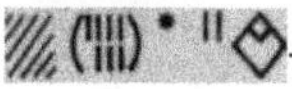7

235

Lothal170A

7229

Lothal171A

Lothal172A

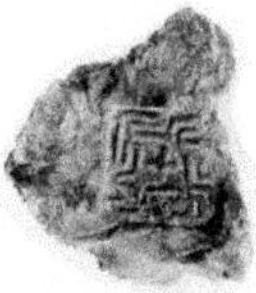

Lothal173A

Lothal174A

Lothal175A

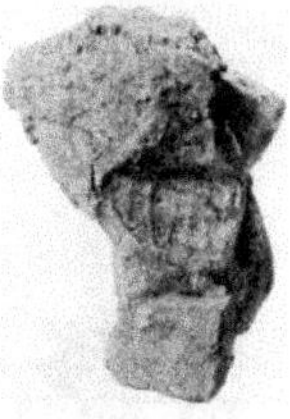

Lothal176A

7216

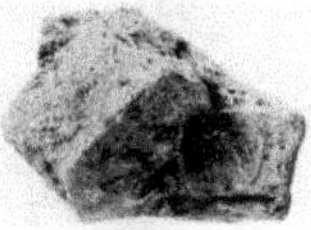

Lothal177A

72

11

Lothal179A

Lothal180A

7

240

Lothal181A

7273

Lothal182A

7238

Lothal183A

Lothal184A

Lothal185A

Lothal186A

7259

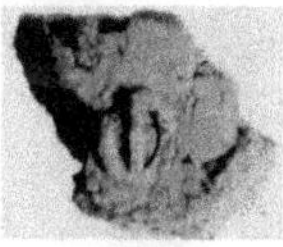

Lothal187A

7209

Lothal188A

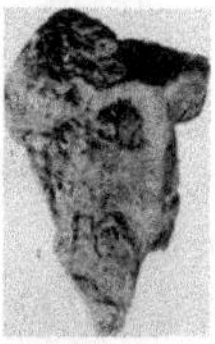

Lothal189A12

Lothal189A34

7217

Lothal190A13

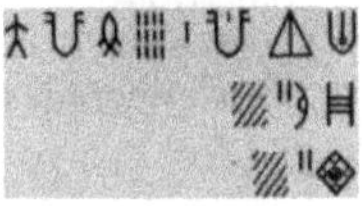

7236

Lothal191A12

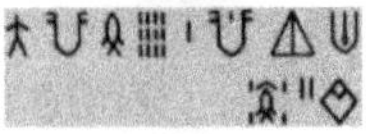

7249

Lothal192A12

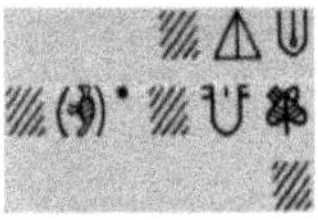

7227

Lothal193A12

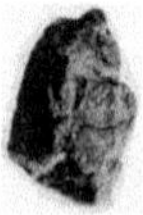

Lothal193A3

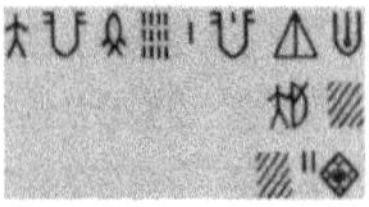

7253

Lothal194A1

Lothal194A2

7251

Lothal195A12

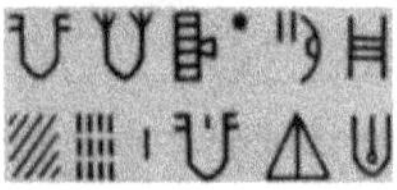

7258

Lothal196A12

7248

Lothal197A12

723
7

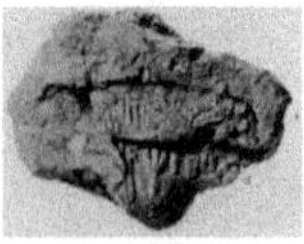

Lothal198A12

7215

Lothal199A12

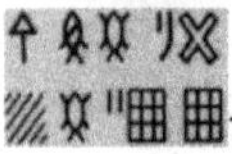

7247

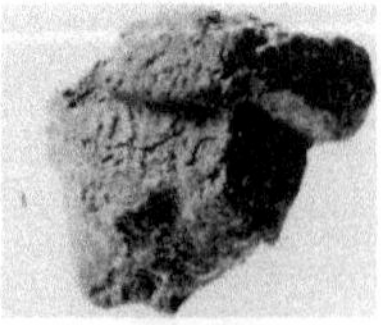

Lothal200A1

Lothal200A2

7219

Lothal201A12

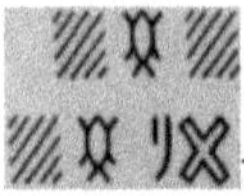

726
3

Lothal202A12

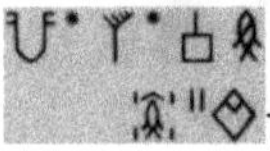

72
67

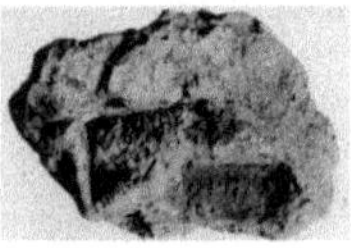

Lothal203A12

7246

Lothal204A

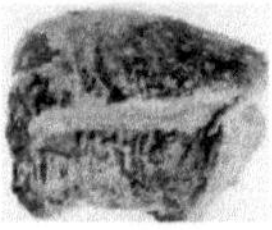

Lothal204F

7275

Lothal205A12

72

18

Lothal206A12

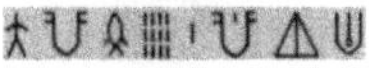

7265

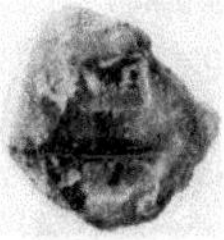

Lothal207A12

7

281

Lothal208A12

Lothal209A12

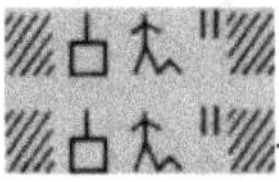

72

62

Lothal210A12

7201

Lothal211A13

7277

Lothal212A12

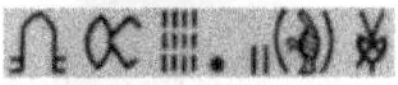

7261

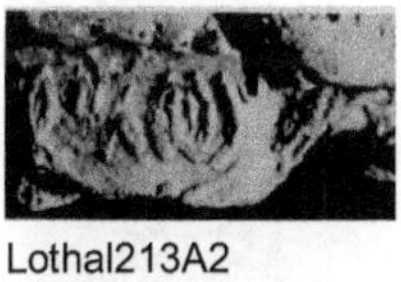

Lothal213A2

7207

Lothal214A12

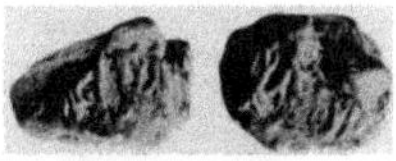

Lothal216D12

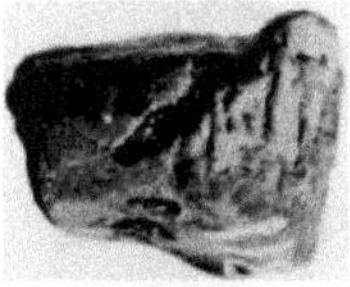

Lothal216E

7283

Lothal217A

Lothal217B

Lothal218A

72

02

Lothal219A

7282

Lothal220A

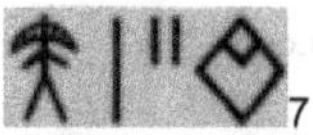

7

278

Lothal221A

Lothal222A

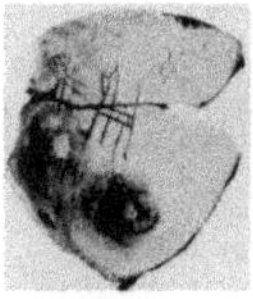

Lothal223A

Lothal224A

Lothal225A

Lothal227A

Lothal229A

Lothal230A

Lothal233A

Lothal246A

Lothal269A

Lothal270A

Lothal272A

Lothal273A

7301

Lothal277A

Lothal280A

Lothal281A

7088

7098

7212

72

32

7233

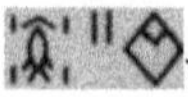
7269

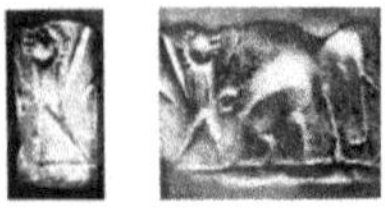

Maski

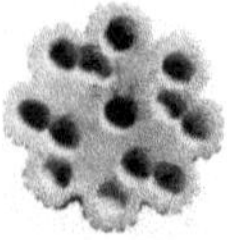

Mehi

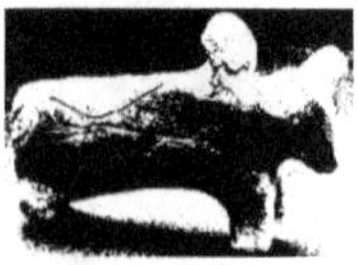

Mehrgarh zebu

Mehrgarh01

Mehrgarh04

Mehrgarh05

Mehrgarh08

Mehrgarh10

Mehrgarh11

Mehrgarh12

Mehrgarh13

Mehrgarh14

Mehrgarh15

Mehrgarh16

Mehrgarh17

Mehrgarh18

m0001a

1067

m0002a

m0003a 

2225

m0004a

3109

m0005

2247

m0006a

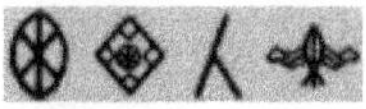

2422

m0007

1011

m0008a

 1038

m0009a 

2616

m0010

1006

m0011

m0012

3031

m0013

 106

9

m0014

1022

m0015

2177

m0016a

1037

m0017

 1

035

m0018Ac

 1548

m0019a

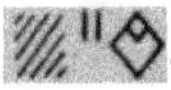 1085

m0020a

1054

m0021a

2103

m0022a

1023

m0023a

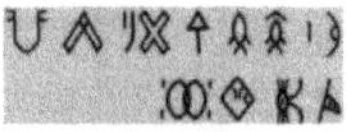

2398

m0024

2694

m0025

 1

056

m0026a

 20

74

m0027a

2084

m0028a

2178

m0029a

2033

m0030a

2396

m0031

2576

m0032a

 2180

m0033a

1042

m0034a

1058

m0035a

2333

m0036a

2455

m0037a

3103

m0039a

1544

m0040

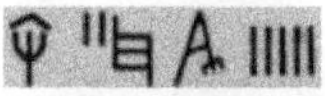

1051 

m0038a

1087

m0041

2271

m0042a

1096

m0043

2584

m0044a

3110

m0045a

1552

m0046a

3089

m0047a

1098

m0048a

1186

m0049a

1047

m0050a

1557

m0051a

1555

m0052a

1540

m0053a

2128

m0054

2307

m0055a

2511

m0056

2406

m0057a

2340

m0058a

2680

m0059a

10

29

m0060a

2124

m0061

m0062

3112

m0063

306

8

m0064

2524

m0065

2

440

m0066AC

1052

m0067

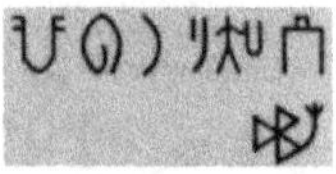

2264

m0068

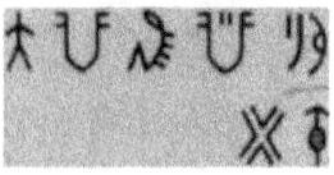

3108

m0069

1

095

m0070

104

8

m0071a

3083 [The second sign from left is an orthographic representation of the thigh of a bovid, perhaps a bull].

m0072a

2085

m0073

1046

m0074

235

3

m0075
1
019

m0076

m0077

311
1

m0078

3
118

m0079a
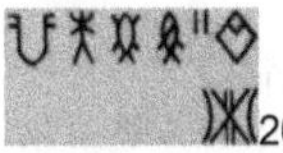
20
83

m0080
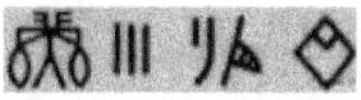
2635

m0081a

1180

m0082

2451

m0083
a

2267

m0084
a

1108

m0085a

2365

m0086

2208

m0087

2148

m0088

1075

m008
9
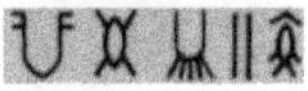
3116

m0090
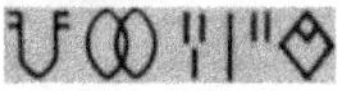
3039

m0091
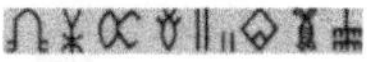
2429

m0092

2407

m0093

2305

m0094
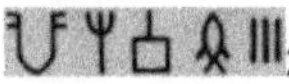
2
594

m0095

265
7

m0096

2698

m0097

2549

m0098

201

2

m009

9  2

475

m0100

1115

m0101

1537

m0102

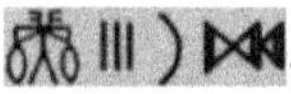
1

129

m0103

1076

m0104

2574

m0105

2337

m0106

2459

m0107

2593

m0108

1110

m0109

1151

m0110

2031

m0111

2029

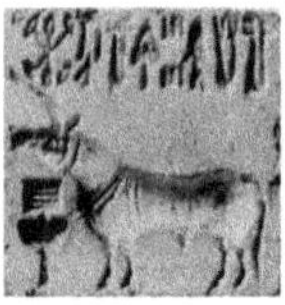

m0112

2099

m0113

2115

m0114

2166

m0115

3087

m0116

2481

m0117

1105

m0118

1104

m0119a

2018

m0120a

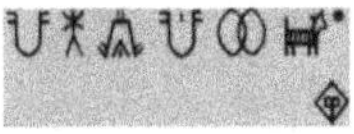

1099

m0121a

1188

m0122a

2015

m0123a

2702

m0124

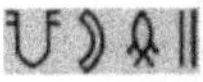

1120

m0125

m0126

2311

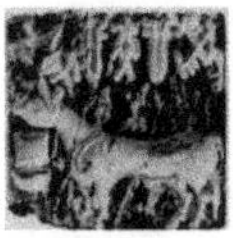

m0127

1119

m0128a

2284

m0129

2193

m0130a

2285

m0131

2263

m0132

2082

m0133a

2052

m0134

2187

m0135

1168

m0136

2233

m0137

 2261

m0138

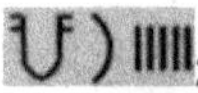 2381

m0139

2185

m0140

2563

m0141

 254

3

m0142

 2630

m0143

2002

m0144

2048

m0145

 1

118

m0146

 1

100

m0147

3097

m0148

 12

45

m0149

1233

m0150

 1236

m0151

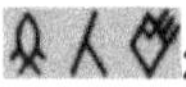 2323

m0152

 2

102

m0153

 2361

m0154

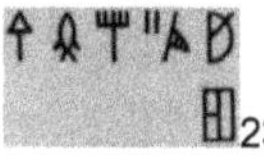 237

3

m0155

 1187

m0156

m0157

2022

m0158

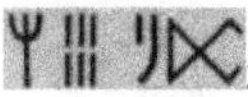219

8

m0159

2355

m0160

2286

m0161

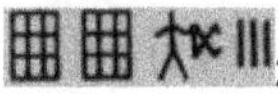20

88

m0162

2486

m0163

1543

m0164

2403

m0165

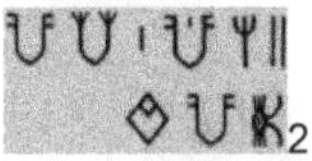2

687

m0166

1080

m0167.

1297

m0168a [The second sign may be an orthographic variant for a thigh of a bovid?]

24

42

m0169

1113

m0170

2237

m0171

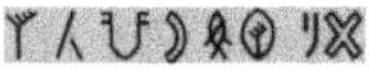

1149

m0172

1071

m0173

1161

m0174

1114

m0175

1291

m0176

1193

m0177

m0178

2354

m0179

m0180

2014

m0181

24

90

m0182

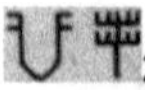2154

m0183

3113

m0184

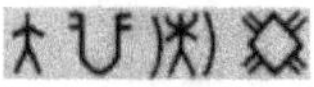

2634

m0185

m0186

2161

m0187

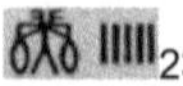2382

m0188

1287

m0189

1195

m0190

1205

m0191

1288

m0192

1206

m0193

2113

m0194

225

4

m0195

2

415

m0196

24

74

m0197

2371

m0198

2363

m0199

2647

m0200

114

8

m0201

2678

m0202

26

25

m0203

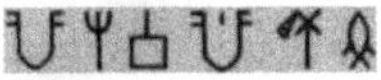
1556

m0204

26

23

m0205

1221

m0206

m0207

2458

m0208

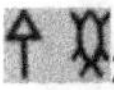
2047

m0209

2375

m0210

2656

m0211

1214

m0212

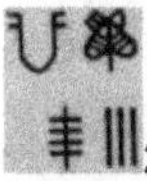
2577

m0213

1150

m0214

2571

m0215

3081

m0216

3036

m0217

20
87

m0218

2175

m0219

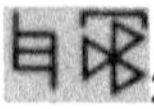2433

m0220a

3093

m0221a

3164

m0222

119
4

m0223

1167 [The sign in front of the one-horned bull may be Sign 162]

m0224

2215

m0225

2199

m0226

2152

m0227 2226

m0228

2502

m0229

3075

m0230.

1295

m0231

24
44

m0232

2234

'Unicorn' with two horns! "Bull with two long horns (otherwise resembling the 'unicorn')", generally facing the standard. That it is the typical 'one-horned bull' is surmised from two ligatures: the pannier on the shoulder and the ring on the neck.

m0233

m0234.

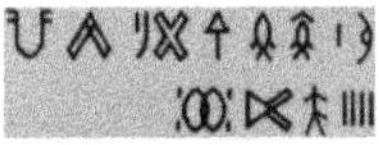

1321

m0235

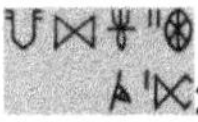
2689

m0236

2123

m0237

m0238AC

2534

m0239

2

238

m0240.

1

324

m0241

1536

m0242

2

216

m0243

2390

m0244

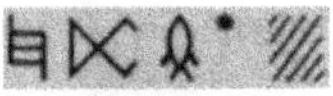

2399

m0245

2290

m0246.

1317

m0247

229

8

m0248.

1310

m0249

2378

m0250.

1308

m0251

23

70

m0252

2423

m0253

2701

m0254

209

0

m0255

2409

[The second sign is diamond-shaped?]

m0256

133

2

m0257

2314

m0258a.

134

0

m0259

213

2

m0260

2567

m0261

2

535

m0262 Zebu

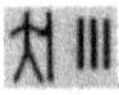2249

m0263

13

36

m0264

2607

m0265

2155

m0266.

1306

m0267 Water-buffalo

22

57

m0268 Water-buffalo

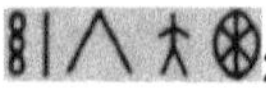24

45

m0269

2663

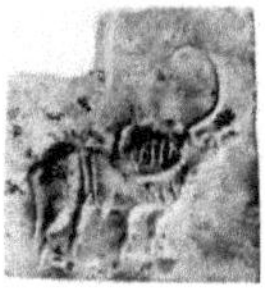

m0270

m0271 Goat-antelope with horns turned backwards and a short tail

m0272 Goat-antelope with horns bending backwards and neck turned backwards

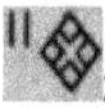2554

m0273 2673

m0274

1342

m0275

2131

m0276AC

312

2

m0277

23

09

m0278

26

48

m0279

3060

m0280

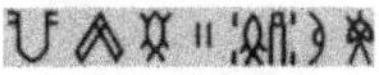

1373

m0281

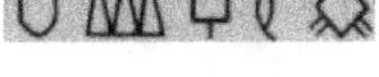

3115

m0282

23

04

m0283

2127

m0284

2195

m0285

1367

m0286

2517

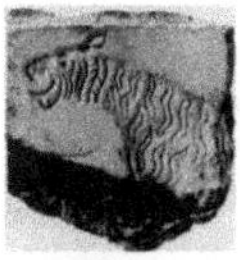

m0287

m0288

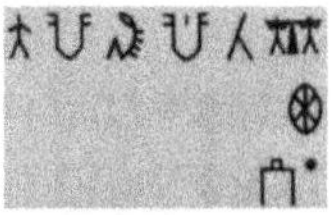

2518

m0289

3121

m0290

2527

m0291 Tiger

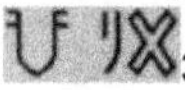3069

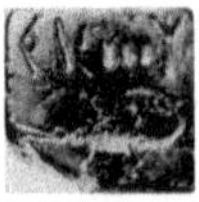

m0292 Gharial

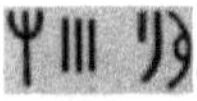
1361

m0293 Gharial

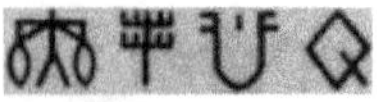

1360

m0294 One-horned bull?; elephant

1376

m0295 Pict-61: Composite motif of three tigers joined together.

1386

m0296 Two heads of one-horned bulls with neck-rings, joined end to end (to a standard device with two rings coming out of the top part?), under a stylized pipal tree with nine leaves.

1387

m0297a Head of a one-horned bull attached to an undentified five-point symbol (octopus-like?)

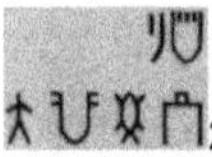
2641

m0298

m0299 Composite animal with the body of a ram, horns of a bull, trunk of an elephant, hindlegs of a tiger and an upraise serpent-like tail.

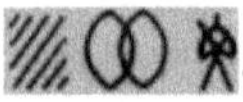
138

1

m0300 Pict51: Composite animal: human face, zebu's horns, elephant tusks and trunk, ram's forepart, unicorn's trunk and feet, tiger's hindpart and serpent-like tail.

2

521

m0301 Composite motif: human face, body or forepart of a ram, body and front legs of a unicorn, horns of a zebul, trunk of an elephant, hindlegs of a tiger and an upraised serpent-like tail.

2258

m0302 Composite animal with the body of a ram, horns of a bull, trunk of an elephant, hindlegs of a tiger and an upraise serpent-like tail.

1380

m0303 Composite animal.

2411

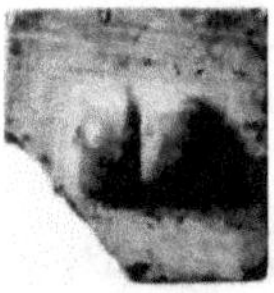

m0304B

m0304AC Pict-81: Person (with three visible faces) wearing bangles and armlets seated on a platform (with an antelope looking backwards) and surrounded by five animals: rhinoceros, buffalo, antelope, tiger and elephant.

2420

m0305AC

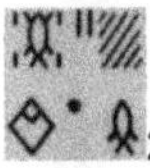

2235

Pict-80: Three-faced, horned person (with a three-leaved pipal branch on the crown with two stars on either side), wearing bangles and armlets.

m0306 Person grappling with two tigers standing on either side of him and rearing on their hindlegs.

2086

m0307 Person grappling with two tigers standing on either side of him and rearing on their hindlegs.

2122

m0308AC Pict-105: Person grappling with two tigers standing on either side of him and rearing on their hindlegs.

2075 [The third sign from left may be a stylized 'standard device'?]

m0309 Pict-109: Person with hair-bun seated on a tree branch; a tiger looks at the person with its head turned backwards.

2522

m0310AC

1355

m0311 Pict-52: Composite motif: body of a tiger, a human body with bangles on arms, antelope horns, tree-branch and long pigtail.

2347

m0312 Persons vaulting over a water-buffalo.

m0313

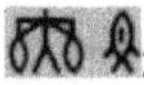

2637

m0314

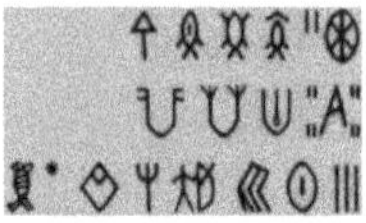

1400

m0315

1395

m0316

240

8

m0317silver

2

016

Mohenjodaro

FEM, Pl.

LXXXVIII, 316

2316

Mohenjodaro

MIC, Pl. CVI,93

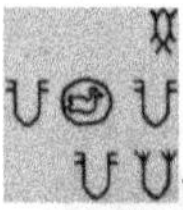

1093

Mohenjo-daro.
Copper seal.
National
Museum, New
Delhi. [Source:
Page 18, Fig. 8A
in: Deo Prakash
Sharma, 2000,
*Harappan seals,
sealings and
copper tablets*,
Delhi, National
Museum].

m0318

m0318B

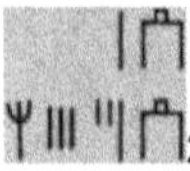

2626

m0319

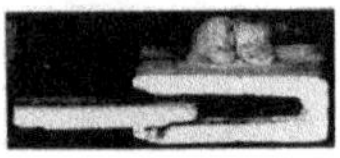

m0319C

2260

m0320

m0320D

2449

m0321

m0321D

2173

m032

2 m0322D

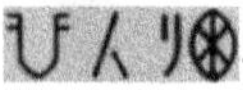

119

2

m0323

m0323D

1

277

m0324A

m0324B

m0324D

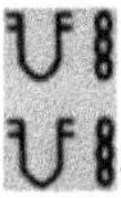

1252

m0325A

m0325B

m0325F

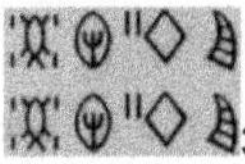

3106

m0326A

m0326B

m0326C

m0326D

m326E

m0326F

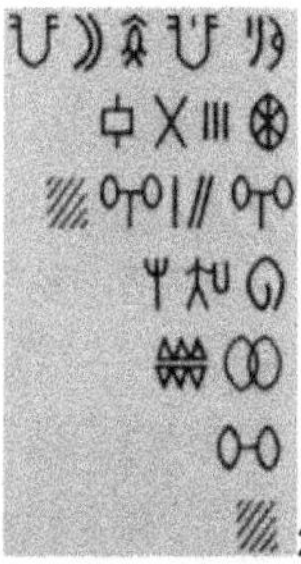

2405

m0327

2631

m0328

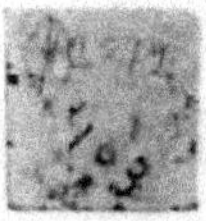

m0328B

2108

m0329

1477

m0330A

m0330B Perforated through the narrow edge of a two-sided seal

1475

m0331A

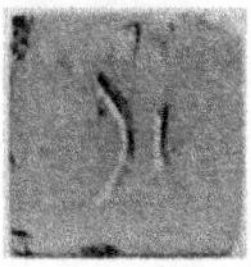

m0331B

m0331D

m0331F Cube seal

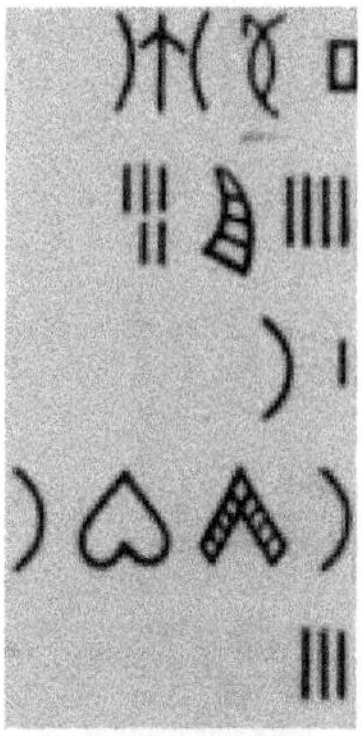

1471

m0332AC

m0333

m0334

m0335
m0336

m0337

m0338

m0339
m0340

m0341

m034
2

m0343
m0344

m0345

m034
6

m0347
m0348

m0349

m0350

m0351

m0352A

m0352C

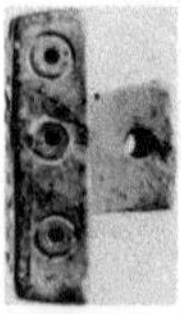

m0352D

m0352E

m0352F

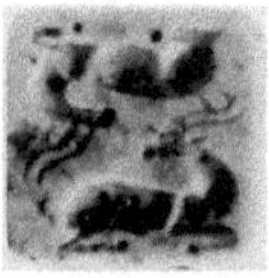

m0353

m0354

1403

m0356

1406

m0357

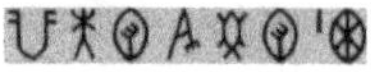

1401

m0358

2297

m0360

3102

m0361

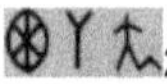
2101

m0362

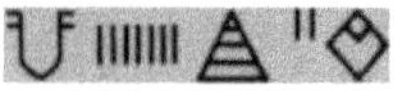

1466

m0363

1
469

m0364

146
5

m0365

2273

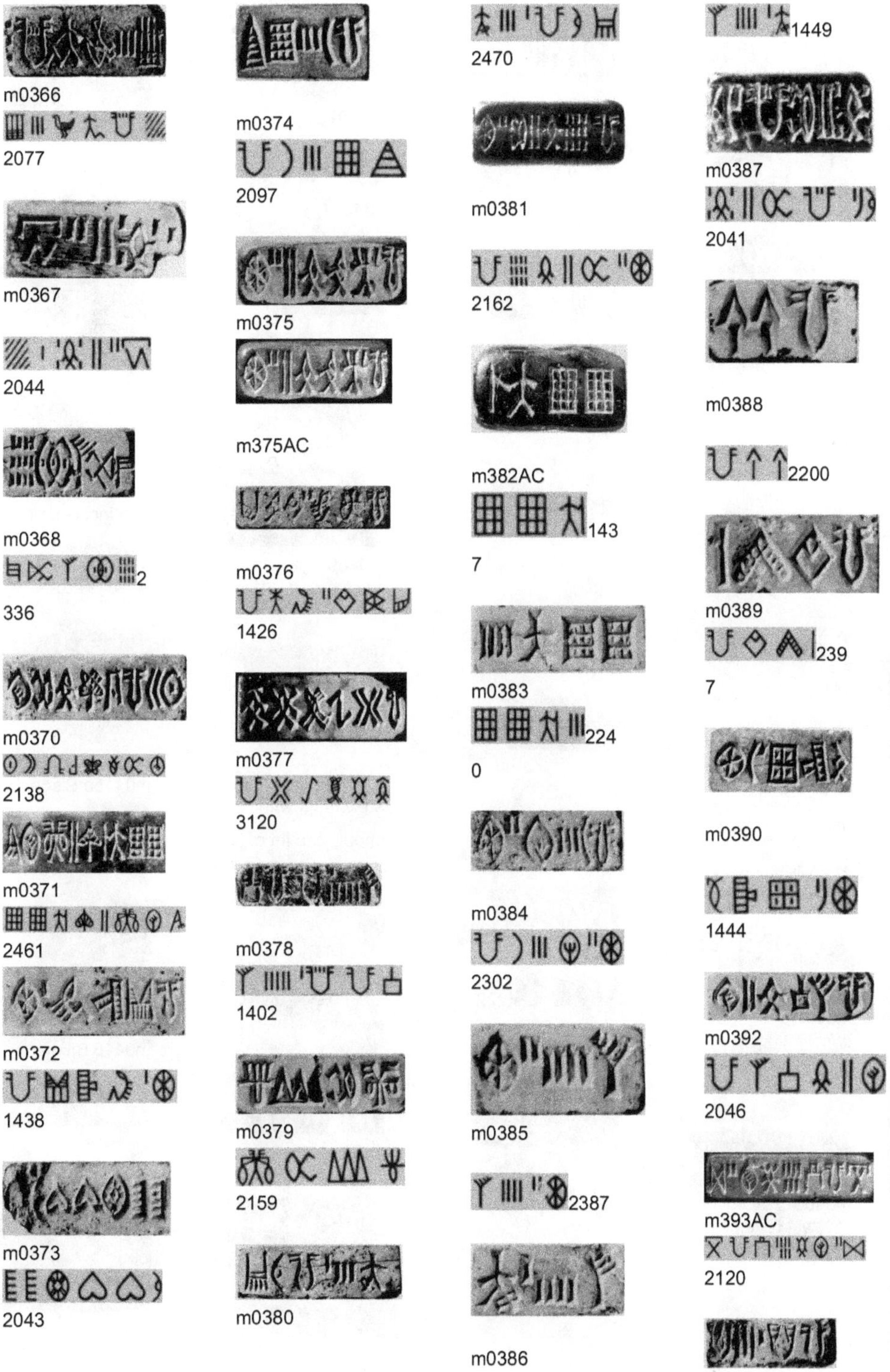
m0366
2077
m0367
2044
m0368
2
336
m0370
2138
m0371
2461
m0372
1438
m0373
2043
m0374
2097
m0375
m375AC
m0376
1426
m0377
3120
m0378
1402
m0379
2159
m0380
2470
m0381
2162
m382AC
143
7
m0383
224
0
m0384
2302
m0385
2387
m0386
1449
m0387
2041
m0388
2200
m0389
239
7
m0390
1444
m0392
2046
m393AC
2120

m0394

2213

m0395

2

183

m0396

1421

m0397

1

415

m0398

2308

m399AC

14

14

m0400

30

88

m0401

2346

m0402

2395

m0403

1410

m404AC

1422

m0405

222

1

m0406

1

399

m0407

2643

m0408

2100

m0409

2699

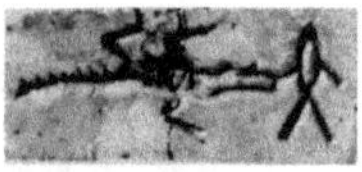

m0410 Pict-64: Gharial snatching, with its snout, the fin of a fish

2133

m0411

1431

m0412

14

50

m0413

2

319

m0414A

m0414B Seal with incision on obverse

2004

m0415a Bison

2500

m0416 Bison .

13

09

m417AC Pict-62: Composition: six heads of animals: of unicorn, of short-horned bull (bison), of antelope, of tiger, and of two other uncertain animals) radiating outward from a hatched ring (or 'heart' design).

1383

m0418acyl

m0419acyl

m0419dcyl

m0419fcyl

m0420A1si

m0420A2si

3236

m0421A1si

m0421A2si

3237

m0422A1si

m0422A2si

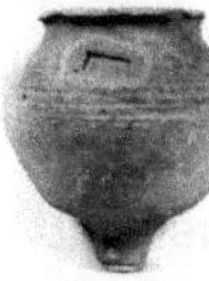

m0423A1si

m0423A2si

3

221

m0424A1si

m0424A2si

m0425A1si

m0425A2si

m0426Asi

m0426Bsi

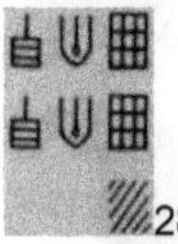2809

m0427t

1630

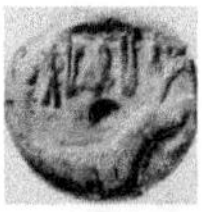

m0428At

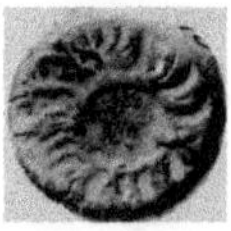

m0428Bt

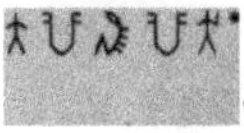160

7 Pict- 132: Radiating solar symbol.

m0429

Text 2862

m0430At

m0430Bt

2862

m0431At

m0431Bt

3

239

m0432At

m0432Bt

162

4

m0433At

m0433Bt

323

3

m0434At

m0434Bt

3248

m0435t

m0436At

m0436Bt

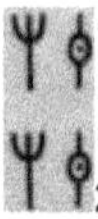

2804

m0437t

2867

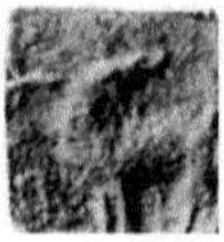

m0438atcopper

m0439t

m440AC

m0441At

m0441Bt

m0442At

m0442Bt

m443At

m443Bt

m444At

3223

m445Bt

m445AC

2821

m446At

m446Bt

2854

m447At

m447Bt

m448t

m449Bt

m449AC

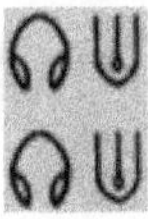
2836

m450At

m450Bt

2864

m0451At

m0451Bt

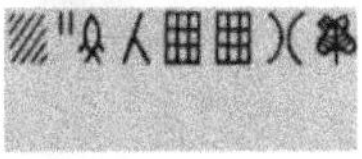
3235

m0452At

m0452Bt

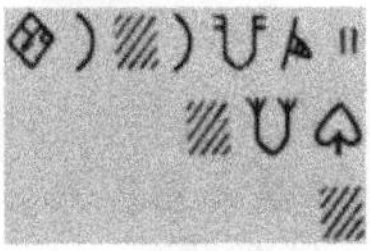
2855

m0453At

m453BC

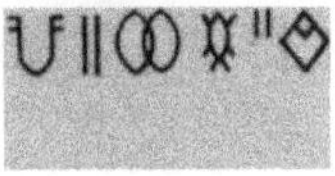
1629 Pict-82
Person seated on a pedestal flanked on either side by a kneeling adorant and a hooded serpent rearing up.

m0455At

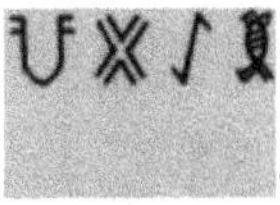
16
19

m0456At

3219

m0457At

m0457Bt

m0457Et

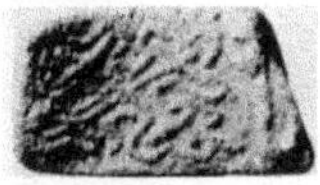

m0458At

m0458Bt

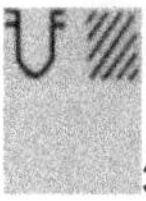
3227

m0459At

m0459Bt

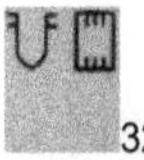
3225

m0460At

m0460Bt

3228

m0461At

m0461Bt

2806 Pict-73: Alternative 1. Serpent (?) entwined around a pillar with capital (?); motif carvd in high-relief. Alternative 2. Ring-stones around a pillar with coping stones in a building-structure as at Dholavira?

m0462At

m0462Bt

3215

m0463At

m0463Bt

2813

m0464At

m0464Bt

3216

m0465At

m0465Bt

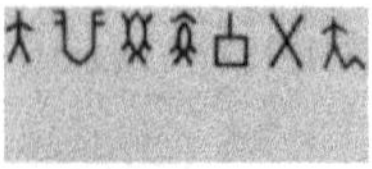
3220

m0466At

m0466Bt

m0467At

m0467Bt

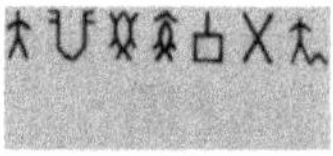
3209

m0468At

m0468Bt

3

249

m0469At

m0469Bt

283

0

m0470At

281

0

m0471At

m0471Bt

3232

m0472At

1615

m0473At

2848

m0474At

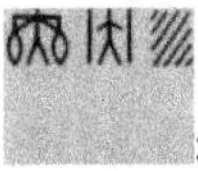

3243

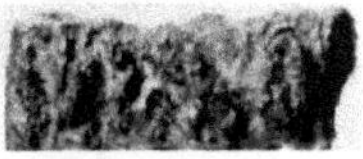

m0475Atcopper

3247

m0476At

m0476Ct

m0477At

m0477Bt

m0477Ct

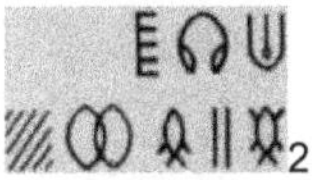2

844

Two rhinoceroses, one at either end of the text (Pict-29).

m0478At

m0478Bt

m0479At

m0479Bt

322

4

m0480At

m0480Bt Tablet in bas-relief. Side a: Tree Side b: Pict-111: From R.: A woman with outstretched arms flanked by two men holding uprooted trees in their hands; a person seated on a tree with a tiger below with its head turned backwards; a tall jar with a lid. Is the pictorial of a tall jar the Sign 342 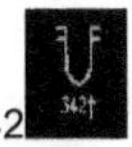 with a lid? Sign 45  seems to be a kneeling adorant offering a pot (Sign 328 )

281

5 Pict-77: Tree, generally within a railing or on a platform.

323

0

m0481At

m0481Bt

m0481Ct

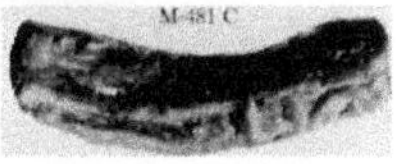

m0481Et

2846 Pict-41: Serpent, partly reclining on a low platform under a tree

m0482At

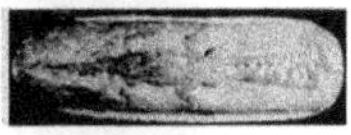

m0482Bt

1620

Pict-65: Gharial, sometimes with a fish held in its jaw and/or surrounded by a school of fish.

m0483At

m0483Bt

m0483Ct

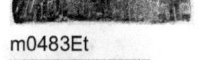

m0483Et

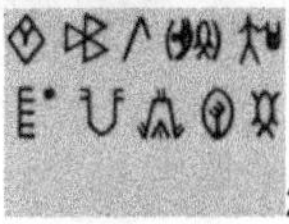

2

866

Pict-145: Geometrical pattern.

m0484At

m0484Bt

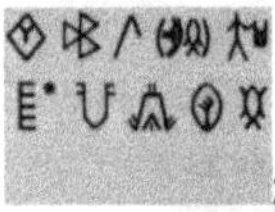

2861

m0486at

m0486bt

m0486ct

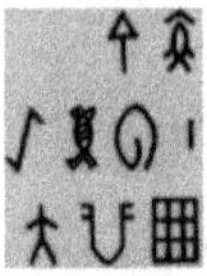

1625

m0487At

m0487Bt

m0487Ct

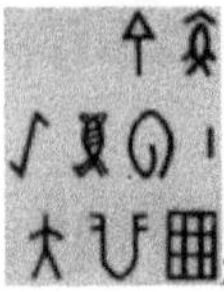

2852

m0488At

m0488Bt

m0488Ct

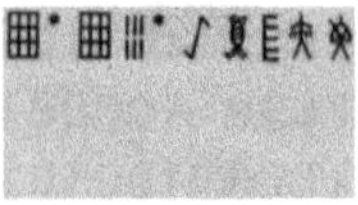

2802 Prism: Tablet in bas-relief. Side b: Text +One-horned bull + standard. Side a: From R.: a composite animal; a person seated on a tree with a tiger below looking up at the person; a svastika within a square border; an elephant (Composite animal has the body of a ram, horns of a zebu, trunk of an elephant, hindlegs of a tiger and an upraised serpent-like tail). Side c: From R.: a horned person standing between two branches of a pipal tree; a ram; a horned person kneeling in adoration; a low pedestal with some offerings.

m0489At

m0489Bt

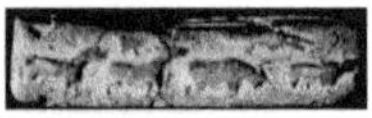

m0489Ct

m0490At

m0490BCt

1605

m0491At

m0491BCt

1608 Pict-94: Four persons in a procession, each carrying a standard, one of which has the figure of a one-horned bull on top.

m0492At

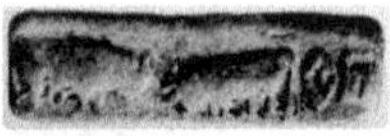

m0492Bt Pict-14: Two bisons standing face to face.

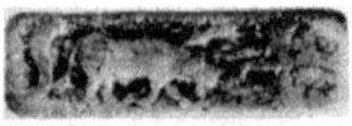

m0492Ct

2835 Pict-99: Person throwing a spear at a bison and placing one foot on the head of the bison; a hooded serpent at left.

m0493At

m0493Bt Pict-93: Three dancing figures in a row.

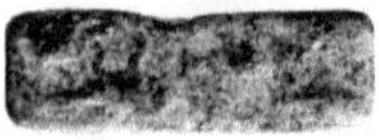

m0493Ct

2843

m0494At

m0494BGt Prism Tablet in bas-relief.

1623

m0495At

m0495Bt

m0495gt

2847b

m0496At

m0496Bt

m0496Dt

m0497At

m0497Bt

m0498At

m0498Bt

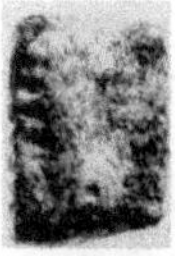

m0498Dt

m0499At

m0500at

m0500bt

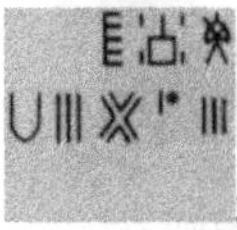

260

4 Pict-76: Tree, generally within a railing or on a platform.

m0501At

m0501Bt

14

12

m0502At

m0502Bt

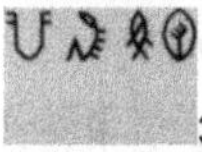

3345

m0503 Text

33

46

m0504At

m0504Bt

332

3

m0505At

m0505Bt

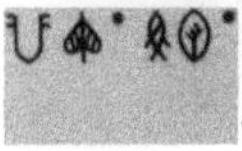

170

2

m0507At

m0507Bt

3350

m0508At

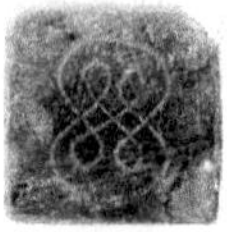

m0508Bt

335

2

m0509At

m0509Bt

33

20

m0510At

m0510Bt

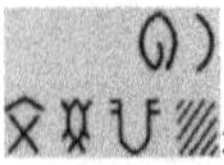

3319

m0511At

m0511Bt

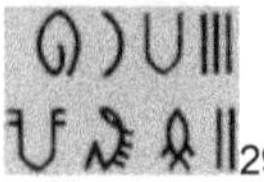

290

5

m0512At

m0512Bt

290

6

m0513At

m0513Bt

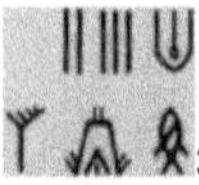

3364

m0514At

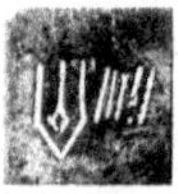

m0514Bt

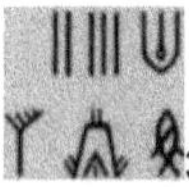

3302

m0515 Text

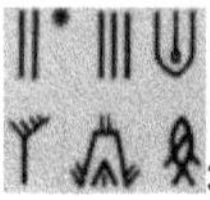

3335

m0516At

m0516Bt

3398

m0517At

m0517Bt

3334

m0519At

m0519Bt

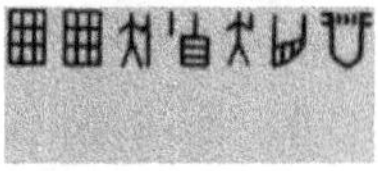

1710

m0520 At, Bt

2916 m0521

34

07

m0522At

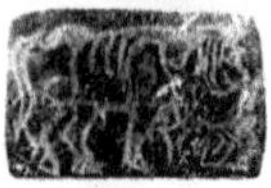

m0522Bt

3378

m0523At

m0523Bt

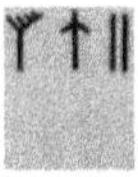
1714

m0524At

m0524Bt

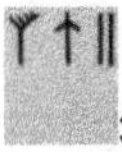
3391

m0525At

m0525Bt

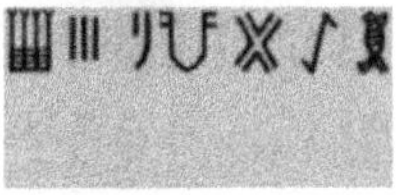
1713 Buffalo

m0526At

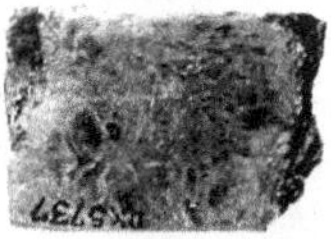
m0526Bt

3329

Buffalo

m0527At

m0527Bt

3336

m0528At

m0528Bt

3368

m0529At

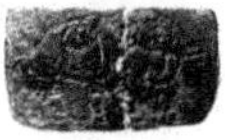
m0529Bt

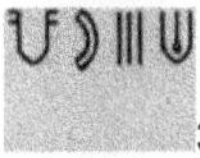
3392

m0530At

m0530Bt

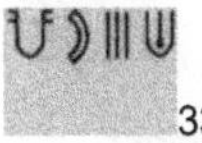
3356

m0531At

m0531Bt

m0532At

m0532Bt

3349

m0534At

m0534Bt

3304

m0535At

m0535Bt

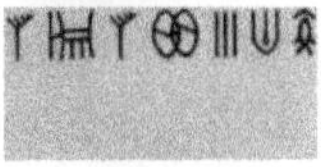
3355

m0536At

m0536Bt

3312

m0537At

m0537Bt

1705

m0538At

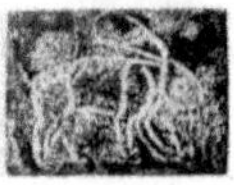

m0538Bt

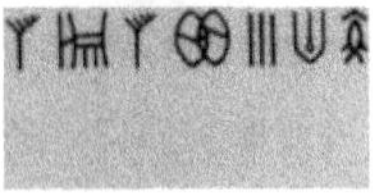

3384

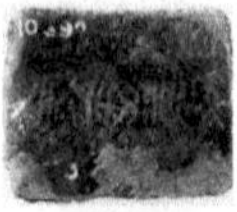

m0539At

m0539Bt

m540t

m0541At

m0541Bt

3331

m0542At

m0542Bt

3326 Hare?

m0543At

m0543Bt

3363 [Note the 'heart' orthograph on the body of the antelope. This is comparable to Sign 323 ]

m0544At

m0544Bt

3357

m0545At

m0545Bt

3301

m0546At

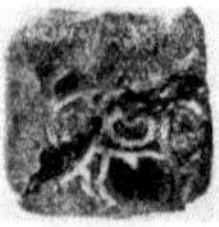

m0546Bt

3383

m0547At

m0547Bt

3303

m0548At

m0548Bt

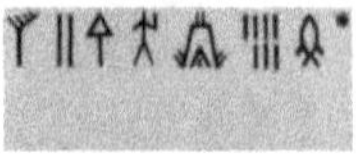

3305

m0549At

m0549Bt

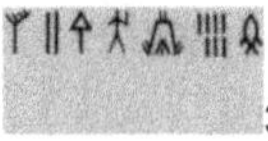

33

73

m0550At

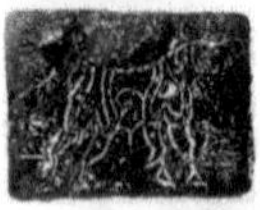

m0550Bt

3351

m0551At

m0551Bt

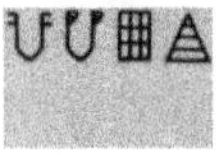

1708

Ox-antelope with long tail.

m0552At

m0552Bt

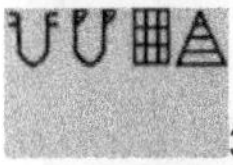

3306

m0553At

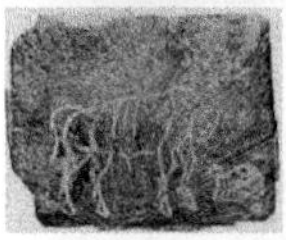

m0553Bt

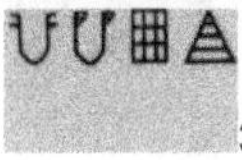

335

3

m0554At

m0554Bt

1712

m0555At

m0555Bt

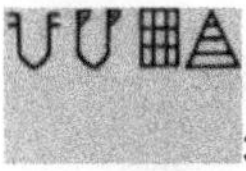

331

4

m0556At

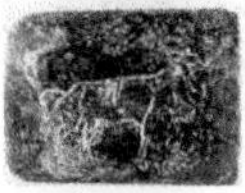

m0556Bt

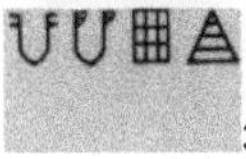

340

4

m0557At

m0557Bt

3341

m0558At

m0558Bt

3342

m0559At

m0559Bt

290

9

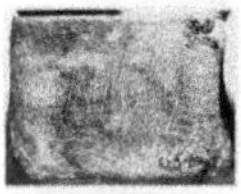

m0560At

m0560Bt

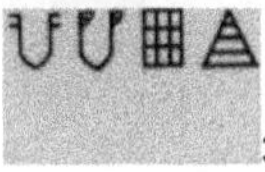

33

86

m0561At

m0561Bt

3339

m0562At

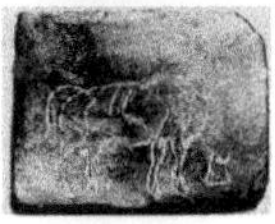

m0562Bt

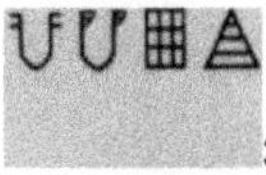

33

61

m0563At

m0563Bt

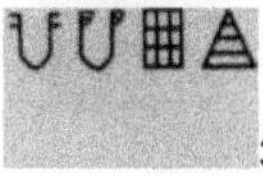

33

79

m0564At

m0564Bt

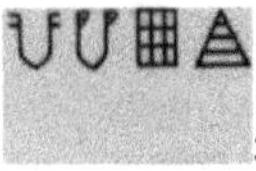

33

71

m0565At

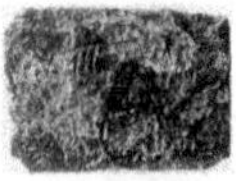

m0565Bt

3

403

m0566At

m0566Bt

335

9

m0567At

m0567Bt

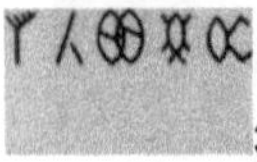

33

22 Bison.

m0568At

m0568Bt

3

332 Tiger.

m0569At

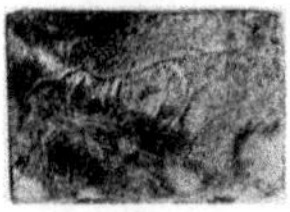

m0569Bt

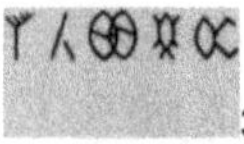

337

2

m0571At

m0571Bt

2913

Horned elephant. Almost similar to the composition: Body of a ram (with inlaid 'heart' sign), horns of a bull, trunk of an elephant, hindlegs of a tiger and an upraised serpent-like tail

m0572At

m0572Bt

3317

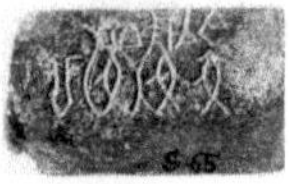

m0573At

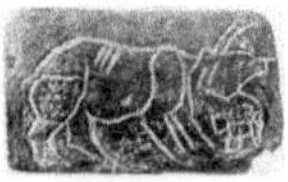

m0573Bt

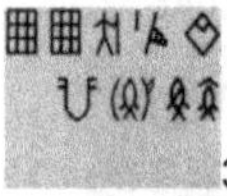

3415

m0574At

m0574Bt

3318

m0575At

m0575Bt

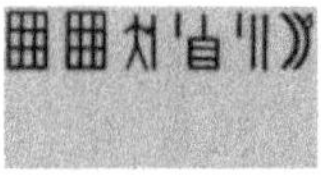

3316

m0576At

m0576Bt

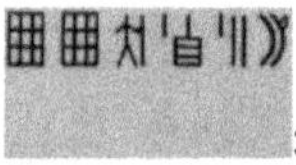

3

344

m0577At

m0577Bt

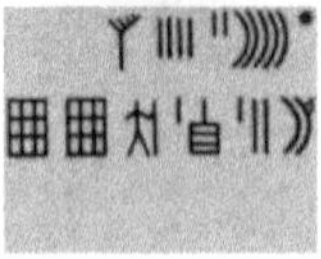

3347

m0578At

m0578Bt

2908

m0580At

m0580Bt

3321

m0581At

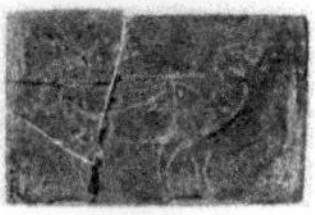

m0581Bt

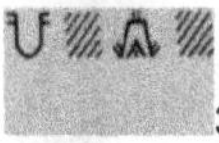

3340

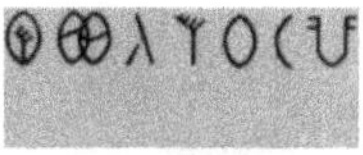

2914

Pict-89: Standing person with horns and bovine features, holding a bow in one hand and an arrow or an uncertain object in the other.

m0582At

m0582Bt

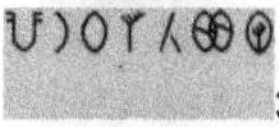

3358

m0583At

m0583Bt

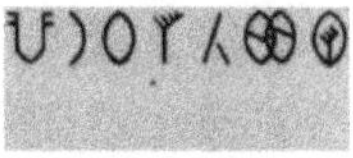

3387

m0584At

m0584Bt

m0585At

m0585Bt

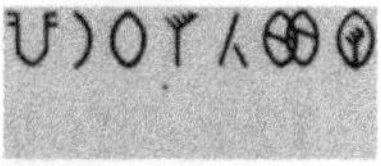

3369

m0586At

m0586Bt

3406

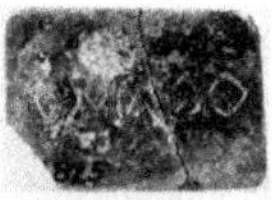

m0587At

m0587Bt

3365 Horned Archer?

m0588At

m0588Bt Horned archer.

m0592At

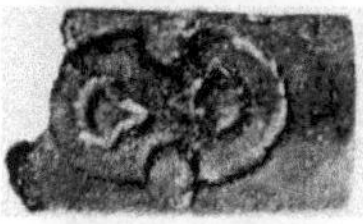

m0592Bt

3413 Pict-133: Double-axe (?) without shaft. [The sign is comparable to the sign which

appears on the text of a Chanhudaro seal: Text 6402, Chanhudaro Seal 23].

m0593At

m0593Bt

3337

m0594At

m0594Bt

m0595A

m0595B

1010

m0596At

m0596Bt

331

3

m0598 Text

3410

m0599At

m0599Bt

3360

m0600At

m0600Bt

33

75

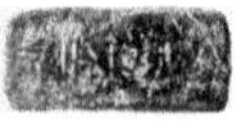

m0601At

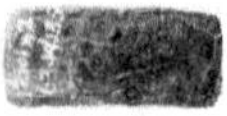

m0601Bt

m0602At

m0602Bt

3414

m0604At

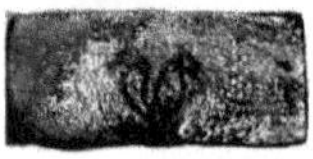

m0604Bt

3315

m0605At

m0605Bt

2

902

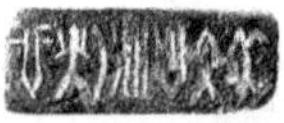

m0606At

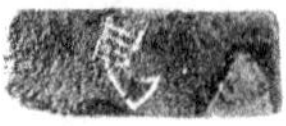

m0606Bt

2918

m0608At

m0608Bt

m0614

1904

m0615

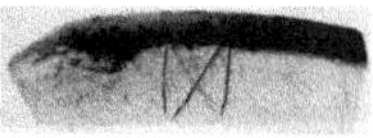

m0618

m0619

2939

m0620

m0621

2367

m0622

m0623

m0624

1015

m0625

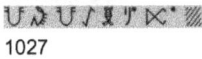

1027

m0626

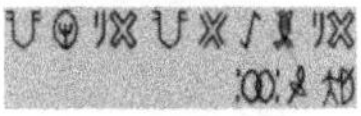
1012

m0627

1004

m0628

1033

m0629

m0630A

m0631

1008

m0632

1017

m0633

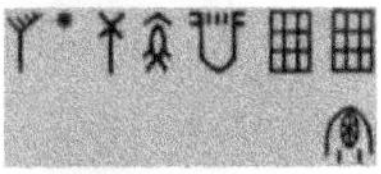
1016

m0634

2069

m0635a

m0636

2019

m0637

1034

m0638 One-horned bull

1404

m0639

m0640

m0641

m0642

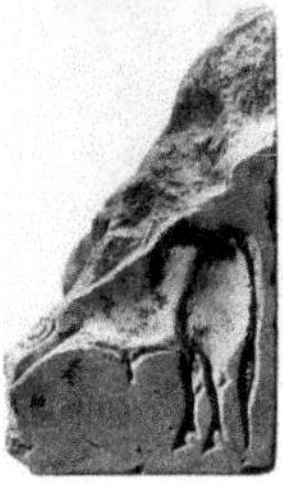
m0643

m0644

1553

m0645

m0646A1

m0646a12

m0646A2

2653

m0647

1024

m0648

3104

m0649

2530

m0650

1032

m0651

2578

m0652

m0653

1057

m0654

2561

m0655

2098

m0656

m0657

2026

m0658

1039

m0659

m0661

2207

m0662

1061

m0663

259
7

m0664

2628

m0665

1139

m0666

2243

m0667

1111

m0668

2032

m0669

26

86

m0670

1

030

m0671

1021

m0672

1040

m0673

1025

m0674

1068

m0675

2197

m0676

m0677

m0678

1066

m0679

m0680A1

m0681

2182

m0682

m0682A2

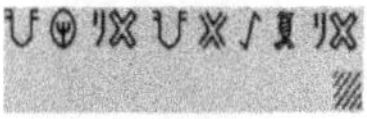

2690

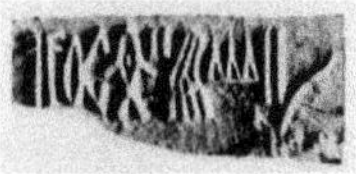

m0683a

m0683A1

m0683A2

2174

m0684

m0685

1276

m0686

2324

m0687

m0688

m0689

m0690

m0691

m0692

1031

m0693

m0694

m0695

m0696

m0697

m0698

m0699

1050

m0700

m0701

1059

m0702

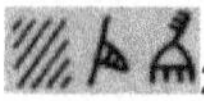
2206

m0703

2438

m0704

2351

m0705

227

2

m0706

1097

m0707

m0708

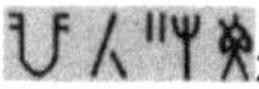
2666

m0709

2071

m0710

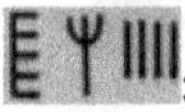 3159

m0711

 1166

m0712

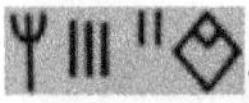 109

1 Note Sign391 ligatured on the animal's neck; this may be a logonym (i.e. two heiroglyphs – rings and spoked circle -- representing the same lexeme) for the rings on the neck?

m0713

 24

32

m0715

2681

m0716

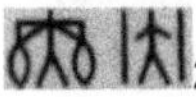 2076

[Are there signs following these two signs?]

m0717

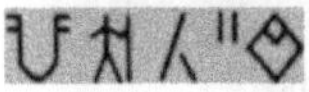

1078

m0714

2446

m0718

 2209

m0719

 2

137

m0720

1082

m0721

 11

65

m0722

1014

m0723

2054

m0724

m0725

m0726

m0727a

m0727A1

m0727A2

2

168

m0728

2691

m0729

1177

m0730

m0732

2

674

m0733

251

9

m0734

15

39

m0735

1060

m0736

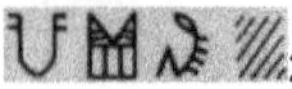
2

562

m0737

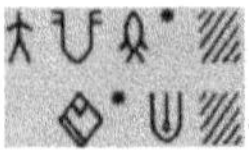
111

2

m0738

2644

m0739

m0740

1090

m0741

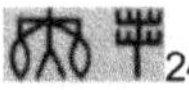
2421

m0742

2595

m0743

m0744

m0745

1175

m0746

1081

m0747

2471

m0748

1135

m0749

2008

m0750

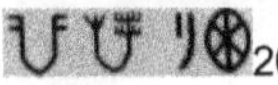
2065

m0751

1102

m0752a

m0753a

m0753A1

m0753A2

2589

m0754

1145

m0755

m0756a

1028

m0757

2507

m0758a

2184

m0759 One-horned bull.

2384

m0760

m0761 One-horned bull.

1417

m0762a

2645

m0763

m0764

m0765

m0766

m0767

m0768

1176

m0769

2034

m0770a

1138

m0771
2676

m0772

2453

m0773

m0774

m0775

m0776

1146

m0777

2536

m0778

2425

m0779

2622

m0780

1178

m0781

22

51

m0782

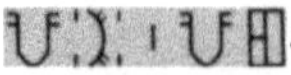

1

122

m0783

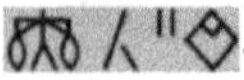

112

7

m0784

1128

m0785

1

181

m0786

1107

m0787

2

503

m0788

m0789

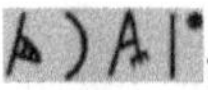

1185

m0790

m0791

m0792

2013

m0793

m0794

2067

m0795

122

8

m0796

2105

m0797

m0798

108

4

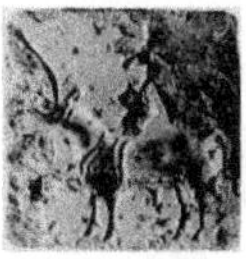

m0799 3015 or

3147

m0800

m0801

21

04

m0802

11

82

m0803

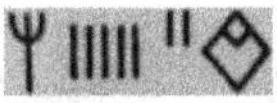11

31

m0804

257

0

m0805

3041

m0806

m0807

2669

m0808

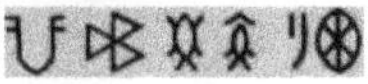

2146

m0809

2548

m0810

2364

m0811

2211

m0812

2629

m0813

m0814

2426

m0815

25

55

m0816

24

24

m0817

243

5

m0818

1089

m0819

2081

m0820

m0821

1238

m0822

1249

m0823

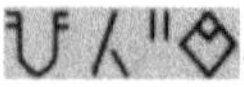

108

6

m0824

1164

m0825

1239

m0826

m0827

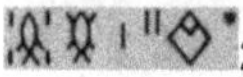

251

3

m0828

2114

m0829

m0830

2274

m0831

2546

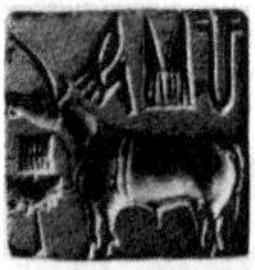

m0832

m0833

2281

m0834

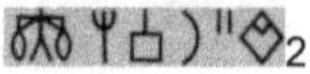

2

569b

m0835

2179

m0836

m0837

3085

m0838

2368

m0839

2
476

m0840

2617

m0841

m0842

2704

m0843

m0844

1290

m0845

2202

m0846

1005

m0847

1156

m0848

2241

m0849

1121

m0850

2533

m0851

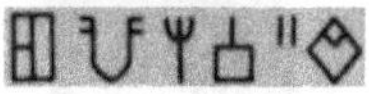
2660

m0852a

2413

m0853

2255

m0854

250
1

m0855

2473

m0856

1211

m0857

209

1

m0858a

2189

m0859

2

063

m0860

m0861

112

3

m0862

225

3

m0863

2621 Is the 'stubble' ligatured glyph a variant of

Sign 162  ?]

m0864

1240

m0865

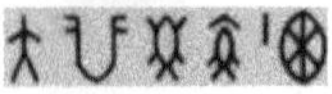

1109

m0866

26

46

m0867

m0868

3160

m0869

m0870

1160

m0871

m0872

m0873

1170

m0874

3092

m0875

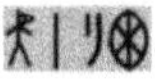1189

m0876

m0877

m0878

1092

m0879

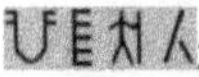2121

m0880

m0881

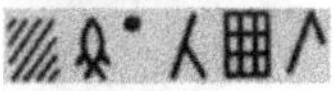
1242

m0882

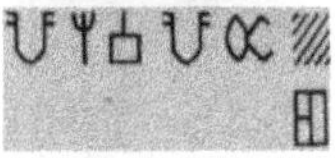
2312

m0883

m0884

3158

m0885

m0886

3072

m0887a

1169

m0888

11
55

m0889

1126

m0890

2
117

m0891

1073

m0892

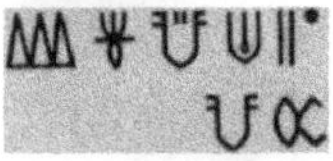
1247

m0893

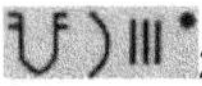2659
One-horned bull.

m0894

2393

m0895

22
62

m0896

213
4

m0897

2545

m0898  21

67

m0899

 2242

m0900

2335

m0901

 227

6

m0902a

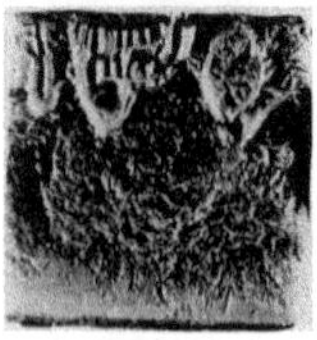

m0903a.

 12

94

m0904

m0905

m0906

m0907

 21

92

m0908

m0909

3028

m0910

m0911

m0914

2143

m0915

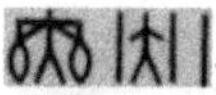 1218

m0916

 1204

m0917

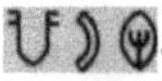 1224

m0918

m0919

2343

m0920

1219

m0921

m0922

 128

2

m0923

m0924

25

91

m0925

1292

m0926

2219

m0927

1171

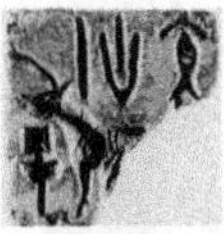
m0928

1202

m0929a

1144

m0930

3020

m0931

3091

m0932

3022

m0933

2160

m0934

11

58

m0935

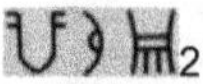
2144

m0936

1197

m0937

2066

m0938

2158

m0939a

2652

m0940a

2060

m0941

2

256

m0942

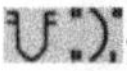
1296

m0943

2282

m0944

2419

m0945

1208

m0946

2358

m0947

2404

m0948

225

0

m0949A

m0949C

1271

Also, Sign 141

m0950a

1013

m0951

1263

m0952

2265

m0953

2582

m0954

12

62

m0955

2

547

m0956

125

1

m0957

1026

m0958

2348

m0959

114

7

m0960

1388

m0961

1163

m0962

307

4

m0963

12

32

m0964

20

10

m0965

1222

m0966

2

070

m0967

2460

m0968

23

00

m0969

2239

m0970a

2116

m0971

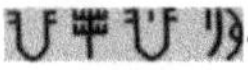
123

4

m0972a

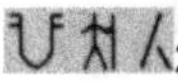
2557

m0973a

2585

m0974a

2650

m0975

2295

m0976

120

3

m0977

3152

m0978

m0979

2564

m0980

2317

m0981

m0982a

2021

m0983

m0984

1143

m0985

m0986a

2341

m0987a

1007

m0988

m0989

m0990

2472

One-horned bull.

m0991 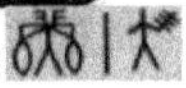 2203

m0992

2464

m0993a

1267

m0994a

2165

m0995

m0996

2299

One-horned bull.

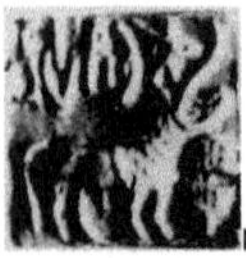

m0997a

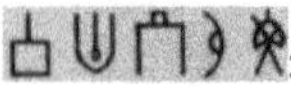3105

m0998

2176

m0999

2452

m1000a

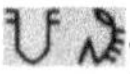1487 One-horned bull.

m1001a

1283

m1002

m1003

1275

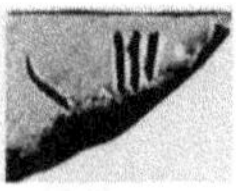

m1004

m1005

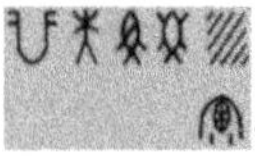1001

m1006

1499

Bovid.

m1007

m1008

m1009

2627

m1010

2672 Bovid.

m1011

m1012

m1013

m1014 One-horned bull?

1397

m1015

m1016.

1348

m1017

13

00

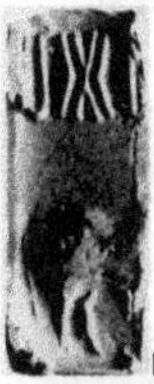
m1018a

24

83 Bovid.

m1019.

1298

m1020

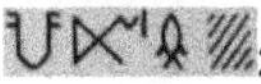
24

96

m1021a.

1

299

m1022

m

1023

m1024

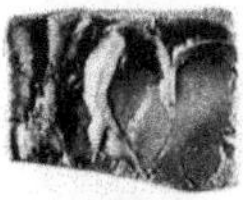
m1025a

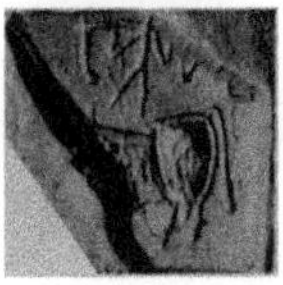

m1026a.

1307

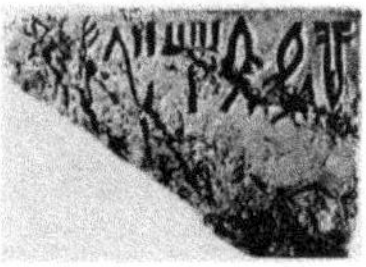
m1027

m1028

2671

Bovid.

m1029

12

65

m1030

3145

m1031

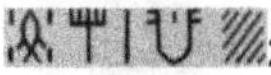
20

53

m103

2

2217

m1033

m1034

2467

m1036

m1037

m1038

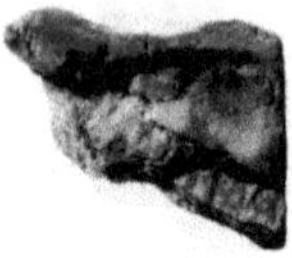

m1039

m1040

m1041

m1042

m1043

m1044a

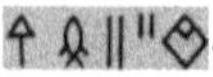1551

Bovid.

m1045

2447 Bovid.

m104

6

305

8

m1047

128

1

m1048

m1049

3032

m1050 119

6

m1051

m1052

3100

m1053

2

163

m1054

24

48

m1055

252

9

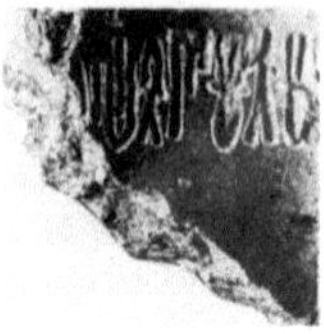

m1057

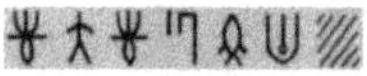

2566

m1058a

1392

m1059

m1060

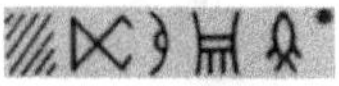

1497

m1061a

1379

m1062

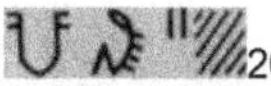208

9

m1063

2357

m1064 1

492

m1065

2151

m1066

1547

m1067a

1496

m1068

m1069

1390

m1070

204

0

m1071

1488

m1072a

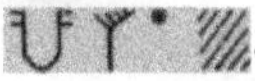144

3

m1073

148

9

m1074

m1075a

1479

m1076

m1077a

2359

m1078

m1079

2655

m1080

154

2

m1081a

2129

m1082.

1349

m1083

m108

4 1316 Bison.

m1085.

1322

m1086a

3070

m1087a.

131

9

m1088

2268

m1089a.

1315

m1090

2675

m1091

m1092

1312

m1093

m1094

m1095

2495 Bison

m1096

241

0

m1097

2313

m1098

1301

m1099

1313

m1100

2201

Bison

m1101

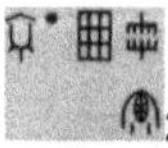2431

Zebu.

m1102

m1103.

1337

m1104

13

35

m1105

m1106

2331

Zebu

m1107a

2306

m1108

1

339

m1109

1327

Zebu

m1110

1334

m1111.

1333

m1112

2366

Zebu.

m1113

244

1

m1114.

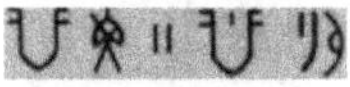

1331

m1115

13

28 Zebu

m1116.

1329

m1117a

2615

m1118

3157

m1119

2463

m112

0

2362

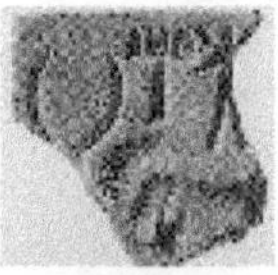

m1122

2610

m1126

2332

m1127

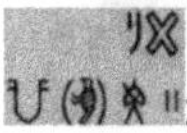2696

m1128a

3163

m1129a

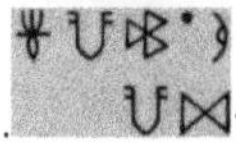130

2 Markhor.

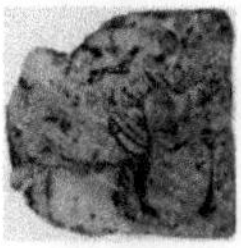

m1130

m1131

m1132

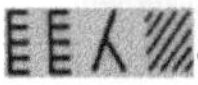1545

Rhinoceros.

m1133

1343

m1134

26

51

m1135

21

40 Pict-50 Composite animal: features of an ox and a rhinoceros facing the standard device.

m1136

m1137

2531

Rhinoceros.

m1138.

1

344

m1139.

1341

m1140a

2

188 Rhinoceros.

m1141

2169

m1142

m1143

m114

4

m1145

m146a

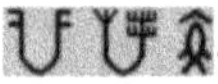
1374

Elephant

m1147

m1148

2590

m1149

136

8 Elephant.

m1150

1

534

m1151

1535

m1152

1369

m1154

1

362 Elephant.

m1155

2573

m1156

1370

m1157a

2

110

m158

m1159

21

71

m1160

205

7

m1161

2504

m1162

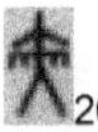2058

m1163

2640

Tiger.

m1164

26

65 Tiger.

m1165a

2064

m1166.

1

351

m1167

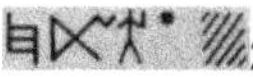248

4 Tiger.

m1168

2360

Seal showing a horned tiger. Mohenjodaro. (After Scala/Art Resource).

Tiger with long (zebu's) horns?

1385

Pict-49 Uncertain animal with dotted circles on its body.

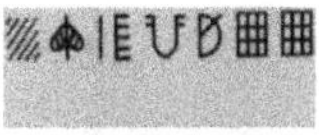

1626

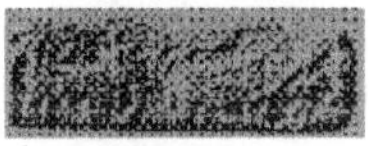

Pict-47 Row of uncertain animals in file.

m1169a

2024

Pict-58: Composite motif: body of an ox and three heads: of a one-horned bull (looking forward), of antelope (looking backward), and of short-horned bull (bison) (looking downward).

m1170a

1382 Compos ite animal

m1171 Composite animal

m1172

m1173

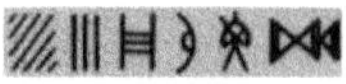

1191

m1175a

2493 Composite animal: human face, zebu's horns, elephant tusks and trunk, ram's forepart, unicorn's trunk and feet, tiger's hindpart and serpent-like tail.

m1176

m1177

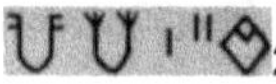

2450 Composite animal: human face, zebu's horns, elephant tusks and trunk, ram's forepart, unicorn's trunk and feet, tiger's hindpart and serpent-like tail.

m1178

2559

m1179

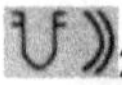

2606 Human-faced markhor with long wavy horns, with neck-bands and a short tail.

m1180a

1303 Human-faced markhor

m1181A

2222 Pict-80: Three-faced, horned person (with a three-leaved pipal branch on the crown), wearing bangles and armlets and seated on a hoofed platform

Padri . Head painted on storage jar from Padri, Gujarat (c. 2800 BCE). Details of body with multiple hands (?) Similar horned-heads painted on jars are found at Kot Diji, Burzhom and Kunal (c. 3rd millennium BCE). [Source: Page 21, Figs. 10A and B in: Deo Prakash Sharma, 2000, *Harappan seals, sealings and copper tablets*, Delhi, National Museum].

m1182a

m1183a

m1184

m1185

Pict-103 Horned (female with breasts hanging down?) person with a tail and bovine legs standing near a tree fisting a horned tiger rearing on its hindlegs.

1357

m1186A

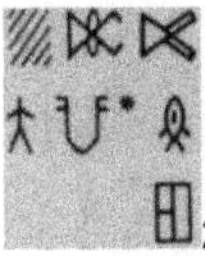

2430

Composition: horned person with a pigtail standing between the branches of a pipal tree; a low pedestal with offerings (? or human head?); a horned person kneeling in adoration; a ram with short tail and curling horns; a row of seven robed figures, with twigs on their pigtails.

m1187

m1188

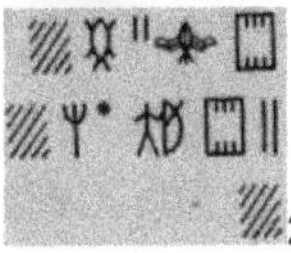

2

228

m1189

1396

m1190

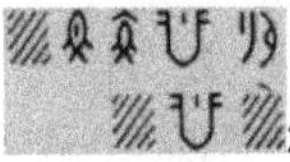

2

558

m1191

1389

m1192

1495

m1193

a  240

1

m1194a

3066

m1195

2181

m1196

m1197

m1198  1482

Silver m1199A

2520

m1200A

m1200C

307

8

m1201

m1202A

m1202C.

1

325 Space on the side of the seal was used to inscribe a third line

m1203A

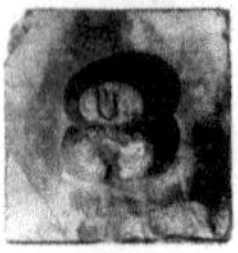
m1203B

1018

m1204

209

5

m1205a

m1205c

m1205f

1293 + Two signs on the sides of the seal.

m1206AE

m1206e1

m1206F

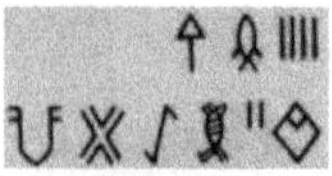
2229 Seal with a projecting knob containing the top

three signs; m1206e is inscribed on the top edge of the lower indented frame which depicts the bison.

m1208

m1221

m1222

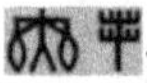
1268

m1223

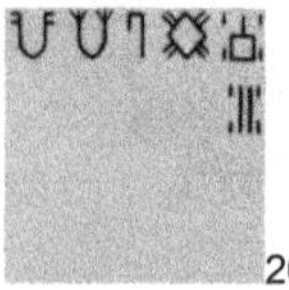
20

45 Pict-40: Frog.

256

5

Pict-37 Goat-antelope with a short tail

m1224A

m1224B

1224

m1224e

Pict-88

1227

Standing person with horns and bovine features (hoofed legs and/or tail).

m1225A

m1225B.

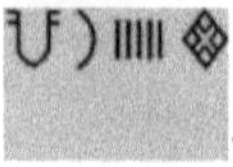
1311

Cube seal with perforation through the breadth of the

seal Pict-118: svastika_ , generally within a square or rectangular border.

m1226A.

1326 Unfinished seal.

m1227

m1228a

1394

m1230a

1358

m1231

2321

Unfinished seal?

m1232a

2497

Unfinished seal

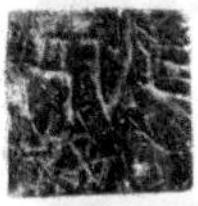

m1233A

m1233B

m1233cd

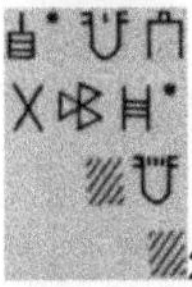2352

m1234a

m1234b

m1234d

m1234e

m1235a

m1235bc

2394

Unfinished seal

m1236

1483

Unfinished seal?

m1239

m1240

m1241

m1242

m1243

m1244

m1245

m1246

m1247

m1248

m1249

m1250

m1251

m1252

m1253

m1254

m1255

m1256

m1257

m1258

m1259

m1260

m1261

m1262

2301

m1263

1391

m1264a

1405

m1265

2227

m1266

1470

m1267

1494

m1268

2288

m1269

m1270

1464

m1271

2603

m1272

m1273

2679

m1274

2106

m1275

3161

m1276

2428

m1277

m1278

2028

m1280a

1462

m1281

2266

m1282

m1283

m1284a

2477

m1285a

2204

m1286

1455

m1287

1454

m1288

3086

m1289

1452

m1290

14

63

m1291a

2688

m1292

1461

m1293a

2388

m1294

2291

m1295

1458

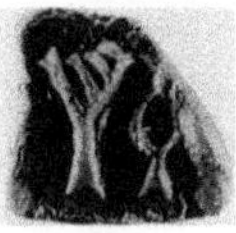

m1296a

3144

m1297

1445

m1298

3037

m1299a

1456

m1300

23

50

m1301

m1302a

1

432

m1303a

1398

m1304

1

423

m1305

2289

m1306

1430

m1307

m1308

2697

m1309

2579

m1310

1418

m1311

248

5

m1312

2318

m1313

2093

m1314a

1439

m1315

2345

m1316a

m1317

3095

m1318

1

416

m1319

m1320

1447

m1321

144

6

m1322a

3079

m1323

20

06

m1324

2682

m1325

211

8

m1326

3143

m1327

14

08

m1328

2392

m1329A

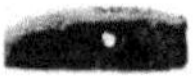

m1329C

2439

m1330

14

09

m1331a

23

03

m1332

m1333

143

4

m1334a

2170

m1335a

2072

m1336a

251

5

m1337

20

55

m1338a

202

0

m1339

2025

m1340

2369

m1341

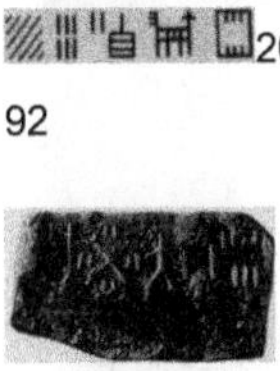

20

92

m1342a

1393

m1343

1433

m1344

2315

m1346a

m1349B

m1349A

m1350

2599

m1351

2142

m1353

1459

m1354a

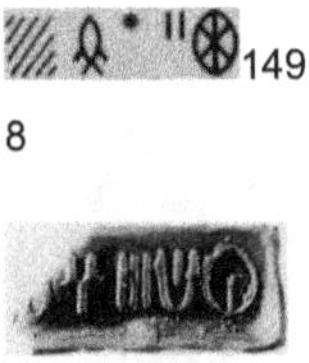

149

8

m1355a

256

8

m1356

m1357

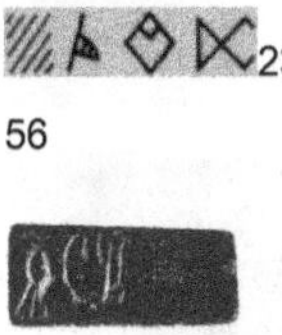

23

56

m1358

m1359

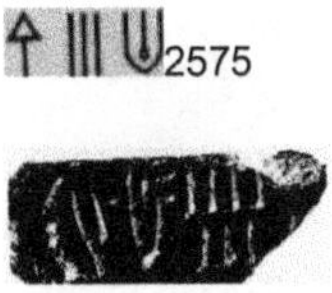

2575

m1360

1442

m1361a

1474

m1362A

m1362C

2230

m1363

2

372

m1364A

m1364C

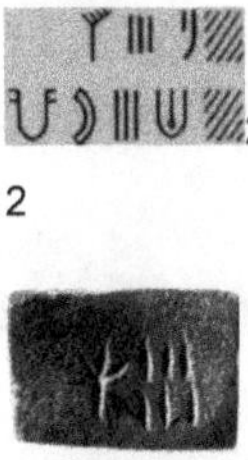

254

2

m1365A

m1365B

2658 Cricket, spider or prawn?

m1366

2

094

m1367a

2661

Two bisons standing face-to-face

m1368

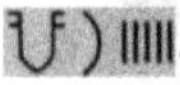1460

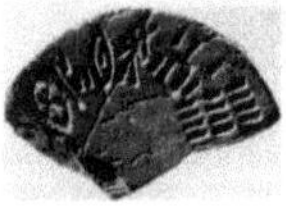

m1369

1478

m1370a

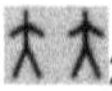2509

Cylinder seal; tree branch

m1371A1

m1371A2

m1372A1

m1372A2

m1373A1

m1373A2

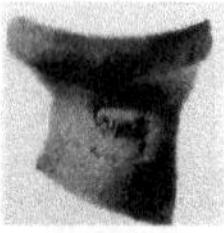

m1374A1

m1374A2

m1375A1

m1375A2

1560

Seal impression on pot

m1376A1

m1376A2

m1378A1

m1378A2

m1379A2

m1380A2

m1381A1

m1381A2

1559

Seal Impression on a pot

m1382A1

m1382A2 Seal impression on a potsherd

3244

m1383

m1384si

m1385A14

m1385A2

m1385A3

m1386si

m1387t

m1388t

2856

m1389t

m1390At

m1390Bt

2868

Pict-74: Bird in flight.

m1391t

2826

m1392t

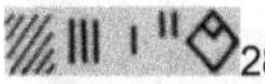2837

m1393t

m1394t

m1395At

m1395Bt

m1396t

m1397At

m1397Bt

m1398t

2807

m1400At

m1400B

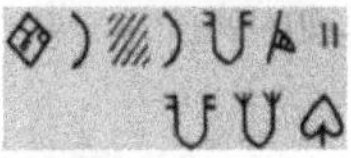

2851

m1401t

2822

m1402At

m1402Bt

m1403At

m1403Bt

m1405At Pict-97: Person standing at the center pointing with his right hand at a bison facing a trough, and with his left hand pointing to the  sign

Obverse: A tiger and a rhinoceros in file.

m1405Bt Pict-48 A tiger and a rhinoceros in file

2841

m1406At

m1406B

2827 Pict-102: Drummer and people vaulting over? An adorant?

m1407At

m1407Bt

m1408At

m1409At

m1409Bt

Serpent (?) entwined around a pillar with capital (?) or ring-stones stacked on a pillar?; the motif is carved in high relief on the reverse side of the inscribed object.

m1410At

m1410Bt

m1411At

m1411Bt

m1412At

m1412Bt

m1413At 

m1413Bt

m1414At

m1414Bt

m1415At

m1415Bt

2825

m1416At

m1416Bt

2818

m1417t

3242

m1418At

m1418Bt

m1419At

m1419Bt

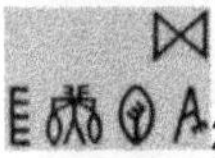
2812

m1420At

2865

m1421At

m1421Bt

m1422At

2845

m1423At

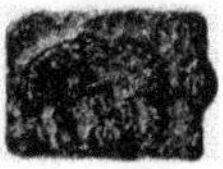

m1423Bt

Elephant shown on both sides of the tablet.

m1424Atc

m1424Btc

3234

m1425At

m1425Bt

m1427At

m1427Bt

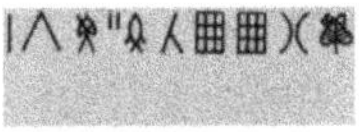

2860

m1428At

m1428Bt

m1428Ct

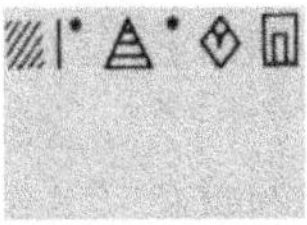

2842

m1426

1621

m1429At

m1429Bt Pict-125: Boat.

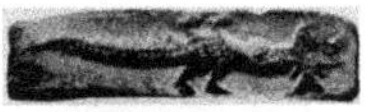

m1429Ct

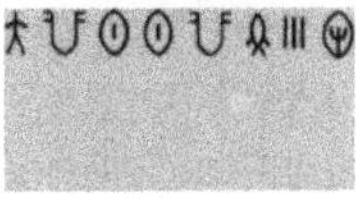

3246 Gharial holding a fish in its jaws.

Pict-100

Person throwing a spear at a buffalo and placing one foot on the head of the buffalo.

2279

m1430Bt

m1430C

m1430At Pict-101: Person throwing a spear at a buffalo and placing one foot on its head; three persons standing

near a tree at the center.

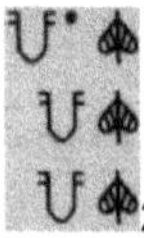
2819

Pict-60: Composite animal with the body of an ox and three heads [one each of one-horned bull (looking forward), antelope (looking backward) and bison (looking downwards)] at right; a goat standing on its hindlegs and browsing from a tree at the center.

m1431A

m1431B

m1431C

m1431E

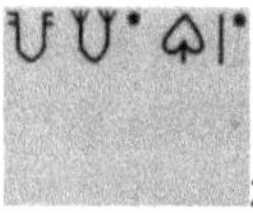
280

5 Row of animals in file (a one-horned bull, an elephant and a rhinoceros from right); a gharial with a fish held in its jaw above the animals; a bird (?) at right. Pict-116: From R.—a person holding a vessel; a woman with a platter (?); a kneeling person with a staff in his hands facing the woman; a goat with its forelegs on a platform under a tree. [Or, two antelopes flanking a tree on a platform, with one antelope looking backwards?]

m1432At

m1432Bt

m1432Ct

m1433At

m1433Bt

m1433Ct

m1436it

m1438it

m1439it

3132

m1440 it

2374

m1441it

m1442it

m1443it

3213

m1444Ait

m1444Bit

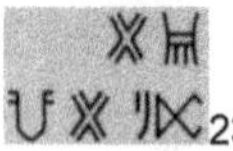
2339

m1445Ait

m1445Bit

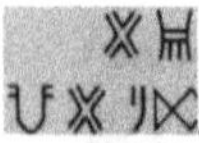
2505

m1447Ait

m1448Act

m1448Bct

m1449Act

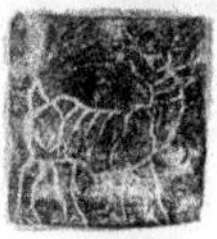

m1449Bct (obverse of inscription) Incised copper tablet (two sides) Markhor with head turned backwards

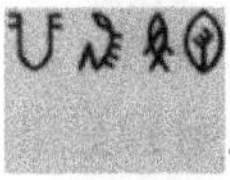

1801

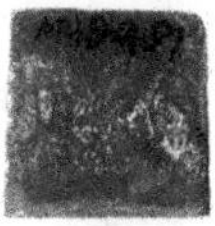

m1450Act

m1450Bct

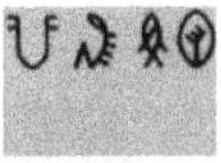

1701

m1451Act

m1451Bct

m1452Act

m1452Bct

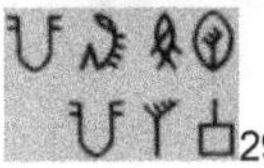

2912

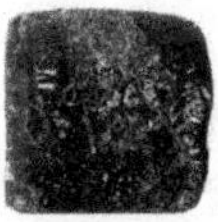

m1453Act

m1453Bct

m1456Act

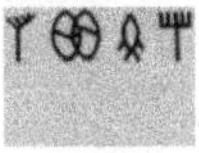

1805

m1457Act

m1457Bct

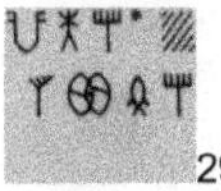

2904

Pict-124: Endless knot motif.

m1458Act

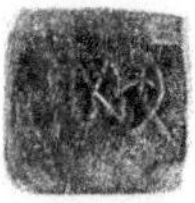

m1461Act

m1462Act

m1463ABct

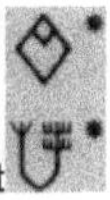

2919

m1465Act

2921

m1470Act

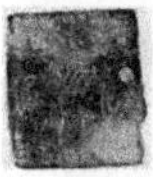

m1472Bct

m1474Act

m1474Bct

m1475Act

m1475Bct

m1476Bct

m1477Act

m1477Bct

m1482Act

m1482Bct

m1483Act

m1483Bct

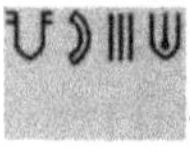

m1484Act

m1484Bct

m1485Bct

m1486Act

m1486Bct

1711

Incised copper tablets.Elephant

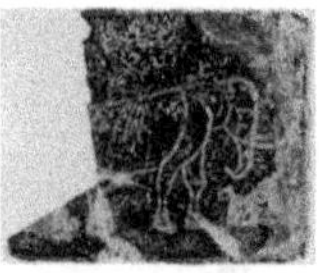

m1488Bct

m1491Act

m1491Bct

m1492Act

m1492Bct

m1493Bct

m1494

1706

Hare

Pict-42

m1497Act

m1498Act

m1498Bct

2917

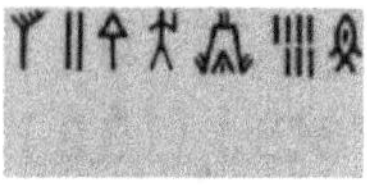

1803

Pict-30

1804

Pict-39 Ox-antelope with a long tail; a trough in front.

m1501Bct

m1502Bct

m1503Act

m1503Bct

m1505Act

m1505Bct

m1506Act

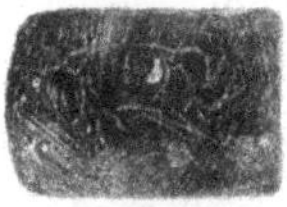

m1506Bct

m1508Act

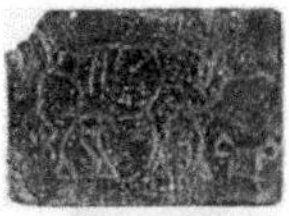

m1508Bct

170

8

m1511Act

m1511Bct

m1512Act

m1512Bct

m1513

171

2

m1514

1715

m1515Act

m1515Bct

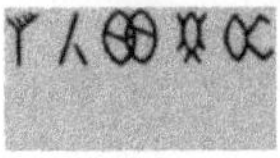

2910

m1516Act

m1516Bct

m1517Act

m1517Bct

m1518

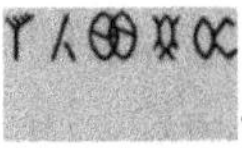

170

9

m1520Act

m1520Bct

290

7

m1521Act

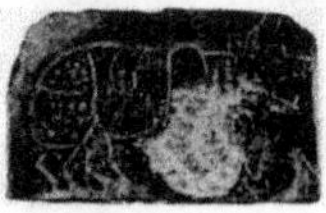

m1521Bct

m1522Act

m1522Bct

m1523Act

m1523Bct

m1524

3396

m1528Act

m1529Act

2920

m1529Bct

m1532Act

m1532Bct

m1534Act

m1534Bct

17
03 Composition:

Two horned heads one at either end of the body. Note the dottings on the thighs which is a unique artistic feature of depicting a rhinoceros (the legs are like those of a rhinoceros?). The body apparently is a combination of two rhinoceroses with heads of two bulls attached on either end of the composite body.

m1535Act

m1535Bct

m1540Act

m1540

m1547Act

1547Bct

m1548A

m1548Bct

m1549Act

m1549Bct

m1563Act

m1563Bct

m1566Bct

m1568Act

m1568Bct

m1569

3333

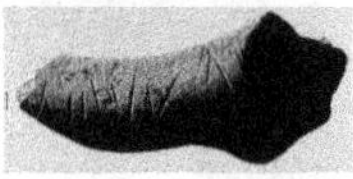

m1575

m1576

m1578

3251

m1591

159

2

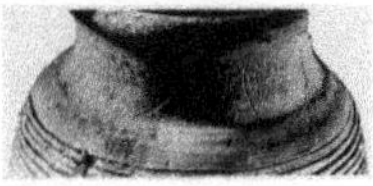

m1597

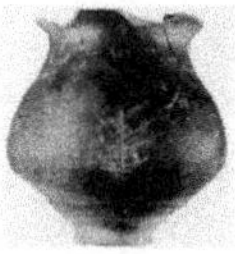

m1598

m1601

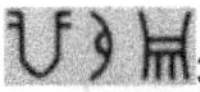
3252

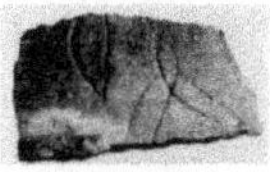

m1603

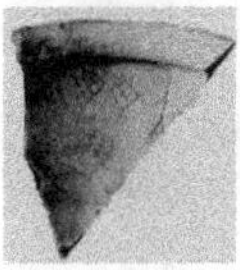

m1609

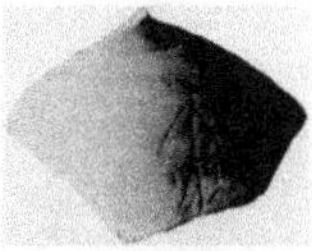

m1611

m1626

3245

m1629bangle

m1630bangle

m1631bangle

m1632bangle

m1633bangle

m1634bangle

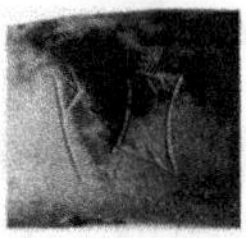

m1635bangle

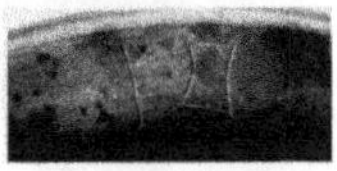

m1636bangle

m1637bangle

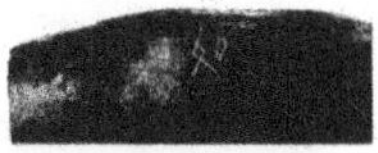

m1638bangle

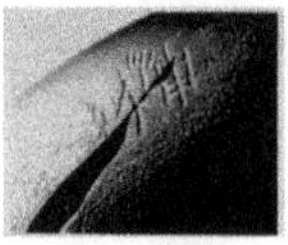

m1639bangle

m1640bangle

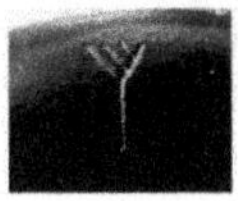

m1641bangle

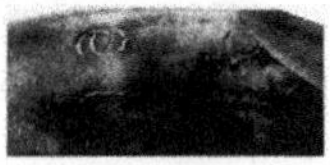

m1643bangle

m1645bangle

m1646bangle

m1647bangle

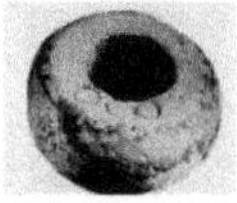

m1648shell

m1649Acone

m1649Bcone

3253

m1650ivory stick

3505

Pict-144: Geometrical pattern.

Pict-141: Geometrical pattern.

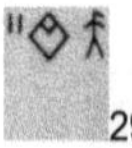
2942

Pict-142: Geometrical pattern.

2943

Ivory or bone rod

Pict-143: Geometrical pattern.Ivory stick

294
8

Ivory rod, ivory plaque with dotted circles. Mohenjodaro. [Musee National De Arts Asiatiques Guimet, 1988-1989, *Les cites oubliees de l'Indus Archeologie du Pakistan.*]

m1652A ivory stick

m1653 ivory plaque

1905

m1654A ivory cube

m1654B ivory cube

m1654D ivory cube

m1655faience ornament

m1656 steatite ornament

m1657A steatite

m1657B steatite

m1658AB etched bead

m1658

2952

Etched Bead

m1659 bangle

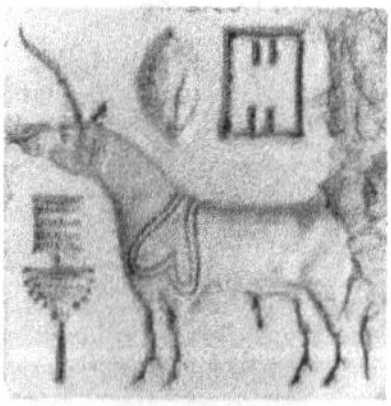
m1660

m1661a

m1662

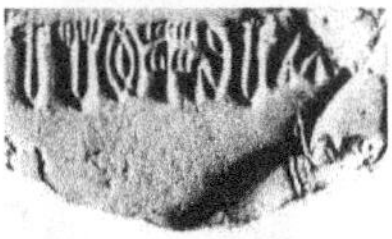
m1663a

m1664a

m1665a

m1666a

m1667

m1668a

m1669a

m1670a

m1671a

m1672

m1673a

m1674a

m1675a

m1676a

m1677a

m1678a

m1679a

m1680a

m1681a

m1682a

m1683a

m1684a

m1685a

m1686a

m1687a

m1688a

m1689a

m1690a

m1691a

m1692a

m1693a

m1694a

m1695a

m1696a

m1697

m1698

m1699a

m1700a

m1701a

m1702a

m1703a

m17054

m1705a

m1706a

m1707a

m1708a

m1709a

m1710a

m1711a

m1712a

m1713a

m1714a

m1715a

m1716a

m1717a

m1718

m1719a

m1720

m1721

m1722a

m1723a

m1724a

m1725a

m1726a

m1727

m1728a

m1729a

m1730a

m1731a

m1732

m1733a

m1734

m1735

m1736a

m1737a

m1738

m1739a

m1740

m1741a

m1742

m1743

m17441

m1745a

m1746

m1747a

m1748

m1749a

m1750a

m1751a

m1752a

m1753a

m1754a

m1755a

m1756a

m1757a

m1758a

m1759a

m1760

m1761a

m1762a

m1763a

m1764a

m1765

m1766a

m1767

m1768a

m1769a

m1770a

m1771a

m1772a

m1773

m1774a

m1775a

m1776

m1777a

m1778

m1779a

m1780a

m1781a

m1782

m1783a

m1784a

m1785a

m1786a

m1787a

m1788a

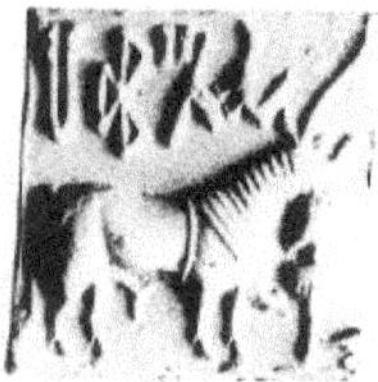
m1789a

m1790a

m1791a

m1792a

m1793a

m1794

m1795a

m1796a

m1797

m1798a

m1799

m1800

m1801a

m1802

m1803a

m1804a

m1805a

m1806a

m1807a

m1808a

m1809a

m1810a

m1811a

m1812a

m1813a

m1814

m1815a

m1816a

m1817a

m1818

m1819

m1820

m1821a

m1822a

m1823

m1824a

m1825a

m1826

m1827

m1828a

m1829a

m1830

m1831a

m1832a

m1833a

m1834a

m1835a

m1836

m1837a

m1838a

m1839a

m1840

m1841a

m1842a

m1843a

m1844

m1845a

m1846a

m1847a

m1848

m1849

m1850a

m1851

m1852

m1853a

m1854a

m1855a

m1856a

m1857

m1858

m1860a

m1863a

m1864

m1865a

m1866

m1868a

m1869

m1872a

m1876a

m1877

m1878a

m1879a

m1880a

m1881

m1882

m1883

m1884a

m1885a

m1886a

m1887

m1888a

m1889

m1890

m1891a

m1892a

m1893

m1894

m1895a

m1896a

m1897

m1898a

m1899a

m1900a

m1901

m1092a

m1903a

m1904a

m1905a

m1906

m1907a

m1909

m1910

m1911a

m1912

m1912

m1913

m1914

m1915a

m1916a

m1917

m1918a

m1919

m1920a

m1921a

m1922a

m1923a

m1923c

m1923d

m1923e

m1927a

m1927b

m1928a

m1928b

m1930A

m1930B

m1931

m1932

m1933

m1934a

m1935

m1936

1937

m1938

m1939a

m1940

m1941a

m1942a

m1943a

m1944

m1945a

m1946

m1947a

m1948

m1950

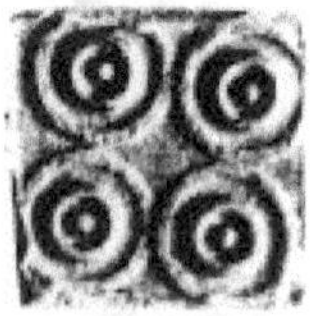

m1951a

m1953a

m1954a

m1955a

m1956a

m1957

m1958

m1959

m1960

m1961

m1962a

m1963a

m1964a

m1965a

m1966

m1967a

m1968A+C

m1969
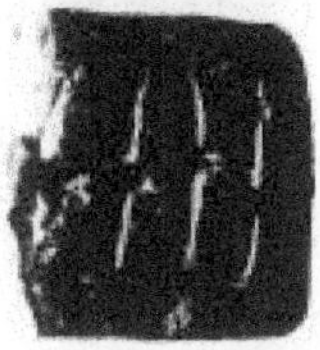
m1970

m1971a

m1972a

m1973a

m1974a

m1975a

m1976

m1977a

m1978a

m1979a

m1980

m1981a

m1982a

m1983a

m1984a

m1985a

m1986a

m1987a

m1988a

m1989a

m1989b

m1990a

m1990b

m1991a
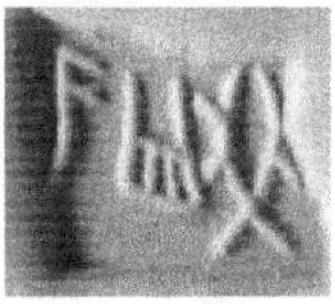

m1992a

m1993a

m1994A

m1995A
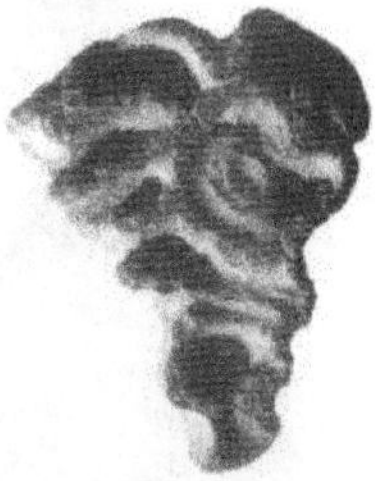
m1996A
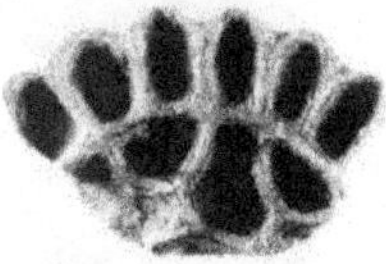
m1997A
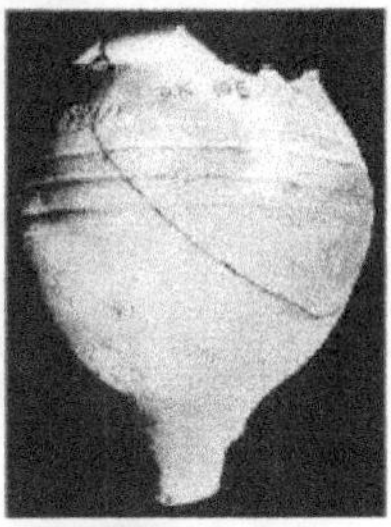
m1998A1

m1998A2

m1999A1

m1999A2

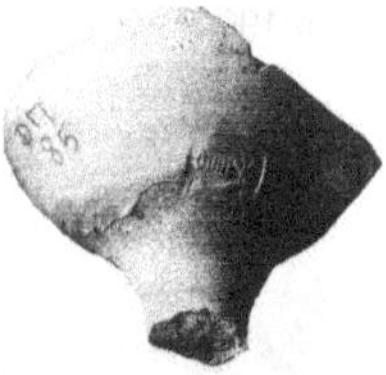

m2000A1

m2000A2

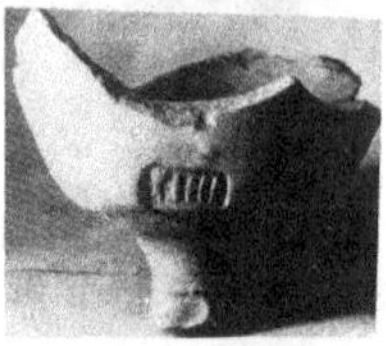

m2001A1

m2001A2

m2002

m2003

m2004

m2005

m2006

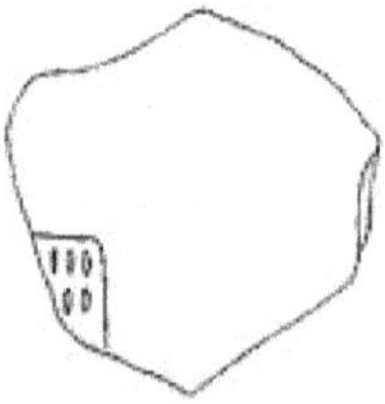

m2007

m2008

m2008B

m2009A

m2009B

m2010A

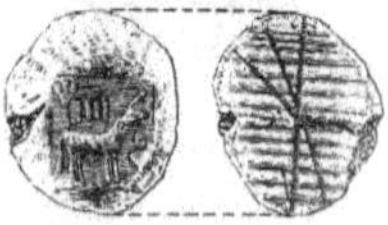

m2010AB

m2011A

m2012A

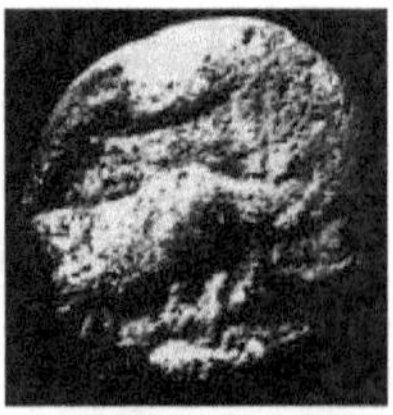

m2013B

m2014A

m2014B

m2015A

m2015B

m2016A

m2017A

m2017B

m2018A

m2018B

m2019A

m2019B

m2020A

m2020B

m2021A

m2021B

m2022A

m2024a
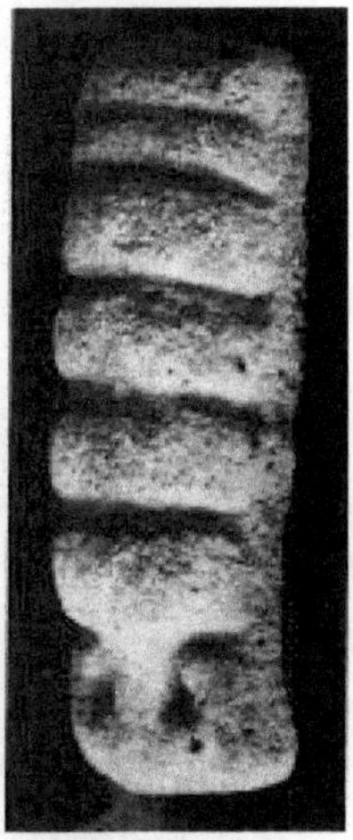
m2025B
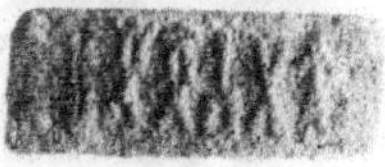
m2026A

m2026B

m2027A

m2027B

m2028A

m2028C

m2029A4

m2029B

m2029B1

m2030A

m2030B

m2032A

m2033A

m20333B

m2033C

m2034c

m2035A

m2035B
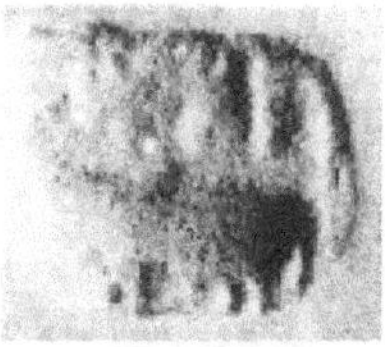
m2035d

m2036A

m2036F

m2037A

m2038F

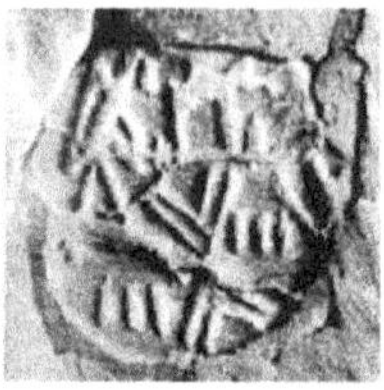
m2039a

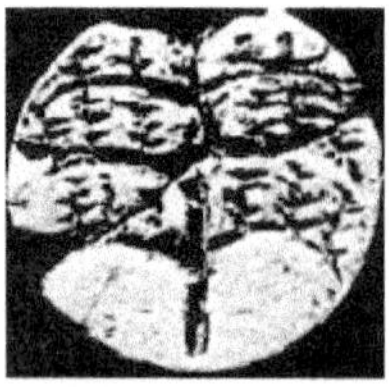
m2039B

m2040a

m2040b

m2041a

m2041b

m2042A

m2042B

m2044B

m2045A

m2045B

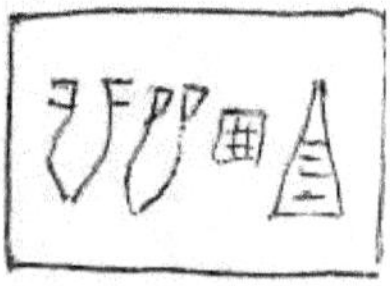
m2046A

m2046B

m2047A

m2047B

m2048A

m2048B

m2049A

m2049B

m2050A

m2050B

m2053A

m2053B

m2054A

m2054B

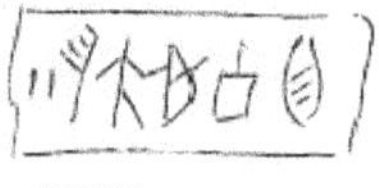
m2055A

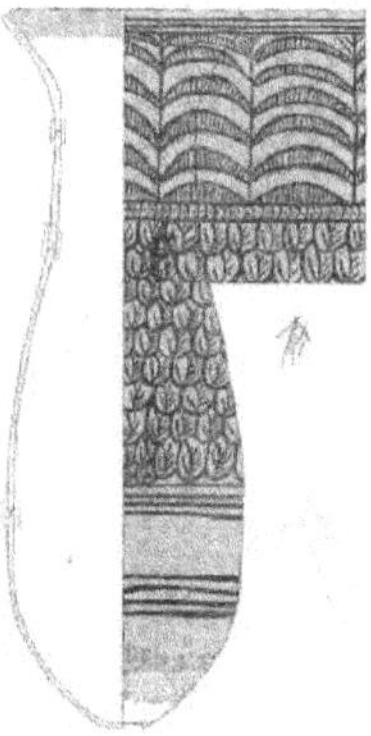
m2059A

m2060A

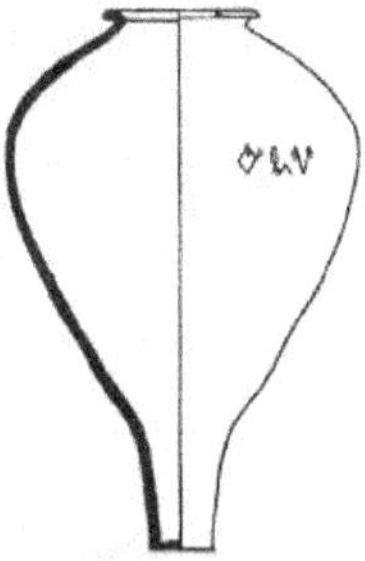
m2060A1+2

m2060b

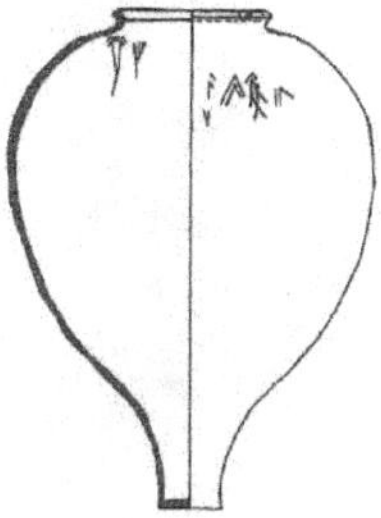

m2061A1+2

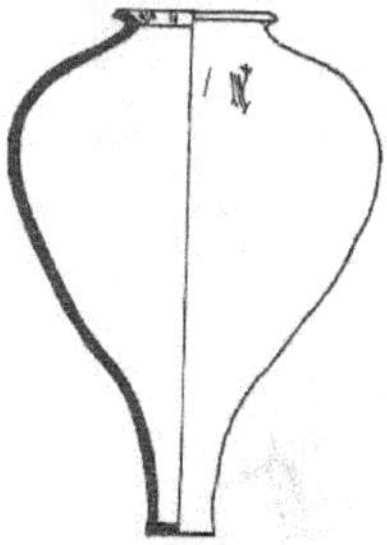

m2062A1+2

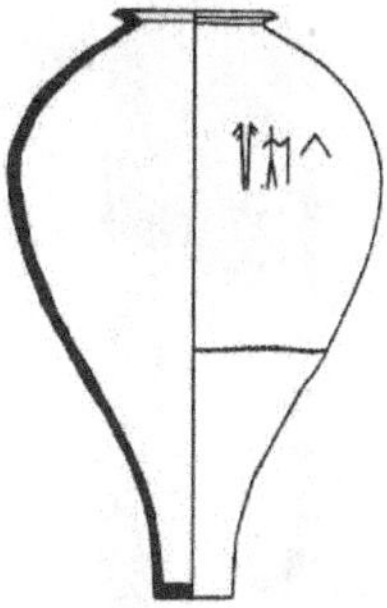

m2063

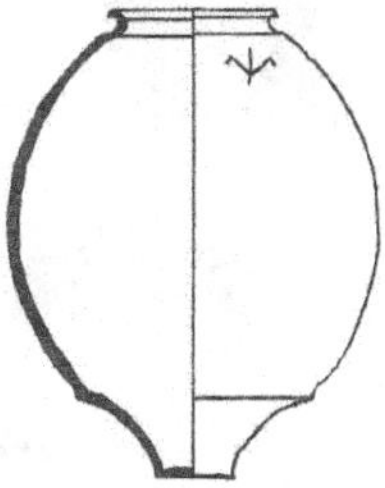

m2065

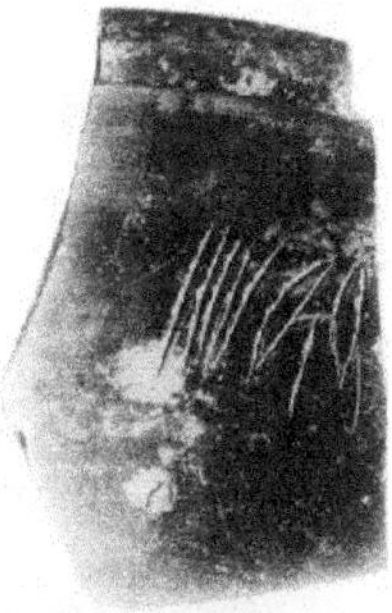

m2065

m2078

m2079

m2080

m2086

m2089A

m2089BC

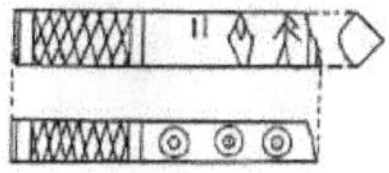

m2090

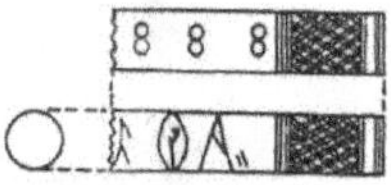

m2091

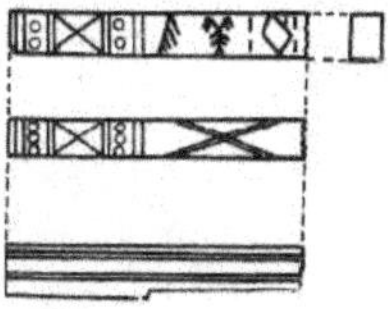

m2092

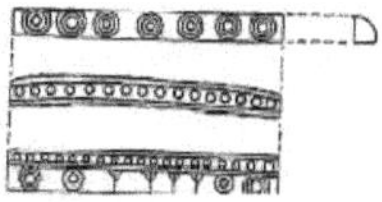

m2093

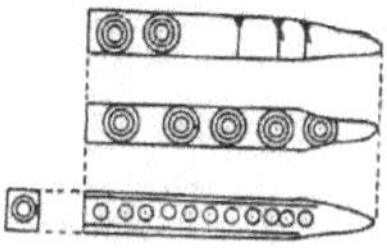

m2094

m2094A

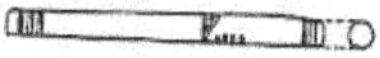

m2095

m2096

m2097a

m2098a

m2099

m2102a

m2103a

m2104a

m2105

m2106D

m2107a

m2108a

m2109a

m2110

m2111

m2112a

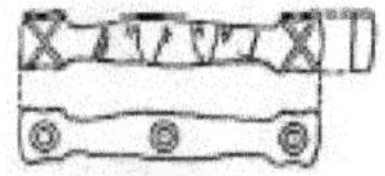

m2113ABD

m2114

m2115

m2116

m2118a

m2118B

m2121A

m2121B

m2123

m2124

m2125

m2125A1

m2128A1

m2129A1

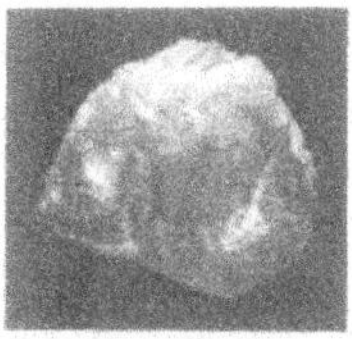

M-2131 A

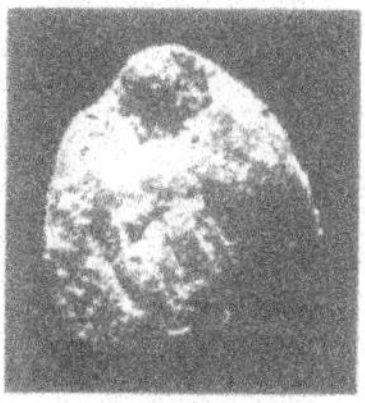

M-2131 B

Photograph from ASI: Sindh series Photo archive of ASI, Janpath, New Delhi. Si. 5:6639, 5:6640. Rattle? Bulla?

Mohenjodaro Texts either not illustrated or not linked with inscribed objects:

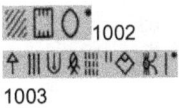

1002

1003

1020

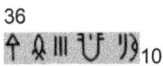

10
36

10
41

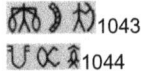

1043

1044

1045

1049

1053

1055

1065

1070

1072

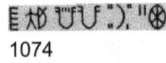

1074

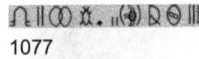

1077

1079

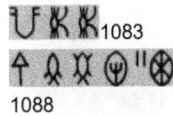

1083

1088

1094

1101

1103

1106

1116

111
7

112
5

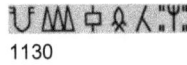

1130

1429

m1651Aivory stick

m1651D

m1651F

2947

1132

1133

1134

1136

1137

1141

1142

115
4

1157

1159

1162

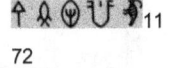

11
72

1173

1174

11
79

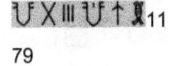

11
83

1190

1198

1199

1200

1201

1207

1209

1212

1213

1215

1217

1220

1225

1226

1229

1231

1235

1237

1243

1244

1246

1248

1253

1254

1255

1257

1260

1261

1266

1269

1270

1272

1273

1274

1278

1279

1285

1286

1289

1305

1314

1318

1320

1323

1330

zebu bull

1338

1345

1346

1347

1350

1365

1366

1372

1407

1411

1419

1420

1424

1425

1427

1435

1436

1441

1448

1451

1453

1457

1467

1468

1480

1484

1486

1490

1491

1527

1529

1530

1531

1532

1533

1538

1541

1549

1550

1554

1558

1561

1563

1602

1604

1609

1610
1611
1613
1616
16
22
1628
1704
1707
18
02
1806
1813
1902
1903
2005
2007
20
23
2027

2035
2038
2039
2042
2049
2050
2051
2056
2061
2068
2073
2079
2080
2107
2109
2111
2112
2119
2125
2126
213
0
2136

2139
2141
21
45
2147
2153
2154
21
57
2164
2186
219
0
2191
2196
2205
2214
2220
2224
2231
2232
2236
2244
22
46
22
52

2269
2270
22
75
22
77
2278
2280
2283
22
92
2293
2294
2296
2310
2322
232
6
2327
2328
2334
2338
2342
23
44
2349
2377
2379

2380
2385
2389
2402
2402
2414
2417
2418
2427
2434
2436
2437
2443
2456
2457
2465
2466
2468
2469
2478
2480
2482
2489
2491
2492
2498
2499
2506
2508
2512
2514
2516
2523
2525
2526
2528
2532
2538
2539
2540
2541
2551
2552
2556
2560
2572
2580
2581
2583
2587
2588
2592
2596
2598
2600
2601
2602
2605
2608
2609
2611
2612
2613
2614
2618
2620
2632
2633
2636
2638
2639
2662
2664
2667
2683
2684
2685

2692

2693

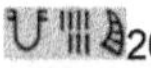
2695

2700

2705

2706

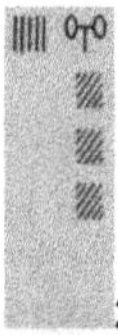
2808

2814

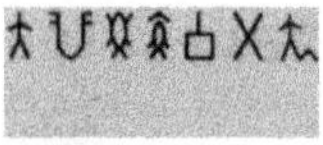
2820

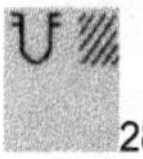
2824

2831

2839

2849

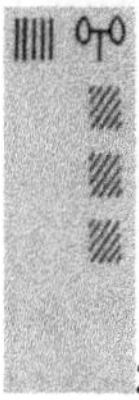
2857

2858

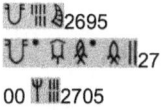

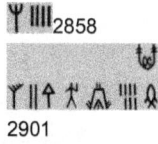

2901
Incised copper tablet

2903 Incised copper tablet

2911 Incised copper tablets. Markhor.

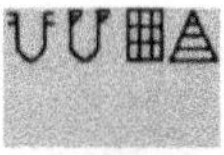
2915

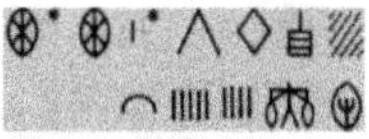
2923
Inscribed bronze implement (MIC Plate CXXVI-2)

2924
Inscribed bronze implement (MIC Plate CXXVI-3)

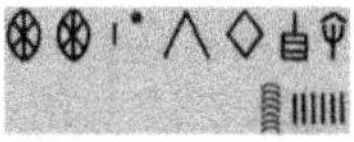
2925
Inscribed bronze implement (MIC Plate CXXVI-5)

2926
Inscribed bronze implement (MIC Plate CXXVII-1)

2928
Inscribed bronze implement (MIC Plate CXXXIII-1)

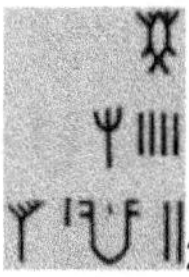
2929
Incised on pottery

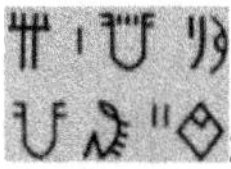
2930
Graffiti on pottery

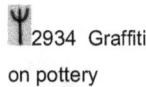

2931 Graffiti on pottery

2934 Graffiti on pottery

2935
Graffiti on pottery

2936 Graffiti on pottery

2937
Seal impression on pot

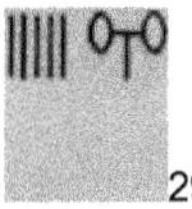
2938Mohenjodaro, Pottery graffiti. Boat.

2940 Ivory or bone rod

2941 Ivory or bone rod Geometrical patterns followed by inscription.

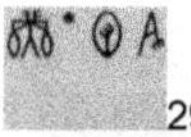
2944
Ivory or bone rod

2945 Ivory or bone rod

2947

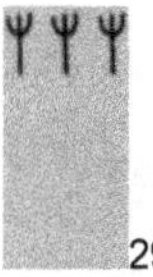
2949 Dotted circles

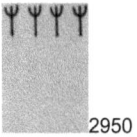

2950

2951

3001

3002

3010

3016

3019

3021

3023

3024

3035

3038

3042

3044

3051

3052

3056

3063

3064

3067

3069

3080

3090

3094

3096

3098

3099

3114

3123

31
51

3153

3154

3155

31
56

3162

3165

3
202

3203

3
206

3207

3217

3218

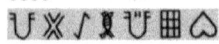

3222

3226

3238

3307

3309

3310

3318

33
25

3326

3328

3343

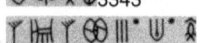

3354

33
62

3367

337
4

3376

3385

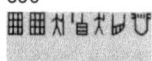

338
8

3
390

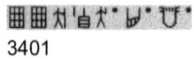

3
393

339
5

3401

3405

35
01

3502

350
3

3504

3506

350
7

3508

350
9

3510

3511

3512

3513

Nindowari-damb01

Squirrel sign

Nindowari-
damb02

Nindowari-
damb03

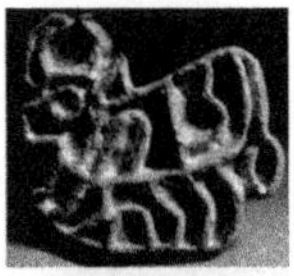

Nausharo01

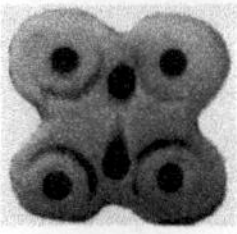

Nausharo02

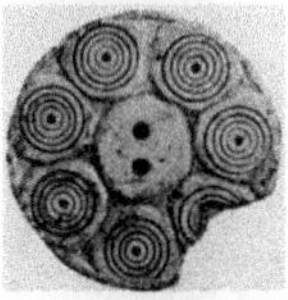

Nausharo03

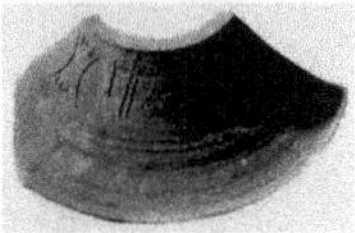

Nausharo04

Nausharo05

Nausharo06

Nausharo07

Nausharo08

Nausharo09

Nausharo10

Naro-Waro-
dharo01

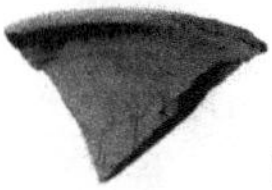

N
aro-Waro-
dharo02

Naro-Waro-
dharo03

Pabumath

Prabhas Patan
(Somnath) 1A

Prabhas Patan
(Somnath)1B

Pirak1

Pirak12

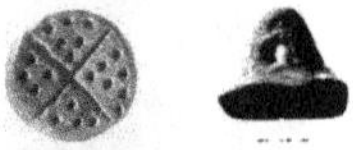

Pirak13

Pirak15

Pirak16

Pirak17

Pirak18

Pirak18A

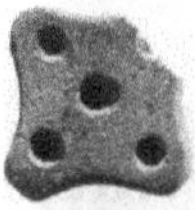

Pirak19

Pirak2

Pirak20

Pirak24

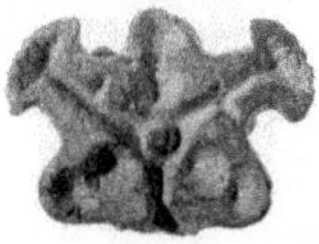

Pirak26Ac

Pirak27

Pirak28

Pirak35

Pirak38

Pirak3 post-harappan

Pirak40

Pirak4

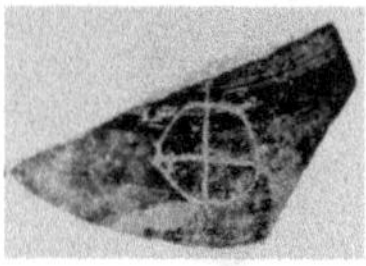

Rangpur

Rakhigarhi1

Rakhigarhi 2

9111

Rakhigarhi 65

Rahman-dheri01A

Rahman-dheri01B

Rahman-dheri120

Rahman-dheri126

Rahman-dheri127

Rahman-dheri150

Rahman-dheri153

Rahman-dheri156

Rahman-dheri158

Rahman-dheri216

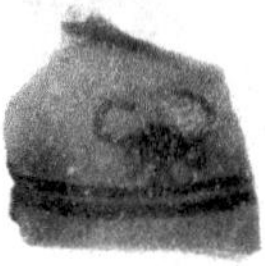

Rahman-dheri241

Rahman-dheri242

Rahman-dheri243

Rahman-dheri254

Rahman-dheri255

Rahman-dheri257

Rahman-dheri258

Rahman-dheri259

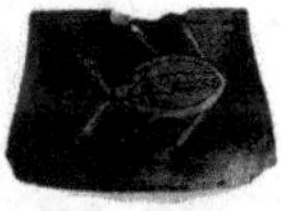

Rahman-dheri260

Rahman-dheri90

Rahman-dheri92

Rohira1

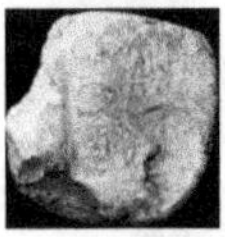

Rohira2

Rojdi

9041

9042

Rupar1A

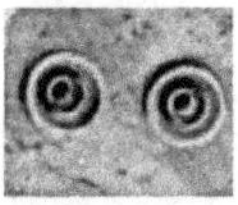

Rupar1B

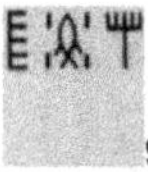

9021

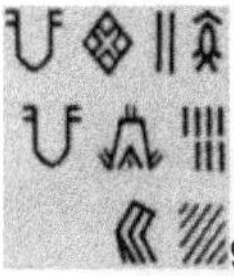

9022

Shahi-tump

Sibri-damb01A

Sibri-damb01B

Sibri-damb02a

Sibri-damb02E

Sibri-damb03a

sibri cylinder seal zebu

Surkotada1

9091

Surkotada 2

9092

Surkotada3c

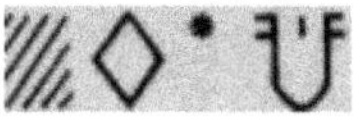

9093

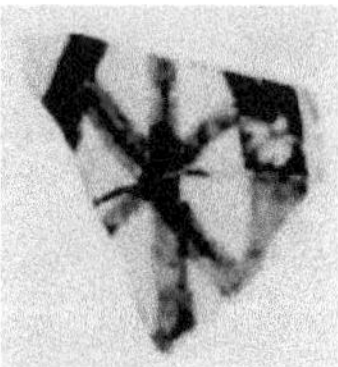

Surkotada 4

9094

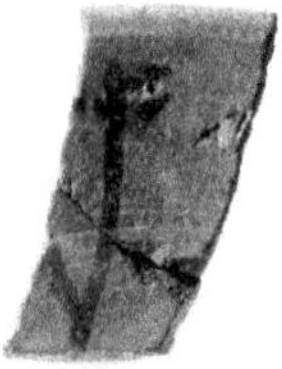

Surkotada 6

9095

Surkotada 7

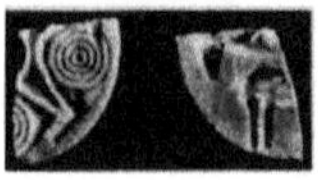

Tarkhanewala-dera1AB

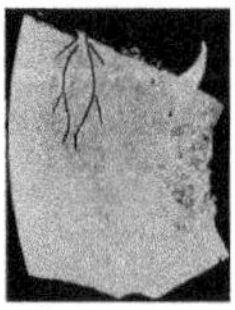

Tarkhanewala-dera 3

9031

Tarakai Qila01A

Tarakai Qila01B

Tarakai Qila02

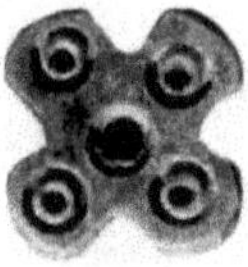

Tarakai Qila03

Tarakai Qila04

Tarakai Qila06

(provenance) unkn01

Lakhonjodaro

unkn02

unkn03

unkn04 unkn05A unkn06

Seau I'nde. Musee des Arts Asiatique, Guimet, France

Mohenjo-daro. Copper tablet DK 11307 (SC 63.10/262).

Mohenjodaro; limestone; Mackay, 1938, p. 344, Pl. LXXXIX:376.

Mohenjodaro; Pale yellow enstatite; Mackay 1938, pp. 344-5; Pl. XCVI:488; Collon, 1987, Fig. 607.

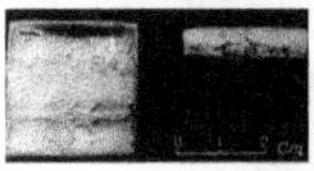

Rakhigarhi: Cylinder Seal (ASI), Lizard or gharial?

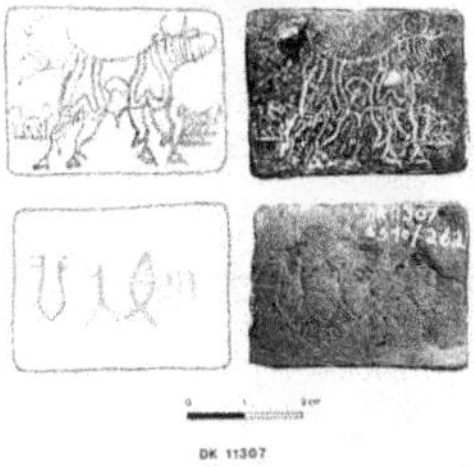

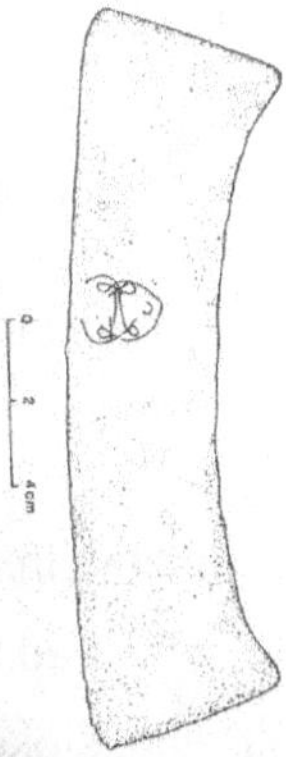

Rojdi. Ax-head or knife of copper, 17.4 cm. long (After Possehl and Raval 1989: 162, fig. 77

 m0355  2654

 m0359  2325

 m0369  2537

 m0391  310

Bibliography

Boas, Franz. 1917. Introduction. International Journal of American Linguistics. (Reprinted: Boas, Franz. 1940.Race, language, and culture, 199-210. New York: The Free Press.)

1920. The classification of American languages. American Anthropologist 22.367-76. (Reprinted: Boas, Franz. 1940. Race, language, and culture, 211-8. New York: The Free Press.

1929. The classification of American Indian languages. Language 5.1-7

Campbell, 1997,.American Indian languages: the historical linguistics of Native America. Oxford: Oxford University Press, 62-6

Campbell, Lyle, 2006 Areal linguistics: a closer scrutiny. In: Linguistic Areas: Convergence in Historical and Typological Perspective, ed.by Yaron Matras April McMahon, and Nigel Vincent, 1-31.Houndmills, Basingstoke, Hampshire: Palgrave Macmillan

Campbell, Lyle, 2006, Areal linguistics. In: Keith Brown (ed.), 2006, Encylopaedia of Languages and Linguistics, 2nd edn., Oxford, Elsevier, pp. 454-460

Campbell, Lyle, and Marianne Mithun. 1979. North American Indian historical linguistics in current perspective. The Languages of Native America: an Historical and Comparative Assessment, ed. by L. Campbell and Marianne Mithun, 3-69. Austin: University of Texas Press

CDIAL Comparative Dictionary of Indo-Aryan Languages

Dales, George F., Jr. 1967, South Asia's earliest writing – still undeciphered, Expedition 9 (2): 30-37

Darnell, Regna and Joel Sherzer. 1971. Areal linguistic studies in North America: a historical perspective.International Journal of American Linguistics 37.20-8

DEDR Dravidian Etymological Dictionary

Durante, Silvio, 1979,"Marine Shells from Balakot, Shahr-i Sokhta and Tepe Yahya: Their Significance for Trade Technology in Ancient Indo-Iran." In South Asian Archaeology 1977, Naples.

Emeneau, MB, 1956, India as a linguistic area, Language 32, 1956, 3-16.

Farmer, Steve, Richard Sproat, and Michael Witzel, 2004, The collapse of the Indusscript thesis: The myth of a literate Harappan Civilization. Electronic Journal of Vedic Studies 11 (2): 19–57

Gould, S.J., 2003, I have landed. Splashes and reflections in natural history, London.

Hunter, G.R., 1934, Script of Harappa and Mohenjodaro and its connection with other Scripts/G.R. Hunter.-London, p. 126

Jakobson, Roman, 1949 (1936), Sur la théorie des affinities phonologiques entre les langues. Actes du quatrieme congresinternational de linguists (tenu a Copenhague du 27 août 1 Septembre, 1936), 48-58. (Reprinted, 1949, as an appendix to: Principes de phonologie, by N. S. Troubetzkoy, 351-65. Paris: Klincksieck.)

1944. Franz Boas' approach to language. International Journal of American Linguistics 10.188-95

Kalyanaraman, S., 1988, *Indus Script: A bibliography*, Manila.

Kalyanaraman, S., 1992, Indian Lexicon, an etymological dictionary of south Asian languages. http://www.scribd.com/doc/2232617/lexicon (ebook)

Kalyanaraman, S., 2008, Sarasvati–Vedic river and Hindu civilization, Chennai, Sarasvati Research and Education Trust (ISBN 978-81-901126-1-1) http://www.scribd.com/doc/7734436/Sarasvati-Book (ebook)

Kalyanaraman, S., 2010, Indus Script Cipher – Hieroglyphs of Indian linguistic area (ISBN 978-0982897102)

Kenoyer, J. M. 1997 Trade and technology of the Indus Valley: new insights from Harappa, Pakistan. World Archaeology 29(2): 262-280.

Kenoyer, J. M. and R. H. Meadow 1999 Harappa: New Discoveries on its origins and growth. Lahore Museum Bulletin XII(1): 1-12.

Kharakwal, J.S., Y.S. Rawat and Toshiki Osada, 2007, Kanmer: A Harappan site in Kachchh, Gujarat, India. PP. 21-137 in: Toshiki Osada (Ed.), Linguistics, archaeology and the human past. (Occasional papers 2.) Kyoto: Indus Project. Research Institute for Humanity and Nature.

P. Kjaerum, 1980, seals of 'dilmun-type' from failaka, kuwait, psas 10: 45-53.

Koskenniemi, Seppo, Asko Parpola and Simo Parpola, 1973, Materials for the study of the Indus script, I. A concordance to the Indus inscriptions, Annales Academiae Scientiaram Fennicae, Ser. B, Tom. 185. xxviii, 528, 55 pp. + errata sheet. Helsinki: [Academia Scientiarum Fennica]

Koskenniemi and Parpola, 1982, A Concordance to the Texts in the Indus Script. Helsinki: [University of Helsinki]. 201pp. Department of Asian and African Studies, University of Helsinki. Research Reports, No. 3., pp. 10-11.

Kuiper, FBJ, 1948, Proto-Munda words in Sanskrit, Amsterdam, 1948

1967, The genesis of a linguistic area, IIJ 10, 1967, 81-102

Lal, B.B., 2002, The Sarasvati flows on: The continuity of Indian culture. New Delhi: Aryan Books International.

Laursen, Steffen Terp, 2010, The westward transmission of Indus Valley sealing technology: origin and development of the 'Gulf Type' seal and other administrative technologies in Early Dilmun, *c.*2100–2000 BC, *Arabian Archaeology and Epigraphy*, November 2010, Volume 21, Issue 2, pp. 96-134.

Mahadevan, Iravatham, 1966, "Towards a grammar of the Indus texts: 'intelligible to the eye, if not to the ears', Tamil Civilization, Vol. 4, Nos. 3 and 4, Tanjore, 1966.

Mahadevan, Iravatham, 1977, The Indus script: texts, concordance and tables. (Memoirs of the Archaeological Survey of India, 77) New Delhi: Archaeological Survey of India.

Mahadevan, Iravatham, 1978, "Recent advances in the study of the Indus script", *Puratattva*, Vol. 9.)

Mahadevan, I., *What do we know about the Indus Script? Neti neti ('Not this nor that'),* Presidential Address, section 5, Indian History Congress, 49th Session, Dharwar, 2-4 November 1988, Madras.

Marshall, J. 1931. Mohenjodaro and the Indus Civilization. Vol. I, II text, Vol. III plates. London: A. Probsthain

Masica, CP, 1971, Defining a Linguistic area. South Asia. Chicago: The University of Chicago Press.

Meadow, R. H., J. M. Kenoyer and R. P. Wright 1997 Harappa Archaeological Research Project: Harappa Excavations 1997, Report submitted to the Director General of Archaeology and Museums, Government of Pakistan, Karachi.

Meadow, Richard and Jonathan Mark Kenoyer, 1997, Excavations at Harappa 1994-1995: new perspectives on the Indus script, craft activities, and city organization, in: Raymond Allchin and Bridget Allchin, 1997, *South Asian Archaeology 1995*, Oxford and IBH Publishing, pp. 157-163.

Meadow, R. H., J. M. Kenoyer and R. P. Wright 1998 Harappa Archaeological Research Project: Harappa Excavations 1998, Report submitted to the Director General of Archaeology and Museums, Government of Pakistan, Karachi.

Meadow, R. H., J. M. Kenoyer and R. P. Wright 1999 Harappa Archaeological Research Project: Harappa Excavations 1999, Report submitted to the Director General of Archaeology and Museums, Government of Pakistan, Karachi.

Meadow, R. H., J. M. Kenoyer and R. P. Wright 2000 Harappa Archaeological Research Project: Harappa Excavations 2000, Report submitted to the Director General of Archaeology and Museums, Government of Pakistan, Karachi.

Meadow, R. H. and J. M. Kenoyer 2001 Harappa Excavations 1998-1999: New evidence for the development and manifestation of the Harappan phenomenon. In South Asian Archaeology 1999, edited by K. R. van Kooij and E. M. Raven, pp. in press. Leiden.

Mughal, M. R. 1990 Further Evidence of the Early Harappan Culture in the Greater Indus Valley: 1971-90. South Asian Studies 6: 175-200.

Mughal, M. R., F. Iqbal, M. A. K. Khan and M. Hassan 1996 Archaeological Sites and Monuments in Punjab: Preliminary report of Explorations: 1992-1996. Pakistan Archaeology 29: 1-474.

Parpola, Asko, 1994, Deciphering the Indus Script, Cambridge University Press, Cambridge, U.K. [Note: A comprehensive bibliography appears.]

Possehl, Gregory L., 1996, The Indus Age: The Writing System, Philadelphia: University of Pennsylvania Press.

Possehl, Gregory and Gullapalli, Praveena,1999, 'The Early Iron Age in South Asia'; in Vincent C. Piggott (ed.).The Archaeometallurgy of the Asian Old World; University Museum Monograph, MASCA Research Papers in Science and Archaeology, Volume 16; Pgs. 153-175; The University Museum, University of Pennsylvania; Philadelphia.

M. A. Probst, Alekseev, G. V., A. M. Kondratov, Y. V. Knorozov, I. K. Fedorova, and B. Y. Volchok, 1965, Preliminary report on the investigation of the Proto-Indian Texts. Academy of Sciences U.S.S.R., Soviet Institute of Scientific and Technical Information, Institute of Ethnography, Moscow

Przyludski, J., 1929, Further notes on non-aryan loans in Indo-Aryan in: Bagchi, P. C. (ed.), Pre-Aryan and Pre-Dravidian in Sanskrit. Calcutta : University of Calcutta: 145-149

Rajagopal, Sukumar, Priya Raju, and Sridhar Narayanan, 2009, Illiterate Indus?, Journal of Tamil Studies, December 2009 issue (#76), pp. 69-88, International Institute of Tamil Studies.

Southworth, F., 2005, Linguistic archaeology of South Asia, London, Routledge-Curzon.

Tewari, Rakesh, 2003, The origins of Iron-working in India: New evidence from the Central Ganga Plain and the Eastern Vindhyas, Antiquity, London http://www.antiquity.ac.uk/projgall/tewari298/tewari.pdf

Trubetzkoy 1939, Gedanken über das Indogermanenproblem Acta Linguistica 1.81-9

Vats, M.S., 1940, Excavations at Harappa, Being an Account of Archaeological Excavations at Harappa carried out between the Years 1920-1921 and 1933-34, Delhi, Archaeological Survey of India

Vidale, Massimo, 2007, The collapse melts down: A reply to Farmer, Sproat & Witzel. East and West 57 (1-4): 333-366. http://www.docstoc.com/docs/8916249/Indus-script-decoded-language----Massimo-Vidale/

About the author

Dr. S. Kalyanaraman is Director, Sarasvati Research Center, President, Ramasetu Protection Movement in India and BoD member of World Association for Vedic Studies. His research interests relate to rediscovery of Vedic Sarasvati River, roots of Hindu civilization, decoding of Indus Script, National Water Grid and creation of Indian Ocean Community. He has a Ph.D. in Public Administration from the University of the Philippines. He is a multi-lingual scholar versed in Tamil, Telugu, Kannada, Sanskrit, Hindi. He was a senior financial and IT executive in Asian Development Bank, Manila, Philippines and on Indian Railways. His 18 publications include: Indian Lexicon - a multilingual dictionary for over 25 Indian languages, Sarasvati in 15 volumes, Indian Alchemy - Soma in the Veda, Indus Script Cipher, Rastram, Indian Hieroglyphs, Harosheth Hagoyim, Indian Ocean Community, A Theory for Wealth of Nations, Sagan Finds Sarasvati (A novel). He is a recipient of many awards including Vakankar Award (2000), Shivananda Eminent Citizens' Award (2008) and Dr. Hedgewar Prajna Samman (2008).

Website: http://sites.google.com/site/kalyan97

About the book

Based on corpora of Indus writing and a dictionary for ancient languages of Indian *sprachbund*, the book validates Aristotle's insight on writing systems. Indus writing is composed using symbols of spoken words. The symbols are hieroglyphs of meluhha (mleccha) words spoken by artisans recording the repertoire of stone, mineral and metal workers. The writing results in a set of catalogs of metalworking of bronze age. Evidence of this competence in metallurgy which evolved from 4th millennium BCE of bronze age, is provided in corpora of metalware catalogs and a dictionary of melluhha (mleccha). Indus writing was a principal tool of economic administration for account-keeping by artisan and trader guilds and did not record literature or, history. Some sacred ideas and historical links across interaction areas between India and ancient Near East, may be inferred from the writing.

Index

A

B

C

D

E

F

G

H

I

J

K

L

M

Mackay, 37, 53, 54, 58, 127, 143, 198, 199, 255, 310, 311, 312, 543

Magan, 63, 182

Mahābhārata, 179, 181

markhor, 85, 86, 112, 165, 248, 274, 276

Marshall, 23, 54, 55, 198, 256, 257, 547

Masica, 547

mason, 6, 24, 109, 155, 219, 231, 232, 250, 273, 295

Meadow, 9

Meluhha, 2, 9, 10, 15, 17, 33, 34, 35, 63, 68, 82, 93, 99, 100, 101, 102, 104, 107, 108, 109, 117, 120, 137, 167, 173, 182, 194, 198, 199, 241, 242, 299

merchant, 6, 8, 16, 18, 19, 22, 47, 71, 82, 97, 98, 101, 102, 105, 138, 142, 143, 144, 150, 154, 155, 193, 194, 195, 217, 219, 221, 227, 232, 246, 248, 275

Mesopotamia, 50

metal, 19, 20, 49, 87, 89, 90, 92, 122, 145, 146, 149, 157, 162, 164, 174, 178, 187, 206, 237, 240, 249, 250, 251, 252, 267, 272, 275, 277, 278, 280, 300

metals, 49, 50

metalsmith, 186, 188, 250

miner, 189, 193, 247

mineral, 5, 6, 11, 13, 14, 19, 20, 22, 73, 82, 92, 104, 112, 113, 116, 123, 149, 153, 154, 157, 158, 185, 191, 206, 221, 222, 235, 238, 241, 248, 258, 275, 551

mine-worker, 300

mleccha, 3, 5, 97, 120, 179, 180, 181, 182, 183, 194, 199, 215, 218, 232, 551

monkey, 40, 63, 285

mould, 212

mountain, 42, 67, 70, 71, 72, 82, 83, 90, 106, 148, 216, 217, 218, 266, 270, 285, 297

Muhly, 93

Munda, 22, 87, 89, 109, 116, 118, 142, 144, 147, 163, 175, 177, 183, 188, 194, 223, 224, 546

N

Narmer, 16

native metal, 8, 66, 87, 89, 146, 162, 167, 185, 186, 201, 209, 277

neck, 6, 27, 39, 43, 115, 143, 162, 167, 183, 184, 211, 214, 222, 248, 249, 264, 269, 270, 271, 273, 274, 276, 278, 293, 296, 311, 417, 447, 449, 450, 475, 496

numeral, 178

O

offering, 278

one-horned, 49

ore, 6, 10, 13, 14, 20, 21, 28, 71, 78, 82, 86, 87, 89, 92, 98, 112, 113, 116, 142, 144, 145, 147, 149, 150, 151, 154, 157, 166, 184, 189, 192, 209, 210, 212, 221, 222, 229, 231, 244, 249, 250, 252, 272, 295

oval, 28, 126, 142, 143, 175, 244, 279, 280, 310

overthrow, 210, 212

T

U

End Notes

---

1 Aristotle, *On interpretation*, tr. by E.M. Edghill http://ebooks.adelaide.edu.au/a/aristotle/interpretation/

2 http://huntingtonarchive.osu.edu/resources/downloads/webPresentations/harappanSeals.pdf

3 Hunter, G.R., *JRAS*, 1932, 476

4 http://indusscriptmore.blogspot.com/2011/08/problematic-13-stroke-signs-in-

indus.html

[5] "The earliest (Indus) inscriptions date back to 3500 BC."
http://news.bbc.co.uk/olmedia/330000/audio/_334517_meadow.ram

[6] DT Potts, 1999, The archaeology of Elam: Formation and transformation of an ancient Iranian state, Cambridge University Press.

[7] Corpora of Indus Writing (March 2013)
http://www.scribd.com/doc/130763262/Indus-Writing-Corpora

[8] E. Cortesi, M. Tosi, A. Lazzari, & M. Vidale, 2008, Cultural relationships beyond the Iranian plateau: the Helmand, Baluchistan and the Indus Valley in the 3rd millennium BCE, Paléorient, Vol. 34-2

[9] http://www.persee.fr/web/revues/home/prescript/article/paleo_0153-9345_2008_num_34_2_5254

[10] J.D. Muhly, 1973, *Copper and Tin*, Conn.: Archon., Hamden; Transactions of Connecticut Academy of Arts and Sciences, vol. 43, p. 221f.

[11] Thornton, C.P.; Lamberg-Karlovsky, C.C.; Liezers, M.; Young, S.M.M. (2002). "On pins and needles: tracing the evolution of copper-based alloying at Tepe Yahya, Iran, via ICP-MS analysis of Common-place items.". *Journal of Archaeological Science* **29** (29): 1451–1460

[12] Babu, T.M., 2003 'Advent of the Bronze Age in the Indian Subcontinent.' In P. Craddock and J. Lang (eds). *Mining and Metal Production Through the Ages.* Pp.174-180.London: The British Museum Press.

[13] After fig. in Rakesh Tewari, 2000, The origins of iron-working in India, http://www.archaeologyonline.net/artifacts/iron-ore.html

[14] http://oi.uchicago.edu/OI/IRAQ/dbfiles/objects/14.htm

[15] After Fig. 7 Holly Pittman, 1984, *Art of the Bronze Age: Southeastern Iran, Western Central Asia, and the Indus Valley*, New York, The Metropolitan Museum of Art, pp. 29-30.

[16] http://cdli.ox.ac.uk/wiki/doku.php?id=uruk_mod._warka

[17] http://tc.templejc.edu/dept/Art/ASmith/ARTS1303/arts1303_2StoneAge2Sumer/Ston2Sumpage022.html

[18] *Catalogue des cylinders orient*, Musee du Louvre, vol. I, pl. xxv, fig. 15. See also J. de Morgan, *Prehistoric Man*, p. 261, fig. 171; *Mem. Del. En Perse*, t.ii, p. 129.loc.cit.,John Marshall, 1931, *Mohenjo-daro and the Indus Civilization*, Delh, AES, Repr., 2004, p.385; pp. 424-425 Note: Five cylinder seals hav since been found at Mohenjo-daro and Kalibangan.

[19] Pierre de talc. Louvre, AO 9036. P. Amiet, Bas-relliefs imaginaries de l'Orient ancien, Paris, 1973, p. 94, no. 274…ils proviendrait de Tello, l'ancienne Girsu, une des cites de l'Etat sumerien de Lagash. Musee National De Arts Asiatiques Guimet, 1988-1989, *Les cites oubliees de l'Indus Archeologie du Pakistan.*

[20] Source: Steffen Terp Laursen, 2010, The westward transmission of Indus Valley sealing technology: origin and development of the 'Gulf Type' seal and other administrative technologies in Early Dilmun, *c.*2100–2000 BC, *Arabian Archaeology and Epigraphy*, November 2010, Volume 21, Issue 2, pp. 96-134

[21] http://en.wikipedia.org/wiki/Zu_(mythology)#cite_ref-1

[22] http://etcsl.orinst.ox.ac.uk/cgi-bin/etcsl.cgi?text=t.1.6.3#

[23] J. Black and A. Green, Gods, Demons and Symbols of Ancient Mesopotamia: An Illustrated Dictionary, London: British Museum Press 1992, s.v. "Tablet of Destinies".

[24] Kramer, Samuel Noah (1963). *The Sumerians: their history, culture, and character.* Chicago: The University of Chicago Press.

[25] http://en.wikipedia.org/wiki/Me_(mythology)#cite_ref-5

[26] BSS III,62-104 describes the steps to construct the falcon-shaped vedi.

[27] S.N. Sen and A.K. Baug, The Sulbasutras of Baudhayana, Apastamba, Katyayana and Manava. Indian National Science Academy, New Delhi, India, 1983. George F.W. Thibaut, Mathematics in the Making in Ancient India, KP

Bagchi & Co., Calcutta, Indiia, 1984 (Repr. Of two articles by Thibaut: On the sulvasutras, J. Asiatic Soc. Bengal, 1875 and Baudhayana Sulva Sutram, Pandit, 1874/5-1877.

[28] Subhash Kak, 2003, The vedic religion in ancient Iran and Zarathushtra http://www.archaeologyonline.net/artifacts/Vedic%20Religion%20in%20Ancient%20Iran.pdf

[29] http://rbedrosian.com/imyth.htm

[30] Loc.cit. http://bharatkalyan97.blogspot.com/2011/11/syena-orthography.html http://www.docstoc.com/docs/104571692/simorgh

[31]

http://www.britishmuseum.org/explore/highlights/highlight_image.aspx?image=ps267036.ipg&retpage=18837

[32] cf. Christensen, A.,1932, *Les Kayanides*. Det Kgl. Danske Videnskabernes Sellskab, Hist.-Filos. Meddelelser XIX.2. Copenhagen). cf. S. Kalyanaraman, 2000, Rgvedic Soma as a metallurgical allegory; soma, electrum is deified.

[33] cited in Needham, Joseph, 1985, SCC, Vol. 5, Pt. II, pp.18-21.

[34] Hopkins, AJ, 1967, Alchemy, pp. 103-104.

[35] Needham, Joseph, 1985, Science and Civilization in China, Vol. 5, pt. II, p.45.

[36] Georges-Jean Pinault, 2006, Further links between the Indo-Iranian substratum and the BMAC language in: Bertil Tikkanen & Heinrich Hettrich, eds., 2006, *Themes and tasks in old and middle Indo-Aryan linguistics*, Delhi, Motilal Banarsidass, pp. 167 to 196.

[37] ibid., p.192

[38] Source:

http://books.google.co.in/books?id=rEpF0GY-vn0C&pg=PR2&dq=kadru+story&source=gbs_selected_pages&cad=3#v=onepage&q=kadru%20story&f=false

[39] Angot, Michel, 2001, *L'Inde Classique, Les Belles Lettres*, Paris.

[40] Excerpted from HW Bodewitz, 1990, The Jyotistoma ritual: Jaiminiya Brahmana I, 66-364, Brill, p. 203.

http://www.docstoc.com/docs/96454517/Rgvedic-Soma-as-a-metallurgical-allegory-soma-electrum-is-deified----S-Kalyanaraman-(2000)

[41] Si. Ara Svaminathan, Indira Gandhi National Centre for the Arts, 2000, *Kaanvashatapathabraahmanam*, volume 3, Motilal Banarsidass, Sanskrit text with English translation, IV.6.2.4-5.

[42] AK Coomaraswamy, Rama P. Coomaraswamy, 2004, 'The Myth' in: The essential Ananda K. Coomaraswamy, World Wisdom, Inc., p.267, p. 273.

[43] http://www.asidehraduncircle.in/uttarkashi.html

[44] McCrindle's Ptolemy, p.110

[45] Manusmriti, 10.20.22

[46] Georges-Jean Pinault, 2006, Further links between the Indo-Iranian substratum and the BMAC language in: Bertil Tikkanen & Heinrich Hettrich, eds., 2006, T*hemes and tasks in old and middle Indo-Aryan linguistics*, Delhi, Motilal Banarsidass, p.192.

[47] http://bharatkalyan97.blogspot.com/2011/09/central-asian-seals-seal-impressions.html

[48] Jim Tyson, South West Maritime Archaeological Group http://www.archaeology.org/1005/etc/artifact.html

[49] Shelly Wachsmann, 1988, *Seagoing ships & seamanship in the Bronze Age Levant*, Ed Rachal Foundation Nautical Archaeology Series, p. 303.

[50] Source: http://sondmor.tripod.com/index-7.html

[51] Source: http://sara.theellisschool.org/~shipwreck/artifacts.html

[52] This artwork is currently on display in Gallery 173 Said to be from Amathus, Cyprus. 1865–1872, found in Cyprus by General Luigi Palma di Cesnola;

acquired by the Museum in 1874, purchased from General Luigi Palma di Cesnola http://www.metmuseum.org/collections/search-the-collections/30000008

[53] Cited in Gregory L. Possehl, The Middle Asian Interaction Sphere, *Expedition*, UPenn, p.41.

[54] http://www.penn.museum/documents/publications/expedition/PDFs/49-1/Research%20Notes.pdf

See: S. Kalyanaraman, 2011, Decoding Indus script Susa cylinder seal: Susa-Indus interaction areas. http://www.docstoc.com/docs/102138513/Decoding-Indus-Scipt-Susa-cylinder-seal-Susa-Indus-interaction-areas-(Kalyanaraman-2011)

[55] Gadd 1 (U.7683; BM 120573); image of bison and cuneiform inscription; length 2.7, width 2.4, ht. 1.1 cm. cf. Gadd, PBA 18 (1932), pp. 5-6, pl. I, no.1; Mitchell 1986: 280-1 no.7 and fig. 111; Parpola, 1994, p. 131.

[56] Gregory L. Possehl,Shu-ilishu's cylinder seal, Expedition, Vol. 48, Number 1, pp. 42-3. http://www.penn.museum/documents/publications/expedition/PDFs/48-1/What%20in%20the%20World.pdf

[57]

http://www.archive.org/download/mmoires01franuoft/mmoires01franuoft.pdf Jacques de Morgan, Fouilles à Suse en 1897-1898 et 1898-1899, Mission archéologique en Iran, Mémoires I, 1990

[58] Department des Antiquites Orienteles, Musee du Louvre, Paris.

http://www.louvre.fr/en/oeuvre-notices/statuette-man-carrying-goat

[59] A.Leo Oppenheim, The Seafaring Merchants of Ur, *Journal of the American Oriental Society*, Vol. 74, 1954, pp. 6-17

[60] C.J. Gadd, Seals of ancient Indian style found at Ur, *Proceedings of the British Academy, XVIII*, 1932; Henry Frankfort, Tell Asmar, Khafaje and

Khorsabad, *OIC*, 16, 1933, p. 50, fig. 22.

[61] L. Delaporte, *Musee du Louvre. Catalogues des Cylindres Orientaux...*, vol. I, 1920, pl. 25(15), S.29. P. Amiet, Glyptique susienne, *MDAI*, 43, 1972, vol. II, pl. 153, no. 1643.

[62] Images courtesy: Maurizio Tosi in an international conference in New Delhi, November 2010 organised by Draupati Trust.

[63] Pierre de talc. Louvre, AO 9036. P. Amiet, Bas-reliefs imaginaries de l'Orient ancient, Paris, 1973, p. 94, no. 274...Ils proviendrait de Tello, Pancienne Girsu, une des cites de l'Etat sumerien de Lagash. Musee National De Arts Asiatiques Guimet, 1988-1989, Les cites oubliees de l'Indus Archeologie du Pakistan.

[64] http://www.louvre.fr/en/oeuvre-notices/cylinder-seal-ibni-sharrum

[65]

(http://www.archive.org/download/mmoires01franuoft/mmoires01franuoft.pdf Jacques de Morgan, Fouilles à Suse en 1897-1898 et 1898-1899, Mission archéologique en Iran, Mémoires I, 1990, p.116).

http://wpcontent.answcdn.com/wikipedia/commons/thumb/5/5c/Goatfishes_Louvre_Sb19.jpg/220px-Goatfishes_Louvre_Sb19.jpg Accession Number Sb 19. Excavated by Jacques de Morgan, 1904–1905

Louvre Museum. Department of Oriental Antiquities, Richelieu, ground floor, room 11 H. 9 cm (3 ½ in.), W. 13 cm (5 in.) Accession Number Sb 2834 Excavations of Jacques de Morgan

[66] http://www.penn.museum/documents/publications/expedition/PDFs/40-2/Life.pdf See also: *Expedition* 40:2 (1998), p. 33, fig. 5b

[67] The Toda mund, from, Richard Barron, 1837, "View in India, chiefly among the Nilgiri Hills'. Oil on canvas.

[68] http://www.louvre.fr/en/recherche-globale?f_search_cles=sit+shamshi

[69] http://en.wikipedia.org/wiki/File:Relief_spinner_Louvre_Sb2834.jpg Source: http://ia600406.us.archive.org/29/items/mmoires01franuoft/mmoires01franuoft.pdf After "Kunst." Barthel Hrouda. Editor. *Der Alte Orient, Geschichte und Kultur des alten Vorderasien.* Munchen. C. Bertelsmann. Verlag GmbH. 1991, p. 360.

[70] After "Kunst." Barthel Hrouda. Editor. *Der Alte Orient, Geschichte und Kultur des alten Vorderasien.* Munchen. C. Bertelsmann. Verlag GmbH. 1991, p. 360.

[71] http://www.oznet.net/iran/elamspin.htm

[72] Scheherezade Qassim Hassan, R. Conway Morris, John Baily, Jean During. "Tanbūr", *The New Grove Dictionary of Music and Musicians*, ed. S. Sadie and J. Tyrrell (London: Macmillan, 2001), xxv, pp. 61-62. "روبنت (ای روبمت /روبنط)". Encyclopaedia Islamica

[73] http://www.columbia.edu/itc/mealac/pritchett/00routesdata/0300_0399/earlyguptacoins/samudracoin1.jpg

[74] Roberts, B. W., C. P. Thornton, and V. C. Pigott. 2009. Development of Metallurgy in *Eurasia.Antiquity* 83:1012–1022.

[75] Frame, L. 2010. Metallurgical Investigations at Godin Tepe, Iran, Part I: The Metal Finds. *Journal of Archaeological Science* 37:1700–1715

[76] Moorey, P. R. S. 1994. Ancient Mesopotamian Materials and Industries: The Archaeological Evidence. Oxford/New York: Clarendon Press

[77] De Ryck, I., A. Adriaens, and F. Adams. 2005. An Overview of Mesopotamian Bronze Metallurgy during the 3rd Millennium BC. Journal of Cultural Heritage 6:261–268

[78] Kenoyer, J. M., and H. M.-L. Miller. 1999. Metal Technologies of the Indus Valley Tradition in Pakistan and Western India. In The Archaeometallurgy of the Asian Old World , edited by V. C. Pigott, pp. 107–152. Philadelphia: The University Museum, University of Pennsylvania.; Lamberg-Karlovsky, C. C. 1972. Trade Mechanisms in Indus-Mesopotamian Interrelations. Journal of the American Oriental Society 92:222–229.

[79] Brett Kaufman, 2011, Metallurgy and ecological change in the Ancient Near East, *Backdirt*, pp.87-89 http://www.academia.edu/1989221/Metallurgy_and_Ecological_Change_in_the_Ancient_Near_East.

[80] It is possible that the rosette Egptian hieroglyph on this 'scorpion macehead' of c. 31st cent. was read *kundan.* Ka? http://www.ancient-egypt.org//kings/01/0101_narmer/scorpion_macehead.html

[81] From:Shaika Haya Ali Al Khalifa and Michael Price, 1986, *Bahrain through the ages, the Archaeology*, Kegan Paul International.

[82] http://arxiv.org/ftp/arxiv/papers/0809/0809.3566.pdf (Amelia Carolina Sparavigna, 2008, Symmetries in images on ancient seals.)

[83] http://en.wikipedia.org/wiki/Narmer_Palette#cite_note-13

[84] *Expedition* 40:2 (1998), p. 31, figs. 3a,b,4,5b

[85] Kenoyer, J.M., 1998, Ancient cities of the Indus Valley civilization, Oxford University Press.

[86] Cf. Randall William Law, 2008, Inter-regional interaction and urbanism in the ancient Indus valley: a geologic provenience study of Harappa's rock and mineral assemblage, University of Wisconsin-Madison http://tinyurl.com/3s22o4m

[87] ṛgveda (ṛca 3.53.12) uses the term, *'bhāratam janam'*, which can be interpreted as 'bhārata folk'. The ṛṣi of the sūkta is viśvāmitra gāthina. India was called Bhāratavarṣa after the king Bhārata. (Vāyu 33, 51-2; Bd. 2,14,60-2; lin:ga 1,47,20,24; Viṣṇu 2,1,28,32).

Ya ime rodasī ubhe aham indram atuṣṭavam

viśvāmitrasya rakṣati brahmedam bhāratam janam

3.053.12 I have made Indra glorified by these two, heaven and earth, and this prayer of viśvāmitra protects the people of Bhārata. [Made Indra glorified: indram

atuṣṭavam — the verb is the third preterite of the casual, I have caused to be praised; it may mean: I praise Indra, abiding between heaven and earth, i.e. in the firmament].

[88] Excerpt from Encyclopaedia Iranica article (Gherardo Gnoli) Originally

Published: December 15, 1993 Last Updated: November 11, 2011

http://www.iranicaonline.org/articles/dahyu-

[89] Śatapatha Brāhmaṇa vol. 2 of 5, tr. By Julius Eggeling, 1885, in SBE Part 12; fn 78-81

[90] Emeneau, MB, 1956, India as a linguistic area, Language 32, 1956, 3-16.

Kuiper, FBJ, 1948, Proto-Munda words in Sanskrit, Amsterdam, 1948

1967, The genesis of a linguistic area, IIJ 10, 1967, 81-102

Masica, CP, 1971, Defining a Linguistic area. South Asia. Chicago: The University of Chicago Press.

Przyludski, J., 1929, Further notes on non-aryan loans in Indo-Aryan in: Bagchi, P. C. (ed.), Pre-Aryan and Pre-Dravidian in Sanskrit. Calcutta : University of Calcutta: 145-149

Southworth, F., 2005, Linguistic archaeology of South Asia, London, Routledge-Curzon.

[91] S. Beal, 1973, *The Life of Hiuen Tsiang*, New Delhi, p 57; cf. NL Dey, *Geographical Dictionary of India*, p. 113 for an identification of Lamgham (Lampakā) 20 miles north-west of Jalalabad.

[92] WF Leemans, Foreign Trade in the Old Babylonian Period, 1960; 'Trade Relations on Babylonia', Journal of Economic and Social History of the Orient, vol. III, 1960, p.30 ff. 'Old Babylonian Letters and Economic History', Journal of

Economic and Social History of the Orient, vol. XI, 1968, pp. 215-26; J. Hansam, 'A Periplus of Magan and Meluhha', Bulletin of the School of Oriental and African Studies, vol. 36, pt. III, 1973, pp. 554-83. Asko and Simo Parpola, 'On the Relationship of the Sumerian Toponym Meluhha and Sanskrit Mleccha', Studia Orientalia,vol. 46, 1975, pp. 205-38.

93 Siddhānti Subrahmaṇya śastri's *New interpretation of the Amarakośa,* Bangalore, Vicaradarpana Press, 1872, p. 330.

94 http://www.hindu.com/fline/fl2712/stories/20100618271206800.htm

95 V. Gordon Childe, 1929, *The most ancient East: the oriental prelude to European history*, London, Kegan Paul, Trench, Trubner and Co. Ltd., Fig. 72b.

96 http: //www.harappa.com/indus/Kenoyer-Meadow-2010-HARP.pdf

97 http://en.wikipedia.org/wiki/File:Barren-Gott,_Enkomi,_12._Jh._v._Chr._C.jpg

98 JM Kenoyer, 1998, Ancient cities of the Indus Valley, Oxford University Press, p. 115.

99 Cf. Diakonoff, I. M. (1985), "Media", *The Cambridge History of Iran*, 2 (Edited by Ilya Gershevitch ed.), Cambridge, England: Cambridge University Press, pp. 36–148. http://en.wikipedia.org/wiki/Medes

100 Donkin, R.A., 1998, Beyond price: pearls and pearl-fishing: origins to the age of discoveries, Philadelphia, American Philosophical Society, Memoir Volume 224, pp.49-50)Full text at http://tinyurl.com/y9zpb5n Note 109. For Sumerian words, see Delitzch, 1914: pp.18-19 (igi, eye), 125 (ku, fish), 195 (na, stone); and cf. Chicago Assyrian Dictionary I/J: 1960: pp.45 (iga), 153-158 (Akk. i_nu), N(2), 1980: p.340 (k), 'fish-eye stones'.Note 110. A.L. Oppenheim, 1954: pp.7-8; Leemans, 1960b: pp.24 f. (IGI-KU6). Followed by Kramer, 1963a: p.113, 1963b: p.283; Bibby, 1970: pp.189, 191-192: Ratnagar, 1981: pp.23-24,79, 188; M. Rice, 1985: p.181.Note 111. A.L. Oppenheim, 1954: p.11; Leemans, 1960b: p.37 (NA4 IGI-KU6, 'fish-eye stones').Note 112. Leemans, 1968: p.222 ('pearls from Meluhha'. Falkenstein (1963: pp.10-11 [12]) has 'augenformigen Perlen aus

Meluhha'. (lit. shaped eyes beads from Meluhha).

[101] http://www.harappa.com/indus4/e6.html

[102] http://www.ling.hawaii.edu/faculty/stampe/aa.html

See http://kalyan97.googlepages.com/mleccha1.pdf

[103] http://www.scribd.com/doc/2232617/lexicon linked at http://sites.google.com/site/kalyan97/indus-writing

[104] [http://huntingtonarchive.osu.edu/Makara%20Site/makara

www.ingramcontent.com/pod-product-compliance
Lightning Source LLC
Chambersburg PA
CBHW071351280326
41927CB00041B/2825
9780982897188